# FREEDOM AND AUTHORITY

SCOTLAND *c.*1050–*c.*1650

Plate 1 Grant G. Simpson. Courtesy of Alan Young

# FREEDOM AND AUTHORITY

## Scotland *c.* 1050–*c.* 1650

Historical and Historiographical Essays presented to
Grant G. Simpson

edited by

TERRY BROTHERSTONE and DAVID DITCHBURN

TUCKWELL PRESS

First published in Great Britain in 2000 by
Tuckwell Press Ltd
The Mill House, Phantassie, East Linton, East Lothian, EH40 3DG
Scotland



ISBN 1 898410 79 8

British Library Cataloguing-in-Publication Data. A catalogue record for this book is available on request from the British Library

Typeset in 10/12 Garamond by
*Aligra* Lancaster
Printed and bound in Great Britain by
The Cromwell Press, Trowbridge, Wiltshire

# Contents

# Tables



# Illustrations

# Contributors

STEVE BOARDMAN is a Lecturer in Scottish History at the University of Edinburgh

TERRY BROTHERSTONE is a Senior Lecturer in History at the University of Aberdeen

SONJA CAMERON is Co-ordinator for History in the CTI Centre for History, Archaeology and Art History at the University of Glasgow

E. PATRICIA DENNISON is Director of the Centre for Scottish Urban History in the Department of Scottish History at the University of Edinburgh

DAVID DITCHBURN is a Lecturer in History at the University of Aberdeen

ELIZABETH EWAN is an Associate Professor of History and Scottish Studies at the University of Guelph, Ontario

ALEXANDER GRANT is a Reader in Medieval British History at the University of Lancaster

MICHAEL LYNCH is Sir William Fraser Professor of Scottish History and Palaeography at the University of Edinburgh

ALASTAIR J. MACDONALD is the Mackie Lecturer in History at the University of Aberdeen

LESLIE MACFARLANE is an Honorary Reader in History at the University of Aberdeen

COLIN MCLAREN is Associate Director and Librarian in the Directorate of Information Systems and Services at the University of Aberdeen

ROBIN MACPHERSON is an Assistant Secretary in the Institute of Historical Research at the University of London

ULRIKE MORÉT is a Curator in the Rare Books Division of the Department of Special Collections at the National Library of Scotland in Edinburgh

CYNTHIA J. NEVILLE is an Associate Professor of History at Dalhousie University, Halifax, Nova Scotia

RICHARD D. ORAM is an Honorary Lecturer in History at the University of Aberdeen

ALEXANDER STEVENSON is an independent scholar, based in Glasgow

KEITH J. STRINGER is a Reader in Medieval British History at the University of Lancaster

JANE THOMAS is an independent scholar, based near Elgin

JENNY WORMALD is V. H. Galbraith Fellow and Tutor in Modern History in St Hilda's College at the University of Oxford

# Acknowledgements

Grant Simpson received the first draft of this volume in a surprise presentation at the end of 1995. Its final appearance may therefore be described as 'long-awaited', certainly by him – and by those contributors whose chapters were delivered within our original schedule. On behalf of the procrastinators we apologise to the expeditious ... and to those enquirers who have encouragingly been pressing us to make the book available. John and Val Tuckwell have been very tolerant but their greatest contribution of all was finally to lose patience. Since their *final* final deadline was applied, the collective effort of all contributors has been marvellous to behold and participate in. The sense of pulling together was indeed a tribute to our respect for the scholar to whom *Freedom and Authority* is presented. We hope that accuracy and nuance have not been sacrificed in the final edit, but we take full responsibility if, in any degree, it has. The book certainly looks and reads much better than it would otherwise have done thanks to Sandy Grant's speedy, efficient and generous assistance with production. We are indebted to him. Hilary Horrocks and Alison Grant helped greatly with the copy-editing, and Linda Fryer compiled the index. Allan Macinnes has been most supportive in his inimitably forceful way – crucially so in his agreement that this project amply merited financial support from the funds provided to Aberdeen University under the will of the late Dr James R. M. Mackie of Glenmillan. Ried Zulager, one of Simpson's distinguished postgraduates, would have contributed a chapter had business commitments in the USA not prevented him: his benevolent interest has been encouraging in other ways. The National Archives of Scotland (formerly the Scottish Record Office – at which Grant Simpson worked for fifteen years), we are very pleased to record, associated itself with the volume by contributing the photographs of charters which illustrate chapter 16. Alan Borthwick was particularly supportive both in this respect and more generally with chapters 16 and 17. Karen Jillings assisted with the initial formatting, while Gillian Brown and Sandra Williams helped with the final processing of some disks. Along with our colleagues in the History Department we regret that this is likely to be the last of our books to which Sandra will have made her cheerful contribution. We wish her health and happiness in her retirement. Norma Sim was extremely tolerant of both us as, at different times, we spread our papers all over her office; and the coffee was a lifesaver. Last, but very far from least, Anne Simpson has been encouraging and helpful throughout.

Terry Brotherstone
David Ditchburn
Department of History
University of Aberdeen
31 July 1999

# Abbreviations

| | |
|---|---|
| *Aberdeen-Banff Ills.* | *Illustrations of the Topography and Antiquities of the Shires of Aberdeen and Banff*, ed. J. Robertson *et al.* (Spalding Club, 1847–69) |
| *Aberdeen Council Recs.* | *Extracts from the Council Register of the Burgh of Aberdeen*, ed. J. Stuart (Spalding Club, 1844–8) |
| *APS* | *The Acts of the Parliaments of Scotland*, ed. T. Thomson and C. Innes (Edinburgh 1814–75) |
| Barbour, *Bruce* | [John Barbour], *Barbour's Bruce*, ed. M. P. McDiarmid and J. A. C. Stevenson (Scottish Text Soc., 1980–5) |
| Barrow, *Bruce* | G. W. S. Barrow, *Robert Bruce and the Community of the Realm of Scotland* (3rd edn, Edinburgh, 1988) |
| BL | British Library, London |
| *CBP* | *Calendar of Letters and Papers relating to the Affairs of the Borders of England and Scotland*, ed. J. Bain (Edinburgh, 1894–6) |
| *CDS* | *Calendar of Documents relating to Scotland*, ed. J. Bain *et al.* (Edinburgh, 1881–1986) |
| *Chron. Bower* (Watt) | *Scotichronicon by Walter Bower, in Latin and English*, ed. D. E. R. Watt *et al.* (Aberdeen and Edinburgh, 1987–98) |
| *Chron. Fordun* | *Johannis de Fordun, Chronica Gentis Scotorum*, ed. W. F. Skene (Edinburgh, 1871–2) |
| *Chron. Knighton* | *Knighton's Chronicle, 1337–1396*, ed. G. H. Martin (Oxford, 1995) |
| *Chron. Le Baker* | *Chronicon Galfridi le Baker de Swynebroke*, ed. E. M. Thompson (Oxford, 1889) |
| *Chron. Le Bel* | *Chronique de Jean le Bel*, ed. J. Viard and E. Déprez (Paris, 1904–5) |
| *Chron. Melrose* | *Chronicle of Melrose*, ed. A. O. Anderson and M. O. Anderson (facsimile edn, London, 1936) |
| *Chron. Walsingham* | Thomas of Walsingham, *Historia Anglicana*, ed. H. T. Riley (Rolls Ser., 1863–4) |
| *Chron. Westminster* | *The Westminster Chronicle*, eds. L. C. Hector and B. F. Harvey (Oxford, 1982) |
| *Chron. Wyntoun* (Laing) | Androw of Wyntoun, *The Orygynale Cronykil of Scotland*, ed. D. Laing (Edinburgh, 1872–9) |
| *Coldingham Corresp.* | *The Correspondence, Inventories, Account Rolls and Law Proceedings of the Priory of Coldingham*, ed. J. Raine (Surtees Soc., 1841) |
| *Coupar Angus Chrs.* | *Charters of the Abbey of Coupar Angus*, ed. D. E. Easson (SHS, 1947) |
| CRO | Cumbria Record Office, Carlisle and Kendal |
| *CSP Scot* | *Calendar of the State Papers relating to Scotland and Mary, Queen of Scots 1547–1603*, ed. J. Bain *et al.* (Edinburgh, 1898– ) |
| CWAAS | Cumberland and Westmorland Antiquarian and Archaeological Soc. |
| *Dryburgh Liber* | *Liber S. Marie de Dryburgh*, ed. W. Fraser (Bannatyne Club, 1847) |
| Duncan, *Kingdom* | A. A. M. Duncan, *Scotland: The Making of the Kingdom* (Edinburgh, 1975) |
| *Dunfermline Reg.* | *Registrum de Dunfermelyn*, ed. C. Innes (Bannatyne Club, 1842) |

| | |
|---|---|
| *Edin. Recs.* | *Extracts from the Records of the Burgh of Edinburgh*, ed. J. D. Marwick (Scottish Burgh Records Soc., 1869–92) |
| *Elgin Recs.* | *The Records of Elgin, 1234–1800*, ed. W. Cramond (Spalding Club, 1903–8) |
| *ER* | *The Exchequer Rolls of Scotland*, ed. J. Stuart *et al.* (Edinburgh, 1878–1908) |
| *Fasti Aberdonenses* | *Fasti Aberdonenses: Selections from the Records of the University and King's College of Aberdeen*, ed. C. Innes (Spalding Club, 1854) |
| Fraser, *Annandale* | W. Fraser, *The Annandale Family Book* (Edinburgh, 1894) |
| Fraser, *Buccleuch* | W. Fraser, *The Scotts of Buccleuch* (Edinburgh, 1878) |
| Fraser, *Carlaverock* | W. Fraser, *The Book of Carlaverock* (Edinburgh, 1873) |
| Fraser, *Douglas* | W. Fraser, *The Douglas Book* (Edinburgh, 1885) |
| Fraser, *Elphinstone* | W. Fraser, *The Elphinstone Family Book* (Edinburgh, 1897) |
| Fraser, *Frasers of Philorth* | A. Fraser, Lord Saltoun, *The Frasers of Philorth* (Edinburgh, 1879) |
| Fraser, *Grandtully* | W. Fraser, *The Red Book of Grandtully* (Edinburgh, 1868) |
| Fraser, *Lennox* | W. Fraser, *The Lennox* (Edinburgh, 1874) |
| Fraser, *Menteith* | W. Fraser, *The Red Book of Menteith* (Edinburgh, 1880) |
| Fraser, *Pollok* | W. Fraser, *Memoirs of the Maxwells of Pollok* (Edinburgh, 1863) |
| *Halyburton's Ledger* | *Ledger of Andrew Halyburton, 1492–1503*, ed. C. Innes (Edinburgh, 1867) |
| HMC | Historical Manuscripts Commission |
| *Holm Cultram Reg.* | *The Register and Records of Holm Cultram*, ed. F. Grainger and W. G. Collingwood (CWAAS, Record Ser., 1929) |
| *Holyrood Liber* | *Liber Cartarum Sancte Crucis*, ed. C. Innes (Bannatyne Club, 1840) |
| *Inchaffray Chrs.* | *Charters, Bulls and other Documents relating to the Abbey of Inchaffray*, ed. W. A. Lindsay *et al.* (SHS, 1908) |
| *Inchaffray Liber* | *Liber Insule Missarum*, ed. C. Innes (Bannatyne Club, 1846) |
| *IR* | *Innes Review* |
| *Kelso Liber* | *Liber S. Marie de Calchou*, ed. C. Innes (Bannatyne Club, 1846) |
| Lawrie, *Annals* | *Annals of the Reigns of Malcolm and William, Kings of Scotland* (Glasgow, 1910) |
| Leslie, *De Origine* | John Leslie, *De origine, moribus, et rebus gestis Scotorum Libri decem* (Rome, 1578) |
| *Lindores Cart.* | *Cartulary of the Abbey of Lindores, 1195–1479*, ed. J. Dowden (SHS, 1903) |
| Mair, *Historia* | John Mair, *Historia majoris Britanniae tam Angliae quam Scotiae* (Paris, 1521) |
| *Melrose Liber* | *Liber Sancte Marie de Melros*, ed. C. Innes (Bannatyne Club, 1837) |
| *Midlothian Chrs.* | *Charters of the Hospital of Soltre, of Trinity College, Edinburgh, and other Collegiate Churches in Midlothian*, ed. D. Laing (Bannatyne Club, 1861) |
| *Moray Reg.* | *Registrum Episcopatus Moraviensis*, ed. C. Innes (Bannatyne Club, 1839) |
| *Morton Reg.* | *Registrum Honoris de Morton*, ed. T. Thomson *et al.* (Bannatyne Club, 1853) |

| | |
|---|---|
| NAS | National Archives of Scotland, Edinburgh |
| *Newbattle Reg.* | *Registrum S. Marie de Nuebotle* (Bannatyne Club, 1831) |
| Nicholson, *Scotland* | R. Nicholson, *Scotland: The Later Middle Ages* (Edinburgh, 1974) |
| NLS | National Library of Scotland, Edinburgh |
| *Peebles Recs.* | *Extracts from the Records of the Burgh of Peebles*, ed. R. Renwick (Scottish Burgh Record Soc., 1910) |
| Pitcairn, *Trials* | *Criminal Trials in Scotland from 1488 to 1624*, ed. R. Pitcairn (Edinburgh, 1833) |
| PRO | Public Record Office, London |
| *PSAS* | *Proceedings of the Society of Antiquaries of Scotland* |
| Raine, *North Durham* | J. Raine, *The History and Antiquities of North Durham* (London, 1852) |
| *RMS* | *Registrum Magni Sigilli Regum Scotorum*, ed. J. M. Thomson *et al.* (Edinburgh, 1882–1914) |
| *Rot. Scot.* | *Rotuli Scotiae in Turri Londinensi et in Domo Capitulari Westmonasteriensi asservati*, ed. D. Macpherson *et al.* (Record Commission, 1814–19) |
| *RPC* | *The Register of the Privy Council of Scotland*, ed. J. H. Burton *et al.* (Edinburgh, 1877– ) |
| *RRS* | *Regesta Regum Scottorum*, ed. G. W. S. Barrow *et al.* (Edinburgh, 1960– ) |
| *RSS* | *Registrum Secreti Sigilli Regum Scotorum*, ed. M. Livingstone *et al.* (Edinburgh, 1908– ) |
| Rymer, *Foedera* | T. Rymer, *Foedera, Conventiones, Litterae et Cuiuscunque Generis Acta Publica* (Record Commission, 1816–69) |
| *St Andrews Liber* | *Liber Cartarum Prioratus Sancti Andree in Scotia*, ed. T. Thomson (Bannatyne Club, 1841) |
| *St Bees Reg.* | *Register of the Priory of St Bees* (Surtees Soc., 1915) |
| *Scone Liber* | *Liber Ecclesie de Scon*, ed. W. Smythe (Bannatyne and Maitland Clubs, 1843) |
| *Scots Peerage* | *The Scots Peerage*, ed. J. B. Paul (Edinburgh, 1904–14) |
| *SHR* | *Scottish Historical Review* |
| SHS | Scottish History Society |
| SRO | Scottish Record Office, Edinburgh |
| Stevenson, *Documents* | *Documents Illustrative of the History of Scotland, 1286–1306*, ed. J. Stevenson (Edinburgh, 1870) |
| Stringer, *Nobility* | K. J. Stringer, ed., *Essays on the Nobility of Medieval Scotland* (Edinburgh, 1985) |
| *TA* | *Accounts of the Lord High Treasurer of Scotland*, ed. T. Dickson and J. B. Paul (Edinburgh, 1877–1916) |
| *TDGAS* | *Transactions of the Dumfriesshire and Galloway Natural History and Antiquarian Society* |
| *TGSI* | *Transactions of the Gaelic Society of Inverness* |
| *Wigtownshire Chrs.* | *Wigtownshire Charters*, ed. R. C. Reid (SHS, 1960) |
| *Yester Writs* | *Calendar of Writs preserved at Yester House 1166–1503*, ed. C. C. H. Harvey and J. Macleod (Scottish Record Soc., 1930) |

# Part One

# Historians and the Uses of History

# 1

# The Steam behind the Spectacles: Grant G. Simpson and *Freedom and Authority*

*Terry Brotherstone and David Ditchburn*

At Glasgow University when the results came out in the summer of 1952, the twenty-two-year-old Grant Simpson had an interview with the head of the History Department, Professor Andrew Browning. 'Ah, Mr Simpson,' said Browning in a rather nasal, West of Scotland accent that his former pupil still imitates with affection, 'it may please you *slightly* to know that although you did not get a first, you were however the *first* of the seconds.' Oral history has its problems as a means of accurate record, but when Simpson tells that story, you are certain that he has remembered each word exactly as it was spoken.

In those days, failure to achieve first-class honours meant that postgraduate research was virtually out of the question, so Simpson's top 'two-one' signified that, after National Service, he would be looking for employment outside the university. But then he himself had not particularly expected a first (though others, he realised, had expected it of him), so it is not, one senses, because of its effect on his career plans that he remembers that interview so clearly. Rather there is a kind of Glasgow gallusness in the way he tells the story: as though he is modestly challenging you to regard being described as 'the first of the seconds' – especially by Browning, whose mind he much admired – as anything but the highest praise.

This notion fits well with Anne Simpson's perception of her husband's greatest contribution to Scottish medieval and early modern history: it lies above all, she suggests, not in his having made headlines, but in his commitment to 'double digging'. There are different approaches to gardening: 'You can double dig, you can single dig, or you can just start planting.' The current pressures in academic life in Britain – with agendas increasingly dominated by the 'mystic formulae' of the Research Assessment Exercise, and intellectual resistance to such imperatives weakened by insecure contracts – mean that many scholars are forced into immediate planting.[1] 'Grant,' says his partner and erstwhile pupil, 'sees the value of ... laying the foundations.'[2] He belongs, in

[1] We borrow the phrase 'mystic formulae' from John D. Hargreaves, Burnett-Fletcher Professor of History at Aberdeen from 1962 to 1985, and Head of Department when Grant Simpson was appointed in 1969. See his 'The Aberdeen History Department in a changing university', *Aberdeen University Review*, lviii, no. 201 (1999), 47. Since the late 1980s, readers outside British universities may not know, RAEs have been conducted at four-yearly intervals to ensure that British academics publish or face damnation. These exercises seriously affect the prestige and research funding of what are now encouraged to regard themselves as – if this is not a contradiction in terms – rival universities. Young scholars are under pressure to meet publishing performance targets if they are to succeed in their probation interviews and/or to be offered other than fixed-term contracts.

[2] Now 'partner' in both senses: the Simpsons were married in 1979; and their company HISTORY IN THE MAKING (Heritage Consultants) was set up in Aberdeen in 1996.

other words, to a generation that understood by 'standards' something more serious than creating whatever can look good in the market place.

In that, of course, he is not alone. Grant Simpson has been associated with a distinguished group of scholars whose work ensured that Scottish history not only survived as a discipline but began to claim parity of status with the history of any other small country. Until the late 1960s when the post-Union period began for the first time to receive serious scholarly attention, that task fell substantially to the medievalists. (The work of Gordon Donaldson – one of Simpson's PhD supervisors – on the Reformation might perhaps be seen as occupying a transitional place in this story.) Secure in the knowledge that they were dealing with a period when Scotland clearly *had* a history of its own, the medievalists were also perhaps less constrained than those interested in the period since 1560 by having to wade their way through justificatory Presbyterian tracts often dressed up with the paraphernalia of scholarship. In that sense, although they are very different people, and very different scholars, the work of Archie Duncan, Geoffrey Barrow, Grant Simpson, Donald Watt and Ian Cowan performed a major service for all subsequent historians of Scotland, not only for their immediate successors as medievalists. And if it is true, as Duncan has suggested, that 'the first modern book on medieval Scottish history' appeared in 1965, then it could also be claimed that it pre-dated the first 'modern' books on post-Union Scottish history by three to four years.[3]

Despite all the external threats to scholarship, moreover, its values *do* survive and have been passed on to new generations. Young historians in Britain at the turn of the twenty-first century face not only new pressures but also new opportunities. In Scotland these opportunities are political, technological and theoretical. They are political in the sense that the establishment of a Scottish Parliament in 1999 has been much spoken of as a 'historic' moment: if, as time passes, the Parliament proves that its establishment did indeed mark a real change in the lives of ordinary Scots, the country's historians will surely be called upon to rewrite its history to make it relevant to what will, therefore, be regarded as a new political period. They are technological in as much as new modes of information transference – while claims for them are often exaggerated – open up the possibility of easier initial consultation of some records and of more rapid, and more international, interchange of ideas. And they are theoretical in the sense that the discounting of academic Marxism – which provided such a major point of reference for historians well into the 1980s – has created a level field on which to replay the contest for the informing methodologies and purposes of historical work in general. This last circumstance provides a particular challenge for Scottish medieval history – often thought of as a preserve of scholarly conservatism – which it is well equipped to meet. Simpson's generation provided a basis of empirical work, and an examplar of how it should be done, which should ensure that there is no danger of the new challenges

[3] Which we take to be W. Ferguson, *Scotland Since 1689* (Edinburgh, 1968); and, especially, T. C. Smout, *A History of the Scottish People* (Glasgow, 1969). Duncan was referring to the first edition of Barrow, *Bruce*: see A. A. M. Duncan, *The Nation of Scots and the Declaration of Arbroath* (Historical Association, 1970), 38.

being met by flights into the realms of epistemological relativism, characteristic of the more extreme 'postmodernists'.

In putting this book together we have tried, in the main, to reflect Simpson's contribution to the future rather than to meditate on his own achievement and reputation. Nearly everyone asked to participate in this celebratory volume – and we apologise both to those distinguished historians (particularly some of Simpson's closest scholarly associates) who were not asked, and to others who volunteered when the lists were already full – is substantially younger than the historian they honour. In the main they have been Simpson's students (usually at postgraduate level), or were examined by him, or simply grew to their intellectual and scholarly maturity conscious of his influence on their chosen field. The most obvious exception to this rule is Leslie Macfarlane, an inspirational scholar *sui generis*: in this volume, Steve Boardman and Macfarlane are the bookends of Aberdeen collegiality supporting the other contributors – the one the last medievalist to be appointed during Simpson's tenure, the other representing those in post when he arrived.[4]

Grant Simpson was born on 24 August 1930 in Glasgow into what he carefully defines as a 'middle-middle-class' family. History was, at a senior level, a discounted subject in the Scottish school curriculum in those days, but the teenage Simpson, a pupil from 1940 to 1948 at Hutchesons' Boys' Grammar School, benefited from some one-to-one tuition from the first master appointed there as a specialist historian. At the University of Glasgow, his initial focus was on English – and his thought was to become a schoolteacher. But his distaste for compulsory Anglo-Saxon and his lack of enthusiasm for T. S. Eliot ('I thought [he] was impossible: [the Glasgow English Department] thought he was the bees' knees ...') were two reasons why he switched to Honours in History. Inspired in different ways by Browning, and by Lionel Stones who later became a research colleague, he developed an interest in scholarship on the one hand and the medieval period on the other.

National Service was in the RAF – as a junior officer in the Secretarial/ Administrative branch – an experience of which Simpson has on the whole positive memories. Then, in 1954, he was appointed as Assistant Keeper in the Scottish Record Office (a civil service post), at that time under the old-fashioned and self-centred leadership of that regular performer in the radio show *Round Britain Quiz*, Sir James Fergusson of Kilkerran. Simpson's decision to do a part-time PhD at the University of Edinburgh met with no encouragement whatsoever from Sir James.

For Glaswegians, a move to Edinburgh is usually a culture shock, and so it was with Grant Simpson. But his love of the cinema – acquired in his teenage years under the tutelage of some ever-arguing, very Tory but broad-minded aunts – provided a lifeline of continuity between the warmth of the West and the chill of the East. He made good use of his years in the Scottish capital, battling away for the modernisation of the Record Office; acquiring his PhD in

4 Boardman left for Edinburgh in 1997. Colin McLaren has also long been a valued Aberdeen colleague, though not in the History Department.

1966; serving as assistant secretary, then secretary of the Scottish History Society from 1956 to 1969; and becoming a fellow of the Society of Antiquaries of Scotland (in 1955), of the Royal Historical Society (in 1962), and of the Society of Antiquaries of London (in 1967). He established himself in these years, too, as a historian of growing repute, with scholarly articles in the *Scottish Historical Review*, the *Innes Review* and elsewhere.

In 1969 came what turned out to be the big decision. Simpson was offered and, after twenty-four hours of doubt, accepted a lectureship in the History Department at the University of Aberdeen. Amongst the first cohort of undergraduates he encountered was one contributor to this volume, Michael Lynch. Soon he was to meet another, Alexander Stevenson, who was to become his first doctoral student. As a lecturer, Simpson was careful and well organised but also, in his own quiet and ironic way, inspiring to students ready to be inspired. He was a kenspeckle figure in the academic gown which, by then, had been abandoned by most of his colleagues. Over the years, he lectured to the second year on Scottish history from 1000 to 1625; and his honours courses included an innovative survey of Scotland's contacts with Europe from the Vikings to the Renaissance, and an introduction to palaeography, taught with Colin McLaren. A special subject on the reign of James VI attracted able students such as Robin Macpherson, whose dissertation – now developed into chapter 12 of this volume – provided the starting-point for a later Edinburgh PhD thesis. And, in a department where research students had been mainly concentrated on African and later modern Scottish history, Simpson ensured that medieval and early modern Scotland more than held their own. Of the twelve Aberdeen postgraduates he supervised, five are contributors to *Freedom and Authority*: in addition to Stevenson (on Bruges), there are Cynthia Neville (on the earldom of Strathearn), Sonja Cameron (on Sir James Douglas), Alastair Macdonald (on warring nobles) and Jane Thomas (on the craftsmen of Elgin) – the diversity of their subjects emphasising the breadth of Simpson's interests. The point is reinforced by reference to the topics of those contributors for whose doctoral theses Simpson was examiner – Sandy Grant (on the fourth earl of Douglas), Elizabeth Ewan (on the women of late medieval Edinburgh), and Ulrike Morét (on medieval and humanist historiography).

Simpson's own output has been equally wide-ranging. He is best known for his studies of the medieval Scottish baronage and its castles, and of 'feudalism' – though the publication of his reflections on this last topic remains eagerly awaited. These interests led him, while still in the Record Office, to found the Scottish Baronial Research Group ('BARG'), which provided the initial impetus behind his contacts with scholars such as Jenny Wormald, Keith Stringer, Sandy Grant and Richard Oram – though, with Wormald, James VI was to become a further mutual attraction. But Simpson has also had considerable influence – as Pat Dennison points out below – on the development of Scottish urban history; and his interest in Scotland's overseas connections governed his choice of themes for the first three Mackie symposia, and the volumes to which they gave rise.[5] His more minute studies – for example on castle gatekeepers and the seal of the minority of Alexander III – though titled in a manner likely to deter all but the most determined specialist, provide surprisingly accessible insights into the broader nature of medieval society.[6]

Much is heard today of the 'star monograph', an astronomical phenomenon forecast much more often by publishers' blurb-writers than recorded by objective observers of actual scholarship. Grant Simpson has not produced such a book; and some critics may hold that this will diminish his legacy. If so, they will miss the point. The main monuments to Simpson's scholarship lie in his use of the paleographical skills he learnt as an archivist to edit complex and difficult texts. This is most notable in the authoritative two-volume edition of documents relating to *Edward I and the Throne of Scotland, 1290–1296* which he and Lionel Stones produced in 1978; but there are also *Scottish Handwriting 1150–1650*, published first in 1973 and in a new edition in 1998, and the indispensable fifth volume of the *Calendar of Documents relating to Scotland in H.M. Public Record Office, London, 1108–1516*, edited with J. D. Galbraith and published in 1986. The appearance of the 1249–1306 volume of the *Regesta Regum Scottorum* – which he is now co-editing with Alan Young, whose Newcastle PhD was another he examined, and with his former pupil, Cynthia Neville – will complete a formidable achievement. It is one for which later generations may be grateful long after some, more headline-grabbing, publications are forgotten.

What additional contribution Simpson might have made to his field – and to the further development of the research culture of the University of Aberdeen – had he been appointed to a chair of Scottish History, will never be known. Such a position was advertised in 1973, when, in British universities, some of the optimism of the expansionist 1960s remained and the dog-days of Thatcherism lurked around the corner still barely perceived. Simpson was one of four serious candidates, but, in the discreetly incandescent words of the historian of the Aberdeen History Department, Doreen Milne (who hints at no preference for any particular applicant), the outcome

> was disappointment, even farce. The inability of the appointing committee to choose between the applicants became a minor *cause célèbre* in Scottish academic circles. The decision to delay a decision for a year, in the hope that a clearer picture might emerge, was overtaken by the increased financial stringency which ended any prospect of an appointment.[7]

5 G. G. Simpson, ed., *Scotland and Scandinavia, 800–1800* (Edinburgh, 1990); idem, ed., *The Scottish Soldier Abroad, 1247-1967* (Edinburgh, 1992); idem, ed., *Scotland and the Low Countries 1124–1994* (East Linton, 1996). Grant Simpson's account of the Mackie Bequest and its value to History at the University of Aberdeen and more generally can be read in *Scotland and Scandinavia*, p. v.

6 G. G. Simpson, '"Claves Castri": the role of the gatekeeper in Scottish medieval castles', *Château Gaillard: European Castle Studies*, v (1992), 319–24; idem, 'Kingship in miniature: a seal of minority of Alexander III, 1249–57', in A. Grant and K. J. Stringer, eds., *Medieval Scotland: Crown, Lordship and Community. Essays Presented to G. W. S. Barrow* (Edinburgh, 1993), 131–9.

7 D. J. Milne, *A Century of History: The Establishment and First Century of the Department of History in the University of Aberdeen* (Aberdeen, 1998), 78.

So a chair around which to centre the development of Scottish history within the generalist work of the Aberdeen department was not to be. Only with the appointment, in 1994, of Allan Macinnes to the Burnett-Fletcher chair and the headship of the department as a whole, did the University find a different way of giving developments in Scottish history professorial recognition. Soon afterwards, Simpson's contribution to creating the situation which had made that a possible, even logical, step to take, was recognised with his rather belated promotion to a Readership.

Grant Simpson's role in the History Department, in the University of Aberdeen, and in the broad scholarly community, though firmly rooted in his own specialism, has not been limited to it. In the later 1980s, he assisted enthusiastically in setting up and running an innovative 'Approaches to History' course, which attempted – in the face of the narrowing of the focus of teaching through staff cuts and then 'modularisation' – to challenge Honours history students to familiarise themselves with historiography, and with a variety of methodologies and theories. He has been a senator, and has served on the University chapel, library, museums and other committees. In 1993, following a period of argument over how historians should respond to new bureaucratic demands – deemed to be required by the unfunded expansion of student numbers, and by a seemingly endless imposition of external quality control exercises – he stood, in a gesture of principle, as a non-management candidate for the Faculty of Arts Advisory Committee. His election caused a few feathers to flutter, though the plumage of university managerialism soon fell back into place.

Since 1970, Simpson has been a member of the Château Gaillard Colloquium (concerned with European castle studies); from 1974 to 1976 he was on the Council of the Society of Antiquaries of London; from 1984 to 1987 he chaired the Scottish Records Association; and, from 1992 to 1994, the Conference of Scottish Medieval Historians, of which he was a founding member and the only one to have attended each of its annual meetings. He has served on the Ancient Monuments Board for Scotland; and on the councils of the Scottish Urban Archaeology Trust and the Scottish Record Society. In the early 1970s he convened the Urban Archaeology Trust of the Society of Antiquaries of Scotland; and more recently has been a consultant for Historic Scotland's Finds Disposal Panel. In 1992 he was elected to the presidency of the Scottish History Society, choosing to deliver his four annual lectures not on medieval history as such, but on aspects of the evolution of Scottish historiography as a whole.

Coming to the early twentieth century in this exercise he found himself drawing inspiration not so much from professional historians as from an early-1930s volume, *Scottish Scene*, by James Mitchell and Christopher Grieve (Lewis Grassic Gibbon and Hugh MacDiarmid).[8] Asked what the careful scholar finds of merit in this rather wayward book, he replies that Grassic Gibbon shows:

[8] Lewis Grassic Gibbon and Hugh MacDiarmid, *Scottish Scene, or the Intelligent Man's Guide to Albyn* (Bath, 1974; first publ. London, 1934).

> incisiveness in some aspects of Scottish history at a point where – in the 1920s and 1930s – the academics, the R. K. Hannays and so on, were off in their fuddy-duddy world editing their texts. The Hugh MacDiarmids and the Grassic Gibbons were being fiery and got through to some fundamentals. But the two worlds I'm sure never met. And yet the one had more to offer perhaps than the other. It comes back to the question, 'what was Scotland about?' To discover that you go back to MacDiarmid and Grassic Gibbon: you don't go to R. K. Hannay.

'But hasn't your own image,' we ask, 'been closer to Hannay than to MacDiarmid?' Simpson responds:

> I'd admit that absolutely, except that a bit of the flash of fire comes out occasionally ... In the days of reforming Register House [one former colleague used to say], 'You should have seen him ... when he got really worked up and the steam came up from behind his spectacles.'

It is an irresistible image, which can be seen in more than one way. Grant Simpson's contribution to history may not have been speedily spectacular; but his work in the power-house of the old technologies has contributed mightily to equipping others to make the most of the new. If a fresh generation can create new spectacles, new streamlined vehicles for the conveyance of Scottish history, they will have cause to be grateful for the Simpsonian steam which has helped keep the traditional engine on track. And if Simpson has not been exactly a firebrand, there has always been a quiet passion, which, when a cause seems to demand it, can fuel a certain intransigence – to the surprise of friend and foe alike. The steam behind the spectacles, when it rises, does so almost imperceptibly: it is enough to make action determined, but not so overwhelming as to blur scholarly vision. We hope that, if the steam rises as Grant Simpson reads the following chapters – which we now present to all our readers, but to him in particular – it will not be because he feels they are unworthy of him.

# 2

# 1320 and A' That: The Declaration of Arbroath and the Remaking of Scottish History

*Terry Brotherstone and David Ditchburn*

When William's Abbey, noble pile,
Stood unsurpassed in Britain's isle,
When vows were ta'en within her wa's
To stand or fa' for freedom's cause –
When Bruce wore bonnie Scotland's crown
And knights and nobles thronged the toon,
'Twas then Arbrothock led the van
'Gainst England's might – Rome's impious ban.[1]

'A declaration I wasn't familiar with': as late in the day of British constitutional history as 23 November 1998, this remark about the Declaration of Arbroath was made by Jeremy Paxman – the well-known presenter, writer and commentator on the English nation.[2] Hosting a radio programme about topical cultural and scientific issues, Paxman quoted the famous passage in the Declaration on resistance to English rule (see page 11 below), suggesting that its citation in the new Museum of Scotland might still be taken as anti-English. The Declaration, responded Museum director Mark Jones, was there because it was 'one of the great constitutional documents of any country's history'. It also marked 'a moment when the Scots affirm their national identity', which, in the context of the fourteenth century, they necessarily had to do in opposition to the English.

The discussion moved on. Could museums be as important in Scotland as they had once been in the definition of national identity in (say) Czechoslovakia or Ireland? The Irish actress Fiona Shaw contributed a definition of museums as being 'about resolution', gatherings of 'the debris of our lives ... [which] should be held for a while until we can make sense of it'. In this chapter we ask: is Scotland yet making sense of a letter dated 6 April 1320 and sent in the name of thirty-nine barons to Pope John XXII in Avignon – the Declaration of Arbroath?

It is appropriate to deal with this topic here. First, the Declaration is a piece of 'debris' from the Middle Ages, which, a growing number of references in the 1990s suggest, can still play a part in contemporary political argument. Age-old events can have a practical resonance across the centuries, and this gives us a focus on the broader question: 'does medieval Scottish history really matter?'

1 A. T. Matthews, quoted in J. Brodie, *About Arbroath: The Birthplace of the Declaration of Scottish Independence – 1320* (Arbroath, 1904), 9.

2 To be precise, 9.25 a.m. (GMT) on Monday 23 November. Paxman was hosting *Start the Week* on the BBC's Radio 4. Over the previous decade or so he had established himself as one of the most acute and well informed of commentators, and penetrating of interviewers, in the British media. See too J. Paxman, *The English: Portrait of a Nation* (London, 1998).

Second, one of Grant Simpson's few forays into historical polemic concerned the 1320 Declaration. This encouraged us, in 1992, to organise in Aberdeen the seminar on the subject we refer to below, and which provided the initial inspiration for this chapter. Third, though we allude to this only briefly, questions about the ways in which medieval history does, or does not, matter took on new significance in the 1990s when a battle of 1389 – at Kosovo Polje – played a political role in the 'justification' of 'ethnic cleansing'. The chapter's three sections deal with the recent interest in the Declaration of Arbroath; with its fate at the hands of modern historians; and with some reflections on the use of such historical references in present-day political debate.

*

Every year thousands of tourists go to Edinburgh Castle, one of Britain's most popular attractions. Many visit a presentation about the Scottish monarchy which culminates in a holy of holies – a case containing the Honours (or crown jewels) of Scotland. These were stored away after the Union of Parliaments in 1707, and rediscovered by Sir Walter Scott and others in 1818. Alongside the Honours, there now lies the Stone of Destiny. This lump of sandstone is said to be the rock upon which the Scottish kings were enthroned until the 1290s (when Edward I took it to London as part of the spoils of war), and it has served at the coronation of British monarchs since 1603. The Stone was repatriated on the initiative of the Conservative government in November 1996 – an ingratiating act which failed to prevent the Tories' unprecedented Scottish electoral whitewash in the general election six months later.

At the entrance to the Honours, beside a reproduction of Cursiter's painting of Elizabeth II receiving the Scottish crown in 1953, a caption announces:

> The Stone remained under the Coronation Chair in Westminster Abbey for almost 700 years. In early 1951 the Stone was absent from the Abbey for four months following its theft on Christmas Eve 1950. It was returned to Scotland and surrendered to the authorities after being symbolically placed in Arbroath Abbey, the location of the 1320 Declaration of Arbroath. For many the inspiring words of that declaration of nationhood echo the spirit of the Stone's significance:
>
> *... for as long as but one hundred of us remain alive, never will we on any condition be brought under English rule. It is in truth not for glory, nor riches, nor honour, that we are fighting, but for freedom – for that alone, which no honest man gives up but with life itself ...*
>
> In 1996 Her Majesty Queen Elizabeth gave her consent to the Stone of Destiny's return to Scotland. The role of the Stone in coronations will continue, for the ancient seat of kingship will be borne to Westminster Abbey for all future ceremonies.

This simple statement, designed to aid tired tourists through a tale of kings and queens reveals, on reflection, some sophisticated political thinking.

It has several ingredients folded skilfully into an apparently smooth mixture which, on consumption, turns out to be rather lumpy. First, there is the history of the Stone of Destiny itself and the fact that, in 1950, it was considered worth stealing from Westminster Abbey as a political gesture.[3] That this was done by Scottish Nationalists is withheld, presumably because the caption is inviting visitors to endorse the political union of England and Scotland. This union, we may infer from the caption, is essentially a monarchical one, maintained today under the authority of a queen who graciously permits objects of national heritage to be displayed in Edinburgh or in London, as she sees fit. Like the 1999 Scottish Parliament itself, the Stone of Destiny, it is implied, has been 'devolved' to Scotland by the British monarch: it has not been repossessed by the Scots.

But for the purposes of this chapter the most interesting aspect of the statement is the way in which the association of the Stone with monarchy, and of its theft with Arbroath, are used to make today's British monarch into the protector of the 'freedom' for which the Scots are supposed to have been fighting in 1320. Yet for many – and notably those who stole the Stone in 1950 – the 'freedom' they seek is that of Scotland from England; and for others the feelings for 'freedom' that swell in the breast when they read the inspiring words of the Declaration relate to an aspiration for a democracy that would have no place for monarchy. To think about what the Declaration of Arbroath says in a context in which it is so publicly quoted is to recognise that this rather distinguished piece of historical 'debris' can disclose very different meanings.[4]

The constitutional reformers who campaigned for the new parliament opened in Edinburgh in 1999 made discreet references to the Declaration when they pointed out, in support of their more practical arguments, that Scotland's distinctive political identity has a long history.[5] Donald Dewar MP, later Scotland's first First Minister, commented in 1995 that its call not to submit to English dominion had considerable resonance 'in Nationalist quarters', but was also 'very familiar at least to those involved in the current constitutional debate'.[6] A more extraordinary political usage, however, came in the tabloid *Sun* newspaper. Its Scottish edition adopted a Nationalist marketing strategy in the early 1990s. On 6 April 1992, with a British general election in full swing, an editorial offered a history lesson. 'Exactly 672 years ago,' readers were informed, 'our nation proclaimed its independence to the world', and, '[l]ike the people of Scotland in 1320, we want to stand on our own two feet ... [and] take responsibility for our own affairs.' And then:

3 See I. R. Hamilton, *The Taking of the Stone of Destiny* (Moffat, 1991; London, 1992) – incorporating material from idem, *No Stone Unturned: The Story of the Stone of Destiny* (London, 1952). Hamilton, one of the political thieves of 1950–1, was amongst the honoured guests present when the queen's second son, Prince Andrew, returned the Stone in 1996.

4 Trade unionists attending a government reception in recognition of the centenary of the Scottish TUC were taken round the exhibit in 1997. Among them was Transport and General Workers' Union leader, Bill Morris, then in dispute with his own members in the Mersey docks over what they saw as his lack of commitment to their long fight for 'freedom' – freedom to have jobs with negotiated conditions, and to fight the unfreedom of over a decade of anti-Trade-Union legislation.

5 See, e.g., O. D. Edwards, ed., *A Claim of Right for Scotland* (Edinburgh, 1989), 3, 194.

6 D. Dewar to T. Brotherstone, 4 Jan. 1995. Dewar recalls a reproduction of the Declaration being in his home as a child; and that his grandfather was an office-bearer in the Scottish Patriotic Association.

> If the brave men gathered at Arbroath saw our country now, they would be horrified ... at the way we have transformed ourselves into a senile, second-class nation. There is no question about the way *they* would cast their vote ... They would ... vote for full independence ... [And as] men of vision ... [who] saw that the nations of Europe had to work in peace and harmony with each other ... they would be enthusiastic about continuing and developing our membership of the European Economic Community.[7]

This extraordinary convergence between the views of the barons of 1320 and the Scottish National Party in the 1990s was endorsed by Edinburgh's most famous son, the Hollywood star Sean Connery who urged the Scots to 'go for independence'. And five years later, at the general election which resulted in a 'new' Labour government at Westminster, committed to devolution, *Sun* readers in Scotland were told that Connery's 'greatest dream' was to read the Declaration of Arbroath at the opening of an independent Scottish parliament. He was not to be asked to do so when the devolved Parliament opened on 1 July 1999 (though he did attend saying it was the proudest day of his life); but he was in the meantime credited with being the only person to inject life into the referendum campaign which had endorsed devolution in September 1997. According to a press report the ninety-second-long intervention at an Edinburgh rally of the 'balding pensioner ... with the physical presence of a volcano' raised the 'roof, along with morale'. And Connery's text, the reader will have anticipated, was 'It is not for glory ... [that we fight] but for liberty alone'. It had been written 677 years ago, he remarked, adding 'I never knew that patience was a Scottish characteristic.'[8]

Meanwhile, Scotland's other international star, the comedian Billy Connolly – a scourge of Scottish nationalism – played a part not so much in the doubtful political use of the Declaration as in spreading misinformation about it. Arbroath, he told television viewers of his stand-up comedy tour is the home of:

> an ancient abbey ... where the Treaty of Arbroath was signed ... [And] Robert Bruce said that as long as a hundred men remained alive they wouldn't bow beneath the yoke of English domination.[9]

Three historical errors (not a treaty, not signed, and Robert I certainly not the acknowledged author of the statement) is a high score. Still, it was a good show.

Between 1992 and 1997, evidence grew that the 1320 Declaration meant something practical to politically engaged Scots. In November 1992, the novelist William McIlvanney quoted it when he addressed one of the largest demonstrations ever seen in Edinburgh – called to demand Home Rule.[10] And Lynda Sinclair of West Pilton, Edinburgh, wrote to the press in 1995:

> In a recent debate on the constitution of Scotland, George Robertson ... for Labour, and Jim Wallace, for the Liberal Democrats, said the Westminster

7 *The Sun*, Scottish edition, 6 Apr. 1992.

8 Ibid., Scottish edition, 28 Apr. 1997; *The Guardian*, 8 Sep. 1997.

9 For Connolly on Scottish nationalism, see, e.g., *The Sunday Herald*, 27 Jun. 1999. For Connolly on Arbroath, see his *World Tour of Scotland* (BBC Television, 1994), available on video.

10 Eyewitness testimony: the reference to 1320 was not widely picked up in the freedom-loving press.

> parliament is sovereign in Scotland. In fact the dispute over sovereignty was finally settled in the reign of Robert Bruce. It is enshrined in the Declaration of Arbroath, which was published inside and outside of Scotland, for all to know, that the Scottish people are sovereign and for all time, while even 100 of us remain alive! ... It is alarming that politicians do not know this ...[11]

She went on, to be sure, to argue that the doctrine of Westminster sovereignty was also contrary to modern ideas of electoral democracy, since the MPs who constitute 'Westminster' at any one time are transient creatures subject to the verdict of the voters. But it is clear from the linkage in her letter that Sinclair regarded the Declaration as part of the prehistory of real democracy, carried forward by the development of modern parliaments but yet to be achieved.

As the 1997 election approached, first use of the Declaration as a political weapon came from a different angle. The Conservatives' Scottish Secretary, Michael Forsyth, told an Arbroath audience that it was 'the definitive exposition of our Scottish identity', amounting to 'an early written constitution'. Other parties would fight the election on 'the constitutional question': Forsyth, in effect, argued that that question had been answered in 1320. Everything that had happened since – including the Union of 1707 – was therefore 'the product of our [the Scots'] history'. Writing in the Glasgow *Herald*, the historian and constitutionalist Owen Dudley Edwards replied that the idea that 'the Declaration ... was conceived as an election address' for John Major's Tory government deserved no more than the kind of giggle reserved for a stand-up comic so desperate for material that he resorts to quoting the pornographic tabloid, the *Sunday Sport*. And political scientist, Malcolm Dickson argued that, while it had been quite natural for the Scottish nobles, after Bannockburn, to claim Scottish sovereignty when appealing to the Pope to withdraw his support from the English king, 'the politics of the fourteenth century had nothing to do with a modern general election'. Forsyth attributed growing scepticism about the Union to deficiencies in knowledge of Scottish history. His real concern was saving the Tories' bacon in seats where the SNP was their main challenger, not raising historical consciousness.[12]

Nevertheless, there is an issue of general historical consciousness in all this. Most of the knowledge about the Declaration we have reported has the air of self-learning rather than the school curriculum. When we carried out an amateur survey of Grampian Region's schools in the mid-1990s, for example, only one was teaching any medieval history.[13] And, of thirty first-year pupils polled at two Dunfermline secondary schools, only one had heard of the Declaration, and

11 *The Scotsman*, 30 Oct. 1995.

12 *The Herald*, 31 Jan. 1997.

13 Survey conducted by Lesley Diack for the Department of History, University of Aberdeen, in March 1995. We are grateful to Mrs Diack for providing us with the results of her survey, which included responses from all secondary schools in Grampian Region. Things may, however, be changing: 'Wallace, Bruce and the Wars of Independence 1286–1328' is to be introduced at Elgin Academy in August 2000 – and no doubt elsewhere – at Intermediate levels 1 and 2 of the new 'Higher Still' syllabus. We owe this information to Fiona Malcolm.

s/he thought that it dated from the eleventh century.[14] Among Scotland's Westminster MPs of the mid-1990s, 35% of respondents to a questionnaire, most of them educated in Scotland and one with a degree in History, acknowledged that they had no clear conception of what the Declaration was and why it was made. Perhaps the surprising statistic is that 65% *did* know something about it.

Some of them learned their history at the end of the late-imperial period of (say) the 1920s to the 1950s. Whereas the usual complaint today is that school students learn little or no Scottish history, then, however crudely chauvinist (in both senses) the history taught, there was a perceived ideological imperative – at least at primary school level – to provide Scottish children with some kind of historical consciousness to explain both their separate historical identity from the English *and* the roots of imperial togetherness. The working-class militant Les Forster reports from his 1920s schooldays in Glasgow:

> vague memories of my Standard School History book. Up front, Robert the Bruce with his wee spider on the cave wall. The derring-do of William Wallace with his colossal sword. Much time was spent instructing our young minds on the wondrous glory of the British Empire [and] there was a chapter devoted to the missionaries, Mary Slessor of Calabar and David Livingstone of Blantyre. It was said they 'civilised' the cannibals, by spreading the Holy Word ...[15]

He mentions no instruction in the Declaration of Arbroath, which might have been far too incendiary for a rebellious young mind on 'Red Clydeside'. But Forster's historical education reflected the perception that *some* connecting links had to be provided to create a sense of Scottish identity, which could encompass both the wars of independence against the English *and* the background to the common slaughter of Scots and English (and Irish) at the Somme.

The late twentieth century in Britain has, in contrast, seen historical consciousness (the 'sense of history') discounted. History tends either to be adapted to the conservative needs of the heritage industry (exemplified in Edinburgh Castle's opportunistic linking of the Declaration of Arbroath to the authority of Queen Elizabeth II); or subordinated to training in 'transferable skills', thought 'useful' in the jobs market. Yet there are two detectable countertrends in which the Declaration of Arbroath has interesting parts to play. First, our evidence of a public sense of the importance of the Declaration suggests a popular idea of history as a politically enabling discourse that could come to challenge the historically ignorant ideologies of contemporary politics.

Second, even in official educational discourses, a theory of the importance of the Declaration exists. The 1990 report of the English National Curriculum History Working Group – in a section on the desirability of the study of the relationship between England and other parts of the British Isles in the Middle Ages – cited the Declaration specifically.[16] The chair of that working party, in

14 We are grateful to Joan Davidson, Jim Pennel, and pupils of Queen Anne High School and Woodmill High School for taking part in the survey.

15 L. Forster, *Rocking the Boat: Memoirs of a Glasgow Socialist and Whistleblower* (Glasgow, 1995), 13.

16 *National Curriculum History Working Group: Final Report* (Dept. of Education and Science, 1990), 60–1. Such idealism, however, was soon lost beneath the fear, reinforced by a survey by

defending its non-anglocentric approach, suggested that if ethnic minorities 'are to be taught that the British identity is made up of a number of individual cultures, it might be easier for them to accept that they are part of this multi-cultural evolution rather than standing outside it'.[17] If, in other words, the Scots were allowed their own antecedents to the aspiration for a community of free citizens in the British Isles – one to be set alongside an English history in which Magna Carta still plays its part – then all those subsequently recruited to this aspiration, whether Afro-Caribbean, Asian or whatever, could see better how both to retain their own history, *and* to be part of the larger identity and *its* history.

The notion that study of the Declaration of Arbroath could play this reconciliatory national role is analogous to the function Fiona Shaw ascribed to museums. But it was not picked up on by our surveyed Scottish MPs, not least, perhaps, because, even amongst those who claimed to know about the Declaration, most had no theory about *why* it matters. Yet, of those who responded, nearly all thought that the Declaration should form part of the history curriculum in Scottish schools, some wanting it to be compulsory. Most agreed it would be desirable for everyone in the United Kingdom to learn something about it.[18] And half the respondents, including all the Nationalists but also some of the Conservatives (perhaps prefiguring Michael Forsyth's 1997 speech), believed that, even if they did not quite know in what way, the Declaration matters not just for itself but also because of its potential to shape political attitudes today.

There is a relatively widespread perception, then, that the 1320 Declaration is of current relevance, not just of historical interest. In 1977 Grant Simpson, in an article we return to below, commented on the evidence of public interest during the previous decade. The Declaration's 650th anniversary, he observed, was celebrated with pageants, poems, popular histories and a postage stamp.[19] But there had also been some more political references, even if nothing quite to compare with those of the 1990s. In 1968, for example, the 1320 Club – a new organisation of radical nationalists (shunned by the Scottish National Party) – had the poet Hugh MacDiarmid speak on 1320 and other matters, prior to its publication, in 1970, of an *Outline of a Scottish Constitution*.[20] The Liberal MP David Steel was historically deliberate in his choice of 8 April 1970 to introduce a parliamentary bill 'to provide for the better government of Scotland'.[21] But the 650th celebrations, commented Simpson wearily, tended to be 'sadly divorced from scholarship'.[22] The political 'revitalising' (Simpson's word) of the Declaration

the magazine *History Today*, xlix(7) (Jul. 1999), that students leave school knowing little history except Stalin and Hitler. Perhaps there is more hope in Scotland: see note 13 above.

17 Letter from the NCC history working party chair to the authors.

18 We are grateful to the MPs who took the time in 1995 to reply to our questionnaire.

19 E.g. D. Morrison, *Sterk Vision: A Poem for the 650th Anniversary of the Declaration of Arbroath* (Edinburgh, 1970); J. Prebble, *The Lion in the North: A Personal View of Scotland's History* (London, 1971), esp. 112–14. The Scottish Record Office published a facsimile of the Declaration; and pageants, taking the Declaration as their theme, were staged at Arbroath every two years from 1947 to the 1960s. Proposals for a one-off school holiday were turned down.

20 H. MacDiarmid, *A Political Speech* (Edinburgh, 1972); *An Outline of a Scottish Constitution* (2nd edn, The 1320 Club, 1970).

21 *Parliamentary Debates (Hansard)*, 5th ser., 799 (1969–70), cols. 551–4.

22 G. G. Simpson, 'The Declaration of Arbroath revitalised', *SHR*, lvi (1977), 12.

in the context of the much-promised, more participative 'new Scottish politics' of the twenty-first century, it is arguable, calls for a more robust academic response.

The Berlin Wall that once separated professional history-writing in Scotland from the comfortable, self-sustaining myths that passed for popular history and nurtured the tourist trade has been substantially eroded, if not torn down. With regard to the Declaration of Arbroath, for example, there have been real efforts to popularise scholars' ideas about it. Geoffrey Barrow's interpretation is seen on the video at Arbroath Abbey and was published in the commercially successful *Sunday Mail Story of Scotland*.[23] Alexander Grant's contribution informed the Channel Four television series *The Making of Britain*; and E. J. Cowan's account enlivened Magnus Magnusson's *Tales of a Grandfather* radio history.[24] Accounts of the Declaration are also in the more serious popular histories, notably John Prebble's *The Lion in the North*, a station bookstall favourite.[25] Elsewhere, however, one finds not so much alternative interpretations as a void: in the still much-sold (though about to be replaced) Penguin *History of Scotland* by J. D. Mackie, for example, there is only one short reference.[26] And guidebooks, even the scholarly ones, vary greatly with regard to the Declaration, both as to facts and interpretation: an amusing short article could be written about the confusion awaiting an earnest traveller who seeks clarification by comparing a selection.[27] In contrast to the Barrow video at Arbroath, moreover, the National Trust for Scotland, at least in its *Bannockburn* illustrated guide, gives up entirely on historical interpretation. The Declaration, it pronounces, is 'probably the most important document in Scottish history'. But then nothing is said to explain why; and the silence is filled with a visual image from the on-site tableau, which shows a noble *signing* the Declaration with a quill pen (rather than affixing his seal).[28] Such is often the way with 'heritage' presentations. Visitors are given the illusion that they have witnessed history. What they have seen is neither accurate, nor remotely challenging to the historical imagination.

23 G. W. S. Barrow, 'The fight for freedom', *The Story of Scotland* (Glasgow, 1988), i, 123–5.

24 A. Grant, 'The Triumph of Scotland', televised on Channel 4, 24 Feb. 1985; cf. L. M. Smith, ed., *The Making of Britain: The Middle Ages* (Basingstoke, 1985), 76–7. E. J. Cowan, in 'Tales of a Grandfather', broadcast on BBC Radio Scotland, 9 Nov. 1998. Sir Walter Scott's *Tales of a Grandfather*, written for children, has nothing to say about the Declaration of Arbroath; but see our conclusion. In a *Scotland on Sunday* article (27 Jun. 1999) on 'historic moments' in the Scottish past, Cowan mentioned the Declaration but did not prioritise its importance before a number of other events. He eschewed any temptation to make a link between the 'freedom' fought for in 1320 and the 'democracy' hoped for in 1999.

25 Prebble, *Lion in the North*, 112–14.

26 J. D. Mackie, *A History of Scotland* (Harmondsworth, 1964), 83. Even the most fastidious scholars, moreover, can err in writing about the Declaration. William Ferguson, in his ambitious *The Identity of the Scottish Nation: A Historic Quest* (Edinburgh, 1998), 41–3, leaves the impression that it was despatched to Rome, not Avignon. And Brotherstone and Ditchburn, over-eager to make a point, wrote in an earlier draft of this chapter that it was not mentioned in the Saltire Society publication, R. Mitchison, ed., *Why Scottish History Matters* (Edinburgh 1991, new edn 1997). It is, on p. 20 (1991 edn), as the author, Sandy Grant, tactfully pointed out. Grant there implies that the 1320 Declaration should be studied by Scots at least as seriously as the Great Charter of 1215 is by the English.

27 One Automobile Association guide, published in 1988, managed to have more errors in it than another, published four years earlier. See *Illustrated Guide to Britain's Coast* (London, 1984), 195; and *Places to Visit in Britain* (London, 1988), 418.

28 National Trust for Scotland, *Bannockburn* (edn current in 1999, Edinburgh, n.d.), 6.

The achievement, in terms of informing public perception, then, is variable. More important still, the lack of encouragement for people to see history as a disputatious discipline requiring thought and not the mere absorption of facts and images remains widespread. The way in which this can be obscured in popularly available sources is perhaps best made by referring to two much-read books – the journalist-historian Andrew Marr's *The Battle for Scotland* and the historian-journalist Christopher Harvie's *Scotland and Nationalism*.

For Marr, the Declaration was 'a sophisticated act of international diplomacy by the aristocracy and church leadership', which proves nothing about why the lost, dumb-to-history schiltroms of Scottish spear-carriers fought at Bannockburn'.[29] Harvie, however, pronounces that the late thirteenth-century English invasion 'made patriots of the mass of the [Scottish] people', generating 'a type of popular nationalism rare before the French Revolution'; and he writes about the Declaration in this context.[30] In one version, the Declaration is a nationalist document of profound significance; in another, it says nothing that might make modern citizens feel a sense of continuity with the fourteenth century. If readers are to draw useful conclusions for themselves, there needs to be some explicit engagement between the rival approaches.

An extreme example of opinion presented as unchallenged truth before a wide audience came at the Edinburgh Festival in 1991 when Robert Silver's play *The Bruce* – to which we refer below – was performed. The perpetrator was not the playwright but the Scottish Nationalist commentator on matters historical and literary, P. H. Scott. In a programme note, he claimed as though it were incontrovertible, not only that the events depicted in the play established Scotland's nationhood, but also that they were important to the world because:

> the Declaration of Arbroath ... was the first assertion of two great principles ... the value of freedom from foreign domination ... [and] the revolutionary idea that sovereignty rests not with a king or a ruler, but with the people themselves.[31]

There is an interesting case to be argued for this point of view, but the problem is that no argument is thought necessary. Scott here exemplifies a historical – or rather ahistorical – method which must be overcome if the Declaration is indeed seriously to enter contemporary debate.

Our light-hearted chapter heading alludes to Burns's chorus 'A man's a man for a' that'; and to the 1930s satire on the history of England's rise and decline as 'top nation', *1066 and All That* by W. C. Sellar and R. J. Yeatman. We refer later to Burns. Sellar and Yeatman did not mention the Declaration in their account of how the Scots cheated the English by exploiting their sense of 'fair play' and turning up at Bannockburn with the weaker team.[32] But in a recent cartoon-history *Scotland for Beginners*, Jeff Fallow does. After Bannockburn, he writes:

29 A. Marr, *The Battle for Scotland* (London, 1992), 11–13.

30 C. Harvie, *Scotland and Nationalism: Scottish Society And Politics, 1707 to the Present* (3rd edn, London, 1998), 8–9.

31 Edinburgh International Festival, 1991, programme for *The Bruce*, 21–2.

32 W. C. Sellar and R. J. Yeatman, *1066 and All That* (paperback edn, London, 1975), 41–5.

> A declaration of independence – the DECLARATION OF ARBROATH – was ... drawn up and signed by Scotland's barons in 1320, for submission to and acceptance by the Pope. To paraphrase it generally states that:
>
> *We have chosen our Prince, Robert, to be our sovereign king ... but should he give up what we have begun and agree to make our kingdom subject to the English, we shall exert ourselves at once to drive him out and choose another king ...*
>
> (This shows an early, if limited, form of democracy, comparable with England's Magna Carta, subjecting the power of the king to that of his followers.)[33]

Here the 1320 letter becomes not simply a baronial declaration of independence from England (as in the nineteenth-century doggerel we began with): it sets the Scots on the road to democracy. We shall return to this idea when we come to ask if 1320 can be seen as a Caledonian 1776.

*

Grant Simpson's 1977 article, asking if 'anything conceivably new [could] be said about a document so well known in Scotland as the Declaration of Arbroath?', provides a useful vantage point from which to view Declaration scholarship.[34] Scholars of the 1960s and early 1970s arguably did more to advance diplomatic analysis and understanding of the Declaration than any generation since that which, after a long sixteenth-century silence, 'rediscovered' the letter in the 1680s.[35] The document was retranslated both by Sir James Fergusson and by A. A. M. Duncan, while Simpson (a critic of the amateurish aspects of Fergusson's scholarship) produced an authoritative analysis of the relationship between the Declaration, earlier drafts of it and later copies. Others concentrated on the significance of the Declaration. The textual and scholarly analysis of this period showed three widely held – and still often repeated – assumptions to be at best uncertain.[36]

Whoever wrote the document, it had been pointed out in the 1940s, knew

33 J. Fallow, *Scotland for Beginners* (New York and London, 1999), 36. On Magna Carta in the history of democracy, see J. C. Holt, *Magna Carta* (2nd edn, Cambridge, 1992), 1–22; and cf. R. Nicholson, 'Magna Carta and the Declaration of Arbroath', *University of Edinburgh Journal*, xii (1965), 140–4.

34 Simpson, 'Declaration of Arbroath revitalised', 11–33.

35 The Declaration was rarely quoted in subsequent constitutional disputes, though several 15th-century writers obtained copies of it: see *Copiale Prioratus Sanctiandree: The Letter-book of James Haldenstone*, ed. J. H. Baxter (London, 1930), 17–18; *Chron. Bower* (Watt), vii, 4–9, 165–6; and *Liber Pluscardensis*, ed. F. H. Skene (Edinburgh, 1877–80), i, 201–5; 252–5. On the significance of this, see D. E. R. Watt, 'A national treasure? The *Scotichronicon* of Walter Bower', *SHR*, lxxvi (1997), 51. For the Declaration's history from the mid-15th until the late 16th centuries, see B. Webster, 'The Declaration of Arbroath and Scottish national identity', *Medieval History*, iii (1993), 162–3.

36 Barrow, *Bruce* (1st edn 1965; 2nd edn 1976; 3rd edn 1988); A. A. M. Duncan, 'The making of the Declaration of Arbroath', in D. A. Bullough and R. L. Storey, eds., *The Study of Medieval Records: Essays in Honour of Kathleen Major* (Oxford, 1971), 174–88; A. A. M. Duncan, *The Nation of Scots and the Declaration of Arbroath* (Historical Association, 1970); J. Fergusson, *The Declaration of Arbroath* (Edinburgh, 1970); R. Nicholson, 'Magna Carta and the Declaration of Arbroath' (1965); Nicholson, *Scotland* (1974). In addition, E. J. Cowan delivered a paper on the Declaration to the Conference of Scottish Medieval Historical Research in January 1975, which formed the basis of his 'Identity, freedom and the Declaration of Arbroath', in D. Broun, R. J. Finlay and M. Lynch, eds., *Image and Identity: The Making and Re-making of Scotland through the Ages* (Edinburgh, 1998), 38–68.

Sallust's *History of the Catiline Conspiracy* and the Vulgate well and adapted quotations from them into the Latin prose rhythms (*ars dictaminus*) favoured by the papal chancery.[37] He (it was certainly a man) was also familiar with political theory, notably the twelfth-century arguments of John of Salisbury.[38] He was, then, a learned man, generally thought to be Robert I's chancellor, Abbot Bernard of Arbroath. But Simpson insisted that we do not actually know this. It could not simply be assumed that an important officer of state 'sat down and sharpened his quill when a particularly important text had to be produced'. Nor did the evidence we have of Bernard's literary style unequivocally support the case for his authorship. Simpson made more than previous commentators of a rambling poem ascribed to the abbot in Bower's fifteenth-century *Scotichronicon*.[39] Could the same quill have produced a rhetorical *tour de force* and an indifferent poem?

If the Declaration was not so assuredly Bernard's work, neither was it quite so completely of Arbroath, nor, indeed, of 6 April 1320. Duncan had analysed the parchment and seals preserved on the Scottish Record Office's copy of the letter and, setting this against his knowledge of contemporary royal government, had shown that the gathering of barons at Arbroath probably never happened. Rather, he suggested, the decision to send the Declaration to Pope John was taken at a council held at Newbattle, near Edinburgh, in March 1320. The text would then have been drafted at the royal chancery in Arbroath, and, probably over a period of weeks, seals would have been sent, or brought personally to be affixed to the document. It followed that the date of the Declaration was purely nominal; and, since the letter did not arrive in Avignon until some time between 16 June and 29 July, it is unlikely that it was dispatched from Scotland before late April.[40]

There has been little academic dispute over the conclusions drawn from such text-centred analyses, though they do not always seem to have been taken on board in the wider discussion. But greater controversy has surrounded the Declaration's political and constitutional significance. One group of scholars, following Andrew Lang's work of 1900, has viewed the Declaration as an evocative expression of Scottish nationalism. For Lang the Declaration sounded, 'perhaps for the first time in many centuries, the classic note of national freedom'.[41] By the 1970s this thesis had been refined, with nationalism seen more as a cause of the Wars of Independence and the Declaration rather than as their consequence. For

37 J. R. Philip, 'Sallust and the Declaration of Arbroath', *SHR*, xxvi (1947), 75–8; T. M. Cooper, 'The Declaration of Arbroath revisited', in idem, *Super Crepidam* (London, 1951), 48–59. See also the letters published in *The Times Literary Supplement* of 9 Jun., 23 Jun., 30 Jun. 1945 and 12 Oct. 1946.

38 Cowan, 'Identity, freedom and the Declaration of Arbroath', 46, 49–50.

39 Simpson, 'Declaration of Arbroath revitalised', 25–6; *Chron. Bower* (Watt), vi, 360–5.

40 Duncan, 'Making of the Declaration of Arbroath', 187; Simpson, 'Declaration of Arbroath revitalised', 19–21.

41 A. Lang, *A History of Scotland from the Roman Occupation* (Edinburgh, 1900–7), i, 230. Of Lang's near contemporaries, Tytler and Hume Brown offer matter-of-fact comments on the Declaration, but Hill Burton considered it 'illustrious among the utterings of national wrongs and appeals for national mercy and justice': P. F. Tytler, *History of Scotland* (3rd edn, Edinburgh, 1845), 332–4; P. Hume Brown, *History of Scotland* (Cambridge, 1899), 164; J. Hill Burton, *The History of Scotland* (Edinburgh, 1905), ii, 283.

William Ferguson the Declaration marked 'the product of a burgeoning nationalism'[42] – a conclusion endorsed in the same author's more recent work referred to above. Geoffrey Barrow, Robert I's biographer, thought that there was 'no clearer statement of Scottish nationalism and patriotism in the fourteenth century' and 'no finer statement of a claim to national independence ... provided in the period anywhere in Europe'.[43] And Ranald Nicholson – who had previously asserted that 'nineteenth-century historians and some of the present century as well were all too prone to see evidence of nationalism in the Scotland of Robert Bruce'[44] – was later converted to the view that the Declaration was 'the most impressive manifesto of nationalism that medieval Europe produced'.[45] In the decade in which the Scottish National Party made its first major strides into Westminster politics, what we may call 'the nationalist school' of the Declaration of Arbroath was in the ascendant.

Dissent was represented, above all, by Duncan and Simpson. Each acknowledged the nationalist sentiment in the Declaration, but neither dwelt on it. Rather than criticise the nationalist school directly, Duncan set a different agenda. He – with Simpson following a similar line – was more concerned with the diplomatic context of the Declaration. Enraged at the blatant disregard Robert I had shown for papal envoys, papal messages and papally imposed truces, John XXII had issued a barrage of threatening bulls against the Scots in 1319 and 1320. A response was needed. Its form (the Declaration) followed a conventional thirteenth-century pattern of a baronial letter to the Pope. Similar, if less rhetorically polished examples, had previously been sent to the *curia* by French, English and (in 1317) Irish barons. For Duncan and Simpson, the Declaration was, primarily, a pragmatic response to a pressing diplomatic difficulty. It was also, since it purported to represent the views of anonymous freeholders as well as barons, an indication of change in the fabric of Scottish society, spawned by the years of warfare with England. These freeholders were the 'middling folk' who, Duncan argued, rose to new prominence by mustering support for William Wallace and Andrew Murray in 1297. Relating this development to the Declaration's grand statements on freedom, it was, in Duncan's words, for 'freedom from [personal] unfreedom' that these men fought.[46]

There were then two opposed views, or at least significant differences of emphasis. It was all too typical of Scottish historiography, however, that the clarifying possibilities of open polemic – between those who interpreted the Declaration's references to freedom in terms of national liberation and those for whom what was important was the idea of being personally free – were avoided. Nicholson, to be sure, argued that both concepts were present in the Declaration – but this merely added a third possibility rather than resolving the dispute.[47]

42 W. Ferguson, *Scotland's Relations with England: A Survey to 1707* (Edinburgh, 1977), 28; idem, *Identity of the Scottish Nation*, 41–3.

43 Barrow, *Bruce* (2nd edn), 430.

44 Nicholson, 'Magna Carta and the Declaration of Arbroath', 142.

45 Nicholson, *Scotland*, 101.

46 Duncan, *Nation of Scots and the Declaration of Arbroath*, 32; Simpson, 'Declaration of Arbroath revitalised', 31–3.

47 Nicholson, *Scotland*, 100.

Disagreements *were* aired, however, about the Declaration's constitutional significance. The discussion revolved around one key passage:

> Yet if he [Robert I] should give up what he has begun ... we [the authors] should exert ourselves at once to drive him out as our enemy and a subverter of his own rights and ours and make some other man who was able to defend us our King.

If this is taken at face value, it is easy to see whence came the now popular notion that the Scottish kings derived their right to rule from 'the people'.[48] Barrow's more circumspect but apparently similar interpretation suggested that the passage implied 'the essence of a theory underlying the community of the realm' and 'a clear statement of the constitutional relationship between the king and the community', but he did not spell out the precise nature of this relationship.[49] And others have disagreed. Nicholson (before his Pauline conversion), thought that this argument mistook 'an emotive appeal abounding in hyperbole for a workaday constitutional treatise'. Simpson held that, in so far as the contentious passage was not just propaganda, it merely stated the conventional view - expounded by John of Salisbury - that action could be taken against an unjust monarch.[50]

Since Simpson's 1977 article appeared, an early draft of the Declaration has been published and translated; the Declaration itself has been translated into Gaelic, Scots and Russian; and it has appeared on the world-wide web.[51] Efforts to place the Declaration in its international intellectual context have also advanced. Cowan, for instance, has shown that the author was familiar not only with Sallust and John of Salisbury, but probably also with Thomas Aquinas and John of Paris.[52] It has been noted too that the Declaration's comparison of the plight of the Scots with that of Judas Maccabeus in the Old Testament has similarities with descriptions of Boleslaw of Poland in the early twelfth century, and of King Wenzel of Bohemia, the Teutonic Order and the inhabitants of Ghent in the fourteenth. The passages adapted from Sallust were also used by Wipo in the eleventh century.[53] Similarly, recent work has compared the Declaration's origin-of-the-Scots legend not only with other legends (from which it differs), but also with mythical lineages found elsewhere in the medieval west.[54] All this may

48 Prebble, *Lion in the North*, 114.

49 Barrow, *Bruce* (2nd edn), 426, 428.

50 Nicholson, *Scotland*, 101; Simpson, 'Declaration of Arbroath revitalised', 30–1.

51 *Chron. Bower* (Watt), vii, 4–9; J. Adam, *The Declaration of Arbroath* (Arbroath, 1993), 14–23; D. Fedosov, 'The Arbroath Declaration of Scottish independence, AD 1320', *Srednie Veka*, lii (1989), 398. Further English translations appear on the following world-wide-web sites. All begin http://www/, followed by: angus.gov.uk/history/decind.htm; angusanddundee.co.uk/fill/index.htm; freescotland.com/decl-arb.htm; geo.ed.ac.uk/home/scotland/arbroath.html; home.clara.net/rabpert/declarat.html

52 Cowan, 'Identity, freedom and the Declaration of Arbroath', 57–8.

53 F. Graus, 'Historische Traditionen über Juden in Spätmittelalter (Mitteleuropa)', in A. Haverkamp, ed., *Zur Geschichte der Juden im Deutschland des Späten Mittelalters und der Frühen Neuzeit* (Stuttgart, 1981), 11; S. Reynolds, *Kingdoms and Communities in Western Europe*, 900–1300 (Oxford, 1984), 293 n. 107.

54 Scottish origin legends are discussed in detail by D. Brown, 'The Scottish Origin-Legend before Fordun' (University of Edinburgh, unpublished PhD thesis, 1988); D. Broun, *The Irish Identity of the Kingdom of the Scots in the Twelfth and Thirteenth Centuries* (Woodbridge, 1999); idem,

question the originality of the Declaration's author. But it reinforces his erudite reputation, and places the Declaration more firmly in the mainstream of contemporary European scholarship. Who the author was remains uncertain. Two new candidates are Alexander Kinninmonth, who delivered the letter to Avignon, and Walter Twynholm, who succeeded Abbot Bernard as chancellor; though Bernard's claims have not been conclusively disproved.[55]

The internationalising of discussion about the Declaration has not, of itself, resolved the debate about its political significance. The nationalist school has drawn some succour from origin-legend analysts. Susan Reynolds argues that 'the myths of the common origins of a people serve to increase its sense of solidarity', and more particularly that the Declaration

> must have been intended to appeal to values and emotions current at the time: the Scottish royal officials who drafted the letter presumably thought that ideas of collective political independence based on a single collective ancestry would seem convincing.[56]

On this basis, it might be argued that evidence of attempts to invent a 'national history' is of itself evidence of the presence of a sense of nationhood or even 'nationalism'. But, against that, Reynolds herself carefully avoids the use of the words 'national' and 'nationalism' in favour of the concept of 'regnal solidarity'. Like Nicholson in his earlier mode and others, she has doubts regarding the propriety of 'nationalism' in a medieval context.

Barrow, on the other hand, has analysed contemporary usage of the word 'freedom', and concludes by rejecting the Duncan–Simpson proposition that this implied primarily personal freedom. He reasserts that it is the freedom of the nation that is being referred to, noting that others, too, detect 'nationalism' in the fourteenth century.[57] With regard to the letter sent by the Irish barons to the Pope in 1317, for example, J. A. Watt cannot find 'any word more accurate than nationalism to describe the principles and emotions in the remonstrance'.[58] The claim of the nationalist school, however, hangs not merely on showing that the Declaration can be described as in some sense 'nationalist', but requires us to

'Defining Scotland and the Scots before the War of Independence', in Broun *et al.*, *Image and Identity*, 4–17; E. J. Cowan, 'Myth and identity in early medieval Scotland', *SHR*, lxiii (1984), 111–35. See also R. J. Goldstein, *The Matter of Scotland* (Lincoln, Neb., 1993), 90–3; S. Reynolds, 'Medieval *Origines Gentium* and the community of the realm', *History*, lxviii (1983), 375–90.

55 G. W. S. Barrow, *Robert the Bruce and the Scottish Identity* (Saltire Soc., 1984), 22–3; idem., *Bruce* (3rd edn), 308; Goldstein, *Matter of Scotland*, 315, reporting A. A. M. Duncan's suggestion of Twynholm. On the careers of Kinninmonth and Twynholm see D. E. R. Watt, *A Biographical Dictionary of Scottish Graduates to AD 1410* (Oxford, 1977), 301–3, 549–50. Sandy Grant tells us he is unconvinced by the arguments against Abbot Bernard as at least the principal author; he points out that medieval chancellors had to write speeches for opening parliaments, and reckons that they are unlikely to have been any more overburdened with routine chores than are heads of History Departments nowadays.

56 Reynolds, 'Medieval *Origines Gentium*', 375, 386.

57 G. W. S. Barrow, 'The idea of freedom in late medieval Scotland', *IR*, xxx (1979), 16–34.

58 J. A. Watt, 'Gaelic polity and cultural identity', in A. Cosgrove, ed., *A New History of Ireland*, vol. II: *Medieval Ireland 1169–1534* (Dublin, 1987), 350. The Irish letter is published in *Chron. Bower* (Watt), vi, 384–403, and is discussed in J. R. S. Phillips, 'The Irish Remonstrance of 1317: an international perspective', *Irish Historical Studies*, cvi (1990), 112–29. On medieval nationalism see the excellent article by K. J. Stringer cited in note 80, below.

be convinced that its grandiloquence makes it a uniquely significant statement of medieval nationalism. Barrow's verdict on documents roughly contemporaneous with the Declaration, and of a supposedly cognate nature, is that the Irish remonstrance is 'lengthy and prolix', and that the 1291 *Bundesbrief* of Uri, Schwyz and Nidwalden is 'sturdy but somewhat stodgy'.[59] The latter in any case is a letter of the forest cantons in 1291 which says nothing of Swiss independence – a point which at the same time questions its relevance to the argument but also supports Barrow's view that there were few, if any, contemporary documents directly comparable to the Declaration.[60]

There has been no major response from the historians sceptical about the concept of 'medieval nationalism', who, moreover, have never fully spelt out their own reasons for downplaying the strongly held feelings of 'Scottishness' which – it is clear from other contemporary sources – existed in 1320 and before. Grounds for a critique of the nationalist view which deserve more exploration have, however, emerged. In 1306–7 Robert I dispatched an appeal for assistance to the Irish chieftains.[61] Seeking Irish aid, the king was at such pains to stress the common Scottish-Irish heritage that he referred to a single Scottish-Irish nation. His letter can be written off as apiece of pure political expediency but, if not,[62] the sentiments in the 1306–7 letter may be interpreted as in line with the idea of some Irish historians that Gaelic Ireland and Gaelic Scotland shared a sense of common identity. If so, this has some implications for the argument that there was an instrumental concept of *Scottish national* identity in the fourteenth century, though the very existence of a Scottish kingdom, and the growing amnesia of some thirteenth-century Scots regarding their Irish origins provide some ammunition for a counter-argument.[63]

The letter to the Irish did not claim (as the Declaration did) to express the views of the barons, freeholders and the whole community of the realm of Scotland: the king was credited with its authorship. Yet, the extent to which the Declaration itself expressed anything more than the prejudices or stylistic hyperbole of the royal clerks and the king has been challenged anew by Duncan. If, as he argued in 1970, the Declaration was drafted in the royal chancery, away from the hullabaloo of a representative assembly, then it could be argued, as he did in 1992, that 'there is a fair possibility that the content of

59 Barrow, 'Idea of freedom', 26–7.

60 Swiss historians are divided as to whether the 1291 pact was a *Landfriedensbündnis* or an alliance against the Habsburgs: *Handbuch der Schweizer Geschichte* (Zurich, 1980), i, 180–2, esp. n. 62. Neither interpretation seems analogous to the Scottish situation.

61 *RRS*, v, no. 564. The dating we adopt is that suggested by S. Duffy, 'The Bruce brothers and the Irish Sea world, 1306–29', *Cambridge Medieval Celtic Studies*, xxi (1991), 64–5.

62 Reynolds warns against 'that curious historical cynicism – almost a sort of inverted naïveté – which is determined not to take any statement of feeling or principle at its face value': 'Medieval *Origines Gentium*', 385–6.

63 E.g. Duffy, 'Bruce brothers and the Irish Sea world', 58–9; idem, 'Medieval Scotland and Ireland: overcoming the amnesia', *History Ireland*, vii(3) (1999), 17–21; S. G. Ellis, 'Nationalist historiography and the English and Gaelic worlds in the late Middle Ages', *Irish Historical Studies*, xxv (1986), 7–8. See also K. Nicholls, 'Celtic contrasts: Ireland and Scotland', *History Ireland*, vii(3) (1999), 22–6; and, for the counter-argument, D. Broun, 'The birth of Scottish identity', *SHR*, lxxvi (1997), 4–22.

the document was not known to the baronage who appeared as its authors'.[64] Where then the high-spirited nationalism of the community of the realm?

Duncan's argument also has implications for those who would read the Declaration as a prototype constitutional treatise. If the community was unaware of the Declaration's content, then the passage which threatened the king with deposition may be nothing more than the rhetoric of royal clerks – endorsed, therefore, by the king himself. This, moreover, *might* explain three rather critical points. First, the Declaration was never explicitly used to justify aristocratic rebellions against the crown in the later medieval period. Second, no explicitly contractual relationship between the crown and the political community – of the sort which did find expression, for example, in the medieval kingdom of Aragon – is to be found in medieval Scotland.[65] And, third, although many of the arguments expounded in the Declaration were elaborated upon by the Scottish delegation during the negotiations held with English representatives at Bamburgh in 1321, the crucial passage regarding the removal of the king was dropped.[66] For the benefit of a distant Pope, the king was apparently willingly to promote the idea that his office was contractual, but he did not want to broadcast such a notion in front of his own representatives and English adversaries.

R. J. Goldstein's critique of the controversial 'constitutional' passage is different. It refers, he argues, to a king unable to perform that fundamental regal duty of defending the realm. *Rex inutilis* is a sobriquet which, in the terminology of Bruce propaganda, might have been applied to King John (Balliol). The Declaration's failure to mention John by name has often been noted, but it is surprising that Goldstein was the first to suggest in print that John is indeed present in all *but* name. If the passage refers to him, then, far from offering a constitutional statement, it might be taken as nothing more than a justification for Robert's seizure of power and the deposition of John. With their eyes set on the past rather than the future, it is doubtful 'that the king and his clerks fully realised how radical the letter's theory might sound to later observers'.[67]

The arguments advanced by the 'constitutional sceptics' seem to require of the 'enthusiasts' that they show both that the community did know the contents of the Declaration, and that the controversial passage does not simply refer to John's deposition. Some have subtly shifted their ground. Barrow, for example, has amended his earlier reference equating the Declaration with a clear statement of the constitutional relationship between the king and the community, by substituting 'mutual' for 'constitutional'.[68] Others simply reassert earlier claims.

64 A. A. M. Duncan, 'The War of the Scots, 1306–23', *Transactions of the Royal Historical Society*, 6th ser., ii (1992), 130–1. A similar point is implied in C. McNamee, *The Wars of the Bruces: Scotland, England and Ireland, 1306–1328* (Edinburgh, 1997), 235.

65 A. MacKay, *Spain in the Middle Ages: From Frontier to Empire 1000–1500* (London, 1977), 104–17.

66 P. A. Linehan, 'A fourteenth-century history of Anglo-Scottish relations in a Spanish manuscript', *Bulletin of the Institute of Historical Research*, xlviii (1975), 106–22. We are grateful to Sandy Grant for this reference.

67 Goldstein, *Matter of Scotland*, 95–7. See also Grant, 'Aspects of national consciousness in medieval Scotland', in C. Bjørn, A. Grant and K. J. Stringer, eds., *Nations, Nationalism and Patriotism in the European Past* (Copenhagen, 1994), 70, 73. Note, however, that Goldstein's argument ignores the grammar of the passage in question, which explicitly refers to Robert I and his successors.

68 Barrow, *Bruce* (2nd edn), 428; idem, *Bruce* (3rd edn), 308.

Matthew MacDiarmid describes the relationship between king and community as 'in brief, nation first and kings in right of the nation'. More eccentrically he concludes that vague 'concepts of nature and the ancient free nation prevailed over merely feudal notions of the kingly function' to the point that the Scottish king was no more than a Guardian.[69] Few historians would go so far, though Norman Reid has come close. For him the community of the realm's self-reliance through the minorities of Alexander III and Margaret, and then 'the nightmare scenario of dynastic collapse' and Edward I's intervention, resulted in the king becoming 'marginalised': increasingly 'he became the servant of the kingdom, the one appointed to guide and safeguard it, through the wielding of the royal dignity which had been bestowed upon him through election and inauguration by the community'.[70] These arguments can only be sustained if the objections of the sceptics are confronted. This MacDiarmid and Reid scarcely do.[71]

Grant, indeed, is almost alone in *engaging* with the constitutional sceptics. Although the Declaration was not (so far as we know) referred to in the arguments of the 1350s and 1360s regarding the royal succession, Grant points out that echoes of it can be heard in the staunch resistance which David II then encountered as he attempted to nominate an English successor. The failure of the king's plans lends support to Grant's view that a 'nationalist theory of popular sovereignty' had developed in the aftermath of 1320.[72] Indeed, it was unnecessary, one might argue, for the Declaration to be quoted chapter and verse in the 1350s or thereafter, because its logic had been accepted by the vast majority of the political community.

E. J. Cowan has further reinforced the potential for a debate – which might stretch from the seminar room to the public arena to mutual benefit. In a recent article he makes a lively restatement of the Declaration's claim to be 'the supreme articulation of Scottish nationhood and constitutionalism'.[73] But by his stress on reading the document as political theory, he also raises new questions – perhaps returning to the spirit of the discourse of the 1940s. The 'legacy of Arbroath', Cowan argues, 'survived in a distinguishable, and distinguished, Scottish political tradition', which was also influenced by 'the inspirational legend of William Wallace'.[74]

Cowan sensibly avoids reference to the 1995 Oscar-winning movie *Braveheart* and its Scottish reception, which veered between the seriously farcical (the aforementioned Michael Forsyth attending the première in, for public purposes

69 M. P. McDiarmid, 'The kingship of the Scots in their writers', *Scottish Literary Journal*, vi (1979), 7–8.

70 N. H. Reid, 'Crown and community under Robert I', in A. Grant and K. J. Stringer, eds., *Medieval Scotland: Crown, Lordship and Community. Essays Presented to G. W. S. Barrow* (Edinburgh, 1993), 208.

71 Their footnotes, indeed, are relatively innocent of references to other points of view.

72 *Knighton's Chronicle 1337–1396*, ed. G. H. Martin (Oxford, 1995), 120–3; A. Grant, *Independence and Nationhood: Scotland 1306–1469* (London, 1984), 30–1. For an at times contrary view of the succession dispute, see A. A. M. Duncan, '*Honi soit qui mal y pense*: David II and Edward III, 1346–52' *SHR*, lxvii (1988), 113–41; idem, ed., 'A question about the succession, 1364', in *Scottish History Society Miscellany XII* (SHS, 1994), 1–57.

73 Cowan, 'Identity, freedom and the Declaration of Arbroath', 39.

74 Ibid, 62–3.

at least, an unprecedented kilt) and the potentially tragic (some of the anglophobic audience reactions observed and commented on internationally).[75] Yet, read in the light of 'Braveheartiness', Cowan's comments suggest the need for clarification of this medieval/early modern political tradition. If there was such a tradition, why was its 'supreme articulation' so little referred to? If the tradition did indeed exist, was it distinguishably *Scottish* (as opposed to *not English*)? And what was its longer-term outcome? The concept of 'medieval nationalism' in Scotland is given much of its vigour by the implication that it relates to some form of nationalism today. But is it actually being suggested that a direct line can be recognised between the nationalism and constitutionalism of the Middle Ages and modern politics? And, if so, can the influence of this tradition – in a Scotland transformed by the Reformation, three centuries of the Union, industrialisation, and globalisation, and by struggles for class, gender and racial equality – still be unproblematically 'distinguished' in Cowan's approbatory sense of the word?

*

At the 1992 Aberdeen seminar we referred to in our introduction Barrow and Simpson rehearsed their views about the 1320 Declaration. Differences were elegantly clarified in a way which demonstrated to some neutral observers at least that the arguments probably cannot be resolved purely on the basis of historical evidence. Perhaps the most significant contribution made by the Aberdeen discussion, indeed, was the intellectual context provided for the main exchange by an American historian, Ferenc Szasz, and the playwright, Robert Silver. Szasz spoke about a less controversially important document, the US Declaration of Independence of 1776. Silver's subject was the relevance of the 1320 Declaration to a politically concerned Scottish dramatist in the twentieth century.[76]

Szasz started with Abraham Lincoln. In 1863 Lincoln famously declared at Gettysburg that '[f]our score and seven years ago, our forefathers brought forth upon this continent a new nation, conceived in liberty and dedicated to the proposition that all men are created equal'. Spoken after one of the bloodiest of Civil War battles, Lincoln's words had little impact at the time, but later entered into the sustaining political rhetoric of the USA. Most obviously, this was because of the conclusion which called for devotion to 'a new birth of freedom' to protect 'government of the people, by the people, for the people' – a phrase often optimistically taken to define western democracy. Szasz argued that Lincoln's first sentence was significant too. One part of it in particular was new.

When Americans had spoken of the concept of human equality as enunciated by the Founding Fathers, they had not customarily used the term: 'dedicated to the proposition that ...' This phrase, argued Szasz, took the 1776 Declaration into the realm of Euclidean geometry. It began from the 'self-evident' truths that men are born equal and have the right to 'life, liberty and the pursuit of happiness', but by making this a Euclidean *proposition*, Lincoln changed its

75 See, e.g., *Newsweek* magazine, 16 Oct. 1995, 31.

76 Szasz's publications include *The Divided Mind of Protestant America, 1880–1930* (Alabama, 1982); and *British Scientists and the Manhattan Project: The Los Alamos Years* (Basingstoke, 1992). Silver (1913–97) was Professor of Mechanical Engineering at Glasgow University from 1967 to 1979.

nature into something to be actively *proved* rather than accepted passively. The self-evidence of the truths of 1776 could no longer simply be taken as read: they required constant reaffirmation. New tasks faced the nation, requiring not new principles, but a new use of old ones. The Declaration of Independence, through Lincoln, had passed one of the key tests for a piece of grand political rhetoric if it is to be of continuing historic significance. Its continuity had been preserved but it had shown itself capable of being redefined for a new period.

Szasz also alluded to the lack of evidence for the notion that the Founding Fathers had the 1320 Declaration in mind when drafting their own. This is more relevant than it might seem in the light of a line of thinking which holds: first, there is a tradition of 'freedom' and popular sovereignty in Scotland (of which the 1320 letter is an early manifestation); second, Scots played a part in drawing up the 1776 Declaration; and, third, it can therefore be inferred that the Scots tradition influenced the later event. 'Scotland's loss has become America's gain,' said Benjamin Franklin of John Witherspoon, a signatory of the 1776 Declaration. And this is glossed by Andrew Lockhart Walker, with the comment that Witherspoon's 'secure niche' in the history of 1776 is 'not totally surprising when one recalls the Scottish constitutional tradition, enshrined in the Declaration of Arbroath ... that the King rules by popular will and for the good of the people'.[77] Provocative speculations of this nature, if they are to be taken seriously, need to be subject to historical critique.

Silver spoke about his play, *The Bruce*, which, written in the late 1940s, had received its first full production at the Edinburgh Festival of 1991.[78] The play, said Silver, had been written when he had great hopes, embodied in the United Nations, for a peace based on mutual respect amongst nations of a manageable size. The struggle in early fourteenth-century Scotland seemed to provide a historical basis for a discussion of such a vision. Whatever they might have meant in the fourteenth century, the words of the Declaration of Arbroath seemed inspirational in a world caught between World War II and the Cold War. That Silver was not alone in this view may be deduced from the fact that it was in this period that the first steps were taken towards bringing the study of the Declaration of Arbroath under the scrutiny of modern scholarship. Silver's modest excitement centred on the hope that renewed interest in his play in the early 1990s might herald a revival of principles of international relations on which, in the 1940s, he had pinned his faith. Subsequent events in the former Yugoslavia cannot have increased his optimism about the fulfilment of such a political programme. But the questions he was trying to raise by historical analogy did prove relevant to the mainstream agenda of the 1990s – more so indeed than in the 1950s.

This provides the occasion briefly to pick up on our introductory allusion to the Kosova (or Kosovo) crisis. Noel Malcolm's recent history, *Kosovo*, shows that the historian's striving for accuracy and the debunking of myth can still involve life-and-death questions. No one, so far as we know, has recently killed,

77 A. L. Walker, *The Revival of the Democratic Intellect* (Edinburgh, 1994), 74.

78 R. Silver, *The Bruce: Robert I King of Scotland* (Edinburgh, 1986); or as *The Hert o' Scotland: A Play* (Aberdeen, 1995). The Declaration is not directly quoted in the play.

or been killed, as a result of a political outlook which pivots around an interpretation of events in fourteenth-century Scotland; and, on that basis, it may sensibly be argued that the medieval history of the British Isles matters less than medieval Balkan history, though here we cannot resist an aside about Ireland. On the Newtonards Road in Protestant Belfast (witnessed in 1996 and in 1999) – and no doubt elsewhere – a street-painting incorporates the following words:

> For as long as one hundred of us remain alive we shall never consent to submit to the rule of the Irish for it is not for glory that we fight but for freedom alone which no man loses but with his life.

While this is a use of history scarcely to be blamed on the Scottish barons of pre-reformed Christendom, it is one which the more promiscuous Scottish Nationalist flirters with the Declaration of Arbroath might perhaps ponder. But our point about Malcolm is more serious. His work is not only an exemplar of high standards of empirical accuracy and fair-mindedness in a particularly tense situation. It also serves to promote a discussion about approaches to history more generally. For Malcolm is not a historian for whom scholarship is a way of life divorced from current issues. He is both committed to the cause of political justice for the Albanian Kosovars and a 'good historian'. Indeed, arguably the objectivity of his history depends on this commitment.[79]

Our point, then, is not that we should draw direct comparisons between Scotland and Kosova – or Northern Ireland. We are not issuing a sensational warning of future 'ethnic' conflict between Scots and English if scholars fail to clarify Scottish medieval history. What we are suggesting is that medieval Scottish history not only matters: it matters enough for it to be discussed in a more open and committed way. We showed at the outset that interpretation of the Declaration of Arbroath is an issue in the public arena; but that an account of perceptions of what it meant, and means now, creates if not a confusion, then certainly a kaleidoscope of ideas. The Declaration can be made to endorse monarchy and to prefigure republican democracy; to define Scottish nationalism and to help reconcile a multi-ethnic Britain. It can serve a turn for a floundering Unionist politician and even embellish the Loyalist cause in Northern Ireland. It can be so important that an international festival audience is informed that it is the fount of all constitutional and revolutionary theory; and it can be so contextualised by historians and journalists that it has no contemporary significance at all. To the extent that what Grant Simpson called the sad 'divorce' between scholarship and public perception plays a part in this, it is worth redoubling efforts to overcome it, not because professional historians have all the answers, but because they could help clarify some of the questions.

Scholarly work on text and context will continue to produce new insights. But broadening the nature of the discussion is at least as important. Lord Cooper sought to do so when he wrote enthusiastically about the Declaration in the 1940s; and Cowan, in the article referred to above, advocates a return to this approach.

79 N. Malcolm, *Kosovo: A Short History* (London, 1998; new edn, 1999).

In this discourse, the ringing rhetoric of 1320 is not merely a point of interest, but the main reason to read the document and debate its ongoing relevance in political theory. But Cooper addressed a limited audience, though one which obviously included Silver, through whose play a certain continuity from the 1940s to the 1990s was created. In the meantime the work of scholars has tended to be very specific and separated from the clarifying possibilities of a more explicitly political discussion. But it is not only to the pupils of Barrow, Duncan and Simpson (and Cowan, Grant and others) that the 'storm over Arbroath' (so far meteorologically a rather minor affair) is of interest. It matters also to citizens involved in the 'new Scottish politics' – be they heritage-site visitors, Connery or Connolly fans, Festival playgoers, or *Sun* readers.

We draw no authoritative conclusions. The Declaration of Arbroath provides a focus for a lively discussion of history and its uses in twenty-first-century Scotland. But the 1320 letter cannot be said so far to have passed the test Szasz applied to the Declaration of 1776: it has been forgotten about too often for too long, and is remembered now too inconsistently, to be the 'Euclidean' proposition with which Scotland's political future is bound up. If it is indeed evidence of something we can meaningfully call 'nationalism' in medieval Scotland, that only opens up the question of what relationship medieval nationalism may have to the nationalism of later centuries.[80] If its talk of 'freedom' still resonates, that is proof of the power of its rhetoric drawn from a broader European culture, not that 'the Scots' as a whole and for all time have some particular claim on the concept. Yet the Declaration's rhetorical resonance is real enough, and those who have revived interest in the Declaration – whether in the 1680s or in the twentieth century – have done so at times when some argument about the nature of political freedom was on the agenda.

There could be many suggestions for 'further research'. One byway – perhaps a highway – not explored in our historiographical peregrinations is that of the political and theoretical considerations which brought about the Declaration's 'rediscovery' in the later seventeenth century. This might also serve to clarify the role of the Declaration both in the Whig interpretation of Scottish history and in Scottish legal history.[81] Another project might be to chart the Declaration's fate in the early struggles for a modern democracy. It would be fascinating to discover a nineteenth-century plebeian tradition of devotion to the rhetoric of

[80] The relationship is discussed in K. J. Stringer, 'Social and political communities in European history: some reflections on recent studies', in Bjørn *et al.*, *Nations, Nationalism and Patriotism*, 9–34.

[81] The former matter is alluded to in C. Kidd, *Subverting Scotland: Scottish Whig Historians and the Creation of an Anglo-Scottish Identity, 1689–c.1830* (Cambridge, 1993), 28–9; but both the rediscovery and the role of lawyers in it (in the 17th century and later) might benefit from further investigation. On the latter, N. McCormick, in P. H. Scott, ed., *Scotland: A Concise Cultural History* (Edinburgh, 1993), 348, in the chapter on 'Law', simply asserts that, 'In relation to the constitutional aspect of the totality of legal relations, one must recall the powerful rhetoric of the Declaration ... repeated in various forms time after time since by spokespersons for Scottish constitutionalism.' T. B. Smith, *Scotland: The Development of its Laws and Constitution* (London, 1962), 50, called the Declaration 'Scotland's most important ancient constitutional document', but did not elaborate. Donald Dewar, also a lawyer, in the letter quoted on page 12 above, also recalled the relevance of the Declaration to the case raised by John McCormick during the controversy over the royal title (Elizabeth *II*) in the 1950s, another matter we have not been able to explore further on this occasion.

1320, but notwithstanding the interesting reference in John Galt's novel *Ringan Gilhaize*, this seems unlikely.[82] In 1920 the Clydeside internationalist, John Maclean asked in his article on 'The Irish Tragedy', 'Why did I visit Arbroath on Saturday, 11 September?' But his answer, though political, was pragmatic in its reference to the Declaration. He was protesting against:

> the hollow mockery of the sex-centenary [*sic*] celebration of the Scottish Parliament's declaration of independence to Pope John XXII, whilst Scottish boys dressed in the garb of the English government were ... daring the Irish to set up a free and independent Irish Parliament elected by the overwhelming vote of the Irish people.[83]

In the name of political balance, we return to the late Enlightenment and two Scots almost as famous as Sean Connery. Robert Burns, whose 'A man's a man for a' that' has less problematic democratic (though not, perhaps, feminist) credentials than has the Declaration of Arbroath, was inspired, if not by the events of 1320, then at least by the story of Wallace. 'This,' he wrote, 'poured a Scottish prejudice in my vein which will boil there till the flood-gates of life shut in eternal rest.'[84] And Sir Walter Scott, Tory and antiquarian, made, an interestingly historical judgement about the Declaration itself. It was, he wrote:

> a spirited manifesto or memorial, in which a strong sense and a manly spirit of freedom are mixed with arguments suited to the ignorance of the age ... Having astounded, as they doubtless conceived, the pontiff with the nation's claim to antiquity, of which the Scots have been at all times more than sufficiently tenacious, they proceeded in a noble tone of independence ...[85]

A right note, perhaps, on which to end. This chapter set out to provide some entertainment as a warm-up for the main programme of *Freedom and Authority*. It acquired its own more serious purpose from the observation that a turning-point in political history – if that is what the new Scottish Parliament signals – is a moment at which the aspiration of professional historians to inform an unprejudiced public can acquire added importance and impetus. By drawing attention to the range of ideas current about the 1320 Declaration – from Paxmanite ignorance to Nationalist hyperbole – we have suggested that it is an important subject for attention.[86] This survey of recent historiography provides a possible starting-point.[87]

82 J. Galt, *Ringan Gilhaize or the Covenanters* (1823), ed. P. G. Wilson (Edinburgh, 1984), 244, 324–7.

83 *The Vanguard*, Nov. 1920; N. Milton, ed., *John Maclean – In the Rapids of Revolution: Essays, Articles and Letters, 1902–23* (London, 1978), 180. Our thanks to James D. Young for the reminder about this reference.

84 For Burns, democracy and 'Scottishness', see, *inter alia*, T. Crawford, *Boswell, Burns and the French Revolution* (Edinburgh, 1990). For Burns on Wallace, see the reference in P. H. Scott, *An Unwon Cause: An Anthology* ... (Edinburgh, 1997), 7. In this book, Scott's historical method is particularly transparent.

85 Walter Scott, *The History of Scotland* (1st edn, 1828; Philadelphia, 1830), i, 138.

86 The aspiration for a historically literate discourse relevant to contemporary culture and politics is evidenced in magazines like *Cencrastus* and *Scotlands*. On the Declaration of Arbroath, see, e.g., C. Kidd, 'The canon of patriotic landmarks in Scottish history', *Scotlands*, i (1994), 1–26.

87 Our thanks are due to Sandy Grant and Duncan Forbes for their comments on two different drafts, and their rather different warnings. They bear no responsibility for our final product.

# 3

# Gold into Lead?
# The State of Early Medieval Scottish History

*Richard D. Oram*

Like Scotland itself in 1286, research on the period before the Wars of Independence appears to face a bleak future. We stand at a historical crossroads. This is not solely a consequence of the retirement of the leading academic figures in the field. It is a situation which has beckoned for many years as changes in the secondary education system influence new generations of university students. To compound the problems, advances in general medieval studies question the constructs and paradigms upon which most interpretations of medieval Scottish society are founded.[1] Each of these factors by itself would have a major impact: together they represent a formidable challenge when the subject is scarcely capable of response. This is not too pessimistic a note. Research on Scotland before the fourteenth century in the Scottish universities is atrophying. Furthermore, with no full-time lecturer in twelfth- and thirteenth-century studies at any of the Scottish universities, a reversal of that trend appears unlikely. It is not too extreme to claim that Scottish history – at least that of the twelfth and thirteenth centuries – again faces a 'strange death'.[2]

Marinell Ash's account of the 'strange death' of Scottish history in the late nineteenth century holds a bitter irony at present.[3] After three decades of growth we risk losing all that has been gained as no new generation of research students emerges to build upon past achievements. The current trend towards development of post-1300 – or more particularly post-1500 – postgraduate research is compounding the problem, for the next generation of research supervisors lies in the present postgraduate community. Whilst there are encouraging signs for the early and later medieval periods, the prognosis for the central middle ages is gloomy. In retrospect, this situation can be attributed to inherent flaws in the system which generated the great advance in scholarship over the last thirty years.

Historiography has travelled far since the 1900s when Lawrie and Anderson produced sourcebooks of charters and annals, thereby stimulating textual criticism which had languished since the demise of the Sir Walter Scott-inspired historical publishing clubs.[4] The study of medieval Scottish history remained,

[1] E.g. E. A. R. Brown, 'The tyranny of a construct: feudalism and historians of medieval Europe', *American Historical Review*, lxxix (1974), 1063–88; S. Reynolds, *Fiefs and Vassals: The Medieval Evidence Reinterpreted* (Oxford, 1994).

[2] The scarcity of entries for Scottish topics falling into the 1100–1300 period in the Institute of Historical Research's lists of theses in progress underscores this point.

[3] M. Ash, *The Strange Death of Scottish History* (Edinburgh, 1980).

[4] A. C. Lawrie, *Early Scottish Charters* (1905); A. O. Anderson, *Scottish Annals from English Chroniclers AD500 to 1286* (London, 1908); idem, *Early Sources of Scottish History AD500–1286* (Edinburgh, 1922).

however, introspective and isolationist and, down to the 1950s, the little work which was published was largely a 'succession of historical kailyards'.[5] This trend was broken in 1956 by the publication of Geoffrey Barrow's *Feudal Britain*.[6] Although not Scottish history *per se*, *Feudal Britain* represented the first successful attempt to escape the kailyard and move into a wider British context and relevance. By dismantling spatial barriers which compartmentalised the component parts of Britain, just as temporal barriers between 'medieval' and 'modern' were being eroded by contemporary research, Barrow demonstrated that developments in one area of these islands could impact on other, far-removed areas. The approach was hardly new: Patrick Tytler had used English sources to elucidate Scottish circumstances as long ago as the 1830s.[7] What was different was that *Feudal Britain*'s general survey of the British Isles took an integrationist approach which moved beyond older, one-dimensional histories of Scotland.

Yet, the publication of *Feudal Britain* proved to be a false dawn for Scottish historiography. Unremarkable by today's standards, its approach was revolutionary for its time, and in an academic world dominated by exponents of traditional, compartmentalised medieval history it made few converts. Indeed, it was not until the 1980s that its pioneering outlook was re-adopted by historians of the twelfth and thirteenth centuries in any significant way. The result was that in the component parts of the British Isles, historians were 'happy enough to cultivate their gardens in isolation' and rarely crossed boundaries to keep abreast of current developments or explore areas of mutual historical contact other than where 'foreign' evidence supported their own theses.[8] Such selectivity of approach led merely to the cultivation of more kailyards.

In part the failure of *Feudal Britain* was due to its author, who subsequently abandoned his synthetic approach to medieval Scottish studies. Whilst Barrow can hardly be labelled isolationist, there was a singular failure to inculcate the broad perspective of *Feudal Britain* within the Scottish universities. Moreover, Barrow himself moved away from the broad-brush approach to 'British' history which made *Feudal Britain* outstanding. However, the still-birth of this first attempt since 1521 to produce 'a genuinely even-handed study of medieval Britain' must be counterbalanced against the revolution in Scottish historiography underway by the 1960s.[9] This produced a radical remodelling of Scottish medieval historical research and the formulation of the principal paradigms which were to govern the subject into the early 1990s. Whilst the opportunity was lost to break the moulds into which were set the four respective national histories, the sacrifice of a distinctively Scottish contribution to 'British History' saw instead a revitalisation and redirection of Scottish medieval studies.

5 Ash, *Strange Death of Scottish History*, 152.

6 G. W. S. Barrow, *Feudal Britain: The Completion of the Medieval Kingdoms, 1066–1314* (London, 1956).

7 Ash, *Strange Death of Scottish History*, 100–15.

8 R. Frame, *The Political Development of the British Isles 1100–1400* (Oxford, 1990), 1.

9 A. Grant and K. J. Stringer, eds., *Medieval Scotland: Crown, Lordship and Community* (Edinburgh, 1993), p. xiv.

Central to this was a revival in charter scholarship. Many primary sources had been published before 1914 but had received minimal editorial treatment. Moreover, with the exception of monastic cartularies published by the historical clubs, most printed sources comprised later medieval and early modern material. New research into the pre-1300 period required provision of soundly edited sources as a basic tool. This regeneration of documentary analysis underpinned the pioneering work of the 'new wave' of scholars – Barrow, A. A. M. Duncan, Grant Simpson and their fellows – and represented the first significant advance since Anderson and Lawrie. The focus for this initiative lay in the *Regesta Regum Scottorum* series, the first two volumes of which were both edited by Barrow.[10] The project had a profound impact on the evolving historiography of the period and the scholarship which underpinned these volumes confirmed the twelfth and thirteenth centuries as Barrow's fief, within which few others presumed to tread.[11]

The principal development from this charter scholarship was the formulation of the 'Barrovian' thesis of the 'feudalisation' of Scotland. Barrow used his familiarity with the charter evidence to examine land-holding based on hereditary tenures, and to elaborate his earlier research on military aspects of the system which developed after 1124. Barrow saw knight-service and the provision of the personnel to perform that obligation as central to the colonising venture which accompanied the introduction of the new tenures. The impact of Anglo-Norman colonisation after *c.*1100 had been explored before, most notably by R. L. G. Ritchie, but the weight of documentary research behind the essays which prefaced the *Acts of Malcolm IV* produced *prima facie* evidence for the scale of the transformation wrought by these incomers and their royal patrons.[12] Backed by the fruits of the new scholarship, arguments for the construction of a 'feudal system' and a sea change in the structure of society could be advanced with confidence: 'Feudal Scotland' became the central tenet of the new historiography.

Given the enormous influence which this thesis gained, it is surprising that Barrow did not publish a monograph articulating his ideas on the subject until the 1980s. Instead, the origin of the 'Barrovian' thesis lay in essays, such as 'The earls of Fife in the twelfth century'; and its more sophisticated exposition first appeared in 'The beginnings of feudalism in Scotland' – published in the same year as *Feudal Britain*.[13] The introductions to the first two volumes of the *Regesta* presented the thesis as it pertained to the reigns of Malcolm IV and William; and publication of a collection of earlier essays in 1973 brought together disparate strands which came the nearest yet to an articulation of the construct of Scottish military feudalism.[14] It was not, however, until publication of *The Anglo-Norman Era in Scottish History* and *Kingship and Unity* that the

10 *RRS*, vols. I and II.

11 See the comments in Duncan, *Kingdom*, 651–2.

12 R. L. G. Ritchie, *The Normans in Scotland* (Edinburgh, 1954).

13 G. W. S. Barrow, 'The earls of Fife in the twelfth century', *PSAS*, lxxxvii (1952–3), 51–62; G. W. S. Barrow, 'The beginnings of feudalism in Scotland', *Bulletin of the Institute of Historical Research*, xxix (1956), 1–31.

14 G. W. S. Barrow, *The Kingdom of the Scots: Government, Church and Society from the Eleventh to the Fourteenth Century* (London, 1973).

mature thesis was presented.[15] While, however, *The Anglo-Norman Era in Scottish History* was a masterly exposition of charter scholarship, it is in *Kingship and Unity* that the governing principles of the theory of the 'feudalisation' of Scotland are expounded in a tightly argued and deceptively simple presentation.

In both volumes Barrow re-staked his 'British history' credentials through an exploration of English (and French) contributions to the development of Scotland. One important theme which emerged in *The Anglo-Norman Era* was the equation of the Scots common law with the contemporary system in England. From this developed the argument that the 'feudal' society expounded in Scottish legal treatises such as *Regiam Majestatem* was directly modelled on the 'classic feudal' institutions established in England after 1066.[16] England was the intermediary through which the 'continental, west European phenomenon' of military feudalism reached Scotland, and it was a wholesale importation of an already highly evolved system.[17] What the Scots imported (along with the colonists to put it into practice) transformed the relationship between a ruler and his greater nobles from one which depended upon traditional exercise of his kingly role, into one which emphasised the proprietary controls governing relationships between landlords and tenants.

The depth to which this thesis penetrated the consciousness of researchers is testimony to the presentational skill of its proponent. 'Barrovian' feudalism – particularly the military aspects of the system which were seen as having strengthened the Scottish crown – lies at the heart of most general histories of Scotland produced between about 1970 and 1990; and it influenced a host of other work which took the 'feudalisation' of Scottish society as a pivotal theme.[18] Moreover, the social reconstructionalism which is an inevitable concomitant of such theoretical constructs imbedded itself deeply in the consciousness of archaeologists.[19] An alien system founded upon the principle of grants of land to foreign colonists in return for service, imposed on Scotland from above by its kings, is a convenient model for explaining the appearance of new phenomena in the archaeological landscape.

Cogent though this construct was, it did not meet with universal acceptance. Before the articulation of the mature thesis, Duncan advanced alternative

15 G. W. S. Barrow, *The Anglo-Norman Era in Scottish History* (Oxford, 1980); G. W. S. Barrow, *Kingship and Unity: Scotland 1000–1306* (London, 1981).

16 T. M. Cooper, ed., *Regiam Majestatem and Quoniam Attachiamenta* (Stair Society, 1947); Barrow, *Anglo-Norman Era*, 118–20. See also H. L. MacQueen, *Common Law and Feudal Society in Medieval Scotland* (Edinburgh, 1993); and idem, 'Canon law, custom and legislation: law in the reign of Alexander II', in R. D. Oram, ed., *Scotland in the Reign of Alexander II* (forthcoming).

17 Barrow, *Kingship and Unity*, 43–4.

18 E.g. R. Mitchison, *A History of Scotland* (London, 1970), esp. ch. 2. More recent work, such as R. A. McDonald's *Kingdom of the Isles: Scotland's Western Seaboard, c.1100–c.1336* (East Linton, 1997) takes a Barrovian line to explain the relationship between Somerled and the Scots in terms of an 'anti-feudal' reaction by a Celtic traditionalist.

19 The influence of basic theories of the feudalisation of Scottish society on archaeological studies of aristocratic settlement can be seen in, e.g., C. J. Tabraham, 'Norman settlement in Upper Clydesdale: recent archaeological fieldwork', *TDGAS*, liii (1977–8), 114–28; idem, 'Norman settlement in Galloway: recent fieldwork in the Stewartry', in D. Breeze, ed., *Studies in Scottish Antiquity* (Edinburgh, 1984), 87–124; P. A. Yeoman *et al.*, 'Excavations at Castlehill of Strachan, 1980–81', *PSAS*, cxiv (1984), 315–64.

interpretations of feudalism in the central Middle Ages. These questioned the basis of relationships between lords and men, which Barrow considered dependent on tenure. Wrestling with indications that property was transferred by sale or by gift, Duncan argued that relationships based on tenure (central to Barrow's thesis) were coincidental to, rather than dependent on, mutual bonds of obligation arising from such tenure. To him, the relationship stemmed from the power and status of the lord and the fact that the knight's lands lay within the territorial sphere of his influence.[20] In effect, Duncan challenged the tidy 'feudal pyramid' which the charter scholarship of the new historiography appeared to reveal, questioning the idea of the neat system of tenure and service, which the formulaic recitation of the documents had fossilised. Where a feudal system existed it was as a mere fig leaf to cover the blushing modesty of a reality far removed from the Barrovian ideal. 'It existed,' wrote Duncan, 'as a form to enable two basic kinds of transaction to take place: sale of land outright, and irredeemable loan of land at a fixed rate of interest, the feu duty.'[21] The charters, viewed as evidence for the spread of feudalism and of the practical workings of the hierarchy of tenures, could now be dismissed as legal safeguards for the respective interests of donors (or vendors) and recipients (or purchasers). The proliferation of secular documentation after about 1170 was neither an accident of survival, nor evidence for an acceleration of knight-service infeftments. It was, instead, a symptom of the increasingly easy alienation of land and the need to record transactions in a form which preserved the spirit of the donor's or vendor's intentions.

It is an irony of charter-based historiography of the period from 1100 to 1300 that such opposed views should spring from different analyses of the same evidence. The root of the differences, however, as revealed to great effect by Grant Simpson in his unpublished study of mainly thirteenth-century non-eleemosynary grants (presented to the Conference of Scottish Medieval Historical Research at Pitlochry in January 1986) lies in the skewing of the evidence marshalled by Barrow. Simpson demonstrated the pitfalls of concentration on the *acta* of the topmost strata of society which moved in a rarefied atmosphere of feudal purity, pointing instead to the parchment records of activity at lower levels amongst individuals directly touched by a messy reality on the ground. His was not a world where feus and knight-service predominated, but rather one in which money governed the relationships between men.

Arguments concerning relationships between lords and men in the 'new' kingdom which emerged after 1124 are more blurred than might be expected after thirty years of research. Indeed, there is a widening gulf between Barrow and his opponents, rather than any convergence of views. Nevertheless, it remains a debate where little heat and less light has been generated with which either to fire the enthusiasm of students or to illuminate them; and this despite the centrality which the understanding of lordship, the means of its exercise, and the structure of relationships between sorts of men holds not just for studies in pre-Wars of Independence Scotland, but for the whole of the medieval and early

20 Duncan, *Kingdom*, 407–8.
21 Ibid., 408.

modern periods. Feudalism has become, as Jenny Wormald observed, a wall of uncertain composition which obscures understanding of what preceded it and also of what followed.[22] The wall of polite silence which greeted Grant Simpson in 1986, and the apparent rejection of Duncan's reappraisal of the evidence, means that 'Barrovian feudalism' still, apparently, holds the ring in Scotland. Sooner or later, however, its adherents will have to engage with Susan Reynolds's monumental assault on the orthodox ideas about European feudalism.

Unconsciously interlinked with arguments for social transformation through the introduction of 'off-the-peg' feudalism runs acceptance of continuity from the pre-feudal past. There is no conflict between these two strands, for they combined to form the hybrid construct which was medieval Scottish society. Nevertheless, there was little attempt to quantify the scale or significance of the contribution which 'continuity' made to the whole.[23] It is a paradox of this peculiar situation that while there was no question in the minds of scholars that what was being recorded in the mid-twelfth century was change, there was no significant effort to determine the nature of the earlier structures which were experiencing that transformation. In part, the charter-based nature of the scholarship militated against such examination, for the documents furnish *prima facie* evidence for widespread innovation but only residual traces of continuity.

Despite efforts to set evidence for novelty alongside that for continuity, much analysis has merely emphasised that the pre-feudal past was transformed. It has avoided wrestling with the problem of how old and new were accommodated together.[24] This reflected an implicit view that in areas that mattered, although old and new intermingled, it was the new that was dominant and allowed Scotland to escape the limitations of the Celtic past.[25] The tunnel vision of the new charter scholarship, dealing as it was with the raw evidence for change, produced still greater marginalisation of arguments for continuity. This is manifest in the first volume of the *Regesta* series, where brief commentaries on native traditions are submerged by detailed analysis of the new mechanisms which evolved, conveying the image of an abandonment of earlier forms in a scramble to 'modernise'.[26]

The historical uncertainties of the pre-'feudal' past remained unexplored ground until the later 1970s. Stimulus for this stemmed from two major studies of early medieval Scotland by Marjorie Anderson and, more relevant in the present context, by John Bannerman.[27] Concerned essentially with pre-Kenneth MacAlpin Argyll, Bannerman's essays, and particularly his detailed study of the *Senchus fer nAlban*, offered insight into social structures in the unified Scoto-Pictish kingdom. This appeared in synthetic form in *The Making of the Kingdom*, but the telling comments made there against the conventional view of the years 1058 to 1124 as a transitional period between the Celtic past are blunted by the

22 J. Wormald, *Lords and Men in Scotland: Bonds of Manrent, 1442–1603* (Edinburgh, 1985), 10.

23 Barrow, *Feudal Britain*, 224.

24 Ibid., 134, 143; Barrow, *Anglo-Norman Era*, 84–6.

25 Barrow, *Feudal Britain*, 224.

26 *RRS*, i, 27–56.

27 M. O. Anderson, *Kings and Kingship in Early Scotland* (Edinburgh, 1973); J. Bannerman, *Studies in the History of Dalriada* (Edinburgh, 1974).

narrative.[28] The conclusion, that 'it may be doubted whether the innovations read into meagre evidence were important either in quantity or quality or, indeed, whether many of them took place in this period at all', heightens the image of dichotomy between the reigns of David I and his predecessors.[29] While Edgar and Alexander I may have been 'content with the framework of the old Scottish state' and the structures inherited from it, that old Scottish state still ends symbolically with consideration of the two kings at the close of Duncan's sixth chapter.

For Duncan and Barrow the reign of David I constituted the moment of change to a brave new world dominated by Anglo-Norman influences.[30] This outlook in Barrow's work in particular cannot be attributed to distortion by his feudal spectacles, for quite simply he was exploring the positive imagery of the new world preserved within the parchment record, rather than the negative reflection of the old. For example, in 'The pattern of lordship and feudal settlement in Cumbria', twelfth-century lordships were projected against a background of Celtic continuity.[31] 'Badenoch and Strathspey, 1130–1312' took a similar approach, where analysis of the 'feudalisation' of the region produced a masterly display of his ability to draw out the evidence from a fragmentary record.[32] Discussion of native continuity, prefaced by the comment that 'in spite of lordships, fiefs and castles much of the *ancien régime* remained in the thirteenth and fourteenth centuries and even beyond', becomes a frustratingly brief coda which scarcely addresses the issues of the nature and level of survival.[33] His treatment of the same forms of evidence in 'The lost Gaidhealtachd of medieval Scotland' emphasises this deliberate bias in his work: continuity is largely taken for granted in an exposition of the dynamics of change.[34]

A consequence of this promotion of 'innovation' by Barrow was understatement of the underlying conservatism and resilience of Celtic Scotland in work influenced by him. The reaction when it came was not anti-Barrovian, but took as its focus his theme of continuity rather than that of change. The result has been more far-reaching than this simple shift in emphasis might suggest: 'feudalisation' now appears as a thin veneer which clouds observation of the material below. Again, the constraints of charter scholarship can be seen to have pushed research in one particular direction, drawing the eye to the changing colonial world where charters were essential records of title to property in circumstances where local lordship was in a state of flux. The newcomers needed security of title by charter, but native lords turned to parchment only once they entered the land market of the later twelfth and thirteenth centuries or where they began to deal with the crown and the new colonial elites.

28 Duncan, *Kingdom* chs. 3–6.

29 Ibid., 132.

30 E.g. G. W. S. Barrow, *David I of Scotland (1124–53): The Balance of New and Old* (Reading, 1985).

31 G. W. S. Barrow, 'The pattern of lordship and feudal settlement in Cumbria', *Journal of Medieval History*, i (1975), 117–38.

32 G. W. S. Barrow, 'Badenoch and Strathspey, 1130–1312, 1: secular and political', *Northern Scotland*, viii (1988), 1–15.

33 Ibid., 9–10.

34 G. W. S. Barrow, 'The lost Gaidhealtachd of medieval Scotland', in W. Gillies, ed., *Gaelic and Scotland: Alba agus a' Ghaidlig* (Edinburgh, 1989), 67–88.

Against the traditional 'feudalising' image of the earl of Fife receiving his earldom as a feu (i.e. change) stands the 'anti-feudal' posture of the earl of Strathearn (i.e. continuity). Cynthia Neville showed the crown's inability – or reluctance – to force the pace of change in Strathearn, with colonisation prevented by a native ruler whose centres of power were fixed in upland zones and rested on the support of a native nobility, a pattern which survived into the mid-fifteenth century.[35] Clearly this is a native landowner perceiving no necessity for new-fangled tenures in his earldom, but where new land came into the possession of the Strathearn family, title was confirmed by charter: new circumstances demanded new responses.[36] Much the same occurred in Galloway, where traditional historiography has presented a confrontational relationship between native lords and feudal colonists, focusing on an 'enforced infeudation' and the destruction of the native nobility.[37] Trappings of change were important to the lords of Galloway, but they moved between the old and new worlds with ease and for all their Anglo-Normanised urbanity continued as native lords who depended on the support of the native community for much of their power.[38] In Galloway the brilliance of the few recorded instances of feudal colonisation has blinded historians to the continuing dominance of native aristocrats.[39]

The most valuable contributions to this trend lie in the festschrift presented to Barrow.[40] Amongst the themes explored by the essays in that volume is 'the interplay between Celtic and feudal influences'.[41] This is 'Barrovian', but its emphasis has switched from concentration on feudal innovation to exploration of the Celtic legacy. In particular, Bannerman's study of 'MacDuff of Fife', by addressing the strong survival of a kin-based, Celtic social structure at the apex of which stood the figure of the earl, demonstrates the superficiality of 'feudalisation' in the first of the native earldoms touched by the mechanisms of feudalism.[42] Whilst Barrow was drawn to the 'feudal' significance of the re-grant to the earl, Bannerman indicated that this infeftment scarcely affected how the earl and his kin functioned within Fife.[43] Indeed, the role which was fulfilled by the MacDuffs as late as the 1290s was that of mormaer of a Celtic province rather than feudal lord of a great feu.[44]

35 C. J. Neville, 'The Earls of Strathearn from the Twelfth to the Mid-Fourteenth Century' (University of Aberdeen, unpublished PhD thesis, 1983), 30, 63; A. Grant, 'The Higher Nobility and their Estates in Scotland, *c.*1371–1424' (University of Oxford, unpublished DPhil thesis, 1975), 232–9. See also chapter 6, below, by Cynthia Neville.

36 E.g. *RRS*, ii, nos. 206, 474; Barrow, 'Badenoch and Strathspey', 5.

37 R. D. Oram, 'A family business? Colonisation and settlement in twelfth- and thirteenth-century Galloway', *SHR*, lxxii (1993), 111–45.

38 See esp. K. J. Stringer, 'Periphery and core in thirteenth-century Scotland: Alan son of Roland, Lord of Galloway and Constable of Scotland', in Grant and Stringer, *Medieval Scotland*, 82–113; Oram, 'Family business', 134.

39 Oram, 'Family business', 134–45.

40 Grant and Stringer, *Medieval Scotland.*

41 Ibid., p. xvi.

42 J. Bannerman, 'MacDuff of Fife', in Grant and Stringer, *Medieval Scotland*, 20–38; and see also the earlier parts of A. Grant, 'Thanes and thanages, from the eleventh to the fourteenth centuries', in the same volume.

43 Barrow, 'Earls of Fife', 54–5.

44 Bannerman, 'MacDuff of Fife', 38.

This radical redirection has occasioned a comparative unresponsiveness in Scottish medievalists to recent developments in 'British' historiography. A redefinition of domestic issues has resulted, for example, in a signal failure amongst Scottish-based historians to contribute in any significant way to the new wave of 'British History' influenced by Rees Davies and Robin Frame.[45] This failure is all the more surprising considering the long-established tradition of Anglo-Scottish studies amongst Scottish historians. The direction of this Anglo-Scottish research, however, has been largely moulded by conventional perspectives which, like Tytler in the 1830s, simply used English sources to illuminate Scottish problems. It is rarely that Scottish historians stepped back from the traditional lines of demarcation to take the wide-angled view prescribed by Frame, producing instead dimly perceived keyhole glimpses of themes within a restricted field of politically oriented study.[46] The latter and preferred approach was essentially that taken by Barrow in *The Anglo-Norman Era*, narrowly focused on aristocratic relationships and governmental development, rather than his broadly-based comparative studies of the *Feudal Britain* tradition. While this saw major advances in understanding of the political relationship between Scotland and England, of Anglo-Scottish cross-border landholding, and of the processes at work in the colonising ventures (characterised by the outstanding work of Keith Stringer), the seminal comparative studies of social structures and institutions produced by Barrow failed to germinate and produce a parallel area of growth.[47]

The self-satisfied assumption that this tradition of research into Anglo-Scottish themes indicates an openness of mind and willingness to embrace 'British History' in contrast to the narcissistic introspection which is often characteristic of English historians is a further facet of the malaise which afflicts Scottish historical research. It is, moreover, self-deception, for, with the notable exceptions of Barrow and Stringer, much recent work is strongly Scoto-centric and gives scant consideration to underlying political and social stresses in England – and elsewhere in Britain – which might affect the Scottish position. This is evident, for example, in the only academic book devoted to the reign of a thirteenth-century Scottish monarch (Alexander III) to be produced in the last thirty years.[48] With the exception of Nicholas Mayhew's essay on the state of the Scottish economy under Alexander, there is an astonishing failure to consider the impact of the relationship with Scotland's southern neighbour on

45 R.R. Davies, *Domination and Conquest: The Experience of Ireland, Scotland and Wales 1100–1300* (Cambridge, 1990); Frame, *Political Development*.

46 Frame, *Political Development*, 3–4.

47 K. J. Stringer, *Earl David of Huntingdon 1152–1219: A Study in Anglo-Scottish History* (Edinburgh, 1985). Many of these themes are explored as 'case studies' in Stringer, *Nobility*. For works by Barrow, see 'Northern English society in the twelfth and thirteenth centuries', *Northern History*, vi (1969), 1–28; 'The pattern of lordship and feudal settlement in Cumbria', *Journal of Medieval History*, i (1975), 117–38; or 'Das mittelalterliche englische und schottische Königtum: ein Vergleich', *Historisches Jahrbuch*, cii (1982), 362–89, translated and expanded to take account of Davies and Frame as 'Kingship in medieval England and Scotland', in *Scotland and Its Neighbours in the Middle Ages* (London, 1992).

48 N. H. Reid, ed., *Scotland in the Reign of Alexander III, 1249–1286* (Edinburgh, 1990).

domestic politics.[49] Indeed, it has taken a non-historian, Roy Owen, in his overview of the reign of William the Lion, to underscore the potential in a broader exploration of Scotland's international relationships.[50]

A similarly one-dimensional approach has blighted understanding of Anglo-Scottish relations in the period from 1000 to 1174. Lynch, in a search for 'the over-arching continuities which give coherence' to free-standing episodes in Scottish history, recognised the continuity of policy towards northern England from the tenth to the twelfth centuries, but failed to address the interplay of responses between Scottish and English kings.[51] This is a consequence of the constraints of a single-volume history, but is also symptomatic of the research upon which his narrative is based. The influence of William Kapelle's study of the transformation of northern English society runs throughout Lynch's analysis, underscoring the failure of Scottish historians of the period to attempt parallel studies for their side of the border.[52] England, as Kapelle demonstrated, was more than an occasional reservoir of inspiration or colonising manpower upon which Scottish rulers could draw: co-operation and collaboration rather than confrontation underpinned the establishment of the pre-1135 Anglo-Scottish frontier.[53]

Significantly, all important - and recent - advances in this context are the work of historians based outwith Scotland. For example, Judith Green has produced a wide-ranging study of Anglo-Scottish relations from 1066 to the Treaty of Falaise, in which she explores the mutual attempts and responses of Scottish and English kings to fill the political vacuum in Northumbria. In particular, she stressed David I's relationship with Henry I before and after his accession in 1124 and the part which the stability which arose from this played in the consolidation of Norman control in northern England and in the origins of cross-border landholding, commonly understated in conventional Scottish interpretations.[54] The most significant contribution, however, is Stringer's reassessment of the reign of King Stephen, where the traditional image of David's involvement in the English civil war has been overturned.[55] Viewed from a Scottish perspective, this was a side-issue whose only lasting consequence was to compromise Scottish independence. The short-lived nature of David's conquests and failure to recognise the degree of his control over them led to a dismissive attitude towards David's 'Scoto-Northumbrian' realm. But Stringer

49 N. Mayhew, 'Alexander III - A Silver Age? An essay in Scottish medieval economic history', in Reid, *Alexander III*, 53–73.

50 D. D. R. Owen, *William the Lion, 1143–1214: Kingship and Culture* (East Linton, 1997).

51 M. Lynch, *Scotland: A New History* (2nd edn, London, 1992), pp. xv, 83.

52 W. E. Kapelle, *The Norman Conquest of the North: The Region and its Transformation, 1000–1135* (London, 1979); Lynch, *Scotland*, 74–6, 79.

53 Kapelle, *Norman Conquest*, 202–13.

54 J. Green, 'Anglo-Scottish Relations, 1066–1174', in M. Jones and M. Vale, eds., *England and her Neighbours, 1066–1453: Essays in Honour of Pierre Chaplais* (London, 1989), 59–65; idem, 'David I and Henry I', *SHR*, lxxv (1996), 1–19; cf. Duncan, *Kingdom*, 134–7, 217–19.

55 K. J. Stringer, *The Reign of Stephen: Kingship, Warfare and Government in Twelfth-Century England* (London, 1993), 28–37; also idem, 'State-building in twelfth-century Britain: David I, king of Scots, and northern England', in J. C. Appleby and P. Dalton, eds., *Government, Religion and Society in Northern England, 1000–1700* (Stroud, 1997), 40–62.

has argued cogently that David's conquests were 'firmly absorbed into the Scottish kingdom', and that 'David ruled them in complete independence of Stephen'.[56] The implications are far-reaching for our understanding of Anglo-Scottish relations from 1157 to 1237, but the integration into the Scottish realm which Stringer posits speaks of the survival of ancient bonds and the forging of new social, cultural and economic links. The need for a Kapelle-style analysis of southern Scotland is now all the more pressing, but equally, perhaps, here we can see most clearly – and explore – the mechanisms at work which were used to bind together the extended realm which David and his heirs established. The question arises, however, of who will undertake such work: where are the Competitors who would rescue Scottish history 'and remede that stad is in perplexytie'?

There is no gainsaying the remarkable achievement of the last thirty years. Few academic subjects have experienced such a renaissance in the truest sense of that word, nor seen such rapid and comprehensive reconstruction of its research base. The achievement is all the more remarkable if the smallness of the group of scholars who carried it through is considered, and in particular that the revolution in our understanding of the period from 1124 to 1296 was largely the product of one man's efforts. Geoffrey Barrow and his fellows effectively resuscitated medieval Scottish History, gave it a philosophy and ethos which established it as a credible independent academic subject. They furnished it with the constructs and paradigms which underpinned research. But it is in the very smallness of the group involved that many of its most life-threatening defects originate. In the drive to create a 'new' history there was a need for closeness and co-operation: without consensus there would have been no revolution. But consensus can also stifle debate and the cosy closeness of co-operation can lead to blandness. This absence of radical discussion and the domination of specialist spheres within the subject has led to stagnation. Without debate there can be no stimulus for advance.

To survive, Scottish medieval historical research needs to move on, to find new impetus and direction. 'Dark Age' studies have perhaps shown the way forward in the willingness of researchers in that field to look beyond traditional temporal and spatial barriers and to embrace the products of related disciplines. This has two dimensions, the multi-disciplinary synthesis represented, for example, in Barbara Crawford's *Scandinavian Scotland*, and the supranational scope which is a characteristic of both that volume and the work of the Committee for Dark Age Studies and the Early Medieval Research Group.[57] The potential for developing similar research on the central Middle Ages has already been demonstrated by Robert Bartlett, whose identification of common themes and responses on a Europe-wide platform has revealed the parochialism of traditional 'national' histories. It is not only Scottish History that has cultivated its own

56 Duncan, *Kingdom*, 222–4; Stringer, *Reign of Stephen*, 35.

57 B. E. Crawford, *Scandinavian Scotland* (Leicester, 1987); idem, ed., *Scotland in Dark Age Europe* (St Andrews, 1994); idem, ed., *Scotland in Dark Age Britain* (St Andrews, 1996); idem, ed., *Conversion and Christianity in the North Sea World* (St Andrews, 1998).

kailyards for too long.[58] At the other extreme, however, there is a need to scrutinise the kailyard ever more closely. Local studies have illustrated starkly the fallacious complacency which has allowed the presentation as 'national' history of generalised results founded on the research of a narrow-based group into what can be seen increasingly as an unrepresentative region. In a scramble to establish its credentials as a viable independent subject, Scottish medieval research leaped for the maturity of 'big idea' history without first passing through an adolescence that would equip it with the experience for survival.

There can be no turning back of the clock, nor should there be. While many interpretations of pre-fourteenth-century Scotland are long past their sell-by date, the charter scholarship upon which interpretation was built remains as fresh and valid as ever. Nevertheless, internal inconsistencies in the traditional image of pre-Wars of Independence Scotland, and in the theses from which this image has been constructed, can no longer be glossed over by generalisations. There is an urgent need for these issues to be re-examined and debated – not least because historiographical developments beyond Scotland have tarnished the gold of the new Scottish historiography of the 1960s to reveal a leaden burden in shabby packaging. This must be jettisoned if scholarship is to advance significantly and if Scottish history is to play any part in the development of medieval studies in general. The legacy of the charter scholarship of the 1960s must not be the present tottering structure, falling down under the weight of its own contradictions. Rather, it must lie in the panoply of edited tools with which the structure can be rebuilt from the foundations. It is an inheritance which could be truly golden. We can but pray that it does not fail through default of heirs.

58 R. Bartlett, *The Making of Europe: Conquest, Colonisation and Cultural Change, 950–1350* (London, 1993).

# 4

# The State of Late Medieval and Early Modern Scottish History

*Steve Boardman and Michael Lynch*

There are few Scottish historians whose work bridges the medieval and the early modern periods.[1] As a result, analysis of the transitions from the fourteenth to the seventeenth centuries has been rarely undertaken; and where it has, it has been confined to specialist areas, such as urban or legal history. And although it is widely acknowledged that the Renaissance welds together fifteenth- and sixteenth-century Scotland, it is striking how few studies of the Renaissance have been written.[2] Instead, the Reformation looms large, and its historians' concern is often to emphasise the break with the past forged in or after 1560 by the reformers. In these historiographical circumstances, important continuities in Scottish history can easily be missed.

This chapter arises from of a dialogue between two historians, one of the late fourteenth and early fifteenth centuries, the other of the sixteenth century. It suggests that historians of the two periods still have much to learn from each other, and that one of the reasons for the many lacunae in historical research on the late medieval and early modern periods is the lack of a common agenda. For the earlier Stewart period, for example, a series of scholarly monographs has steadily beaten a path through difficult territory; yet whole reigns in the later period – notably that of James VI – have as yet received no satisfactory account. On the other hand, the history of many spheres of the medieval Church is virtually unknown; and this contrasts sharply with the number of studies of the post-Reformation Church. There is, for instance, no equivalent for the earlier period to the various handlists of the post-Reformation ministry. It is also the case that relatively little work has been done on rural society, and less still on the royal court, in the fifteenth century. These topics, in contrast, have been growth areas among sixteenth-century scholars.

In part, perhaps, this chasm owes something to the grim and unappealing terms in which late medieval Scotland has traditionally been portrayed. Until the second half of the twentieth century, it was represented as a blighted land in the iron grip of a 'dark age', characterised by the decline or stagnation of the kingdom's government, economy, Church, legal system and cultural life.[3] The inability of the crown to dominate and control the great magnates of the realm was seen to be the root cause of the political disorder and endemic lawlessness which was assumed to have afflicted the kingdom throughout the fourteenth

1 Grant Simpson being amongst the exceptions: hence the nature of this book.

2 J. MacQueen, ed., *Humanism in Renaissance Scotland* (Edinburgh, 1990); A. A. MacDonald, M. Lynch and I. B. Cowan, eds., *The Renaissance in Scotland: Essays presented to John Durkan* (Leiden, 1994).

3 For a discussion of this legacy, see J. M. Brown, 'Introduction' and 'The exercise of power', in J. M. Brown, ed., *Scottish Society in the Fifteenth Century* (London, 1977).

and fifteenth centuries.[4] In the last twenty years, however, there has been a significant revision in historical attitudes towards the late medieval kingdom.

One of the areas in which historians have been most active and productive is in their examination and assessment of the kingdom's politics and political structure. Many of the most important advances revolve around the work of Alexander Grant and Jenny Wormald. In a series of articles and general studies, they have argued persuasively against the dual assumption that late medieval royal government was a failure and that the Scottish kingdom experienced unusually high levels of political violence. Instead, a new and generally positive model of the way in which the king and the political establishment worked to defend the kingdom and to maintain law and order in the localities has emerged.[5] At the core of this new view is a re-evaluation of the political strength of fourteenth- and fifteenth-century Scottish kingship and of the role of aristocratic lordship. The work of Wormald and Grant has laid great stress on what they see as the essentially co-operative nature of crown–magnate relations and the relatively low-key nature of political violence and dispute in late medieval Scotland.[6] The critical role of the aristocracy in the successful operation of government, justice and warfare has been emphasised. The reckless, ambitious and independent-minded lords who were emblematic of the older 'dark and drublie days' interpretation have been replaced by responsible men who generally acted in concert with the king and his administration, and who sought to advance themselves and their families through royal favour and patronage.

The interpretative framework advanced by Wormald and Grant may involve bending the stick too far in its overall re-evaluation of political structures and crown–magnate relations. But it was never intended simply to provide a political narrative for the fourteenth and fifteenth centuries: it was meant to stimulate and invigorate scholarly debate.[7] The rejection of the older political framework was an integral part of a wider movement which sought to rescue and rehabilitate the later Middle Ages as an area for research in a variety of interests and specialisms. Recent studies on law, towns and prices attest to the broadening themes pursued by scholars working on the period.[8] Nevertheless, the greatest body of recently published work on the later Middle Ages still deals with what some regard as the 'traditional' areas of government, crown–magnate relations and baronial politics. The publication of biographies of the first six Stewart kings, covering the trials and triumphs of their dynasty from 1371 to 1513, has transformed our understanding of the political interrelationship

4 See J. Wormald, 'Taming the Magnates?', in Stringer, *Nobility*; A. Grant, 'Crown and nobility in late medieval Britain', in R. A. Mason, ed., *Scotland and England, 1286–1815* (Edinburgh, 1987).

5 See Brown, 'Exercise of power'; Wormald, 'Taming the magnates?'; Grant, 'Crown and nobility'; A. Grant, *Independence and Nationhood: Scotland 1306–1469* (London, 1984), esp. chs. 5–7 (the rest of this book deals with some of the other themes discussed below).

6 This reassessment of the role of the Scottish nobility was at least partly inspired by the work of K. B. McFarlane on the medieval English aristocracy. See K. B. McFarlane, *The English Nobility in the Later Middle Ages* (Oxford, 1973); idem, *England in the Fifteenth Century* (London, 1981).

7 Brown, 'Introduction' [to *Scottish Society*], 7–9.

8 H. L. MacQueen, *Common Law and the Feudal Kingdom* (Edinburgh, 1995); E. Ewan, *Townlife in Fourteenth-Century Scotland* (Edinburgh, 1990); E. Gemmill and N. Mayhew, *Changing Values in Medieval Scotland: A Study of Prices, Money and Weights and Measures* (Cambridge, 1995).

between crown and aristocracy and the way in which royal power was successfully exercised, or lost, in the fourteenth and fifteenth centuries.[9]

The evidence uncovered and the conclusions reached by these studies of the policies and aims of individual monarchs and magnates has built on, and to some extent modified, the political overview of the kingdom provided by Grant and Wormald. Michael Brown's recent review article 'Scotland Tamed?' is a lucid exposition of the key points raised by such research.[10] His major contention is that Grant and Wormald have replaced a simplistic model of chronic political instability with a pattern of stable local lordship and crown–magnate co-operation which imposes its own distortions. While the 'new orthodoxy' has properly stressed the decentralised and unbureaucratic nature of kingship, and the importance of local lords and lordship in the governance of the realm, it has overstated the benefits flowing from this situation, particularly in terms of the suppression of political conflict in the late medieval kingdom. Brown's thesis is that aristocratic competition and violence remained an integral and natural part of late medieval society, as indeed did a measure of political tension between the crown and some of its subjects.[11] The major political and social crises of the fifteenth century did not drop like thunderbolts from a clear blue sky, disrupting an otherwise stable and self-regulating 'political community', but were produced by deep-rooted tensions and conflicting ambitions within that society.

The debate over crown–magnate relations which has so preoccupied historians of the late Middle Ages has not, generally, excited the same interest amongst sixteenth-century historians. This may reflect the alternative attractions provided by an age which saw rapid religious, cultural, social, economic and intellectual changes, all of which seem to carry a greater long-term significance than the bruising and petty battles of political faction and local feud. Moreover, these wider changes are seen to have made the political situation in sixteenth-century Scotland more complex, and no longer adequately described by, or comprehended within, a simple analysis of aristocratic interests and the personal relationship between the king and the great magnates of the realm.[12] The recent marginalisation of political dispute and tension as a significant factor within the late medieval kingdom has also reinforced the view that sixteenth-century Scotland saw unprecedented levels of disorder and disruption. The natural tendency has been to seek out 'new' economic and religious factors which might explain the 'uniquely' violent and traumatic events of the early modern age.[13]

Our argument, then, is that a largely artificial sense of discontinuity has emerged in the study of the political life of late medieval and sixteenth-century Scotland; and that this has proved unhelpful to historians of both periods. There is still a need for sixteenth-century historians to address in a sustained and direct fashion

9 N. Macdougall, *James III* (Edinburgh, 1982); N. Macdougall, *James IV* (Edinburgh, 1989); C. McGladdery, *James II* (Edinburgh, 1990); M. Brown, *James I* (Edinburgh, 1994); S. Boardman, *The Early Stewart Kings: Robert II and Robert III, 1371–1406* (East Linton, 1996).

10 M. H. Brown, 'Scotland tamed? Kings and magnates in late medieval Scotland: a review of recent work', *IR*, xlv (1994).

11 Ibid.

12 See M. Lynch, *Scotland: A New History* (London, 1991) , chs. 11–12.

13 Ibid.

the way in which particular political crises developed, and the specific motivations and interests of those involved. Even in a reign so apparently familiar as that of James VI many blank spots remain and even the basic configurations of politics remain unclear. Late medieval specialists, on the other hand, should perhaps give greater weight to the fact that many of the long-term factors which are seen to be critical in explaining the upheavals of sixteenth-century society, such as the 'rise of the middling sort' and the emergence of financially acquisitive and bureaucratised royal government, also had their effect in the earlier period.

There has, in contrast to the systematic analysis of late medieval crown-magnate relations, been remarkably little examination of the political structure in the early modern period. While the attention given to Mary's reign has served to obscure the normal patterns of politics, satisfactory political studies of the reigns of James V and James VI are only now appearing.[14] Nonetheless, Wormald detected continuity in crown-magnate relations across the chronological divide, suggesting that they were essentially co-operative.[15] The reign of James VI, she argued, was the epitome of a culture of '*laissez-faire* kingship' which linked the reigns of most Stewart monarchs. This interpretation was a refinement of the orthodox view of the sixteenth century, first advanced by Gordon Donaldson, which held that the politics of the period, at least on the part of the monarchy and responsible elements of churchmen, were characterised by a pursuit of 'moderation'.[16] Donaldson found the 'moderates' amongst his chosen monarchs and a particular sort of churchmen: Wormald detected them more generally, amongst kings and their great nobles.

Both views may have passed too lightly over the competitiveness which lay at the roots of a society which, in the long reign of James VI, saw more noble creations than in any other period since the twelfth century. 'Responsible men ... who sought to advance themselves and their families through royal favour and patronage' abound in sixteenth-century Scotland.[17] Their behaviour has scarcely been explored, nor has the milieu in which they operated. There are very few published analyses of major nobles or noble families in that period since the pioneering work of Maurice Lee almost forty years ago.[18] At least as many nobles resorted to rebellion – or, rather, as the vocabulary of the new orthodoxy of late medieval historians insists, were provoked into 'protests' – in the sixteenth century as in the fifteenth. Yet the careers and motives of nobles such as the fourth earl of Argyll, the fourth and sixth earls of Huntly, the second earl of Arran (Châtelherault), and the first and second earls of Gowrie remain obscure. The enigmatic Francis Stewart, fifth Earl Bothwell, however, has recently found his

14 J. Cameron, *James V: The Personal Rule, 1528–1542* (East Linton, 1998); J. Goodare and M. Lynch, eds., *The Reign of James VI* (East Linton, 1999).

15 J. Wormald, *Lords and Men in Scotland: Bonds of Manrent, 1442–1603* (Edinburgh, 1985); idem, *Court, Kirk and Community: Scotland 1470–1625* (London, 1981).

16 G. Donaldson, *Scotland: James V to James VII* (Edinburgh, 1965).

17 See above, page 45.

18 M. Lee, *John Maitland of Thirlestane and the Foundation of Stewart Despotism in Scotland* (Princeton, 1959). See M. Kelley, 'The Douglas Earls of Angus: A Study in the Social and Political Bases of Power of a Scottish Family from 1389 until 1557' (University of Edinburgh, unpublished PhD thesis, 1973); E. Finnie, 'The house of Hamilton: patronage, politics and the Church in the Reformation period', *IR*, xxxvi (1985); and G. Hewitt, *Scotland under Morton, 1572–80* (Edinburgh, 1982).

historian – who contributes to this volume.[19] It is difficult to establish the *mentalité* of the period until more of such basic groundwork is done.[20] By the time of James VI's majority, it is becoming clear, much of the competition was channelled though the court, where the issue of access to the king became contentious.[21] The king's departure in 1603 provided a solution to that problem, although it was to have disastrous consequences in little more than a generation. This is one example of a key difference between the reign of James VI (and perhaps also the personal reign of Mary) and the earlier period: the patterns of politics, preferment and power were increasingly based on institutions rather than the old informal means.[22] If 'personal kingship' still existed – and the bulk of late sixteenth-century historians seem to think that it did – it worked in quite different ways from those of a century before. One sign of this was the nobility's increasing anxiety, felt from the reign of Mary onwards, about its 'ancient blood'. Another, which suggests a later break with the past, lies in the fact that James VI did not spend his time travelling round his kingdom in the manner of all his Stewart predecessors, except James III. As late as the 1560s Mary virtually governed from the saddle, as she worked hard to make personal contact with local magnates as far distant as Inverness and Whithorn.[23] James VI also spent much time in the saddle, but he was hunting: the localities came to him.[24]

James VI's parliaments passed more legislation than those of any previous reign. The business of the Privy Council expanded hugely in the later 1580s and the 1590s. Yet the finances of Stewart monarchy remain, with some specialised exceptions, largely unexplored.[25] Both taxes and customs duties sharply increased during James's reign and a permanent exchequer (part of a formidable and largely new apparatus of state power) reorganised royal finances. This suggests that James's reign marked a decisive turning-point.[26] It is difficult, in the light of this evidence, to see how James can remain in the ranks of *laissez-faire* Stewart kings who ruled through a combination of goodwill towards co-operative leading nobles, intense personal ferocity towards dissident nobles, and a genial indifference to most of what nobles got up to in their own localities. In turn, this suggests that the reigns of his mother and grandfather have more in

19 R. Macpherson, 'Francis Stewart, 5th Earl Bothwell, *c*.1562–1612: Lordship and Politics in Jacobean Scotland' (University of Edinburgh, unpublished PhD thesis, 1998); and see chapter 12, below. Macpherson's interest in Bothwell began while he was a student of Grant Simpson.

20 But see K. Brown, *Bloodfeud in Scotland, 1573–1625* (Edinburgh, 1986).

21 J. Goodare and M. Lynch, 'James VI: a universal king?', in Goodare and Lynch, *Reign of James VI*.

22 This theme is explored in detail in J. Goodare, *State and Society in Early Modern Scotland* (Oxford, forthcoming, 1999), esp. in the chapters, 'State power' and 'The absolutist state'; see also idem, 'The nobility and the absolutist state in Scotland, 1584-1638', *History*, lxxviii (1993).

23 P. G. B. McNeill and R. Nicholson, eds., *An Historical Atlas of Scotland, c.400–c.1600* (St Andrews, 1975), 86–7, 198–9; E. Furgol, 'The progresses of Mary, Queen of Scots, 1542–8 and 1562–8', *PSAS*, cxvii (1987).

24 Goodare and Lynch, 'Universal king?'.

25 See, e.g., A. L. Murray, 'The Comptroller, 1425–1488', *SHR*, lii (1973); J. Goodare, 'Parliamentary taxation in Scotland, 1560–1603', *SHR*, lxviii (1989).

26 J. Goodare, 'The finances of the Scottish state, 1560–1637' (Royal Society of Edinburgh project, 1993); two of the results of this research are: idem, 'Thomas Foulis and the Scottish financial crisis of the 1590s', in W. M. Ormrod and R. Bonney, eds., *Crises, Revolutions and Self-Sustained Growth: Essays in Fiscal History, 1130–1830* (Woodbridge, 1996); and idem, '"Ane breiff information for the thesaurer", 1616', *Scottish History Society Miscellany XIII* (SHS, forthcoming).

common with fifteenth-century arrangements, reproducing, for example, much the same ramshackle financial patterns of earlier Stewart kings.

Historians of the fifteenth century are inclined to suspect that there were new levels of disorder and disruption in the sixteenth century and to deduce that they must be connected to a novel factor, the introduction of religious dissension into what had hitherto been a stable political system. Yet such suspicions sit uneasily with what has been a widely accepted nostrum of sixteenth-century politics – that the pull of kinship and loyalty to the crown usually counted for more than religious partisanship.[27] One difficulty is that relatively little work has been done on the nobles in their unaccustomed post-Reformation role as Christian magistrates, and the findings as yet seem inconclusive. Assessment of individual localities where the new gospel spread early, however, seems to suggest that the landed elite continued to exercise a stabilising function in what remained an essentially conservative society.[28] These suspicions of late medieval historians may in part stem from the extensive work done on the sixteenth-century bloodfeud by Keith Brown, which produced a plethora of citable gory examples; or they may have been deduced from the crackdown on violence in both the Borders and the Highlands by the government of James VI from *c.*1587. Either assumption, however, could be flawed. The extent and seriousness of bloodfeud is more likely to have been conspicuous in a period when there was an active land market, such as marked the sixteenth century from at least the 1540s onwards. Neighbourhood and boundary disputes were favourite flashpoints. Yet, without the evidence to produce a comparative perspective illuminating fifteenth-century patterns of violence, it is difficult to deduce much more than this.

As for the new-found 'problem' of violence in the localities detected by James VI's Privy Council in the 1580s, it needs to be remembered that the government's attention was both discriminating and opportunistic. It was first directed to the Borders in the early 1580s, when a league with England was in prospect, and to the Highlands with any seriousness only in the mid-1590s, when a frantic search for new sources of crown rents became imperative.[29] If a novel factor existed, it is likely to have been at best only indirectly connected to the Reformation. It is more possible that it lay in the added opportunities afforded by an active land market in the wake of wholesale secularisation of Church property, either before the Reformation in the form of feuing of kirklands or, after 1560, in a tussle for lay commendatorships. The former has been amply investigated, but the latter has scarcely been touched.[30]

Meanwhile, the development of later medieval religious life has been similarly neglected. Relative inactivity in this area is all the more disappointing given the

27 G. Donaldson, *All the Queen's Men: Power and Politics in Mary Stewart's Scotland* (London, 1983).

28 K. M. Brown, 'In search of the Godly Magistrate in Reformation Scotland', *Journal of Ecclesiastical History*, xl (1989); J. Wormald, 'Princes and the regions in the Scottish Reformation', in N. Macdougall, ed., *Church, Politics and Society: Scotland 1408–1929* (Edinburgh, 1983) (and an unexpectedly large amount of ecclesiastical patronage exercised by the fifth earl of Bothwell is also detailed in Macpherson, 'Earl Bothwell'); F. D. Bardgett, *Scotland Reformed: The Reformation in Angus and the Mearns* (Edinburgh, 1989), 156–8, 165–7.

29 Goodare and Lynch, *Reign of James VI*, chs. 11–12.

30 M. Sanderson, *Scottish Rural Society in the Sixteenth Century* (Edinburgh, 1982).

sources made available to the current generation of historians by those scholars involved in the Vatican archive project. It is to be hoped that recently completed doctoral research on the secular clergy and on the Dominicans – which made extensive use of these sources – will encourage increased use of the voluminous papal records to illuminate medieval social and religious life.[31] The material contained in the Vatican archives is now supplemented by the translated edition of Walter Bower's *Scotichronicon*, a work which contains a wealth of incidental and explicit observations on religious belief and custom.[32]

There are clearly many insights available into the society and culture of the medieval kingdom through an examination of the vitality of the cults of local and international saints, and of their changing fortunes. At the highest political levels the evolution of the cult of St Margaret was of great significance. The development of a specifically 'royal' cult focused on Margaret began in the mid-thirteenth century with the successful campaign for her canonisation. Thereafter, Dunfermline Abbey became the 'cult centre of Scottish kingship for a century'.[33] Tracing the evolution of St Margaret's reputation in the disturbed conditions of the sixteenth century would be an interesting and illuminating exercise. How did reformers reconcile their hostility to St Margaret as the focus for a saintly cult with her critical role in the iconography of the royal dynasty and her historical importance in the origin legends of a succession of aristocratic families?

A proper assessment is required of the fifteenth-century Church, its triumphs and failings; and of the nature of popular piety, patronage, devotion and dissent. Meanwhile, the more vigorous historical debate over religious affairs in the sixteenth century has to be based on untested supposition as to the nature of medieval spirituality. This means that long-term trends and continuities, and the origins and attractiveness of radical religious reform remain obscure. Sanderson's recent study of early sixteenth-century Ayrshire argues (as A. G. Dickens did for parts of England over thirty years ago) that there was a tangible connection between late medieval Lollardy and early Protestantism.[34] But this is a localised example of a community with distinct idiosyncrasies and little or no spill-over effect outside itself. The extent of appropriation of benefices in Ayrshire was appreciably higher than the average. The impact of religious orders (with only one significant house within it) was probably less than elsewhere and the impact of diocesan administration, based in distant Glasgow, was muted. Furthermore,

31 E. Williamson, 'Scottish Benefices and Clergy during the Pontificate of Sixtus IV (1471–84): The Evidence in the *Registra Supplicationum*' (University of Glasgow, unpublished PhD thesis, 1998); J. Foggie, 'The Dominicans in Scotland, 1450–1560' (University of Edinburgh, unpublished PhD thesis, 1998). See also idem, '*Archivium Sacrae Pænitentiariae Apostolicae* in the Vatican Archives as a source for Scottish Historians', *IR*, xlvii (1996); and chapter 14, below, by Leslie Macfarlane.

32 *Chron. Bower* (Watt).

33 John Barbour, *The Bruce*, ed. A. A. M. Duncan (Edinburgh, 1997), 756. As Duncan points out, Alexander III and his first wife, and Robert I and his queen, Elizabeth, were all buried in Dunfermline, while David II was born there. Despite the implication that, thereafter, the royal lineage showed less affection for the abbey as a burial site, there remained some significant connections. David II and his second wide, Queen Margaret Drummond evidently planned to be buried at Dunfermline before their acrimonious divorce in 1368 (*ER*, ii, 300, 348). Robert III's wife, Annabella Drummond, *was* buried in the abbey and may well have deliberately chosen Dunfermline as the location for the birth of her third son, James (the future James I) in 1394: *Chron. Bower* (Watt), viii, 37.

34 M. Sanderson, *Ayrshire and the Reformation: People and Change, 1490–1600* (East Linton, 1997).

the early Protestant movement had, to an unusual extent, a lay character, composed of nobles, lairds and burgh office-holders. The role of local magnates and lairds was probably magnified by the locality's relative geographical isolation and the lack of local leading clerical activists. The absence of a major, or even second-rank, early preacher is striking, although there were prominent visitors such as George Wishart in 1545, John Willock (the ex-Dominican from Ayr) in 1559; and, more frequently after 1555, John Knox. It seems clear from Foggie's work on the Friars Preacher, who took an active role in the towns where their houses were located, that they came, overwhelmingly, from local, usually burghal, families, not often from the upper echelons of society. This may cast some doubt on Sanderson's picture of the pre-Reformation secular clergy as a 'Church of working subordinates', unable or unwilling after 1560 to take on new levels of responsibility.[35] In both the social make-up of the pre-Reformation clergy and in their local outlook there was probably considerable continuity in the generations before and after 1560, and these things may go some way towards explaining the motivation behind conformity to the new, Protestant Church.

The conundrum of how late medieval devotion apparently turned into attachment to evangelical reform has often tempted historians to easier answers than are warranted. This is perhaps because evidence for the nature of devotion is more difficult to root out than that for the corruption and unpopularity of the late medieval Church. It is only one example of how historians – of both periods, it must be admitted – tend merely to scan the boundaries of their own period to explain earlier and later events. Yet it is distinctly curious that the role of nobles as Christian magistrates surfaces in the literature only for the years after 1560. There is for example – in a distinguished collection of essays on the medieval nobility by several hands – scarcely a passage devoted to religious patronage in the late Middle Ages, apart from a recognition that there is some connection between the emergence of the new class of lords of parliament in the mid-fifteenth century and the sharp rise in the number of foundations or refoundations of collegiate churches.[36]

This exception is, however, significant for our argument, since it explains certain post-Reformation developments and makes them seem less novel. The resort of many post-Reformation nobles to family burial aisles, sepulchres and mausoleums circumvented some of the original reformers' desire for public worship but also continued in the tradition of the collegiate church, which was often intended as a private chapel as well as a familial resting-place.[37] The godly actions of lairds like Robert Campbell of Kinzeancleuch, who, because of his dissatisfaction with provision by local ministers, made a nightly examination in the 1560s of his immediate family and servants and a weekly examination of his tenantry, may come to seem less singular. It is possible that this was merely a return to past practice, when the grant made by the papal Penitentiary of a

35 Ibid., 109.

36 Stringer, *Nobility*; cf. I. B. Cowan and D. E. Easson, eds., *Medieval Religious Houses: Scotland* (2nd edn, London, 1976), 213–30.

37 See R. Fawcett, 'Church archaeology in Scotland and Man, AD 1200–1600', 87, 92, 94, 97, and J. G. Dunbar, 'The post-Reformation church in Scotland', 130–2: both in J. Blair and C. Pyrah, eds., *Church Archaeology: Research Directions for the Future* (Council for British Archaeology, Research Report 104, 1996).

licence to a family chaplain for a portable altar made private worship possible.[38] The wholesale 'dechristianisation' of the medieval nobility is a curious and implausible creation of modern historians.

Apart from Macfarlane's magisterial study of Bishop Elphinstone, and a sizeable pot-pourri of articles, mostly in the *Innes Review*, there is little, other than useful overviews, to act as a guide through the complex and overlapping structures of the medieval Church.[39] The systematic exploitation of material found in the archives of the Roman *Rota* and the Sacred Penitentiary in the Vatican by a team of researchers headed by Ian Cowan and James Robertson should produce significant new data on which to base sounder judgements. Recent work on the religious houses shows how unsound generalisations about the state of the Church can be. Mark Dilworth has shown that significant differences existed in each religious order and, at times, even in the different individual houses within an order.[40]

Medieval historians have, on the whole, tended to know and care more about ecclesiastical politics – particularly about disputes over benefices and tussles for the control of various religious houses – than about religion. Piety has not been a conspicuous interest of pre-Reformation scholars. Donaldson, indeed, berated some of them for their lack of understanding of sin. He, however, seems to have had only a limited grasp of late medieval patterns of piety, or knowledge of relevant comparative evidence from outside Scotland, crucially that from Flanders and the Rhineland. The tension which he detected between the cults of the Passion and the Virgin Mary within one of the key documents of late medieval Passion poetry in Scotland, Arundel MS 285,[41] led him to generalise that 'clerical eyebrows must have raised' by such lines and to find in them a forerunner of early Protestant devotion. But this evidence needs to be counterbalanced by other, more representative sources, drawn from both Scotland and beyond. The cult of Mary as the mother of Christ was a favourite theme of the Dominicans, unlikely as it may seem to those accustomed to viewing them either as front-line troops in the future battle against heresy or as a recruiting ground for early Protestants. And the Fetternear Banner, crafted for the Edinburgh merchant guild in the 1520s and showing the direct influence of the Flemish cult of the Holy Blood, as well as being a prime example of the cult of the Passion, was a penitential exercise devoted to the Virgin Mary. Rosaries abound in its fringes.[42]

There is much to suggest that the fifteenth century and early part of the sixteenth saw a renewed interest or even, some might say, an obsession with new habits of piety and fresh, large-scale investment in some areas of religious provision. Post-Reformation historians are often content to point out the distaste felt by those inclined towards Protestant reform for cults such as the

38 See David Calderwood, *History of the Kirk of Scotland* (Wodrow Soc., 1842–9), iii, 312. We are grateful to Janet Foggie for the point regarding licences for portable altars, discovered by her in an exploration of Penitentiary records.

39 See also the recent work, A. D. M. Barrell, *The Papacy, Scotland and Northern England, 1342–1378* (Cambridge, 1995).

40 M. Dilworth, *Scottish Monasteries: Monastic Life in the Sixteenth Century* (Edinburgh, 1995).

41 G. Donaldson, *Faith of the Scots* (London, 1990), 61–2; idem, *Queen's Men*, 9.

42 M. Lynch, 'Religious life in medieval Scotland', in S. Gilley and W. J. Sheils, eds., *A History of Religion in Britain* (Oxford, 1994).

shrine at Loreto. But this is only one side of the coin. The early Protestant earl of Glencairn was one of the most vocal critics of this new shrine, and the reason for his dislike of it may well have been its popularity, both at the royal court and outside it. The lack of work on late medieval piety and worship is unfortunate, for the successes and failures of the new Church can be realistically assessed only when cast in the context of the successes and failures of its predecessor. The sins of the one may not have been visited on the other, but many of its shortcomings are likely to have been. This argument applies also to the lack of overviews of the culture and society which produced the works of the great makars of the late fifteenth and early sixteenth centuries. The late medieval world we have yet to reclaim is a cultural as well as a religious one. As Roger Mason recently argued, it has 'languished for too long in the shadow of the Reformation' and a Protestant-dominated historiography, with 'no wish to recognise the richness of the material and literary culture which the Reformation destroyed'.[43]

Sixteenth-century historiography has, however, laid great stress on the importance of the royal court as a cultural, social, political and intellectual focus for the kingdom. Particular attention has been paid to the uses of courtly ceremony, mythic history, chivalric ideology and spectacle, and architectural display as a means of building a 'cult' of monarchy, closely tied to expressions of national identity, which both overawed and embraced the greater aristocracy.[44] Combined with this has been a concern to examine the way in which the royal establishment conceptualised, expressed, and promoted its role in the kingdom's legal, political and administrative structure and encouraged the growth and acceptance of these ideas amongst its subjects.[45] Historians of the fifteenth century have, thus far, paid little attention to this aspect of the enhancement of royal power, tending to concentrate on explaining the physical growth of the crown's fiscal and territorial resources through a series of tactical political triumphs by individual kings over powerful aristocratic opponents.[46] In recent years, however, a number of scholars with a background in the study of the intellectual and literary life of the sixteenth century, notably Roger Mason, Sally Mapstone and Carol Edington, have begun to explore the political and social conventions and ideologies of crown and nobility in late medieval Scotland.[47] In particular, Mason has outlined the establishment and advance of a dominant aristocratic ideology, which he summarises as one of 'patriotic

43 R. A. Mason, *Kingship and the Commonweal: Political Thought in Renaissance and Reformation Scotland* (East Linton, 1998), 105–6.

44 Edington, *Court and Culture*; M. Lynch, 'Queen Mary's triumph: the baptismal celebrations at Stirling in December 1566', *SHR*, lxix (1990), 1–21; R. A. Mason, 'Chivalry and citizenship: aspects of national identity in Renaissance Scotland', in R. A. Mason and N. Macdougall, eds., *People and Power in Scotland: Essays in Honour of T. C. Smout* (Edinburgh, 1992); M. Lynch, 'A nation born again? Scottish identity in the sixteenth and seventeenth centuries', in D. Broun, R. J. Finlay and M. Lynch, eds., *Image and Identity: The Making and Re-making of Scotland through the Ages* (Edinburgh, 1998), 83–4, 86, 93–4.

45 R. A. Mason, 'Scotching the Brut', in Mason, *Scotland and England*; idem, 'Kingship, tyranny and the right to resist', *SHR*, lxvi (1987).

46 Nicholson, *Scotland*, chs. 11, 13–14, 17–18; Brown, *James I*; McGladdery, *James II*.

47 S. Mapstone, 'The Advice to Princes Tradition in Scottish Literature, 1450–1500' (University of Oxford, unpublished DPhil thesis, 1986); C. Edington, 'Scottish nobility and chivalry in the later Middle Ages', *Proceedings of the Harlaxton Seminar* (forthcoming).

conservatism'. Mason suggests that fifteenth-century political elites were encouraged to view the monarchy as a guarantee of, and synonymous with, the political independence of the Scottish kingdom and the 'common weal' of the kingdom's subjects, an identification made more explicit by the events and pressures of the Wars of Independence in the early fourteenth century.[48] It has been argued that, with this powerful and widely accepted ideological underpinning, the fifteenth-century monarchs possessed a crucial psychological and political advantage in any confrontation with their subjects, who could find few ways to justify sustained opposition to a legitimate king.[49]

Mason's arguments are broadly persuasive, although in the second half of the fourteenth century the identification of *individual* monarchs with the preservation of the 'common weal' was by no means automatic. The reigns of Robert II (1371–90) and Robert III (1390–1406), for example, were marked by a series of guardianships which removed power from adult kings or royal lieutenants against their will. In 1384 the elderly Robert II was pushed from power by his son and heir John, Earl of Carrick, who became guardian of the kingdom in a bloodless coup which was linked to a propaganda campaign depicting Robert as a man incapable of organising warfare against the English. In 1388 Carrick was himself replaced as guardian by his brother Robert, Earl of Fife, an appointment which was explicitly justified by the supposed inability of both the king and Carrick to defend the kingdom against an expected English invasion in 1389.[50]

Overall, it could be argued that the nature of early fourteenth-century political and military struggles encouraged the view that the defence of the kingdom and the 'common weal' was a duty which had been shared and discharged by the entire aristocratic community, and not simply the 'royal' dynasty. During the second half of the fourteenth century, then, the ideology and rhetoric of 'patriotic conservatism' seems to have been a two-edged weapon. It *was* used to augment the political and social standing of the royal dynasty, but it could also be employed by cadet branches of the royal family, backed up by powerful regional lords, to support and justify attempts to confront or curb those exercising royal power. New research on the later medieval parliament will illustrate how far political tension and friction in the changed conditions of the second half of the fifteenth century came to rest on the interplay between the increasing demands of the crown and the rights of the crown's subjects to resist them.[51] Despite the rising tide of demands made by monarchs of their subjects from the reign of James V, and the recurrence of minorities involving different kinds of regency or governorship, there has, by contrast, been little or no systematic analysis of the strains imposed on 'patriotic conservatism' in the sixteenth century.

Another interesting area which has not been addressed in a sustained way by scholars of the late Middle Ages is the military, political and administrative

48 Mason, 'Kingship, tyranny and the right to resist'.

49 Ibid.

50 Nicholson, *Scotland*, ch. 8; Grant, *Independence and Nationhood*, 178–84; Boardman, *Early Stewart Kings*, 119–24, 152–3.

51 E.g. R. Tanner's essay on the 15th-century Scottish parliament, in T. Thornton, ed., *Social Attitudes and Political Structures in the Fifteenth Century* (Stroud, forthcoming).

significance of the royal household and the king's court. In England a series of studies has emphasised the importance of the king's personal affinity in the conduct of war and the governance of the kingdom. The knights of the English king's household formed the core of royal armies and were a powerful factor in domestic politics.[52] Moreover, the loyalty of this group to the figure of the king was vigorously promoted by their participation in a variety of courtly ceremonies (both secular and sacred) and chivalric spectacles centred on the monarch. In fourteenth-century Scotland the reign of David II is likely to be a profitable starting-point for any examination of the development of the royal household.

Although more work has been done on the sixteenth-century royal court than on its earlier counterpart, it is still one of the key under-explored issues of that century. There are isolated incidents which suggest that it may have exercised a dynamic role in politics - or, at least, that monarchs supposed so.[53] With two important exceptions very little has been done to analyse court politics, although Ried Zulager's thesis goes some way towards establishing a *Who's Who* of the king's government in the first half of the long reign of James VI.[54] The route which the king's servants took towards preferment is, as a result, much easier to trace. Most often, at least in James VI's reign, it was through the chamber.[55] And it is clear that, for many well-informed contemporaries, politics by the 1590s was predominantly a dispute between council and chamber. It is difficult, in the absence of studies of earlier Stewart courts, to be sure that this was a wholly new phenomenon since, in a sense, there had also been a divide between the household and council in the personal reign of Mary, though for rather different reasons.[56] The huge inflation of honours during the reign of James VI, who created two dukes, two marquises, twenty-seven earls, six viscounts and twenty-nine lords, tends to suggest that friction was the inevitable result, here reflecting the obsession of nobles, old and new, with status.

In another important respect, however, the quest for status was nothing new. The fifteenth and sixteenth centuries were linked by a cult of honour and the difference between the two periods lay in the fresh outlets found for it. One of the best-selling works to come off Scottish printing presses in the last quarter of the sixteenth century was the fifteenth-century chivalric romance, *Graysteil*, itself a translation into Scots of a French verse romance. The period after 1585 also saw an increasing formalisation of the riding of parliament. The Honours of Scotland,

52 E.g. M. Prestwich, *War, Politics and Finance under Edward I* (London, 1972); C. Given-Wilson, *The Royal Household and the King's Affinity: Service, Politics and Finance in England, 1360–1413* (London, 1986).

53 C. Edington, *Court and Culture*, 89–114; Lynch, 'Queen Mary's triumph'; M. Lynch, 'A royal progress: court ceremony and ritual during the personal reign of James VI', in Goodare and Lynch, *Reign of James VI*.

54 C. Edington, *Court and Culture*; A. Thomas, 'Renaissance Culture at the Court of James V, 1528–42' (University of Edinburgh, unpublished PhD thesis, 1997); R. Zulager, 'A Study of the Middle Rank Administrators in the Government of King James VI of Scotland, 1580–1603' (University of Aberdeen, unpublished PhD thesis, 1993). There are, however, important passages, mostly pertaining to the reign of James VI, in Brown, *Bloodfeud*, 116–21; and in N. Cuddy, 'The revival of the entourage: the bedchamber of James I, 1603–1625', in D. Starkey, ed., *The English Court: From the Wars of the Roses to the Civil War* (London, 1987).

55 This should be made clearer by the current doctoral research on James VI's household by Amy Juhala.

56 Donaldson, *Queen's Men*, 76–7.

borne in procession before each parliament, in a much more formal ceremony than the equivalent in England, were another feature of the growing cult of honour. So was the vogue for family histories, elaborate armorials and expensive sepulchres. Yet most of these were intended as a parade of noble antiquity, real or imagined: the link with the past was the epitome of the cult of honour. What may have been new in it was the emergence of a triumphal element.[57]

The chivalric ideal encompassed, in ever-growing elaborate rituals of power, both royal dynasty and noble house. One of the focal points of James VI's formal entry into his capital in 1579 was the series of portraits depicting Stewart kings from James I to V, probably displayed at the Tron. The message could hardly have been clearer: the continuity of kingship was as powerful an image in the sixteenth century as at any time in the Middle Ages. The cult of honour is a subject which needs further exploration, in the fifteenth century as well as in the sixteenth and early part of the seventeenth. Amongst that parade of Stewart monarchs featured in 1579, there can be little doubt that James III is the king whose reputation has suffered most in the historical writing of the past generation. This applies not only to his effectiveness as a ruler but also to the cultural milieu which obtained during his reign. The courts of James I, II and IV have all been acknowledged in recent work, but that of James III has been all but passed over. This is a curious omission for a king who was the first to settle his administration in a 'capital' and for one who had an influential mother, with a background in the Burgundian court. James, furthermore, had a formidable extended family for whom he might have been expected to find niches at court. The possible effect of this neglect of James's court may be illustrated by two inconclusive examples. The survival of an account, by Somerset herald, of the triumphal entry of Queen Margaret into Edinburgh in 1503, has tended to accentuate the attention given to the court of James IV – yet certain parts of that ceremony and of later royal entries, including that of Queen Anne in 1590, suggest Burgundian or French influences which date from the third or fourth quarters of the fifteenth century.[58] Second, the template of a royal, processional route through the king's capital is more likely to have been laid down in the reign of James III than that of James IV. Recent excavation at Stirling Castle suggests that some work previously ascribed to James IV's reign may have an earlier date.[59] Often cultural developments may belong to the reign *before* that to which they are usually ascribed.

There is more to be discovered about the *mentalité* of the reign of James III; and MacDonald's provocative essay also focusing on the chivalric cult of St Andrew provides a new starting-point.[60] The cult of honour also raises, in stark terms, the issues of political continuity. One of the accusations made against the

57 Edington, *Court and Culture*, 114; D. Bentley Cranch, 'Effigy and portraiture in sixteenth-century Scotland', *Review of Scottish Culture*, iv (1987).

58 See the Danish account of the entry, printed in D. Stevenson, *Scotland's Last Royal Wedding: The Marriage of James VI and Anne of Denmark* (Edinburgh, 1997), 107–22; particular prominence was given to the earlier marriage of a Danish princess to a king of Scots – James III.

59 See N. Macdougall, '"It is I, the Erle of Mar": in search of Thomas Cochrane', in Mason and Macdougall, *People and Power*: Cochrane, one of the despised, low-born favourites of James III, may have been the architectural designer of the Great Hall, completed in the reign of James IV.

60 A. A. MacDonald, 'The Chapel of Restalrig: royal folly or venerable shrine?' (forthcoming).

Black Douglases in the reign of James II was that they 'held court'. In the 1580s so did leading nobles such as Bothwell and Huntly. The difference between the periods, however, was that James VI's major nobles mostly held court in Edinburgh. They were forced to behave like political lobbyists at a time when even some of the major burghs had employed permanent agents in the capital to look after their interests. Again, what was really new about James VI's reign was simply that the localities had come to the centre.

Fifteenth-century historical studies of the localities and the kingdom have, thus far, tended to focus on the problems and interests of one group, the great aristocrats of the realm. There has been little or no reference to other sectors of society, their distinctive views and concerns and their role in the political and social life of the kingdom. It seems more than likely that issues familiar to sixteenth-century historians, such as the impact of growing burghal prosperity and self-confidence on the rest of the kingdom, the 'rise of the middling sort' and the establishment of an Edinburgh-based legal elite, could be profitably studied in the later medieval period.[61]

There are other 'communities' which have received scant attention from the historians of either period. For example, the history of the peasantry and of the experience of women in both the late medieval and early modern periods remain, with one or two notable exceptions, unexplored.[62] Given the finite nature and relative paucity of documentary and literary record, the opening up of these areas will probably rest on comparative studies and the application of new interpretative methodologies to existing sources. Some of these techniques have already been used in two full-scale monographs concerned with fourteenth- and fifteenth-century Scotland, by Goldstein and Fradenburg.[63] Both works are, however, uneven, alternating between genuine insights and obscure jargon-ridden analysis.

Another 'community' which has been ill served by medieval and early modern historians is that of Gaelic-speaking Scotland. Many histories of late medieval 'Scotland', reflecting their focus on the affairs of the crown and the regional bias of the chronicle and record sources on which they are constructed, happily equate the kingdom with Lothian, Fife and the north-eastern Lowlands. Most work on Gaelic Scotland in the medieval period has created a different imbalance by concentrating on that icon of independent cultural identity, the MacDonald Lordship of the Isles.[64]

61 Lynch, *Scotland*, chs. 10–11.

62 J. J. MacGavin, 'Robert III's 'Rough Music': charivari and diplomacy in a medieval Scottish court', *SHR*, lxxiv (1995); E. Ewan and M. Meikle, eds., *Women in Scotland, c.1100–c.1750* (East Linton, forthcoming); also chapter 9, below, by Elizabeth Ewan. See too T. Brotherstone, D. Simonton and O. Walsh, eds., *Gendering Scottish History: An International Approach* (Glasgow, 1999).

63 R. J. Goldstein, *The Matter of Scotland: Historical Narrative in Medieval Scotland* (Nebraska, 1993); L. O. Fradenburg, *City, Marriage, Tournament: Arts of Rule in Late Medieval Scotland* (Wisconsin, 1991).

64 E.g. *Acts of the Lords of the Isles, 1336–1493*, ed. J. and R. W. Munro (SHS, 1986); J. Bannerman, 'The Lordship of the Isles', in Brown, *Scottish Society*; A. Grant, 'Scotland's "Celtic Fringe" in the late Middle Ages: the MacDonald Lords of the Isles and the kingdom of Scotland', in R. R. Davies, ed., *The British Isles, 1100–1500* (Edinburgh, 1988). A rather different geographical perspective is evident in M. MacGregor, 'A Political History of the MacGregors before 1571' (University of Edinburgh, unpublished PhD thesis, 1989). MacGregor's recent appointment to a post in the Department of Scottish History, University of Glasgow, should do much to ensure the continued vitality of research into Gaelic society and culture in the 15th and 16th centuries.

Yet, even at the height of its power, the political and cultural influence of the Lordship of the Isles covered only a part of Gaelic-speaking Scotland, and the Lordship's eventual fate – confrontation with the crown ending in persecution and destruction – was only one of the routes taken by aristocrats who dominated Gaelic-speaking areas during the late medieval period. The durability of native aristocratic families and their domination of large areas of the kingdom outwith the Hebrides is a phenomenon which has been little studied. Similarly, the long-term assimilation and integration of the leaders of Argyllshire, Perthshire and Galwegian kindreds into crown service and the ranks of the wider Scottish nobility is a historical process deserving investigation. Given the attention devoted by medieval historians to the Lordship of the Isles (if not to Gaelic lordship as a whole), the sixteenth century – although it has prominence in contemporary Gaelic literature as the 'century of the forays' – has, until very recently, been *terra incognita*.[65] This neglect has allowed an unbalanced view of the extent of the power and authority of the crown to gain currency. Sixteenth-century historians might learn from medievalists' scepticism on this issue.

By the sixteenth century the evidence suggests – although it has not been fully exploited as yet – that the locality was being redefined. The introspective local society of Easter Ross survived the potential disturbance caused by the Reformation through the comparatively easy progress made by the abbots of Fearn to lay landlords, with their influence unimpaired.[66] On the other hand, the authority of the sixth Lord Hume in Berwickshire and the Merse was progressively undermined in the last quarter of the sixteenth century by the rise of more assertive minor lords or greater lairds within his kinship network. The Humes of Wedderburn and Manderston outflanked him both in the locality and at court.[67] Despite this there was a clear appreciation of the ties which bound lordship and locality. When David Hume of Godscroft wrote his *History of the House and Race of Douglas* in the early seventeenth century – a work amended for publication in 1644 – he thought that the Douglas bonds of alliance and manrent were important enough to be listed in a separate index.[68]

The best known example of a local study is Donaldson's on the 'conservative north'.[69] Yet what was meant here was less a coherent locality than a sprawling region – the 'conservative' *north-east*, ranging from the Mounth to Moray. This was an area which even the magnate family of Gordon found difficult to contain with consistency. The contrasting area of the 'radical south-west',

[65] See MacGregor, 'Political History of the MacGregors'; J. Dawson, 'The origins of the 'Road to the Isles': trade, communications and Campbell power in early modern Scotland', in Mason and Macdougall, *People and Power in Scotland*; idem, 'Two kingdoms or three? Ireland in Anglo-Scottish relations in the mid-sixteenth century', in Mason, *Scotland and England*.

[66] *The Calendar of Fearn: Text and Additions*, ed. R. J. Adam (SHS, 1991), passim.

[67] M. Meikle, 'Lairds and Gentlemen: A Study of the Landed Families of the Eastern Anglo-Scottish Borders, 1540–1603' (University of Edinburgh, unpublished PhD thesis, 1989).

[68] See F. Gilfillan, 'David Hume of Godscroft: His Life and Work' (University of Edinburgh, unpublished PhD thesis, 1994); the list occurs in a recently rediscovered manuscript copy of the History; for the text and commentary, see *David Hume of Godscroft's The History of the House of Douglas*, ed. D. Reid (Scottish Text Soc., 1996).

[69] G. Donaldson, 'Scotland's conservative north', as reprinted in idem, *Scottish Church History* (Edinburgh, 1985), 191–203.

though also remote, was a more coherent locality.[70] The continuing intractability, in terms of the crown's authority, of large areas of the mainland is suggested by the repeated failure of Campbell earls of Argyll and Gordon earls of Huntly as lieutenants of the kingdom. Both families were increasingly conspicuous at court during the sixteenth century, but in the same century each was also provoked into rebellion.

All this suggests that the study of interaction between central authority and local powerbases requires greater nuance. The Reformation should perhaps be treated in the way the seventeenth-century Civil War has been by historians of England – as an opportunity for lifting the veil which usually conceals the secret workings of society.[71] The new reformed order worked best, it has been argued, where it conformed to the existing 'political culture' of the locality: the lairds and feuars of Monifieth, for example, ran their kirk session not like a Genevan consistory, but like a baron court – the institution which they knew best.[72]

The period between about 1450 and 1600 saw the conspicuous emergence of the 'middling sort'. Some of its layers have been treated more fully than others. The lairds, despite their new-found prominence in at least local politics have attracted surprisingly few definitive studies, and the character of their new role remains unresolved.[73] The professions have been treated more fully. The new breed of churchmen – ministers of the reformed Church – have received detailed study, though not always of a systematic kind; and the various branches of the medical profession have recently found their historian.[74] Yet the treatment of the lawyers has been patchy; more work has been done on their origins in the fifteenth century than on the explosion in their numbers in the second half of the sixteenth.[75]

The fate of the different 'middling sorts' is symptomatic of the links so far forged between medieval and early modern historians and of the opportunities which greater dialogue might open up. A mid-1990s conference on the nobility in the medieval and early modern periods, for example, allowed for a coherent discussion of the economic context in which the fortunes of the landed classes shifted across the centuries.[76] This provided a salutary lesson about what has not been done and a welcome harbinger of things to come. For sixteenth-century historians, who have to explain complex evolution rather than abrupt change, the challenge is to draw a clearer picture of the provenance of the key push and pull factors in their period. For medievalists the most pressing need is to extend their agenda beyond politics and lordship and to work towards a more complete account of Scottish society as a whole.

70 S. Adams, 'The making of the radical south-west: Charles I and his Scottish kingdom, 1625–1649', in J. Young, ed., *Celtic Dimensions of the British Civil Wars* (Edinburgh, 1997).

71 A. Everitt, *The Community of Kent and the Great Rebellion* (Leicester, 1966), 1.

72 F. Bardgett, *Scotland Reformed*, 147, 157–8.

73 M. Meikle, 'The Invisible Divide: the greater lairds and the nobility of Jacobean Scotland', *SHR*, lxxi (1992).

74 H. M. Dingwall, *Physicians, Surgeons, and Apothecaries: Medicine in Seventeenth-Century Edinburgh* (East Linton, 1995).

75 A significant start, however, has been made in J. Finlay, 'Professional Men of Law before the Lords of Council, *c.*1500–*c.*1550' (University of Edinburgh, unpublished PhD thesis, 1998).

76 Hosted by the Department of Scottish History, University of Edinburgh.

# 5

# Historians and Languages: Medieval and Humanist Views of Celtic Britain

*Ulrike Morét*

From the late fourteenth century Scots considered themselves to be divided into two groups, each with its own distinctive language and culture: the Gaelic-speaking Highlanders, and the Scots-speaking Lowlanders. Although there was much contact and cultural exchange between these groups, written sources also give ample evidence of mistrust and prejudice between the two and of the mutual formation of stereotypes. It is mainly with the attitudes of the Lowlanders that this essay is concerned.

Before Hector Boece published his *Scotorum historia a prima gentis origine* in 1527, Lowland views of Highlanders were characterised by disrespect. In poetry Lowlanders tended to satirise their neighbours as savages who spoke incomprehensibly in either Erse or faulty English and who were prompted by inferior motives. Early Lowland historians raised the criticism to a more serious level. Scholars such as John of Fordun, Walter Bower and John Mair regarded the Highland lifestyle as something that ought not to be found in a civilised country. They were worried about Highland hostility towards Lowlanders and they explained their antagonism as having been caused by the linguistic barrier between the two parts of Scotland. Fordun, for example, wrote that the 'people' (*gens*) of the Gaelic Scots were 'hostile to the English people and language, but also towards their own nation'.[1] This was confirmed by Mair.[2]

While Fordun and Mair clearly described Scotland as a country of two different peoples, languages and cultures, these early Lowland authors did not attempt to explore the historical roots of this situation. The origins of Scotland, England and Wales had been muddled in the origin legend produced by Geoffrey of Monmouth in the twelfth century. This had featured the legendary Trojan Brutus and his three sons, who had inherited respectively England, Scotland and Wales. The eldest had acquired England, and the English kingdom thus gained a hegemony in the island. This tale was repeatedly used for political purposes by later English monarchs, most notoriously by Edward I. Against this, the Scots advanced their own origin myth, which involved the Greek Gathelos and the Egyptian Pharaoh's daughter, Scota, who had settled in Scotland with their respective followers.[3] In Fordun's words:

> But because this people of mixed race derived its origin from the Greeks and Egyptians, they adapted the names of these peoples to form their own,

1. *Chron. Fordun*, i, 24; ii, 38.
2. 'Nor are they very fond of us, because of our English language and different customs': Mair, *Historia*, bk. IV, cap. 20.
3. For a study of the English and Scottish origin myths, see W. Matthews, 'The Egyptians in Scotland: the political history of a myth', *Viator*, i (1970), 389–406.

> in case the memory of their former rulers might by chance disappear from the world in the long passage of time. So the Greeks called themselves Gaels after their ruler Gaythelos, and ... the Egyptians ... called themselves Scots after Scota. Later on, and still at the present time, both peoples are proud to use this last name alone. Hence someone has written:
>
> The Scots derive their name from Scota
> and all Scota is derived from the Scots,
> while increased use of the name
> of the leader Gaythelos is forbidden.[4]

Fordun noted, then, that the name of *Gathelenses* (or Gaels) who never seem to have made up more than half of the population, had been abandoned – indeed forbidden – as a name for the Scots.[5] However, Fordun did not explain why this had happened. Moreover, if we are to understand from him that the *Gathelenses* spoke Gaelic, what language did the *Scoti* speak? Surely Fordun did not imagine that it would have been Egyptian. Later, in his well-known passage about the differences between the Gaelic-speaking Highlanders and the Scots-speaking Lowlanders, Fordun wrote that the latter speak a [*lingua*] *Theuthonica*, while the Gaels speak the [*lingua*] *Scotica*.[6] This means that the former *Gathelenses* now spoke the language of the former *Scoti*, while the *Scoti* had adopted another language that was not previously connected with them.

Hector Boece partly disentangled the confusion. In Fordun's account the 'Egyptian' Scots or non-*Gathelenses* emerged as the more important part of the population whose name was adopted by all: Boece turned this around. He no longer minimised the importance of the Gaels in the ancestry of the Scots but instead put special emphasis upon it. He presented the Highlanders as the original Scots who had preserved the ancient Scottish language and culture which had long since been abandoned by Lowland Scots. Rather than describing them as anachronistic barbarians whose resistance to civilisation was an embarrassment to the whole nation, Boece presented the Gaels as conscious preservers of a precious Scottish tradition which had once been common to both Highlanders and Lowlanders. Their modesty and austerity, he held, was admirable and worthy of imitation.[7] Boece thus added a new historical dimension to the description of Highlands and Lowlands. He gave the Highlanders an immense cultural and national importance. Scotland's cultural roots were shown to be Gaelic, and later authors drew on Boece to remove all doubt that the country possessed a distinct cultural identity. Moreover, the archaic customs of the Gaels seemed to tie in well with Boece's argument that the Scots were the most ancient nation on the island. On a political level, however, Boece had nothing new to say about the Gaels. He did not excuse their hostility or their lack of commitment to king and government and, just as before him John Mair

4 *Chron. Fordun*, i, 24; translation from *Chron. Bower* (Watt), i, 67.

5 Gaels is the translation of *Gathelenses* given in Watt's bilingual edition.

6 Cf. *Chron. Fordun*, i, 24; ii, 38.

7 For a more detailed study of the views of Hector Boece and Scottish humanists after him, see U. Morét, 'Gaelic History and Culture in Mediaeval and Sixteenth-Century Lowland Scottish Historiography' (University of Aberdeen, unpublished PhD thesis, 1993).

had marginalised the Highlanders when he wrote, 'Yet the weight and government of the whole reign is almost entirely with the civilised Scots', so Boece neglected the Gaelic involvement in Scotland's history, and criticised what he considered to be the Gaels' rebellious tendencies.[8]

Boece's interpretation of Highland culture, which had been prompted by antiquarian enthusiasm and a typical humanistic interest in primitive but noble peoples, was taken up by subsequent Lowland historians, most notably John Leslie and George Buchanan.[9] It also appealed to the learned public on the Continent. At the same time, however, most Lowlanders seem to have clung to old prejudices, and most still considered the Gaels to be barbaric and dangerous. Even though Boece believed that the key to the original Scottish culture might lie in the Gaelic language,[10] among Lowland poets the tradition of treating it as an object of ridicule remained strong. To a king like James VI Gaelic seemed to be the source of many Highland troubles, prompting him to devise measures, such as the 1609 Statutes of Iona, which were designed to eliminate the language.[11]

The testimonies of outsiders also show the small extent to which the scholarly perception of Highlanders had been adopted by the rest of Lowland Scotland. The Welsh scholar Humphrey Llwyd, for example, found Lowlanders to be contemptuous of Gaelic Scots, and criticised them for it.

> That the Scots are descended from the Irish is well known to themselves as well as to everybody else, and they are referred to by the same name by our people [the Welsh], that is 'Gwyddyl'. That they came from there seems to be well proven by the fact that they share the same language and customs with the Irish, and are given the same name by British speakers. For the southern Scots are not true Scots, but are descended from the English, of whom a great multitude arrived in Scotland whilst fleeing from William Duke of Normandy, and to this day they glory in their English origins; at the same time both they and the English look upon the true Scots as barbarians and uncivilised people.[12]

Llwyd attributed these superior Lowland attitudes to their English descent. His statement that all Lowlanders were of English origin, although a popular contemporary perception is, of course, as much of an oversimplification as Boece's conviction that all Lowlanders were originally Gaels who had unlearned

8 Mair, *Historia*, bk. I, cap. 8.

9 Cf. John Leslie, *De Origine*; G. Buchanan, *Rerum Scoticarum historia* (Edinburgh, 1582).

10 'Nos vero qui in confinio Angliae sedes habemus sicut Saxonicam linguam per multa commercia bellaque, ab illis didicimus nostramque deseruimus: ita priscos mores omnes reliquimus, priscusque nobis scribendi mos vt & sermo incognitus est. At qui Montana incolunt vt linguam ita & caetera prope omnia arctissime tuentur.' See Hector Boece, *Scotorum historia a prima gentis origine* (Paris, 1527), fo. 19v.

11 Cf., e.g., William Dunbar's poem *Fasternis Even in Hell,* ll 109–20, or Alexander Montgomerie's *Ane Answer to ane Helandmanis Invective*. An earlier example of the same tradition can be found in Richard Holland's work, *The Buke of the Howlat*, ll. 794–806.

12 Humphrey Llwyd, *Commentarioli Britannicae descriptionis fragmentum* (Cologne, 1572), 31r–v. (my translation). This work was written much earlier but only published after Llwyd's death in 1568.

their language and customs.[13] However, Llwyd's belief that the English, or Englishness as such, were responsible for Lowland attitudes, deserves closer consideration. The Gaelic Scots were not the only non-English-speaking people in the British Isles. An examination of how other Celtic peoples – primarily the Welsh and Cornish – were viewed by contemporaries makes for an interesting parallel with the Highland–Lowland polarity in Scotland.

The sources available for such a comparison include topographical descriptions and historiographical works of the sixteenth and early seventeenth centuries. While topographical descriptions are of obvious relevance to such a study, historiographical works are useful because they often contain descriptions of peoples and countries. These descriptions – found mostly at the beginning of such works – are of a significance that goes beyond mere geographical interest. To write a national history was a means of consolidating a people's national identity, and the description of a country's physical features and inhabitants was, like a map, designed to convey an image of the country as a complete and clearly outlined unit with which one could more easily identify. The various parts and inhabitants of a country were often described with respect to the way in which they fitted into the whole and often the components were judged accordingly.

Gaelic, of course, was only one of several non-English languages spoken on the British Isles in the sixteenth and early seventeenth centuries. Speakers of English, or its earlier forms, had in fact arrived on the scene rather late. When in the fifth century the Angles, Saxons and Jutes first settled in what was to become England, the Britons, speakers of a P-Celtic language, had been established on the island for centuries. They had lived under Roman occupation for more than three centuries and had themselves superseded a Bronze Age people about whom very little is known. After the departure of the Romans the Britons, divided into numerous small kingdoms, had been unable to resist the attacks of the Picts from the north and the Scots from Ireland. The Germanic tribes – not entirely unfamiliar with the terrain because of a long tradition of piratical activity – helped the Britons fight these enemies; but subsequently they occupied the land which they had come to rescue. Within a relatively short time the Germanic tribes had conquered roughly the area of modern England. Seven kingdoms were formed, the supremacy over which was held by several individual kingdoms in turn until it finally passed to Wessex. The name of one tribe, *Angli* (Old English: *Englisc*), was assumed as a national name, while the native Britons, who did not speak their language, were called *wealas* ('foreigners') or *Brytwealas* ('British foreigners'). The countries to which the Britons mainly retreated came

[13] It can also be found in William Camden: 'Tunc enim omnis Septentrionalis Britanniae plaga in Scotorum nomen concessit, vna cum citeriori illa regione citra Cluidam, & Edenburgh frith. Illam enim Northumbriae partem fuisse, & a Saxonibus possessam nemo repugnat; & hinc est quod omnes qui orientalem Scotiae partem tenent, & Lawlandmen, id est, inferiores vocantur, sint origine Anglo-Saxones, & Anglice loquantur. Vero qui Occidentalem oram incolant, Hetchlandmen dicti, id est, superiores, sint Scoti, & Hibernice loquantur, infestissimique sint illis inferioribus, qui Anglico idiomate vtuntur.' See W. Camden, *Britannia sive florentissimorum regnorum, Angliae, Scotiae, Hiberniae, et insularum adiacentium ex intima antiquitate chorographica descriptio* (3rd edn, London, 1600), 95.

to be known by names which reflect the perception of their inhabitants as outsiders: the elements '-wall' in 'Cornwall', as well as the words 'Wales' and 'Welsh', are derived from the Anglo-Saxon word for foreigners. While Britain and the outside world adopted the terms coined by the Anglo-Saxons, the names by which the Britons referred to their own countries and languages came to be used only by Celts. It remains to add that the Celts had their own way of referring to the people who had invaded their land. While elsewhere all of the Germanic invaders came to be known as 'Angles', the Britons and the Gaels, after the same principle, lumped them together as 'Saxons'.

Scotland, too, had been the scene of drastic linguistic developments. Following the settlement of Scots from Ireland in Dál Riata around the middle of the fifth century both the Pictish language and the Cumbrian language of Strathclyde ultimately vanished, as Gaelic came into general use, except in Lothian. A Scandinavian element was added after the Viking incursions. Then Gaelic gradually gave way to Scots. In Scotland, as in England, one part of the population came to be known as 'foreigners' to another, though in Scotland it was the Gaels, speakers of the older language, who called the intruding Lowlanders 'foreigners'. In 1521 John Mair reckoned that the numerical balance between Scots and Gaelic in Scotland was about equal.[14]

In the later Middle Ages, then, a variety of languages were spoken in England, Scotland, Wales and for that matter in Ireland too. The remainder of this chapter will focus on two of these languages, Cornish and Welsh – the two languages with which the English were in closest geographical contact.

Before roughly the end of the fifteenth century, neither the Cornish language nor the Cornish people receive much attention in histories, or in other works which contain descriptions of the island. The Celtic-speaking population of Cornwall was descended from the British Dumnonii, whose kings had ruled over Cornwall and modern Devon. The Dumnonian kingdom had emerged in the fifth century, after the end of the Roman occupation, and disappeared in the early tenth century, when it was finally subjugated by King Æthelstan. Anglo-Saxon settlement in Cornwall caused the retreat of the Cornish language to the west of the peninsula.

Incorporated within the English kingdom since Anglo-Saxon times, the Cornish no longer acted as a nation in the way that the Welsh and Scots did. Cornwall was *de iure* a part of England, with the status of a shire, and in 1337 it was erected into a duchy. It was marginal to mainstream English political developments, but maintained close contact with Brittany which, having become home to British emigrants from the British Isles, spoke a language very similar to Cornish.

The Cornish language was an issue of importance to the Church. The bishops of Exeter, in whose diocese Cornwall was located, seem to have been careful that those Cornish people who did not speak English were properly catered for and taught in their own language.[15] The appointment of clergymen in Cornwall often depended upon their linguistic ability. In the Cornish mystery plays and

14 'Vna Scotiae medietas Hibernice loquitur': Mair, *Historia*, bk. II, cap. 8.

15 Cf. P. B. Ellis, *The Cornish Language and its Literature* (London and Boston, 1974), 33–4.

religious prose literature the Cornish language was the vehicle by which the essence of the Christian faith was popularly conveyed. Apart from this, Cornish as a language was hardly noticed, even by historians. There is, for example, no mention of it in Higden's influential *Polychronicon*, written in the fourteenth century, even although Higden was interested in language and the results of linguistic interaction.[16]

In 1387 Higden's translator, John Trevisa, added nothing on the subject, despite often including his own observations in Higden's text.[17] It seems curious that Trevisa, himself a Cornishman who possibly had some knowledge of Cornish, should not have acknowledged the existence of the language. It has been suggested that he did not consider Cornish to be 'worthy of special mention';[18] but he and Higden were much preoccupied with the fortunes of the English language, which had only recently emerged from the threat to its existence posed by French. However, their silence on Cornish explains why William Caxton, who published a *Description of Britain* in 1480 which was closely based on Higden, did not mention its existence either.

The later fifteenth century saw an increase in Cornish political activity. During the closing stages of the Wars of the Roses, Cornwall and Wales had largely supported Henry Tudor. Henry had strong Welsh connections and had raised hopes of liberation among the conquered Welsh. Once victorious, he rewarded his former supporters in Wales and Cornwall and attracted many Welshmen and Cornishmen to his court; but disillusionment soon followed. Henry did not promote the Welsh cause as had been expected. Instead, he treated Wales and England as a single kingdom which he ruled from London. In the south-west, Cornwall's secluded status too was invaded by the policies of a new centralist government. In 1497 Perkin Warbeck's revolt led to two unsuccessful Cornish insurrections which 'thrust Cornwall forward into the gaze of the English administration in an unfavourable light. It was the beginning of the end of Cornwall's separate existence.'[19] English became the only language of the Cornish church following the Reformation and, despite the Cornish rising of 1549 in protest at the newly monolingual church, the use of Cornish in churches was abandoned. This dealt the most severe blow to the language and caused its rapid decline.

Nevertheless, references to Cornish are more frequent from the sixteenth century. In 1521 John Mair still counted only three languages on the island of Britain – Welsh, Gaelic and English. Of Welsh, however, he wrote: 'Towards the south there is the Welsh language, which the British-speaking Britons use.'[20] Although he did not mention Cornish specifically, neither did he state expressly that Welsh was spoken only by the Welsh, apparently keeping an open mind as to the identity of the 'British-speaking Britons'.

Further references to Cornish and the Cornish people appear in Andrew Borde's

16 Cf. *Polychronicon Ranulphi Higden, Monachi Cestrensis*, ed. C. Babington and J. R. Lumby (Rolls Ser., 1865–86), ii, 156–63.

17 Ibid.

18 M. F. Wakelin, *Language and History in Cornwall* (Leicester, 1975), 94.

19 Ellis, *Cornish Language*, 57.

20 Mair, *Historia*, bk. II, cap. 4.

small and eccentric book, published in the 1550s under the title *The Fyrst Boke of the Introduction of Knowledge. The which doth teache a man to speake parte of all maner of Languages, and to knowe the usage and fashion of al maner of countreys.* This work was addressed to the English people, accusing them of boorishness and a lack of interest in anything except fashion, and exhorting them to improve their general knowledge. Borde himself had travelled extensively and had lived in a number of different countries, including Scotland. His book contains brief descriptions of various nations in Europe, but also of the peoples closer to his home:

> In Englande and under the dominion of England be many sondry speches beside englyshe there is frensh used in england specially at Calys, Gernsey, and Jersey: In Englande the walshe tongue is in wales. The Cornyshe tongue in Cornewall, and Iryshe in Irlande, and Frenche in the Englysshe pale. There is also the Northen tongue, the whyche is trew Scotysshe, and the Scottes tongue is the Northen tongue.[21]

Borde's section on Cornwall begins with a number of versed lines which imitate the Cornish dialect of English,[22] and then refers to the bilingual situation in Cornwall: 'In Cornwal is two speches, the one is naughty englyshe, the other is Cornyshe speche. And there be many men and women which cannot speake one worde of Englyshe but all Cornyshe.'[23] It has been pointed out recently that the number of monolingual Cornish speakers was probably not as high in the Middle Ages and sixteenth century as was believed by contemporary English-speaking authors.[24] Borde, however, was certainly under the impression that they were numerous and he decided to teach his readers some of the language. As with most other languages of which he gives samples, he renders the Cornish words and phrases in his own English orthography. The beginning of his list of phrases, for example, reads like this:

> God morow to you syr – Dar day dew a why serra.
> God spede you mayde – Das zoa de whi math tath.
> You be welcome good wyfe – Welcom a whe gwra da.
> I do thanke you syr – Dar dala de why da.[25]

Borde's attitude towards the Cornish does not seem to have been one of great respect, but he was possessed of a humorous and good-natured, if also very idiosyncratic, approach to examining the various nations that he described. The Scots alone he disliked because Scots did not like him.[26] About the Cornish he

21 Andrew Borde, *The Fyrst Boke of the Introduction of Knowledge* ... (London, 1542), ch. 1.

22 Ibid. Borde's book is very valuable for linguistic research. It contains the earliest recorded specimen of the Cornish dialect of early modern English; his other samples of languages as he encountered them in the sixteenth century are also highly interesting.

23 Ibid.

24 Cf., e.g., Wakelin, *Language and History*, 82–3.

25 Borde, *Fyrst Boke*, ch. 1. In the Welsh chapter he apologises for the way he writes the Welsh words: 'And where that I do not wryte true welshe I do write it that euery man may rede it & understand it without any teachynge': See ch. 2.

26 'Also it is naturally geuen, or els it is of a deuyllyshe dysposicion of a scotysh man not to loue nor fauor an englishe man. And I beyng there and dwellynge amonge them was hated but my sciences & other polices did kepe me in fauour that I did know theyr secretes': ibid, ch. 4.

knew next to nothing, but since he was fascinated with languages and their diversity, he listened closely to their speech, and most of his chapter about them deals with their language. Borde did not, however, subject the language to scholarly analysis and he was not apparently aware that Cornish was closely related to Welsh, with which he dealt in the next chapter. The connection is, however, made by other sixteenth-century scholars.

Even in the Middle Ages much more was known about Wales than about Cornwall. Until the sixteenth century the main authority on all matters concerning Wales and the Welsh was Giraldus Cambrensis, who at the end of the twelfth century had written two works about Wales, *Itinerarium Cambriae* and *Descriptio Cambriae*. Giraldus was partly Welsh and began to call himself 'Cambrensis' in order to emphasise this link. His depiction of Wales was accepted widely by both English and Welsh. Humphrey Llwyd, for example, concluded a passage on contemporary Welsh customs by noting: 'So much for the modern customs of the Welsh: you may learn about the ancient customs from Giraldus.'[27] Medieval perceptions of Wales and its history were closely linked with the fictitious history of Brutus, and with Arthurian confusion and mythological muddle. As late as 1480, for instance, Caxton was only able to enlighten his readers as follows:

> But because this people of mixed race derived its origin from the Greeks and Egyptians, they adapted the names of these peoples to form their own, in case the memory of their former rulers might by chance disappear from the world in the long passage of time. So the Greeks called themselves Gaels after their ruler Gaythelos, and ... the Egyptians ... called themselves Scots after Scota. Later on, and still at the present time, both peoples are proud to use this last name alone.

In the following century, however, Polydore Vergil, an Italian cleric who spent much time in England, made an important etymological statement. In his *Anglica Historia*, first published in 1534, he observed that 'Wales' and 'Welsh' were simply names for the Britons coined by the Anglo-Saxons, for no better reason than that they could not understand the British language, adding: 'This is the true explanation and origin of the Welsh name, which to my knowledge nobody has found out before me. And whoever thinks that the country is named after some king or queen is doubtless hallucinating.'[28] In fact, this point had already been made by Giraldus Cambrensis. However, after centuries in which misguided etymological explanations, such as that offered by Caxton, had gone uncontradicted, Vergil was probably the first to reintroduce this piece of knowledge into the discussion. It made him very unpopular. Some took ill the fact that it was a foreigner who had made the rediscovery. Now in their own works Vergil's critics pretended that they had known all along where the word 'Wales' came from because they had read Giraldus Cambrensis, while Vergil, who had not done so, had merely shown his foolishness and ignorance. Some of the criticism was personal and unpleasant, and it continued even after Vergil's

27 Llwyd, *Commentarioli*, 50v.
28 Polydore Vergil, *Anglica Historia* (3rd edn, Basel, 1555), 8.

death in 1555.[29] Although it was now established that the word *Wales* was of English origin, explanations of the Celtic word *Cymru* – *Cambria* in Latin sources – remained far-fetched:

> The third sonne [i.e. of Brutus] Camber had to his part all that which remained vndiuided, lieng within the Spanish and the Irish seas, and separated from England, with the riuers Seauerne and Dee, and this part was after his name called Cambria, and the inhabitants thereof Cambry, and their language Camberaec, and so are at this daie.[30]

What mattered most, however, was the realisation that the Welsh had preserved the language of the ancient Britons: 'The Welsh speak the British language, and are descendants of the Britons.'[31] Their language was the same as that which was used in British times:

> Which is an euident token that this is the same language which the Brytaines spake at the beginning: for the works of Merdhyn and of Taliessin, who wrote aboue 1000. yeares past, are almost the same words which they vse at this daie, or at the least easie to be vnderstanded of euerie one which knoweth perfectlie the Welsh toong, especiallie in Northwales.[32]

The addendum 'especiallie in Northwales' refers to the division between the Welsh-speaking north and the southern part of the country where the language was used to a lesser extent. But while Borde stated with his usual directness that 'Sowth Wales is best, but for all the variaunce of the premisses they can not speke .x. wordes to gither of Welsh', the point seems to have been underemphasised by the Welsh themselves.[33]

Now that the ground was prepared, the Cornish too were included in the discussion and their status as ancient Britons was acknowledged, even if the fact that Cornish and Welsh were similar but not quite the same initially led to misunderstanding. Vergil, for example, believed that the Cornish originally came from France and that, although Welsh and Cornish had many words in common, their grammatical structures were different.[34] Again this earned him criticism, marked by allusions to his 'ignorance'.[35] Llwyd, as a Welsh speaker, wrote from a more informed position:

[29] E.g. David Powell, a Welsh author, first repeats exactly what Vergil had written, but then adds: 'Neither is this anie new inuention, although Polydore Virgil with an Italian brag dooth glorie himselfe to be the first that espied it out, for diuers ancient writers doo alledge the same cause of the name of Wales, of whom Syluester Giraldus is one, who wrote in the time of Henrie the second after the conquest, before 380. yeares passed: which is an euident token, that the said Polydore did either neuer see nor read the ancient histories of this realme, or dissembleth the same to the aduancement and praise of himselfe and his countrie': see David Powell, *The historie of Cambria, now called Wales ... written in the Brytish language aboue two hundreth yeares past: translated into English by H. Lhoyd Gentleman: corrected, augmented and continued ... by Dauid Powel* (London, 1584), 2.

[30] Ibid.

[31] Cambri lingua utuntur Britannica, gnesiique Britanni sunt': Llwyd, *Commentarioli*, 41v.

[32] Powell, *Historie of Cambria*, 4.

[33] Borde, *Fyrst Boke*, ch. 2.

[34] Cf. Vergil, *Anglica Historia*, 9.

[35] Cf. Llwyd, *Commentarioli*, 15v.

> The last of all is Cornwall, which by its inhabitants and by ourselves is called Kernow, and by the English Corwall. The Saxons had driven the remainder of the Britons into these confined places, and because they were using the British language, which they could not understand, they called them 'Cornwalas', that is, the Cornish Welsh, in the same way as they also called us 'Brytwealar', the British Welsh. This is the true etymology of the name ... They use the British language, and almost all their words can be found to be similar to ours, although in their syntax there seem to be some insubstantial differences.[36]

David Powell confirmed this, and included the third British-speaking country, Brittany:

> Besides this, where at this daie, there doo remaine three remnants of the Brytaines, diuided euerie one from other, with the seas which are in Wales, Cornewall (calles in Brytish Cerniw) and little Brytaine, yet almost all the particular words of these three people are all one, although in pronunciation and writing of the sentences they differ somewhat, which is no maruell, seeing that the pronunciation in one realme in often so diuers, that one can scant vnderstand the other.[37]

Finally, in 1586, William Camden, the great English antiquarian, consolidated the Britons' cause with further and deeper research in his *Britannia*; and by 1602, when Richard Carew, a Cornish gentleman and scholar, wrote his *Survey of Cornwall*, Camden's work had become a standard handbook of British antiquities which yielded quotable information of the highest scholarly value: 'Touching the personall estate of the Cornish Inhabitants, to begin with their name in generall, I learned by master Camden ... that Ptolomy calleth them Damnonii, Strabo, Ostidamnii, and Artemidoros, Cossini.'[38] The close affinity between Welsh and Cornish too was by now firmly established, and presented by Carew from an interesting insider's point of view:

> And as the Cornish names hold an affinity with the Welsh, so is their language deduced from the same source, and differeth only in the dialect. But the Cornish is more easie to bee pronounced, and not as unpleasing in sound, with throat letters, as the Welsh.[39]

Although this essay has dealt only with references to language, and not with references to manners and customs, it is nevertheless possible to come to some conclusions. It appears that the perception of Welsh and Cornish speakers held by English authors was different from the perception of Gaelic speakers by Lowland Scottish authors. Yet it might be added that the perception of Gaelic Scots among many English was not essentially different from that held by Lowland Scots. The *Chronicle of John Hardyng*, for example, referred to the

36 Ibid.

37 Powell, *Historie of Cambria*, 4.

38 Richard Carew, *The Survey of Cornwall* (London, 1602), fo. 54v.

39 Ibid., fo. 55r.

Highlanders as the 'wilde Scotrie'.[40] Borde wrote of the Highlands: 'And the people of that parte of Scotland be very rude and vnmanered & vntaught'.[41] Moreover, it is difficult to say who was influencing whom on the question of the Gaelic Scots. Llwyd seemed to think that English influence caused Lowlanders to treat Highlanders with contempt, but in many cases the opposite is more likely. Both Hardyng and Borde had visited Scotland and, like other foreign travellers, they had presumably collected their information from Lowland Scots.[42] Other more scholarly authors may have had access to the works of the Scottish historians: Vergil's description, for example, of the Highland–Lowland situation is reminiscent of Fordun and Mair.[43] It seems likely, then, that differences in the perceptions of the Celtic peoples of Britain were linked less to an author's country of origin and more to the public image attached to the individual Celtic peoples themselves; and here, two major points can be made.

The first is historical. The Welsh and Cornish were fortunate in that they could trace their origins to the ancient Britons. The Britons had been glorified in the writings of Geoffrey of Monmouth and some of their glory and nobility was transferred to those who still spoke their language. English kings, especially the Tudors, went to great lengths to trace their lines of descent to King Arthur and other celebrated Britons. Arthur was a glorious ancestor, useful principally because he had ruled over the whole of the island. He thus gave strength to English claims of island-wide overlordship. That English kings sought to establish a close link between themselves and the British past gave respectability to the Welsh, and to some extent the Cornish – even though there were many, like Borde, who continued to see them as highly-strung cheese-roasting harp-players, or worse.[44]

The British language also had a special status, in that it was the oldest language on the island. This had been a unifying factor among the original insular inhabitants, distinguishing them from later intruders. Supposedly indeed, British had once been spoken all over England, Cornwall and Wales, and even by the Picts.[45] By the sixteenth century it was spoken too by Welsh humanists like Humphrey Llwyd and learned by William Camden.[46] But it was not for this reason alone that Gaelic, by comparison, seemed inferior. Gaelic was not an ancient British language. It was the language of newcomers who had arrived at the same time as the Anglo-Saxons. Boece had sought to establish a Scottish past that began centuries before anyone else set foot on the island, but his account was received with scepticism, and was seriously attacked by Llwyd

40 *The Chronicle of John Hardyng ... together with the continuation by Richard Grafton*, ed. H. Ellis (London, 1812), 420.

41 Borde, *Fyrst Boke*, ch. 4.

42 Further examples can be found in P. Hume Brown, *Early Travellers in Scotland* (Edinburgh, 1891).

43 Cf. Vergil, *Anglica Historia*, 7.

44 Cf. Borde, *Fyrst Boke*, ch. 2.

45 Camden, *Description of Britain*, 146.

46 In contrast, the only Scottish humanist who was a Gaelic speaker, George Buchanan, said that he did not like the language and would be happy to see it disappear: Buchanan, *Rerum Scoticarum historia*, i, fo. 2v.

and Camden. That the Scots came from Ireland, and that some still spoke the Irish language, was of no benefit either; for Ireland was now a conquered and troublesome country and English propaganda referred to the native Irish in a critical and often contemptuous fashion.[47]

The second point relates to attitudes. Welsh and Cornish noblemen were endowed with high posts at Henry VII's court and Welsh humanists were among the greatest scholars of the time. The Welsh contributed significantly to the scholarly discussion of British antiquities and according to Llwyd the general standard of education among the Welsh made them popular with the English nobility.[48] While upholding their own language – for instance by printing a bible and prayers in Welsh – the Welsh were respected for the scholarly service which they provided to the English. They 'played the game', while the Gaelic Scots generally did not. Llwyd, for example, recorded proudly that the Welsh 'learn very quickly the manners of the court'.[49] Although many Welsh were doubtless hostile to the English court, their general attitude seems to have been different from that of the Scottish Gaels. Among the latter, as John Leslie noted, the adoption of courtly manners and dress was not looked upon kindly.[50]

Resentment of English speakers and all aspects of Englishness, and an unwillingness to communicate with the English, was evident in all the Celtic nations of the British Isles. Instances are recorded where Celtic speakers, out of hostility, created an artificial linguistic barrier. Carew, for example, wrote of the Cornish:

> Most of the Inhabitants can no word of Cornish; but very few are ignorant of the English: and yet some so affect their owne, as to a stranger they will not speake it: for if meeting them by chance, you inquire the way or any such matter, your answere shalbe, *Meea nauida cowza sawzneck*, I can speake no Saxonage.[51]

More important than hostility, though, were differences in culture. These made for a much greater degree of inaccessibility in the case of the Gaels than in the case of the Britons. While, for the Welsh, the English court was the centre of

47 See, e.g., B. Bradshaw *et al.*, eds., *Representing Ireland: Literature and the Origins of Conflict, 1534–1660* (Cambridge, 1993); A. Hadfield and J. McVeagh, eds., *Strangers to that Land: British Perceptions of Ireland from the Reformation to the Famine* (Gerrards Cross, 1994).

48 'Vnde fit ut paucos per totam Angliam invenies nobiles quorum famulitii (qua in re Angli omnes gentes superant) magna pars non sit de Cambria oriunda ... Hac tamen in re eos [i.e. Anglos] vincentes, quod nullus sit adeo pauper quin liberos suos aliquo tempore scholae ad litteras discendas tradit, & qui studio proficiunt, in academias mittentes, Iuri civilii pro maiori parte operam dare compellunt. Vnde evenit, quod maior pars eorum qui in hoc regno Ius civile aut Pontificum profitentur Cambri natione sunt. Paucos etiam ex rudiori populo invenies qui legere & scribere proprium sermonem, cytharamque suo more pulsare nesciunt: Nunc etiam & Sacra Scriptura & preces ecclesiasticae in hac lingua impressari habentur.' Llwyd, *Commentarioli*, 50v.

49 Ibid.: 'aulicos ... mores citissime discentes'.

50 'They preserve completely unchanged the ancient form of dress and lifestyle, and they are so assiduous about it that their lords and sub-kings, when they go to the King's court and dress themselves in more elegant and refined clothes after the manner of the court, always on return to their own people strip off this courtly elegance and dress according to their native style as quickly as possible unless they want to incur the hatred of all, and the gravest insults': Leslie, *De Origine*, i, 59–60 (my translation).

51 Carew, *Survey of Cornwall*, 56r.

culture and power, in Scotland the royal court faced strong competition from that of the Lord of the Isles. To the Gaels the latter was a cultural centre and focus of power that made them less inclined to look eastwards. It is possible that if a king with strong Highland connections had succeeded to the Scottish throne, much as Henry VII had become king of England, the Gaelic Scots might have found the Scottish court and communication with the Lowlands more attractive. As it was, their orientation and interest lay in the opposite direction. They accepted the political link which tied them to the Lowlands, and professed themselves to be loyal to the king of Scots, but cultural and linguistic similarities linked them to Ireland. On the whole they did not think highly of the Lowlanders and satirised them in poetry as kail-growing weaklings. They also looked upon the Lowlanders with bitterness, regarding them as intruders who, with their foreign language and culture, were destroying the culture of a land where once only Gaelic had been spoken. Yet they rarely seem to have raised these issues with Lowlanders. Apart from rare occasions such as the *Flyting of Dunbar and Kennedy*, in which the Gaelic-speaking Kennedy passionately described the Highlanders' view of the Scottish past, Gaelic Scots seem normally to have expressed their feelings on this subject in their own language, and thus kept their opinions to themselves.[52] It was a Lowlander, Hector Boece, who first introduced a more Gaelic-oriented view to Lowland audiences. When Lowland humanists finally began to extol the Highlanders as preservers of Scotland's ancient culture, and when English and Welsh humanists stated that they were the only real Scots, the Gaels still did not respond.

But while they did not speak, there had always been others who spoke for, or rather about, them. These were the Lowland historians, some of whom felt under no obligation to speak kindly of their own compatriots. In the Middle Ages and the Renaissance, their works, as well as travellers' reports, were the main sources of information about Gaelic Scotland. Thus the image of the Gaels was not created by themselves, but by others whose opinions were distorted by prejudice and lack of information. The result was that a predominantly negative view of Highlanders was shared by English and Scottish writers. In England, on the other hand, a more positive view of the Welsh and Cornish developed; and this was substantially because the political and mythological situation encouraged the Welsh to take matters into their own hands and to discuss, improve and broadcast their own image.

52 Cf. lines 345–52, ed. P. Bawcutt (Glasgow, 1998). Unfortunately his opponent Dunbar, whilst richly abusing Kennedy otherwise, has absolutely nothing to say in answer to this particular point. For a study of Gaelic views on the subject, see J. MacInnes, 'The Gaelic perception of the Lowlands', in W. Gillies, ed., *Gaelic and Scotland: Alba agus a'Ghaidhlig* (Edinburgh, 1989), 89–100.

# Part Two

# Authority and Freedom in Country and Town

# 6

# A Celtic Enclave in Norman Scotland: Earl Gilbert and the Earldom of Strathearn, 1171–1223

*Cynthia J. Neville*

In the year 1200, before an assembly of clerics, noblemen and family members, Earl Gilbert of Strathearn set his seal to a charter establishing an Augustinian priory on a site in Perthshire known as the Isle of Masses.[1] The contents of the charter are a fine example of the rhetorical penmanship and pious sentiment that inform many of the documents issued to religious houses by the Anglo-Norman baronage of the later twelfth and early thirteenth centuries: it begins with an invocation of the Holy Trinity, endows the new house with generous gifts, and calls down dire consequences on any who might dare disturb the possessions of the community. But the charter is also remarkable for its peculiarities. The hand in which it was written was already in 1200 being abandoned by royal and baronial scribes as old-fashioned, and the irregular shape and layout of the parchment original suggest an unfamiliarity with current diplomatic practice.[2] Latin was the usual language of Scottish baronial charters of this period, and the Strathearn scribe conformed to practice in this respect, but there is much evidence in his rendition of Celtic personal and place-names of a difficulty in translating these words into appropriate Latinate form. Thus, the little priory known to Gilbert and his Gaelic-speaking familiars as *innis aifrion*[3] was roughly, if eloquently, translated as *insula missarum*.

The unique features of Gilbert's foundation charter clearly attest the distinct characteristics of the earldom of Strathearn in the last decades of the twelfth century and the first of the thirteenth. His was a lordship historically based on the pre-Norman division of the kingdom north of Forth into seven provinces, where Gaelic remained the language of everyday use, tenurial relationships were very often only vaguely defined, and officials whose designations harked back to the early Middle Ages conducted business on behalf of a lord once known as the mormaer. But Strathearn was also becoming, under Earl Gilbert, recognisably Norman in flavour. The knight's feu, hallmark of the classical 'feudal system', made its appearance in the region, the writ-charter became popular as a deed of conveyance (especially with ecclesiastical beneficiaries), and the earl began to involve himself closely with the royal court. In many respects, then, the period 1171–1223 may be regarded as

1 Dupplin Muniments (Kinnoull Trustees, *penes* Messrs Condie, Mackenzie and Co., Perth) no. 108 (printed in *Inchaffray Chrs.*, no. 9).

2 G. G. Simpson, *Scottish Handwriting 1150–1650* (Edinburgh, 1977), 4–5. Compare too the shape of the charters of King William I and Earl David of Huntingdon, described in *RRS*, ii, 84, and K. J. Stringer, 'The charters of David, Earl of Huntingdon and Lord of Garioch: a study in Anglo-Scottish diplomatic', in Stringer, *Nobility*, 79.

3 From the Gaelic *innis* ('island') and *aifrionn*, itself a Gaelicised version of the Latin *offerendum*, 'offering' or 'mass'. See W. J. Watson, *The History of the Celtic Place-Names of Scotland* (Edinburgh, 1926), 354–5; J. B. Johnston, *Place-Names in Scotland* (London, 1934), 206–7.

one of transition in the earldom of Strathearn, of its gradual integration into the administrative structure of Scotland refined by King William I.

The process was as yet gradual and piecemeal. In 1223 there was much in the earldom that was still recognisably Celtic, and despite the efforts of two kings to establish firm control over it, Strathearn remained essentially insular and largely independent of the crown. Real integration would not be complete until after 1250. Gilbert's tenure as earl is therefore of some importance in the history of Scottish 'Normanisation', for it reveals – at numerous levels – the continuity with the Celtic past that until the mid-twentieth century scholars too easily dismissed.

With Gilbert's succession as earl around 1171 something of a 'dark age' in the history of Strathearn gives way to a more enlightened period. Gilbert's immediate predecessors, Malise and Ferteth (who died in 1171), are noted only fleetingly in the early Scottish chronicles, and seldom appear in the witness lists of royal charters.[4] Certainly, neither was anxious to emulate the policy of infefting Anglo-Norman newcomers which David I had inaugurated, and which his successors and their barons perpetuated elsewhere in the kingdom. The prestige of the native earls of Strathearn ensured their standing among the Scottish baronage as a whole, but in contrast with other great men – including the native earls of Fife – the lords of Strathearn were remote and probably little known figures at the royal court.

Gilbert established his first links with the wider political community in Scotland early in his career. Between 1171 and 1200 he appeared numerous times as a witness to baronial and royal deeds.[5] His occasional presence in the king's entourage, such as the royal visit to several northern burghs in 1196–7, indicates that in the early part of his life at least, Earl Gilbert was more active at the royal court than either of his predecessors had been.[6] He also played an important role in the governance of Scotland in this period as justiciar of Scotia.[7] The appointment to a prestigious public office was designed to forge links between the crown and one of its most important native landowners. It served to bring the earl of Strathearn directly within the orbit of royal influence. Other bonds were also created. Shortly after he became earl, Gilbert assigned sizeable Perthshire estates to his brother, Malise, to be held for the service of one knight, a grant that was quickly ratified by King William.[8] In the last decade of the century the earl

4 The activities of the earliest earls are examined in C. J. Neville, 'The Earls of Strathearn from the Twelfth to the Mid-Fourteenth Century, with an Edition of their Written Acts' (University of Aberdeen, unpublished PhD thesis, 1983) [hereafter Neville, 'Thesis'], i, 46–54. The relative scarcity of the native earls from north of the Forth among the witnesses to royal charters is noted in G. W. S. Barrow, *David I of Scotland (1124–1153): The Balance of Old and New* (Reading, 1985), 16.

5 *St Andrews Liber*, 147, 277; *Dunfermline Reg*., nos. 147–8; *Inchcolm Chrs*., 126; *Scone Liber*, no. 32; *RRS*, ii, nos. 128, 137–8, 149–53, 159, 171, 188, 190, 197–8, 203–5, 207–10, 214, 223, 236, 242, 251, 261, 271–4, 278, 281–4, 295, 302, 321–4, 327–8, 333–9, 344–6, 350, 355–6, 359–62, 364, 373, 375, 388, 391–2, 394, 405, 421; *Lindores Cart*., no. 2, App., p. 284; *Inchaffray Chrs*., no. 7; *APS*, i, 387.

6 *RRS*, ii, nos. 350, 356–7, 359–62, 388, 391, 393–4. In 1174, moreover, Gilbert had accompanied William I to France as a prisoner of Henry II of England: Lawrie, *Annals*, 194, 196; Duncan, *Kingdom*, 230.

7 *RRS*, ii, no. 337; G. W. S. Barrow, 'The justiciar', in idem, *The Kingdom of the Scots* (London, 1973), 105–6; Duncan, *Kingdom*, 203.

8 *RRS*, ii, no. 136.

himself became a tenant of the king's brother, Earl David of Huntingdon, for the lands of Kinnaird in Fife.[9] Simultaneously, Gilbert became a tenant-in-chief in three separate estates. These grants are important, for they constitute the first evidence of a direct tenurial relationship between the earl and the crown.

The first royal grant was made between 1175 and 1185, and assigned to the earl the lands of Kinveachy in Inverness-shire – to be held heritably 'as freely and quietly as he holds the earldom of Strathearn'.[10] No military or annual return of any kind was specified. The ambiguity of William's terminology is remarkable: it has been observed that it stands 'in marked contrast ... with the precisely worded conditions of contemporary knight-service charters'.[11] Perhaps most noteworthy is the implication that the native earl governed his territories as something distinct from the feus of other tenants-in-chief. The evidence of a much later period is instructive here. When, in 1343, David II granted the earldom of Strathearn to Sir Maurice Murray, he stipulated that the honour should be held 'as Malise held it'.[12] A later earl, David Stewart, was styled 'earl palatine'.[13] Both the holding clause and the title suggest a breadth of authority that was as unusual in the fourteenth century as it had been in the twelfth.

The second royal grant, made in the late 1180s, bestowed upon Gilbert the land of Madderty, 'with all its lawful appurtenances, in sake, soke, toll, team and infangenthief, to be held ... in feu and heritage, freely and quietly, fully and honourably, for the service of one knight'.[14] The inconsistency of these terms of tenure with the vague conditions implied in the earlier grant is, at first glance, confusing. But the charter reveals that the lands of Madderty did not originally constitute a portion of Gilbert's possessions as earl of Strathearn. They had been held by a royal official and forfeited during the MacWilliam rebellion of 1179–87.[15] The king had been accustomed to receiving military service from his tenant in Madderty and it was expected that he would wish that to continue when he granted the lands to another party. No such precedence could be demanded of the earl of Strathearn in respect of the lands of his earldom proper, or for the newly created feu in Inverness-shire. Barrow has aptly noted that the deliberate ambiguity of some early royal charters to native earls conveys the impression that for the king to have claimed anything more than the traditional requirement to perform forinsec service would have been 'an exceptional burden', and thus an uncustomary, and possibly unlawful, demand.[16]

9 K. J. Stringer, *Earl David of Huntingdon 1152–1219: A Study in Anglo-Scottish History* (Edinburgh, 1985), 269–70.

10 *RRS*, ii, no. 206.

11 G. W. S. Barrow, 'The beginnings of feudalism in Scotland', *Bulletin of the Institute of Historical Research*, xxix (1956), 21.

12 *RRS*, vi, no. 77. The Malise referred to was Earl Malise V, the last of the native family to hold the title. He was forfeited in 1344.

13 *RMS*, i, nos. 389, 526, 666; *Morton Reg.*, ii, no. 121; *Inchaffray Chrs.*, no. 138. Nicholson, *Scotland*, 187, argues that the grant of the earldom in regality 'may have been compensation' for the preference King Robert II had shown the sons of his first marriage, but the broad powers thus bestowed may have been intended to emphasise, in 14th-century terms, the kind of authority historically wielded by the native earls of Strathearn.

14 *RRS*, ii, no. 258.

15 Ibid.

16 Barrow, 'Beginnings of feudalism', 22.

The distinction between the feudal requirements that the king might impose on tenants-in-chief and the largely honorary and independent terms under which the native earl of Strathearn held his lands is well exemplified in the third of William's grants to Gilbert. Around 1214 the king confirmed to the earl the Strathtay estates of Meikleour and Lethendy, which the earl's brother, Malise son of Ferteth (who had no heirs), had gifted to him. The clause that outlined the conditions of tenure states that the lands were to be held 'in feu and heritage ... with sake and soke, pit and gallows, toll, team and infangenthief, freely and quietly, fully and honourably, for the service of one knight, as the charter which granted it to Malise bears witness'.[17] Here, as with the Madderty estates, the crown exacted from a new tenant-in-chief the same service it had been accustomed to receive from the old. The exhaustive *sicut* clause, however, recalls the kind of authority already exercised by the earl elsewhere in his territories. A commonplace jingle in contemporary knight-service charters to royal tenants, it was deliberately intended here to cloak that authority in recognisably feudal terms.

William's designs to bring Gilbert into a direct feudal relationship with the crown were undertaken only in part by establishing him as a tenant-in-chief. Any attempt to enforce formal ties might provoke overt resistance, for there existed no customary means of so doing. But those designs might also be pursued by less aggressive measures, notably by fostering familial ties between the native earl and the Anglo-Norman aristocracy that constituted the foundation of William's administration in Scotland. Two important marriages, approved if not planned by the king, brought the comital family within the large royal entourage. Gilbert's first wife was Maud d'Aubigny, daughter of Sir William d'Aubigny *Brito* and Maud de Senlis, who was cousin to both Malcolm IV and William I.[18] The earl's introduction into the rarefied world of the Norman nobility was expected to open channels through which English and continental ideas might flow into Strathearn. The second important marriage occurred in the 1190s, when a match was arranged between Gilbert's daughter, Maud, and Malcolm, son and heir of Earl Duncan of Fife.[19] The native earls of Fife had a tradition of close relations with the Scottish crown that was already well established by the time of King William, and the linking of the ancient earldoms of Fife and Strathearn brought together two of the oldest families in the realm. Gilbert himself may have welcomed his introduction to the prestigious circle of the king's closest friends and advisors, but he demonstrated little intention of entrenching these men deep in his own territory. Malcolm obtained as a tocher substantial lands within Strathearn, but it is significant that all were situated in the eastern and southern limits of Gilbert's possessions, far from the administrative centre of the earldom. Just as caution and care had tempered the acceptance and dissemination of Anglo-Norman feudal influences by his predecessors, so did

17 *RRS*, ii, no. 524.

18 G. W. S. Barrow, 'The earls of Fife in the twelfth century', *PSAS*, lxxxvii (1952–3), 56–7; idem, *The Anglo-Norman Era in Scottish History* (Oxford, 1980), 89. Gilbert's father-in-law was a substantial landowner in England. See *Early Yorkshire Charters*, ed. W. Farrer (Yorkshire Archaeological Soc., Record Series, Extra Series, 1914–16), i, 460–3; G. E. C[okayne], *The Complete Peerage*, rev. V. Gibbs *et al.* (London, 1910–59), iv, 93–4.

19 Barrow, 'Earls of Fife', 60–1.

Gilbert remain reticent in his own practice of introducing new men and new ideas.

The closing years of the twelfth century mark a turning-point in Earl Gilbert's history. From then until his death in 1223 he withdrew almost entirely from the national scene. He continued, on occasion, to witness royal and baronial charters and deeds and he was present in a formal capacity at public events, such as the funeral of William I in 1214 and the ceremonies that accompanied the enthronement of Alexander II.[20] The absence of the native earl of Strathearn from such honourable gatherings would have been highly unusual. But increasingly the earl confined his presence at public meetings to burghs situated close to his own lands: Perth, Edinburgh, Stirling. Between the years 1171 and 1200, Gilbert's name appears in the witness lists of over eighty charters and deeds; by contrast, the years 1200 to 1223 saw him attest a mere seventeen acts. More than half these later charters related to lands situated within the boundaries of Strathearn.

Gilbert's abrupt withdrawal from the national scene and the focus of his attentions on his own territories are difficult to explain, but it is perhaps no coincidence that the year 1200 also marked the establishment by the earl and his countess of the small priory of Inchaffray in the heart of the earldom, hard by one of the comital residences. For many years on the Isle of Masses there had been a community of brethren, probably secular priests, dedicated to St John the Evangelist.[21] Around 1194 Gilbert made a modest grant to the house of three acres at Fowlis.[22] A few years later he confirmed (or regranted) to it the church of St Chattan of Aberuthven, which his parents had gifted, and further added to the possessions of the brethren by giving to them the church of Madderty and a teind of his cain in wheat, meat, malt, cheese and fish.[23] In the autumn of 1198 Gilchrist, the eldest son of Gilbert and Maud d'Aubigny, had died and been interred in the chapel at Inchaffray. Grief at the loss of his heir may account for the earl's decision in 1200 to establish a priory on the burial site, and may also have contributed to his withdrawal from public life. In the deed by which the house was founded it is possible to read sincere devotion and sorrow.[24]

Inchaffray was never a wealthy house, but Earl Gilbert proved a generous patron. Altogether, he granted to the community some eleven parish churches, the revenues of several estates, crofts, tofts and acres in half a dozen touns, considerable shares in mills, fishing, fowling, venison and timber and, finally, a great variety of gifts in kind and money from his cain and the profits of comital justice.[25] He also took an interest in the affairs of nearby Lindores Abbey,

20 *RRS*, ii, nos. 405, 519; *Moray Reg.*, no. 17; *St Andrews Liber*, 319; *Dunfermline Reg.*, no. 148; *Coupar Angus Chrs.*, i, no. 11; *Chron. Fordun*, i, 280. Gilbert was also one of four arbiters who presided over a session of the court convened in Edinburgh in 1213, in which a settlement was made between the heirs of the earldom of Menteith. See Fraser, *Lennox*, ii, nos. 7–8; *CDS*, i, nos. 2275–6.

21 I. B. Cowan and D. E. Easson, *Medieval Religious Houses in Scotland* (2nd edn, London, 1976), 48.

22 MS cartulary of Inchaffray Abbey, fos. 11v–12r (*Inchaffray Chrs.*, no. 2); *Inchaffray Liber*, nos. 18.

23 Dupplin Muniments, nos. 13, 118, 131 (*Inchaffray Chrs.*, nos. 3–5).

24 Dupplin Muniments, no. 106 (*Inchaffray Chrs.*, no. 9). In 1220–1 the priory was raised to the status of an abbey.

25 These grants are discussed in Neville, 'Thesis', i, 65–9.

possibly as a result of his contacts with the earl of Huntingdon.[26] But in spite of his close ties to the priory of Inchaffray, Gilbert's patronage of the Scottish church was, on the whole, conservative. It was, moreover, highly local and paternalistic in character. His gifts to the brethren on the Isle of Masses, if numerous, were confined to a house which had been established by his own charter, and which he endowed with few lands outside the earldom. Moreover, Inchaffray was a community over which the earl exercised strict and exacting control: the business of the house was seldom undertaken without Gilbert's approval, and sometimes only with his express consent.[27]

The claim of the fifteenth-century chronicler, Walter Bower, that Gilbert gave the bishopric of Dunblane one-third of his possessions, was long ago dismissed as spurious, but relations between Strathearn and the see manifested little of the influence of the Hildebrandine reform movement that was apparent in larger episcopal centres.[28] Dunblane bishops appear under the special protection and patronage of the earl, and episcopal dignitaries are frequently referred to by the name of Strathearn, rather than that of the diocese.[29] There was no formal chapter at Dunblane in the time of Earl Gilbert, and the Gaelic personal names of several episcopal ministers are evidence of the tenacity of Celtic influences within the cathedral's precincts.[30] Reform was on the horizon at Dunblane in 1223, but in the earlier part of the century it had yet to take firm hold.

In spite of the great influx of foreign families into the kingdom of the Scots in the course of the twelfth century and the dominating role that these individuals came to play in the king's court and the royal administration, Strathearn remained largely untouched by change. The tenurial position of the earl in relation to royal authority was left undefined in written record, and the independence enjoyed by Gilbert was not generally shared by the Anglo-Norman barons. The question of rendering knight service to the crown was never clearly addressed. The earl was undoubtedly responsible for making available to the king a common army made up of able-bodied men of the region, as his predecessors had been.[31] But there is no indication that anything other

26 *Lindores Cart.*, nos. 42–3. Gilbert's brother, Malise, was married to Earl David of Huntingdon's natural daughter, Ada. In addition, Gilbert appears to have been a tenant of Earl David for the lands of Kinnaird in Fife: Stringer, *Earl David*, 269–70.

27 The instances are numerous, but see, e.g., Edinburgh University Library, Laing Charters, no. 13 (*Inchaffray Chrs.*, no. 34). Here, the earl grants to the brethren of Inchaffray licence to build a second mill, and a small parcel of land beside his own mill upon which to do so. But the charter stipulates that the canons must build a stank to service both the mills of the priory and his own, and that they must grind no grain reaped from demesne lands.

28 *Chron. Bower* (Watt), iv, 458–9; J. H. Cockburn, *The Medieval Bishops of Dunblane and their Church* (Edinburgh, 1959), 143–4. The influence of ecclesiastical reforms in the later 12th century is discussed in Duncan, *Kingdom*, 256–77. The son of Bishop Abraham of Dunblane caused something of a scandal at the papal court in the early 1210s: see note 62 below.

29 See, e.g., *Inchaffray Chrs.*, nos. 3, 11, 13, 33–4, 39.

30 Duncan, *Kingdom*, 201, noting that the early bishops depended for counsel upon 'a motley but canonical group'. Lists of the Dunblane clerics mentioned in formal record are compiled in Cockburn, *Medieval Bishops of Dunblane*, 237–9.

31 In 1138, e.g., Earl Malise I and an army from Strathearn joined the royal host at the Battle of the Standard: Ailred of Rievaulx, *Relatio de Standardo*, in *Chronicles of the Reigns of Stephen, Henry II, and Richard I*, ed. R. Howlett (Rolls Ser., 1884–90), iii, 189–90.

than the traditional render of foot-soldiers was expected or demanded of Gilbert, nor indeed ever given by him; the service of two knights due from the estates of Madderty, Meikleour and Lethendy was only temporarily vested in him. These lands, together with the military obligation they carried, were granted by the earl to his son, Fergus.[32]

Immunity from strict royal control was perhaps most markedly manifested in the judicial rights that the earl exercised within his territories. The ancient Scottish judicial office of the *judex* was preserved in Strathearn long after it had disappeared elsewhere. That the *judex* was the earl's man rather than the king's is indicated by the fact that when his lands are specifically referred to in charters, the *judex* is always identified with the province of Strathearn, not a royal sheriffdom.[33] The men who held office under Gilbert, all of whom were of Celtic origin, performed a variety of duties on behalf of their lord. One of the most common was the formal perambulation of boundaries; in Strathearn the *judex* is found either among the 'true and good men' appointed to undertake such extents, or is counted among the important men of the locality who witnessed boundary marking.[34] Macbeth *judex* was also present at a large assembly convened in the church of Strageath shortly before Gilbert's death, where the earl's heir pledged himself to safeguard the interests of Inchaffray Abbey.[35] The profits of justice, however, remained the prerogative of Earl Gilbert.

The early earls of Strathearn apparently never sought royal confirmation of the broad judicial powers they exercised, for the same reason that they never looked to the king of Scots for explicit recognition of the wide authority they wielded within their territories. Such powers they exercised by virtue of their historic status in Scottish society. Gilbert granted to the canons of Inchaffray the chattels of any of the priory's tenants who might be convicted in his court.[36] Around 1220 he further gave to the house licence to convene a court of its own, though he reserved to himself the execution of convicted felons. In the charter that records this act, instructions are issued to bailies that 'when asked by the canons they should without delay go to the prior and canons and hold their court even as they would his own'.[37] In the realm of ecclesiastical jurisdiction Gilbert claimed and exercised similar authority. His gifts of parish churches and teinds to the abbey of Inchaffray were made without recourse to episcopal approval and, indeed, with the endorsement of two bishops.[38] Under the vigorous reforming leadership of Bishop Clement (1233–58) the first challenges to comital interference in Dunblane would disturb relations with Earl Robert of Strathearn, but Clement's predecessors were Gilbert's docile servants.

An examination of the household and retinue of Earl Gilbert confirms the impression of conservatism and continuity with an earlier age so evident

32 See below, page 91.

33 G. W. S. Barrow, 'The *Judex*', in *Kingdom of the Scots*, 71; W. D. H. Sellar, 'Celtic Law and Scots Law: survival and integration', *Scottish Studies*, 29 (1981), 3.

34 NAS, GD24/5/1/1. A cartulary copy of the original is printed in *Inchaffray Chrs.*, no. 46.

35 MS cartulary of Inchaffray Abbey, fos. 10v–11v (*Inchaffray Liber*, no. 16).

36 Dupplin Muniments, no. 39 (1) (*Inchaffray Chrs.*, no. 25).

37 NLS, MS Adv. Ch. B1354 (*Inchaffray Chrs.*, no. 43; see also no. 44).

38 *Inchaffray Chrs.*, nos. 10, 30–1.

elsewhere in Strathearn. The comital household was very different from those of contemporary Anglo-Norman barons, such as Earl David of Huntingdon and Roger de Quincy, earl of Winchester.[39] Within Gilbert's entourage there mingled what Duncan has termed a 'collection of overlapping household dignitaries'.[40] Some reflected current Norman models, but others represented the persistence of older Celtic influences: they included Gillenem *dapifer*, the steward Malise, Brice and Macbeth *judices*, Robert *dispensarius*, Henry *rennarius*, Constantine *pincerna*, Anecol *theinus*, as well as clerks, chaplains and a cook.[41]

The official most frequently mentioned in Gilbert's charters is the steward. Until 1200 the term *dapifer* was used almost exclusively in witness lists to describe him; for twenty years thereafter, it appears to have been interchangeable with *senescallus*. If the scribes who drafted the charters intended to imply a distinction between the duties assigned to each of these ministers (as occurred, for example, with respect to the households of both King William and Earl David of Huntingdon), such a nuance has long been lost.[42] It seems likely that the older term *dapifer* was gradually being displaced by the more widely used *senescallus*, and that the choice between the two reflected simply the discretion of the scribes. But in Gilbert's time, household and estate duties were concentrated in a single office.

The surviving records attest the importance of the steward in Gilbert's household. Of the twenty-seven original charters extant from his period as earl, Gillenem the steward witnessed fifteen, his son and successor, Malise, sixteen. Their names almost always appear at the head of those of household dignitaries.[43] The steward was entirely responsible for managing the earl's financial affairs as well as customary renders from his estates, for there is no evidence of a chamberlain in the Strathearn household until the middle of the thirteenth century.[44] Under Earl Gilbert the office of steward was hereditary and as yet no more than honorific. Gillenem was succeeded between 1214 and 1218 by his son, Malise, but the family did not acquire its lands of Tullibardine until after 1223.[45]

The steward and the *judex* are the lay officials whose names occur most frequently in early Strathearn record. But Gilbert's immediate entourage counted a host of other ministers, both lay and ecclesiastical. Two men, one designated by the Latin term *dispensarius*, the other by the old Gaelic name *rannaire*, held office simultaneously.[46] No clear distinction can be made between their duties,

39 Stringer, *Earl David*, 149–76; G. G. Simpson, 'The *familia* of Roger de Quincy, Earl of Winchester and Constable of Scotland', in Stringer, *Nobility*, 102–29.

40 Duncan, *Kingdom*, 432.

41 Neville, 'Thesis', i, 172–94.

42 *RRS*, ii, 34–5; Stringer, *Earl David*, 150.

43 Precedence in witness lists is generally accorded to ecclesiastical dignitaries. In Gilbert's charters the scribes usually allot next place to the comital family: countess, brothers, sons and daughters. Lesser ecclesiastics are then listed. Thus, the steward's name does not usually appear at the top of the list, but it is given prominence among the earl's household ministers.

44 The first mention of a chamberlain occurs in a charter of Malise II, dated 1257: Dupplin Muniments, no. 146 (i) (*Inchaffray Chrs.*, no. 86). Nicholas the chamberlain was the cousin of Earl Malise II.

45 See *Inchaffray Liber*, App., no. 10.

46 Robert was succeeded in his office by a man named Theobald.

and both appear to have been charged with the division and distribution of food within the household. Where the two offices appear together in comital charters, precedence is given to Henry *rannaire*, which may suggest the subordination of one to the other, though the dangers of placing too much emphasis on the order in which the witnesses of baronial *acta* are listed are well known.[47] The duplication of domestic duties by one official with a traditional Gaelic designation and another with a Norman name is a good illustration of more than merely vestigial customs in Strathearn, for the office of *rannaire* had disappeared from the royal household in the 1170s, and is not found among the domestic staff of the Anglo-Scottish earls of Huntingdon and Winchester. The charters do not reveal whether the positions were hereditary but, unlike the steward's, these offices appear to have been more than merely honorary. Theobald the dispenser held the toun of Pitlandy, a tenement situated close to Fowlis, in the centre of Strathearn, which he may have been given as a reward for service to his lord.[48] Henry the *rannaire*, too, was a landholder of modest degree in the toun of Kintocher.[49]

The offices of butler (designated by the old-fashioned title of *pincerna*) and marshal were also included among the earl's lay household ministers. The charter evidence offers little information about the status or duties of these men, but it is noteworthy that their personal names, Constantine and Gillecolm, indicate Celtic origins. In fact, most of the laymen who served the earl of Strathearn were of Celtic, rather than Norman, background. The traditional – and unusual – composition of Gilbert's entourage is evident, too, in the place occupied within it by Anecol the thane. Recent historical work has traced the origins of many thanages to pre-feudal Scotland, and has noted the existence of both royal and comital thanes.[50] The thane of Dunning was Gilbert's man. In several charter witness lists he is referred to as *theinus meus*, and the earl's grant of the church of Dunning to Inchaffray Abbey was made irrespective of any rights Anecol may have enjoyed there.[51] The lands of the thanage of Strowan, near Crieff, may also have been under direct comital control. The nature of the relationship between the earl and these men is difficult to discern, but the freedom with which Gilbert and, later, his great-grandson, Malise III, disposed of lands in Dunning and Strowan lend credence to Barrow's argument that it was ministerial or serviential, rather than tenurial.[52] A chirograph dated 1283 notes that the thanes of Dunning were accustomed to rendering conveth to their lord in respect of their lands.[53] Elsewhere north of Forth the traditional

47 See, e.g., *Documents Illustrative of the Social and Economic History of the Danelaw*, ed. F. M. Stenton (London, 1920), p. civ.

48 Between 1226 and 1234 Theobald made a small grant of land from Pitlandy to Inchaffray Abbey: *Inchaffray Chrs.*, no. 56.

49 Ibid., no. 55. Henry was the son of Tristram of Gorthy, a tenant of the earl.

50 G. W. S. Barrow, 'Pre-feudal Scotland: shires and thanes', in *Kingdom of the Scots*, 7–68; A. Grant, 'Thanes and thanages, from the eleventh to the fourteenth centuries', in A. Grant and K. J. Stringer, eds., *Medieval Scotland: Crown, Lordship and Community* (Edinburgh, 1993), 39–81.

51 Dupplin Muniments, nos. 6, 131; MS cartulary of Inchaffray Abbey, fos. 4v–5v, 43r–43v (in *Inchaffray Chrs.*, nos. 4, 14, 16–17); ibid., nos. 20–1.

52 Barrow, 'Shires and thanes', 47.

53 Dupplin Muniments, no. 110 (*Inchaffray Chrs*, no. 113).

obligation of offering hospitality was similarly linked to thanages.[54] But in contrast to royal tenants, neither of the Strathearn thanes enjoyed criminal jurisdiction within the boundaries of the earldom. This was a privilege reserved to, and jealously guarded by, Earl Gilbert.[55]

Clerks and chaplains constituted a large body in the *familia* of Earl Gilbert, but their identities are not easily discovered. Charter witness lists include the names of only three of the former, but an examination of the handwriting of these documents reveals that at least seven different men were employed as scribes.[56] These individuals played an essential role in the household, not only as drafters of comital acts, but also as 'a reserve of literate and perhaps educated men', whose skills were needed in financial and administrative business.[57] Unlike the royal household and those of some of the Anglo-Norman magnates, there was no formal chancery in Gilbert's time, although some scribes were particularly favoured for their secretarial abilities, and were commissioned to draft comital charters on several occasions.[58] The background of these men is, for the most part, obscure, an indication perhaps of the *ad hoc* nature of their duties within the household.[59] The prevalence of French personal names (three Williams and a John), a general clumsiness in rendering Gaelic place-names into Latin, and the heavy predominance of deeds in favour of the ecclesiastical house on the Isle of Masses, however, are all hints that the clerks were of French rather than Celtic background. Possibly they were brethren of Inchaffray Abbey, which, if so, provided a permanent pool of secretarial personnel for the earl.[60]

Chaplains, too, are generally shadowy figures in Gilbert's entourage. Comital deeds include notice of four chaplains, while a charter of his brother, Malise son of Ferteth, makes mention of two priests who may also have resided there.[61] Abraham is the only one of these for whom a brief history may be compiled. After serving the earl and his family for several years, around the year 1212 he was elected bishop of Dunblane, an office which he held until after Gilbert's death.[62] Parsons, rectors and vicars of the parish churches of Strathearn also

54 Barrow, 'Shires and thanes', 47; *RRS*, ii, 52–3.

55 Gilbert's brother, Malise, exercised the right of pit and gallows over his tenants, but this is the only example of such authority within Strathearn other than the earl's.

56 Neville, 'Thesis', i, 323–38.

57 W. E. Wightman, *The Lacy Family in England and Normandy, 1066–1194* (Oxford, 1966), 106.

58 See, e.g., William de la Hay and the unnamed Scribe A3 in Neville, 'Thesis', i, 338–9.

59 An exception might be the William de la Hay (see note 58 above), who may have been a cadet of the important family of the same name.

60 The chronicler Walter Bower claimed that Earl Gilbert brought canons from Scone to the house he founded at Inchaffray: *Chron. Bower* (Watt), iv, 458–9. The diplomatic skills required to draft writ-charters in the Anglo-Norman style may thus have been introduced to Strathearn by means of the older establishment.

61 Abraham: Dupplin Muniments, nos. 2, 10, 13, 118, 125, 131, 139 (i), 139 (ii), 149; MS cartulary of Inchaffray Abbey (Dupplin Muniments, T102), fos. 43r–44v (*Inchaffray Chrs*., nos. 3–5, 11–15, 25, 27). 'Cungi', John and Richard: NLS, MS Adv. Ch. B1354 (*Inchaffray Chrs*., no. 43). Richard also in MS cartulary of Inchaffray Abbey, fos. 11v–12r; Edinburgh University Library, Laing Charters, no. 13 (*Inchaffray Chrs*., nos. 2, 34). Elias: *Lindores Cart*., no. 29; the other priest's name is unknown.

62 The Pope admonished Bishop Malvoisin of St Andrews for his 'great audacity and presumption' in confirming the election without dispensation, for Abraham was the son of a priest, and himself the father of a son named Arthur. Nevertheless, the bishop of Dunblane went on to enjoy a distinguished

played a ubiquitous, but probably transitory role in the comital household. At least one was simultaneously a canon and a dignitary of the cathedral church of Dunblane; others were attached to the chapel of Inchaffray Abbey.[63] Their functions were of the spiritual kind: they acted as priests and confessors to Gilbert, his countess and the *familia* in general.

Despite the *lacunae* in surviving records, a clear division of personnel along cultural lines is discernible in the comital household. While the earl's ecclesiastical entourage was made up largely (but not solely) of individuals who bore French names, his lay *familiares* were virtually all Celtic in origin.[64] They included the officials reviewed above, and also family members. Both countesses of Strathearn, Maud d'Aubigny and Ysenda (whom Gilbert married late in life), were of Norman background, but he bestowed on five of his seven sons the purely Gaelic names of Gilchrist, Ferteth, Fergus, Malise and Gilbert. Daily life in the earl's residences was apparently marked by a blend of two very different linguistic cultures, though it seems to have overwhelmingly retained an atmosphere of traditionalism characteristic of an earlier age.

In Gilbert's time comital revenues were still paid chiefly in kind. Charter evidence is rich in references to cain rendered in wheat, oats, rye, meal, malt, cheese, fowl, 'and everything else that is owed to us in food and drink'.[65] Cain also came into the earl's residences in the shape of wild game. Mentions of licence to hunt and hawk are plentiful in early thirteenth-century *acta*. They indicate that Gilbert permitted general freedom to take foodstuffs from his forests, a privilege that had been traditional in pre-feudal Scotland, but one that was highly unusual in the royal and baronial lands of his contemporaries.[66] Other revenues were derived from the earl's mills and fisheries, and from his woodlands.[67] Conveth is not mentioned in records during Gilbert's period as earl, but given the extent of the territories that constituted the earldom, it is likely that this too was a prerogative which the earl found convenient to collect in kind.[68] Finally, profits accruing from fines and amercements levied in the comital courts provided a regular, considerable, and perhaps even a cash, revenue. Early in the thirteenth century Gilbert granted to the religious of Inchaffray the chattels of all criminals sentenced in his courts of law and found to be dwelling on priory lands,[69] and

career in the Scottish Church. He died around 1225. See *Vetera Monumenta Hibernorum et Scotorum Historiam Illustrantia*, ed. A. Theiner (Rome, 1864), no. 6; *Inchaffray Chrs.*, no. 26; Cockburn, *Medieval Bishops of Dunblane*, 36–40.

63 Dupplin Muniments, no. 139 (ii) (*Inchaffray Chrs.*, no. 27).

64 One of the earl's chaplains was called 'Cungi', possibly a corruption of the name Conghal. More noteworthy here is the fact that at the time of its foundation, the new priory on the Isle of Masses was entrusted to Malise, 'presbyter and hermit': Dupplin Muniments, nos. 106, 139 (iv) (*Inchaffray Chrs.*, nos. 9, 44).

65 Dupplin Muniments, nos. 3, 13, 106 (*Inchaffray Chrs.*, nos. 5, 9, 16).

66 J. Gilbert, *Hunting and Hunting Reserves in Medieval Scotland* (Edinburgh, 1979), 24–6, 226–7.

67 MS cartulary of Inchaffray Abbey, fos. 16v–17r; Edinburgh University Library, Laing Charters, no. 13; Dupplin Muniments, no. 6 (*Inchaffray Chrs.*, nos. 16, 19, 34).

68 In 1283, however, the tenants of the thanage of Dunning were accustomed to render conveth to Earl Malise III. By then the obligation had been commuted to a monetary payment of 4 merks annually. Dupplin Muniments, no. 110; MS cartulary of Inchaffray Abbey, fos. 8v–9v (*Inchaffray Chrs.*, nos. 113–14).

69 Dupplin Muniments, no. 139 (i) (*Inchaffray Chrs.*, no. 25).

shortly thereafter he made them a gift of a teind of judicial profits. But within a few years, he had exchanged the latter for revenues from the toun of Rahallo.[70] Neither of the charters that describe these donations reveals the value of the privileges bestowed, but they were considerable, for the prior and canons were anxious to secure permission to hold courts of their own.[71] Feudal incidents such as relief, wardship and marriage receive no mention whatsoever in Gilbert's charters. There can be little doubt, given the far-ranging authority he exercised in other aspects of baronial perquisites, that the earl also maintained close control over the conduct of his tenants in such matters as the disposition of Strathearn lands. In Gilbert's day, however, that authority continued to rest largely, if not exclusively, on ancient custom alone, and as such, it was not amenable to definition in the feudal language of written charters.

Gilbert's landed followers were a small, tightly-knit group, far less sophisticated than the circle surrounding contemporary Anglo-Norman lords. Only the most important of the earl's household officials were counted among those who regularly advised their lord, and who met with him in informal sessions to discuss matters of importance. Charter witness-lists constitute valuable sources of information for the study of the comital entourage. In spite of the dangers inherent in placing too much reliance upon this type of source material, it is clear that Gilbert surrounded himself with men with whom his relationship was primarily ministerial and personal, rather than tenurial.[72] The names of sixty-two men are enrolled in the testing clauses of the twenty-seven deeds that have survived in complete texts.[73] Ten of these had their names appended to comital deeds ten times or more. A further eight witnessed between four and eight times. *Table 1* presents a list of these individuals, together with a figure representing the number of times their names appear in testing clauses. Taken alone, these figures do not disclose much reliable information. Moreover, they are open to criticism on the basis that the notoriously untrustworthy rate of charter survival makes them quantitatively unsound.[74] Yet the intimacy evident in the 'inner circle' of Gilbert's *familiares* is noteworthy. This circle was predominantly made up of members of his own family and included only two important officials. Such persons were humble indeed compared to the witnesses of the *acta* of Gilbert's contemporary Anglo-Normans, David of Huntingdon and Roger de Quincy. They were, for the most part, prominent men in their own right, or the sons of families who had tenurial links to the crown or the wider community of the Anglo-Norman baronage. The most striking contrast between the witness lists of Strathearn

70 Dupplin Muniments, no. 109 (*Inchaffray Chrs*., no. 39).

71 NLS, MS Adv. Ch. B1354 (*Inchaffray Chrs*., no. 45).

72 E. L. G. Stones, 'Two points of diplomatic', *SHR*, 32 (1953), 47–51. See also Simpson, '*Familia* of Roger de Quincy', 105; Stringer, 'Charters of David, Earl of Huntingdon', 93.

73 This figure does not include bishops, abbots, priors, deans or archdeacons. Although the bishop of Dunblane and the prior and abbot of Inchaffray maintained regular contact with the earl, their ties were manifestly of a spiritual nature. They are not here considered members of the comital household or of the group of men who looked to the earl as their overlord.

74 See the warnings of Simpson, '*Familia* of Roger de Quincy', 107, and Stringer, *Earl David*, 153–4.

**Table 1. Witnesses to Earl Gilbert's Acta**

| 'INNER CIRCLE' | | 'OUTER CIRCLE' | |
|---|---|---|---|
| Malise, son of Gillenem the steward from *c.* 1211 × 1214 | 16 | William, son of the earl | 8 |
| Gillenem the steward | 15 | Fergus, son of the earl | 7 |
| Malise, son of Ferteth | 14 | Duncan, son of Malise the steward | 7 |
| Robert, son of the earl | 13 | Henry *rennarius* | 6 |
| Constantine *judex* of Strathearn | 13 | Gilbert, son of the earl | 5 |
| Maud d'Aubigny, countess of Strathearn | 11 | Gilchrist Gall | 5 |
| Ferteth, son of the earl | 11 | Malise, son of the earl | 4 |
| Brice, parson of Crieff | 11 | Gilbert *miles, socius comitis* | 4 |
| Anecol, thane of Dunning | 10 | | |
| Abraham, chaplain of the earl | 10 | | |

charters and those of Gilbert's contemporaries is the exclusivity in the latter of men of English and Anglo-continental origin: their word 'was generally thought to carry greater weight' than those of their Scottish fellows.[75] Gilbert's trust was placed more firmly in persons of local origin and Celtic descent. Moreover, in Strathearn the word of women was deemed as binding as that of men. The earl's wife was often a witness to his deeds.[76]

*Table 2* represents the social position of these same sixty-two witnesses. The names are classified according to the nature of their links with Earl Gilbert, the last group ('others') including individuals who had a connection with the earls in terms other than those of kinship, tenure or administration. Representation by clerics is, on the whole, modest. The figures suggest a baronial household in which comital business was conducted chiefly by a circle of persons who had strong personal links with their lord. The impression is reinforced by an examination of the identity of men classed as 'others'. These were men who, if they did not maintain frequent or direct contact with the household, were nevertheless linked to it indirectly: they included Duncan son of Malise the steward, Gilchrist son of the *judex* of Strathearn (Gilchrist Gall), Anecol thane of Dunning and Duncan thane of Strowan. Some were the children of local clerics, such as Malise son of Brice parson of Crieff. Still others were men identified as knights, but who were not attached to particular estates. They were

75 Stringer, 'Charters of David, Earl of Huntingdon', 93; Simpson, '*Familia* of Roger de Quincy', 122.

76 Gilbert's daughter, Maud, also witnessed two charters: see Dupplin Muniments, nos. 10, 149 (*Inchaffray Chrs.*, nos. 11–12).

| *Table 2. Social Standing of Witnesses to Earl Gilbert's Acta* | |
|---|---|
| Family | 10 |
| Tenants | 7 |
| Lay household officials | 6 |
| Both tenants and lay household officials | 2 |
| Clerics | 16 |
| Others | 21 |

the household knights found in so many thirteenth-century baronial entourages, though there is no evidence that Gilbert's men were in receipt of the *fiefs-rentes* allocated to such men elsewhere in the realm.[77] Gilbert 'the knight' witnessed an early grant to the religious on the Isle of Masses; in two slightly later deeds he is designated *socius comitis*.[78]

There is no evidence in surviving Strathearn records of a baronial council, distinct from the circle of friends, tenants and household officials who witnessed the earl's *acta*. Comital business of all kinds was conducted by a small core whose ranks were swelled by a varying group of local visitors to the household, probably in informal fashion. In this respect, Gilbert's management of Strathearn stood in some contrast to the kind of lordship exercised by David of Huntingdon and Roger de Quincy. As noted above, the Anglo-Norman barons maintained a distinction between domestic and estate affairs. David was advised by an embryonic council that consisted largely of important tenants, and which Keith Stringer has likened to the private councils of late medieval English magnates. Roger de Quincy's advisers were a more amorphous group, but it appears to have included tenants and estate stewards.[79] Both magnates, of course, wielded authority over estates scattered far and wide across Scotland and England, and the diversity of territorial interests that preoccupied them required some sophistication of administration. Gilbert's lands were, for the most part, situated within compact territorial boundaries, and relative ease of communication made it unnecessary for him to erect artificial distinctions between landed and purely personal affairs. Nevertheless, the style of lordship he exercised over his earldom was of a remarkably informal and intimate nature.

A sense of conservatism and resistance to the influence of Norman feudal ideas characterised the relationship between Earl Gilbert and his tenants. One of the most troublesome problems in the reconstruction of Strathearn history is the poor representation in the records of charters to lay persons. Indeed, the

77 Simpson, '*Familia* of Roger de Quincy', 122; Stringer, *Earl David*, 167, 172–3. See also Barrow, *Anglo-Norman Era*, 123–6.

78 Dupplin Muniments, nos. 10, 131, 149 (*Inchaffray Chrs*., nos. 4, 11–12).

79 Stringer, *Earl David*, 176; Simpson, '*Familia* of Roger de Quincy', 105–22.

only complete text of a grant by Gilbert in favour of a lay beneficiary is the record of a gift of land made to his daughter and son-in-law at the time of their marriage, and this survives only in two very late copies.[80] Even given the poor rate of survival of medieval private *acta*, the paucity of the Strathearn material is suspicious. It seems likely that within the earldom the charter as a deed of conveyance was accorded less significance by Gilbert's lay tenants than it enjoyed elsewhere. Grants of land to laymen may simply not have required the authority of the written word in order to be considered definitive. Here, a form of 'kindly' tenancy may not only have been customary, but still common and still widely accepted in the early thirteenth century.

Gilbert's 'chartered' tenants, then, consisted almost exclusively of the religious of Inchaffray Priory and, later, Abbey. But he was also the lord of several lay families. Only two, and possibly three, were of non-Celtic origin. The foundation charter to the priory on the Isle of Masses is witnessed by Nigel de Dalpatrick, a man who later appears with the surname Luvetot. Nigel was probably a cadet of the family that has been traced to Normandy (*département* Seine Maritime, *arrondissement* Yvetot, *canton* Caudebec), and perhaps a descendant of Nigel son of Richard de Luvetot, lord of Worksop and Hallam.[81] The family came to Scotland in the train of Earl Gilbert's countess, Maud, whose mother, Maud de Senlis, had taken as her second husband Richard de Luvetot.[82] In the late twelfth century Nigel de Luvetot held the toun of Dalpatrick, but the nature of the services he owed the earl remains unknown. In Gilbert's early thirteenth-century circle, moreover, was a man with the French name Tristram, which – in the light of other recorded family names – attests its Breton origins. It has been suggested that, like the Luvetots, Tristram came to Strathearn in the company of Countess Maud d'Aubigny.[83] He was granted the lands of Gorthy shortly after 1200, and was succeeded by his son, also named Tristram.[84]

The most substantial of Earl Gilbert's tenants was a family which took its surname from the lands it controlled. Sir Richard first appears as the 'knight of Kinbuck' in the early thirteenth century; thereafter he witnessed other comital charters.[85] His background is obscure, but he began his career in Gilbert's entourage as a household knight. In addition to the lands of Kinbuck, Sir Richard's father, Lugan, had an interest in the toun of Abercairny.[86] Control of this estate reverted to the earl sometime after 1210, when he married Richard's sister, Ysenda.[87] The families of Luvetot, Gorthy and Kinbuck constitute the

80 Barrow, 'Earls of Fife', 60–1, transcribed from John Skene's MS Notebook; Robert Sibbald, *The History, Ancient and Modern, of the Sheriffdoms of Fife and Kinross* (new edn, Edinburgh, 1803), 229, transcribed from a MS of Sir James Balfour of Denmilne.

81 L. C. Loyd, *The Origins of Some Anglo-Norman Families*, ed. C. T. Clay and D. C. Douglas (Harleian Soc., 1951), 55–6; Farrer, *Early Yorkshire Charters*, iii, no. 1268. See also Barrow, *Anglo-Norman Era*, 124–35 and n. 44; C. Clay and D. E. Greenway, eds., *Early Yorkshire Families* (Yorkshire Archaeological Soc., Record Ser., 1973), 53–6.

82 Barrow, *Anglo-Norman Era*, 125 and n. 44; idem, 'Earls of Fife', 57 and n. 8.

83 Duncan, *Kingdom*, 449.

84 MS cartulary of Inchaffray Abbey, fos. 36v–37r (*Inchaff.ray Chrs.*, no. 59).; Duncan, *Kingdom*, 448–9.

85 Dupplin Muniments, no. 139 (ii) (in *Inchaffray Chrs.*, no. 27); *Lindores Cart.*, no. 30.

86 Neville, 'Thesis', i, 272.

87 The countess gifted five acres of land and common pasture from her toun of Abercairny to the

only documented examples of the infiltration of foreign settlers into Strathearn in the late twelfth and early thirteenth centuries. If, as Duncan has suggested, King William had hoped that the native earls of Scotland would emulate royal practice in installing new families as feudal tenants in their territories, he must have been disappointed with Gilbert's performance. Foreign penetration into the earldom was only superficial, and Anglo-Norman tenants remained very much a rarity in his time. Gilbert did not overtly reject a policy of subinfeudation, but in his grants to lay persons he sought to avoid disruption of the traditional social and legal structure of the earldom. His most important vassals were, in fact, members of his family. Malise son of Ferteth held of him a number of estates in the parishes of Comrie, Muthill, Blackford and Dunning.[88] On Malise's death they reverted to the earl, but soon after 1215 they were given to Gilbert's son, Sir Fergus. The latter also received from his father the lands of Meikleour and Lethendy in eastern Strathearn, which had belonged to Malise. Gilbert's youngest son, also named Gilbert, received the lands of Kinveachy and Glencarnie in Inverness-shire which had been granted to the earl by King William.[89] These estates were located far from Strathearn and had probably proven difficult to manage effectively from a distance. They constituted an excellent feu for a younger son, who could otherwise have expected to inherit much less from the patrimonial lands.[90] Finally, Earl Gilbert's sons-in-law were also his tenants: Malcolm of Fife in Glendevon, Aldie, Fossoway, Dalkeith, Cambo and 'Pethven';[91] and Walter son of Alan in Coulgask.[92]

The pattern of land tenure by lay tenants in Strathearn reflected little of the immense changes that occurred elsewhere in the kingdom, in which new men acquired estates by charters of infeftment as a matter of course. Gilbert was conservative in his gifts, preferring to base tenurial relationships on already strong personal foundations. Nor did he welcome the wholesale displacement of native customs by Norman legalisms. The feudal concept of land held in return for specified military services was largely absent from the earldom, and Gilbert is known to have enjoyed the service of only a single knight from among all his lay tenants.[93] Similarly, the practice of conveying property by sasine and charter was implemented only gradually, and almost exclusively on the initiative of the earl's ecclesiastical beneficiaries. The nature of the relationship between lord and man recalled that of an earlier age. Gilbert took counsel from his kinsfolk (including his wife and daughters) and trusted servants. The 'important men' of the earldom of Strathearn were small fry compared to those of other Scottish lordships: for the most part they were modest native landowners whose interests

canons of Inchaffray Abbey just prior to her husband's death: NAS, GD24/5/1/1 (*Inchaffray Chrs.*, no. 46). The charter also mentions Geoffrey of Gask, a brother of Sir Richard and Ysenda.

88 *RRS*, ii, no. 136.

89 *RRS*, ii, nos. 206, 474. See also above, page 77.

90 Gilbert of Glencarnie established a wealthy and powerful lordship in Inverness-shire. The fortunes of the family are reviewed in Neville, 'Thesis', i, 76–7.

91 Barrow, 'Earls of Fife', 60–1.

92 Notice of Gilbert's grant to Walter survives only in a charter of confirmation sealed by Earl Robert after his father's death: NAS, RH6/19 (*Inchaffray Liber*, App., no. 8).

93 *RRS*, ii, no. 136. The tenant was his brother, Malise son of Ferteth.

did not extend beyond the boundaries of Strathearn. The basis of lay land tenure in this period is difficult to define with precision, but it appears to have been less the written deed of conveyance and the formal act of homage, than the mutual trust and the customary promise of protection and favour that the Celtic mormaers had traditionally offered their tenants and followers.

Comital charters, by their very nature, provide only an incomplete picture of the social and tenurial structure of early thirteenth-century Strathearn. They are, however, a trustworthy guide to the wider changes that were occurring within the earldom. The frequent inclusion of Gilbert's family members among witness lists, for example, reveals that at the very heart of the comital entourage, Norman customs were beginning to compete with traditional Celtic ways. Two of Gilbert's seven sons, the second and the fourth, were given the 'foreign' names of William and Robert so common among the English and continental newcomers to Scotland. Similarly, two of his three daughters bore the Norman names of Maud and Cecilia; and only that of the youngest, Ethen, commemorated a personal name once borne by a Celtic countess of Strathearn.[94] The arrangements that Gilbert made for his children's well-being were designed with an eye to the future and the changing social structure of the Scottish baronial order. He established his son Fergus as a significant landowner within the earldom, and his youngest son Gilbert in Inverness-shire, and in so doing made it possible for them to achieve the status of knighthood so highly valued in feudal society.[95] Within Sir Fergus's newly erected lordship the feudal customs of knight service, aid and the honorial court were firmly entrenched in family territory.[96] The marriages of Gilbert's daughters brought the Strathearn women into close contact with the wider community of the Scottish baronage. As noted above, Maud was married to Malcolm son of the earl of Fife, a family whose links to the royal court were already of long duration. Cecilia's husband, Walter son of Alan (1204–41), came from a family who had acquired the lands of Ruthven in Perthshire, and whose descendants would become earls of Gowrie.[97] The last daughter, Ethen, seems to have been the first wife of Sir David de la Hay of Erroll, a family which had been part of the 'tidal wave of Norman immigration into Scotland' which occurred in the twelfth century.[98] The two oldest daughters brought to their husbands lands in Strathearn, and on these estates feudal customs competed with, and eventually eclipsed, older ways.

The comital charters themselves attest the growing popularity of Norman diplomatic practice within the earldom. Many of the features of the 'classical' baronial writ-charter, including the holding and warranty clauses, do not appear in Strathearn deeds on a regular basis until after Gilbert's death.[99] And yet, the

94 Earl Ferteth's wife had been named Ethen.

95 Neville, 'Thesis', i, 74–7.

96 See, e.g., *Lindores Cart.*, nos. 24, 28; Muniments of the Earl of Moray, Darnaway Castle, Moray Charters, Box 32, Division IV, Bundle 1, no. 21, calendared in *Coupar Angus Chrs.*, i, no. 35.

97 Duncan, *Kingdom*, 432; *Complete Peerage*, vi, 40–2.

98 G. W. S. Barrow, 'Scotland's "Norman" families', in *Kingdom of the Scots*, 325, 332.

99 The standard analysis of baronial charters remains the kind of study pioneered many years ago by French scholars. See A. Giry, *Manuel de diplomatique* (Paris, 1894), and A. de Boüard, *Manuel de diplomatique française et pontificale* (Paris, 1929–48). This analysis has been applied to Scottish *acta*

presence of other standard features, notably the *sicut* and corroboration clauses, and the use of a comital seal to authenticate the written deeds, suggest an intention on the part of both donor and beneficiary to conform to current practice in the composition and redaction of these all-important documents. While the demand for written deeds of conveyance remained confined almost exclusively to ecclesiastical houses, the lay tenants of Gilbert's successor, Robert, and those of his landholding sons, Fergus and Malise, were anxious to secure them. It is surely no mere accident that the survival rate of written charters to lay persons is significantly greater for the period after 1223 than it is for the years of Gilbert's tenure of the earldom.[100] In comparable fashion, while Gilbert's written deeds make little distinction in terminology between the dispositive clauses of grants and confirmations, or between instruments such as notifications and letters patent (as do those of some of his contemporaries),[101] the surviving *acta* of his sons and other lay tenants begin to demonstrate the use of formulae that define clearly the intentions of these deeds. By the middle of the thirteenth century such distinctions had become common, and Strathearn documents display the rich variety of form and content found elsewhere in the realm.

If Earl Gilbert's charters are windows through which significant new influences within the earldom may be glimpsed, they nevertheless conceal much that was unchanged, and it would be unwise to ignore Sellar's warning that 'the forms of feudalism could be used to camouflage and, on occasion, legitimate, older practice'.[102] Evidence of a varied nature conveys the unmistakable impression that below a façade of conformity with new styles of lordship and land exploitation introduced to Scotland by the Normanising kings, and despite the profound social and economic consequences of these innovations, the earldom of Strathearn in Gilbert's time remained an enclave of Celtic conservatism. Moreover, the fortuitous survival of a large family of sons ensured that, for another generation after 1223 at least, the traditions that were giving way to change elsewhere in the kingdom would remain entrenched in the heart of old Scotia. [103]

by historians such as E. L. G. Stones, G. G. Simpson, G. W. S. Barrow and K. J. Stringer. A lengthy study of Strathearn charters using the methods refined by these Scottish scholars is undertaken in Neville, 'Thesis', i, 352–97, on which the following paragraphs draw heavily.

100 See the edition of 'Additional Charters' in Neville, 'Thesis', ii, Appendix B.

101 Simpson, e.g., notes a distinction of form between instruments of notification, letters patent, precepts and bonds in the acts of Roger de Quincy. See G. G. Simpson, 'An Anglo-Scottish Baron of the Thirteenth Century: the Acts of Roger de Quincy, Earl of Winchester and Constable of Scotland' (University of Edinburgh, unpublished PhD thesis, 1965), 172–5. Barrow notes a tendency for deeds to become at once more formulaic and more identifiable by type as the reign of William I progresses (*RRS*, ii, 69, 79). A handlist of the *acta* of Alexander II emphasises the differences between grants, general confirmations, letters patent and brieves of various kinds. See J. M. Scoular, *Handlist of the Acts of Alexander II* (Regesta Regum Scottorum, 1959), passim.

102 Sellar, 'Celtic Law and Scots Law', 7.

103 I am very grateful to the Social Sciences and Humanities Research Council of Canada for its generous financial assistance in funding research for this essay.

# 7

# Medieval Scottish Associations with Bruges

*Alexander Stevenson*

The topography of the Bruges area has been almost entirely changed since the Middle Ages by the processes of inundation and silting, which – along with centuries of drainage and dredging – gave rise to Bruges's international traffic and then destroyed it.[1] Gone today is the Zwin estuary, which once linked Bruges with the sea. Altered beyond recognition are the many islands and shoals which rendered much of the Scheldt delta hazardous to medieval shipping and long impeded the growth of Antwerp. What was once the greatest port in northern Europe now underlies fields stretching between the towns and villages of Damme, Hoeke, St Anna ter Muiden, Sluis and Cadzand – districts now divided between Belgium and the Netherlands. Yet in the Middle Ages the Zwin, sheltered by the island of Cadzand at its mouth, provided one of the finest harbours in the Low Countries. Lying south-west of the Zeeland archipelago, it flowed directly into the North Sea and was closer to Berwick and Leith (successively Scotland's premier ports) than were most other major medieval ports, including London.[2]

Ease of access meant Scottish trade must have come early to Bruges – though lack of early Scottish commercial records, and the destruction of the Bruges archives in 1280 when a famous belfry burned down, have left few traces before the late thirteenth century. The earliest surviving Bruges records show that wool from England, Scotland, Ireland and Flanders (in that order of quality and possibly also of quantity) was used exclusively in Bruges's primary cloth manufactures, as it was in other parts of Flanders.[3] They show too that the marshal of Flanders, Syger de Bailleul, received letters from the Bruges authorities when on a mission to Scotland in 1284;[4] that there was a 'Scotland street' in the town; and that a quay along the principal canal in central Bruges was known as the Schottendijk – the only section of the medieval Reie with a foreign territorial name.[5] Whether these names are indicative of a Scottish community in thirteenth-century Bruges remains unclear. Only one Scottish *poorter* (burgess)

1 S. T. Bindoff, *The Scheldt Question* (London, 1945); A. M. Lambert, *The Making of the Dutch Landscape* (London, 1971); C. T. Smith, *An Historical Geography of Western Europe before 1800* (2nd edn, London, 1978), 385, 388–91; A. Duclos, *Bruges, histoire et souvenirs* (Bruges, 1910), 5–14.

2 Approximate distances by sea from Leith: Veere, 375 miles; Sluis, 385 miles; Amsterdam, 390 miles; St Omer, 405 miles; Bergen, 405 miles; Antwerp, 415 miles; London, 415 miles; Dieppe, 440 miles; Hamburg, 495 miles; Copenhagen, 610 miles.

3 G. Espinas and H. Pirenne, eds., *Receuil de documents relatifs à l'industrie drapière en Flandre* (Brussels, 1906–20) [hereafter Espinas and Pirenne, *Industrie drapière*], i, 396.

4 E. Wyffels and J. de Smet, eds., *De Rekeningen van de Stad Brugge, 1280–1319* (Brussels, 1965), 71, 77, 110–11; L. Gilliodts-van Severen, *Cartulaire de l'ancien grand tonlieu de Bruges* (Bruges, 1908) [hereafter Gilliodts, *Tonlieu*], i, 31.

5 L. Gilliodts-van Severen, ed., *Inventaire des archives de la ville de Bruges* (Bruges, 1871–82) [hereafter Gilliodts, *Inventaire*], intro., 439; ii, 123; v, 383.

of Bruges is identifiable at this date: Walter the Deacon, also a burgess of Perth, who acted as a factor for the countess of Fife in the early 1290s.[6] It seems likely, however, that Flemish merchants and ships dominated Scotland's overseas trade until the Wars of Independence;[7] and that the Zwin was their principal destination for much of the thirteenth century.[8]

During the final decade of the thirteenth century Scotland and Flanders suffered grievously in wars which resulted from the expansionist ambitions of the English and French kings. Both countries sought to remain neutral, but neutrality was denied them. Both were subjected to military occupation and to the overthrow of their rulers.[9] That this gave rise to a strong emotional bond between Scotland and Bruges is demonstrable from the refusal of the Flemish authorities to comply with English demands that they desist from trading with, or sheltering, Scottish 'rebels'. It was through Bruges that most Scottish contacts with the outside world were maintained during the Wars of Independence (1296–1328) and that most military supplies for the Scottish resistance were channelled. It was only in 1302 – in the aftermath of the 'Matins of Bruges' when the French were massacred and Flanders rose in revolt – that Scottish goods were seized. Yet Flemish hopes of English support did not materialise and in 1305 the Flemings made peace with the French king. Thereafter Bruges seems to have maintained almost unbroken support for the Scots until the fifteenth century. Meanwhile, Flemish antipathy towards the English steadily grew as the English government diverted wool exports to non-Flemish ports and increased the customs duties on English wool, thereby promoting English cloth manufactures in direct competition with the Flemish cloth industry. As a result, the security of English merchants was often threatened in Flanders and the sale of English cloth was banned there.[10] The English presence in Bruges was accordingly limited. By contrast, in the fourteenth century Bruges came to dominate Scotland's overseas trade to an unparalleled extent.

By the 1330s, when higher duties were introduced by the Scottish government on exports by aliens, all but 15% of recorded exports were shipped by Scottish merchants.[11] Wool was then Scotland's most valuable export and Flanders was

6 Stevenson, *Documents*, i, nos. 131, 234.

7 Duncan, *Kingdom*, 502–18; A. W. K. Stevenson, 'Trade with the south', in M. Lynch, M. Spearman and G. Stell, eds., *The Scottish Medieval Town* (Edinburgh, 1988), 186–7. Flemish merchants dominated the much better documented overseas trade of England until a breakdown of Anglo-Flemish relations in 1270, which did not concern Scotland. The resulting vacuum was filled by Italians and Germans, most of whose exports were sold in Flanders. English merchants did not secure primacy until the early 14th century: T. H. Lloyd, *The English Wool Trade in the Middle Ages* (Cambridge, 1977), 2–143.

8 A French panegyric extols the excellence, wealth and world-wide trade of the port of Bruges around 1213, the year of the earliest reference to a Bruges ship trading with Scotland: L. Gilliodts-van Severen, *Cartulaire de l'ancienne estaple de Bruges* (Bruges, 1904–6) [hereafter Gilliodts, *Estaple*], i, no. 32; *Rotuli Literarum Patentium in Turri Londinensi asservati*, ed. T. D. Hardy (Record Commission, 1835), i, 106.

9 A. W. K. Stevenson, 'The Flemish dimension of the Auld Alliance', in G. G. Simpson, ed., *Scotland and the Low Countries* (East Linton, 1996), 32–5.

10 Lloyd, *Wool Trade*, passim; E. M. Carus-Wilson, *Medieval Merchant Venturers* (2nd edn, London, 1967), xxii, 239–64.

11 Stevenson, 'Trade with the south', 188.

its only significant market until the late fifteenth century, as it was for cowhides and woolfells, the only other goods on which export duty was levied in Scotland until the reign of James I.[12] Most of Scotland's trade became focused upon Bruges, its concentration there accentuated by the uncertain reception Scots found elsewhere, since the English government did its utmost to prevent other countries from trading with the Scots. In other circumstances commercial restrictions abroad would have necessitated greater self-sufficiency at home. But, in the fourteenth century, the Flemish focus of Scottish trade coincided with the peak of Bruges's international prestige and prosperity. With the rapid expansion of seaborne trade, the hub of western commercial activity had shifted from the fairs of Champagne, in eastern France, to Bruges.[13] Consequently, Bruges provided a ready market not only for most of Scotland's exports but also for most of its import requirements, as Scottish trade became increasingly concentrated in the hands of a small Scottish merchant elite and foreign merchants largely withdrew from active trade in Scotland.[14]

Between 1313 and 1323 the English government directed the export of all English wool, hides and woolfells to a staple at St Omer,[15] driving the Scots out of their only other significant market for such goods. This event may explain why a Scottish staple was formally established at Bruges – whereby, in return for protection and privileges, the Scottish government directed that Scottish wool, hides and woolfells were to be exported exclusively to Bruges. There is circumstantial evidence that Bruges was already well established as the Scottish staple in 1321.[16] Though in 1347, after a breakdown in relations with Flanders, it was proposed to remove the staple to the town of Middelburg in Zeeland,[17] the Scots returned to Bruges the following year.

The earliest surviving staple agreement dates from 1359;[18] and a series of such agreements followed – in 1387, 1394, 1407, 1427 and 1470. These agreements, and related records, provide a vivid picture of Scottish trading practices.

On arrival off Sluis, possibly in convoy with other ships from Scotland, Scottish vessels were directed to designated anchorages. As many as four ships might be

12 Ibid., 190, 193, 196, 198–201; D. Ditchburn, 'Trade with northern Europe', in Lynch *et al.*, *Scottish Medieval Town*, 166–7.

13 Smith, *Historical Geography*, 356–9, 379, 387–8; R. de Roover, 'The organisation of trade', and C. Verlinden, 'Markets and fairs', in M. M. Postan *et al.*, eds., *The Cambridge Economic History of Europe*, vol. III (Cambridge, 1963), 70–102, 106–15, 126–36; L. A. Warnkoenig, *Histoire de la Flandre et de ses institutions civiles et politiques, jusqu'à l'année 1305* (Brussels, 1835–6), ii, 513–16; *The Libelle of Englyshe Polycye*, ed. Sir G. Warner (Oxford, 1926); P. Dollinger, *The German Hansa* (London, 1970); J. Finot, *Relations commerciales et maritimes entre la Flandre et l'Espagne* (Lille, 1898); M. Mollat, *Le commerce maritime normand à la fin du moyen age* (Paris, 1952); H. Tochard, *Le commerce maritime breton à la fin du moyen age* (Paris, 1967); J. Finot, *Relations commerciales entre la Flandre et la république de Gênes* (Paris, 1906); R. Cessi, 'Le relazioni commerciali fra Venezia e le Fiandri', *Nuovo Archivio Veneto*, xxvii (1914), passim.

14 A. W. K. Stevenson, 'Trade between Scotland and the Low Countries in the Later Middle Ages' (University of Aberdeen, unpublished PhD thesis, 1982) [hereafter Stevenson, 'Thesis'] 6–12.

15 Lloyd, *Wool Trade*, 106–15.

16 *RRS*, v, no. 190.

17 Ibid., vi, nos. 110–11; Gilliodts, *Estaple*, nos. 272–4.

18 Gilliodts, *Estaple*, i, nos. 272–4, 309; M. P. Rooseboom, *The Scottish Staple in the Netherlands* (The Hague, 1910), App. 10.

tied together in rows abreast or astern.[19] There they were inspected by the Sluis water bailiff and his officers, who levied tolls and transit fees on all vessels, supervised the loading and unloading of cargo, and enforced (often officiously) the laws and customs of the port and anchorages of the Zwin.[20] These laws and customs were jealously guarded by the Bruges authorities in order to prevent the direct transhipment of goods from Sluis to other Netherlandish markets. Initially all but staple goods might be sold at Sluis or Damme, but from the late fourteenth century the authorities insisted that all Scottish goods should be taken to Bruges itself. Scottish cargoes were therefore transferred into lighters and taken by water directly to Bruges.[21]

While cargo was strictly supervised, travellers were free to go as they pleased. Many probably stayed in Sluis when waiting for a ship to Scotland. In recognition of this, in 1456, James II appointed Lawrence Pomstrat, a Sluis innkeeper, as 'host and receiver' of all Scots visiting Sluis. Pomstrat was guaranteed Scottish business in return for looking after Scottish interests.[22] This must have been a valuable concession, as Sluis was then the continental gateway for most Scottish travellers. In 1470 the Scottish 'consul' at Sluis was further empowered by the Bruges authorities to arbitrate in disputes over lighter fees, which had been revised in negotiations with the Bruges guild of lightermen and extended to cover boat traffic from Sluis to Zeeland, Antwerp and Bergen-op-Zoom.[23] Only then did the Bruges authorities agree that Scottish-owned goods might be taken from Sluis to the increasingly important Brabantine fairs (the Pentecost and St Bavo fairs at Antwerp and the Easter and winter fairs at Bergen-op-Zoom), without first being taken to the Bruges staple.[24]

By then many Scottish ships were docking at Veere on the island of Walcheren, thirty miles north-east of Bruges and four miles from Middelburg.[25] Veere offered not only easier access to other Netherlandish towns than did Sluis, but also greater safety from the hazards created by the continual silting of the Zwin.[26] This perhaps explains why in 1457 the famous cannon Mons Meg, having been transported by river and canal from Lille to Sluis, was taken to Veere and there loaded aboard a Dutch vessel for shipment to Scotland.[27] Doubtless a similar route was taken, at least as far as Sluis, by most of the Tournai-stone sepulchral slabs of the thirteenth to the sixteenth centuries that are scattered across Scotland from Iona to Roxburgh.[28] The same route may also

19 Ibid., App. 14, cc.2, 3.

20 Ibid., Apps. 8 c.10, 9 c.10, 14 c.7, 15 c.2, 26 c.2; Gilliodts, *Estaple*, ii, nos. 1144–5; Stevenson, 'Thesis', 174–8.

21 Gilliodts, *Inventaire*, iii, 427–34.

22 Aberdeen City Archives, Council Registers, vol. V(2), 792.

23 Gilliodts, *Inventaire*, vi, 41–3.

24 Gilliodts, *Inventaire*, vi, 39–40; Rooseboom, *Scottish Staple*, App. 26 c.7.

25 Stevenson, 'Thesis', 202–9.

26 J. A. van Houtte, *Bruges: essai d'histoire urbaine* (Brussels, 1967), 77–81; Finot, *Relations entre la Flandre et l'Espagne*, 229–31.

27 C. Gaier, 'The origin of Mons Meg', *Journal of the Arms and Armour Society*, v (1967), 425–31.

28 J. Bertram, *Lost Brasses* (London, 1976), 69; Royal Commission on the Ancient Monuments of Scotland, *The County of Roxburgh* (Edinburgh, 1956), i, 246.

have been taken by the tomb of Robert I, which was brought from Paris to Dunfermline via Bruges.[29]

Between Sluis and Bruges – as described by the Spanish traveller Tafur in 1438 – the water-flow was regulated by a series of 'sluice-gates, as of water mills', to take advantage of the considerable tidal range. 'When the tide rises,' he noted, 'the [lighters] are laden and travel with their cargoes from Sluis on the tide. When the water reaches its highest point they lock it up, and those [lighters] which had been unloaded and filled with fresh cargoes return with the same water which carried them upstream, travelling down again with the falling tide.'[30] All foreign-owned goods were subject to customs duty (something which Tafur does not mention) before proceeding through the lock at Damme. Here, by the mouths of the Reie canal to Bruges and the Lieve canal to Ghent, was the main comital customs post, which levied duty in accordance with a table of tariffs established in 1252 'for merchants of the Empire and other foreigners'.[31] These rates of duty seem to have persisted until 1425, when some were sharply increased, causing bitter dispute with Scottish and Hanseatic merchants. The Scots were in the stronger position, having removed their staple to Middelburg in 1423 following numerous disputes with the Flemish authorities. One of the conditions of their return to Bruges in 1427 was a reversion of these tariffs to their former rates.[32] By contrast, it seems that the Hanse failed to secure any redress.[33] A further customs increase in the 1460s was one cause of the next withdrawal of the Scottish staple in 1467. A condition of its return in 1470 was that the revised lighter tariffs for Scottish traffic, agreed as part of a general settlement, were to be inclusive of the Damme customs.[34]

During the thirteenth century, when it had been the principal Zwin port, Damme had acquired staple privileges. It retained these even after silting led to its replacement as the chief Zwin port by Sluis in about 1290. The wine staple, for instance, remained at Damme. French, German, Spanish, Italian and Greek wines were to be found here; as were Flemish, Dutch and German beers.[35] Here too was the main international outlet for the renowned copper and brass wares of Dinant.[36]

From Damme lighters travelled some three miles up the Reie before entering Bruges at the Speipoorte, a long-vanished complex of land and water gates. Here, as at all Flemish town gates, Scottish merchants and their servants were entitled to enter or leave at any time of the day and night, in accordance with a privilege granted by Philip the Bold, duke of Burgundy, in 1387.[37] Beside the town walls the Reie joined the Iperleet (reconstructed and widened in the

29 *ER*, i, 214.

30 M. Letts, *Bruges and its Past* (2nd edn, Bruges and London, 1926), 140.

31 Warnkoenig, *Histoire de la Flandre*, 444–55.

32 Gilliodts, *Inventaire*, v, 301 c.5; Stevenson, 'Thesis', 178–9.

33 Gilliodts, *Estaple*, i, no. 740.

34 Stevenson, 'Thesis', 85–6, 93, 96–7, 179–80; Gilliodts, *Inventaire*, vi, 37, 42.

35 J. Craeybeckx, *Les vins de France aux anciens Pays-Bas* (Paris, 1958), passim; Warnkoenig, *Histoire de la Flandre*, 513; Dollinger, *German Hansa*, 250.

36 H. Pirenne, 'Les marchands-batteurs de Dinant au XIVe et au XVe siècle', *Vierteljahrsschrift für Social- und Wirtschaftsgeschichte*, ii (Leipzig, 1914), 442–9.

37 Rooseboom, *Scottish Staple*, App. 11, c.5.

nineteenth century as the Ostend canal), a canal system which linked most of western Flanders with Bruges, much as the Lieve linked Bruges with eastern Flanders.[38] Beyond this junction a wooden boom was set across the canal so that tolls on all foreign-owned goods could be collected on behalf of the lord of Ghistelles, who possessed hereditary rights to the Bruges tolls.[39] The tolls paid, lighters proceeded for about three-quarters of a mile before reaching the international quarter of Bruges, where the Reie divided to form a great quadrangle through the trading centre of the town.

It was here that the Scottish district was located, straddling both sides and forks of the canal. Here was the Schottendijk, now St Annarei.[40] A bridge spanning the Reie at this point (now St Annabrug) was called the Stocvischbrugge, stockfish (dried cod) being a major Scottish export particularly associated with Aberdeen before the Wars of Independence.[41] The bridge linked the Schottendijk with the Schottenplaats, a small part of which still bears its alternate medieval name of St Maartensplein – the rest having been demolished in 1619 to make way for a Jesuit church (now St Walburgakerk).[42] Hereabouts also were various other Scottish streets and houses.

In medieval Bruges there appear to have been more place-names associated with Scots than with any other nationality.[43] The sole survival is Schottinnenstraat, a short side-street between St Gilliskerk and the Augustijnenbrug (the finest medieval bridge in Bruges, built in 1391), whose alternate medieval name was the Schottenbrugge.[44] Nearby were both the house of the Scottish burgesses, first noted in 1439, on Nieuw Straete – now Gouden-Handstraat, where Jan van Eyck had his home – and the Schotillepoorte ('little Scottish gate'), the entrance to the new churchyard of St Giles.[45] In 1406–7, following a brief removal of the Scottish staple, the Bruges authorities granted the princely gift of £3,000 *parisis* to Scottish ambassadors upon the return of Scottish merchants and their goods to St Giles parish 'where they were wont to be'.[46] St Gilliskerk – where the decorated timber ceilings are remarkably similar to those of King's College chapel in Aberdeen – had two Scottish altars in the fifteenth century. One was in the south aisle of the nave. Dedicated to St Ninian and probably associated with Scots in humbler occupations, such as labourers and tailors, it was reassigned in 1474 to the corn porters and measurers. The other Scottish altar was in the north aisle. Dedicated to St Andrew, in 1462 it belonged to the 'Scottish brokers'. It is perhaps surprising that there should have been sufficient brokers of Scottish origin to form their own fraternity – though the altar's relics suggest that the fraternity was both numerous and affluent. It encompassed all

38 Duclos, *Bruges, histoire et souvenirs*, 544.

39 Ibid., 544–5; Gilliodts, *Tonlieu*, i, passim, ii, 360.

40 Duclos, *Bruges, histoire et souvenirs*, 557.

41 Stevenson, 'Trade with the south', 185–6; H. Pirenne, *Histoire de Belgique* (5th edn, Brussels, 1929), i, 265 n.2; *Munimenta Gildhallae Londoniensis, Liber Albus*, ed. H. T. Riley (Rolls Ser., 1859–60), i, 376.

42 Duclos, *Bruges, histoire et souvenirs*, 554.

43 Gilliodts, *Inventaire*, ix, 379–412; Marc Gheeraerts, *Town Plan of Bruges* (Bruges, 1562).

44 Duclos, *Bruges, histoire et souvenirs*, 527.

45 Gilliodts, *Inventaire*, intro., 500, 502 n.4, 504; Letts, *Bruges and its Past*, 156.

46 Ibid., v, 302–3 note.

Bruges burgesses of Scottish origin, whose lodge may latterly have been only a short distance away. By 1511, however, the 'workpeople of the Scottish nation' had gone and relics associated with the St Andrew altar (fragments of the True Cross and of the Column of Flagellation and oil of St Andrew) had been deposited elsewhere.[47]

Brokers made their money as middlemen, acting as factors and organising bulk sales and purchases. All brokers were burgesses of Bruges and foreign merchants were obliged to deal through them. This caused bitter resentment. The Scottish embassy of 1407 complained about the excessive charges levied by both porters (who monopolised the carriage of goods and who were also burgesses) and brokers. To secure the return of the Scottish staple, the Bruges authorities undertook to investigate porterage and brokerage charges and to punish offenders as an example to others. They also agreed to allow Scottish merchants to trade on their own account, 'like German merchants and others', without employing brokerage services.[48] That this undertaking was not always observed is apparent from its reaffirmation in the staple settlement of 1470, when Scottish merchants also secured the right to choose their own porters, apparently for the first time, so long as they were burgesses of Bruges.[49]

Many brokers were also innkeepers, providing board, lodging, storage and banking facilities. The broker-innkeepers formed a patriciate which dominated the mercantile life of Bruges. Among the most prominent were members of the Metteneye family, which had close Scottish associations for much of the fourteenth and fifteenth centuries.[50] As early as 1328 a royal debt to Paul Metteneye was settled against the Berwick customs. In 1361 his executors were paid 160 marks for the redemption of jewels pawned by David II, and a further £92 sterling was paid to Adam Metteneye between 1361 and 1363.[51] There is then a gap in the record until 1416, when, as 'host of the Scots', Jan Metteneye stood surety in a case of letters of marque which nearly caused another temporary removal of the Scottish staple to Middelburg. The judicial records intermittently available thereafter constantly refer to representation in Scottish cases first by Jan Metteneye, then by Jacob Metteneye and later by Jacob's son, also Jan.[52] Presumably the family's Scottish connections grew from its role as broker-innkeepers, much as those forged by Lawrence Pomstrat in Sluis. The Metteneyes were perhaps lessees of the inn on the Schottendijk, recorded in the Bruges accounts from 1302 – when the freehold of the inn apparently passed to the town council, following the 'Matins of Bruges'.[53]

47 E. Rembry, *De bekende pastors van Sint-Gillis te Brugge, 1311–1896, met aanteekeningen over kerk en parochie* (Bruges, 1890–6), pp. xvii–xx; W. H. Finlayson, 'The Scottish Nation of Merchants in Bruges' (University of Glasgow, unpublished PhD thesis, 1951), 185–6.

48 Rooseboom, *Scottish Staple*, App. 15 c.6.

49 Ibid., *Staple*, App. 26 cc.5, 8.

50 For the Metteneye family, see R. de Roover, *Money, Banking and Credit in Medieval Bruges* (Cambridge, Mass., 1948), 13, 171, 282, 287 n.39; Gilliodts, *Inventaire*, passim.

51 *ER*, i, 98; ii, 79–80, 90–1, 128.

52 Gilliodts, *Estaple*, i, nos. 622, 683, 842, 889; Bruges, Stadsarchief, Civiele Sententies, i, fos. 61r, 66r, 71v, 90v, 116r, 123v, 143r, 326r; ii, fos. 17v, 30r, 52v, 55r–v, 58v, 82r, 92r–93r, 159r, 222v, 265v, 339v, 371v, 379r, 382v.

53 Gilliodts, *Inventaire*, intro., 383.

While Scots resident in Bruges may have worshipped in St Gilliskerk, visiting Scots worshipped mainly in the Carmelite church, adjacent to the Schottendijk, on Carmersstraat. The friary was destroyed in 1578, during the Dutch Revolt. Here land was leased by a Scottish confraternity in 1366, in order to build an aisle chapel dedicated to St Ninian on the south side of the church, and to provide a burial ground.[54] In 1369 a papal indulgence was granted to support building work then in progress. By the fifteenth century the chapel was supported in Edinburgh and Aberdeen (and probably elsewhere too) by a levy on all wool exports.[55] The value of one woolsack from each ship arriving from Scotland in Flanders, Holland or Zeeland, was paid to the Scottish chaplain in Bruges, and it was on this basis that the grant was confirmed by royal decree in 1442 and reconfirmed by the Scottish parliament in 1467 (with minor modifications) and in 1487.[56] The chaplaincy was a royal appointment, at least until the reign of James V – though in 1538 the Carmelites claimed that the chapel had not been properly maintained for forty or fifty years.[57] The concern to provide adequate funds for the St Ninian's aisle doubtless reflected the international standing of the Carmelite church. Scottish pride was at stake, for here also were chapels of the German Hanse, the English Merchant Adventurers and the Catalans.[58] Until the construction of the Oosterlingenhuis in 1478 the refectory of the Carmelites was used for official assemblies by the Hanse; and the Catalans also held their assemblies here. It is likely that so too did the Scots.[59]

Little is recorded about the regulatory arrangements of the Scottish staple. Unlike other foreign communities in Bruges, the Scots had no accredited governor until the later years of the Bruges staple and there may never have been a Scottish consulate. Although the duke of Burgundy agreed to the appointment of a 'Conservator of the Scottish Privileges' in 1407 (an office which survived, in name at least, until 1847 and whose holder was charged with regulating the Scottish community and representing Scottish interests throughout Burgundian territories), there is no further mention of a Conservator until 1466.[60] But the dearth of cases between Scots in the judicial records of Bruges, combined with frequent references to the Metteneyes representing both Scots in the Bruges courts and the Bruges authorities on embassies to Scotland, suggests that Jan Metteneye, his son and grandson successively acted as conservators of the Scottish privileges from 1407 onwards.[61] Presumably the Scots reasoned

54 J. Marechal, *Europese aanwezigheid te Brugge* (Bruges, 1985), ch. I-3, 'De devotie te Brugge tot Sint-Ninian, bisschop van Whithorn in Schotland, 1366–1548', 51–62 (at 54, summary of the original deed of 6 July 1366).

55 *Edin. Recs*, 5 (1438), 66–7 (1494); Aberdeen City Archives, Council Register, v(2), 680 (before 1444).

56 *APS*, ii, 57, 87 c.4, 178 c.15.

57 Finlayson, 'Scottish Nation of Merchants', 180; *RSS*, ii, pp. xxiii–iv, no. 2722 (1538); Marechal, *Europese aanwezigheid te Brugge*, 59–61.

58 Finlayson, 'Scottish Nation of Merchants', 178; Letts, *Bruges and its Past*, 109; van Houtte, *Bruges: essai d'histoire urbaine*, 64.

59 van Houtte, *Bruges: essai d'histoire urbaine*, 61, 64.

60 Gilliodts, *Estaple*, i, nos. 540 cc.5–6, 543 c.4; Rooseboom, *Scottish Staple*, 11–12, 237, Apps. 14–15.

61 For the Metteneyes' involvement in Bruges court cases, see note 52 above; for Metteneye ambassadors to Scotland, see: *Chron. Bower* (Watt), viii, 257; N. Geirnaert, ed., *Het Archief van de familie Adornes en de Jeruzalemstichting te Brugge* (Bruges, 1987–9), ii, nos. 184–6; Gilliodts,

that, as members of one of the most powerful families in Bruges, the Metteneye were better placed to uphold Scottish interests than any conservator of Scottish origin.

Growing dissatisfaction with trading conditions in Bruges led to a change of policy. Probably in 1465, Master Stephen Angus, possibly the St Ninian's aisle chaplain, was appointed conservator.[62] Two years later the Scots withdrew from Bruges. In the staple agreement of 1470 the Bruges authorities undertook to ensure that Angus was 'honoured, respected and obeyed by the merchants and subjects of the [Scottish] nation', presumably because until then he was not.[63] At the same time a Scottish consulate was allegedly constructed on the Schottenplaats, although the only authority for this seems to be an eighteenth-century Bruges antiquary.[64] Yet Angus's position remained unsatisfactory and in 1472 he was replaced by Anselm Adornes. Adornes's remarkably successful diplomacy had secured the return of the Scottish staple in 1470, winning him the unique appointment of councillor to both the duke of Burgundy and the king of Scots.[65]

Unlike those of earlier conservators, Adornes's commission has survived.[66] Significantly, it specifically revoked the appointment of all previous conservators, suggesting that the Metteneyes' replacement by Angus had never been generally accepted. The commission gave Adornes plenary powers throughout Burgundian territories to uphold and defend, through the courts if necessary, all privileges and liberties granted to the Scottish nation. He was further empowered to judge lawsuits, disputes and altercations (civil and criminal) between Scottish merchants, other Scots and sectional interests among the Scottish burghs. In this judicial capacity the conservator was, by a statute of 1503, to be assisted by at least four and preferably six 'prudent and trustworthy' Scottish burgesses.[67] His salary was set some time previously, by agreement of the Scottish burghs, as a proportion of the value of all Scottish exports (presumably to Flanders, Holland and Zeeland).

To avoid the fate of other associates of the Burgundian Duke Charles the Bold, killed in 1477, Adornes fled Flanders after a short period of imprisonment. He settled in Scotland where, once more ill-starred in his patronage, he was

*Inventaire*, iv, 485; O. Delepierre, ed., *Précis analytique des documents des archives de la Flandre Occidentale*, ii (Bruges, 1844), 29–30; Gilliodts, *Estaple*, ii, no. 1146.

62 Stevenson, 'Thesis', 85–7, 191–2; Bruges, Stadsarchief, Civiele Sententies, iii, fo. 10r; Gilliodts, *Estaple*, ii, no. 1044 (summary, misquoting date and source). Angus may have been the Scottish chaplain in Bruges as early as 1443, when a copy of the original title deeds of the chapel was made on his behalf; he was a graduate of Louvain and former treasurer of Brechin: Marechal, *Europese aanwezigheid te Brugge*, 57–8; J. H. Baxter, 'Scottish students at Louvain University, 1425–1484', *SHR*, xxv (1929), 328–4 (matriculated 1436); Angus Council, Montrose Burgh Court Book, 1458–76, fo. 3v (1461).

63 Rooseboom, *Scottish Staple*, App. 26 c.4.

64 Duclos, *Bruges, histoire et souvenirs*, 554; Marechal, *Europese aanwezigheid te Brugge*, 27.

65 For the remarkable career of Anselm Adornes, see: *Nationaal Biografisch Woordenboec*, vol. XII (Brussels, 1987), 2–13; M. E. de la Coste, *Anselme Adornes, sire de Corthuy, pélerin de Terre Sainte, sa famille, ses voyages et son temps, récit historique* (Brussels, 1855); Comte de Limburg Sterum, 'Anselme Adornes, ou un voyageur Brugeois au XV^e^ siècle', *Messager des sciences historiques*, xlix (1881), 1–43; Stevenson, 'Thesis', 91–6; Geirnaert, *Archief van de familie Adornes*, i, nos. 18–37, ii, nos. 183–270. A recent Scottish summary, unfortunately marred by various inaccuracies, is A. Macquarrie, 'Anselm Adornes of Bruges, traveller in the East and friend of James III', *IR*, xxxiii (1982), 15–21.

66 Gilliodts, *Estaple*, ii, no. 1169; Rooseboom, *Scottish Staple*, App. 29.

67 *APS*, ii, 244 c.32.

murdered in the aftermath of the coup at Lauder bridge against James III. Adornes's heart was later returned to Bruges by his son (a canon of Aberdeen cathedral) and laid to rest in what must surely be the strangest and best-preserved medieval church in Belgium.[68] The Jeruzalemkapel, still owned by Anselm's descendants, was founded by his father and uncle and modelled on the church of the Holy Sepulchre. It still retains its medieval stained glass and altarpieces, the reliquary of the True Cross that it was built to house, and a reconstruction of the Holy Sepulchre itself, complete with plaster effigy of the entombed Christ. The tomb of Anselm Adornes and his wife dominates the lower chapel. To emphasise the circumstances of Anselm's death, the point of a sword protrudes from the right side of his effigy. In the heraldic glass above, the chivalric order bestowed upon Anselm by James III (the earliest known antecedent of the Order of the Thistle) is represented by a collar composed of elaborate interlinking knots from which hangs a unicorn.[69] The collar is also represented on Anselm's effigy. Parts of the adjoining Adorneshof also survive. It was there that James III's sister Mary and her husband (the forfeited earl of Arran) stayed after the fall of the Boyd government, until Anselm returned Mary to Scotland in 1471–2.[70] In a park between the Jeruzalemkapel and the Schottendijk – where St Annakerk now stands – once stood the Hof ter Veere, the Bruges mansion of the Borsselen family, lords of Veere, into which James II's sister (another Mary) married in 1444 and where she may have died in 1466.[71]

Some 500 yards down the south-western branch of the Reie, in Jan van Eyckplein, is the former toll-house and magnificent business headquarters of the Luxembourgs (Mary of Guise's maternal ancestors), heirs of the lords of Ghistelles. The present building dates from 1477. Over the years various negotiations were conducted here between the Scots and the toll officials. In the staple negotiations of 1394 the Scots complained specifically about the 'rummaging' of bales and other baggage by toll officials. They proposed instead that the contents should be verified by the word of the 'hosts of the merchants or their servants' – a clear indication that most Scottish business was then transacted through broker-innkeepers. Not surprisingly, this was refused. Instead, the lord of Ghistelles was persuaded by the Bruges authorities to bear the cost of repacking, if goods were found to be in order.[72] Further disputes arose in the 1460s, notably concerning charges on the export of clothing.[73] This particular issue was singled out in the staple settlement of 1470, when the 'Four Members of Flanders' (Bruges, Ghent, Ypres and the Franc of Bruges – which acted

68 Jan Adornes succeeded his brother Anthuenis as a canon of Aberdeen in March 1482: Geirnaert, *Archief van de familie Adornes*, ii, nos. 258–9, 305.

69 C. J. Burnett, 'The collar of the most ancient and most noble Order of the Thistle', *Orders and Medals*, xxvi (1987), 149–58.

70 W. H. Finlayson, 'The Boyds in Bruges', *SHR*, xxviii (1949), 195–6. Within the Adorneshof there are various representations of the Order of the Unicorn carved in wood and stone: Marechal, *Europese aanwezigheid te Brugge*, figs. 3–5.

71 Duclos, *Bruges, histoire et souvenirs*, 557; G. W. Watson, 'Wolfart van Borssele, Earl of Buchan', *Genealogist*, new ser., xiv (1898), 10–11; ibid., xvi (1900), 136; A. I. Dunlop, *The Life and Times of James Kennedy, Bishop of St Andrews* (Edinburgh, 1950), 66.

72 Rooseboom, *Scottish Staple*, Apps. 8 c.8, 9 c.8, 12, 13 c.6.

73 Stevenson, 'Thesis', 93; Bruges, Stadsarchief, Archief Adornes, 23, fo. 3v.

as a Flemish assembly) undertook to pursue the matter through the Burgundian courts and to absolve Scottish merchants of all expenses in the affair.[74]

The Ghistelles also had feudal control over the four Bruges weigh-houses. All large transactions by weight had to be conducted at a weigh-house, since no weights in excess of sixty pounds were permitted elsewhere in the Bruges area, including the Zwin towns. With this too, the Scots had various grievances. When the English staple was established at Bruges in 1359 (it remained there until 1362 and returned again only after the loss of Calais), English merchants had been granted exclusive use of what was already known as the English weigh-house, at 16 Engelse Straat.[75] There was another weigh-house on St Jansplein associated with the Spaniards.[76] In 1394, although no other nation apparently then possessed exclusive privileges, the Scots demanded a weigh-house of their own. This was refused, but the lord of Ghistelles agreed to give Scots priority over others at whichever of the four weigh-houses they nominated – a remarkable indication of the importance attached to Scottish trade. They chose the English weigh-house, probably because it was situated on the edge of the Scottish district – there was a house called 'Schotlant' beside that weigh-house and another of the same name close-by, on Koningstraat.[77] Since this was also the weigh-house most accessible to the English district (which lay immediately to the west), the Scottish choice probably inconvenienced English merchants most, doubtless to the delight of the Scots.

Fraud was a further concern at weigh-houses. In 1394 the Scots demanded that weighmen caught with their hand on the balance should be dismissed. In 1407 they protested that both hands and feet should be kept off the balance. Finally, in 1470 the Bruges authorities agreed to pay the weighman at the English weigh-house an annual fee for weighing Scottish goods, so that he had no incentive to cheat them.[78]

Another weigh-house was situated near the Tolhuis at the western edge of the German district, by St Jansbrug (the bridge being demolished in the late eighteenth century, when the Reie was covered over from this point to the Halle). The fourth weigh-house was further down the Reie beside the great medieval crane, on what is still Kraanplein.[79] Between these lay the northern part of the Spanish district and the Italian district, the banking and exchange centre of Bruges – and most of northern Europe until the early sixteenth century.[80] Here, as the ledger of Andrew Halyburton shows, much Scottish ecclesiastical business was transacted: papal dues were channelled through the Italian banking houses and papal bulls and dispensations, and other ecclesiastical correspondence, were carried by the regular courier services which the banks

74 Rooseboom, *Scottish Staple*, App. 26 c.9.

75 Lloyd, *Wool Trade*, 209–10; Marechal, *Europese aanwezigheid te Brugge*, 19.

76 Gilliodts, *Tonlieu*, i, 55–6, ii, 380–2.

77 Gilliodts, *Estaple*, i, no. 304 c.20; Rooseboom, *Scottish Staple*, Apps. 8, 9, 12; Duclos, *Bruges, histoire et souvenirs*, 554.

78 Rooseboom, *Scottish Staple*, Apps. 12, 15; Gilliodts, *Tonlieu*, i, 55–6, 57–8, 95–6.

79 Gilliodts, *Tonlieu*, i, 56; ii, 380–2.

80 de Roover, *Banking in Medieval Bruges;* J. Marechal, *Bijdrage tot de geschiedenis van het Bankwegen te Brugge* (Bruges, 1955).

provided to and from Italy.[81] Here, too, initial instalments were raised for the ransoms of David II and James I, and doubtless many other Scottish loans.[82] The focal point of the Italian district was the Inn of the Three Purses, the precursor of all continental *bourses*, on what is now Beursplein. Two medieval trading houses still stand on Beursplein: the Huize ter Beurze (1453), on the site of the eponymous inn, and the Genoese consulate (1399).

Beyond lies the Markt, on which still stands the great medieval Halle with its octagonal belfry, where merchants from all parts of Flanders sold their cloth. Nearby was the wool-house, at the end of Wollestraat beside what is now the St Jan Nepomuk Brug, which served a similar function for wool. It seems that the Scots resented the charges levied here by the Danwilt family. They may also have found the location of the wool-house inconvenient after the ban imposed on the use of Scottish wool in the cloth manufactures of Bruges, and other prestigious cloth towns, during the final decade of the fourteenth century – although Scottish wool was still generally employed in the so-called *nouvelles drapéries*.[83] At some point in the late fourteenth century Scottish merchants and brokers ceased to bring their wool and woolfells to the wool-house. 'After many years' they were taken to the comital court, which upheld the Danwilts' feudal rights. To resolve complaints, the Bruges council bought the wool-house in 1415 and abolished the charges previously levied.[84] Even then it is probable that, like other Scottish goods, wool and woolfells were sold from cellars and storehouses in the Scottish district. Although no general Bruges property register has survived, early sixteenth-century evidence from Bergen-op-Zoom indicates that both resident and visiting Scots owned or rented houses with storage facilities.[85] This may also have been the case in Bruges once the brokers' monopoly was lifted in 1407, for Halyburton recorded receipt of a large consignment of wool 'in my hous in Brugis'.[86] Further storage facilities were available in the inns and with the many brokers.

The wool-house was situated across the Reie from the Romanesque basilica of the Holy Blood. This is the oldest building in modern Bruges and the only surviving portion of the early comital Burg. It houses the venerated phial said to be of Christ's blood, brought back from the Second Crusade by Count Thierry of Flanders.[87] It seems perverse that only after the Scots abandoned the wool-house did the cult of the Holy Blood sweep through Scotland. Much as each craft had its patron saint, so Scottish merchants came to venerate the Holy Blood. From the fifteenth century Holy Blood plays, processions, masses, altars and confraternities were established by the merchants of Aberdeen, Ayr, Dundee, Dunfermline, Edinburgh, Haddington, Irvine, Lanark, Linlithgow, Montrose,

81 *Halyburton Ledger*, passim.

82 *ER*, ii, xli–iii; *APS*, ii, 6.

83 O. Delepierre and M. P. Willems, eds., *Collections des keuren ou statuts de tous les métiers de Bruges* (Ghent, 1842), 42; Espinas and Pirenne, *Industrie drapière*, i, 49, ii, 307, iii, 637.

84 Gilliodts, *Inventaire*, v, 211–13.

85 A. W. K. Stevenson, 'An early sixteenth-century Scottish colony at Bergen-op-Zoom', *IR*, xxvi (1975), 50–2.

86 *Halyburton Ledger*, 169.

87 Duclos, *Bruges, histoire et souvenirs*, 453, 457–9.

Perth, St Andrews, and doubtless elsewhere. In Edinburgh the remains of the Holy Blood aisle (now the Moray chapel) in St Giles and the Fetternear banner bear testimony to the cult, as do the many *Arma Christi* to be found across eastern Scotland.[88] The Scottish community as a whole was probably a fervent participant in the annual Holy Blood procession through Bruges, although only the participation of eminent ecclesiastics is recorded, including various visiting Scottish bishops and abbots.[89]

Beside the Holy Blood basilica stands the magnificent Stadhuis, constructed between 1376 and 1420, where council business was transacted, staple agreements were negotiated, civic receptions were held for visiting notables and embassies, and civil cases were heard before the *schepens* (aldermen) – the second highest civic office in Bruges. The Metteneyes were all *schepens* at different times and Anselm Adornes held the highest office of all, that of burgomaster, in 1475–6.[90] The Burg having been transferred to civic functions, the palace of the later counts of Flanders and the dukes of Burgundy was moved to the south, beyond the Markt. It occupied much of the area between Noordzandstraat, Geldmuntstraat, Geerwijnstraat, Moerstraat and Ontwangersstraat, but all that survives is the name Prinsenhof, on a street and square which occupy the sites of a former gateway and courtyard. Mary of Guelders spent part of her childhood in the Prinsenhof and it was there that a great feast and tournament were held in her honour in June 1449, on the eve of her departure to marry James II.[91]

Between the Prinsenhof and the Markt was the goldsmiths' district, now the shopping centre of Bruges. A significant proportion of medieval Scottish gold and silverware probably came from here. Although none of the little that has survived is identifiably Flemish, the standard of the Bruges goldsmiths was adopted as the legal standard for all Scottish silverwork in 1489.[92] At the turn of the sixteenth century Halyburton exported a wide variety of silverware and signets to Scotland, though by then most came from Antwerp.[93] Perhaps it was in this district too that the monumental brass workshops were located. Several notable brasses survive in Bruges. Halyburton recorded the purchase of six brasses from Bruges, including those of Archbishop Scheves and James, Duke of Ross – which seem to have been among the largest ever made.[94] In this district also were to be found the booksellers, scriptoria, illuminators and (from 1474) printers, who may have supplied many of Scotland's early books.[95] McRoberts

88 D. McRoberts, 'The Fetternear banner', *IR*, vii (1956), 69–86; G. Hay, 'The late medieval development of the High Kirk of St Giles, Edinburgh', *PSAS*, cvii (1975–6), 242–60; C. Carter, 'The *Arma Christi* in Scotland', *PSAS*, xc (1956–7), 116–29.

89 Bruges, Confraternité du Saint-Sang, Registres.

90 Gilliodts, *Inventaire*, iii, 425, v, 32, 133, 345.

91 G. F. de Beaucourt, ed., *Chronique de Mathieu d'Escouchy* (Société de l'histoire de France, 1863), i, 175–6; Gilliodts, *Inventaire*, v, 498; Dunlop, *Bishop Kennedy*, 100.

92 *APS*, ii, 221 c.13.

93 *Halyburton Ledger*, passim.

94 M. Clayton, *Victoria and Albert Museum: Catalogue of Rubbings of Brasses and Incised Slabs* (London, 1968), 226; *Halyburton Ledger*, 7, 47, 69, 215–16, 250; D. McRoberts, 'The glorious house of St Andrew', in idem, ed., *The Medieval Church of St Andrews* (Glasgow, 1976), 90–1.

95 Most 15th-century books of Scottish provenance were printed in Paris, Venice, Louvain, Cologne, Nuremburg, Antwerp, Basel and Strasbourg. Only one was printed in Bruges. However, the international nature of the early book trade is demonstrated by an inscription in a book published

believed that one of the most famous Bruges illuminators, Sanders (Alexander) Bening, was Scottish. His evidence was circumstantial, but both names were common in Scotland, while exceptionally rare in Flanders. Halyburton employed one Richard Bening as an assistant and married Sanders's daughter.[96] Flemish artistic influences were pervasive in late medieval Scotland.[97] Many Flemish altarpieces, sculptures and pictures were imported. Few remain, apart from the Trinity Panels by Hugo van der Goes, a close associate of Sanders Bening.

The only other places in Bruges with recognisably medieval Scottish associations are the Gruuthuse museum, the Church of Our Lady, Wapenmakersstraat and Minderbroedersstraat. The Gruuthuse museum occupies the surviving portion of the fifteenth-century mansion of the hereditary governors of Bruges. It was largely rebuilt in the late 1460s by Lodewijk van Brugge, lord of Gruuthuse, brother-in-law of Wolfert van Borsselen and Mary of Scotland, and a Burgundian ambassador to Scotland in 1461.[98] The Church of Our Lady, to which the museum is linked, was the meeting place of the aristocratic Confraternity of Our Lady of the Snow. Several Scots were members, including at least two members of the Bonkil family, whose coat of arms is depicted in the Trinity Panel. As its name implies, Wapenmakersstraat, which links St Jansplein with the Burg, was the centre of the armourers' district. Between the thirteenth and fifteenth centuries Bruges was Scotland's main supplier of armaments of all descriptions and was thus a vital link in Scottish defences.[99] The links with Minderbroedersstraat are more tenuous but hereabouts were carved the choir stalls of Melrose Abbey (modelled on those of the Flemish abbeys of Ter Duinen and Thosan), which were stored for some years in the refectory of the long-since-demolished Franciscan friary, until a dispute over payment was

in Basel in 1492, to the effect that it was bought in Bruges in 1495: J. Durkan and A. Ross, 'Early Scottish libraries', *IR*, ix (1958), 5–167 (Bruges references at pp. 118, 153). Halyburton shipped books by the case from the Low Countries to Scotland: *Halyburton Ledger*, 6–7, 100–1, 254, 273.

96 D. McRoberts, 'Notes on Scoto-Flemish artistic contacts', *IR*, x (1959), 91–6; *Halyburton Ledger*, passim. Lorne Campbell adduced further corroborative evidence, while maintaining that Sanders's origin was an unproven contention: C. Thompson and L. Campbell, *Hugo van der Goes and the Trinity Panels in Edinburgh* (Edinburgh, 1974), 50 n.6.

97 Ibid., 50 n.5, 53–4; McRoberts, 'Scoto-Flemish artistic contacts'; *Halyburton Ledger*, 9, 189, 254; G. Hay, 'A Scottish altarpiece in Copenhagen', *IR*, v (1956), 5–10; R. Fawcett, 'Late Gothic architecture in Scotland: considerations on the influence of the Low Countries', *PSAS*, cxii (1982), 477–96; idem, *Scottish Architecture from the Accession of the Stewarts to the Reformation, 1371–1560* (Edinburgh, 1994). Richard Fawcett emphasises the strength of architectural links with the Low Countries but underplays specific links with Bruges. The probable derivation of the ceiling of King's College chapel from those in St Gilliskerk has already been noted. Marc Gheeraerts's town plan of 1562 indicates a strong resemblance between the west front of the Dominican church in Bruges and the burgh church of Haddington and between the tower of the old St Walburgakerk and that of Dundee.

98 Duclos, *Bruges, histoire et souvenirs*, 348, 497–8; Dunlop, *Bishop Kennedy*, 214–15, 217. I am grateful to Lorne Campbell for this information.

99 Stevenson, 'Flemish dimension of Auld Alliance'; *APS*, ii, 9 c.2, 100 c.6; *ER*, iv, 677–81 (a miscellany of armaments and luxury goods bought in Flanders for James I), vi, 308–10; *Chron. Bower* (Watt), viii, 263. Although it focuses mainly on the 16th century, when France was Scotland's main supplier of armaments, see also D. H. Caldwell, 'Royal patronage of arms and armour making in fifteenth- and sixteenth-century Scotland', in idem, ed., *Scottish Weapons and Fortifications, 1100–1800* (Edinburgh, 1981), 73–89.

settled in 1441.[100] It has often been suggested that the stalls of King's College chapel, Aberdeen, are Flemish. There is no documentary evidence for this, but, at about the time they were made, five chairs of state were commissioned in Bruges for James IV's wedding.[101]

There can, then, have been few parts of Bruges unfrequented by medieval Scottish merchants, and the *Poorterboeken* indicate that more Scots became burgesses of Bruges during the fifteenth century than did any other foreign nationality apart from the French.[102] Close links persisted until the early sixteenth century, when Bruges was still the most frequently recorded place of business in Halyburton's ledger, but the Scottish staple at Bruges was already irreparably damaged by the 1460s. Increasingly Veere became the principal port of entry for Scottish vessels and a more evenly distributed pattern of trade developed with Bruges, Middelburg, Bergen-op-Zoom and Antwerp. Political problems also had their effect. One consequence of the anarchy that enveloped Bruges after the death of Charles the Bold in 1477 was that the Scottish staple was suspended. Most of the Scottish community withdrew to Middelburg and did not return. While the Scots were amongst the first 'nations' to leave Bruges, their departure was part of a long-drawn-out process of commercial decline, consequent on the silting up of the Zwin and the rise of Antwerp. By 1553 only the Spaniards remained.[103]

100 O. Delepierre, 'A document preserved among the records of West Flanders, relating to the carved stalls of Melrose abbey church', *Archaeologia*, xxxi (1846), 346–9.

101 *TA*, ii, 227–8. As for the weddings of David II and James III (*ER*, i, 119, 149, vii, 658–9, 662–5), it was in Flanders that most purchases were made for the wedding of James IV: *TA*, ii, 227–42.

102 R. A. Parmentier, *Indices op de Brugsche Poorterboeken* (Bruges, 1938); Finlayson, 'Scottish Nation of Merchants', 189–93, 254. Merchant burgesses are not recorded, although some (such as Alexander Bonkil) can be separately identified.

103 Marechal, *Europese aanwezigheid te Brugge*, ch. VI-13, 'Le départ de Bruges des marchands étrangers (XV^e et XVI^e siècles)', 180–93. The brief Scottish references are inaccurate, but this essay provides the best general summary available.

# 8

# Sir James Douglas, Spain, and the Holy Land

*Sonja Cameron*

When, in early 1329, Robert I knew that he was dying, the affairs of his realm appeared settled and secure. In 1328, after forty-four years of warfare, peace had been agreed with England, and the English king had renounced his claims to the kingdom of Scotland. A ten-year papal interdict on the Scottish realm had recently been lifted. More importantly, there was a direct male heir to the throne, in the person of the future David II, who had been born in 1324. Although David's age meant that a lengthy royal minority would probably ensue, a solution had already been formulated: a tailzie of 1326 designated Robert's nephew, Thomas Randolph, Earl of Moray, and failing him Sir James Douglas, as regent. With these tried and trusted veterans in charge of a realm newly at peace, there would seem to have been little to worry about. It was against this background that Robert made dispositions for his heart to be buried at Melrose. The reference to 'cor nostrum' ('our heart') in this document, dated about a month before he died, suggests that Robert had by then already decided that his heart would be separated from his body, and carried into battle against the infidel by a selected champion, before being committed to its final resting-place.[1]

This was neither an unheard-of, nor unreasonable, desire.[2] Both Robert's father and grandfather had taken the cross.[3] And while Robert himself, preoccupied with his own enemies, never found time to crusade against the enemies of Christ, he appears to have been a religious man. He may have felt the burden of his repeated excommunications and of the killings he had both committed and authorised. Pilgrimage and crusade were accepted methods of atoning for sin, benefiting the soul, and expressing love of Christ. Moreover, a crusade (however personal) was guaranteed international acclaim. Robert's inability to go in person was no obstacle. Sending a proxy was a perfectly legitimate alternative.

In his epic poem *The Bruce*, John Barbour claimed that Robert had left the choice of proxy to the barons.[4] But this seems doubtful, since the proxy selected was Sir James Douglas, one of the kingdom's most able military leaders, who was also included in the plans for the regency. It is difficult to understand how a committee would choose him for a venture which would entail a lengthy absence from Scotland at a critical juncture. Le Bel's claim that Bruce had made the decision sounds more plausible;[5] and it is remarkable that none of the more detached witnesses should have attempted to stop him.

1 *RRS*, v, no. 380. There used to be debate concerning the reliability of this document, but Duncan's analysis has shown it to be authentic.

2 The matter of heart-burials is discussed further in G. G. Simpson, 'The heart of King Robert I: pious crusade or marketing gambit?', in B. Crawford, ed., *Church, Chronicle and Learning in Medieval and Renaissance Scotland* (Edinburgh, forthcoming).

3 A. Macquarrie, *Scotland and the Crusades 1095–1560* (Edinburgh, 1985), 58–9.

4 Barbour, *Bruce*, iii, 246 (XX, ll. 191–6).

5 *Chron. Le Bel*, i, 83.

Why, then, did the king choose Douglas? Chroniclers claimed that he justified his choice on the grounds that Douglas was the 'most worthy' of men and 'the most loyal champion in all his wars'.[6] Moreover, they added, Douglas's 'bounte' made Robert long to give him this commission, and the king knew of no one in the realm more suited to undertake the task. [7]

These are personal, not rational reasons, and the search for more pragmatic explanations is frustrated. John Mair, critical of the decision to dispatch Douglas overseas, attempted to provide one which went beyond mere sentimentality. He suggested that Robert I may have feared that, after his death, rivalry between Thomas Randolph and James Douglas might lead to civil war in the realm, and that he therefore decided to send Douglas abroad.[8] But Mair and subsequently John Leslie were unhappy with this interpretation.[9] Besides, although the notion that serious rivalry existed between Douglas and Moray originated in one passage in *The Bruce*, it is even there contradicted by other passages.[10] There is no corroborating evidence of such rivalry.[11] Douglas and Moray had co-operated to dazzling effect for over a decade, and their partnership would surely have been shorter and less successful, had it been strained by serious rivalry. We might also ask why, if Robert feared Douglas's ambitions, he nominated him for a role in the regency. Douglas was not closely related to the royal house.[12] He could not, in justice, have complained had he been overlooked for the regency in the first place. The fact that Bruce chose him to act as guardian shows that he trusted Douglas's integrity and his ability to work with Moray.[13]

Alan Macquarrie has suggested a different interpretation of these events. He points out that Douglas was part of 'a new generation [which] had grown up in an atmosphere of intermittent war and constant hostility', and argues that, in 1330, 'when the country was looking forward ... to a long period of peace', it may have been best to remove 'incorrigible belligerents' from the kingdom.[14] This builds upon his earlier contention that Douglas 'had probably become so inured to fighting through a quarter of a century that he had little skill or experience at anything else'.[15] Several of these judgements may be questioned. Experience seemed to have taught the Scots that treaties with England would

6 *Chron. Le Baker*, 42; *Chron. Bower* (Watt), vii, 65.

7 Barbour, *Bruce*, iii, 247 (XX, ll. 222–5); *Chron. Le Bel*, 84.

8 Mair, *Historia*, V, ix, fo. 96v. 'Sed forte dices oculatissimus erat Robertus: sentiensque quod non capit fortuna duos quando illi sunt æquales: quemadmodum istos [i.e. Douglas and Moray] iudico, propterea honestissima occasione habita Iacobum Douglassum extra regnum misit. [Q]uod si ita fecerit non est factum eius improbabile: bella enim ciuilia timens non multum inprudenter egit ...'

9 Leslie, *De Origine*, VIII, 17, p. 13. Sir Herbert Maxwell, however, espoused this interpretation enthusiastically: see H. Maxwell, *The House of Douglas* (London, 1902), i, 62.

10 Barbour, *Bruce*, iii, 152 (XVII, ll. 52–60); cf. iii, 25, 31–2 (XI, ll. 637–57; XII, ll. 105–29).

11 The impression conveyed by contemporary sources is hyperbolically eulogised in David Hume of Godscroft, *The History of the Houses of Douglas and Angus* (Edinburgh, 1644), 39.

12 He was probably Walter Stewart's cousin (cf. *Melrose Liber*, no. 408), which would make him remotely related to Robert Stewart, now second in line to the throne.

13 Finally we may enquire what, if Mair's hypothesis be true, Bruce expected to happen when Douglas returned from his crusade. For sending him away would just have been postponing the problem. Or would we have to assume that Bruce hoped for Douglas's death on his mission?

14 Macquarrie, *Crusades*, 79–80.

15 Ibid., 75.

last only as long as they appeared able to defend themselves. A royal minority was in this respect a handicap, and men such as Douglas were the closest to a deterrent against English aggression that the Scots possessed. It is also simplistic to argue that Douglas – merely because he belonged to the war generation and happened to be a successful warrior – enjoyed nothing but fighting and was good at nothing but fighting. Indeed, Douglas was involved in the administration of the realm in times of peace.[16] He played a major part in negotiating the treaty of Edinburgh, and supervised the arrangements for the marriage of David Bruce and the English princess Joan.[17] It appears, then, that Macquarrie's evaluation of Douglas's activities is based on the rather one-dimensional image of him in Barbour's *Bruce*. Of course, Douglas 'possessed elements of a rough soldier' – but so did Moray, whom Macquarrie contrasts with Douglas as the 'accomplished diplomat and statesman'.[18] Moray, too, had spent most of his life fighting, and so, for that matter, had most of Bruce's trusted companions. It is unreasonable to assume that Douglas's military abilities disqualified him from more peaceful activities, and unrealistic to believe that during a royal minority many would not have been grateful for his presence.

This brings us back to the less than rational motives suggested by the chroniclers. Robert selected Douglas for neither religious nor political reasons, but rather because he liked and trusted him. In a similar spirit, Douglas – also ignoring the demands of common sense – accepted the mission. It might have been difficult to refuse the king's wish in any case, but the impression given by the chronicles is that Douglas responded with enthusiasm rather than resigned acquiescence.[19] Le Bel has Douglas offer 'cent mille mercys de la grand honeur que vous me faites'.[20] And it was a 'great honour' which brought Douglas into conflict with the Church. Boniface VIII's bull *Detestandae feritatis abusum* of 1299 condemned tampering with the bodies of the dead, and decreed automatic excommunication for those who did so.[21] Douglas was duly excommunicated for his role in removing the king's heart from his body and this sentence was lifted only in 1331, a year after Douglas's death and following a petition submitted to the Pope by Moray. Had Douglas been a deeply religious man, certain excommunication might have caused him some uneasiness. However, Douglas's known involvement in organised religion was businesslike rather than fervent, and even his final bequest

16 He attended parliaments, and was a member of Bruce's council. Bruce entrusted to Douglas the business of his special protégé, the monastery of Melrose (*RRS*, v, nos. 108, 169), indicating the king's good opinion of Douglas's management abilities. Even more significantly, someone devoid of administrative competence could hardly have been designated prospective regent of Scotland.

17 Barbour, *Bruce*, iii, 241–2 (XX, ll. 67–72, 80–4). English chronicles name him as the chief representative on the Scottish side: *Adam Murimuthensis Chronica sui Temporis*, ed. T. Hog (English Historical Soc., 1846), 57; *Chron. Le Baker*, 41; *Chron. Walsingham*, 190.

18 Macquarrie, *Crusades*, 74–5.

19 *Chron. Le Bel*, 85; cf. also Barbour, *Bruce*, iii, 247–8 (XX, ll. 233–44). Le Baker portrays Douglas as enthusiastic not only about the honour but also about the prospect of death in battle against the infidel: *Chron. Le Baker*, 41–2.

20 *Chron. Le Bel*, 85.

21 *Regesta Pontificum Romanorum*, ed. A. Potthast (Berlin, 1874–5), ii, no. 24881: 'Statuit et ordinat, ut, cum quis diem de cetero claudet extremum, circa corpora defunctorum nullatenus observetur abusus ille, quo nonnulli fideles corpora in remotas terras transferenda aqua ferventissima decoqui, concide vel exuri consueverunt, cum id a pietate christiana abhorreat.

to Newbattle Abbey suggests a conventional, rather than a pious, outlook.[22] While one commentator has accepted the statement on Douglas's safe-conduct that he went to Spain 'inflamed with the love of the cross',[23] it is safer to regard this wording as formulaic. Douglas went to Spain not to serve God, but to please Bruce, and as a consequence he incurred excommunication.

Robert I died on 7 June 1329. By 1 September Douglas had acquired from Edward III a seven-year safe conduct and a personal recommendation written on his behalf to Alfonso XI of Castile.[24] Alfonso was then fighting the Muslims on the frontiers of Granada, this latest instalment of *reconquista* having begun in 1328.[25] His campaigns attracted support from many different countries, and Castile was an obvious and accessible destination for those seeking to participate in a crusade.

Douglas left Scotland in the spring of 1330. He travelled to Flanders and remained on his ship off Sluis for twelve days, refusing to touch land but inviting guests on board and holding court in luxury 'as if he were the king of Scotland'.[26] It seems that Robert had instructed Douglas to raid the treasury and equip himself in such a manner that all would realise that he was carrying the late king's heart.[27] From Sluis Douglas sailed south to Castile, probably landing at Seville, where he was received by Alfonso XI. Barbour claims he was placed in command of a whole division of the Castilian king's host.[28] It is more likely that Douglas remained in charge of his own retinue alone, though he may have been joined by individual volunteers. This is perhaps what Barbour meant when he stated that all the foreign knights were put under Douglas's command.[29] It was probably, therefore, as captain of a small body of volunteers, and not as a major commander, that Douglas took up his position with Alfonso's army outside the walls of Teba de Ardales on 7 August 1330.[30]

The setting of Douglas's final battle was described in the *Crónica del Rey*. A Muslim army came to relieve the town and struck camp at Turón, a few miles away. Between the Christian and Muslim camps, and half a mile from Teba itself, lay the river Guadalteba, at which the Christians watered their animals. The Muslims launched minor attacks on the Christians during these visits, forcing the Christians to defend themselves with cavalry. One day Alfonso was informed that the Muslims intended to divide their army, using one half in the daily diversion at the river while the remainder was to attack the main Christian camp. Alfonso accordingly divided his own army. Both at the river and at the camp the Muslims

22 Except in the choice of beneficiary. For a more detailed examination of Douglas's encounters with religion see S. Väthjunker, 'A Study of the Career of Sir James Douglas – The Historical Record *versus* Barbour's *Bruce*' (University of Aberdeen, unpublished PhD thesis, 1992), 131–5.

23 B. Krauel Heredia, 'Sir James Douglas's death in Spain, 1330', *SHR*, lxix (1990), 89–90.

24 T. Rymer, *Foedera, Conventiones, Litterae et Cuiuscunque Generis Acta Publica* (Record Commission, 1816–69), ii (2), 771 (1 Sep. 1329).

25 Ibid., 770 (1 Sep. 1329).

26 'Comment ce fust roy d'Escoce.' *Chron. Le Bel*, 86–7; cf. also Barbour, *Bruce*, iii, 252 (XX, ll. 345–7).

27 *Chron. Le Bel*, 84.

28 Barbour, *Bruce*, iii, 254 (XX, ll. 410–11). This appears particularly unlikely since the leaders of the other two divisions were Alfonso himself and the master of Santiago, both of whom were of higher standing than Douglas: ibid., 254–5 (ll. 413–15).

29 Ibid., l. 412.

30 A. G. Soler, *Don Juan Manuel: Biografía y estudio critico* (Zaragoza, 1932), no. CCCCLXXXVII.

were routed, and their leader sent those who had attacked the camp to the aid of those who were fleeing from the river. However, Alfonso reorganised his men, and his combined forces chased the combined Muslim armies back to Turón. The day's events so demoralised the Muslims that Teba fell shortly afterwards.[31]

Douglas's precise role in these events is uncertain, though it is clear that he died during an armed confrontation. He and the men in his charge found themselves isolated from the main host, and, faced with a multitude of enemies, they were overpowered.[32] How this could have happened, and whether it occurred during the battle described above, remains a matter of controversy. The view that Douglas's death occurred in the decisive battle appears to be supported by Fordun, whose account of it matches that of the *Crónica del Rey* in indicating that the Muslim force was split in two:

> James of Douglas and the king of Spain ... warred down the Sultan, and numberless Saracens with him; and when these had been overcome and put to flight ... the said king went back safely with his army. But the aforesaid James alas! kept a very few with him, as his army; and as this was by no means hidden from another sultan, who was lurking in an ambush, the latter with his men, started out from his hiding-place, and challenged James to battle. No sooner had the said James recognised his army and banners afar off, than, in his fearlessness, he dashingly charged them with his men. A great many Saracens were slain; and James ended his days there in bliss ...[33]

This account was supported by Barbour. He claimed that Douglas put the Muslims to flight, and then outrode the rest of the army, before being surprised by Muslim reinforcements.[34] Both Fordun and Barbour suggested that Douglas did not keep enough men by his side. Bower added that these events occurred 'at the castle of Teba'.[35] Piecing together the Scottish and Castilian evidence, it seems that Douglas was with the first division at the river, and that he fell in the interval between the appearance of Muslim reinforcements and Alfonso's arrival with the rest of the Christian army. That means Douglas was initially successful – but possibly too successful, because he had ridden so far ahead of the main host that he was unable to reach safety when the Muslim reinforcements arrived. His death was therefore due to over-enthusiasm, or to 'chivalrous emulation [which] overbore his habitual prudence'.[36] This, in essence, is the traditional version of events last championed by Macquarrie.[37]

31 Fernán Sánchez de Valladolid, *Crónica del rey don Alfonso el Onceno,* ed. D. Catalán (Madrid, 1953), pp. lxxxiv–lxxxviii; *Obras del Padre Juan de Mariana*, ed. D. F. P. y M. (Madrid, 1909–31), i, 15, 21.

32 Maxwell's interpretation is limited to these basic factors: Maxwell, *House of Douglas*, i, 63.

33 *Chron. Fordun*, i, 353; ii, 345–6. Barrow concluded from this that Douglas and his men, 'deceived by the Moorish tactics of making a feint attack ... found themselves cut off from the main body' (Barrow, *Bruce*, 324). Hume's statement that 'hee was there inclosed by an Ambush of the Enemie, and lost his life' (Hume of Godscroft, *Douglas*, 57) seems similarly based upon Fordun's account. However, all Spanish sources agree that the Muslims' intention to divide their forces was known to the Christians, who successfully took precautions.

34 Cf. Barbour, *Bruce*, iii, 256 (XX, ll. 435–55).

35 'apud castrum Tibris': *Chron. Bower* (Watt), vii, 71.

36 Maxwell, *House of Douglas*, i, 63.

37 Fraser, *Douglas*, i, 180; I. M. Davis, *The Black Douglas* (London, 1974) 163–4; Macquarrie, *Crusades*, 78–9.

Blanca Krauel Heredia's more recent interpretation, based on a different set of sources, differs notably.[38] She refers to Le Bel whose account describes Douglas taking up position on a flank so that he could better demonstrate his prowess. When he saw Alfonso's division move a little, he mistook this for the signal to attack. Since he was eager to be amongst the first into the battle, he charged with his division straight up to the Muslim lines, thinking that the entire Christian host was behind him. However, no attack took place that day, and Douglas and his entire division were surrounded by enemies and killed.[39] This, Krauel Heredia argues, tallies with an account in the *Gran Crónica* which states that

> one day at [the river] there was a big battle in which a foreign *conde* died, who had left his country to serve God and try his strength in battle against the enemies of the Cross ... [H]e died through his own fault because, leaving the Christian lines, he inopportunely attacked the Moors in a way that he should not have done.[40]

Krauel Heredia claims that

> this account, which coincides strikingly with Le Bel's, indicates that Douglas was killed on the day before the Christian victory at Teba, and not during the battle itself. It is true that the *Gran Crónica* does not mention Douglas by name, but the way in which it portrays the foreign count or earl tallies with the circumstances which brought Lord James to Spain.[41]

She therefore concludes that Douglas's death was the result of a misunderstanding which led him to attack the enemy when no one else did and when no one else even intended to.

Krauel Heredia's analysis is offered as the definitive version of what happened at Teba. It is, however, open to a number of criticisms. While she used the narrative *Crónica del rey* for her account of much of the campaign, she dismissed the narratives of Fordun and Barbour (which broadly agree with the *Crónica del rey*), on the grounds that they were 'written half a century later'.[42] This is unfortunate because the source which she eventually preferred (the *Gran Crónica*) was 'written between 1376 and 1379' – at much the same time as Barbour's *Bruce* and just before Fordun's chronicle.[43] She also argues that, since Le Bel mentioned no earlier battle, Douglas fell in the first battle of the campaign.[44]

38 Krauel Heredia, 'Douglas's death', 89–90.

39 Douglas 'se trahy à ung des costez pour mielx faire sa besongne et mielx monstrer son effort. Quant il vist toutes les batailles rengier et vist colle du roy ung poy esmouvoir, il cuida qu'elle alast assembler. Il qui mielx amoit estre des premiers que des derrains, feri des esperons à toute sa compaignie et ala jusques à la bataille du roy de Guernade, et pensoit bien que le roy et toutes ses batailles le syewissent, maiz il en fut lourdement deceus, car oncques ce jour ne s'esmurent; ains fut ledit messire Guillaume et toute sa compaignie enclos des anemis que oncques ung seul n'en eschappa qu'ilz ne fussent tous tuez ...': *Chron. Le Bel*, 88.

40 *Gran Crónica de Alfonso XI*, ed. D. Catalán (Madrid, 1976), i, 477.

41 Krauel Heredia, 'Douglas's death', 89.

42 Ibid., 88. She also claims that Barbour merely mentions that Douglas found himself surrounded, ignoring his full account of the initial success and pursuit of the fugitives which matches the picture given in *Crónica del rey don Alfonso el Onceno*.

43 Krauel Heredia, 'Douglas's death', 89.

44 Ibid., 88.

But Le Bel was not primarily concerned with charting the wars against the Moors. His interest was in the figure of Douglas. Not one of the non-Spanish chroniclers (except Le Baker who generalises about 'many victories'[45]) mentions a battle before Teba. Concerned primarily with Douglas, there is no reason why they should have done.

A further problem is that Krauel Heredia appears to consider it beyond dispute that the *conde* of the *Gran Crónica* can, indeed, be identified as Douglas. If so, the description of him is curious. For one thing, Douglas was not a count (that is, an earl) but a knight, albeit a powerful and famous knight. More puzzling still is her contention that 'the way in which [the *Gran Crónica*] portrays the foreign count or earl tallies with the circumstances which brought Lord James to Spain'.[46] This is precisely not the case. What the *Gran Crónica* states is that this *conde* 'departed from his country to serve God and prove his body against the enemies of the Cross'.[47] Arguably, these were the circumstances in which every foreign volunteer joined a crusade – and in 1330, as usual, there would have been a considerable number of foreigners fighting against the Muslims, a point implied by Krauel Heredia herself.[48] But Douglas's was a special case. He bore a silver casket with the heart of the internationally well-known king of Scots around his neck, and he was on the crusade as proxy for that king. Le Bel claimed that it was Bruce's express command to Douglas that 'par tout où vous vendrez, qu'on sache que vous portez comme message le cueur du roy d'Escoce, puis qu'ainsy est que le corps n'y poeut aler'.[49] Le Bel also described how Douglas had kept court in the king's name at Sluis. Barbour suggested that he did the same in Spain.[50] It is unlikely that Douglas pretended he was there for purely personal reasons, thereby defeating the purpose of his mission. The conventional motives ascribed to the 'foreign count' in the *Gran Crónica* do not accord with what we know of Douglas's mission.

Still, these criticisms alone are not conclusive. The half-century which elapsed between the events and the writing of the *Gran Crónica* could account for errors of this kind. If, however, we accept for the moment that the *conde* of the *Gran Crónica* is indeed Douglas, it is worth examining more closely what the chronicle really says about his fate, and comparing this with Le Bel's account. Almost immediately, we encounter problems.

The author of the *Gran Crónica* stated that one day at the river there was a big battle (*muy gran contienda*) in which the *conde* was killed.[51] Le Bel, however, claimed that on the day Douglas died the armies did not move (*ne s'esmurent*).[52] This makes it difficult to argue that the two accounts 'coincide strikingly'.[53] In this regard, the

45 *Chron. Le Baker*, 41.

46 Krauel Heredia, 'Douglas's death', 89.

47 'saliera de su tierra pere fazer a Dios seruiçio e prouar su cuerpo contra los enemigos de la Cruz': *Gran Crónica de Alfonso XI*, i, 477.

48 Krauel Heredia, 'Douglas's death', 85. Barbour had Douglas put in charge of the strangers, implying that there were quite a few of them; cf. Barbour, *Bruce*, iii, 254 (XX, l. 411).

49 *Chron. Le Bel*, 84.

50 Barbour, *Bruce*, iii, 252–3 (XX, ll. 364–9).

51 *Gran Crónica de Alfonso XI*, i, 477.

52 *Chron. Le Bel*, 88.

53 Krauel Heredia, 'Douglas's death', 89.

*Gran Crónica* resembles more closely the *Crónica del rey*, Fordun, and Barbour's *Bruce* – that is, the sources used by Macquarrie. Yet it is the idiosyncratic Le Bel upon whom Krauel Heredia relies in arguing that Douglas attacked when he should not have done, and that he died before any major battle took place.

The crux of the matter appears to lie in the *Gran Crónica*'s claim that the *conde*, 'leaving the Christian lines ... inopportunely attacked the Moors in a way that he should not have done'. 'Inopportunely' (*a desora*) is the term on which Krauel Heredia seems to base her argument that the *Gran Crónica* matches the account of Le Bel – who stated that Douglas attacked when nobody else did. This supposed agreement, Krauel Heredia adds, proves that Le Bel's account of Douglas's actions was essentially correct. However, we have already seen that in all other details the account in the *Gran Crónica* corresponds not with Le Bel's, but with the *Crónica del Rey*, Fordun, and *The Bruce*. It is doubtful whether such broad agreement should be disregarded on the basis of two words. It seems more likely that either the *conde* of the *Gran Crónica* was not Douglas at all; or that the accounts of Le Bel and the author of the *Gran Crónica* are incompatible. In the latter case, the traditional account, broadly supported by three chronicles, would seem most plausible. On balance, the evidence suggests that there was a full-scale battle; and that the *conde* (whoever he was) was involved in an impetuous charge in which he outdistanced everyone else. In describing Douglas's death, Fordun and Barbour suggest a similar version of events.

In brief, we may accept either the 'traditional' account of Douglas's death, based on one Spanish chronicle of the 1340s and two Scottish accounts written in the 1370s and 1380s, or an interpretation based on a French source of the 1350s and an ambiguous Spanish source of the 1370s, the latter of which, if it really does refer to Douglas, might actually be interpreted as supporting the traditional version of events.[54] According to the first accounts, Douglas's death was due to his personal recklessness in pursuing the fleeing Muslims. Alternatively, his death was the result of a foolish misunderstanding.[55] Both interpretations fit uneasily with Douglas's considerable military experience and competence. But it is just about conceivable that, acutely conscious that he was representing his king, Douglas may have overreached himself. This would at least provide some explanation for a reckless chase.

Since Le Bel wrote, some have assumed that Douglas, by falling in battle in Spain, failed to carry out his intended mission of taking Bruce's heart to Jerusalem. According to Le Bel, Robert had expressed the wish that his heart be taken to the Holy Sepulchre.[56] Such a destination is also suggested by the safe conduct for travel

54 The English chroniclers have nothing of importance to add. Le Baker stated simply that Douglas 'post multas victorias ... simul contra v. Saracenos solus dimicans, v. letalibus wlneribus ab ipsis est occisus' (*Chron. Le Baker*, 41) – which can be used to support either view because he does not say how Douglas arrived in that uncomfortable situation. Knighton records Douglas's death, and no more: *Chronicon Henrici Knighton, vel Cnitthon, monachi Leycestrensis*, ed. J. R. Lumby (Rolls Ser., 1889–95), i 460.

55 Le Bel's statement that Douglas's death 'fut grande dommage et grand deffault pour les Espaignolz' [*Chron. Le Bel*, 88] is probably not to be taken to imply that the Spanish were to blame. *Deffault pour*, rather than meaning *the fault of*, as Krauel Heredia has it (Krauel Heredia, 'Douglas's death', 90), can be translated as *loss for*.

56 *Chron. Le Bel*, 84, 87. This version was accepted by Fraser, who claimed that there is 'good

to the Holy Land which Douglas received from Edward III of England.[57] Le Bel further claimed that it was while at Sluis, on his way to Jerusalem, that Douglas first heard about Alfonso's Castilian campaign; and that he then resolved to make a detour via Spain. However, Edward III had provided Douglas with a letter of recommendation for Alfonso XI on the same date as the safe conduct was issued.[58] If Spain was indeed a diversion from the original destination, then Douglas had planned it well in advance, and long before he reached Sluis.

There are, then, considerable doubts about Le Bel's reliability. His account of Douglas's journey to Spain is a minefield of half-truths and misinformation. He claimed that Douglas set sail from Montrose – which is nautically unlikely.[59] He claimed that Douglas heard about Alfonso's crusade in Sluis – which is demonstrably incorrect. He claimed that Douglas's assault on the Moors was an isolated incident – which is contradicted by every other source. And finally he claimed that Douglas intended to journey to the Holy Land. Le Bel's work was incorporated in the widely disseminated history written by Froissart, and his 'Holy Land theory' was then adopted by the Scottish historians Wyntoun, Boece and Leslie. Interestingly, they all claimed that Douglas did travel to Jerusalem and that he stopped in Spain on the way back, having completed his mission.[60] Some later writers believed that Douglas buried Bruce's heart at the Holy Sepulchre.[61] This is manifestly wrong; and would also have been in contravention of Bruce's wish, expressed a month before his death, for his heart to be buried at Melrose.[62]

Nevertheless, while this appears to have been the accepted version of events in the fifteenth and sixteenth centuries, none of the fourteenth-century chroniclers, apart from Le Bel, refers to the Holy Land. They seem to have been unaware that Jerusalem played a part in Bruce's or Douglas's plans. Neither Fordun nor Barbour considered anything amiss in Douglas's exploits in Spain and in Barbour's epic Robert simply asked Douglas 'on Goddis fayis my hart to ber'.[63] Le Baker had Douglas carry Bruce's heart 'against the enemies of Christ at the Granadan frontier',[64] and Thomas Gray referred to the Granadan journey, pointing out that Douglas had 'undertaken that holy voyage *according to the request of Robert Bruce his king*'.[65] Lastly, the Pope's absolution for Douglas,

evidence of Bruce's real desire that his heart should be taken to Palestine': Fraser, *Douglas*, i, 176, 178–9. The theory has even found its way into the most authoritative study of Robert Bruce: Barrow, *Bruce*, 323.

57 *Foedera*, ii(2), 770 (1 Sep. 1329).

58 Ibid., 771 (1 Sep. 1329).

59 *Chron. Le Bel*, 80.

60 Leslie, *De Origine*, VIII, 17, p. 13; *Chron. Wyntoun* (Laing), iii, 375–6 (VIII. 22, ll. 3121–3); Hector Boece, *Scotorum Historiae a prima gentis origine* ... (Paris, 1526), XV, fol. 323v. The Pluscarden chronicle ingeniously manages to combine Spain and Jerusalem by making Douglas journey to the Holy Land in the company of Alfonso XI: *Liber Pluscardensis*, ed. F. J. H. Skene (Edinburgh, 1877–80), i, 263–4.

61 E.g., this was accepted by David Hume (Hume of Godscroft, *Douglas*, 57).

62 *RRS*, v, no. 380.

63 *Chron. Fordun*, i, 353; Barbour, *Bruce*, iii, 246 (XX, l. 195).

64 *Chron. Le Baker*, 42.

65 'enpris cest saint veage *od le quere Robert de Bruys lour roys*' (my italics): *Scalacronica, by Sir Thomas Gray of Heton, knight. A Chronicle of England and Scotland from AD MLXXI to AD MCCCLXII*, ed. J. Stevenson (Maitland Club, 1836), 163.

probably requested by Moray during Douglas's absence, stated that Bruce's heart 'had been carried to Spain against the Saracens by the late James Douglas, a Glaswegian knight, *according to the wish of that king*'.[66] Granada, surely, was always the intended destination. It fits with Edward III's letter of recommendation to Alfonso XI (if not with his seven-year safe conduct). It is contradicted by neither Fordun nor Barbour, the two earliest Scottish sources. It is implied by Le Baker, and expressly stated by Gray.

This view was supported by Sir Herbert Maxwell, who argued that Bruce had no specific location in mind when he made the arrangements for his heart, and that although 'it was at Jerusalem where [infidels] could most constantly be found', Spain at the time offered a viable alternative.[67] Others have pointed out that, following the fall of Acre (the last Christian outpost in the Holy Land) in 1291, there was little possibility of launching a crusade in the Middle East during the early fourteenth century.[68] Crusading activity, such as it was, was by then confined to Cyprus (directed against Turkish pirates) and to Rhodes (where the conquest of the Knights of St John was gradually consolidated). But travel to the Middle East was not essential, since 'the concept of the Holy War against the heathen continued' in places like Granada.[69] From a pragmatic point of view, Spain also appears a more plausible destination for Douglas's mission. Had he looked after himself, Douglas might have been expected to have returned to Scotland within a couple of years of his departure. A mission to Palestine would have taken considerably longer. If the king insisted that Douglas should be his champion, he may at least have envisaged that the undertaking would have been completed within a reasonable time span.

To sum up this European episode. There are no grounds for assuming that Douglas was sent on his mission for other than sentimental reasons. The theory that Douglas was a dangerous rival to the regent Moray, and that Douglas had therefore to be removed from the kingdom, does not stand up to examination. The hypothesis that Douglas was unsuited to peaceful activity, because he had the misfortune to grow up during a prolonged period of warfare, is untenable. The precise circumstances of Douglas's death can probably never be ascertained for sure, but, on balance, Krauel Heredia's contention that Douglas fell in an isolated and unplanned encounter is doubtful. Whatever the cause of Douglas's death, it occurred in the context of a major battle. Finally, it seems clear that, contrary to later mythology, Douglas's destination was from the beginning Spain, and not Jerusalem. In the less than pragmatic decision to send him abroad, it seems that care was at least taken to ensure that Douglas's absence would be as short as possible.[70]

66 'per quondam Iacobum de Dunglas, militem Glasguensem, in Ispaniam contra ... Sarracenos *iuxta voluntatem ipsius Regis* ... deportatum' (my italics): *Vetera Monumenta Hibernorum et Scotorum*, ed. A. Theiner (Rome, 1864). 251.

67 Maxwell, *House of Douglas*, i, 62–3.

68 Davis, *Black Douglas*, 155; Macquarrie, *Crusades*, 69.

69 Ibid.

70 In 1996, a heart which may be Robert I's, was unearthed during excavations in the chapter house at Melrose Abbey. It was officially reburied at the site by Historic Scotland in June 1998. See Simpson, 'Heart of King Robert I'.

# 9

# Profit, Politics and Personality: War and the Later Medieval Scottish Nobility

*Alastair J. Macdonald*

Why on earth did the Scots continue to attack England throughout the later Middle Ages? The usual answers to this question have come in the form of throwaway comments and sound-bites. The issue has not, until recently, been seriously addressed in any detail.[1] Historians have sifted through the carnage of Flodden and come up with verdicts which hint that the personality of an otherwise capable king may perhaps have been fatally suspect. This, however, hardly accounts for the enthusiastic involvement in the Flodden campaign of the Scottish nobility, a large section of which perished with James IV in 1513. Neither does it explain intermittent, but sometimes intense, Anglo-Scottish conflict throughout the fifteenth century; nor, even more certainly, the fierce border warfare of the later fourteenth century, which occurred after the 'Wars of Independence' are supposed to have ended – let us say, at the latest, in 1357.[2]

These traditional time-scales for the duration of the wars are, as I argue in detail elsewhere,[3] unsatisfactory in many ways. The main focus of this essay will be on the fifty years or so after 1370, and the obvious explanation for Anglo-Scottish warfare in these years is that the 'Wars of Independence' had not, in any meaningful sense, come to an end at all. For much of this period, the Scottish government, in pursuit of precise diplomatic objectives, underpinned the military endeavours of the nobility. The very concept of 'government' is of course a difficult one at a time when the reigns of power in Scotland were regularly not in the king's hands.[4] Nonetheless, Scottish military offensives, until 1402 at any rate, featured a marked degree of central organisation and control. Scottish attacks were carefully co-ordinated and featured the involvement of forces well beyond the resources of any individual magnate. Offensives were launched with a sophisticated eye on developments in international politics: England was attacked at times of Anglo-French war or when it was experiencing political disturbance. Diplomatic manoeuvres and the conduct of war were

1 The recent exception is M. Brown, *The Black Douglases: War and Lordship in Late Medieval Scotland* (East Linton, 1998), to which I refer below.

2 The 'Wars of Independence' are traditionally taken as having ended in 1328: e.g. E. M. Barron, *The Scottish War of Independence* (London, 1914); R. L. Mackie, *A Short History of Scotland* (Oxford, 1930), 114–39; W. C. Dickinson, *Scotland from the Earliest Times to 1603* (3rd edn, rev. A. A. M. Duncan, Oxford, 1977), 154–74. Recent work tends to see continuities between the earlier period of Anglo-Scottish struggle and that of the 1330s and 1340s, with a coherent phase in Anglo-Scottish relations having come to an end by 1346 or 1357: e.g. G. W. S. Barrow, 'Wars of Independence', in G. Menzies, ed., *The Scottish Nation* (London, 1972), 15–29; A. Grant, *Independence and Nationhood* (London, 1984), 3–31; M. Lynch, *Scotland: A New History* (London, 1992), 30–1.

3 See note 5 below.

4 See S. Boardman, *The Early Stewart Kings: Robert II and Robert III* (East Linton, 1996), for a convincing account of political developments to 1406.

carefully linked. In essence the Scottish war effort during the reigns of Robert II and Robert III expressed familiar 'national' themes current earlier in the century during the Wars of Independence proper. The Scottish crown, when opportunities arose, utilised all its resources in the attempt to force recognition of its independence from England through military pressure.[5]

The Scottish attempt, during the later fourteenth century and beyond, to force recognition of the realm's independence ultimately proved futile. It could scarcely have been otherwise: the diplomatic triumph of Robert I in 1328 was based upon a temporary military predominance abetted by chronic political problems in England. Even in these circumstances a peace treaty with the Scots which conceded their major diplomatic demand (independence) was regarded as a craven submission. Rioting London crowds prevented the return to Scotland of the symbols of the kingdom's sovereignty; and the regime responsible for the concession was ousted shortly afterwards by Edward III.[6] Nevertheless, the Scottish government's persistent sponsorship of warfare in the pursuit of its diplomatic aims is an essential framework for understanding Anglo-Scottish warfare in the period from *c.*1370.

This essay attempts to recognise such a governmental or 'national' perspective,[7] while at the same time re-examining ideas about the individual motivations of magnates. Interpretations of Scottish military activity in the later Middle Ages have focused almost exclusively on the latter. I will not argue that a national emphasis should supersede such studies; but rather that there is no contradiction in an analysis based on the importance of both approaches; and on how national diplomacy and the magnates' particular objectives intermingled. Historians dealing with English involvement in the Hundred Years War have no difficulty examining both particular motivations and national objectives;[8] and a similar method needs to be developed with regard to Scottish warfare in the later fourteenth century, and beyond.

There is a long-standing orthodoxy which accounts for post-'Wars of Independence' Scottish attacks on England. This interpretation suggests that magnate motivations were entirely personal, having little to do with the

5 These themes are outlined in detail in A. Macdonald, 'Crossing the Border: A Study of the Scottish Military Offensives against England *c.*1369–c.1403' (University of Aberdeen, unpublished PhD thesis, 1995) [hereafter Macdonald, 'Thesis'], passim. They are further developed in my forthcoming monograph, provisionally titled *Crossing the Border: Scotland and England at War, 1369–1403* (East Linton, 2000).

6 E. L. G. Stones, 'An addition to the *Rotuli Scotiae*', *SHR*, xxiv (1950), 34–5; R. Nicholson, *Edward III and the Scots* (Oxford, 1965), 54.

7 See Grant, *Independence and Nationhood*, 39–45; idem, 'Disaster at Neville's Cross: the Scottish point of view', in D. Rollason and M. Prestwich, eds., *The Battle of Neville's Cross* (Stamford, 1998), esp. 15–21; idem, 'The Otterburn war from the Scottish point of view', in A. Goodman and A. Tuck, eds., *War and Border Societies in the Middle Ages* (London, 1992), 30–64; and Macdonald, 'Thesis', passim, for attempts to establish such a perspective.

8 There is extensive work on the motivations for English soldiers in the Hundred Years War period. See, e.g., K. B. McFarlane, *The Nobility of Later Medieval England* (Oxford, 1973), 19–40; idem, 'War, the economy and social change: England and the Hundred Years War', *Past and Present*, xxii (1962); A. Tuck, 'Why men fought in the Hundred Years War', *History Today*, xxxiii(4) (Apr. 1983), 35–40; A. Ayton, 'War and the English gentry under Edward III', *History Today*, xlii(3) (Mar. 1992), 34–40; and M. Prestwich, *Armies and Warfare in the Middle Ages: The English Experience* (New Haven, 1996), 83–114.

national concerns that had been predominant earlier in the fourteenth century. In 1965 James Campbell placed the emphasis on 'the prospect of plunder', while Ranald Nicholson in 1974 referred to a late fourteenth-century 'war of chivalry' on the Anglo-Scottish marches.[9] Both writers used their chosen labels pejoratively: the impression is that the 'overmighty magnates' involved in carrying warfare to England had selfish motives at heart, in contrast to the altruistic nationalism which had driven earlier military activity.[10] This vision was of individualised and shapeless conflict bringing turmoil to the Borders from around 1370 onwards: 'the selfish and disjointed expeditions of an aristocracy whose principal objects were plunder and military adventure'.[11] Nicholson and Campbell were by no means the first to suggest that random self-interest underlay Scottish military activity at this time. They were the heirs of a long historiographical tradition; and their viewpoint remains the dominant one in non-academic approaches to the Anglo-Scottish warfare of the period.[12]

In attempting to deal with the 'overmighty magnate' thesis as an explanation for Scottish attacks on England, it is perhaps useful to split the suggested motivations into their two main categories – that is chivalry and the desire for profit – and deal with the profit motive first. There can be little doubt that financial gain through warfare was important to the Scottish magnate, just as it was to his English and continental counterparts. The methods employed by the Scots in raiding England would suggest that material gain was an objective of the forays: booty was seized, prisoners were taken, and blackmail was demanded.[13] During the largely successful Scottish offensives of the late fourteenth century we might imagine that fortunes could be made. In addition, lands in the Borders were retaken and substantial sums of money from France, aimed at encouraging the war effort, were distributed. To suggest that material concerns were of overwhelming concern to the Scottish magnate in his pursuit of war is, however, problematic. Scottish armies were unpaid, in contrast to the situation on the Continent, where lucrative military employment was available. Richer prizes of war were also available there; and there is evidence to suggest that the really serious money in the late fourteenth century, for Scots as for other nationalities, was to be made abroad.[14] Yet it would be difficult to deny that the pursuit of profit was one of the factors that motivated Scots in their military activities.

9 J. Campbell, 'England, Scotland and the Hundred Years War', in J. R. Hale, J. R. L. Highfield and B. Smalley, eds., *Europe in the Later Middle Ages* (London, 1965), 213; Nicholson, *Scotland*, 194.

10 For the suggestion of powerful patriotic motivations earlier in the century see, e.g., Barron, *War of Independence*; Barrow, *Bruce*; and B. Webster, 'Scotland without a king, 1329–1341', in A. Grant and K. J. Stringer, eds., *Medieval Scotland: Crown, Lordship and Community* (Edinburgh, 1993), 223–38.

11 P. F. Tytler, *The History of Scotland from the Accession of Alexander III to the Union* (Edinburgh, 1864), i, 333; cited in Nicholson, *Scotland*, 194.

12 See George Ridpath, *The Border History of England and Scotland* (London, 1776) for an early description of the 'randomness' of border warfare. The version currently sold to tourists is similar: '[Otterburn, 1388] was of no importance, a useless carnage which had no military or political results': F. Graham, *Famous Northern Battles* (Rothbury, 1988).

13 See D. Hay, 'Booty in border warfare', *TDGAS*, 3rd ser., xxxi (1952–3), 145–66.

14 For a discussion of these points, see Macdonald, 'Thesis', 177–83.

Rather more difficult to pin down in this sense is the more nebulous concept of chivalry as a motivating factor. The word itself has no easy definition, but, for current purposes, two elements commonly present in definitions of the chivalric ethos may usefully be isolated: first, the desire to attain glory and renown through martial feats; and, second, an intrinsic enjoyment of military activities. Both of these factors are surely evident in the appearance of thirty freelance French knights in the Scottish raids on England in 1384. Froissart, whose works suggest that martial values were highly regarded on their own account in fourteenth-century aristocratic society, reckoned that these men sought glory and adventure.[15] Certainly, it seems unlikely that they came to the poor hunting-ground of Scotland in search of material gain.

Chronicle accounts of warfare in this period are quite consistent: men fought with an eye on their status and prestige, and they enjoyed the sheer excitement of military endeavours. Glorious and successful feats of arms are lauded as much for their own sake as for any beneficial results following from them. Never mind the Scottish victory at Otterburn in 1388. English chroniclers were still keen to praise Henry Percy in defeat for his valiant conduct during the battle.[16] The problem with all this, for those attempting to examine the motives of men who fought in the later medieval period, is that chronicles are pieces of literary artifice. They do not describe warfare 'realistically'. And chroniclers routinely attribute chivalric motivations – the pursuit of honour, glory and so on – to military figures of whom they approve.[17] Twentieth-century historians cannot, of course, accept that this stereotyping gets us inside the minds of the warriors of the later Middle Ages. Neither, though, can we reject outright the power of the chivalric ethos. There has been a long recognised gap between later medieval 'reality' and chivalric artifice and display, but there is substance in chivalry nonetheless.[18] The very fact that so many chroniclers used chivalry as their standard of judgement is telling, since there is obviously a link between literary works and attitudes in the wider society from which they came. The relationship is a complex one but we can surely say that chivalry, given the consistency with which it is advanced as a laudable attribute, was approved of in the chroniclers' audience.[19]

Chivalric ideas were certainly powerful in the mental world of the secular and clerical aristocracy. Proving that nobles fought precisely because of the chivalric ethos is, however, a rather different matter. Other reasons can usually be found for involvement in war and battlefield behaviour. The suicidal charge of Sir John Swinton and Adam Gordon is a case in point. At the battle of

15 *Oeuvres de Jean Froissart*, ed. K. de Lettenhove (Brussels, 1867–71), x, 228.

16 *Chron. Knighton*, 506; *Chron. Walsingham*, ii, 176; *Chron. Westminster*, 348.

17 For a discussion in a Scottish context of the treatment of one chivalric model, see S. Väthjunker, 'A Study of the Career of Sir James Douglas – The Historical Record versus Barbour's Bruce' (University of Aberdeen, unpublished PhD thesis, 1992).

18 J. Barnie, *War in Medieval Society: Social Values and the Hundred Years War* (London, 1974), 56–7; M. Keen, 'Huizinga, Kilgour and the decline of chivalry', *Medievalia et Humanistica*, new ser., viii (1977), 1–20.

19 For the huge influence of chivalric modes of thought on later medieval chronicle-writers, see, e.g., A. Gransden, *Historical Writing in England*, vol. II: *c.1307 to the Early Sixteenth Century* (London, 1982), passim.

Humbleton in 1402 the invading Scottish army was being cut to pieces by English archery. In Walter Bower's account Swinton urged his fellows to seek honour by launching a charge at the English forces. Gordon, previously a mortal enemy, responded to the call, begged forgiveness for their previous enmity, received knighthood at Swinton's hands, and joined him in leading a small band of Scots to their deaths in a hail of arrows.[20] This account would appear to be accurate in its essentials, and a final grand chivalric gesture is certainly in keeping with the character and career of Sir John Swinton.[21] Yet we cannot know absolutely that Swinton, Gordon and their fellows chose a glorious death on the battlefield. They possibly believed that the battle could be turned by their actions. Chroniclers repeatedly place chivalric leanings at the heart of aristocratic military behaviour and as a key causative factor in the prevalence of war. But in war other, more concrete, factors can usually be found that might serve to undermine the importance ascribed to the ethos of chivalry.

The power of chivalry as a motivating force is, perhaps, examined more fruitfully by turning to jousts, tournaments and duels rather than war itself. These forms of pseudo-warfare were certainly highly popular in the later Middle Ages.[22] It is much easier, here, to establish that nobles participated in these activities because they enjoyed martial endeavour and because they sought a pathway to honour and renown. Other motivations seem to be secondary: profit, for instance, might come the way of star tournament performers via royal largesse, but this could hardly be relied upon to defray the considerable expenses of jousting.[23] Personal animosity was clearly an element in judicial contests, the more so as the protagonists, in Anglo-Scottish duels, seem frequently to have formed their grievances during real warfare in the Borders.[24] That such figures, though, felt it appropriate to settle their disputes publicly and by force of arms continues to give weight to the ethos of chivalry in explaining their actions. The numerous Scots who participated in the gamut of peacetime feats of arms surely did so for motives that can be termed chivalric – love of the military chase, prestige, glory, fame.

For such intangible rewards the later medieval nobility was willing to take risks. The game of jousting was a serious business, especially when, as on the Anglo-Scottish Border, 'jousts of war' were undertaken – that is jousts *à outrance* with full combat weaponry.[25] One celebrated encounter, fought at Berwick probably early in 1342, featured picked bands of Scottish and English knights

20 *Chron. Bower* (Watt), viii, 46.

21 Bower's account fits well with other evidence: Walsingham also recounts a fragmentary Scottish charge (*Chron. Walsingham*, ii, 251) and Gordon is indeed posthumously referred to as a knight: see *Scots Peerage*, iv, 517. For one of Swinton's previous chivalric escapades, see A. Goodman, *John of Gaunt* (Harlow, 1992), 217.

22 R. Barber and J. Barker, *Tournaments: Jousts, Chivalry and Pageants in the Middle Ages* (Woodbridge, 1989); G. Neilson, *Trial by Combat* (Glasgow, 1890).

23 See S. Lindenbaum, 'The Smithfield Tournament of 1390', *Journal of Medieval and Renaissance Studies*, xx (1990), 1–20, for one example of royal interest in the tournament, including rewards for participants.

24 C. J. Neville, 'Keeping the peace on the northern Marches in the later Middle Ages', *English Historical Review*, cix (1994), 14; Macdonald, 'Thesis', 127–8, 130.

25 Barber and Barker, *Tournaments*, 34.

under the leadership of Sir Alexander Ramsay and Henry, Earl of Derby, respectively. At least three fatalities resulted.[26] Individual combats were even more dangerous, whether judicial duels or challenges designed simply to measure the prowess of those involved. We do not know the outcome of many such Anglo-Scottish encounters which were planned in the late fourteenth century. Sir William Inglis, though, certainly killed his English adversary in a duel of 1396; and as prominent a figure as John Dunbar, Earl of Moray was wounded, perhaps fatally, in a combat with Thomas Mowbray, Earl of Nottingham in 1390 or 1391.[27] In this form of combat the body count was certainly high. Single combat was a much more dangerous form of martial activity than warfare itself.

An understanding of this element of risk makes it easier to link chivalric motivations to warfare proper. Scottish nobles were willing to take grave risks, when real war was unavailable, to engage in the nearest equivalent. Such activities offered the likelihood neither of significant material reward, nor of benefit to the realm in the context of Anglo-Scottish struggle. The motivations of importance in this context were chivalric ones – relish of martial activity for its own sake, and the quest for fame and honour. Nobles who were prominent in feats of arms were, of course, the same figures who led the Scottish forces in open war. If they were powerfully in thrall to chivalric ideas in times of peace, it may be assumed that such impulses did not suddenly lose their force in times of war. Chivalry, we may be fairly certain, had a strong influence in making the prospect of war attractive to the later medieval Scottish nobility.

The factors looked at so far – the profit-motive and adherence to an ethos of chivalry – are the two selfish motivations for war suggested in the traditional approaches to later medieval Scottish baronial militarism.[28] But we can go much further than this. One motivating factor that has been given little credence in the period from around 1370 is individual patriotism. To an extent this is perhaps understandable: to prove, in an absolute fashion, that there were nationalistic causes in individual incidents in the Scottish war effort is as difficult as it is to be certain about chivalric motivation.[29] Scottish warfare was certainly conducted with a savagery that might seem to be expressive of national animus, but a widespread process of burning and devastation was the only means available to the Scots of exerting pressure on England in pursuit of diplomatic objectives. So, when in 1377 Roxburgh (then in English hands) was burned by George Dunbar, tenth Earl of March, the destruction – seemingly directly contrary to Scottish economic interests – was not necessarily a product of ferocious nationalism.[30] We may doubt whether diplomatic aims were always uppermost in the minds of the Scottish nobility as they led their forces on a trail of destruction on English soil, but we can hardly prove that they were not.

26 *Chron. Bower* (Watt), 136; *Chron. Knighton*, 38.

27 Neilson, *Trial by Combat*, 219–24; Macdonald, 'Thesis', 127–8.

28 Nicholson, *Scotland*, 194, 222; Campbell, 'England, Scotland and the Hundred Years War', 213–15.

29 Although for warfare earlier in the 14th century historians have had no trouble identifying a strong patriotic impulse (see works cited at note 9 above), this factor has recently been accorded little relevance in M. Brown, 'The development of Scottish border lordship, 1332–58', *Historical Research*, lxx (1997), 1–22.

30 For the value to local Scots of the fair at Roxburgh, see *Chron. Wyntoun* (Laing), iii, 9.

Accounts of seemingly motiveless atrocities perpetrated on English inhabitants of the Borders – the killing of suckling infants and old, decrepit men – can be read at least partly as anti-Scottish propaganda which cannot be wholly relied upon.[31] The lurid descriptions offered tend to be formulaic with little sense of reportage. Even the murder by their Scottish captors of the crew of a Grimsby ship taken in 1377 – potentially valuable in terms of ransoms – may attest to the problems of conveying prisoners by sea rather than a murderous anti-Englishness.[32]

As they do with chivalry, the chronicle sources place patriotic motivations in a position of prominence as a spur to the later medieval Scottish war effort. We must again assume that the chroniclers' audience approved of the repeated anti-English sentiments, and that there was a shared belief that these were proper and fitting reasons for embarking on military activity.[33] Evidence of animosity towards England can be seen from the very start of the Wars of Independence. In 1297, for instance, Sir Robert Clifford's expeditionary force was taunted by locals with cries of 'tailed dogs' as it pushed into south-western Scotland.[34] This anecdote acquires the character of innocent banter when compared to the more virulent outpourings of later Scottish chroniclers. Abbot Walter Bower, writing in the 1440s, is at times almost hysterical in his abuse of the English. They are snakes at the breast, rats in a bag, satanic satellites.[35] Numerous evils and treason, no matter how unlikely, are recounted. Equally unlikely Scottish triumphs are reported with glee: Henry V, campaigning in France, dies due to the curse of St Feargus the Scot, and resignedly announces on his deathbed that 'wherever I pursue Scots alive or dead, I find them in my beard.'[36] And of course Bower complacently informs us that all those entitled to be called Scots will enjoy his book.[37] He is very confident of his editorial line.

Bower was not an unusual case or a uniquely bitter individual. His concrete allegations against the English monks of Coldingham in Berwickshire were not the product of his fevered imagination. They were taken from the official case presented by Dunfermline Abbey in an attempt to secure the expulsion and replacement of the English monks. The Dunfermline plea – a supposedly rational legal document – blithely refers to 'the tyranny and cruelty of the English', known the world over.[38] Certainly people throughout Christendom were aware of the special hatred which the Scots held for the English. We can find this sentiment expressed by Froissart, the archbishop of Armagh, two Popes (Martin V and Pius II) and others.[39] Those involved in the framing and

31 For examples of the genre in English chronicle and record sources, see *Chron. Knighton*, 526, and *Calendar of Close Rolls* (London, 1902– ), *1385–89*, 610.

32 *Calendar of Close Rolls, 1377–81*, 39.

33 The link between chroniclers' patriotism and the attitudes of their audience is discussed in A. Grant, 'Aspects of national consciousness in medieval Scotland', in C. Bjørn, A. Grant and K. J. Stringer, eds., *Nations, Nationalism and Patriotism in the European Past* (Copenhagen, 1994), 73–4.

34 *The Chronicle of Walter of Guisborough*, ed. H. Rothwell (Camden Soc., 1957), 307.

35 *Chron. Bower* (Watt), vi, 68–70.

36 Ibid., viii, 122.

37 Ibid., viii, 340.

38 Cited in R. B. Dobson, 'The last English monks on Scottish soil', *SHR*, xlvi (1967), 5. For the full Dunfermline pleading, see *Coldingham Corresp.*, 246–55.

39 Macdonald, 'Thesis', 190–1.

execution of Scotland's foreign policy, unsurprisingly, reflected the prevalent anti-English spirit. In March 1364 a parliament was convened to consider an English proposal for Edward III's succession to the Scottish throne should David II die childless.[40] Arguments for and against this proposal were framed by William Spyny, the future bishop of Moray, for transmission to the assembled representatives of the three estates of the realm. What Spyny clearly felt – and he wrote as if this was very much a shared set of attitudes – was a deeply felt animosity towards the English and a distrust of their motives. Potentially disastrous war was a looming possibility for the Scots in 1364, yet their policy-makers were expected to be swayed by arguments which stated that the English would not feel safe until all the Scots were dead; that the king of England would seek excuses to condemn Scots to death so that he would be able to redistribute their lands; that English merchants were perennially dishonest; and that English people were by nature cruel.[41]

There is no reason to believe that, at the highest level, such sentiments were untypical. At border truce negotiations in 1401, for instance, the attitude of the Scottish diplomatic party was hostile and intransigent.[42] There is a tone of rudeness and recrimination in a letter to Henry IV sent by Archibald, fourth Earl of Douglas in 1402, while Archibald's younger brother Sir James Douglas wrote with similar belligerence to the English king, justifying the burning of Berwick by the Scots in 1405 and challenging the English right to the town.[43] In 1396 the Scottish crown granted a barony in Peeblesshire to Sir William Inglis because he had killed the Englishman Sir Thomas Strother in one of the judicial combats already referred to.[44] Even in the civilised arena of diplomatic discourse sentiments of national animosity seem to have been strong enough to provoke violence. In 1391 a brawl apparently broke out between English and Scottish representatives at a Border March Day.[45] Anti-Englishness was manifestly a powerful component of the Scottish psyche in the later Middle Ages. We must, I think, allow that it had a role to play in spurring the magnates on into war policies.

We can go further still in the attempt to list factors that may have contributed to Scottish belligerence in the period under consideration. Personal antipathy was clearly a factor at times. The famous (although much exaggerated) feud between the houses of Douglas and Percy hints at personal as well as territorial animosity.[46] There was clearly a personal element to the judicial combats already discussed. Such conflicts came about because one party made allegations against another of such a serious nature that they had to be settled by force of

40 The diplomatic niceties surrounding David II's ransom and the succession issue are discussed in A. A. M. Duncan, '"Honi soit qui mal y pense": David II and Edward III, 1346–52', *SHR*, lxvii (1988), 113–41; and idem, 'A question about the succession, 1364', *Scottish History Society Miscellany XII* (SHS, 1994), 1–23.

41 Ibid., 39, 41–2, 47.

42 For these negotiations, see *Anglo-Scottish Relations 1174–1328: Some Selected Documents*, ed. E. L. G. Stones (repr. Oxford, 1970), 173–82.

43 BL, MS Cotton, Vespasian F vii, fos. 17, 88.

44 *Peebles Recs.*, 206–7.

45 Neville, 'Keeping the peace on the northern Marches', 13.

46 The place of the Douglas/Percy feud in Anglo-Scottish conflict as a whole is discussed in Macdonald, 'Thesis', 32–5, 103.

arms.[47] This is suggestive of some level of personal hostility. Similar animosities surely played their part in the incident of 1391 in which Sir William Douglas of Nithsdale was killed in Königsberg by English fellow crusaders. On this occasion, when a dispute between Douglas's party and that of Sir Thomas Clifford over their religious allegiances in the context of the Great Schism spilled into violence,[48] it is hard not to see personal antipathy – in addition to national and religious animosity – as vital in transforming latent into open conflict. A judicial combat was previously to have been held between Douglas and Clifford.[49] Even at the governmental level, moreover, personal animosities often appear to be important in causing conflict. One reason for Henry IV's invasion of Scotland in 1400 was the allegedly slanderous letters about him dispatched by a Scottish magnate to France and intercepted by English naval forces.[50] The magnate was presumably David, duke of Rothesay who, while besieged in Edinburgh Castle by the invading English force, added another dimension to the personal element by challenging Henry IV to combat along with selected knights on either side.[51]

We cannot even, in the Latin West, discount religion as a factor which spawned Anglo-Scottish warfare. During the period 1378–1419 Scotland determinedly adhered to the Avignon Papacy while the English allegiance was to the Roman Popes. Thomas de Rossy, Bishop of Galloway was moved to challenge Henry Despenser, Bishop of Norwich to a duel because of their differing allegiances in the Great Schism.[52] Despenser, for his part, organised a crusade to Flanders in 1383 ostensibly aimed at schismatic adherents of the Avignonese Popes. The venture attracted widespread support in England and enthusiastic involvement in the resultant campaign.[53] In the context of Anglo-Scottish warfare, religious institutions do seem to have been targeted more readily by both sides in their military activities during the Schism period.[54] The clergy was in a powerful position to form and influence attitudes in the medieval world. Religion cannot be ruled out as one of the complex of factors which caused warfare and for the Schism period it seems at least to have been an intensifying force in Anglo-Scottish conflict.

We must also embrace other, even less historically demonstrable, factors in an attempt to explain fully the individual motivations which led the Scottish nobility to go to war in this period. It has long been accepted by psychologists

47 *Rot. Scot.*, ii, 39, 103.

48 *Chron. Westminster*, 474–6; *Chron. Bower* (Watt), vii, 446–8. An accurate account of the fracas is given in D. Ditchburn, 'Merchants, Pedlars and Pirates: A History of Scotland's Relations with Northern Germany and the Baltic' (University of Edinburgh, unpublished PhD thesis, 1988), 446–56.

49 *Rot. Scot.*, ii, 105–6.

50 *Chron. Bower* (Watt), viii, 36; 'Annales Ricardi Secundi et Henrici Quarti', in *Johannis de Trokelowe et Henrici de Blaneforde monachorum S Albani, necnon quorundam anonymorum, Chronica et Annales*, ed. H. T. Riley (Rolls Ser., 1866), 332–3.

51 T. Rymer, ed., *Foedera, Conventiones, Litterae et Cuiuscunque Generis Acta Publica* (original edn, London, 1704–35), viii, 157.

52 H. McEwan, '"A Theolog Solempne": Thomas de Rossy, bishop of Galloway', *IR*, viii (1957), 28–9.

53 N. Housley, 'The bishop of Norwich's crusade, May 1383', *History Today*, xxxiii(5) (May 1983), v, 15–20.

54 A. Goodman, 'Religion and warfare in the Anglo-Scottish Marches', in R. Bartlett and A. Mackay, eds., *Medieval Frontier Societies* (Oxford, 1989), 256.

that certain individuals have a greater propensity than others towards violent behaviour.[55] Individuals with excessively violent tendencies exist. We might surmise that they existed in later medieval Scotland too; and that their psychological make-up inclined them more than usually to involve themselves in Anglo-Scottish warfare. At a broader level, studies on the nature of war, largely ignored by medieval historians, have long addressed the question of why men (in particular) fight. It is accepted by sociologists and psychologists that a range of impulses lead to war, certainly far beyond the obvious and historically visible considerations of defence against an enemy and the acquisition of wealth, territory and power through military endeavour.[56]

Such insight into aggression and war derive largely from studies which relate to modern examples. In the context of the later Middle Ages psychological and sociological factors should be even more strongly stressed, despite the fact that their impact in promoting military activity is even harder to quantify for the distant past. Huizinga's great insights into later medieval mentalities retain, in their general tenor, the ring of authenticity. We should not disregard his masterly account of the violence of emotions – and the violence of behaviour – in which life was steeped in the later Middle Ages.[57] Life was far cheaper; how could it not be in the age of the Black Death and repeated recurrences of pestilence? With this context in mind, we can perhaps begin to understand why in later medieval England levels of homicide were vastly higher on a *per capita* basis than is the case now, and why crimes against property, on the basis of jury convictions, were regarded as being more serious than those that resulted in death.[58] We can scarcely contemplate how much more ready people were, in such a climate, to kill and to risk death in warfare. But we must nevertheless admit of these unquantifiable factors in any attempt to examine the engine which drove later medieval warfare.

From the individual perspective, then, a complex of motivating factors must be weighed to explain Scottish military activity in the period under consideration. In mainstream academic historical work, however, a different explanation for later medieval Anglo-Scottish conflict has recently been offered. In a challenging thesis Michael Brown has suggested that the Scottish nobility, as best exemplified by the great house of Douglas, consciously utilised warfare as a means to acquire and maintain political power in the south of Scotland. This personal political imperative was, to Brown, overwhelmingly the motive force for Anglo-Scottish warfare from the 1330s onwards.[59] In this assessment the military motivations of the Scottish nobility remained individualistic and selfish, as represented in the traditional approach espoused by Nicholson and Campbell.[60] The difference is

55 Among many works, see, e.g., R. A. Baron and D. R. Richardson, *Human Aggression* (New York, 1994).

56 See, e.g., L. Bramson and G. W. Goethals, eds., *War: Studies from Psychology, Sociology, Anthropology* (New York, 1964).

57 J. Huizinga, *The Waning of the Middle Ages* (Penguin edn, Harmondsworth, 1955), esp. 9–30.

58 B. A. Hanawalt, 'Violent death in fourteenth- and early fifteenth-century England', *Comparative Studies in Society and History*, xviii (1976), 302, 315–17.

59 Brown, 'Development of border lordship'; idem, *Black Douglases.*

60 See references at note 8 above.

that in Brown's interpretation magnate individualism involved a rather more focused self-interest than had been allowed in the older approach. The theory of war lordship in the Borders is an enticing one. It offers a coherent and consistent explanation of later medieval warfare in the Anglo-Scottish Borders, and places understandable human motivations of survival and self-advancement at the heart of the causative process.

One figure whose military career is explained by Brown in terms of this political approach is Archibald, fourth Earl of Douglas, often involved in warfare between 1398 and 1424. Douglas's very active engagement in war in Scotland, England and France is remorselessly explained as the expression of political ambition.[61] By another reading, though, Douglas's military activities suggest much more than simply the rational pursuit of political power. That international trait of the aristocracy – a relish of warfare for its own sake – and that Scottish trait – hatred of the English – seem to be equally attested in the sources. The Douglas involvement in the brief English civil war of 1403 when the Percy family rebelled against Henry IV remains an enigmatic episode.[62] A much neglected explanation was provided by Bower: one of the Scots present in the Douglas retinue at the battle of Shrewsbury, Sir Robert Stewart of Durisdeer, advocated involvement because the deaths of English nobles would result.[63] When Douglas engaged the English in his final battle at Verneuil in France in 1424 he issued orders that no quarter was to be given or received in the encounter.[64] No political objectives can have been served by this edict, which ensured that even in victory the ransom bonanza would be limited. For the call of 'no quarter', the most obvious motivation is the primal one of hatred.

A relish for fighting also seems evident in the career of Douglas. Numerous sources attest to his bravery in battle. This can be seen in Scottish and English accounts of the battle of Shrewsbury as well as continental chronicles which deal with the defeat at Verneuil.[65] At the latter encounter Douglas had to cajole his French allies into fighting the English, who had long since demonstrated their superior battlefield capability, not least against the earl himself.[66] Douglas was ferocious in border warfare; yet burning Roxburgh (1398), Bamburgh (1401), Penrith (1415) and Alnwick (1420) cannot have provided material enrichment for his followers. There is little sign, either, of the pursuit of clear diplomatic aims in these activities.[67] Douglas continued to lead personally in war, seemingly undeterred by the loss of an eye at Humbleton in 1402 and the loss of a testicle at

61 Brown, *Black Douglases*, 95–118, 214–24.

62 For explanations stressing political expediency, see Grant, 'Otterburn War', 55 n.9; and Brown, *Black Douglases*, 106.

63 *Chron. Bower* (Watt), viii, 58. A similar motive for Scottish involvement in this episode is suggested in *Chron. Wyntoun* (Laing), iii, 90–1.

64 *Chron. Bower* (Watt), viii, 126.

65 Ibid., 58; *The Chronicle of Adam of Usk 1377–1421*, ed. C. Given-Wilson (Oxford, 1997), 170; Brown, *Black Douglases*, 222.

66 A recent account of the English edge on the battlefield can be found in Prestwich, *Armies and Warfare*, 318–23.

67 PRO, E39/95/2; *Royal and Historical Letters of Henry IV*, ed. F. C. Hingeston (Rolls Ser., 1860), i, 58–65; Macdonald, 'Thesis', 136–7, 149–50; *Chron. Bower* (Watt), viii, 84, 116; E. W. M. Balfour-Melville, *James I King of Scots, 1406–1437* (London, 1936), 63.

Shrewsbury the following year.[68] The totality of the earl's military career cannot be accounted for by reference to political drive alone. Douglas was indeed a glutton for power. He was also a glutton for money.[69] It is entirely in keeping with his character that he revealed himself a glutton for war as well.

The career of Douglas also raises wider questions about the linkage between warfare and Scottish border lordship. For, despite the great power wielded by Douglas in the South – to Brown the hosts raised by the earl represented 'the culmination of ... militarised lordship' – he was perennially a failure in his war-making.[70] This was not only the case in the set-piece battles of Humbleton, Shrewsbury and Verneuil which brought only financial loss and death to the Douglas following. Failure is evident in the full range of the earl's military activities. In the early fifteenth century Douglas was singularly unable to protect the Scottish border communities. In the conflict that from 1400 onwards was very much his war, southern Scotland suffered repeatedly from the forays of English forces energised by a newly resurgent northern leadership.[71] Later, with Douglas again free from captivity, his burning of Penrith in 1415 led only to the traditional English response of putting Dumfries to the flames.[72] In 1417 Douglas was in charge of the Scottish siege of Roxburgh, while the duke of Albany besieged Berwick. Both forces in this, the 'Foul Raid', melted away in the face of an English invasion.[73] The unopposed English army ravaged the Scottish central Borders, the first of a number of successful English raids of the next couple of years, which included highly effective naval attacks.[74]

In sum, there are strong arguments for suggesting that the fourth earl of Douglas enjoyed political dominance in the south of Scotland in spite of, rather than because of, his military activity. Douglas's regional dominance was based, rather, on his great territorial inheritance, strong links of lordship and kin, and continuing political acumen.[75] A deterioration in his local position prior to his departure for France in 1424 may have had much to do with continued military failure causing discontent in the Borders.[76] Certainly, major Scottish armies were now reluctant even to cross the Border. Douglas had no option but to seek

68 *Chron. Bower* (Watt), viii, 58.

69 See B. G. H. Ditcham, '"Mutton Guzzlers and Wine Bags": foreign soldiers and native reactions in fifteenth-century France', in C. Allmand, ed., *Power, Culture and Religion in France c.1350–c.1550* (Woodbridge, 1989), 6–7; it is hard to disagree with Ditcham's assessment of the earl of Douglas, that his 'hunger for money was matched only by his military incompetence'.

70 Brown, *Black Douglases*, 153. The 'irony' of Douglas's drastic military record is rather reluctantly mentioned (ibid., 223), but more is made of his one victorious skirmish on the Borders, which is depicted as demonstrating his ability to lead and defend the Scottish marchers in war (ibid., 141, 145). The victory was not of enough moment to appear in any English account.

71 Macdonald, 'Thesis', 139–60; 236–8.

72 *Chron. Bower* (Watt), viii, 84; *Rot. Scot.*, ii, 152.

73 *Chron. Bower* (Watt), viii, 86; *Chron. Walsingham*, ii, 325. Even the patriotic Bower says the Scottish leaders of these attacks went home in disgrace.

74 P. J. Bradley, 'Henry V's Scottish policy: a study in realpolitik', in J. S. Hamilton and P. J. Bradley, eds., *Documenting the Past* (Woodbridge, 1989), 189.

75 See chapter 18, below, by Alexander Grant, for an analysis of the *acta* of the fourth earl of Douglas which shows the importance of inheritance, lordship and kinship in Archibald's powerful territorial base in southern Scotland.

76 See Brown, *Black Douglases*, 116–17, although unsuccessful militarism is not cited as a possible explanation.

foreign fields in which to indulge his favourite hobby of war, and to seek that last great battle against the English.

The career of the earl of Douglas shows us that the link between war and border lordship is not as neat as it has been portrayed. For a further demonstration we could turn to the career of the greatest Scottish warrior of the era, Douglas's rival, George, tenth Earl of March. His phenomenal military success between 1370 and 1403 did not stop him losing many of his lands as a result of being politically outmanoeuvred at court.[77] Both figures demonstrate also that a trenchantly monocausal approach cannot be taken in attempting to explain Scottish military activity in the later Middle Ages. The pursuit of local political dominance can help to explain Scottish militarism in the Borders.[78] But we must also take account of many other factors in the keenness of later medieval Scottish magnates to go to war. They willingly involved themselves in governmental attempts to seek diplomatic gains, even in the period after 1370. Certainly, the magnate class sought profit; but it was also imbued with the international ethos of militarism that we call chivalry, and in thrall to seemingly nebulous concepts such as honour and renown. Finally, Scottish magnates at war were individuals whose personalities helped to shape their military behaviour. Embracing this truth does not help us reach neat and overarching explanations; but, no matter how untidy the results, we do a disservice to the historical record by shying away from the complex motives that drive human beings to war.

77 March's military career is discussed in Macdonald, 'Thesis', passim.

78 The case is quite convincing for William Douglas, lord of Liddesdale, active in the mid-14th century: see Brown, 'Development of border lordship'.

# 10

# Mons Meg and Merchant Meg: Women in Later Medieval Edinburgh

*Elizabeth Ewan*

In 1457 James II received a gift of the great cannon Mons Meg – an instrument of war. The consequences of war affected the townsfolk who lived below the walls of Edinburgh Castle, where the cannon was kept and where it can still be seen today. After the death of many townsmen at Flodden in 1513, much of the responsibility for maintaining community life fell on the women of Edinburgh. The burgh council ordered widows to provide for the town's defence, and told women not to neglect their work for public grieving.[1] But it was not only in crises that women were crucial to the functioning of the town. Women played an integral role in the urban economy, but one largely ignored by contemporaries and by urban historians.[2] There is no monument to 'Merchant Meg'.

Most work on medieval towns has focused on the prominent merchant and craftsmen burgesses who governed the community. As the most influential members of urban society, the burgesses figure prominently in the surviving records. The impression given by these records is of a well-regulated economy ruled by the wise actions of the good men of the town.[3] And they were men: women did not hold municipal office. However, the urban environment was not shaped by the male elite alone. The unenfranchised also contributed to burgh life, though their actions are harder to uncover. This essay will examine the types of work undertaken by one unenfranchised group (women) in the later fifteenth and early sixteenth centuries. In so doing, it seeks also to assess the contribution of the female work-force to the urban economy as a whole.

1 *Edin. Recs.*, i, 143–4.

2 The role of women in Edinburgh is briefly discussed in D. Robertson and M. Wood, *Castle and Town: Chapters in the History of the Royal Burgh of Edinburgh* (Edinburgh, 1928), 266–7; and M. Sanderson, *Mary Stewart's People* (Tuscaloosa, 1987), 91–102. Some recent works on 17th- and 18th-century Edinburgh have included further discussion of women: see H. M. Dingwall, *Late Seventeenth-Century Edinburgh: A Demographic History* (Aldershot, 1994); and R. A. Houston, *Social Change in the Age of the Enlightenment: Edinburgh 1660–1760* (Oxford, 1994). Works focusing specifically on women include E. Sanderson, *Women and Work in Eighteenth-Century Edinburgh* (Basingstoke, 1996); and A. Mann, 'Embroidery to enterprise: the role of women in the book trade of early modern Scotland', and H. M. Dingwall, 'The power behind the merchant? Women and the economy of late seventeenth-century Edinburgh', both in E. Ewan and M. Meikle, eds., *Women in Scotland c.1100–1750* (East Linton, 1999). Studies of medieval urban women in other countries include E. Uitz, *Women in the Medieval Town* (London, 1990); M. Wiesner, *Working Women in Renaissance Germany* (New Brunswick, 1986); and P. J. P. Goldberg, *Women, Work and Life Cycle in a Medieval Economy: Women in York and Yorkshire c.1300–1520* (Oxford, 1992).

3 E. Ewan, *Townlife in Fourteenth-Century Scotland* (Edinburgh, 1990), ch. 2. For the focus on the burgh elite, see the essays in M. Lynch, M. Spearman and G. Stell., eds., *The Scottish Medieval Town* (Edinburgh, 1988). The interest of earlier historians in political and constitutional history led to a similar focus. See, e.g., W. M. Mackenzie, *The Scottish Burgh* (Edinburgh, 1949); and D. Murray, *Early Burgh Organisation in Scotland* (Glasgow, 1924).

Late medieval Edinburgh was not a typical Scottish town. It contained several institutions of central government, political leaders spent a good deal of time there, and it was the setting for several dramatic political events. Edinburgh was Scotland's largest town by far, with a population of about 13,000 in the early sixteenth century. It dominated the Scottish economy, controlling most of the country's export trade.[4] In this unusual environment, women were excluded from formal political power. Although they might become burgesses and members of certain gilds, in 1508 the council specified the conditions on which a burgess daughter could obtain burgess rights and gild membership.[5] With few exceptions, women could not hold office. They gained no practical experience of government and failed to organise formally even in occupations where they predominated.[6]

Historians have identified several characteristics typical of women's work in the Middle Ages. Because most women had to timetable paid work around housework and childcare, female work tended to be flexible, short-term, lacking formal political organisation, and based largely on domestic skills.[7] However, a woman's work pattern changed as she moved through her lifecycle, from childhood, to an adolescence usually spent in domestic service, to marriage, motherhood and widowhood. Single women were strongly encouraged by the authorities to join households, generally as servants.[8] Above all, the female work-force had to be adaptable to changing personal circumstances.

A woman's legal position changed with marriage, when she lost her legal independence. Her husband controlled all her property and was responsible for her debts. She could not enter into contracts without his consent, nor could she act as cautioner for anything given away or sold.[9] The ability of women to

4 M. Lynch, *Edinburgh and the Reformation* (Edinburgh, 1981), 1–66; L. Fradenburg, *City, Marriage, Tournament: Arts of Rule in Late Medieval Scotland* (Madison, 1991), chs. 2, 4; M. Lynch, 'The social and economic structure of the larger towns, 1450–1600', in Lynch *et al.*, *Medieval Town*, 269–70.

5 *Edin. Recs.*, i, 112–13. Alison Duscoll was made a gild member in 1407 (ibid., i, 2). For the burgess Isabel Williamson, see note 23 below. For women burgesses in other towns, see *Peebles Recs.*, 113, 133, 197; and *The Burgh Records of Dunfermline 1488–1584*, ed. E. Beveridge (Edinburgh, 1917), 70, 87, 89.

6 Women did, however, act as custumars in Edinburgh and elsewhere in 1514 and 1515 after the death of many husbands at Flodden: *TA*, i, pp. ccxc–ccxcii; *ER*, xiii, 52–7, 102–8, 199–205, 267–8). For the relationship between gilds and women, see M. Kowaleski and J. Bennett, 'Crafts, gilds and women in the Middle Ages', in J. Bennett *et al.*, eds., *Sisters and Workers in the Middle Ages* (Chicago, 1989), 11–38.

7 M. Kowaleski, 'Women's work in a market town: Exeter in the fourteenth century', in B. Hanawalt, ed., *Women and Work in Pre-industrial Europe* (Bloomington, 1986), 155–7. See E. Newlyn, 'Of "vertew nobillest" and "serpent wrinkis": taxonomy of the female in the Bannatyne Manuscript', *Scotia*, xiv (1990), 7, 10–11, for the primacy assigned to motherhood in medieval women's lives.

8 Increasingly single women living alone were viewed as a moral, as well as an economic, problem. Authorities in Scotland and elsewhere tried to force 'masterless' women into households. In 1530 the Edinburgh council ordered that rooms should not be rented to poor women who did not have a husband to earn a living: *Edin. Recs.*, 11, 40; see also Lynch, 'Social and economic structure', 277–8; R. A. Houston, 'Women in the economy and society of Scotland, 1500–1800', in R. A. Houston and I. D. Whyte, eds., *Scottish Society 1500–1800* (Cambridge, 1988), 132–4. For similar views elsewhere in Europe, see M. Wiesner, *Women and Gender in Early Modern Europe* (Cambridge, 1993), 62, 99.

9 *Regiam Majestatem*, ed. T. M. (Lord) Cooper (Stair Soc., 1947), 291; G. C. H. Paton, 'Husband and wife: property rights and relationships', in idem, ed., *An Introduction to Scottish Legal History* (Stair Soc., 1958), 99–101.

market goods was affected by these restrictions – but, in practice, many evaded them. They could, for instance, be negated by the provisions of a marriage contract, and husbands could grant their wives full administrative rights over their goods. In 1493 Henry Naper gave his wife Marion all his moveables with full power to dispose of them at her will.[10] Widows generally had more freedom of action than did wives, but also more responsibilities. On a husband's death, a wife regained her legal independence, and Edinburgh burgess widows found themselves responsible for the duties of their late husbands. In 1529 Isabell Kyle, widow of a cordiner, petitioned the king for exemption from her husband's duties of providing defence for the burgh and paying local taxes. A local ordinance also made it clear that female heads of households were expected to have the rule and governance of those with whom they resided.[11] A large proportion of Edinburgh households were headed by single women, most of them probably widows.[12]

These legal changes meant a woman might work at one trade as a child, another during domestic service in her teens, a third when married, and a fourth if widowed or remarried. Elizabeth Douglas, for example, wife of a baker in 1510, appears as the wife of a barber in 1513.[13] The extent of a woman's participation in any one of her career stages also depended upon the age of her children. But since flexible, short-term and temporary work suited women's lifestyles, women rarely received the apprenticeship training commonly available to craftsmen's sons – though female apprenticeship did exist in some crafts, such as the bonnetmakers.[14] As a result, most women were unlikely to form the strong work identity common among medieval men. Girls generally learned their skills from parents or while working as domestic servants, and most female occupations developed from domestic skills. Meanwhile, domestic work itself was crucial to the economic and social functioning of the household, even though it rarely appears in the records. Some, at least, recognised that women's domestic responsibilities did not make for an easy life. In one contemporary poem a man attempts to exchange duties with his wife. He concludes that if he went on with the arrangement the entire household would be wrecked.[15]

In reality, however, the household was an economic unit and marriage was an economic partnership of husband and wife. A merchant wife often saw to tasks such as bookkeeping, or carried on her husband's business in his absence. The

10 *Protocol Book of James Young 1485–1515*, ed. G. Donaldson (Scottish Record Soc., 1952), no. 578; E. Ewan, 'Scottish Portias: women in the courts in mediaeval Scottish towns', *Journal of the Canadian Historical Association* (1992), 32–43.

11 *RSS*, ii, no. 246; *Edin. Recs.*, i, 106.

12 In a 1635 survey of Edinburgh, single women or widows headed 22% of households: Lynch, 'Social and economic structure', 263. This proportion is comparable to other European cities: Wiesner, *Working Women*, 4–5.

13 Edinburgh City Archives [hereafter ECA], Calendar of the Protocol Book of Vincent Strathauchin, nos. 37, 146. It is possible that there were two women named Elizabeth Douglas.

14 *Edin. Recs.*, i, 199–200; Wiesner, *Women and Gender*, 83–4. For a potential female apprentice in Peebles, see *Peebles Recs.*, 254–5.

15 Newlyn, 'Taxonomy of the female', 8–9, discussing *The Wif of Auchtermuchty*. This is a common theme in medieval Europe; the presence of a Scottish version suggests that the message was familiar. See P. Bawcutt, *Dunbar the Makar* (Oxford, 1992), 366, for attitudes to women's work.

craftsman's wife often took an active role in the craft, supervising workmen, participating in some craft processes, and marketing the manufactured product. Many a widow took over her husband's business and ran it successfully, suggesting she had been familiar with the enterprise while he was alive. In Edinburgh women worked, both alongside their husbands and alone, at every level of the economy from overseas trade to hawking wares on the street.

The wealthiest Edinburgh townswomen were the wives of overseas merchants and leading craftsmen.[16] Apart from domestic duties of raising children, provisioning the household, and supervising servants (whose numbers increased with the family's wealth), some merchant wives participated in trade. In the 1360s Margaret Hogg accompanied her husband Roger on foreign trips and acted as a merchant. When he died, she married John Peebles, her late husband's business partner. Margaret was not unusual in her conduct of business activities. Indeed, it was routinely assumed that merchant wives could act on their husband's behalf, and both goods and cash were often delivered to a merchant's wife in her husband's absence.[17] Since overseas merchants were frequently absent, many wives effectively worked jointly with their husbands, supervising business affairs at home while the husbands were away – though some, like Margaret Hogg, also travelled abroad. In 1530 Elizabeth Carkettill, from a prominent mercantile family, was unable to appear in a court case because she was 'furth of the country'.[18]

Merchant wives were, however, more commonly to be found in Edinburgh itself. Many ran shops and booths. Agnes Cockburn, widow of the printer Walter Chepman, built a shop on her property, and several women owned booths, either singly, or sometimes together with a husband. Some were rented from the town: Janet, widow of William Scott, rented a tolbooth shop for 45s. in 1457. Other women inherited booths: Agnes Gibsoun inherited hers from her father, the skinner John Gibsoun.[19] The monarch's presence in the town ensured regular business for all merchants, and some merchant wives also supplied the royal household: John of Burgone's wife, for instance, was paid for cloth delivered for the royal wedding in 1503. Several purchases of cloth were also made from Henry Atkinson's wife in 1495, but only one from Henry himself.[20] It is not clear whether these women were in business for themselves or working in partnership with their husbands. The designation *femme sole*, which in some countries indicated a married woman with a business legally independent of her husband, was not used in Edinburgh – though the examples given may be evidence that such people existed in practice. Certainly, widows of overseas merchants often carried on their husbands' business. Margaret, widow of William Rynd, traded in partnership with her son Robert. Janet Paterson was

16 Merchants' wives were generally the elite of Edinburgh society. This was not the case in some other towns, such as Perth, where the declining export trade gave craftsmen greater importance relative to the merchants: Lynch, 'Social and economic structure', 270–2.

17 *Halyburton's Ledger*, 32–3; for Margaret Hogg, see Ewan, *Townlife*, 81.

18 ECA, Gild Court Records, 1529–1557 [hereafter GC], fo. 4v.

19 ECA, GC, fos. 35v, 23r, 26v, *Edin. Recs.*, i, 17; National Register of Archives, Scotland, Duke of Roxburghe Papers, no. 76.

20 *TA*, i, 391; ibid., 227, 256, 258, 262; ibid., 226.

involved in overseas trade after the death of her first husband, John Carkettill, in 1494. Not all such women were prosperous. In 1489 Jonet Bridy, unsure if her husband William Broune was alive – he had left Scotland because of poverty – sold a tenement to Thomas Gilmour and invested the money in Gilmour's overseas commercial venture with her son Robert Broune.[21]

By contrast, Isabel Bras or Williamson, widow of Thomas Williamson was a prominent merchant widow. She appeared as 'Thomas Williamson's wife' in 1473, but after this was recorded as Isabel Williamson, suggesting she had become a well-known merchant in her own right. Other widows were often described in relation to their husbands rather than by their own name alone. Isabel was active in selling fine cloth to the royal household. She appeared as an Edinburgh burgess before the Lords of Council in 1490, and was involved in financial transactions with many of Scotland's powerful figures.[22] Her son John followed in her footsteps: in 1473 the royal household bought cloth from 'Isabel Williamson's son'. Indeed, John became a prominent merchant, serving as town treasurer in 1494 and supplying goods to the crown.[23]

Among the crafts, it was also assumed that wives would work with their husbands. Craft gild ordinances indicate that female websters and candlemakers were allowed to exercise their crafts, if they were married to a craftsman. In the later Middle Ages, however, some gilds began to exclude single women. In 1517 the candlemakers voted to expel all women from their craft, unless they were wives of freemen. Margaret Atkynson fell foul of these rules in 1520 and was ordered to cease her activity.[24] Other gilds, such as the websters, expressed doubts about women's skill, but allowed them to continue working. Others still continued to admit women members in their own right: Jonet Watsoun was listed among leading members of the bonnetmaker craft in 1530 and other bonnetmakers included Jonet Polton and Katherine Graham.[25] The masons may also have had women members; and there were female carders, spinsters, and tailors.[26]

Some craft women may not, however, have undertaken manual labour themselves. Women admitted to gilds may often have been employers and sellers of the finished products manufactured by journeymen in workshops. Indeed, some gilds required craftsmen to give up manual work before they were

21 *Halyburton's Ledger*, 168, 183, 191; 8, 51–2, 57; *Protocol Book of James Young*, nos. 178, 197.

22 *Edin. Recs.*, i, 39; *TA*, i, 19–27, 31–2, 34–8, 41–2, 55, 58, 60–3; *The Acts of the Lords of Council in Civil Causes*, ed. T. Thomson *et al.* (Edinburgh, 1839–), i, 142, 200; *The Acts of the Lord Auditors of Causes and Complaints*, ed. T. Thomson (Edinburgh, 1839), i, 85. See R. Marshall, *Virgins and Viragos: A History of Women in Scotland from 1080–1980* (London, 1983), 50, for a description of Isabel's business. For Isabel's life, see 'Isabel Williamson', in *New Dictionary of National Biography* (Oxford, forthcoming). Isabel was unusual among Scottish women in using her husband's surname; this may reflect the established nature of the mercantile enterprise she took over.

23 *TA*, i, 40, 219–20, 303; *RMS*, ii, no. 2237.

24 *Edin. Recs.*, i, 34, 171, 197.

25 Ibid., i, 199, ii, 22–4. The bonnetmakers were the precursors of the later knitting trades which involved many women: H. M. Bennett, 'The Origins and Development of the Scottish Hand-Knitting Industry' (University of Edinburgh, unpublished PhD thesis, 1981), 170–2.

26 *Registrum Cartarum Ecclesiae Sancti Egidii de Edinburgh*, ed. D. Laing (Bannatyne Club, 1859), App., no. 8 (which refers to the 'brothers and sisters' of craft of masons and wrights); *Edin. Recs.*, ii, 40; *TA*, i, 212, 215.

admitted to membership,[27] and it seems likely that women's main contribution to the crafts may have been selling the finished product. Because of the life they led, this was the branch of craft activity which best suited them.

The skill of retailing was easily adaptable to different crafts. Having learned the ways of the market-place from her mother, the new craft wife could bring her knowledge to bear in selling the products of her husband's workshop. Overseas merchants' wives might be familiar with the conditions and characteristics of the export trade, but the wives of craftsmen were equally familiar with local market conditions: the best place to sell, seasonal fluctuations in demand, trustworthy customers and suppliers (an important consideration when so many transactions involved credit). Female friendship networks meant that women could learn as much, or more, about local needs as their husbands could at town or gild meetings.[28] The power of gossip should never be underestimated, and was put to good use in the market-place.

Women dominated the brewing trade, both as brewers and as tapsters or sellers of ale. In 1499, 110 female brewers are recorded, and in 1529–30 there were almost 400 of them.[29] Although in 1529 the council attempted to limit brewing to those who were 'honest and substantial persons', then attempted in 1545 to register ale sellers and, the next year, to insist that all tapsters and brewers were married or widows, Edinburgh's brewers were socially diverse. They included merchant wives, poor widows and ex-servants.[30] Indeed, since ale was a staple of diet, most who wanted to brew were normally allowed to do so, with council interventions restricted mainly to the regulation of prices and quality. Brewing suited the female lifestyle. It developed from domestic skills. Most adult women brewed ale for their own household, and brewing equipment was often inherited, obviating the need for capital investment. Alternatively, it could be hired readily. Brewing was a lengthy process and, since ale spoiled quickly, brewing for sale as well as for domestic consumption made good sense. Brewing was thus an intermittent activity for many women, though some brewed regularly enough to be considered professional alewives,[31] and might even be hired to brew ale for workers employed on government projects. In 1529, for example, Katherine Reid and Widow Layng provided ale for construction workers at Holyrood. In Leith women were also active as brewers, selling to visiting sailors and merchants, and to their Edinburgh neighbours.[32]

27 One burgess was told off for engaging in manual labour: Robertson and Wood, *Castle and Town*, 262.

28 M. Wiesner, 'Paltry peddlers or essential merchants? Women in the distributive trades in early modern Nuremburg' *Sixteenth-Century Journal*, xii (1981), 4, 7.

29 *Edin. Recs.*, i, 75; ii, 20–1, 25–6, 43–4; ECA, GC, fos. 60r–78r. See E. Ewan, 'Whatever ales ye: women as consumers and producers in late medieval Scottish Towns', in Ewan and Meikle, *Women in Scotland*.

30 *Edin. Recs.*, ii, 8, 117, 124. In Aberdeen different prices were set for ale brewed by wives of freemen and unfreemen: *Aberdeen Council Recs.*, i, 157–8, 436.

31 *Edin. Recs.*, ii, 27; *Leges Burgorum*, c.116, in *Ancient Laws and Customs of the Burghs of Scotland*, ed. C. Innes and R. Renwick (Scottish Burgh Records Soc., 1868–1910; *Aberdeen Council Recs.*, i, 408; J. Bennett, 'The village ale-wife: women and brewing in fourteenth-century England', in Hanawalt, *Women and Work*, 20–36; Ewan, 'Whatever ales ye', 129–30.

32 *Accounts of the Masters of Works*, ed. H. M. Paton *et al.* (Edinburgh, 1957– ), i, 19, 26–7; *Edin. Recs.*, ii, 15.

For most women, however, brewing was an occasional means of supplementing household incomes. That it was normally part-time work is implied by an Aberdeen ordinance of 1507 which decreed that craftsmen's wives use different lades for brewing and for other crafts. Since this decree was addressed especially to the wives of dyers and cordiners, who steeped their raw materials in urine, the council's concern is perhaps understandable. Nevertheless, burgh councils were anxious to ensure that adequate supplies of ale were available for purchase, and there were periodic attempts to force women to brew all year round.[33] However, it may also have been recognised that allowing women to carry out work of a temporary nature was one means of supplementing the family income – thereby keeping a household off charity.[34]

Because ale was a staple of diet, the brewers' trade was heavily regulated. Most towns regularly proclaimed a set price (or 'assize') for bread and ale. In 1450 the Edinburgh council set sixpence and eightpence as the maximum price for different ales. Town-appointed ale-tasters tested its quality and those who broke the statute were to have their cauldron taken to the market cross and the bottom struck out. There were also attempts to protect the trade of Edinburgh brewsters. In 1529 the council forbade Edinburgh people to buy ale from Leith brewers for two months.[35] And, in 1494, the council decreed that twelvepence was to be raised from every brewster and tapster to fund repairs of the common wells, since brewers were frequent users.

Despite the importance of their product, there is no evidence of brewers establishing a formal organisation, although they may have acted together occasionally and were sometimes treated collectively by the urban authorities. It seems possible that the 110 brewster-wives who broke the ale assize in 1499 were co-operating in raising their prices; and in 1507 the council blamed brewsters and tapsters for hurting the poor by overcharging. The council was more often concerned with the prices charged by the crafts and, on a number of occasions included the brewsters along with the cordiners, smiths, baxters and sellers of food and salt amongst those whose activities it sought to regulate.[36]

Women did not only brew ale. Some also made and sold whisky, although forbidden to do so by the barbers craft in 1505. In 1557 Bessie Campbell was convicted of illegally making whisky, but the barbers were evidently prepared to licence some women manufacturers, as the council suggested Bessie apply for admission to their craft.[37] Whisky-makers provided only limited competition for brewsters, but the increasing popularity of hop-brewed beer in sixteenth-century Scotland was a more serious threat. Foreign beers had been sold in Scotland since the fifteenth century, but beer soon began to be brewed in

33 *Aberdeen Council Recs.*, i, 437; *Fragmenta Collecta*, nos. 41–2, in *Ancient Laws and Customs of the Burghs of Scotland.*

34 Kowaleski, 'Women's work in a market town', 156.

35 *Edin. Recs.*, i, 12, 62; ii, 5. Scottish towns do not appear to have imposed the annual fines common in England: see E. Gemmill and N. Mayhew, *Changing Values in Medieval Scotland: A Study of Prices, Money, and Weights and Measures* (Cambridge, 1995), 52–3. For England, see J. Bennett, *Ale, Beer and Brewsters in England: Women's Work in a Changing World, 1300–1600* (Oxford, 1996), 4, 100, 161–2.

36 *Edin. Recs.*, i, 67, 111; ii, 265–6.

37 Ibid, i, 101–4, ii, 262.

Scotland too. Because it could be preserved, it could be produced in much larger quantities than ale. This required capital, which explains why the brewing of beer was a male-dominated trade. Indeed, the formation of the Company of Brewers in 1596 probably had an adverse effect on the traditional ale-brewing trade of women.[38]

Lack of capital also disadvantaged women in trades such as baking. Although there were female bakers, the activity tended to be dominated by men. Few women could afford the construction of an oven or a bakehouse. Moreover, other outlays of capital were required: some Edinburgh bakehouses employed up to nine workers.[39] Unlike brewing, baking also required uninterrupted attention – and time was a commodity few women possessed. Women bakers seem to have been restricted to small-scale activities, such as the baking of oatcakes – which could be baked over a hearth-fire. They could be prosecuted for cake-baking since this was regarded by the authorities both as wasteful of scarce supplies of flour and as unwelcome competition for bakers.[40] The frequency with which cake-bakers were prosecuted suggests that the activity was carried on regardless, in part no doubt because there was a ready market among those too poor to buy bread – perhaps most of whom would be women themselves.[41] Indeed, women played an important role more generally in provisioning the poor. Much of the distribution network for the necessities of life, both in the market-place and beyond, lay in female hands.[42]

By the late fifteenth century Edinburgh's trade had grown to such an extent that its traditional market sites were becoming congested. In 1477 fifteen locations were established around the town for the selling of different goods.[43] In these bustling, noisy and often rambunctious markets, women were active participants. Burgesses could sell goods without paying toll, but for a fee – in 1479, of two shillings *per annum* – non-burgesses could obtain the status of stallanger and the right to set up a market stall. Since female burgesses were rare, this concession was particularly useful for women – especially once the council insisted that all who worked in the burgh (including brewsters, and regraters of fish, butter, cheese, eggs, wild fowl and all other things bought and sold within

38 *ER*, vi, 117; M. Lynch, *Scotland: A New History* (London, 1991), 176–7; Robertson and Wood, *Castle and Town*, 264.

39 *Edin. Recs.*, 129–30, 214; Robertson and Wood, *Castle and Town*, 263–4; Lynch, 'Social and economic structure', 278. See Bennett, 'Village ale-wife', 21 n.4. There were women bakers in other towns, but they appear to have been few in number: P. Symms, 'Social Control in a Sixteenth-century Burgh: A Study of the Burgh Court Book of Selkirk 1503–1545' (University of Edinburgh, unpublished PhD thesis, 1968), 117; *Aberdeen Council Recs.*, i, 276.

40 *Edin. Recs.*, i, 97–8. No Edinburgh cake-bakers are named, but most of those prosecuted for the offence in Aberdeen were women: e.g. Aberdeen City Archives, Council Register, i, fo. 328; v(1), fo. 682. See also Gemmill and Mayhew, *Changing Values*, 38.

41 Payments of alms in the Canongait in 1564–7 were made to 111 women and 102 men: *The Buik of the Canagait 1564–1657*, ed. A. B. Calderwood *et al.* (Scottish Record Soc., 1961), 7, 52–3, 58, 66–7. Twice as many women as men were listed among the poor in several Scottish parishes in early modern Scotland: R. Mitchison, *Coping with Destitution: Poverty and Relief in Western Europe* (Toronto, 1991), 20. Women made up a large proportion of the poor in most European countries: Wiesner, *Women and Gender*, 94. See also Symms, 'Social Control in Sixteenth-century Selkirk', 117; and Gemmill and Mayhew, *Changing Values*, 38.

42 Wiesner, 'Paltry peddlers', 12–13.

43 *Edin. Recs.*, i, 34–6.

the burgh) must be of either burgess or stallanger status.[44] Many women sold foodstuffs. While some came from the countryside, town-dwellers often went to rural areas to purchase goods and some may have offered their services as market-sellers to country people.[45] Knowledge of local conditions and needs made urban women useful to those with produce to sell – and women can be found selling butter, cheese, eggs, fruit, tar, tallow, salt, malt, poultry, game and even livestock. Market women thus provided an essential service for the town, the small-scale nature of their enterprise being reflected in the following contemporary poem:

For I, a wyfe, with sempill lyfe,
Dois wyn my meit ilk day,
For small auaill, ay sellinȝ caill,
The best fassoun I may.[46]

Fish, too, was commonly sold by women, many of them from Leith. Dunbar paints a vivid picture of the fish market with its 'stink of haddockis and scaittis ... cryis of carlings and debaittis [and] fensum flyttingis of defame'.[47] The fish sellers were taxed to pay for the cleansing of the High Street from the dirt of their market.[48]

As well as foodstuffs, women sold other goods, often of little value (such as pins or ribbons), and second-hand articles. A second-hand goods market was established in front of the Greyfriars in 1477, though it was regarded suspiciously as a convenient place to sell stolen goods.[49] If placing it in front of the Greyfriars was meant to deter such activity, it probably failed. Indeed, illegal trading practices more generally often involved women. Numerous cases before the burgh court concerned women 'disturbing the town'. In the competitive atmosphere of the market, accusations of bad faith by both buyers and sellers readily arose. Appropriately, in 1503 the council ordered persons convicted of scolding to be punished at the market cross. Agnes Wright was put in irons at the cross 'that all the people might see', and her crime was openly proclaimed before she was banished. In 1548 the council ordered that all women found arguing on the High Street, especially fruit sellers, be put in the pillory for six hours.[50]

The market was supervised closely by the town. Burgh officers found many instances of poor goods – adulterated wine, watered-down ale, stinking fish, reheated pies, goods measured or weighed with false measures – despite many regulations to the contrary, some of which (such as measuring meal) were supervised by women.[51] The most effective way of ensuring regular supplies for

44 Ibid, i, 36, 40–41.

45 Ibid, i, 105–6.

46 Robert Sempill, *Maddeis Proclamatioun*, in *Satirical Poems of the Time of the Reformation*, ed. J. Cranstoun (Scottish Text Soc., 1889–90), i, 149, ll. 17–24.

47 William Dunbar, *To the Merchantis of Edinburgh*, in *The Poems of William Dunbar*, ed. J. Kinsley (Oxford, 1979), 201–3; ll, 8–11; P. Bawcutt, 'Images of women in the poems of Dunbar', *Etudes Ecossaises*, i (1991), 49–50.

48 *Edin. Recs.*, i, 124, 135.

49 Ibid, i, 35; Wiesner, 'Paltry peddlers', 9.

50 *Edin. Recs.*, i, 97; ii, 88, 141; ECA, Burgh Court Records, May–Sep. 1507 [hereafter BC], fo. 29.

51 *Fragmenta Collecta*, nos. 45, 47–8; *Edin. Recs.*, i, 133; ii, 15.

the burgesses, adequate quality, and payment of tolls was to centralise trade in the markets. Forestalling (buying goods before they came to market) was therefore prohibited, as was selling goods privately in houses. But sellers often found means of circumventing these decrees. In 1529 the council enacted legislation against those who evaded tolls by hiding poultry under their cloaks and gowns.[52]

In part these problems arose because many goods were sold wholesale and few could afford them. Hucksters and regraters – who in most medieval towns included women – provided a solution to this problem by retailing commodities in small quantities, which the poor could afford.[53] However, the burgh authorities tried to regulate them by limiting their access to the market to certain hours. In 1515 those regrating meal were not allowed to purchase supplies until after three o'clock. Margaret Clapane was banished for a week for buying fish to regrate outside the stipulated hours.[54] The time restrictions meant that regraters were left to purchase what remained in the market once more privileged households had bought their supplies. This was to the town's advantage as it allowed sellers to dispose of poorer-quality stock and also ensured a supply of cheap goods for the poor – though periodically the council cracked down on regraters, blaming them for food shortages and high prices. In 1517 regraters of meal were charged with causing 'the greitt exorbitant derth that is rissin' and on other occasions regraters of game, poultry, cheese, eggs, butter, oats and hay were targeted. In 1524, for example, Helen Bayne was banished after being convicted of regrating eggs.[55]

Like brewing, regrating suited the female lifestyle. It could be part-time, carried out while also providing for a woman's own household. It required little capital and made use of familiar marketing skills. It was flexible work entailing the purchase of different products and the sale of household surpluses. It was also sociable work, affording regular contact with other women. What concerned the council about such activity was the scope for private or door-to-door sales of products made by the vendors or produce bought in the countryside. This offended against market regulations designed to ensure fair prices. It also enabled regraters to evade market tolls – though private or door-to-door selling suited women's working conditions, allowing them to make use of their social networks. In 1530, for example, Isobel Bowy and Kate Boyd, confined to their house by plague, opened a feather bed, and persuaded Besse Anderson to sell the feathers.[56]

Goods of all description were often bought on credit. Women of all social classes, from merchant wives to servants, were involved in pawning and money lending.[57] Wedwives who pawned goods performed an essential service for the poor. The goods pawned were usually household articles, such as spoons, sheets,

52 Ibid, ii, 6.

53 Kowaleski, 'Women's work in a market town', 148. In 1515 a list of meal regraters included nine women and one man: *Edin. Recs.*, i, 156–7.

54 *Edin. Recs.*, i, 157; ii, 8–9, 11. See also ibid, ii, 10.

55 Ibid, i, 156–9, 172–3, 217; ii, 26–7.

56 Ibid, i, 112; ii, 42.

57 Ibid, i, 96, 106–7; ii, 28–9; Sanderson, *Mary Stewart's People*, 91, 98–101; W. C. Jordan, *Women and Credit in Pre-Industrial and Developing Countries* (Philadelphia, 1993), 24–42.

and blankets, or articles of clothing. In 1504 Jonet Kinnaird laid a silver belt in pledge to Jonet Freland which she did not redeem for three years. Women even extended credit to the king. James Lamb's wife was paid 13s. 4d. to redeem the king's French saddle.[58]

There were many other essential services which women also performed for the town. They acted, for example, as midwives and wet-nurses. Agnes Preston, wife of John Turing, wet-nursed the future James IV, and was rewarded with a land grant. Some wet-nurses were single mothers, supporting themselves and their children, and some boarded with their charge's family, in order to save enough money to establish their own household afterwards.[59] Other women acted as nurses or teachers.[60] Yet others entered domestic service. Many families had a maid, and in craft households the maid might undertake craft work in addition to domestic chores such as fetching water, laundering and helping her mistress brew ale. Wages were paid in both money and goods, usually clothes.[61] Most women probably spent several years in service before marriage, as this would allow them to build up a dowry.[62]

Much work of this sort was an extension of child-rearing duties and several other female occupations, like brewing and regrating, were an extension of other domestic chores. Similarly, many women provided accommodation for people and animals. The wife of Snowdon Herald was paid for the expenses of Windsor Herald visiting Edinburgh on a diplomatic mission, but women also rented rooms to lodgers on a long-term basis, though not always profitably. Helen Baty was forced to pursue her lodger, a chaplain, for four years of rent arrears and a silver cup which he had stolen.[63] While the council regulated stablers, it protected their livelihood by giving them a monopoly on the sale of oats and hay to visitors – though in 1529 five women regraters broke this monopoly.[64]

Many women also ran taverns. Christina Gammyll bequeathed hers to her daughter. Marion Law probably ran the tavern which she and her husband owned jointly.[65] Even in taverns run by men, women did much of the work. In

58 ECA, BC, fos. 6, 16, 35; *TA*, i, 330.

59 After 1560 supervision of midwives increased when the Kirk ordered them to report illegitimate births: Calderwood *et al.*, *Buik of the Canagait*, 10, 28, 35. On wet-nurses, see *Edin. Recs.*, ii, 27; *RMS*, ii, no. 1796; and R. K. Marshall, 'A history of wet-nurses in Scotland 1500–1800', *Review of Scottish Culture*, i (1984). For the employment of single mothers as wet-nurses in the 17th century, see G. DesBrisay, 'Wet nurses and unwed mothers in seventeenth-century Aberdeen', in Ewan and Meikle, *Women in Scotland.*

60 *Edin. Recs.*, i, 76; *Liber Conventus S. Katherine Senensis prope Edinburgum*, ed. J. Maidment (Abbotsford Club, 1841), 66–7.

61 ECA, BC, fo. 41. In 17th-century Edinburgh, domestic service was the most common occupation for women: Dingwall, *Late Seventeenth-Century Edinburgh*, 28, 132–4.

62 See I. D. and K. A. Whyte, 'The geographical mobility of women in early modern Scotland', in L. Leneman, ed., *Perspectives in Scottish Social History* (Aberdeen, 1989), 84, 92–4; P. J. P. Goldberg, 'Female labour, service and marriage in the late medieval urban north', *Northern History*, xxii (1986), 18–38; and E. Ewan, 'Mercantile power? Female domestic servants in late medieval Scottish towns' (paper presented at the International Medieval Congress, University of Leeds, July 1994).

63 *TA*, i, 53; NAS, GD172/188.

64 ECA, BC, fo. 24; *Edin. Recs.*, i, 117–18, 153, ii, 9–10. Banishment did not last for long; one of the women was able to return after five days, another after two weeks: ibid., 12–13.

65 *Protocol Book of John Foular 1501–28*, ed. W. Macleod and M. Wood (Scottish Record Soc., 1930–53), i, no. 507; ECA, GC, fo. 41r; M. W. Stuart, *Old Edinburgh Taverns* (London, 1952), 9–10.

1520 the body regulating the wine trade forbade taverners' wives and women servants from going to Leith to buy wine directly from ships. A list of fifty-one taverners compiled in the 1560s included seventeen women.[66] Some taverns and inns were regarded as haunts of thieves and prostitutes. Prostitution was common in medieval towns – there was at least one brothel in Edinburgh by 1530 – and was viewed as a necessary evil where there were large numbers of unmarried apprentices and clergy.[67] Many prostitutes were probably poor women who had migrated to the town or ex-servants dismissed for pregnancy.[68] The fear of syphilis led to attempts to control prostitution, and in 1497 all infected persons were ordered to Inchkeith Island. In Aberdeen, the council ordered all 'light women' to work at another trade or be banished.[69] While no similar statute is known in Edinburgh, one act against beggars insisted that all vagabonds (men and women) find work or face banishment. In 1505 the council forbade anyone to rent houses to men or women who could not support themselves through their labour and in 1529 Jonet Heriot was ordered to cease begging and start working for her living.[70] Medieval authority expected women to work for their living.

Women, then, lacked formal political power but were nonetheless important in urban life. Official attempts to regulate their activities suggest authorities viewed them as troublesome, but necessary. Many urban historians take a similar view. The occupations of women are troublesome: they do not fit into neat categories, and they make description of the urban economy more complex. But women are as necessary to historians as they were to medieval Edinburgh. How can we truly understand the nature of medieval towns unless we examine the whole economy, not just the trade which lined the pockets of the elite? To return to the point from which this essay started: Mons Meg, some years ago, was moved indoors, and new signs now direct tourists to its site. It is now time for historians to remove the women of Edinburgh from their private worlds of home and family and to locate them in the public sphere of market and street. Mons Meg's contribution to Scottish history has been recognised and celebrated. The challenge now is to do the same for Merchant Meg.[71]

66 *Edin. Recs.*, i, 201–2; *Roll of Edinburgh Burgesses and Guild-Brethren 1406–1700*, ed. C. B. B. Watson, i, 3.

67 J. Rossiaud, *Medieval Prostitution* (Oxford, 1988), 3–10. For Dunbar's description of Edinburgh prostitutes, see Bawcutt, *Dunbar the Makar*, 214.

68 *Edin. Recs.*, ii, 27; Kowaleski, 'Women's work in a market town', 154–5. In York several prostitutes were surnamed Scott, suggesting that they may have migrated south: Goldberg, *Women, Work and Lifecycle*, 152.

69 *Edin. Recs.*, i, 71–2; *Aberdeen Council Recs.*, i, 425.

70 *Edin. Recs.*, i, 97, 107, 204, 214.

71 I would like to thank the Social Sciences and Humanities Research Council of Canada for financial support for the research for this essay, Alan McDonald for his research assistance in the Edinburgh Archives, and Pat Dennison for her helpful and insightful comments on the burgh community in Scotland.

# 11

# The Craftsmen of Elgin, 1540–1660

*Jane Thomas*

Early modern Elgin was a town of moderate size. With a population of about 2,000–2,500 by 1660, it was probably the largest town in Moray, and had long been the seat of the local diocese and a centre of local government.[1] In national tax rolls Elgin figured frequently among the twenty most heavily taxed burghs.[2] Clearly the town enjoyed some economic prosperity even though its geographical location – some six miles from the coast and still further from navigable waterways – ensured that it was remote from lucrative markets. It seems unlikely that commerce was the basis of Elgin's success. More probably the town's wealth owed more to its craftsmen than to its merchants. An occupational survey of 1,775 men recorded in the town's records between 1540 and 1660 confirms the importance of crafts: 56.7% of the work-force were craftsmen, and only 17.4% merchants.[3] Craftsmen evidently formed the backbone of the urban work-force and, in this, Elgin was not unusual among provincial towns – though in larger centres, such as Aberdeen, the merchant population was dominant.[4] The contribution of craftsmen to the society, economy and government of these smaller towns merits further examination.

The range of crafts practised in Elgin was extensive. Forty different trades are recorded over the period (see *Table 3*), though many – such as that of the solitary golf-ball maker, George Watson – occur rarely. There was, however, a more numerous core of between ten and fifteen crafts, based around the leather, clothing and textile industries and the food trades. Among these, the largest number of craftsmen was employed in the leather trades. Indeed, the proportion of craftsmen employed in leather working (34.5%) was apparently higher than that in many other towns.[5] Skinners and cordiners each accounted for 8% of the burgh's total work-force, and they figured among the four or five most numerous crafts groups recorded in each decade of the period. Other leather workers were less significant, though the glovemakers, who accounted for just over 2% of the total work-force over the period, are first recorded only in the 1640s. All leather workers were, however, fortunate in that the raw materials required for their trades were abundant locally. Elgin's rural hinterland included extensive grazing

1 J. E. Thomas, 'The Burgh of Elgin in Early Modern Times' (University of Aberdeen, unpublished MLitt thesis, 1990) [hereafter Thomas, 'Thesis'], 16–17, n.15.

2 *Records of the Convention of the Royal Burghs of Scotland*, ed. J. D. Marwick (Edinburgh, 1866), passim.

3 For further details see Thomas, 'Thesis', 29–31.

4 I. D. Whyte, 'The occupational structure of the Scottish burghs in the late seventeenth century', in M. Lynch, ed., *The Early Modern Town in Scotland* (London, 1987), 227. It is estimated that merchants made up about 74% of the burgess population in Aberdeen: M. Lynch, 'Continuity and change in urban society, 1500–1700', in R. A. Houston and I. D. Whyte, eds., *Scottish Society, 1500–1800* (Cambridge, 1989), 107.

5 Whyte, 'Occupational structure', 230. Only 11 of the 37 burghs investigated there have 20% or more employed in the leather trades, and most are closer to 10–15%.

*Table 3. The Crafts of Elgin, 1540–1660*

| OCCUPATION | NOS. EMPLOYED | OCCUPATION | NOS. EMPLOYED |
|---|---|---|---|
| Skinner | 145 | Aqua vitae maker | 4 |
| Cordiner | 143 | Brewer | 4 |
| Tailor | 124 | Glasswright | 4 |
| Weaver | 118 | Potter | 3 |
| Flesher | 74 | Tinker | 3 |
| Maltman | 47 | Bonnetmaker | 2 |
| Smith | 44 | Gunsmith | 2 |
| Mason | 41 | Horner | 2 |
| Glover | 39 | Pewterer | 2 |
| Wright | 34 | Thatcher | 2 |
| Litster | 28 | Turner | 2 |
| Baxter | 27 | Barber | 1 |
| Cooper | 25 | Barrowman | 1 |
| Saddler | 20 | Bowster | 1 |
| Miller | 17 | Carpenter | 1 |
| Armourer | 13 | Cartmaker | 1 |
| Cutler | 11 | Gartermaker | 1 |
| Goldsmith | 6 | Limeman | 1 |
| Slater | 6 | Lorimer | 1 |
| Walker | 6 | Golf-ball maker | 1 |

land, though some inhabitants also maintained herds in the Highlands, and cattle from fairs in Inverness and Dornoch supplemented local supplies.[6] Ox and cow hides were most commonly used by leather workers, but wether, lamb, kid, and even dog skins were periodically used. All these could have been found locally.[7]

Demand for the leather manufactures was generally buoyant. As well as supplying Elgin itself, treated and untreated hides were among the town's exports, and trade in these items may have increased from the 1580s.[8] In the latter part of the period, leather gloves also entered the export market.[9] It was undoubtedly demand from outwith the town which helped to support the large number of leather workers in Elgin, though it is possible that the attractive prices paid for hides elsewhere led to periodic shortages in Elgin itself: in 1572 and 1581 the council decreed that barked (treated) hides were to be offered for sale to the burgh first, at reasonable prices, before being removed for sale

6 Moray Record Office, Forres [hereafter MRO], Elgin Burgh Court Book [hereafter EBCB], ii, 408, 422, 431, 1107.

7 MRO, EBCB, ii, 69.

8 *Elgin Recs.*, i, 32-3, 37, 39–40; MRO, EBCB, ii, 88. Elgin's customs tax of 1587 was, at 1.6%, higher than its usual assessment of 1.4%: M. Lynch, 'Continuity and change', 96.

9 *The Statistical Account of Scotland, 1791–99*, ed. D. J. Withrington and I. R. Grant (Wakefield, 1982), xvi, 598.

elsewhere.[10] From at least 1570, the prices of hides, boots and shoes were fixed annually by the council, suggesting similar concerns.[11] The only other commodities subject to such regulation were basic foodstuffs, tallow and candles.

The importance of leather to the urban economy was reflected in the wealth and status of the leather workers themselves. Among them, the skinners were pre-eminent. The job of treating animal skins involved removing wool or hair from them, then barking (or tanning) and/or salting the hides. This work was evidently lucrative and many were keen to practise the trade, though council restrictions prevented this. In 1546, 1548 and 1572 unfreemen were barred 'fra all occupasioun of this craft' other than as servants to burgesses, and in 1570 only those with a council licence were permitted to treat hides for the market.[12] Skinners clearly formed a major part of the craft aristocracy and had considerable status in the burgh, which possibly helped them to persuade the council to enact these regulations. They were one of only three crafts known to have been represented on the council over the entire period, and they also supplied more craft elders on the kirk session than did any other trade.[13] They may also have been allowed admission to the merchant gild as, following the foundation of that body in the 1640s, some of its members were described as merchant skinners.[14]

Elsewhere too, skinners figured among the leading urban craftsmen.[15] It was perhaps more unusual that in Elgin the skinners enjoyed certain trading privileges. From at least 1550 they possessed the right 'to us salt or dry hidis in m[er]chandice as stapill guid and pay custum th[ai]rfor'.[16] This right was shared with merchants and was strictly overseen by the provost and bailies. It was a valuable concession, nonetheless, and probably continued throughout the period: the skinners' right to sell treated hides within Scotland was confirmed in February 1658 by the council, which simultaneously confirmed the exclusive right of merchants to sell untreated skins and to export hides.[17] The privileged position of the skinners probably owed much to the importance of leather among the town's exports. Indeed, this is implied by the noticeable decrease in the number of skinners following the national decline in exports from the later sixteenth century.[18] There may have been a further slump in exports in the 1650s as the burgh's maintenance rolls show a marked decline in the fortune of skinners between 1646 and 1652; and this was still evident in the rolls of 1658.[19]

10 MRO, EBCB, ii, 132, 750.

11 MRO, EBCB, ii, 16.

12 MRO, EBCB, i, 202, 227; ii, 16, 132.

13 Thomas, 'Thesis', 103, 152–3.

14 E.g. MRO, EBCB, iv, 147; A699/646/1.

15 M. Lynch, *Edinburgh and the Reformation* (Edinburgh, 1984), 25; idem, 'The social and economic structure of the larger towns, 1450–1600', in M. Lynch, M. Spearman and G. Stell, eds., *The Scottish Medieval Town* (Edinburgh, 1988), 266.

16 MRO, EBCB, i, 286.

17 MRO, Elgin Town Council records [hereafter ETC], i, 247–9; A37/6/3.

18 Lynch, *Edinburgh and the Reformation*, 276; T. C. Smout, *Scottish Trade on the Eve of the Union, 1660–1707* (Edinburgh, 1963), 236.

19 MRO, C62/646/1–3; C62/651/2; C62/652/1, 2, 5; C62/653/3, 5; C62/654/1; C62/655/1; C62/656/1; C62/657/1, 3; C62/658/2, 4.

Nevertheless, in spite of their waning fortunes, the skinners remained among the most influential of Elgin's craftsmen.

Of the other leather-based craftsmen, saddlers were among the wealthiest by the 1640s and 1650s and, although they were never numerous, their specialist skills probably attracted many rural inhabitants to Elgin in search of their manufactures. In the 1640s the saddlers were joined at the top of the craft hierarchy by leather glovemakers. Although they had made their first appearance in the records only a few years previously, by 1646 the glovers were the second wealthiest craft according to the maintenance rolls, following only the litsters or dyers. The glovemakers grew rapidly in number and wealth thereafter. By 1658 they constituted the second largest craft group represented on the maintenance roll and they paid almost 6% of the total maintenance and just under one quarter of the craft contribution. Their status rose as gloves began to appear among the town's exports.[20] In contrast to fellow craftsmen, they were producing finished goods which, since they were for export, we may assume were of high quality.

The remaining group of leather workers, the cordiners, were numerically strong throughout the period. Chiefly engaged in the manufacture of boots and shoes, the cordiners also treated their own hides which they were then permitted to sell.[21] In spite of their numbers, there seems to have been a shortage of boots and shoes for much of the period in Elgin, and nationally too, from the early seventeenth century. As early as 1548 the council gave licence to unfreemen to practise the trade of cordiners if freemen could not meet the burgh's needs at reasonable prices – prices which the council regulated from at least 1570.[22] The number of unfree cordiners was substantial throughout the period, suggesting that the freemen's production regularly fell short of the burgh's needs. Nevertheless, although unfree competition was apparently permitted throughout, it was resented by the cordiners, who in 1657 persuaded the council to impose restrictions on unfree practitioners of the trade. These included the stricter enforcement – by the dean of gild and two cordiners – of licensing procedures and quality controls.[23]

Nevertheless, unfree competition, or maybe a slump in trade, significantly affected the fortunes of the cordiners. By the later 1650s they were the middling group of Elgin taxpayers, whereas they had figured much closer to the top on the maintenance rolls of 1646 and 1652. The cordiners were not, however, without influence in the burgh. They were one of only three crafts represented on the council in the period, albeit by only one member, for one year – that following the death of many councillors at the battle of Pinkie in 1547. They also managed in 1658 either to secure or to confirm the right to sell their boots, shoes and barked hides within Scotland 'als freelie as the merchands' by agreement of the council.[24] It would seem that the demand for their manufactures

20 Withrington and Grant, *Statistical Account*, xvi, 598.
21 MRO, EBCB, ii, 55, 67, 150, 155, 373, 819; ETC, i, 247–9.
22 MRO, EBCB, i, 228; ii, 16.
23 MRO, EBCB, ii, 132; ETC, i, 229–30.
24 MRO, ETC, i, 247–9; A37/6/3.

gave the cordiners, like the skinners, sufficient economic muscle to obtain commercial privileges, even if it did not make them wealthy.

After the leather workers, the largest group of tradesmen were those engaged in the cloth industries, who between them accounted for 27.7% of the craft population. Like the leather workers, cloth workers benefited from a rich source of local supply – in their case, wool. The most influential of the cloth workers was the relatively small group of litsters. Only twenty-eight are known of over the entire period, but their influence was disproportionately large. Litsters were one of only three crafts to be represented on the council and they also provided the second highest number of craft elders on the kirk session. The reason for their status and influence in early modern Elgin is not entirely clear, though elsewhere, even in the thirteenth century, the expensive products with which dyers worked, and their specialised skills, ensured that litsters were men of wealth and influence. By the early modern period they held a position of importance not only in Elgin, but also among the crafts of Aberdeen, Dundee and Perth.[25] Their wealth presumably reflected a strong demand for their expensive products, and by the 1640s the litsters of Elgin were by far the richest craftsmen recorded on the maintenance rolls. Their average tax payments exceeded those not only of all the other crafts but also of many merchants. Indeed one litster, William Robertson, figured alongside local landowners as one of the town's top ten taxpayers.[26]

The majority of other cloth workers were either tailors or weavers who each accounted for around 7% of the labour force. Both were considerably less wealthy than the litsters, figuring only in the middling group of taxpayers. As a consequence they were probably less influential. Little is known about either group, though the weavers apparently encountered considerable unfree competition in the latter part of the period, mainly from men working in the cathedral college, which was technically outwith the burgh's jurisdiction. Much locally produced cloth would have been sent for fulling to the walkmill of Linkwood, which was advantageously located for the college weavers. The burgh weavers petitioned the council at least twice in the 1660s alone for greater powers to counteract this competition, but to no avail.[27]

The food traders constituted the next largest group of Elgin's craftsmen. Over 40% of these were fleshers who had a rich source of supply in the local herds – perhaps passing on some of the valuable hides to the skinners and cordiners for processing. The fleshers had their own market, the Schemill or Shambles, at which they were obliged to pay tolls called 'schemill maills'. These were so valuable to the burgh that when some fleshers were made burgesses it was on condition that they continued to pay these tolls.[28] The maltmen of the burgh formed a further sizeable group. Malt, used to make ale, began to figure

25 Duncan, *Kingdom*, 490–1; E. Bain, *Merchant and Craft Gilds: A History of the Incorporated Trades of Aberdeen* (Aberdeen, 1887), 116, 292–3; Lynch, 'Social and economic structure', 266, 272; M. Verschuur, 'Merchants and craftsmen in sixteenth-century Perth', in Lynch, *Early Modern Town*, 38.

26 See note 19 above.

27 MRO, A37/6/15; A37/6/20.

28 MRO, EBCB, ii, 419.

among the town's exports towards the end of the seventeenth century.[29] The fertile Laich of Moray again proved invaluable as a source of supply and helped to make the maltmen some of the burgh's wealthier craftsmen. By contrast, other food traders – brewers and bakers – were among Elgin's poorest inhabitants. Some were stallangers – small traders who did not possess burgess status but who paid a fee for the privilege of trading at urban markets – but much brewing and baking was carried out domestically, on a part time basis, and rarely features in official records. A large proportion of brewers and bakers moreover were women: they do not appear in the occupational survey in *Table 3*, so their numbers, while uncertain, would be greater than indicated there. Nevertheless, in later years the vast majority of brewers and bakers mentioned in the town's records were women. Many too were stallangers – small traders who did not possess burgess status, but who paid a fee for the privilege of trading at urban markets.

Aside from the food trades and the leather- and cloth-based industries, there were few crafts of any size in early modern Elgin. The town's metal workers seem mainly to have served basic daily needs. Most were the smiths. Theirs was perhaps not such skilled work as that undertaken by some other craftsmen, though it was still a sufficiently lucrative occupation for some smiths to figure among the middling group of taxpayers in the 1640s and 1650s. Most of their fellow metal workers were similarly placed – even the goldsmiths. They were frequently to be found working with base metals, making poor tokens in 1601 and 1620, as well as mending the town knok (clock) in 1610 and making the burgh seal in 1615.[30] But, while elsewhere goldsmiths enjoyed a position of some importance, in Elgin they were no more than moderately wealthy. Indeed, no new goldsmiths appear in the town's records after the 1600s and most of the burgh's inhabitants were probably content to look further afield to purchase fine metalwork.

Besides the goldsmiths, other metalworking specialists in Elgin included armourers, cutlers and gunsmiths, whose skills were highly prized beyond as well as within the town, as well as tinkers, pewterers and a lorimer. Each trade makes only rare appearances in the records. In the timber and construction trades, only the wrights, masons and coopers appear consistently. Others, such as thatchers, glasswrights, slaters, turners and cart makers, are only occasionally referred to. It is readily understandable why coopers feature so consistently, since barrels were used for storing and transporting foodstuffs, as well as for maturing ale and *aqua vitae*: they can rarely have been short of work.

The opportunities for construction workers were enhanced by several major building projects undertaken in Elgin during the period. A new tolbooth and knok house was begun in 1601 (even though the previous building had been unserviceable since about 1580) and completed around 1612. Meanwhile, the first stone bridge over the River Lossie was built in 1630, paid for by burgh

29 E.g. MRO, EBCB, ii, 267, 351, 414, 476, 846.

30 Lynch, 'Social and economic structure', 277; Veerschuur, 'Merchants and craftsmen', 38; MRO, Elgin Kirk Session records [hereafter EKS], ii, 143, 147; iii, 297; Elgin Burgh Accounts [hereafter EB.Accts], 251, 329.

Plate 2 Charter of Uhtred and Gunnilda of Galloway to Holyrood Abbey. By permission of the Earl of Dalhousie

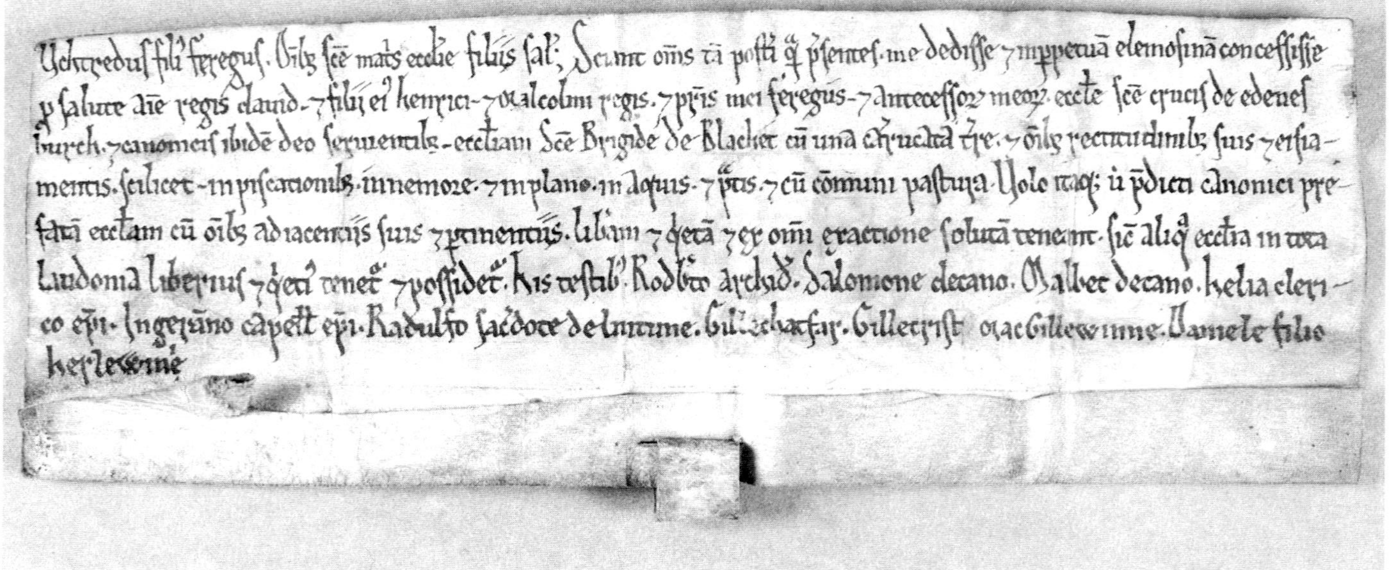

Plate 3 Charter of Uhtred of Galloway to Holyrood Abbey. By permission of the Keeper of the Records of Scotland

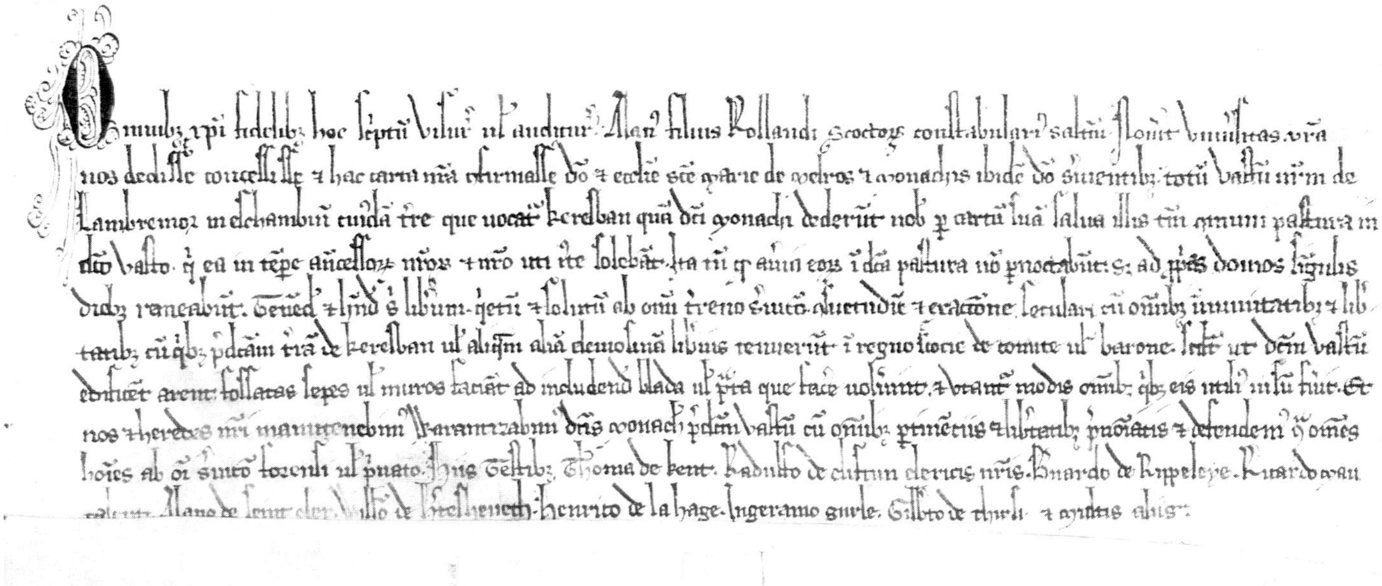

Plate 4 Charter of Alan Galloway to Melrose Abbey. By permission of the Duke of Buccleuch

Plate 5 A view of Kirkcaldy from the air. By permission of the Royal Commission on the Ancient and Historical Monuments of Scotland

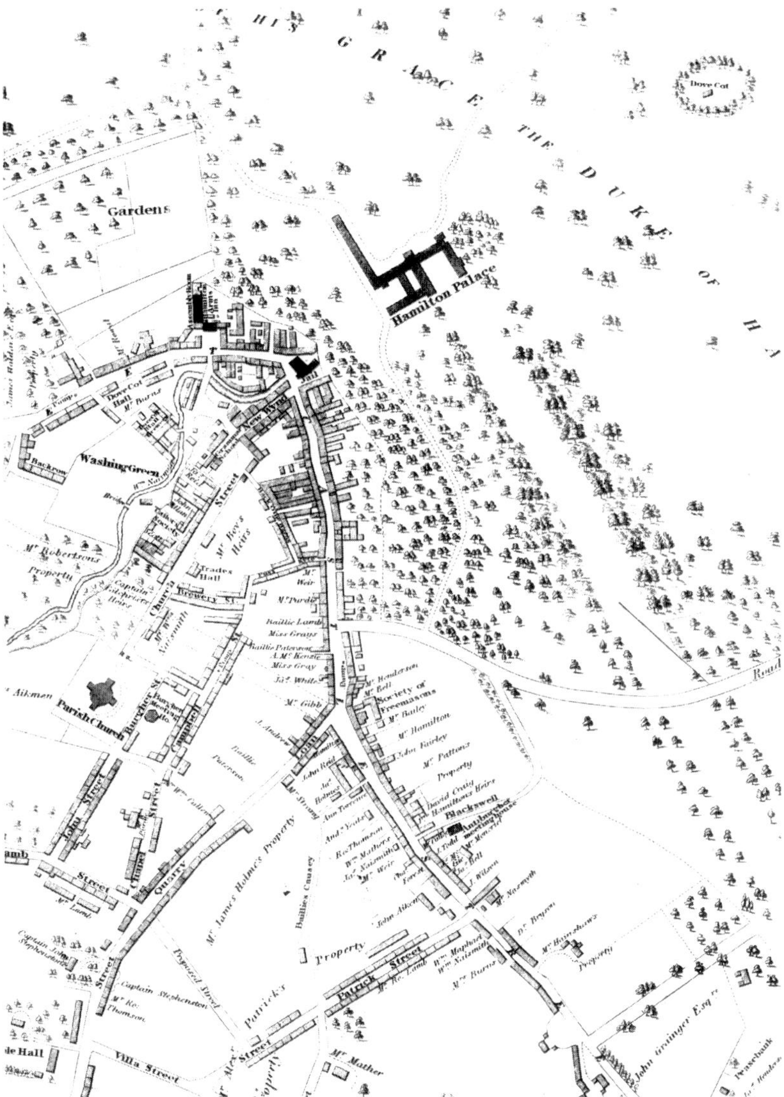


Plate 6 John Wood's plan of Hamilton. By permission of the Trustees of The National Library of Scotland

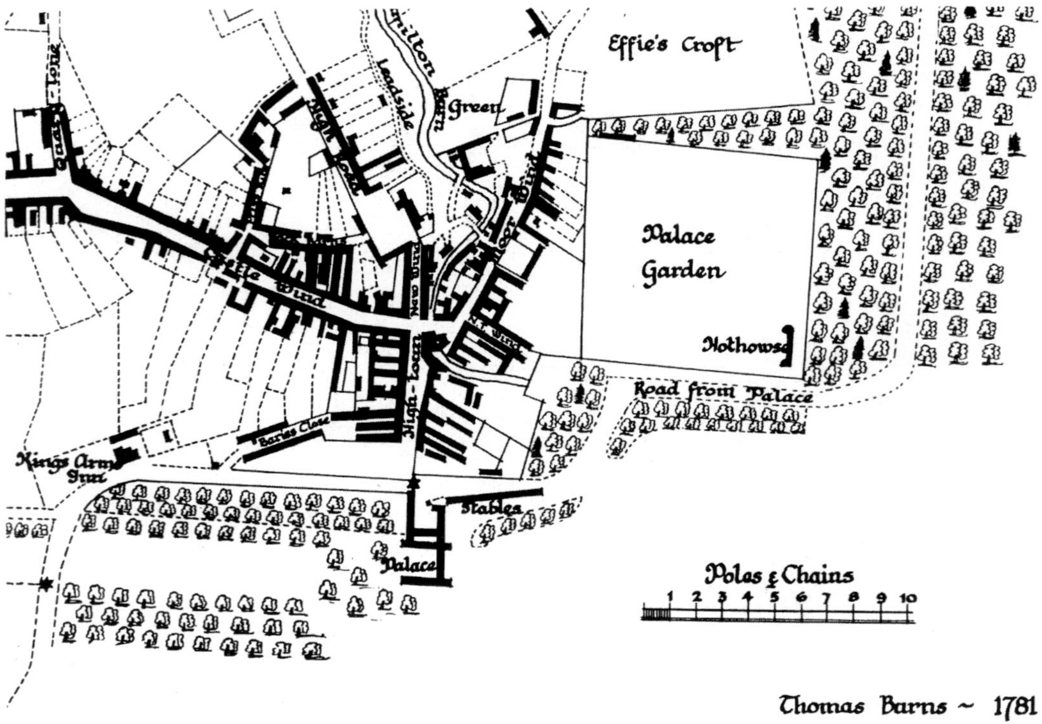


Plate 7 Thomas Barn's plan of Hamilton. By permission of Hamilton District Library

Plate 8 Slezer's engraving of Dunfermline. Private collection

Plate 9 A nineteenth-century view of Kirkcaldy from the north. By permission of Kirkcaldy Art Gallery

stent.[31] The bridge still stands, as does The Tower, a fine town house which was also constructed at around this time. In addition, a new song school was built in 1676 and a new grammar school in 1694.[32] There was abundant local stone and the skills employed in building and maintaining the Cathedral must have survived to some extent. Yet, despite the demand for their skills, construction workers were not among the wealthiest or most influential craftsmen. However, it is perhaps significant that in 1660 the deacon of the wrights, Alexander Russell, was influential enough amongst his own kind to lead the craftsmen in revolt.[33]

It is evident, then, that there was a craft hierarchy – from the skinners, glovers and litsters at the top to the baxters and brewers at the bottom. The most successful craftsmen were those who used local resources and/or catered for specialist needs, and who either found a market outside the burgh for their manufactures or a wealthy market within. But how did the craft wealth relate to that of other sectors of urban society? The maintenance rolls, available for the period 1646–58, suggest that the average Elgin merchant was wealthier than the average craftsman – despite the town's unfavourable geographical position for trading purposes.[34] Although merchants made up only 30–33% of the working population on the tax rolls, they paid 42–47% of the tax. On the other hand, the crafts, who accounted for 57–59% of the working population, paid a similar share of 43–47%. These average figures do not reveal the whole picture, for although merchants were among the most numerous of the higher taxpayers (discounting the landowners), many of the individual craft groups paid amounts more than, or similar to, those paid by the merchant group. In these tax rolls the average payments by merchants were always lower than those made by litsters, and by glovers and saddlers. Sometimes skinners and maltmen paid only marginally less. The position of the merchants, moreover, was if anything more favourable by the time of these tax rolls than earlier in the period as there seems to have been a local upturn in trade at that time.[35] Meanwhile, the average of payments made by litsters, and occasionally by some other craftsmen too, also exceeded those made by notaries who formed possibly the most influential group in the burgh.

While elsewhere it was not unusual for some craftsmen to attain as much wealth as some merchants, it was perhaps unusual for so many of Elgin's craftsmen to have attained such a degree of affluence.[36] Although trade was important to Elgin, as the number of craftsmen producing for export seems to attest, it is probably Elgin's relatively small volume of overseas trade which explains the comparative parity of wealth between the merchant and (certain) craft communities.[37] Indeed, the similarity of income between the two groups

31 MRO, EB.Accts, 171–2, 176–8, 180, 185–6, 194, 198, 203, 207, 222, 229, 242, 251–2, 255, 265, 267; A37/2/10.

32 *Elgin Recs.*, i, 406, 408.

33 MRO, A37/6/14.

34 As note 19 above.

35 Thomas, 'Thesis', 35.

36 E.g. Lynch, *Edinburgh and the Reformation*, 52–3. Perth, for which see Verschuur, 'Merchants and craftsmen', 38, was an exception.

37 For further details, see Thomas, 'Thesis', 39–52.

may also explain why Elgin's craftsmen and merchants did not form distinct and separate social units. There was considerable intermarriage between the two groups. The sons and daughters of even the most notable merchants frequently married into craft families, and not just those which constituted the craft aristocracy. For example, Isabel Hardie, the daughter of the merchant Robert, married Alexander Innes, a skinner burgess, in 1644; the early seventeenth-century merchant James Douglas was the second husband of Grisell Urvell, a flesher's daughter; and William Robertson, a skinner, married Bessie Leslie, whose father Alexander was a merchant.[38] There was, however, less intermarriage between the craft and notarial families – the latter preferred to mix with the landowning classes rather than with other members of the urban community. Social interaction was facilitated by the absence of distinctive, occupation-based residential areas. A voluntary stent of 1630 and the maintenance rolls of the 1640s and 1650s demonstrate that craftsmen were living in all quarters of the town, though there were fewer in the affluent south-west.[39] But there is evidence of children from craft families attending the local school, and they may well have walked there with their neighbours from merchant families. Indeed the extent of adult literacy amongst the crafts by the seventeenth century was noteworthy.

While it seems likely that there were no clear socio-economic barriers between the crafts and the rest of the urban community, social interaction did not extend to politics. A total of 154 men are known to have served on the burgh council during the period examined and the occupations of ninety-nine of these are known. Forty-six were merchants, twenty-one were notaries, twelve were landowners, fourteen were craftsmen and six were clerics.[40] The craftsmen were all drawn from the upper echelons of the craft hierarchy: there were nine skinners, four litsters and one cordiner. Most served in the period before 1600, only five doing so thereafter and none, so far as is known, during the 1610s. Two of the three craft councillors who served after the merchant gild emerged in 1643 were known as merchants and skinners: they may have renounced their craft on joining the gild, to facilitate their election. While some craftsmen may be concealed among those councillors of unknown occupation, it is clear that the crafts were always under-represented on the council, and especially so after 1600. This weakening of the craft position coincided with a strengthening of mercantile interests on the council.

The diminution of craft influence is confirmed by a more detailed examination of council service. On average, merchant councillors served around nine years, notaries sixteen years, landowners around twelve, but craft councillors served an average of only seven years, with only four serving for ten years or more. Whilst all the notaries, forty-one (89%) of the merchants, and ten (84%) of the landowners on the council held high civic office, only eight (57%) of the craft councillors did so, most serving as bailies. Merchants, however, provided two

38 MRO, EKS, vi, 194; iii, 384; v, 369.

39 MRO, A37/2/10; see also note 19 above.

40 For a detailed examination of Elgin's notaries, see J. E. Thomas, 'Elgin notaries in burgh society and government, 1540–1660', *Northern Scotland*, xiii (1993), 23–30.

provosts in the period, notaries three, and landowners eight. There were no craft provosts. But while only a few craftsmen gained admittance to the political community of the burgh, perhaps only a minority sought office. Many might not have welcomed the responsibilities of office, and there is no evidence that craftsmen were dissatisfied with the situation.

Council membership was broadly reflected in kirk session membership. Details of this are available from 1585: of 157 elders, the occupations of 116 are known. Almost half (fifty-seven) were merchants, and mercantile domination was particularly marked from the 1610s. Twenty-nine, by comparison, were craftsmen – though eight of these were designated as skinner merchant, pewterer merchant, etc., and these may well have been craftsmen who had been accepted into the merchant gild. Of the rest, twenty-one were notaries and nine were landowners. Again skinners and litsters dominated craft representation on the session, with fourteen skinners (including five designated skinner merchant) and seven litsters. Apart from two smiths, other groups provided just one representative – a miller, a saddler, an armourer, a tailor merchant, a cordiner merchant and a pewterer merchant. As on the council, most of the craft elders served for relatively short periods. Just over half (52%) served for five years or more, compared with two-thirds of merchants and 57% of notaries. Although more craftsmen than notaries served as elders, the proportion of notaries on the session each year was greater because each notary served for a longer period. It was quite unusual for the session to boast more than one craftsman at any one time.

If the crafts played little part in the political or religious government of Elgin, what of their self-government? Even though they were not formally incorporated until the mid-seventeenth century, the crafts appear to have maintained a limited organisational existence for some time. Before the Reformation many craft groups collectively patronised altars in the parish church of St Giles. There were craft deacons too in the 1540s and 1550s, though they were apparently illegal by 1570.[41] In May of that year five craftsmen – a cordiner, a flesher, a smith, a tailor and a skinner, two of whom were non-burgesses – were censured by the burgh court for accepting the office of deaconry. They were accused of acting contrary to the Acts of Parliament, but it is likely that the court was responding to the craft revolt which had taken place on Trinity Sunday in 1570.[42] The nature of this revolt remains obscure, though the appointment of deacons perhaps lay at its heart. Whatever lay behind the revolt, the rebel deacons were punished severely, through confiscation of their goods, imprisonment and loss of burgess-ship.

After 1560 there is no indication of craft organisation in Elgin, except of an informal nature, until incorporation. A decree of June 1619 apparently regulated the crafts, at least in relation to their respective precedence at wappenshaws, though unfortunately it no longer survives.[43] We know too of a skinners' pinsell, or banner, mentioned in 1640, and that in 1641 the skinners gained permission to build their own desk in the parish church: they, at least, clearly

41 MRO, EBCB, i, 57, 202, 293.
42 MRO, EBCB, ii, 4.
43 MRO, A3/659/1.

acted as a distinct body, however loosely organised.[44] But the lack of formal organisation meant that even matters such as apprenticeships, which surely would have been regulated by craft bodies had they existed, were instead dealt with by the burgh court.[45]

The first step towards the establishment of formal craft organisations came in the 1650s – at around the same time as the merchant gild was formalising its powers.[46] In May 1652 the crafts delivered certain demands for consideration to the provost, a bailie, the dean of gild and two councillors.[47] The nature of these demands remains unclear, but five years later the cordiners complained again about unfree competition, and the council agreed to their request that two or three cordiners be allowed to visit the shoe market with the dean of gild to check the standard of manufactures on sale.[48] The final step towards incorporation came in July 1657 when members of twelve crafts drew up a band pledging to ask for liberties which craftsmen elsewhere enjoyed, such as the right to appoint deacons.[49] It was in direct response to this that a Condescendence was drawn up between the crafts and the council in October 1657.[50] The burgh of Perth was apparently consulted in the drafting of this document and its laws were used as a framework for the agreement reached in Elgin.[51] Briefly, this permitted each craft with seven or more practising burgesses the right to appoint a deacon. The deacons were to be chosen annually by the magistrates from a leet of two or three submitted by the craft. Each deacon was to be assisted by six craft councillors, and one deacon was chosen annually as deacon convener by the magistrates and council. The duties of deacons in regulating their members were also laid down. These were exciting new privileges for the crafts, even though the council still retained a large degree of control over their affairs.

In the event, seven craft bodies emerged: the Hammermen, the Glovers, the Tailors, the Cordiners, the Weavers, the Fleshers and the Wrights and Masons. Neither the skinners (despite their sizeable number and prominent role in the band of 1657) nor the litsters were incorporated, though the skinners may have been included amongst the Hammermen or Cordiners, and the litsters may have joined the Weavers, as they did in Aberdeen.[52] Alternatively, the litsters may have remained unincorporated as they did in Dundee and Perth.[53] Meanwhile, it appears that those craftsmen who were too few in number to merit a deacon, or those who were too poor to acquire burgess-ship, remained under the direct control of the magistrates, as others had before incorporation.[54]

44 MRO, ETC, i, 56; EKS, vi, 67.
45 MRO, EBCB, ii, 725, 942.
46 Thomas, 'Thesis', 49–51.
47 MRO, ETC, i, 177, 179.
48 MRO, ETC, i, 229–30.
49 MRO, A37/6/1.
50 MRO, A37/6/2; ETC, i, 235–7.
51 W. E. Watson, 'The convenery of the six incorporated trades of Elgin' (Elgin Library, unpublished typescript, n.d.).
52 E.g. Bain, *Merchant and Craft Gilds*, 194, 197, 292.
53 M. Lynch, 'Introduction: Scottish towns 1500–1700', in Lynch, *Early Modern Town*, 11; Veerschuur, 'Merchants and craftsmen', 38.
54 MRO, ETC, i, 258.

Despite incorporation, one particularly vexed issue remained unresolved: the demarcation line between craft and merchant activity. It was clarified in February 1658.[55] The agreement reached defined in detail the appropriate activities of saddlers, skinners, smiths, metal workers, cordiners, weavers and fleshers *vis-à-vis* merchants. The position of the cordiners was apparently settled on the basis of precedents established in Perth, Dundee and Aberdeen. It was dealt with in great detail, as was that of the skinners, suggesting that boundaries between the crafts and the merchants in the leather trades had been particularly hazy.[56]

Nevertheless, despite the Condescendence of 1657 and the agreement of 1658, the craftsmen's newly won privileges proved short-lived. Their status was clearly under threat by April 1660 when several crafts formed a band to protect the 'fredome and libertie of deackonrie within our bruch of Elgin'.[57] In May of that year, an incomplete council document tells of the craft revolt, referred to above, led by Alexander Russell, deacon of the wrights, which had led to the appearance of a 'mutinous band' and a bloody disturbance.[58] Although several craftsmen pleaded that they had been coerced into joining the disturbance, the crafts suffered a wholesale loss of privileges.[59] During May and June 1660 individual craftsmen came before the council and 'willinglie laid doune thair deaconrie', and a glover, Archibald Bonyman, was imprisoned until he produced the copy of the indenture and Condescendence between the crafts and the magistrates which he had left at Perth.[60] The advice of the Perth craftsmen had clearly been sought directly.

In the aftermath of the revolt and the suppression of the crafts, the skinners and weavers both complained of the hardship they were suffering as a result of losing the right to regulate work.[61] Several more pleas were made in 1667–8, in joint supplications by all the crafts, for overseers and/or deacons to check and standardise work and to regulate unfree competition which, if the complaints are credible, was increasing. These requests fell on deaf ears, even though the craftsmen had promised to maintain their own poor and not to threaten the power of the gildry in return for the restoration of their privileges.[62] Only in 1675 did the council once again permit the crafts to have their deacons along with a deacon convener, who henceforth was granted a seat on the council, in the hope that he would improve the understanding between the crafts and the council and achieve the 'quiet and peace of the people'.[63] But it was not until September 1700 that the terms of the 1657 agreement were restored in full.

Formal craft organisation came relatively late to Elgin, and even then it was granted reluctantly. Yet the relative lateness of the original craft incorporations,

55 MRO, ETC, i, 247–9; A37/6/3.

56 Elsewhere, especially in the 15th century, disputes between craftsmen and merchants frequently concerned hides: Lynch, 'Social and economic structure', 264.

57 MRO, A37/6/11–13.

58 MRO, A/37/6/14; and see above, page 151.

59 MRO, ETC, ii, 3–6, 10; A3/660/1; A37/6/18–19.

60 MRO, ETC, ii, 3–6; A37/6/16.

61 MRO, A37/6/15, 17, 20.

62 MRO, A37/6/21–3.

63 *Elgin Recs.*, i, 320–1.

in 1657, is less surprising when it is remembered that Elgin's merchants also had no formal organisation until 1643. That these organisations developed at all was partly a consequence of the increasing awareness of structures in other towns, to which both craftsmen and merchants periodically made reference.[64] More immediately occupational organisations were perhaps also a result of growing merchant resentments towards some notably affluent craftsmen and growing craft fearfulness of unfree competition. Yet, despite their strength of numbers, the real power of the crafts in Elgin remained minimal. Although the wealthier craftsmen mixed and married with the merchant families, and their children probably sat together at school, most craftsmen would still have been regarded as social inferiors by their merchant neighbours. While there was craft representation on the council and kirk session, this was restricted to a few individuals, and it declined over the period. Although the contribution of the crafts to the urban economy was substantial – occupationally Elgin was a craft town – the crafts were excluded from real power, and denied even the right to supervise the quality of their own production.

[64] MRO, ETC, i, 102; A37/6/1, 11.

# 12

# Francis Stewart, Fifth Earl Bothwell, and James VI: Perception Politics[1]

*Robin Macpherson*

James Hepburn, fourth Earl Bothwell and third husband of Mary, Queen of Scots, died on 14 April 1578. He ended his colourful life in a Danish dungeon, arguably insane.[2] The earldom was inherited by Hepburn's nephew, Francis Stewart.[3] Many historians have questioned Stewart's sanity too, suggesting that he was 'a little mad', 'of schizophrenic personality', and 'verging to the edge of insanity'.[4] He was not. Rather he has been the victim of the same historians' disease which, in a different way, has afflicted the reputation of his cousin, James VI. By 'reading history backwards' historians have inaccurately superimposed the lacklustre characteristics displayed by James in later life upon a man who had displayed considerable political energy and shrewdness in his youth.[5] Similarly, Francis Stewart's inconsistent actions in 1594 – when he was desperately trying to resurrect a flagging political career – too often are regarded as typifying a complex public career which stretched from the summer of 1582 (when Stewart returned to Scotland from continental study) until 1595 (when he left Scotland for voluntary exile in France). The depiction of Stewart as a desperate, broken man – an image which latterly he cultivated himself[6] – is too simplistic as an assessment of his whole career. This depiction also serves to perpetuate the reputation of James as a king who represented the virtues of justice, consistency and fairness. In reality James was rarely consistent or fair in his dealings with Francis Stewart.

James VI has always proved a difficult character to understand. On balance, William Ferguson may have come closest to the true persona of the monarch when he wrote that James was 'an enigma: learned, opinionated, vulgar and uncouth, he was susceptible to flattery; weak, and conscious of his weakness, he strove to be masterful but merely succeeded in being capricious.'[7] These

1 My work on Francis Stewart started with my University of Aberdeen MA dissertation, completed under the guidance of Grant Simpson in 1992.

2 Hepburn was already considered dead by this time: *RSS*, vii, 1113; *Dictionary of National Biography* (Oxford, 1917), ix, 592. For fuller details of Hepburn's life, see F. Schiern, *James Hepburn, Earl of Bothwell* (Edinburgh, 1880); and R. Gore-Brown, *Lord Bothwell* (London, 1937).

3 For more in-depth discussion, see R. Macpherson, 'Francis Stewart, 5th Earl Bothwell, *c.*1562–1612: Lordship and Politics in Jacobean Scotland' (University of Edinburgh, unpublished PhD thesis, 1998).

4 W. McElwee, *The Wisest Fool in Christendom* (London, 1958), 72; C. J. Tabraham, *Crichton Castle* (Edinburgh, 1987), 23; J. and J. Keay, *Collins Encyclopedia of Scotland* (London, 1994), 901.

5 M. Lee, Jr, *Great Britain's Solomon* (Illinois, 1990), 129.

6 In September 1594, in a letter to David Black, minister in St Andrews, Stewart described his 'endless misery': 'My Friends hanged, slain or beggared; our Lands distributed and possessed by our enemys ... we know not where to goe, not one hour suretie of our Lives from hostility might be saved yet have no monies to fill our emptie bellies, yea within a few days ... we will scarcely have to cover our shamefullness.' Quoted in David Calderwood, *The History of the Kirk of Scotland*, ed. T. Thomson (Wodrow Soc., 1842–9), viii, 289.

7 W. Ferguson, *Scotland's Relations with England* (Edinburgh, 1977), 100.

ambiguities did not, however, prevent James from fulfilling the role traditionally expected of a Scottish monarch. Throughout his reign he tried to promote royal control and political stability in the peripheral regions of his kingdom. He sought to pacify the Borders and so to lessen the prospect of embarrassing confrontation with England's March wardens; and he aimed to subdue and civilise the West Highlands, first by threatening military invasions of the region and then by encouraging Lowland migration and plantation. On one occasion, though ultimately the scheme came to nothing, he even suggested that Francis Stewart exchange his lands in Liddesdale for the Isle of Lewis.[8] James also tried to curb the influence of recalcitrant nobles by attempting to settle their feuds and accommodate their differences, most noticeably during the 'Love Feast' of 15 May 1587.[9] To achieve all this James used the full panoply of the law. But when legal measures proved inadequate, he was prepared to govern his kingdom by threat, bribe, and ultimatum.[10]

The fifth Earl Bothwell's character is no easier to discern than is that of the king. One of the earl's contemporaries, the English emissary Thomas Fowler, noted that 'there is more wickedness, more valour and more good parts in him than in any three of the other noblemen'.[11] Although a cultured and highly intelligent man, Bothwell suffered periodically from impatience and political naïveté. By temperament he too was a traditionalist, though his traditionalism was different from the king's. The earl sought political prominence, patronage, influence and respect. These he considered his traditional noble rights, and he sought to acquire them by almost any means possible (including, when the situation allowed, by dominating the king's person).

These rival perceptions of ancient rights – royal and noble – were scarcely compatible, and, when strongly and persistently advocated in the tight-knit political community of sixteenth-century Scotland, tensions developed. Both the king and his chief councillor, John Maitland of Thirlestane, were astute judges of character. They saw advantage in using Stewart's status and skills, on occasion, for delicate political tasks, but they also recognised the limitations of his character and abilities and were ready to exploit them for the benefit of the crown.

The relationship between James and Francis was grounded in their family ties and boyhood acquaintance, and was initially close. The erudite earl, educated at St Andrews, Angers, Paris, and perhaps in Italy too, made a strong impression on the young king, and at first this was to be to Stewart's significant political advantage.[12] On returning from the Continent in July 1582, he was immediately welcomed at court. James VI (aged sixteen) was attempting to establish himself as a powerful

[8] M. Lee, Jr, *John Maitland of Thirlestane and the Foundation of the Stewart Despotism in Scotland* (Princeton, 1959), 217.

[9] *The Historie and Life of King James the Sext*, ed. T. Thomson (Bannatyne Club, 1825), 229.

[10] D. Gregory, *The History of the Western Highlands and Isles of Scotland* (1836; Edinburgh, 1975), 263–70.

[11] *CSP Scot.*, ix, no. 563.

[12] For Stewart's studies, see *Calendar of the Laing Charters 854–1837*, ed. J. Anderson (Edinburgh, 1899), 934; J. Durkan, 'The French connection in the late sixteenth- and early seventeenth-centuries', in T. C. Smout, ed., *Scotland and Europe 1200–1850* (Edinburgh, 1986), 37; *Calendar of State Papers, Foreign 1582*, 74, 87, 136; and *RSS*, vii, 1575.

figure, and throughout the early 1580s there was a turbulent period of shifting influence and guarded motives. Stewart seems to have weathered this political storm well. Before the Ruthven coup of 23 August 1582, both the king and his then favourite Esmé Stewart, Duke of Lennox, recognised the potential of the earl and sought his support for their floundering administration.[13] Several rebel lords, however (among them members of Francis Stewart's wife's family, the Douglases), also recognised the opportunities afforded by making use of Francis as a more loyal, more Protestant and more controllable replacement for the king's pro-French, profligate, dubiously Protestant and dangerously intimate favourite.[14]

Whilst one of the pretexts for the Ruthven Raid may have been pecuniary – as Treasurer, John, fourth Lord Ruthven, was anxious to end the spiralling expenditure of the royal court – the coup of 1582 also had a strongly Protestant motif.[15] The Ruthven Raid occurred at a powerful time in the fledgling Protestant calendar. The fifteenth anniversary of the acceptance of the regency (after the deposition of Mary, Queen of Scots) by the noted Protestant champion, James Stewart, Earl of Moray, fell on 22 August. And 24 August was the anniversary, not only of the massacre of French Protestants on St Bartholomew's Day in 1572, but also of the act of the Reformation Parliament in 1560 which abrogated papal authority in Scotland.

Those planning the religiously cloaked insurrection of 1582 hoped for support from Bothwell's family. Francis Stewart's mother, Jean Hepburn, sister to the duke of Orkney, had married three times. Her first husband, and Francis's father, was John Stewart, Lord Darnley and commendator of Coldingham. Darnley was an illegitimate son of James V and court favourite of his half-sister Mary, but he played little role in the upbringing of his son, dying at Inverness in October 1563.[16] Darnley was, however, like his half-brother, the earl of Moray, a well-known Protestant from an early stage.[17] In 1566 Jean Hepburn married again, this time John Sinclair, Master of Caithness.[18] She bore him a son (George, fifth Earl of Caithness), a boy brought up and tutored by John, fourth Lord Ruthven.[19] Jean Hepburn's final marriage linked her to the most powerful family in Scotland, the Douglases. Although Archibald Douglas, brother of the laird of Whittingham, was not of the same political stature as Jean's previous husbands, he was nevertheless a significant influence on her son's upbringing.[20] Sometime after the exile of the duke of Orkney, following Queen Mary's

13 *CSP Scot.*, vi, nos. 162, 168, 195, 336, 405, 476; *CBP*, i, no. 158.

14 *CSP Scot.*, vi, nos. 627; ibid., vi, no. 155 (Sir George Carey to Lord Burghley, 5 Aug. 1582), a letter which conveys a confused picture of the events. Bothwell is a 'great friend to the Duke', yet has 'subscribed ... a bond ... against the Duke and Arran'. This perhaps indicates that Bothwell was, in fact, already playing a duplicitous role in affairs of state.

15 M. Lynch, 'A royal progress: court ritual and ceremony during the personal reign of James VI', in M. Lynch and J. Goodare, eds., *The Reign of James VI* (East Linton, 1999).

16 M. Dilworth, 'Coldingham Priory and the Reformation', *IR*, xxiii, 127.

17 P. Anderson, *Robert Stewart, Earl of Orkney* (Edinburgh, 1982), 42.

18 *Scots Peerage*, ii, 161.

19 Ibid., ii, 342.

20 Douglas was effectively an unofficial ambassador at the English court from July 1581. Despite indications that he intended to divorce his wife (*CBP*, i, no. 102), he and Bothwell remained in communication.

surrender at Carberry in June 1567, Francis was placed under the tutelage first of Regent Moray, then of James Douglas, the fourth earl of Morton. During the 1570s, with his tutor as regent of the kingdom, Francis Stewart began to play a more prominent role in public affairs.[21] His family and kinship links meant that by 1580 Stewart was deemed a suitable choice for 'calling home' in order to 'balance' his cousin's court.[22] It seems unlikely, however, that James VI summoned Stewart merely as a result of family affection: the long-awaited ratification of Bothwell's titles by the Privy Council and Parliament of November 1581 (whilst he was still abroad) re-emphasised his significance.[23]

The principal objective of the Ruthven Raid was to remove Esmé Stewart, Duke of Lennox from the king's company. Who better than Francis Stewart to offer as substitute for the king's favouritism? Francis was of royal blood, and thus entitled to a prominent position at court. His overseas education and experience also suggested that he was an eminently suitable character for such a position. Moreover, the disgruntled nobility could be forgiven for believing that, in sharp contrast to Esmé Stewart, Bothwell's political and religious credentials – guaranteed by his upbringing – were impeccable. Indeed, Stewart's actions immediately after his return to Scotland were aimed at confirming this view. Yet his expression of allegiance to the Protestant faith, followed by his rapid appearance at court, might hint that he was being cynically orchestrated by others.[24] It is still difficult to judge the motives behind these events from the scant evidence which survives, but, as Bothwell matured, it is clear that he was rarely a man in control of his own destiny. In 1582, not yet twenty, he was attempting to secure a prominent role which older and wiser heads appreciated would be of wider political benefit, but which could leave the earl dangerously exposed should things go wrong. Bothwell, unaware of the strength of the political undercurrents, gratefully accepted James's favour. He was prominent in the royal bedchamber in the three weeks prior to the Ruthven Raid, during the ten months of the 'Ruthven regime' which followed, and, perhaps surprisingly, within a month of the fall of that regime – when a more 'balanced' government was established.

Another illustration of the ambiguities in Bothwell's actions is afforded by his participation in a second palace coup – the Stirling raid of April 1584. Then, the same basic group of rebel lords who had supported the Ruthven coup (including the earls of Mar and Angus and the master of Glamis) failed in a second attempt to seize power. As they fled for England, they were aware that they retained many sympathisers in Scotland. Among them was Bothwell, even though he appeared loyal to the king and had raised 2,000 men to pursue the rebels.[25] The earl tried to construct an elaborate ruse to fool the king, to hide his

21 Grants to and from Stewart occurred regularly during the regencies of both Moray and Morton: *RMS*, iv, nos. 1905, 1966, 2652; *RSS*, vi, 97–8, 616, 1137, 1239, 2169, 2530, 2806; vii, 56, 1066, 1383, 1514, 1874, 1888, 1987.

22 *CBP*, i, no. 109.

23 *RPC*, iii, 371.

24 Calderwood, *History of the Kirk of Scotland*, iii, 364, 634; *CSP Scot.*, vi, no. 140.

25 *Historie of James the Sext*, 213; *CBP*, i, no. 215; R. Gordon, 'The Political Career of Francis Stewart, 5th Earl of Bothwell' (University of Aberdeen, unpublished PhD thesis, 1952), 244.

complicity with the rebels and to preserve his position of favour.[26] Whatever the full story, Bothwell proceeded to Stirling, whereupon he was ordered to return whence he had come and 'scale' his forces.[27] While this might be interpreted as a gesture of dismissal and rejection, it was in fact an attempt by the king to secure his Borders against English incursion in the aftermath of the revolt. The laird of Cessford received similar instructions, and some of Bothwell's horse were left behind and recognised as the 'chief strength with the king' in the crisis.[28] A fortnight later, the threat abated, Francis Stewart was back at court and still in favour.[29]

Any reinterpretation of Bothwell's career must also grapple with the earl's untrustworthy and abrasive character.[30] He resented those in the positions of power to which he aspired. In the early 1580s, James Stewart of Bothwellmuir, created earl of Arran in April 1581, was perhaps the most significant of the *arrivistes* of whom he was suspicious and resentful. Such resentment was problematic for a king ever more intent on reconciling his factious nobles following the botched coup of 1584. James strenuously sought to reconcile his Stewart kin, most notably the earls of Arran and Bothwell.[31] His attempts failed, for Arran's appointment as Lord Chancellor in May 1584 fuelled Bothwell's dissatisfaction. By July 1584, Bothwell had left court and renewed a previous request to leave the country.[32] He was, therefore, already estranged from the king, when, in October 1585, Mar, Angus and the master of Glamis attempted to gain political influence for the third time. The appearance of the rebels at Bothwell's southern residence in Kelso left the earl with a dilemma. Although ostensibly loyal to the king, loyalty had consistently failed to win him the recognition or the reward he coveted. Bothwell temporised but eventually marched north with the rebels against Arran, if not yet against the king.

Initially James remained unsure of the extent of Bothwell's disaffection. He forced the issue by instructing Bothwell to leave the rebels. Angus, however, ordered him to stay – and Bothwell was once again caught in the agony of indecision between compliance with his cousin or his brother-in-law.[33] Ultimately, upbringing, kinship and dislike of Arran meant more to the earl than loyalty to the crown and he remained with the rebels. Arran fled to the west and the king duly accepted the situation by returning the rebels to favour and admitting them on to his Privy Council – with the sole exception of Bothwell.[34] James felt bitter towards a favourite who had so publicly defied him.

Trust between earl and monarch was, however, slowly re-established between

26 Fraser, *Douglas*, i, 350.

27 *CBP*, i, no. 215.

28 Ibid., no. 217.

29 *CSP Scot.*, vii, no. 118.

30 *CBP*, i, no. 589, 'noman trustes hyme'; *CSP Scot.*, vii, nos. 304, 308; Lee, *Maitland of Thirlestane*, 79.

31 *CSP Scot.*, vii, no. 118.

32 Ibid., nos. 12, 18, 200.

33 Fraser, *Douglas*, ii, 356.

34 John Spottiswoode, *History of the Church of Scotland*, ed. M. Russell and M. Napier (Bannatyne Club, 1851), ii, 333.

1585 and 1589. Whilst never as close to James as before, Bothwell did steadily acquire greater responsibility and influence, though there were limits to his rehabilitation. James refused, for example, to appoint Bothwell captain of Edinburgh Castle – prompting another outburst of hot-headedness.[35] In the meantime, while attempting to strengthen his position at court, Bothwell was simultaneously seeking to establish a reputation for himself on the Border, where he was keeper of Liddesdale. Although he rarely complied with governmental wishes in this area, he was praised for his activities with respect to cross-border raiding, and on one occasion the earl of Angus complained bitterly that Bothwell received more respect in the south of the kingdom than he did as Lieutenant of the Marches.[36] During the later 1580s Bothwell was clearly not alone in trying to secure favour with the Scottish establishment. Following Arran's flight, James himself attempted to establish a more prominent and personal role in the running of his realm. This went alongside – and was sometimes interconnected with – the meteoric political rise of John Maitland of Thirlestane, whose character was similar to that of his king. He was calculating, intelligent and particularly mindful of the long-term implications of policy decisions. Bothwell considered Maitland a 'puddock stool of the night' in contrast to himself, a 'tall oak' of the ancient nobility: his resentment of the early 1580s towards Arran had now found a new and equally potent target.

The relationship between Bothwell and Maitland is as confusing and variable as that between the earl and the king. At times they seemed sufficiently close to plot together against fellow nobles; but on other occasions Bothwell had little hesitation in viewing Maitland as an adversary worthy of assassination.[37] In the mid-1580s the two men were locked in dispute over the rights and revenues pertaining to the priory of Coldingham, a long-running disagreement on a comparatively minor matter which reflected more deep-seated rivalries.[38] By 1587 Maitland had not only resolved most of these differences to his advantage, but he had also advanced spectacularly in royal favour. Although Bothwell had been the chief commissioner at the signing of the Anglo-Scottish peace treaty in July 1586, and one of the king's initial choices as ambassador to plead for his mother's life in December of that year, it was Maitland who was created Chancellor and Maitland whose views were seen to represent the wider sentiments of the Scottish nobility following Queen Mary's execution in February 1587.[39]

Whilst Francis Stewart would have preferred greater Scottish intervention over his aunt's execution, he caused little trouble beyond involving himself in the almost habitual, but localised, confrontations which characterised sixteenth-century cross-border society.[40] Though once a supporter of the English party, he had for some time been adopting a more neutral position in Anglo-Scottish

35 *CBP*, i, no. 388.

36 T. Rae, *The Administration of the Scottish Frontier* (Edinburgh, 1966), 245; *CBP*, i, no. 574.

37 Lee, *Maitland of Thirlestane*, 71; K. Brown, *Bloodfeud in Scotland* (Edinburgh, 1986), 128.

38 Dilworth, 'Coldingham and the Reformation', 128–31.

39 *The Warrender Papers*, ed. A. I. Cameron (SHS, 1931–2), i, 245; *CSP Scot.*, ix, nos. 160, 185, 227; Gordon, 'Political Career of Frances Stewart', 74.

40 *CBP*, i, nos. 493, 499, 501, 522.

relations.[41] It would be premature, however, to detect at this point either a pro-Spanish or a Catholic stance in his attitudes.[42] Indeed, Bothwell was appointed lieutenant of the army to counter the prospect of any Spanish invasion in August 1588.[43] In spite of this appointment, once the Spanish Armada had floundered off the coasts of Scotland and Ireland, Bothwell found himself once again politically detached from his monarch. If his political manoeuvring had hitherto been designed to acquire an important position in court politics, his involvement in the Brig o'Dee affair of April 1589 – a rebellion against James VI by those traditionally seen as having had Catholic sympathies – seems more like the work of an increasingly marginalised maverick. As the earls of Huntly, Montrose, Errol and Crawford raised their forces in the north, Bothwell did likewise in the south. His objective was to march on Edinburgh and capture Maitland, the man whom he perceived to be responsible for his marginalisation.[44]

The government's response suggests that it viewed Bothwell as a potent threat. His revolt was greeted with a sense of panic. James felt that the earl constituted a greater threat than Huntly, and Maitland rapidly made conciliatory gestures to Bothwell. Indeed, the extent of these was staggering: the Chancellor offered to demit office, to leave court and also to pay Bothwell 10,000 crowns, provided the earl did not join the northern lords in revolt.[45] Bothwell, the government perhaps correctly construed, was working to an agenda which was different from that of the northern lords. This worried his northern confederates too and, as it transpired, with good reason. While Bothwell waited for the northern lords to march south, his own planned assault on Edinburgh never materialised and his support drifted away.[46] He had persuaded the border lairds to back him through a mixture of anti-English and patriotic rhetoric, though it soon became apparent that in reality Bothwell's northern allies were pro-Spanish and pro-Catholic.[47] This was unacceptable to many of his border allies. The Brig o'Dee rebellion also demonstrates Bothwell's major weakness: ultimately he possessed neither a sufficiently broad base of political support, nor sufficient manpower to constitute the substantial threat which he at first seemed. Bothwell consistently negotiated as if from a position of strength which in reality he did not hold.

Only in the aftermath of the royalist success at Brig o' Dee did the Chancellor come to appreciate the extent of political discontent within James's realm. Like the king, he now considered it crucial to win noble support in order to bolster the regime. Maitland therefore sought anew to convince Bothwell to co-operate with the king. Given his embarrassing setback in the 1589 revolt, Bothwell had little option but to accept; and so, only weeks after the rebellion, he was working with other members of the nobility (principally the earl of Moray) in

41 Alexander Hay, *Estimate of the Scottish Nobility during the Minority of James the Sixth* (Grampian Club, 1873), 51; *CSP Scot*, ix, no. 164.

42 Hay, *Estimate of the Scottish Nobility*, 51.

43 *CBP*, i, no. 627.

44 *CSP Scot.*, x, no. 28.

45 *CBP*, i, no. 642.

46 *CSP Scot.*, x, no. 34.

47 Ibid., ix, no. 28.

ways beneficial to royal policy and contrary to the policies of Huntly and his confederates.[48] This timely reconciliation had been facilitated by Patrick, Master of Gray, a cunning schemer and a relative of Bothwell[49] – and it explains too the earl's appointment, six months later, as assistant governor of the realm once James and his chancellor left the country to bring home the king's prospective bride from Denmark.

Nevertheless, the underlying motives behind Bothwell's appointment remain contentious. It is conceivable that the appointment was orchestrated by Maitland, who – adopting the guise of a Scottish Machiavelli – bestowed on Bothwell not only high office, but also with enough rope to hang himself. Alternatively, the Danish expedition could have been a calculated manoeuvre by the king to remove Maitland – the focus of much baronial discontent – from the realm, thereby paving the way for a royal reconciliation with other magnates.[50] But both suggestions seem far-fetched. More probably Bothwell was chosen as assistant governor because he was the most suitable candidate for the post. Lacking immediate family, James placed his two closest heirs in positions of authority: the teenage duke of Lennox was made governor and Lord Hamilton became lieutenant of the Borders, responsible for the important matter of Anglo-Scottish relations.[51] By nominating Bothwell as assistant governor James, in effect, made his cousin a mediator between his two closest heirs.[52] Moreover, apart from his royal lineage, Bothwell possessed ties of kinship unmatched by any other noble.[53] Religiously too, he could appear to be an enthusiastic Protestant and he possessed sufficient personal wealth to bear the costs of governmental responsibility.[54] The rebellion of 1589 had even served to demonstrate that Bothwell possessed some degree of support in the eastern Borders – which he might enlist to quell dissent, should it arise while the king was abroad. And there was one further factor which may have influenced the king's decision: Bothwell's political experience. Although other members of the nobility were more mature, only the earl of Mar could rival Bothwell's recent attendance record in the Privy Council.[55] Mar, however, was a noted Anglophile who lacked military and financial backing and was considerably less popular than Bothwell.[56] In the event, whatever calculations lay behind Bothwell's appointment, it proved successful. Signs of discontent were infrequent while

48 Brown, *Bloodfeud in Scotland*, 149.

49 Both men were descended from Adam Hepburn of Dunsyre, father of Patrick, first earl of Bothwell: *Scots Peerage*, ii, 148–73; iv, 276–81.

50 C. Bingham, *James VI of Scotland* (London, 1979), 120.

51 *RPC*, iv, 423.

52 The only other descendant of James V (Robert Stewart, Earl of Orkney) was then in Orkney (Anderson, *Robert Stewart*, 118).

53 *Scots Peerage*, ii, 151–73.

54 Lee claims that Maitland tried to split the Protestants in Spanish pay from the Catholics in Spanish pay prior to going to Denmark: Lee, *Maitland of Thirlestane*, 168. This may account, in part, for the reconciliation with Bothwell. For Bothwell's 'great wealth through his wife', see Hay, *Estimate of the Scottish Nobility*, 34.

55 *RPC*, iv, sederunts, passim.

56 Hay, *Estimate of the Scottish Nobility*, 48–9; J. Elder, *Spanish Influences in Scottish History* (Glasgow, 1920), 135.

James was abroad, and those which did surface – such as the continued lawlessness of Clan Gregor – were ably dealt with by the governors.[57]

Nevertheless, while there was no breakdown in order while James was overseas, there is cause to believe that, consciously or otherwise, the underlying stability of the realm was undermined. Bothwell made no secret of his dealings with the northern earls; and his approach to the Spanish through the duke of Parma was widely known of in court circles. At the same time, a caucus of Stewart kin, potentially hostile to the king, drew ever more closely together.[58] On returning from Denmark, James could have been forgiven for believing that he faced the beginnings of a situation not fundamentally dissimilar to that encountered by his predecessor James I when he returned from English captivity in 1424 to find his kingdom dominated by Stewart relatives. Moreover, Bothwell's *laissez-faire* attitude to government may also have alarmed James. Faced with responsibility, and charged to remain close to Lennox, Bothwell had frequently absented himself from court: indeed, he is found in only three of the nineteen recorded Privy Council sederunts of the period.[59] The king and his cousin were certainly to quarrel over the legacy of the period, James expressing a particular distaste for Bothwell's overly close contacts with outlaws and excommunicants.[60] As tension between the two men again escalated, Bothwell retired to his estates and James, urged on by Maitland, imposed stricter rules on the procedures of his court.[61]

For a little over a year Bothwell remained in political limbo. Refused close contact with James and permission to travel abroad, he became more and more defiant of royal power.[62] However, it was not until 1591 that his downfall commenced. In April was implicated in the North Berwick witch trials for allegedly seeking the witches' opinion on whether James would survive his Danish voyage and whether the new queen would produce an heir.[63] In truth, it was probably immaterial whether Bothwell was innocent or guilty of these charges, for it was not solely this event which sealed his fate. In June 1591 the earl escaped from Edinburgh Castle, where he had been warded following the accusations, and headed for his estates. He had now defied the crown once too often. The events which followed are the stuff of comic legend. In spite of the government's attempts to apprehend him, the forfeited earl frequently rode to the gates of Edinburgh and verbally abused those within. Three times he entered the grounds of the royal palaces of Holyrood and Falkland and threatened the court with fire and sword.[64] On another occasion he gained admittance to the

57 *RPC*, iv, 453.

58 *CSP Scot.*, x, nos. 372, 391.

59 *RPC*, iv, 423–78.

60 *CSP Scot.*, x, no. 403.

61 Gordon, 'Political Career of Francis Stewart', 138–9.

62 *CSP Scot.*, x, nos. 104, 404. The height of this defiance was in January 1590/1 when Bothwell broke into the Edinburgh tolbooth and removed a prisoner while King James was working in the next room: W. C. Dickinson, *Scotland from the Earliest Times to 1603* (3rd edn, rev. A. A. M. Duncan, Oxford, 1977), 378).

63 E. J. Cowan, 'The darker vision of the Scottish Renaissance', in I. B. Cowan and D. Shaw, eds., *Renaissance and Reformation in Scotland* (Edinburgh, 1983), 125–41.

64 *CBP*, i, nos. 740, 753, 775, 865.

king's bedchamber and found the king in a state of undress.[65] Sword in hand, Bothwell fell to one knee, offering the blade to his monarch. He begged for pardon or, failing that, decapitation.[66] James opted for the less violent option, despite previous boasts that he would shoot the earl, even if he came crawling on his knees for mercy.[67]

The reconciliation proved short-lived. The government continued in its attempts to apprehend Bothwell, often with James in the vanguard. However, since both Elizabeth I of England and the Scottish Church found uses for this noble miscreant, and since a significant proportion of the nobility regarded the crown's attempts to detain Bothwell as the thin end of an anti-noble wedge, the actions proved unsuccessful.[68] As a consequence the government was forced to change tack. Bothwell's allies were welcomed back into the political fold and some were even offered governmental office and new lands - though ministers of the Kirk who continued to speak out against the king were deprived of their livings.[69] Meanwhile, the government initiated an active correspondence both with Elizabeth and with Kirk ministers, pleading with them to see sense.[70] It was a war of attrition, and it paid off. After four years Bothwell left his border heartland for Caithness, Orkney and the Continent, retracing almost exactly his uncle's route to exile of a quarter of a century earlier.

In his final years of continental exile Bothwell was evicted from France and, in Spain, hunted by the Inquisition for his profligate lifestyle and uncivilised behaviour.[71] He persistently planned invasions of Scotland - from Spain, Ireland and the Low Countries - both in the cause of Catholicism to which he had converted, and for baser reasons. It was not to be. In 1612 he died a pauper in Naples, having spent his last years performing magical tricks and illusions.[72] It was a peculiarly apt demise for a man often perceived as the greatest threat to order in Jacobean Scotland, but whose character deficiencies ensured that he was never really a substantive threat at all.

65 Cowan, 'Darker vision', 133.
66 Calderwood, *History of the Kirk of Scotland*, v, 256–7; *CBP*, i, no. 872.
67 *CSP Scot.*, xi, no. 94.
68 *RPC*, v, 280.
69 Lee, *Maitland of Thirlestane*, 276, 280; George Ridpath, *Border History of England and Scotland* (1776; Edinburgh, 1979), 471.
70 For an example, see *Letters of James VI and I*, ed. G.P.V. Akrigg (Berkeley, 1984), 120.
71 Elder, *Spanish Influences*, 280, 313.
72 *Scots Peerage*, ii, 171.

# 13

# The Witches, the Devil and the King

*Jenny Wormald*

Burns's great poem *Tam O'Shanter* contains a marvellous description of a coven: the frenzied dancing in the ruined kirk, the corpses in the opened coffins and the dead infants, the devil – the 'Machiavellian' Old Nick – presiding over the fun with fiendish delight. Witchcraft and the compact with Satan were no longer legally recognised or officially believed in when this late eighteenth-century Ayrshire poet was writing; but clearly their distinctive features were still common knowledge. The only thing missing is the traditional stereotype of the witch, the old, ugly, impoverished, perhaps senile woman. One does not normally think of a witch as Burns's Cutty Sark, an attractive young lassie in a mini-skirt. But Burns had a point. The witch who revealed the existence of one of the most famous covens in the history of witchcraft, the coven at North Berwick which featured so largely in the first great witch persecution in Scotland, in 1590–1, was a young servant girl called Geillis Duncan who provided the music for the dancing, playing, as she leapt and skirled, on a Jew's harp. Here is a second account of a coven:

> The devill as God's Ape, counterfeites in his servantes this service & forme of adoration, that God prescribed and made his servants to practise. For as the servants of GOD, publicklie uses to conveene for serving of him, so makes he them in great numbers to conveene (though publickly they dare not) for his service. As none conveenes to the adoration and worshipping of God, except they be marked with his seale, the Sacrament of Baptisme: So none serves Satan, and conveenes to the adoring of him, that are not marked with that marke ... As the Minister sent by GOD, teacheth plainely at the time of their publick conventions, how to serve him in spirit & truth: so that uncleane spirite, in his owne persone teacheth his Disciples, at the time of their conveening, how to worke all kinde of mischiefe: And craves compt of all their horrible and detestable proceedinges passed, for advancement of his service. Yea, that he may the more viuelie counterfeit and scorne God, he oft times makes his slaves to conveene in these verrie places, which are destinat and ordeined for the conveening of the servantes of God (I meane by Churches).[1]

It sounds infinitely less enjoyable. But it was written by a man who was certainly in a position to know all about witches and their doings: James VI, king, scholar and, as Satan's 'greatest enemie in the world' as the devil himself described him, intended victim of a monstrous international diabolic plot. Understandably, he took the subject seriously.

1 James VI, *Daemonologie*, in *Minor Prose Works of King James VI and I*, ed. J. Craigie with A. Law (Scottish Text Soc., 1982), 25.

The diabolic plot was of course a *cause célèbre* – and Scotland was among the major witch-persecuting societies of early modern Europe. But what especially marks out the Scottish persecution is that supposedly it all began with a king. So while the general problems of identifying the causes of witch-hunting remain, and the debate will continue about whether they were inspired by the local communities in which the witches were operating or provoked by authority, periodically seized by collective paranoia about Satan and his works, there is allegedly no doubt about the cause of the 1590–7 outbreak. If a king is involved, one needs look no further.[2]

What, then, began it all? As the orthodox account has it, witchcraft did exist in Scotland before 1590, but examples of it were sporadic in the extreme, and, crucially, there was absolutely no awareness of the demonic pact. The Witchcraft Act was passed in 1563, but it was exceedingly brief, simply pronouncing it a capital crime to practise witchcraft or to consort with a witch. It was merely one of a list of acts passed by parliament in response to the request by the General Assembly of the Kirk to the Privy Council that something had to be done about matters which formerly would have come before the pre-Reformation ecclesiastical courts. Then, in 1589–90, the situation changed completely. James's bride, Anne of Denmark, set sail for Scotland in the autumn of 1589, but was forced back by violent storms at sea, taking refuge in Oslo. The romantic James then went to Oslo – foreign travel in search of brides seems to have appealed to the Stuarts – married Anne, and spent the winter in Denmark. And there he learned for the first time about the demonic pact, from discussions with the great astronomer Tycho Brake, and with Nils Hemmingsen and other Lutheran theologians. In the spring of 1590, his head stuffed with this fascinating new idea, James brought Anne back to Scotland. Despite renewed violent storms, they arrived safely on 1 May, only to find subsequently that the storms which they had survived had been produced by the devil and his minions, witches in Copenhagen and Scotland. The theory was true. It was being put into practice in his own kingdom.[3]

Much of our knowledge about it comes from a pamphlet called *Newes from*

2 Witch-hunting went on in Scotland throughout the 17th century, reaching peaks of ferocity in 1629–30, 1649–50 and 1661–2; the last execution, of Janet Horne at Dornoch, took place in 1727, only eight years before the repeal of the Witchcraft Act in 1735. On this subject, the unrivalled expert is Christina Larner; see her two masterly works, *Enemies of God: The Witch-hunt in Scotland* (London, 1981), and *Witchcraft and Religion* (Oxford, 1984); and also the invaluable *A Source-Book of Scottish Witchcraft*, comp. C. Larner, C. H. Lee and H. V. McLachlan (University of Glasgow, 1977). Larner has reduced the lurid estimates of the numbers who died as witches, which varied from 3,000 to 30,000 to something between 1,000 and 2,000; it is still a lot: Larner, *Enemies of God*, 65; idem, *Witchcraft and Religion*, 28.

3 This paragraph is a brief synopsis of the thesis put forward by Larner, 'James VI and witchcraft', in A. G. R. Smith, ed., *The Reign of James VI and I* (London, 1973), 74–90; it is reprinted in Larner, *Witchcraft and Religion*, 3–22. Challenging any of Larner's views on witchcraft is a rash undertaking; it is only on this point, and not on her analyses of the witch-hunt as a whole, that I have the temerity to do it. Since this article was written, P. G. Maxwell-Stuart has looked closely at the circumstances of James's visit to Denmark and Norway, and has argued strongly against the theory that he picked up continental ideas of witchcraft while he was there: P. G. Maxwell-Stuart, 'The fear of the king is death: James VI and the witches of East Lothian', in W. G. Naphy and P. Roberts, eds., *Fear in Early Modern Society* (Manchester, 1997), 209–13. I am delighted that we have independently come to the same conclusion.

*Scotland*, printed in London in 1591 or 1592, 'according to the Scottish Coppie'; and a fearsome tale it told.[4] The affair came to light because of the suspicions of one David Seaton, bailie depute in Tranent, about his maidservant Geillis Duncan, a girl with unusual powers of healing, who 'used secretlie to absent and lie furth of hir maisters house every night'. Seaton asked her about all this, and getting no satisfactory answer, tried other means:

> [Seaton] did, with the help of others, torment her with the torture of the pilliwinkes [thumbscrews] upon her fingers, which is a grievous torture, and binding or wrinching her head with a cord or roape, which is a most cruell torment also; yet would she not confess anie thing. Whereupon they, suspecting that she had been marked by the Devill (as commonly witches are) made diligent search about her and found the Enemie's marke to be in her fore crag [front of the neck] which being found, shee confessed that al her doings was done by the wicked allurements and entisements of the Devil, and that she did them by witchcraft.[5]

And having thus begun to talk, nothing would stop her. She accused 'Agnes Sampson, the eldest witche of them all, dwelling in Haddington; Agnes Thompson of Edenborough; Dr Fian, alias John Cunningham, master of the schoole at Saltpans [Prestonpans] in Lowthian ...; George Nott's wife, dwelling in Lowthian; Robert Griersoun, skipper', and many others. So witchcraft was rife in the little towns of East Lothian, practised mainly by women but also by a man of education, the schoolmaster Fian, a less usual witch-type. Not just rife, in fact: positively crawling with the evil. In its lengthy description of Fian, the *Newes* recounts how, wanting to seduce a village girl, he had persuaded her brother, by promising to teach him in future without beating him, to get for him three of her pubic hairs. But the boy got a beating anyway, from his mother, when his sister understandably complained that he was troubling her dreams; so he confessed to his mother who, being a witch herself (which is mentioned with a sort of casual inevitability), thoughtfully provided him with three hairs from a cow, with the predictable result; one of the woodcuts in the *Newes* duly portrays Fian with his embarrassingly persistent and adoring heifer.[6]

Geillis's most spectacular charges were laid against two women of quite different stamp: Barbara Napier, wife of an Edinburgh burgess, Archibald Douglas, brother of a laird; and Euphame McCalzean, daughter of Thomas, Lord Cliftonhall, Senator of the College of Justice, and wife of Patrick Moscrop, son of an advocate. This was aiming high, right into the gentry and legal circles of Edinburgh; and indeed, according to Geillis, the witches themselves had aimed high. Barbara had bewitched to death Archibald, Earl of Angus, and Euphame had, by the same means, disposed of her father-in-law and tried to get rid of her husband. Worse, both were known friends of that

4 *Newes from Scotland: Declaring the Damnable life and death of Doctor Fian, a notable Sorcerer, who was burned at Edenborough in January last 1591* (London, ?1591). It is reprinted in Pitcairn, *Trials*, i(3), 213–23, unfortunately without any reproduction of the splendid woodcuts in the original. Citations are made to this edition.

5 Ibid., 215.

6 Ibid., 215–16, 220–1.

aristocratic rogue elephant and constant source of trouble to the king, Francis Stewart, Earl of Bothwell. But they were not alone in implicating Bothwell; the common theme of the confessions was the attempt on the king's life, by the devil, the witches and the earl of Bothwell – a formidable combination which one might have expected to succeed. This, then, was no ordinary outbreak of witchcraft, involving small people. And not surprisingly, it was brought to the attention of the king. The first great Scottish witch-hunt had begun.

For the principal participants, it was a protracted affair. Fian was tried and condemned on 26 December 1590, and Agnes Sampson on 27 January 1591; but Barbara Napier was not tried until 8 May 1591, and Euphame McCalzean on 9 June. And another major figure particularly connected with Bothwell, Richie Graham, languished until his eventual trial on 29 February 1592. Four of the five were executed. Barbara Napier, however, was acquitted of all practice of witchcraft and convicted only of consorting with witches; and although this was legally a capital offence, the jury was reluctant to pass sentence of death, for no-one had actually died for it hitherto and, in any case, she claimed to be pregnant. This produced a violent reaction from the king. In a particularly chilling passage in a letter to Chancellor Maitland, James ordered: 'Trye by the medicinairis aithis gif Barbara Nepair be vith bairne or not. Tak na delaying ansour. Gif ye finde sho be not, to the fire with her presentlie and cause bouell her publicclie.'[7] And the jurors found themselves up on a charge of wilful error, heard on 7 June, when they were harangued by James at considerable length before he accepted that their error was ignorant rather than wilful.[8]

No doubt one reason was Bothwell's involvement.[9] He was summoned before the Privy Council on 15 April 1591 and warded in Edinburgh Castle, but escaped, whereupon under a suspended sentence of May 1589 he was proclaimed traitor. Naturally he denied the charges. For him the villains of the piece were Chancellor Maitland, that 'puddock-stoole of a night', and the 'deboshed Richie Graham', as he called them in a letter to the ministers and elders of Edinburgh written just before Graham's execution.[10] The fact that he was writing to the ministry is an indication of the problem for James; it was exceedingly difficult to deal with Bothwell because, however irresponsible and dangerous he was (and there is no doubt about the danger of a man who *inter alia* twice tried to break into the palace of Holyrood with the intention of seizing the king), he managed to retain the support of another group of James's critics and opponents, the extreme Presbyterians, as well as a certain backing from fellow aristocrats such as Lord Hume who, like himself, hated the Chancellor, John Maitland of Thirlestane.

7 *CSP Scot.*, x, 510; *Letters of King James VI and I*, ed. G. P. V. Akrigg (Berkeley, 1984), 114; M. Lee Jr, *John Maitland of Thirlestane and the Foundation of the Stewart Despotism in Scotland* (Princeton, 1953), 231n., corrects the dating of this letter (April, in *CSP Scot.*, 'Spring' in Akrigg) to 14–19 June.

8 *CSP Scot.*, x, 523–5.

9 It is because of his involvement that Larner has described this witch-hunt as the last of the old style, when sorcery and treason were linked together – though in fact the evidence for earlier examples of this in Scotland is tenuous in the extreme: Larner, *Witchcraft and Religion*, 10.

10 David Calderwood, *The History of the Kirk of Scotland*, ed. T. Thomson (Wodrow Soc., 1842–9), v, 153, 156.

This is reflected in the contemporary *Historie of King James the Sext* – which could fairly enough be called the *Hostile History of James VI*, being consistently favourable to Bothwell and probably written by one of his supporters, John Colville. For the *Historie* insists that the North Berwick witches merely intended to prevent Queen Anne from coming to Scotland; and Bothwell's part was only to consult Agnes Sampson about 'his awin estait and wardlie succes'. But the wicked Maitland persuaded James that Bothwell intended 'sum evill aganis his person' and so the king wrote to all the nobility ordering them to convene for Bothwell's trial. But all refused, knowing that there was no case other than that devised by the Chancellor; and in any case, the account goes on:

> Indeid the municipall law of Scotland beris, That whosoever salbe fundin to consult with sorceres, witches or suthesayers, thay sall dee the death. Bot this law was never heirtofore put in practice, and tharefore the nobilitie thoght, that thay would not begin a preparative upon a member of thair awin.

It sounds very much like a conflation with the Barbara Napier trial.[11]

The *Historie*'s claim was of course grotesquely exaggerated, and in the event even Bothwell's closest associates, Hume and others, ultimately submitted to the king. Nevertheless, the chance to get at Bothwell through all these convenient witches, prattling on about being diabolically inspired, is a major theme in the 1590–1 witch-hunt, which principally serves to confuse and complicate it. The other is divine right monarchy. Larner sees James's belief in divine right as being 'well illustrated in the speech which James made to the recalcitrant jurors on their acquittal of Barbara Napier'.[12] Stuart Clark, who agrees with this, and with Larner's theory of the discovery of diabolism in 1589–90, has argued that James regarded the *Daemonologie* which was the theoretic outcome of that discovery as 'one of his most important works' because 'both in genesis and in content the *Daemonologie* may be read as a statement about ideal monarchy'. For what it represents is argument by antithesis; the order maintained by God's lieutenant and obedient subject on earth is highlighted by considering the very reverse, the inversion of order: 'The devil, of course, *was* disorder, the first rebellious subject who tried to bring chaos to Heaven and succeeded in bringing it to man'; and 'the Devil's style of government was universally acknowledged to be tyranny, the antithesis of true kingship'. So the witches of Scotland in the early 1590s were the vehicle for the expression of paternalistic, divinely ordained kingship and 'The *Daemonologie* was in this sense only one of the earliest of a long line of royal textbooks', a fore-runner of the much better known *Basilikon Doron* and *The Trew Law of Free Monarchies.* Clark acknowledges, of course, that James's attitude to kingship existed independently of witches.[13] But it is surely a little bizarre to suggest that the hundreds of men and women who met frightening and frightful deaths were, for James, little more than fodder for a theory.

11 *The Historie and Life of King James the Sext*, ed. T. Thomson (Bannatyne Club, 1825), 241–2.

12 Larner, *Witchcraft and Religion*, 13.

13 S. Clark, 'King James's *Daemonologie*: witchcraft and kingship', in S. Anglo, ed., *The Damned Art: Essays in the Literature of Witchcraft* (London, 1977), 156–81.

Is it then enough to see the first great witch-hunt in Scotland as the product of the over-fertile brain of a king obsessed with the demonic pact, divine right kingship and the earl of Bothwell? There are grounds for suggesting otherwise. To begin with, although of course the difference in scale was immense, it is a thesis which underplays witchcraft before 1590. From Larner's list of trials, we find references to witches in Elgin in 1560, and to two named witches at Stirling in 1562. Then in 1563, the year of the Witchcraft Act, the number goes up to fifteen. Between then and the end of 1589 there are a further nineteen names, and references to 'witches' executed at St Andrews and Dundee in 1569, and to 'unnamed witches' whose fate is unknown in 1586.[14] More dramatically, that strenuous reformer John Erskine of Dun's pursuit of witches in Angus and the Mearns in 1568 led to nearly forty accusations (not listed by Larner). In 1569, Regent Moray apologised to the General Assembly for having been less expeditious than he would have wished in doing justice to witches as well as those suspected of adultery and incest, but he had a reputation as a persecutor. This is not witch persecution on the scale of the 1590s and subsequent outbreaks. But it is certainly not negligible. Witches were around, in various parts of the country, long before the North Berwick case came to light.[15]

Moreover, the reformed church was certainly exercised by witchcraft – and by the lack of zeal on the part of the state. One unfortunate witch was 'set upe at a pillar' to be 'delt [with] from the pulpit' by John Knox, as her last experience on earth.[16] Knox himself believed that the wife of the Catholic earl of Huntly, dying mysteriously in rebellion against Mary, Queen of Scots in 1562, kept tame witches. He describes how they prophesied Huntly's death, and how the Countess, when she heard of it, 'blamed her principal witch, called Janet; but she stoutly defended herself (as the devil can ever do) ... [the Countess] was angry and sorry for a season, but the Devil, the Mass, and witches have as great credit of her this day as they had seven years ago.' And later, he recounts the burning of two witches in 1563, of whom 'the eldest was so blinded with the Devil that she affirmed "That no Judge had power over her"'.[17] These references do not add up to a demonic pact. But Knox does seem to have believed in a link between witches and a personalised devil roaming the earth. More generally, the General Assembly complained to the king in 1583 'that there is no punishment

14 Figures taken from Larner *et al.*, *Source-Book of Scottish Witchcraft*, 3, 61, 172–3.

15 For Erskine, see A. H. Williamson, *Scottish National Consciousness in the Reign of James VI* (Edinburgh, 1979), 56. Williamson exaggerates when he claims that this can be equated with 'the great witch craze as late as February 1591', but the numbers are certainly impressive. For Moray, *The Booke of the Universall Kirk of Scotland: Acts and Proceedings of the General Assemblies of the Kirk of Scotland from the year MDLX*, ed. T. Thomson (Bannatyne Club, 1839–45), i, 153; Calderwood, *History of the Kirk of Scotland*, ii, 501–2. Robert Lindesay of Pitscottie, *The Historie and Cronicles of Scotland*, ed. A. J. G. Mackay (Scottish Text Soc., 1899–1911), ii, 217–18, anticipates the 1590 diabolic conspiracy against King James when he describes the burning of William Stewart, Lyon Herald, in 1569 for his part in conspiring Moray's death, and recounts the burning of two witches in St Andrews and two in Dundee 'and uthiris plaices to the nomer often or thairby quha pronunsticat at thair deid that my lord regent sould be slaine be the schot of poulder and that because he pat downe the puire vitches' – as indeed happened in Jan. 1570.

16 *The Autobiography and Diary of Mr James Melvill*, ed. R. Pitcairn (Wodrow Soc., 1842), 58.

17 *John Knox's History of the Reformation in Scotland*, ed. W. C. Dickinson (Edinburgh, 1949), ii, 61, 85–6.

for incest, adultery, witchcraft, murders, abominable and horrid oaths, in such sort that daily sin increaseth and provoketh the wrath of God against the whole country'. In 1596 they launched another broadside against the state for 'universall neglect of justice both in civill and criminall causes, as namelie, in granting of remissions and respitts for blood, adulteries and incests'.[18] Witchcraft was not mentioned. For in 1596, the year when the second great outbreak of persecution began, the state was satisfying the Kirk.

The pre-1590 evidence is indeed patchy. But out of that patchiness comes an impression that the witch was already a frightening figure in Scotland well before 1590. And there is something else. The first detailed indictment which survives is that of Janet Boyman, tried and executed in 1572. She described the demonic power which she invoked as a whirlwind, 'and thairafter came the shape of ane man and stood on the other side of the wall'. Who was the man? Larner doubts that Janet was talking about Satan but the probability surely lies the other way;[19] no human man was going to give the witch her power. Is there a difference between this witch and the witches of North Berwick to whom the Devil, in the shape of a man, preached? Or does the demonic pact indeed predate 1590, and is it lack of evidence, rather than lack of existence, which explains why we hear so little about it?

If that remains a question, what is certain is that James's interest in witchcraft existed before he had his winter's instruction in Denmark. A case which finally reached the court of justiciary in July 1590 was that of the northern laird Hector Munro of Foulis, accused of consorting with witches, notably one Marioun McIngurach, 'ane of the maist notorious and rank wichis in all this realme'. In 1589, while the witch was staying with Munro, James, to his considerable embarrassment, turned up in Aberdeen and demanded to see and examine her. Marioun attempted to transfer Hector's fatal illness to his half-brother George; and George's death in April 1590, along with the counter-witchcraft being practised against Hector by his stepmother, Katherine, lady of Foulis, brought both of them to the dock on 22 July, producing the extraordinary situation whereby Hector joined the public prosecutor to bring a private prosecution against Katherine; and then, when her trial was over, he moved into the dock himself while the public prosecutor continued his work. Perhaps not surprisingly, these singularly well-born practitioners of witchcraft both got off.[20] A year earlier, no-one had yet died and James was showing no more than interested curiosity. But the interest was there.

The preconditions of the 1590 outbreak, therefore, are undoubtedly more serious than has been suggested. The events of 1590 itself force further questions. Was the persecution indeed started by the king? And what does it tell us about his attitude to kingship? The answer to the first, at least, is straightforward: it was not started by the king. The trials of Katherine and Hector Munro of Foulis in July 1590 uncovered a whole batch of witches in Ross-shire, all caught up in the affair, and at least some of them executed. There is no evidence at all that James

18 Calderwood, *History of the Kirk of Scotland*, iii, 736; v, 411.

19 Larner, *Enemies of God*, 147.

20 Pitcairn, *Trials*, i(2), 191–204.

was still involved. Nor is there any evidence of royal involvement in the ten trials in Aberdeenshire in August. And there is a third group, mentioned in a letter by the English diplomat Robert Bowes to Burghley on 23 July: 'Sundrie witches were arraigned yesterdaie in this towne [Edinburgh], and are found giltie of odious crimes: chefelie that some of them made in wax the image of the yong lard of Wardhouse, and rosting the image the gentleman pined awaie by sweate as the wax melteth before the fier.'[21] This is good, classic witchcraft – but not in any way linked to the king. So apart from the North Berwick witches, there were three other groups, two in the north and one in Edinburgh, which had no connection with North Berwick, nor with King James. Thus it does appear that at least some of the witch-hunting of 1590 came from within local communities and was not inspired from above. So even in this most notable year of 'authority'-provoked persecutions, 'authority' does not provide the whole explanation. Because there is far less evidence about these three cases than about the much more dramatic North Berwick one, it may never be possible to explain what caused them. All one can do is say quite clearly what did *not* cause them.

There is a further problem. The famous 'North Berwick witches' were actually a very small group – a smaller group than those who apparently danced on the sands at North Berwick. The same people turn up in all the sources: Fian, Sampson, Graham, Napier, McCalzean and Geillis Duncan. But over *sixty* people were involved in legal processes at Prestonpans, three-quarters of them in 1590, the rest in 1591; it was this East Lothian town – home, be it remembered, of Fian – which was the centre of the persecution. At this point we stumble across a rather shadowy figure, James Carmichael, minister of nearby Haddington. In the *Memoirs* of James Melville of Halhill, there is a reference to Carmichael having 'ther [the witches'] history and haill depositions'.[22] Rhodes Dunlap has suggested that it was Carmichael who wrote some of the marginalia and textual amendments to the manuscript of the *Daemonologie* now in the Folger Library; and he quotes a later letter in apparently the same hand, written by Carmichael to James in March 1615, which refers to the king directing him 'to attend sestein monethes upoun the examinationes of divers witches'. Sixteen months would have taken him through the whole period of the persecution. But it was 1590 which was the bad year; there were more prosecutions then than in 1591. Yet only one of the five main North Berwick witches was tried in 1590, and that at the end of December. In other words, much was happening in the first year of the hunt, happening to East Lothian witches to be sure, but not to ones prominent in the particular horror story of conspiring the king's death. And it seems that before the king's involvement, we have a minister who was intensely interested in witchcraft; indeed Dunlap's theory that his 'history' was that 'Scottish Coppie' which became the *Newes from Scotland* as printed in London seems more convincing than Larner's suggestion that it was a tract written 'directly for an English reading public'.[23] Is it possible, then, that 'authority' did

21 Larner *et al.*, *Source-Book of Scottish Witchcraft*, 5, 173; *CSP Scot.*, x, 365.

22 James Melville of Halhill, *Memoirs of His Own Life*, ed. T. Thomson (Bannatyne Club, 1827), 396.

23 R. Dunlap, 'King James and some witches: the date and text of the *Daemonologie*', *Philological Quarterly*, liv (1975), 43; Larner, *Witchcraft and Religion*, 15.

have a great deal to do with the 1590 outbreak – but was it the authority of that watchful, worried and very devil-conscious body, the Kirk, in the person of the local minister, which was the initial mover, and not the king?

What then of that inner group, the conspirers of the king's death? Melville, in his balanced and factual account, singled out Agnes Sampson, 'ane renowned midwyf', who affirmed that with nine other witches, she met the devil at Prestonpans, where she gave him 'a body of wax schaipen' which she had made and wrapped in linen; and when the devil had 'pronounced his verde', he returned it to Agnes and it was then passed round the group, each saying 'this is K. James the sext, ordonit to be consumed at the instance of a noble man Francis erle Bodowell'. Subsequently they met at North Berwick, 'wher the devell, cled in a blak gown with a blak hat upon his head, preachit unto a gret nomber of them out of the pulpit', asking what harm they had done, how many they had converted, and what success they had had with the image since their last meeting. To this 'ane auld sely pure plowman callit Grey Meill' said that 'nathing ailit the King yet, God be thankit', which earned him 'a gret blaw' from the devil. They all marvelled that their devilry was not harming the king, as it had done others, and the devil answered 'Il est un home de Dieu.' Then we get a very full description of the devil, who 'caused all the company to com and kiss his ers, quhilk they said was cauld lyk yrn; his body was hard lyk yin, as they thocht that handled him; his faice was terrible, his noise lyk the bek of an egle, gret bournyng eyn, his handis and legis wer herry, with clawes upon his handis and feit lyk the griffon, and spak with a how voice' – exactly as he is portrayed in one of the *Newes* woodcuts.[24]

James, however, appears only once in Melville, examining Richie Graham because of his connection with Bothwell, although 'his Maieste [was] not willing to credit [Bothwell's] devellische accusers'. Nor does he have a major role in the *Historie*'s account of the witches; that was reserved for his unjust treatment of Bothwell. The *Historie* does, however, confirm Melville's picture of Agnes Sampson, 'the wyse wyff of Keyth'. Spottiswoode also highlights Sampson, 'commonly called the wise wife of Keith ... a woman not of the base and ignorant sort of witches, but matron-like, grave and settled in her answers, which were all to some purpose'. She described her familiar spirit, whom she could summon at will, using the words he taught her 'Holla Master'; but she could criticise her 'Master' and did, because of his failure to do away with James, which, when challenged, he admitted was not in his power, 'speaking words that she understood not, but, as she did take them, the words were 'Il est homme de Dieu.'[25]

These accounts clearly derived from the source with which I began, the *Newes from Scotland*. Here, the schoolmaster Dr Fian is very prominent; the *Newes* has great fun describing Fian's cow, his phenomenal acrobatics in front of the king, the tortures to which he was subjected (which still produced no confession, but only silence, unbroken until the other witches helpfully pointed out that it was

24 Melville, *Memoirs of His Own Life*, 395–7.

25 *Historie of James the Sext*, 241; John Spottiswoode, *History of the Church of Scotland ... to the end of the reign of James VI*, ed. M. Napier and M. Russell (Spottiswoode Soc., 1847–51), ii, 411–12.

caused by two pins stuck through his tongue by the devil, joining it to the roof of his mouth), his renunciation of Satan and then his relapse. And Geillis Duncan played her Jew's harp, or trump, to the king. But still the leading character was Agnes Sampson. It was she who gave him the full story, and amazing it was. Twice the witches had gone to sea to raise storms, in the most remarkable fashion. On one occasion, a whole flotilla of sieves put out into the North Sea, each bearing a witch. On another, they all went 'in a boit like ane chimnay', piloted by the devil – diabolic steampower apparently anticipating the human variety by more than two centuries. And Agnes herself had not only made the image of the king, but hung up a black toad by the heels for three days, collecting its venom which she would have used had her efforts to persuade one of James's attendants to procure for her any of the king's 'foule linen' not failed.[26]

The *Newes* is in fact the only source which brings us firmly into the presence of the king, and makes his interest and involvement clear. It is therefore a crucial text, however problematic. But we cannot use it as evidence for King James's imposition on his Scottish witches of the Danish theory of the diabolic pact. Not only is its emphasis on what the witches told the king about the devil. It also contains a direct, if neglected, statement which shows that long before James was brought into the affair, there was at least one Scotsman who knew all about the demonic pact: that bailie depute in Tranent, David Seaton. That is the significance of the passage quoted earlier, describing his investigation and torture of Geillis Duncan. Throughout the whole period of witch persecution, witch-hunters sought for the devil's mark, for only then would the witch confess. That is precisely what happened to poor Geillis, whose master needed no instruction from a king who had picked up ideas about continental daemonology. And unless we are to reject the whole story of how these witches were discovered – and no one, so far as I know, has ever suggested any good reason why we should – we have here a piece of very clear evidence, to add to the case of Janet Boyman in 1572, which shows that diabolism in Scotland existed without reference to James VI.

Thus the diabolically inspired Agnes forced her story on the king. The dramatic climax came when Agnes described how the witches had asked the devil '"why he did beare such hatred to the kinge?" Who aunswered, "By reason the King is the greatest enemie he hath in the world."' This was an important moment. It was an appeal to James's vanity, and James should have succumbed and been convinced. Remarkably, it was not the case. For it was *after* this highly flattering statement, as the *Newes* tells us, that James said 'They were all extreame lyars.' That was the critical moment; for it provoked from the stately Agnes the indignant response that

> she would not wish his Majestie to suppose her wordes to bee false, but rather to beleve them, in that shee would discover much matter unto him as his Majestie should not in any way doubt of. And therupon taking his Majestie a little aside, shee declared unto him the verie wordes which passed between the kinges Majestie and his Queene at Upslo in Norway, the first night of mariage, with the answere ech to other; wherat the Kinges Majestie wondered

26 Pitcairn, *Trials*, i(3), 218; the 'steamboat' was described by Agnes at her trial: ibid., 240–1.

> greatly, and swore by the living God that he believed all the devils in hell could not have discovered the same, acknowledging her words to be most true; and therefore gave the more credit to the rest than is before declared.[27]

What does one make of this? Seeking desperately for a rational explanation for the thing which persuaded a rational king, one might speculate about the possible role of that shadowy group, the Danish witches, or Agnes's acquaintance among those who served the king, who might provide a link. But in the end there is no rational explanation, only the fact that a hitherto sceptical king changed his mind – and was clearly terrified. And with terror came savagery, the savagery which produced the letter to Maitland about Barbara Napier's claim to be pregnant, the reaction to the jurors' acquittal of her, and the brutality of the death of Euphame McCalzean, burned alive rather than 'wirrit' (strangled) first. This was by any standards extremely unpleasant.

It was, however, also understandable, both in human terms and in its immediate political context. That being so, is it really necessary to argue that it added a further plank to the platform of divine right monarchy? The speech to the jurors in the Napier case, cited in support of that claim, seems positively to contradict it. James went to some lengths to justify what he was doing, acknowledging that it was against custom; and this was hardly the attitude of an arbitrary king. With cheerful indifference to historical fact, he floundered around with the idea that his predecessors had not personally presided over criminal cases because early death prevented them. He was more successful when he divided criminal causes into two sorts:

> Upon crymes touching men's lyves – as adultery, murder, theft, rebellion – yf the prince should sit in person it might be a note of rigour. And therefore it is forbidden in the civile law. But of errour or such like, which concerne only men's goodes, and not their lyves, it is lawfull by that law.

Then he went on to complain that men put support of their friends above impartial justice, in terms very like those he was later to use in *Basilikon Doron*. But the author of the *Historie* said something very similar and he was certainly no supporter of divine right. Furthermore, James continued:

> Yet this I say, that ... I am innocent of all injustice in these behalfes, and for my parte my conscience doth set me cleare, as did the conscience of Samuel, and I call you to be my judges heerein. And suppose I be your King, *yet I submit myselfe to the accusacions of you my subjects in this behalfe, and let any one saie what I have done* [my italics]. And as I have thus begonne, so purpose I to goe forwarde: not because I am James Stuard, and can comaunde so many thousandes of men, but because God hath made me a King and judge to judge righteous judgments.[28]

It is possible to detect in the last sentence the idea of divine right, but it is questionable whether one would do so were it not uttered by the king who, as everyone knows, was the arch-exponent of divine right; for it is an utterly

27 Ibid., 217–18.
28 *CSP Scot.*, x, 523–4.

unexceptional and traditional statement of one of the greatest responsibilities of kingship, which could have been said by any of James's predecessors – or Charlemagne, or Alfred, or Edward I. And it is quite impossible to see any kind of divine right at all in the submission to the judgement of subjects. So far from the witch craze bringing out James's ideas about divine right monarchy, we are faced with the astonishing – and much more interesting – fact that it brought out precisely the opposite.

This remained the case six years later, when James wrote his book about witches. There is no clear statement in the *Daemonologie* to parallel the 1591 remark about the people as his judges. Yet neither was there any attempt to set God's lieutenant on earth, to whom utter obedience was due, against the horrors of obedience to Satan, despite his use of the antithetical style. Indeed, there could not have been. James made it clear enough that he was writing from personal experience. He dismissed, for example, the idea that witches were all self-deluded melancholics, because he had known 'sume of thame riche and worldlie wise, sum of thame fat or corpulent in thair bodies, and maist part of thame altogether gevin over to the pleasours of the flesche, continuall hunting of companie, and all kynde of mirrines baith laufull and unlawfull'; he had a definite candidate for his three categories, writing beside each the initials EM (Euphame McCalzean), RG (Ritchie Graham or possibly Robert Griersoun) and BN (Barbara Napier).[29] And one thing which conversation with Scottish witches had made all too obvious was that they never offered Satan the inverted, diabolic obedience which in the ideal world true subjects would offer truly divine right kings. Far from it: when they were dissatisfied, they complained directly to the devil, just as James's subjects in Scotland complained directly to him. Agnes Sampson had no hesitation in asking Satan why he had failed; Robert Griersoun, the sea captain whose expertise was so useful to sea-going witches, bluntly told the devil that he had not kept his promise to give them the king's image to be roasted.[30] Respect for authority was not a marked feature of the witches. And one could add to that respect for ecclesiastical authority as well, for a coven was not the inversion of a Calvinist congregation. Scottish witches did not put up with long sermons from their devil.

In the late 1590s James would indeed assert monarchy by divine right, in part as a reaction against the contractualist teachings of Buchanan, but much more as the reaction to the extreme claims of the division of church and state advanced by the Melvillians. The witches of North Berwick, and even the *Daemonologie*, show how difficult it is to date that back into the earlier 1590s. There we find in full measure that style of kingship advocated by Melville of Halhill, attributed to James by the English visitor Henry Wotton in 1601, and claimed by the king himself in his self-portrait to the English in 1604: kingship based on consent, the willingness of the king to seek advice and to listen.[31] Despite the theorising, that style remained with James throughout his life. What James's witches show is

29 New York, Folger Shakespeare Library, Folger MS V.a.185, 39.

30 Pitcairn, *Trials*, i(3), 250–1.

31 Melville, *Memoirs of His Own Life*, 378–90; L. Pearsall Smith, ed., *The Life and Letters of Sir Henry Wotton* (Oxford, 1907), i, 314–15; PRO, SP14/8/93.

that the idea of his early adherence to divine right theory cannot be sustained. That, surely, is the most dramatic consequence of considering the theme of the king and the witches.

There was, however, another consequence of the 1590–1 witch-hunt. On 26 October 1591, James set up a commission of the Privy Council to search out, examine and torture witches. On 8 June 1592 he went further, establishing local standing commissions which would co-operate with the General Assembly on a range of matters, including witchcraft.[32] But by that time, the initial frenzy had died down; indeed, James himself had calmed down, to the extent that, as a matter touching his honour and conscience, he was prepared to restore at least part of Euphame McCalzean's forfeited estates to her three daughters.[33] What, then, lay behind the 1592 arrangement?

The answer lies in the divergence between the first and second commissions. The first was Edinburgh-based, and in that sense both 'central' and also very local. It was a single commission, comprising the justice clerk, the advocate, two ministers, and the provost and a burgess of Edinburgh; and the responsibility of this group, or any three of them, was exclusively cases of witchcraft – cases, presumably, in Edinburgh and its environs. The second was on an altogether larger scale. Its inspiration, however, quite clearly came not from the king, but from the Kirk. The General Assembly had directed commissioners 'to travel and tak ordour in all thingis that may serve to the glorie of God and advancement of his trew religioun'; and the king, 'willing that the saidis commissionaris directit be the General Assembly sall not be disobeyit', and by advice of the council, ordered privy council commissions, which contained blanks for 'names of noblemen, baronis, gentilmen and magistratis of borrowis to be insert thairin at the chois and discretioun of the saidis commissionaris of the Generall Assembley, makand thame his Hienes justiceis and commissionaris in that parte'. These local commissions would deal with a whole range of matters, from the repairing of kirks and the stipends of ministers to vagabonds and idle beggars and witches. This was a massive sell-out to the Kirk. The list is very reminiscent of that list of acts passed in the interests of the Kirk in the Parliament of 1563. More immediately, it was reminiscent of a series of acts passed three days earlier, on 5 June 1592, a series which included the 'Golden' Act, the colour referring to Melvillian, not royal pleasure, for it gave legal backing to the presbyteries.[34] In other words, James was giving way to the Kirk at a moment of real royal weakness, when the Melvillians were ruthlessly in the ascendant. Once again, if we are searching for a motivating force beyond that of immediate local tensions for the persecution of witchcraft, we come up against not a witch-hunting king, but the witch-haunted Kirk.

Thus was the machinery for witch-hunting put into place; and four years later, it was used to the full in the next great outburst of persecution in 1596–7. This had none of the exceptional features of 1590–1; the witches were 'normal' witches, practising their *maleficium* within local communities. Why it happened

32 *RPC*, iv, 680, 753–4.
33 *APS*, iii, 608–10.
34 Ibid., iii, 541–54.

is as yet as inexplicable as the initial stages of the first hunt. But its effect on the king is very clear. The first signs of his concern about what was going on are seen in his intervention in the frenzied witch-hunting in Aberdeen in the spring of 1597; on 14 April he quashed the proceedings against two suspected witches, Isobel Burnett and her daughter, Elspeth Forbes, in particular pronouncing their visit to the midwife Margaret Bane a matter of 'ordinare confort and supple, as the haill remanent wemen of all estaitis in the countrey did'.[35] Then in the summer there was a particularly nasty case, involving one Margaret Aitken, who confessed to being a witch herself, and, on the grounds that she could identify other witches because 'they had a secret mark ... in their eyes, whereby she could surely tell', offered 'to purge the country of them so she might have her life preserved ... and in this she was so readily believed, that for the space of three or four months she was carried from town to town to make discoveries in that kind'. This was all too successful, 'especially in Glasgow, where divers innocent women, through the credulity of the minister, Mr John Cowper, were condemned and put to death'. But not everyone was so credulous; for the fraud was discovered when the same people whom on one day she pronounced guilty, 'the next day being presented in another habit she cleansed'.[36] Above all, one person who was not credulous was the king. On 12 August 1597, 'understanding that' their existence meant that 'grite danger may ensue to honnest and famous personis', James – now in a much stronger position *vis-à-vis* the Kirk than he had been in 1592 – revoked the standing commissions.[37] The date of this revocation is all the more remarkable because James himself was apparently plagued by witches that summer. Curiously, there is no record of this in any Scottish source. But reports from Robert Bowes to Burghley in July and August, and 'Advices from Scotland' sent to England in September, describe his involvement in the examination of 'many thousand' witches. Indeed, it almost appeared that 1591 was come again; for one group set out to drown the king in the Tay when he was going to the General Assembly. But this was not North Berwick. This time James's approach was such that 'hereat all estates are grieved and specially the church, affirming that the form of proceeding is neither conform to the law of God or man'. As he also sacked Andrew Melville as regent of St Andrews, publicly interrupted Robert Wallace's godly sermon, and caused further 'great grief' by instructing four ministers to preach on the 'essential power of Satan either by permission or power of God' in his presence and that twelve other ministers summoned to 'censure that doctrine and reason the cause', the Kirk's bitter frustration can be readily imagined. The second great witch-hunt of the reign was fizzling out in the face of determined royal scepticism. And in that year James published the *Daemonologie.*[38]

35 *Miscellany of the Spalding Club* (Aberdeen, 1841–52), i, 163–4; for the Aberdeen witch trials, 82–193.

36 Spottiswoode, *History of the Church of Scotland*, iii, 66–7.

37 *RPC*, v, 409–10.

38 *CSP Scot.*, xiii(1), 56, 73, 78–9. Calderwood, *History of the Kirk of Scotland*, v, 648–51, writes with predictable fury about the onslaught on the St Andrews ministers, but has nothing to say about the witches. The English accounts are tantalising in their lack of detail; but the attitudes of the king and Kirk come through clearly enough.

It is a very short book, much shorter than the works of those great sceptics Weyer and Scot, whom James was setting out to refute. It is a dialogue between Philomathes who asks the questions and Epistemon, who gives all the right answers; and it is divided into three parts, the first on magic, the second on sorcery and witchcraft, and the third on the world of spirits. Almost the only original thing in it is the idea that although witches can fly through the air, this can only be done for the duration of a single breath – which seems remarkably restrictive. But there is also an extent to which James sees his witches as the victims of delusion. In his treatise, this leaves them firmly as Satan's creatures; in reality, the idea was to be increasingly used as the basis for the king's later scepticism about witchcraft which was to perplex his English subjects, and somewhat undermine the point of the two great witch scenes by Shakespeare and Thomas Middleton in *Macbeth*.

The text itself is also revealing. Two holograph fragments of the first draft survive, in which the characters are simply called A and Q; and the As stand out much more clearly than the Qs, which may be an indication of how James's mind was working. He was writing in dialogue form, but he really wanted to get on with making his case.[39] Then there is a complete manuscript, with corrections partly in the king's hand and partly in another, possibly Carmichael's. In this, spaces were left for the names of the characters, which were written in only in the heading and at the first four speeches.[40] Yet remarkably, the manuscript is far more accurate than the printed version, which has erroneous speech divisions and words misspelled or omitted. This was very unusual. James normally cared very much about accurate printing. Dunlap, who argues for an early date for the writing of the *Daemonologie*, concludes from this that by the time it was printed in 1597 James was already thinking about his next work, *The Trew Law of Free Monarchies*.[41] This is surely unconvincing. He was not likely to have forgotten, by 1597, the events of 1590–1. And what author is indifferent to the state of his present work, even if ideas for a future one are already buzzing in his head? It is far more likely that the reason for the shoddy condition of the printed text, and the reason why it was never corrected by its author in subsequent editions, can be found in the very unusual motive he had for writing it. It was written partly for self-reassurance and partly as a signing-off by a man who still believed in witchcraft and diabolic power, but who found it increasingly impossible to believe that the hundreds of women condemned in 1596–7 were all witches. It was done in a hurry. In 1597 the fragments of the first draft are much cleaner than James's usual first drafts, which are full of scorings-out and rewriting. This time, he was not so concerned with his normally vivid and compelling prose style; this time, he was getting something out of his system. We know that he turned to writing to ease and clarify his mind. This, surely, is the supreme example of it. The Preface tells us that his intention was to resolve doubting hearts. Perhaps the most doubting heart was that of the author.

Nevertheless, the fact that James was sickened by the events of 1596–7 is not

39 Oxford, Bodleian Library, MS Bodley 165, fos. 76r–80r.

40 New York, Folger Shakespeare Library, Folger MS V.a.185.

41 Dunlap, 'King James and some witches', 44–5.

quite the end of the matter. We may not believe that witches were scurrying round the North Sea in sieves. But perhaps we might think further about the modern tendency to assume that in this age of witch persecution, indeed witch obsession, the only people who actually knew that it was all rubbish were not the rational, educated elite, but the poor, ill-educated women condemned for witchcraft. The evidence shows that witchcraft was genuinely practised and that many of these women did have sufficient knowledge of herbs and potions – handed down from mother to daughter – to be able to reinforce their curses. Tensions within local societies were not just tensions between irrational accusers and their innocent victims. The trial evidence in 1590–1 reveals a terrifying network of witchcraft, interconnection between the witches, as they aided one another to do harm. I come back to Agnes Sampson, that stately matron who insisted, in the teeth of the king's initial disbelief, that she was indeed a witch and that what she said was true. That does not mean that we can understand or explain the things she claimed to have done.[42] But I am prepared to believe that witchcraft had a reality, and that she practised it.

Part of our modern scepticism comes from the fact that twentieth-century medical knowledge explains so much that in the medieval and early modem age was attributed to the miraculous or the diabolical. We tend to forget, therefore, that the medicine of the mind is in as much a state of infancy today as the medicine of the body in the sixteenth century. And until we know a great deal more about the mind as well as the body we are unwise to discount as mere invention or superstition something so powerful as the impression that the witches of North Berwick made on one of the most intelligent and intellectually curious minds of his age.[43]

42 It is worth pointing out that her claims went far beyond the attempt to kill the king. There were 53 items on her indictment, almost entirely related to more usual forms of witchcraft. Notably, the North Berwick affair did not appear until item 50. Perhaps that is symbolic of the balance between typical Jacobean witchcraft and the very specific case of James and the witches. See Pitcairn, *Trials*, i(3), 230–4.

43 I am very grateful to Robin Briggs, James Sharpe, Clive Holmes and Conrad Russell for their valuable comments on an earlier version of this paper; to Sally Mapstone for her help with this one; and to Patrick Wormald, for his cheerfulness while I wrestled with doom ...

# Part Three

# Sources and the Uses of Sources

# 14

# The Vatican Archives as a Source for Scottish Medieval Historians: An Update

*Leslie Macfarlane*

The Vatican Archive is one of the most important repositories of ecclesiastical material in the world. Its opening for public consultation by Leo XIII in 1881 provided a unique opportunity for scholars of many nationalities to augment the sources available to them at home concerning their own countries' relationship with the papacy from the ninth century onwards.[1] True, from 1815, a number of European countries, including Britain, had already been given permission to have copies made of Vatican documents which were thought to be important to their political and ecclesiastical history. As far as Britain was concerned, by 1828 the papal archivist had compiled some forty-eight volumes of transcripts from records extracted from the departments of the papal chancery, camera, datary and secretariat of state ranging from the eleventh to the eighteenth century.[2] But piecemeal selections like these, some of which were mere summaries, were not a substitute for a systematic exploration of all those registers which were made available for inspection by Leo XIII's decision. Sooner or later each country which had maintained extensive business with the papacy in the Middle Ages found the need to establish schools and institutes in Rome, whose scholars calendared systematically entries relating to their native countries – pontificate by pontificate – from Innocent III's reign onwards. France, Austria, Germany, Belgium, Hungary, Poland and Spain were soon sending out their scholars to the Vatican to calendar their own material;[3] and in like manner, in 1889, the British government authorised the Deputy Keeper of the Public Records to send the English scholar W. H. Bliss to Rome. Bliss was instructed 'to provide an English Calendar of all the entries in the papal registers of the Middle Ages which illustrate the history of Great Britain and Ireland'. At the time neither he nor the PRO could have realised the magnitude of the task – a task which continues to this day.[4]

1 For the history of the Vatican Archives and its losses through the centuries, see L. E. Boyle, *A Survey of the Vatican Archives and of its Medieval Holdings* (Toronto, 1972), 7–15; L. Macfarlane, 'The Vatican Archives with special reference to sources for British medieval history', *Archives*, iv (1959), 29–44, 84–101.

2 BL, MSS Add. 15,351–15,401 (the Marini Transcripts with two volumes of indexes). For lists of other transcripts and microfilms of British and Irish material extracted from the Vatican Archives and later deposited in the PRO in London, the NAS in Edinburgh and the National Library of Ireland, see I. B. Cowan, 'British research in the Vatican Archives', in P. Vian, ed., *L'Archivio Segreto Vaticano e le Ricerche Storiche* (Rome, 1983), 154.

3 Their major series of Calendars are listed in Boyle, *Survey*, 15–18.

4 For the history of this enterprise to 1994, see B. S. Jackson, *Papal History and the Public Record Office: An Exhibition to mark the Centenary Year of the Publication of Volume One of the Calendar of Entries in the Papal Registers relating to Great Britain and Ireland* (London, 1994), 1-14. For further details, see L. Macfarlane, 'The centenary of the Calendars', in *Calendar of Entries in the Papal Registers relating to Great Britain and Ireland*, ed. W. H. Bliss *et al.* (London, 1893– ), xvii(1), *Alexander VI, 1495–1503*, pp. vii–ix.

Although not conceived on so grand a scale, the systematic search for Scottish material in the Vatican Archives proved to be no less successful in its undertaking and development. For a number of years in the 1920s, R. K. Hannay had been studying the underlying causes of the struggle between the Scottish crown and the papacy in the fifteenth century. These struggles appeared to centre largely on patronage rights over provisions to ecclesiastical benefices, and on the various means employed by the papal *Curia* to increase its income at the expense of the Scottish clergy. These moves in turn prompted the crown to adopt anti-papal legislation. An opportunity to examine this struggle more closely came in 1928, when Annie I. Cameron, who had studied under Hannay, was given the opportunity to work in the Vatican Archives. There she systematically transcribed all the entries relating to Scottish benefices in the records of the Apostolic Camera from 1418 to 1488. As a result, when this work was published in 1934, Cameron was able to show how and why the papacy increasingly resorted to the expedient of reserving benefices to its own collation throughout the later Middle Ages, why this practice was so strongly resented, and why the struggle had to be seen within its European context: it had come about as a result of the Schism, the serious loss of income from the papal states which this occasioned, and the opposition of the conciliarists to the ensuing imposition of clerical taxes such as common services and annates. At the same time the secular rulers of Europe were beset by fiscal problems too – caused by falling land values, the shortage of bullion, and the constant drain on their own currencies occasioned by war.[5]

Following these early years in the Archives, Cameron then began to turn her attention to the systematic exploration of Scottish entries in the registers of supplications which are held in the department of the datary, and which begin in 1418. This enormous series contained the records of petitions to the Pope for dispensations or graces of every sort: for provisions to benefices, whether simple, plural or expectative; for promotions to higher dignities; for absolutions sought for defect of birth and dispensations from marriage irregularities; for the erection of collegiate churches; for release from pilgrimage vows; for permission to found universities and dispensations to read civil law therein, and for much else besides. There is a wealth of information here on places and persons, which reflect every facet of religious life in the later Middle Ages. This source is especially valuable for Scottish medieval historians, given the great loss of Scottish parochial and diocesan records at the Reformation. Given also that the information to be found in the registers of supplications was in quantity second only to that in the great series of letters and bulls in the Vatican and Lateran registers of the papal chancery, perhaps it was not surprising that Annie Dunlop (as she became on her marriage in 1938) decided to devote the remaining forty years of her distinguished career to extracting all the Scottish entries from the registers of supplications up to 1479.[6] Such dedication, and the generosity with which she shared her findings with others, could not fail to inspire younger

[5] A. I. Cameron, *The Apostolic Camera and Scottish Benefices, 1418–1488* (Oxford, 1934).

[6] For which see *Calendar of Scottish Supplications to Rome*, ed. E. R. Lindsay *et al.* (Edinburgh and Glasgow, 1934–97), vols. i–v.

medieval scholars not only with the resolve to continue her work on supplications through to 1560, but also to consider exploring the publicly accessible records of other departments of the papal *Curia* for Scottish entries. This possibility became a reality when the Ross Fund Committee (which governed an endowment made to Glasgow University by Herbert Ross under the terms of 'collecting material from abroad relating to the history of Scotsmen and Scottish influences abroad') decided to adopt a policy of funding scholars in Rome. They were charged with working 'systematically through the holdings of the Vatican Archives, identifying relevant documents and ordering microfilm of such material for deposit in the Department of Scottish History at the University of Glasgow'.

This decision was to have a profound effect on the direction and content of ecclesiastical research. In 1961 the first of these scholars, Charles Burns, began a systematic search for the Scottish entries in the *Instrumenta Miscellanea* series of records, and then in the registers of Clement VII among the Avignon Archives.[7] On its successful completion, a team of scholars led by Ian B. Cowan began in 1963 the huge task of extracting and microfilming the Scottish entries up to 1560 to be found in the registers of each of the remaining departments of the papal *Curia* to which they had access; and by 1969 Cowan was able to publish the first invaluable list of those entries already microfilmed and deposited in the University of Glasgow, together with their accompanying inventories and indexes, and with notes of those entries which had already been published in calendar form or which existed in transcript elsewhere.[8] Since then, despite Cowan's tragic death in 1990, and with it the loss of all the inspiration and energy he had given to the whole enterprise, the work of improving the accessibility of the collection with further inventories and indexes has steadily continued. The collection has also been enlarged by the ongoing addition of material drawn from the archives of the Tribunal of the Sacred Roman *Rota* and of the Penitentiary.[9]

The records of these two bodies have already become an important new source for scholars working in the fields of medieval history and law. In the first place, we have to remember that throughout the Middle Ages, the Roman *Rota* was the highest court of appeal in the Latin West for all ecclesiastical causes, whether civil or criminal, save those which had been specially reserved for other

[7] C. Burns, ed., 'Sources of British and Irish History in the *Instrumenta Miscellanea* of the Vatican Archives', *Archivium Historiae Pontificiae*, ix (1971), 7–141; *Calendar of Papal Letters to Scotland of Clement VII of Avignon, 1378–1394*, ed. C. Burns (SHS, 1976), which includes a memoir of Annie I. Dunlop by I. B. Cowan, pp. ix–xviii. See also *Calendar of Papal Letters to Scotland of Benedict XIII of Avignon, 1394–1419*, ed. F. McGurk (SHS, 1976), also completed under the terms of the Ross Fund.

[8] I. B. Cowan, 'The Vatican Archives: a report on pre-Reformation Scottish material', *SHR*, xlviii (1969), 227–42.

[9] J. J. Robertson, 'Scottish legal research in the Vatican Archives: a preliminary report', *Renaissance Studies*, ii (1988), 339–46; J. P. Foggie, 'The *Archivium Sacrae Pænitentiariae Apostolicae* in the Vatican Archives as a source for Scottish historians', *IR*, xlvii (1996), 110–26. The author is very grateful for the assistance provided by James Kirk, Eila Williamson and Professor E. J. Cowan, when he examined all this Vatican Archival material in the Scottish History Department in the University of Glasgow.

jurisdictions. In consequence of this, litigants flocked to the *Rota* from all over Europe. In addition, as far as the Scottish Church was concerned, we have to remember that each Scottish diocese had been a *filia specialis* of the Holy See since 1189, so that Scottish litigants had long been accustomed to appeal directly to the *Rota* when judgements had been given against them at the diocesan level. This procedure was not abandoned even after 1472 when St Andrews was raised to metropolitan status, a status which bestowed the right to hear appeals from its suffragan courts. The collection, then, of 374 Scottish causes dating from between 1464 and 1560, which James Robertson has gathered from the *Manualia*, the official records of the Roman *Rota*, has opened up an exciting new source in a previously little known area of late medieval Scottish legal history. The majority of these causes concerned disputes over the provision of church benefices. Most of them were conducted before the auditors of the *Rota* by Scottish procurators who either lived in Rome, or who travelled out with litigants and witnesses compelled to compear personally at the *Rota* or to provide notarial instruments of their evidence. Some 1,500 Scots involved in these causes have already been identified. And lawyers will be interested to know that the procedures followed by the civil courts in Scotland from the Reformation to the beginning of the nineteenth century closely mirrored those conducted by the auditors of the *Rota* in the late Middle Ages.

The external forum of the Apostolic Penitentiary, on the other hand, dealt with the granting of dispensations by the Cardinal Penitentiary for breaches or irregularities in canon law in matters of public importance. Its records began in 1404, and some 155 volumes have been examined up to 1560, revealing about 2,000 Scottish cases, which have been microfilmed and deposited in the Ross Fund collection. A large number of these are dispensations for irregular marriages contracted within the forbidden degrees of consanguinity, affinity or spiritual relationship. Many others concern Scots of illegitimate birth seeking legitimisation in order to be admitted to clerical orders, while some 270 entries show that permission had been granted for the feuing of monastic lands in Scotland after 1520. A number of entries also refer to Scots seeking dispensation from excommunication for having committed acts of violence resulting in the death or serious injury of clerics. Unlike litigants seeking redress at the *Rota*, however, appellants to the Penitentiary were not required to appear personally.

Between 1432 and 1560, from the examples noted by Robertson, and from the 313 case histories examined by Janet Foggie, it is clear that when added to the evidence emanating from other departments of the papal *Curia*, there is important evidence here reflecting some of the serious difficulties facing the Scottish Church in the later Middle Ages. There is evidence too which illustrates graphically the feudal structures, habits and customs of Scottish society. And these examples enable us to see also how the tribunals of the Roman *Rota* and the Apostolic Penitentiary sought to cope with righting wrongs, restoring order, and healing some of the wounds in the fabric of a Church no longer able to satisfy the demands of the rapidly changing social and economic order of western Europe in the fifteenth and early sixteenth centuries.

So, medieval historians now have on microfilm, and freely available in the Scottish History Department of Glasgow University, a unique collection of Scottish entries from the early fourteenth century to 1560 drawn from the records of all the departments of the papal *Curia* open to scholars in the Vatican. This is an invaluable archive in its own right covering a wide spectrum of information, some of which has already been published in calendar form, but most of which still awaits exploitation. Scholars searching for a specific piece of information – such as the identification of the holder of a benefice, or the details of a charter confirming which abbey had feued out which of its lands and to whom – can make a preliminary scan of either Cowan's 1969 Report, Robertson's 1988 Report, or Foggies's 1996 article on the Apostolic Penitentiary, together with the back up of Leonard Boyle's *Survey of the Vatican Archives*. This should soon enable them to select the microfilm(s) they need to examine. It may also be useful to remember that palaeographical and transcriptional aids apart, the identification of almost unrecognisable personal or place names can sometimes be achieved by referring to the massive indexes of the *Calendar of Entries in the Papal Registers relating to Great Britain and Ireland*, especially those for Volume XV onwards, which offer many alternative spellings. Clearly this Glasgow archive still has much to offer those looking for fresh information on the late medieval Scottish Church, particularly those interested in the pontificates of Leo X, Adrian VI, Clement VII, Paul III, Julius III, Paul IV and Pius IV, from 1513 to 1565.

If, however, scholars wish to understand the fundamental reasons for the deepening malaise affecting the Scottish Church in the later Middle Ages, they will need to balance the factual information which the administrative records of the papal *Curia* provide against society's perceptions of the Western Church and the Church's actual relations with the secular rulers of Europe, some indicators of which it may be suggested here. In the first place we have to realise that the growth of a sophisticated body of canon law from the thirteenth century onwards had given legal expression to the fact that by then the Church had become a state within every state.[10] Emperors and kings had initially noted this development with circumspection, but they came increasingly to challenge it, especially when the papacy, in virtue of its spiritual office, insisted on claiming the plenitude of power. The classic example of such a challenge came when King Philip IV of France, demonstrating the limitations of papal claims, arranged for the abduction of Pope Boniface VIII in 1303. Indeed, it is clear that from then on the papacy fought a losing battle to establish its authority over Europe's secular rulers, not only in its theoretical claims, but also in what might be considered legitimate ecclesiastical business, such as the right to nominate bishops and abbots to their sees and abbeys. From the fifteenth century in particular the chancery and cameral records in the Vatican Archives are littered with the debris of these lost papal principles. Innocent VIII's indult to James III is a notable example and subsequently, as the papal records demonstrate, it was

10 The literature on canon law and the development of its corpus in the Middle Ages is vast; but see the introductory survey of J. A. Brundage, *Medieval Canon Law* (London, 1995).

ruthlessly exploited by the king's son and grandson.[11] By their reigns the long struggle to control the patronage of ecclesiastical benefices had finally been won by the secular rulers of the Latin West. This was their answer to where the plenitude of power really lay.

Even more disturbing in its practical effect on the Church was the catastrophic loss of income from the papal states in the later Middle Ages.[12] It was not that the rulers and princes of Europe objected to a papal monarch having temporal lands of his own. That, after all, was the normal structure of their society. They accepted that lands in central Italy had been 'gifted' to Pope Stephen II by the Frankish king Pippin in 756, and that the papacy had not only acquired its firm legal ownership over them in the course of time, but had also controlled them through a network of local governors and vicars temporal. Such an administrative structure had brought into the Apostolic Camera a considerable annual income by way of custom dues, wine and salt taxes, and tallages of the sort enjoyed by secular rulers and landowners everywhere. But the papacy's move to Avignon between 1305 and 1378 seriously weakened its control over the papal states, which gradually fell into the hands of Italian *signori*. By Martin V's pontificate in 1417, a number of these lands, including the Marches of Ancona, Spoleto, Umbria, and the communes of Perugia and Bologna, had virtually been dismembered.[13] The fact that, from then until the pontificates of Julius II (1503–13) and Leo X (1513–21), the papacy spent much of its time and energy trying to regain control of the papal states has to be seen in the context of papal finances: the papacy had lost more than half of its annual income as these states slipped from its control. Secular rulers, meanwhile, were also strapped for cash as they sought to pay for increasingly expensive and regular wars with each other. As a consequence the monarchs of Christendom blocked the papal demand for an increased flow of clerical taxes to Rome with anti-papal legislation. This being so, Renaissance Popes, from Eugenius IV (1431–47) onwards, had to find some other means of supporting their army of secretaries, scriptors, abbreviators, treasurers and the rest who had to deal with the tens of thousands of petitions pouring into the *Curia* every year demanding resolution of one kind or another.

Between 1471 and 1492 Sixtus IV and Innocent VIII believed that they had solved the problem of this shortfall between their annual income and expenditure: they instituted offices within the *Curia* which could be bought and sold. This had the immediate advantage of bringing in large sums of money to a near bankrupt papacy anxious to shore up its administrative and political needs. But windfalls like these could not be repeated once a new class of officeholder had been created, since the office, when vacated, could only be sold to a third party. Moreover, these creations brought in a major shift to the career structure of the papal *Curia* itself, in that by offering to buy their offices as a means of ensuring

11 *CPR*, xiv, 4, dated 20 Apr. 1487.

12 P. Partner, 'The budget of the Roman Church in the Renaissance period', in E. F. Jacob, ed., *Italian Renaissance Studies* (London, 1960), 256–78.

13 P. Partner, *The Papal State under Martin V* (London, 1958); idem, *The Lands of St Peter* (London, 1972).

themselves a safe career, papal notaries and the like were now effectively restricting entry into the *Curia* to men with capital and the expertise to invest. In addition, it encouraged banking houses like the Medici to become more closely involved in papal finance, even to the extent of taking over work previously handled by the Apostolic Camera. Moves like these could not fail to be seen as yet further proof that by now the papal *Curia* was over-secularised.[14] A system which allowed clerics to supplicate for incompatible benefices now encouraged an unseemly scramble for them. More seriously, litigational delays at the *Curia* told against the cure of souls in every diocese, both at the parish and cathedral level. In short, however intelligible the system of non-residence, plural and expectative benefice-holding may once have been, it was now seen as a fiscal device calling for an urgent overhaul. But how to achieve this, given that secular rulers were quite content to go along with a system which allowed many of their higher civil servants, as clergy, to be paid from church benefices, while a pool of highly qualified graduate clerics was ready to supplicate for offices whenever a vacancy occurred? The truth was that by then the papacy had been forced down a blind alley. It needed to reappraise fundamentally its position in society and to establish a more realistic agreement with secular rulers on the nature and limits of their respective powers. But as the papacy then saw it, the threat of an ascendant secular monarchism, and then of Protestant heresy, made it entirely inappropriate to initiate reform. Hence the deadlock which was only resolved by the Reformation.

Historians who wish to understand more fully the deep malaise affecting the later medieval Scottish Church might well consider studying the records now at their disposal in Glasgow. It will help them to recognise the long drawn out patterns of exploitation, compromise and failure which were a part of the struggle between the papacy and Scottish kings and, indeed, all the secular rulers of Europe – over the two seemingly irreconcilable principles of 'rendering unto Caesar the things which [were] Caesar's, and unto God, the things which [were] God's'. Much of the basic work of understanding this struggle, and placing it in its Scottish context, has been assimilated in our more recent text books thanks to the pioneering labours of scholars like Dunlop and Cowan.[15] But much still remains to be done – and *can* now be done – if we are to get a clearer picture of the state of the Scottish nation when, in 1560, its decision-makers decided to break with Rome.

14 P. Partner, *The Pope's Men: The Papal Civil Service in the Renaissance* (Oxford, 1990).

15 See, e.g., A. Grant, *Independence and Nationhood: Scotland 1306–1469* (London, 1984), 89–119; L. Macfarlane, 'Was the Scottish Church reformable by 1513?', in N. Macdougall, ed., *Church, Politics and Society: Scotland 1408–1929* (Edinburgh, 1983), 23–43; J. Wormald, *Court, Kirk and Community: Scotland 1470–1625* (London, 1981), 75–94; M. Lynch, *Scotland: A New History* (London, 1991), chs. 7, 12; and esp. I. B. Cowan, *The Medieval Church in Scotland*, ed. J. Kirk (Edinburgh, 1995).

# 15

# Visiting the Charter Chest: The Early Records of the University and King's College, Aberdeen[1]

*Colin McLaren*

On 6 February 1495 Bishop William Elphinstone presented to Pope Alexander VI a supplication for the foundation of a university in the north of Scotland, sited in the town of Old Aberdeen. Elphinstone had composed the supplication, but it was made in the name of King James IV. Cogently argued – Elphinstone had emphasised the remoteness of the region and 'almost barbarous' nature of its inhabitants – the supplication won the Pope's approval.[2] Four days later he issued the Foundation Bull.[3] This authorised the establishment of a university, modelled on those of Paris and Bologna, with faculties of theology, canon and civil law, medicine and the liberal arts, awarding degrees up to the grade of doctor.[4]

The Foundation Bull is the first of a sequence of documents (papal, royal and episcopal) which defined the constitution of the university and of the college which housed its staff and students, eventually to be known as King's College. The bull was accompanied by a mandate for its publication, but this was delayed, allowing Elphinstone to place his foundation on a secure financial basis; the act of publication was eventually recorded in 1497.[5] In the same year James granted to the university the privileges given by French kings to the university of Paris and by Scottish kings to the universities of St Andrews and Glasgow, Aberdeen's predecessors; and in 1498 he included the university in the privileges which he had previously granted to the burgh of Old Aberdeen.[6] Also in 1498 Alexander approved the creation of a new parish encompassing the residential and mercantile quarters of Old Aberdeen, which Elphinstone subsequently attached to the university: its church, built soon afterwards, was dedicated to St Mary of the Snows; and in 1500 he issued a bull conserving the

1 From the 1970s to 1990s Grant Simpson regularly brought classes to the University Library to see and handle the early records of the university. This contribution is loosely based on the talks I gave then.

2 The definitive account of the origins and early development of the university to 1514 is L. J. Macfarlane, *William Elphinstone and the Kingdom of Scotland, 1431–1514: The Struggle for Order* (Aberdeen, 1985), ch. 7. As it describes in detail the foundation and other early records of the university, I have limited archival descriptions to items outwith its scope.

3 Aberdeen University Library, MS K 256/43/1. All documents cited are from this source. The prefix OCC (Old Charter Chest), used in references to Aberdeen University archives in Macfarlane, *Elphinstone*, has since been replaced by the prefix K 256.

4 The Foundation Bull and most of the archives and manuscripts described below have been printed in full or sampled, with summaries in English, in *Fasti Aberdonenses*. A full translation of the bull by G. Donaldson is in F. C. Eeles, *King's College Chapel, Aberdeen* (Edinburgh, 1956), App. 5.

5 MS K 256/43/2, 3.

6 MS K 256/44/1. A transcript of the charter of 1498 survives in part in a 16th-century compilation of foundation documents of the university; see note 15 below.

privileges of the university.[7] Finally, in 1505 Elphinstone himself issued the Foundation Charter of the college he had built for his community of thirty-six teachers, students, prebendary priests and choristers. This was confirmed the following year by a bull of Pope Julius II.[8]

Elphinstone was chancellor of the university until his death in 1514. For almost twenty years he strove to win the financial support essential to the university's survival. He contributed generously from his own purse and from the resources at his disposal as bishop and Keeper of the Privy Seal. In addition, he secured endowments of lands and rents from the king, from his friends and relatives and from local lairds and townsfolk. His efforts generated the eighteen series of charters and instruments which form the bulk of the university's early archives. They range from sixteen documents (including five bulls) representing the attenuated annexation of the lands and revenues of the hospital of St Germain in the diocese of St Andrews (the first major endowment of the university) to the comparatively simple acquisition (four charters) of the patronage of the church of Slains; from the grant of a modest rent from an Aberdeen tenement by Robert Blindsell (the first donation by a local layman) to the lands, superiority of lands and annuity granted by Andrew Elphinstone of Selmys, the bishop's kinsman.[9]

If Elphinstone felt gratified at his success in raising funds, his feelings were doubtless shared by those who, through their office or personal relationship with him, or both, appear as witnesses in the final protocols of the accumulating writs. Thomas Myrton, a protégé of the bishop, was one.[10] As a notary public, Myrton certified the publication of the Foundation Bull; and, in the same capacity and as canon of Moray, he participated in two stages of the annexation of St Germain's hospital (1497), the transactions by which the university acquired the patronage of the parish church of Slains (1498–9), the union of the parish of St Mary of the Snows (1499) with the university and, four years later, the grant of two small bells from the cathedral to its new church. As diocesan treasurer, he witnessed the grant of the lands of Balnakettle and Adziel and of the annuity from the lands of Utoch by Andrew Elphinstone (1504), and a grant of half of the lands of Adziel by William Cumming of Inverallochy (1506). As archdeacon of Aberdeen, he witnessed a grant from the fermes of the royal fishings on the Water of Deveron in Banffshire by Alexander Ogilvie of Deskford, and a grant by William Elphinstone of Clatt, another of the bishop's kinsmen, from the lands of Mill of Crimond (both in 1512). Finally, as archdeacon and rector of Auchindoir, he was party to the college's annexation of that parish. He then became a prebendary of the college.[11]

The principal writs of each endowment, together with the Foundation Bull, mandate and instrument of publication, and the Foundation Charter, were transcribed in a cartulary, known by the eighteenth century as 'the Parchment

7 MS K 256/17/3; K 256/43/4.

8 MS K 256/48/2; K 256/43/9.

9 MS K 256/28/1–16; K 256/1/1–4; K 256/15/4; K 256/6/1–5, K 256/3/12; K 256/20/11.

10 Macfarlane, *Elphinstone*, 219–20.

11 *Fasti Aberdonenses*, 9, 18–19, 21–2, 25, 27, 29, 31, 44–5, 47, 69–70, 72, 74.

Chartulary'.[12] Of the eight-two documents it contains, sixty-eight appear to have been written by one hand; the latest of these are dated 1512 and the cartulary may, therefore, have been compiled shortly before or around the time of Elphinstone's death. The arrangement is roughly chronological until the early 1500s, when it follows the progress of writs relating to particular lands. Spaces apparently left for the insertion of documents in sequence have been filled by transcriptions of documents dating from 1490 to 1549 by eight other hands.

By 1514 Elphinstone had prepared a second Foundation Charter for King's College, increasing its size and augmenting its revenues. The document remained unpublished and unimplemented in the two-year interregnum following his death and under his successor as bishop and chancellor, the ailing Alexander Gordon. On succeeding to both offices in 1518, Gavin Dunbar saw the need to publish Elphinstone's charter, and to put it quickly into effect before any of the proposed augmentations were lost by default. When this took place, it inaugurated a second sequence of foundation documents. This second sequence begins in 1526, when Dunbar granted to the college the land on which it stood, together with ground across the High Street, which Elphinstone had chosen for the mediciner's manse. Two years later, possibly at Dunbar's request, James V confirmed the grants made by his father to the university. Meanwhile, the university staff, sharing their chancellor's fears that Elphinstone's unfulfilled intentions might be thwarted, had supplicated the Pope, Clement VII, to rectify the situation. Clement responded early in 1527 with a bull empowering Dunbar to hold a formal enquiry into the matter.[13] The resulting document, initially dated 18 December 1529, is one of the more complex of the early archives of the university. After a brief introduction, it rehearses Clement's bull, Elphinstone's charter of 1505 and the bull confirming it. Next it describes the form of the enquiry: the summoning and examination of witnesses – 'intimate familiars' of the deceased bishop – who produced documents 'made in [his] name ... yet not wholly completed ... by reason, as they alleged, of his premature death'; and the

12 MS K 89 (formerly K 256/41/22). The cartulary measures 32.5 × 22.5 cm and consists of ten quires, each of eight leaves; it has been paginated from fo. 4r to fo. 79r, giving pp. 1–151. The first and final folios were pasted to the inside front and end covers. The cover itself is of coarse vellum, sewn over cords. The bulk of the volume seems to have been written by a single scribe, distinguished by his crude but not unpleasing ornamentation of capitals, ascenders (on the top line) and descenders (on the bottom line); spaces for decorated initials at the beginning of each text have been left unfilled. The scribe left three leaves blank then wrote through the first seven quires, leaving some sides wholly or partly blank (pp. 33–5, 54–5, 74–5, 104–6); he left three blank leaves in the eighth quire (pp. 107–12) then wrote through to the end of the ninth quire, leaving more blanks (pp. 127–30, 134–5). The final quire is ruled like the rest but the scribe has left the first half blank and has filled only two of the remaining leaves (pp. 147–50). The transcriptions in quires one to eight cover the years 1495–1506; the first in the ninth quire is the Foundation Charter of 1505, the rest are from 1506; those in the tenth quire are of documents dated 1512. Transcriptions inserted on the blank leaves are of documents dated 1490 (pp. 105–7), 1518 (pp. 107–8), 1541 (pp. 108–11), notarised 1549 (p. 111), 1556 (pp. 127–9), 1549 (p. 130), 1523 (pp. 139–40), 1538 (pp. 141–4), 1516 (p. 145), around 1547 (p. 151); in three cases the scribes identify themselves as James Watson (p. 108), William Davidson (p. 111) and Martin Howeson (p. 151), notaries public; two of the transcriptions are of documents not found in the university archives (pp. 107–8; 141–4).

13 MS K 256/34/5–6; K 256/44/2; K 256/43/11.

comparison of these with other, corroboratory evidence. It ends with an instrument containing the 'uncorrupt and inviolate tenor' of Elphinstone's proposals. The changes planned by Elphinstone were extensive – the number of staff and students was increased to forty-two – and the legal formalities took a further eighteen months. Only in June 1531 was the document sealed and signed by twenty-one members of the cathedral chapter and the college. Fourth in the list is Archdeacon Thomas Myrton, involved in yet another stage of the university's development.[14] The text of the Second Foundation Charter is also preserved in part in a compilation of the foundation bulls and charters of the university, transcribed and elaborately decorated by a single hand between 1538 and 1548. The collection is of particular interest since it contains three items which are not now among the university archives.[15]

Over the next thirty years the university attracted further endowments, although not as many as it probably wished. The first flowering of humanist learning under Principal Hector Boece, his circle and their immediate successors was beginning to fade, and the university was entering a period of decline. In 1562, when Queen Mary visited Old Aberdeen, an English observer commented disparagingly on the size of the university – one college with fifteen or sixteen students.[16] Nevertheless, such lands as the university possessed had to be managed and its rights exercised, defended and enforced. As a result, records of endowments are extended by chains of charters, confirmations, sasines, resignations and tacks. Of obvious importance for studying the social composition and economic structure of Old and New Aberdeen and their hinterlands, these records have been sadly under-used.

As in the original endowments, recurrent names catch the eye. One is Beroald Innes, reader of the parish of St Machar from around 1576. In 1586 he

14 MS K 256/48/3. The codex measures 47 × 34.5 cm and is composed of five folio vellum leaves, formerly sewn together by two vellum thongs. It was described in 1638 as having 'two seals appended', but when it was repaired in 1948 by Cockerell it had only one (Bishop Dunbar's) on heavy silk cords.

15 MS K 90. The compilation is a codex, measuring 36 × 26 cm. It contains 26 leaves, which cannot now be collated, as the volume has been badly damaged by damp in the margins and extensively repaired; two leaves, fos. 10 and 11, are missing. Fos. 1–25 were foliated by the scribe, and fos. 1–8 have ruled margins; fo. 26 does not seem to have been foliated but it is ruled like the earlier leaves and may therefore be misplaced. The compilation contains: the Foundation Bull (fos. 1r–2r); bulls of Alexander VI, 1500, K 256/43/4, 6 (fos. 2r–3v); bull of Julius II, 1506, K 256/43/10 (fos. 3v–4r); charter of James IV, 21 Aug. 1498, not in the university archives (fos. 4r–5r); charter of James IV, 19 Aug. 1498, not in university archives (fos. 5r–6v); bull of Paul III, 11 Oct. 1538, not in the university archives but printed in *Fasti Aberdonenses*, no. 71, pp. 109–10, where it is said to be from the original (fos. 6v–7v); Foundation Charter (fos. 8r–9v, incomplete); bull of Julius II, 1506, K 256/43/9 (fos. 12r–12v, incomplete); and Second Foundation Charter, excluding the Foundation Charter and bull of confirmation (fos. 13r–25v). On fo. 26r is an inscription: *1548 rectore Alexandro Galloway canonico Aberdonensi, Iuramenti prestandi forma per inquisitores in visitacione novi collegii Aberdonensis infra universitatem eiusdem. In verbo dei et hec sacra dei evangelia, quod super hiis que scitis vel creditis esse in hac universitate et collegio eiusdem reformanda tam in capite quam in membris necnon super observacione fundacionis presentis collegii, exceptis occultis terminibus, meram et plenam dicetis veritatem.* It seems that the compilation was made between 1538 (the date of the latest transcript) and 1548, possibly for the visitation of that year.

16 John Lesley, *The History of Scotland* (Bannatyne Club, 1830), 159; *CSP Scot.*, i, 649; *Fasti Ecclesiae Scoticanae*, ed. H. Scott (Edinburgh, 1915–50), vi, 26.

had an arrangement with the college by which he took in students as boarders, since – as the college itself admitted – facilities for living and studying were inadequate. The college sold Beroald a manse called Chaplains' Chambers, which stood in the burial ground to the north of the chapel and was formerly the residence of the sacrist and the cantor.[17] In the same year, Beroald became 'economus' (steward) of the college. In that capacity he enforced the college's rights, as in 1589, when he obtained a precept of poinding (seizure of goods) against the tenants of Haltoun of Belhelvie for failing to pay the annuity due to the college for the past six years.[18] Soon afterwards, Beroald acquired more college land for himself – the Regents' (or College) Crofts, which lay on the east side of the college, between the burial ground and the college butts, and stretched south to Powis Burn. In 1599 he extended his holdings to the other side of the burn with the acquisition of Tarbert's Croft. Finally, in 1604 he added Strachan's Croft to his lands on the north side of the college. Beroald became a notable figure in the Old Town and served as baillie in the years 1604–6. The Chaplains' Chambers and the Regents' Crofts remained in the possession of his family until his grand-daughter resigned them in favour of the college in 1651. Their site is indicated by the path called Beroald's Wynd shown on Gordon's plan of 1661.[19]

Endowments were made for the most part to provide bursaries for students attending the university. There are few records among the early archives which show the bursary system in action. Those which do, relate to bursaries in canon and civil law. Elphinstone himself had created these, associating them with three chaplaincies – in St Mary of the Snows (canon law), St Nicholas, Aberdeen, and St Machar's cathedral (civil law). He described their apportionment in the Second Foundation Charter. A series of collations (presentations) to these chaplaincies survives among the early archives, and others are to be found among the documents relating to the endowments themselves. The holders of the bursaries before 1514 have been named elsewhere.[20] The civil law students presented to the chaplaincy at St Machar's after 1514 were Alexander Milne (1517–20), John Hay (1520–4), Alexander Stevenson (presented in 1554), William Cable (*c.*1563), Walter Gordon (presented in 1563) and Andrew Anderson (presented in 1572). Meanwhile, John Cuming held the chaplaincy in St Nicholas after 1514. Following his resignation in 1516, he was followed by Thomas Clerk, vicar of Rayne. Clerk's letters of collation survive only in the 'Parchment Chartulary'. They were issued by Thomas Myrton, in his capacity as archdeacon of Aberdeen, as the see was still vacant. Clerk was succeeded in

17 MS K 256/35/16. The sacrist's and cantor's residences originally lay south of the Powis Burn (Macfarlane, *Elphinstone*, 339). I have found no record of a change of site.

18 MS K 256/4/9; the tenants of Belhelvie were notably recalcitrant where the annuity was concerned: Hector Boece, as principal, took out letters of poinding against them in 1531, as did David Rait, principal in 1609 (MS K 256/4/10–11).

19 MS K 256/35/18; K 256/10/11,12; K 256/35/15; K 256/35/31; *Records of Old Aberdeen*, ed. A. M. Munro (New Spalding Club, 1899–1909), i, 34, 37, 41, 59, 113; James Gordon, *Abredoniae utriusque descriptio: A description of both touns of Aberdeen* (Spalding Club, 1842), frontispiece.

20 Macfarlane, *Elphinstone*, 377–8.

1518 by Hector Myrton, who occupied it until his death in 1563, when he was replaced by John Kennedy.[21]

Hector Myrton was guilty of non-residence, failure to carry out his duties as chaplain and neglect of his studies. His shortcomings were revealed during a visitation of King's in 1549. Annual visitations of the college by the rector and four assessors to 'inspect the faults thereof ... as well in persons as in affairs' were an important element of Elphinstone's Foundation Charters. The visitors were required to present a written report to the chancellor. None has survived, but the findings of the 1549 visitation are recapitulated in a series of orders issued afterwards by the chancellor, Bishop William Gordon. They provide a unique opportunity to contrast the aspirations of the founder with the reality of life some fifty years later. The result is something less than impressive: the visitors found much to criticise in the conduct of staff and students alike. Over fifty orders were required to remedy the neglect and abuses which they had uncovered.[22]

An earlier visitation, in 1542, left no records of its proceedings, but it did generate one of the most illuminating of the early archives, an inventory of the contents of the college chapel (in Latin), the hall, the kitchen quarter and the residential block (in Scots). The text has been printed and translated, and the sections on the chapel, the hall and the chambers have been analysed in depth.[23] The kitchen and its appurtenances, however, have received less attention. The kitchen itself lay behind the common school and hall, on the east side of the college, on the site later occupied by King's College Library (from 1870), now King's College Conference Centre. It was furnished with a cupboard (almery) made of fir, and an oak block (stok) on which meat was dressed. It was equipped with a large gridiron (brandar) and a smaller one (roast-iron). There were five large spits, four of them large and set in racks. For boiling and braising food, there were six pots and five pans, all of different sizes; a marginal note of 1543 added 'ane gret beif pot'. Utensils consisted of a pair of tongs; two mortars and pestles, one of stone, the other of brass (donated by Boece) and a board on which dough was kneaded (ane bakein buird). Dishes kept in the kitchen comprised a large, flat dish (chargeour); six dishes with handles (luggit); six round platters (trunscheouris) and four square, or oblong (nukit). There were nineteen plates (twenty-one the following year); the inventory does not say what they were made of, but those kept in the hall for use on special occasions (*extra quotidianum usum*) were mainly of pewter (*vasa stannea*). The kitchen had a loft, presumably used for storage, since it had a lock. Its contents are not listed.

After the kitchen the inventory deals with the pantry (*panarium*), brewhouse (literally 'barley house', *domus polentaria*), larder (*lardanaria*), grain store

21 MS K 256/26/7–11; K 256/2/13, 16; MS K 89, p. 145.

22 MS K 256/23/2; *Fasti Aberdonenses*, 264.

23 MS K 200 (formerly K 256/23/1); Eeles, *King's College Chapel,* 4–69; Macfarlane, *Elphinstone*, 330–8. In 1504 Gilbert Piot ran a brewery which served King's (ibid., 360). The plenishings of the brewhouse suggest that brewing had also gone on there: possibly the 'second ale' served at meals (*Fasti Aberdonenses*, 578).

(*granarium*) and ale store (*penu cervisiarium*). The pantry had a cupboard with a lockable double door and twelve vessels of various measures (stoups, ane chopin). The brewhouse was equipped with tubs for the principal stages of brewing: one for the mash - the infusion of grain and water (mask fatt); a cooling (skeill) tub; a fermenting tub (gyle fatt) and a cauldron. The larder had six tubs and two barrels (boweis) for meat, and two chopping (hackein) blocks. The grain store had two wooden, lidded barrels (girnals), one for meal and one for malt and five casks (dry pypis) for grain, one of which was out of use; there were grain measures (firlot and peck), a balance (schele) and a stick for levelling the portion to be measured (straik). The ale store contained six upright casks (standis) and two barrels, probably resting on the two supports (gantrees) of oak. Like the kitchen, the larder and the stores for grain and ale were lockable, the larder and the grain store made doubly secure with an inset lock (inlok) and a padlock (hingand lok).

There are brief references to catering in the college at this time. The Second Foundation Charter refers to the provisor (steward), who was to receive from the procurator (the member of staff responsible for the college finances) money to buy food and drink. In addition, he was to keep a garden in which he was to grow herbs and vegetables: it still survives, on the south side of the college. The visitation of 1549 is more specific: the procurator was to provide the provisor with fresh food - meal, bread, ale, meat and fish - according to the season. But the women who sold ale and oat-bread (*brasitrices, pistatrices panium avenarum*) to the college were no longer to be allowed beyond the gate, unless they were accompanied by a servitor. The buying in of bread and ale suggests that home brewing and baking were no longer a serious function of the college kitchen. The provisor was to keep daily accounts and a stock book (*liber rationum*): the earliest surviving volume with this title dates from thirty years later.

The *Liber Rationum* contains both accounts and stock for September 1579–October 1583, January 1629–July 1632 and September 1651–March 1653.[24] The entries of the sixteenth and early seventeenth centuries differ in format from those in the 1650s: the former show the amounts purchased and consumed each day, the latter adds the numbers at each table and the amount consumed at each of the three meals, breakfast, dinner and supper. In the sixteenth-century accounts purchases are listed on the right of the page and the food consumed on the left. When he began the accounts on Tuesday 1 September 1579, the steward had seven loaves of white bread in hand. He bought three more that day, making ten, of which five were consumed. On Wednesday he bought three more loaves, making eight, but they were all consumed that day. On Thursday, therefore, he bought twelve. Four were consumed, leaving eight, so on Friday he bought three more loaves, topping up the stock to eleven.[25] The steward seems to have paid most of his suppliers on delivery; the baker, however, was paid periodically: 'Deliverit to the baxter xxi lib. ii s. in compleit payment of all byganes to this day inclusive and so begynnis our new compt 2 October 1580.'

[24] MS K 2, fos. 1–223; 224–359; 360–576.
[25] Ibid., fos. 6r–7r; *Fasti Aberdonenses*, 578–9.

At fairly regular intervals the steward himself would be recompensed by the procurator: 'at quhilk tyme the stewart payit and iii lib. advancit to hym'.[26]

The accounts show what kind of provisions were purchased, and when. In 1582, for example, the steward bought white bread, eggs, milk, ale and malt throughout the year together with haddocks and herrings (small fish), skate, crabs (partans) and mussels. He bought meat at intervals: beef in January, from April to July, and from October to December; mutton in January and February, from July to October, and in December; and veal in January and February, and from April to June. Other commodities were clearly seasonal: codling in January, March and December; cockles from March to May; lobster from September to December; and trout in October and November. The choice of meat and fish widened between March and July with the addition of lamb, capons, chicken and moorfowl; coalfish (podleys), turbot and flounder (fluke). Some commodities appeared only briefly: hens in February and November; salmon and lump-fish (padill) in April; and smoked haddock (findons) in September. The steward bought onions in January and carrots (murins) in January and February, and from September to December. He bought no fruit, except damsons (plumdames), in April, June, October and November. Presumably he grew other fruit, herbs and vegetables in the kitchen garden. He did, however, buy spices and preservatives: vinegar throughout the year; mustard in February and March; fine (small) salt in April and May; coarse (great) salt in July; saffron and pepper together in July and December.[27]

The importance of the *Liber Rationum* lies not only in the light it sheds on food prices and diet, but in the miscellaneous expenditure entered from time to time at the foot of a page. Some entries relate directly or indirectly to the college table: 'Naipre xii serviettis ii towallis; to ane flescher that slew the marts [cattle fattened for slaughter] xx s.' Some relate to the kitchen: 'Item for ii stoppis iiii s.; item for nailis to mende the almris iiiis.' Others are of a more general nature: 'Item for marbell [marl] and clay to the chalmers viii s.'; 'item for laying the flooris'; 'item for mending the loftis'; 'item to the mason to mend the chymnais'; and 'to Andrew Gilgour officier to pass to Slains to arrest Jhone Hous geir and summond otheris xiiii s.' In the seventeenth century casual payments of this kind appear in the accounts of the procurators, under the heading 'discharge extraordinar'. The *Liber Rationum*, written some seventy-five years earlier, contains, in effect, the earliest surviving record of daily expenditure in the college.[28]

The sixteenth-century section refers throughout to 'the stewart', but a note on its penultimate leaf supplies a name.

> The stewart payit for aucht dayis burd of James Irwing, Master Peter Udny, Thomas Burnet, Baroell Innes and him self and for all uther byganes in this boke. In testimonie of the quhich he hes subscryvit this present uith his hand befoir witnes Thome Scot Alexander Lullie David Leper and utheris. Master James Spittall with my hand.

26 MS K 2, fos. 62r, 54r.
27 Ibid., fos. 127v.–179v.
28 Ibid. fos. 74r., 42r., 118r., 28r.

The note was probably written in October 1583 (the accounts end on 13 October), at which time Udny was humanist, or teacher of Latin. (Irving and Burnet have not been identified.) Just over two years later, however, Innes was to replace James as *economus*.

The early archives of the university have enabled historians, notably Leslie Macfarlane, to describe Elphinstone's aims in depth; to explain in detail how he achieved them; and, by drawing on the ancillary evidence of books owned and written by the first teachers and on the practice of the universities on which Aberdeen was modelled, to reconstruct the nature of teaching and learning there. Nevertheless, in the absence of rectorial and faculty act-books, the management of college affairs, the daily life of staff and students, the identity of some of the staff and most of the students, remain obscure. It is clear from the foundation documents and the visitation of 1549 that other series of records were created but have not survived. The Second Foundation Charter stipulated that the procurator was 'to render account, reckoning and payment of his receipts' twice yearly, and that he was to 'give up an account' of the management of funds from vacant burses. A 'common bursar' was to receive the burses of those to be advanced in each faculty and to 'render an account and reckoning' of them. If the records of the visitation of 1549 reflect the general practice, then the principal and staff were to present an account of their management of the property of the college, in particular of the money set aside for repairs to the fabric; and the staff-member responsible for the administration of bursaries in the faculty of arts (in 1549 it was the subprincipal) had to give in an account of his receipts. The orders which followed from that visitation increased the paperwork: the procurator was in future to render his accounts each quarter and to prepare an annual statement, which was to be audited by the rector and his assessors before it was formally recorded; and the steward was to keep daily accounts. As we have seen, of these financial records, the steward's alone survive and those only from a later period. There is no apparent explanation for the loss of these materials, although it is possible that some, at least, shared the fate of the treasures and service books of the chapel, which were dispersed at the Reformation to protect them from plunder, and never retrieved.[29] In one case, at least, loss or dispersal was not permanent. An inscription on the 'Parchment Chartulary' reads: *Librum hunc recuperavit et Collegio Regio Universitatis Aberdonensis dono dedit Magister Thomas Sandielandius a Crabstoun et Commissarius Aberdonensis 8 Junii 1669*.[30]

In a few cases, contemporary or later descriptions and copies describe the form and content of missing items. Thomas Gordon – who served the college in various capacities from 1734 to 1797 and chronicled its history in the *Statistical Account* – made use of an 'old paper chartulary', describing it as 'containing abstracts of college charters and productions of progresses'.[31] In addition a single leaf survives of a reconstruction of the rental of the college 'when Master

29 D. Stevenson, *King's College, Aberdeen, 1560–1641: From Protestant Reformation to Covenanting Revolution* (Aberdeen, 1990), 14.

30 MS K 89, fo. 3v.

31 J. Sinclair, *Statistical Account of Scotland* (Edinburgh, 1791–9), xxi, 51–104; MS K 35, p. 241.

Alexander Arbuthnot entered principal the 11 of July 1569'. It appears to date from the 1590s and may be related to another fragmentary rental of 1593.[32]

Most important of all are the surviving texts of the *Nova Fundatio* of 1587. The New Foundation was a product of the Reformation, when radical ideas about the aim, form and content of higher education, originating abroad, were introduced into Scotland by reformers such as Andrew Melville. These ideas were reflected in new constitutions imposed on the universities of Glasgow and St Andrews and created for Aberdeen. The obscure history of Aberdeen's New Foundation and the bitter internecine strife which it provoked in the first half of the seventeenth century form the core of David Stevenson's study of King's from 1560 to 1641.[33] The original document was deliberately destroyed around 1619 but not before it had been secretly copied.[34] The history of this copy is as problematic as that of the original. It existed in 1638, when its authenticity was challenged by supporters of the Old Foundation (of 1529–31), but it does not appear in the earliest surviving inventory of the college archives (1657).[35] Nevertheless, at a visitation of King's in 1664, the staff produced 'ane coppie of the fundatione be king James 6t' and in 1696, Principal George Middleton declared that 'he had heard ther was a new fundatione, which by report was said to have been destroyed, but he hath ane paper, which is said to be a double thereof'.[36] No further references to it have been found. In the eighteenth century, however, Thomas Gordon transcribed the text of the New Foundation. His is the earliest surviving version and is assumed to derive directly or indirectly from the seventeenth-century copy.[37] Gordon did not simply transcribe the text. He collated it with the Foundation Charter of Marischal College – Aberdeen's second university, founded in the New Town in 1593, and an institution of impeccably Melvillian origin.[38]

Despite the loss of act books and accounts, and of individual items such as the New Foundation, the early records of the University and King's College comprise a major resource for the study of the intellectual, cultural, economic and social history not just of northern Scotland but for the kingdom as a whole. The wonder is that so much has survived. From 1600 to 1860 King's and Marischal were often in contention over issues of status and precedence, while King's itself was repeatedly divided by internal and external wrangles which erupted into litigation.[39] There were, as a result, frequent forays to the Charter Chest. Of the Charter Chest itself, there is no early record. Originally the archives were probably held by the principal, who had responsibility for the

32 MS 2379/1/10.

33 Stevenson, *King's College, Aberdeen*; it contains a translation of the New Foundation by G. P. Edwards.

34 Ibid., 88, 90, 93.

35 *Fasti Aberdonenses*, 287, 300, 302.

36 Ibid., 317, 377.

37 MS K 35, pp. 181–213.

38 *Fasti Academiae Mariscallanae Aberdonensis, 1593–1860*, ed. P. J. Anderson (New Spalding Club, 1889–98), i, 39–77; G. D. Henderson, *The Founding of Marischal College* (Aberdeen, 1947).

39 C. A. McLaren, 'Enlightened men at law: litigation at King's College in the eighteenth century', in J. J. Carter and J. H. Pittock-Wesson, eds., *Aberdeen and the Enlightenment* (Aberdeen, 1987), 129–35.

college books. He may have kept them in the locked box which contained money set aside for the repair of the fabric, or in the Scorpio Chamber high in the south-east tower, which housed the college library. Later they were transferred to the jewel house erected by Bishop Stewart on the south side of the chapel between 1532 and 1545.[40]

The first reference to the Charter Chest and an inventory of its contents dates from the 1630s, when the internal management of King's was overhauled by the chancellor, Bishop Patrick Forbes. In 1634 it became the practice for each rector to deliver to his successor copies of the foundation documents and an inventory of the writs, together with an inventory of the college property, a rental and a catalogue of the library. The system seems to have broken down in the 1640s. In 1637, when the mediciner, William Gordon, served as procurator and simultaneously took a leading part in the dispute over the Old and New Foundations, he withdrew documents from the chest and was with some difficulty forced to return them. Thereafter, staff were instructed to remove and replace documents from the chest systematically, according to the inventory. As an additional precaution, surrogate copies were made of certain items, 'in speciall the auld foundatioun of the college'; and the following year the three keys to the chest were distributed among the rector, the principal and the new procurator.[41]

The structure of the Charter Chest is revealed by the earliest surviving inventory, compiled in 1657 by the energetic Principal John Row. It was a 'cabinet' with fifty-one 'shuttles' (*capsulae*) – long narrow drawers, in which the bulls, charters and other records were placed, tightly folded. They carry the marks of compression to this day. Shuttles 1–22 held documents relating to specific endowments: shuttle 1, those relating to the patronage of the church of Slains; shuttle 2, the chaplaincy of St Mary Madgalene in the church of St Nicholas; shuttle 3, the annuity from the lands of Utoch granted by Andrew Elphinstone of Selmys; and so on. The voluminous documentation of the annexation of the hospital of St Germain filled shuttle 22 and overflowed into shuttle 28. Shuttles 23–31 held documents arranged by type: shuttle 23, visitation records; shuttle 24, tacks; shuttle 26, collations. Of the rest, six held records of (mostly) later endowments; shuttle 43 held papal bulls; shuttle 44, royal confirmations; shuttle 51, the Foundation Charters. Nine shuttles remained empty. Subsequently – possibly in 1665, when the staff found 'severall writs misplaced and many uthers wraped up confusedlie together so that they could not make ane perfect accompt of quhat wreitts wer missing' – the royal confirmations of individual grants were put into the empty shuttle 41, leaving confirmations of privileges in number 44. The Foundation Charters were moved to shuttle 48.[42]

From the later seventeenth century until the early 1800s 'visiting' the Charter Chest became an established, if infrequent, part of college management. The principal, with two or more colleagues, would inspect its contents, set it in

40 Macfarlane, *Elphinstone*, 338, 358; Gordon, *Description of Aberdeen*, 24.
41 MS K 36, fos. 6v, 19r, 21v, 23v, 24v, 25r, 27r, 33v, 36v, 39r.
42 MS K 103/1.

order, revise the inventory, then wait for their colleagues to disrupt it again.[43] In the eighteenth century these visitations led to some improvements. In 1718 the procurator paid a local advocate and his clerk 23 guineas to make a fresh inventory, and in 1720 the Charter Chest was repaired. In 1721, moreover, a second chest was made at a cost of £33 6s. 8d., initially, at least, for accounts and vouchers. Thereafter, the two chests were known as the 'Old' and the 'New'. In 1729 they were moved into the new library.[44]

In 1737, when King's took Marischal to court in a dispute over their respective rights under the Copyright Act of 1709, notarised copies of the foundation documents were despatched to the Court of Session. This was the first of several occasions when the early records were copied for legal purposes. An entry in the accounts of 1763 suggests that clerks did not find it a simple task: 'To copying and deciphering from a very old hand Latin precept Jacobi quarti ...'[45] In 1747 the question of access to the early records was raised by Thomas Gordon, then the college humanist (teacher of Latin). He sought permission to borrow the original Foundation Charter, in connection with a proposed Widows' Fund. His colleagues maintained that the document was too important to be lent out, and that he should consult it in the library. Thomas replied that the library was too cold in the evening to do so; when they remained unmoved, he declared that their refusal was 'an encroachment upon the common right which all the members have in the college papers'. The issue of access arose again in 1761, during a dispute over the management of college affairs. This time the staff demanded free access to the records in the Charter Chest, but the question remained unresolved. It arose for a third time when William Ogilvie, who had succeeded Gordon in the role of embattled humanist, was in dispute with his colleagues. He did little to help his case by removing items and retaining them for long periods. The view of his colleagues was that the principal had, *ex officio*, charge of the college records.[46]

In 1766 a new inventory of the Old Charter Chest was planned but not executed. The order adopted in 1718, which made few changes to that established in the seventeenth century, remained in force until 1898 and is still retained in a large measure today. In 1771 both chests were repaired; a bookcase with pigeonholes was acquired for current papers; and the first inventory of the New Charter Chest was made.[47] In 1787 a threatened union with Marischal College led to the preparation of more copies of the Foundation Bull, James IV's charter of 1497 and the Second Foundation Charter. Finally, in January 1793 there was a visitation of the Old Charter Chest: notes of missing documents still survive and are occasionally referred to. The exercise was repeated in 1795.[48]

The precise location of the charter chests at the beginning of the nineteenth century remains uncertain. It is assumed, but nowhere stated, that they were

43 MS K 37, fos. 10v, 25v, 26v; K 43, pp. 46, 275; K 44, p. 25.

44 MS K 41, fo. 24r; K 57/1–2, 5; K 257/1/4/38; K 257/2/1/53; K 257/2/2/3, 18; K 257/3/3/29. The prefix K 257 identifies records from the New Charter Chest.

45 MS K 43, p. 51; K 257/31/29/8; K 257/8/1/36; K 257/8/5/29, 49; K 58, p. 193; K 257/8/6/40

46 MS K 43, pp. 280–1; K 44, pp. 201–2; K 47, pp. 153, 204.

47 MS K 105; MS K 257/8/6/55; K 59, pp. 65–6; K 257/9/5/30; K 257/20/11/3, 6.

48 MS K 257/11/7/30; K 48, fos. 34v, 69v.

moved with the library into the west end of the chapel in 1775. Wherever they were, their location caused Principal Roderick Macleod concern: he hoped, he said in 1808, that a more convenient place for them could be found. In 1809 he referred to their 'irregular, confused state' and ordered a visitation; another, also on a substantial scale, took place in 1826.[49] It was not until 1844, however, that the chests found a new home in the Round Tower, the south-east tower which had housed the library when the college was first built. They were placed in a 'new Safe Room' constructed by Barry, Henry and Co., at the Aberdeen Iron Foundry.[50]

In the meantime, the early records of the university were made available to the Parliamentary Commission of 1826 and were printed with other evidence submitted to it; the 'Parchment Chartulary' was also sent to Edinburgh, but only for inspection.[51] In 1834 the question of access to the chest arose again, when thirty-three students demanded to see the Foundation Charter and other documents relating to their right to elect a rector, an issue which was, as the Senatus observed, a subject of 'agitation'. Once the students had adopted a less challenging tone, the Senate appointed two professors to 'exhibit to them such deeds and records as may appear proper to them and in such a way as may be completely consistent with the safety of these documents'.[52]

The Senate responded more gracefully to a request of a different sort in 1850: 'It was agreed to lend to Professor Innes of the University of Edinburgh, who has undertaken to edit the History of the University at the instance of the Chancellor, such books and documents in the Library and Charter Chest as he may require for the purpose': the chancellor was the Earl of Aberdeen, sponsor of the volume.[53] *Fasti Aberdonenses* appeared in 1854. For the first time, the early records of the university were readily accessible and, for the most part, intelligible. This work has been the first resort of all those who have explored the history of the university, from the magisterial P. J. Anderson, at the time of the Quatercentenary, to the authors of the Quincentennial Studies in the 1990s. There is every reason to believe that it will serve the same purpose when the university celebrates its six hundredth anniversary on 10 February 2095.[54]

49 MS K 49, pp. 196, 213, 215–16; K 103/2.

50 MS K 51, p. 366; K 255, Box 1.

51 *Alidene ... received by the Commissioners ... for visiting the Universities of Scotland* (London, 1837), i, 129–51; MS K 89, fo. 3v.

52 MS K 51, pp. 46–7, 50–1.

53 MS K 52, pp. 7–8.

54 In 1887 the charter chests were moved to the Crown Tower and set in order by P. J. Anderson. His revised inventories (1898) are still in use: C. A. McLaren, 'P. J. Anderson and the history of the university', in *Aberdeen University Review*, li (1985–6), 83–101. The chests merit the attention of a furniture historian. How much, if anything, of the original wood survives is difficult to say, as they were extensively remodelled, probably in 1889; the original numbers and inscriptions, just visible on the shuttles, show how they have been interchanged and cannibalised.

# 16

# Acts of Lordship: The Records of the Lords of Galloway to 1234

*Keith J. Stringer*

Grant Simpson's pioneering doctoral thesis on Roger de Quincy, Earl of Winchester and Constable of Scotland, was based on the meticulous editing and interpretation of Earl Roger's written *acta*, of which no fewer than seventy-nine were found to have survived as full texts, including forty-three originals.[1] The following collection for the native lords of Galloway, over a period of almost a century, supplies more modest totals. This does not mean that in contemporary Scottish Gaeldom magnates were unfamiliar with (to use Robert Bartlett's phrase) 'the scratch of the quill, the curl of the parchment and the smell of hot wax'.[2] To a large degree the explanation lies rather in serious archival losses. Thus it can readily be deduced from other sources that the Galloways were munificent founders and patrons of monasteries in south-west Scotland, where they established, or helped to establish, as many as seven or eight religious houses;[3] but none of these has left a surviving cartulary and practically all their early records have perished.[4] Nevertheless, no systematic attempt has hitherto been made to gather together the extant records of the Galloways' grants, confirmations and injunctions; and, meagre though it is, the corpus that results is by no means lacking in interest. Moreover, since Earl Roger married as his first wife the eldest daughter of Alan of Galloway, and shared in her right in the partition of the huge Galloway inheritance in 1234–5, it seems especially appropriate that these *acta* should be collected in this festschrift.

The collection comprises sixty-five entries, of which the vast majority are charters or references to charters, and is arranged in approximate chronological order. It covers both the lordship of Galloway and lands beyond it, most notably the extensive estates acquired by the Galloways in 1196 from the Morvilles, hereditary constables of Scotland and one of the most powerful Anglo-Norman families in the twelfth-century kingdom. The acts known to

1 G. G. Simpson, 'An Anglo-Scottish Baron of the Thirteenth Century: The Acts of Roger de Quincy, Earl of Winchester and Constable of Scotland' (University of Edinburgh, unpublished PhD thesis, 1965). Two further full texts have since been located: idem, 'The *familia* of Roger de Quincy, Earl of Winchester and Constable of Scotland', in Stringer, *Nobility*, 130.

2 R. Bartlett, *The Making of Europe: Conquest, Colonization and Cultural Change, 950–1350* (London, 1993), 284.

3 R. A. McDonald, 'Scoto-Norse kings and the reformed religious orders: patterns of monastic patronage in twelfth-century Galloway and Argyll', *Albion*, xxvii (1995), 187–219.

4 G. R. C. Davis, *Medieval Cartularies of Great Britain* (London, 1958), overlooks a roll of 12 deeds, copied in 1504 from the cartulary of Whithorn Priory before it was lost, now in the Ellesmere Collection (Derby Papers) of the Huntington Library, San Marino, California. This important source, while of no assistance for present purposes, includes three *acta* of King Alexander III, on which see G. G. Simpson, *Handlist of the Acts of Alexander III, the Guardians and John, 1249–1296* (Edinburgh, 1960), nos. 157, 171–2.

have survived as full texts, including those with missing witness-lists, number thirty-seven. Only nine originals have been traced (see *Plates 2–4* for examples), though to these may be added a facsimile engraved for James Anderson and published in 1739. In addition, notices are given of twenty-eight 'lost acts', each introduced by an asterisk.[5] Eight charters are printed in full because previous editions are seriously inadequate or (in one case) particularly difficult to obtain, and wherever witness-clauses survive, these are fully recorded. The scribes' punctuation and capitals have been retained in editing original texts; elsewhere, punctuation and capitals are editorial. Many acts have of necessity to be assigned broad date-limits, and a number of dating-points are employed without justifying them every time they appear. Thus it is assumed, albeit with some reservation, that Uhtred did not issue *acta* concerning (eastern) Galloway until after the death of his father Fergus on 12 May 1161;[6] and none of Uhtred's charters seems likely to belong to a date later than about May 1174.[7] The main dating-points for Roland son of Uhtred's acts are 1176 or thereabouts, when he probably gained control in eastern Galloway;[8] 1186, when he became sole lord of the entire province;[9] 1196 (after 31 July), when his wife Helen, on the death of her brother William de Morville, brought him the Morville lordships and the office of constable of Scotland;[10] and November 1200, when he left Scotland for good, dying at Northampton on the following 19 December.[11] The basic criteria for dating Alan son of Roland's acts are his recognition as constable of Scotland and take-over of the family estates – say January 1201 if we allow for a time-lag of about two weeks for the news of Roland's death to reach Scotland – and his own death on or about 2 February 1234.[12]

A detailed analysis of the *acta* is beyond the scope of this introductory essay, but some aspects can briefly be dealt with. Broadly speaking, these records illustrate in microcosm the varied responses of Gaelic-speaking potentates to the major challenges brought by the twelfth century, challenges that can be summarised as the arrival of new European concepts of power, authority and culture. The use of Latin charters was itself a major aspect of the Galloways' capacity for adaptation to novel norms. They adopted them apparently no earlier than the 1140s, and it is

5 'Lost acts' comprise either references to actual missing *acta*, or references to transactions that are specifically recorded and were probably, but not certainly, the subject of individual written record. Almost all fall into the former category. Other *acta* can more or less reasonably be inferred from the sources, but these have not been listed.

6 Lawrie, *Annals*, 67. For a recent suggestion that Uhtred and his brother Gilbert may have controlled much of Galloway from 1156, see J. G. Scott, 'The origins of Dundrennan and Soulseat Abbeys', *TDGAS*, 3rd ser., lxiii (1988), 40, 44.

7 Uhtred campaigned in northern England from Jun. to early Jul. 1174; he rebelled immediately after King William I had been taken at Alnwick on 13 Jul.; and he was then at war with his brother Gilbert. Captured on 22 Sep., he was mutilated by his enemies and died soon after: Lawrie, *Annals*, 189–92.

8 Duncan, *Kingdom*, 184.

9 Lawrie, *Annals*, 265.

10 *Chron. Bower* (Watt), iv, 413, 582.

11 Lawrie, *Annals*, 323–5.

12 *Chron. Bower* (Watt), v, 147, 261. Though Alan did not formally succeed to the Morville estates until Helen de Morville's death in 1217, it is clear that he exercised with her a joint lordship over them in the period 1201–17 [Nos. 30, 36–8, 51–2].

surely significant that written administration seems to have followed hard on the heels of the expansion into Galloway of the reformed continental religious orders, equipped as they were with the necessary technology and literate mentality.[13] Although Fergus was the outstanding figure in the history of his family, this collection scarcely does justice to the place he occupied and his role as a 'moderniser'.[14] None of his charters survives, though we have authentic evidence of *acta* issued in his name for the Knights Hospitallers and Holyrood Abbey [Nos. **1**, **2**]. By failing to appear in the collection at all Gilbert, Fergus's elder son and his successor in western Galloway, seems to live up to his traditional reputation as an arch-conservative unable to adjust successfully to new forces. On the other hand, Gilbert's brother Uhtred, lord of eastern Galloway, has twelve entries over a thirteen-year period (1161–74) – luckily three of his *acta* are surviving originals – and this perhaps suggests that in his milieu documentary habits were already becoming ingrained. Although Fergus was accorded the title 'king of the Gallovidians' [No. **1**], his successors had gradually to come to terms with changing political realities as the Scottish crown became a stronger European-style monarchy, in itself the greatest innovation experienced by elite society in twelfth-century Scotland. The process left a vivid mark in Roland's employment from 1196 of the charter style 'constable of the king of Scots', a title also paraded by Alan, though (like his successor Roger de Quincy) he normally called himself 'constable of Scotland'. Nevertheless, political adjustment was made on terms that allowed the Galloways to preserve as much as possible of Fergus's authority and independence, and in fact they for long retained a residual 'royalty'. A regal emphasis distinguishes the phraseology of one of Uhtred's charters [No. **6**]; while his apparent use – at least in this instance – of the county court at Carlisle for transacting business concerning Galloway drives home the ambiguous nature of its political status despite Malcolm IV's conquest of 1160. A qualified sense of attachment to the Scottish state could easily justify rebelliousness, and the impact of the major uprising that began in Galloway in 1174 can be glimpsed, notably with regard to the disruption of ecclesiastical rights [Nos. **15**, **30**]. About twenty-five years later Roland adopted royal language when he took those monks and servants of Kelso Abbey who resided in Galloway under his firm peace and protection [No. **27**]. Later still Alan referred, albeit in a Cunningham context, to 'the expedition of our army' [No. **61**] – a phrase that not only evokes his formidable military capacity, but seems to imply that he took for granted the right to wage 'private' war.

What can be seen with even greater clarity, however, is the importance of the year 1196 in expanding the family's horizons and giving it a leading place within the Anglo-Norman world. From this point some 60% of the collection concerns the mighty complex of estates formerly held by the Morvilles. The largest constituents were the great regional fiefs of Lauderdale (Berwickshire) and Cunningham with Largs (Ayrshire). Other Scottish gains included Eddleston

13 Cf. D. Broun, *The Charters of Gaelic Scotland and Ireland in the Early and Central Middle Ages* (Cambridge, 1995), passim.

14 See, e.g., D. Brooke, 'Fergus of Galloway: miscellaneous notes for a revised portrait', *TDGAS*, 3rd ser., lxvi (1991), 47–58.

(Peeblesshire), Saltoun (East Lothian), and urban holdings belonging to the constableship to provide accommodation in royal burghs for attendance at court [Nos. **37–8**, **48–9**]. The nature of Alan's territorial priorities was revealed when he relinquished properties in Lauderdale in order to buttress his position in Galloway [Nos. **30**, **63**], which was evidently still perceived as the chief stronghold of family influence. Even so, we are left in no doubt that from 1196 the Galloways were by far and away the greatest magnates in southern Scotland as a whole, and that in this broader context they played an ample and well-recognised role. Moreover, several acts point to their significance as landowners in England and underline their ability to turn in English society [Nos. **10**, **28**, **32**, **51**, **53**, **55**, **57**]. Their biggest English properties came to them as successor lords to the Morvilles; and one very important charter [No. **53**] shows that in 1216–17 Alan recovered temporary possession of the lordship of North Westmorland, originally granted to his great-grandfather Hugh I de Morville by King David I. No act relates to Alan's extensive Ulster estates – though such a gap perhaps should not surprise, for in Ulster, as Alan himself admitted, he was unable to impose an effective hegemony.[15]

Despite the loss of many relevant records, the strength of the Galloways' support for the reformed European Church is manifest. Forty-five of the *acta* are directed to seventeen different ecclesiastical recipients, almost all monastic houses. The chief beneficiaries of almsgiving were the Cistercians and Augustinians; the native 'Celtic' church figures merely as a spent force, as when Iona Abbey was deprived of endowments in Galloway in favour of the reformers [No. **14**]. Glenluce Abbey and the priory of St Mary's Isle are the only monasteries of Galloway to appear [Nos. **22**, **24**, **41**]. The family's gains from the Morvilles included the patronage of Dryburgh Abbey, which is represented by four surviving texts [Nos. **26**, **39**, **40**, **56**]. The abbeys of Holyrood, Kelso, Melrose and Holm Cultram, also a Scottish royal foundation despite its Cumberland location, all attracted particular interest. Other religious in England received gifts, and even the Cluniacs of far-distant St Andrew's Priory at Northampton were endowed in Scotland – explained by the fact that this house was Roland's burial-place [Nos. **42–3**]. The property conveyed to ecclesiastical tenants often comprised local churches and their appurtenances, and in a series of grants between *c*.1160 and 1174 no fewer than eleven churches in Galloway passed to the Augustinians of Holyrood [Nos. **2–4**, **11**, **12**, **14**]. It is probably no coincidence that the earliest warrandice clauses appear in charters issued for the Church either during or immediately after the rebellion of 1174–85, which seriously questioned the Galloways' ability to give 'good lordship' [Nos. **15**, **17**, **23**]. And few if any of the houses known to have received charters from Alan would have seen him as a major benefactor: usually his support extended only to granting confirmations of his predecessors' and tenants' gifts, or to settling outstanding disputes. No doubt one important reason for this was that by the early thirteenth century the amount of property already given by the Galloways in

15 K. J. Stringer, 'Periphery and core in thirteenth-century Scotland: Alan son of Roland, lord of Galloway and constable of Scotland', in A. Grant and K. J. Stringer, eds., *Medieval Scotland: Crown, Lordship and Community* (Edinburgh, 1993), 85–7, 92–4.

alms left limited scope for further generosity. *Pro anima* clauses show a characteristic anxiety for the spiritual well-being of kith and kin; they might also express concern for the souls of members of the Scottish royal house [Nos. **6**, **12**, **23**]. Two acts betray a sense of urgency to free dead relations of their responsibility for specific sins [Nos. **30**, **38**]. It may be added that by virtue of confraternity the family secured a full share in the prayers and good works of Kelso Abbey [No. **30**]. The abbots of Dundrennan, Dunfermline, Holm Cultram, Jedburgh, Melrose, Stirling (Cambuskenneth), and Tongland are found attesting charters; but the senior churchman occurring most often is the bishop of Whithorn, who occasionally travelled with the lord's household outside Galloway [Nos. **6**, **7**, **9**, **15**, **28**, **30**, **50**, **54**].

Just as the Galloways bolstered their position in partnership with reform churchmen, so they sought to strengthen their lordship over local society in alliance with Anglo-Norman settler families. Fourteen of the lay *acta* focus attention on 'feudal' settlement in Galloway, Lauderdale and Cunningham. One military tenant owed a full knight's service; two held fractional knight's feus [Nos. **9**, **35**, **60**]. A fair number of the knights who figure (if only as witnesses) were men of more than local prominence, holding feus of other lords and sometimes of the crown itself. So advanced were the processes of Normanisation (or Anglicisation) in Lauderdale and Cunningham by 1196 that most of the Galloways' vassals in these districts had been established there by the Morvilles. But two families who would become especially prominent in Scottish history, the Maitlands and the Randolphs, made their first appearance as landowners north of the Tweed under Alan's patronage in Berwickshire.[16] Restricted though our field of vision is, it would be quite wrong to imagine that Anglo-Norman colonisation did not involve considerable adaptation to local conditions. Thus several texts 'belong to a border zone where the newly-imported feudalism meets that older regime for which historians have no convenient name'.[17] One tenant's obligation to render knight service was apparently deferred until the customary dues owed to both the king of Scotland and the lord of Galloway were rescinded [No. **9**]. One Cunningham deed, which records an infeftment for habergeon service, has special interest in showing explicitly how an age-old obligation to hosting could be interwoven with 'feudal' practice [No. **61**]. A similar entwining can be seen when a Cunningham tenant was required not only to pay an annual rent of one unmewed sparrowhawk but to meet the forinsec service due from one ploughgate of land – in other words, to provide manpower for the Scottish 'common army' in proportion to the size of his feu [No. **59**]. A religious house, Holm Cultram Abbey, was a rent-paying tenant for a substantial establishment in eastern Galloway. In this case, however, any extra burden was deemed inappropriate, and the lord undertook to discharge all service owed to the king of Scots [Nos. **7**, **15**].

16 Richard Maitland from Northumberland, the first of the Maitlands of Thirlestane, attests No. **63**; Thomas son of Ranulf from Cumberland-Westmorland, progenitor of the Randolphs, attests No. **53**. I hope to return to the early history of these families on another occasion.

17 G. W. S. Barrow, *The Anglo-Norman Era in Scottish History* (Oxford, 1980), 139–40.

The most basic purpose of a great estate was to provide for the immediate needs of the lord and his family. An endowment had to be found for Alan's bastard son [No. **62**], whose rights of inheritance under native customary law no longer sufficed to guarantee his succession as lord of Galloway. The food-rents and other supplies consumed by the lord and his household at Kirkcudbright are mentioned [No. **22**], and some hint is given that in Galloway as a whole the ancient tribute dues of cain and conveth were major sources of maintenance [Nos. **3, 9, 31**]. Woefully sparse though they are, we cannot afford to ignore the special importance of such references as a much needed reminder that the economic underpinning of power depended very heavily on 'Celtic' aspects of lordship and control. Woods and forests were a primary landed resource. Hunting rights might be granted out [No. **9**]; Holyrood Abbey received a tenth of the lord's venison (and of his cain and profits of justice) in the easternmost part of Galloway [No. **3**]. Other charters emphasise concern to preserve game for the lord's sport in Cunningham [Nos. **58–9, 61**]. References are made to parks at Lauder and at Whissendine, one of the family's English manors [Nos. **51, 64**]. Easements in the demesne woods of Galloway were often allocated to religious houses, not least for pasturing pigs, the chief woodland dwellers [Nos. **7, 15, 31**]. Problems and controversy might arise, as with Melrose Abbey concerning rights in the royal forest between the Gala and Leader Waters [No. **64**]. A series of charters highlights the importance of the Solway salt-industry [Nos. **7–9, 15, 17, 21, 23, 27**];[18] and a new initiative was taken in Galloway when the monks of Holm Cultram turned Kirkgunzeon into a grange [Nos. **15, 23**]. Encouragement was given to reclamation of the waste of Lammermuir in Berwickshire [No. **63**]. Nor is there any denying the amount and quality of the pasture at Eddleston in upper Tweeddale, where a grant of land carried with it common pasture for 700 sheep and their lambs, as well as other animals [No. **38**].

Some light is thrown on the bureaucracy for managing the lord's affairs and enforcing his superiority, and the pattern as revealed by the charters is essentially a 'feudal' one. While this remains an important point, it is unfortunate that traditional practices are virtually undetectable – indeed, but for other records we would be entirely ignorant of the mairs or serjeants of Galloway, and almost equally ignorant of Galloway's native *judices*.[19] No. **44**, which stipulates an annual payment out of Alan's *camera*, preserves what is very probably the earliest direct reference in surviving Scottish record to a magnate's chamber. The context may suggest a fully-fledged financial office, and the fact that Walter the chamberlain became bishop of Whithorn in 1209 appears to confirm that the chamberlainship was one of the most important posts in Alan's household.[20] The only estate official to be named as such in the *acta* was the

18 More generally, see G. Neilson, *Annals of the Solway until AD 1307* (repr. Beckermet, 1974), 44–8.

19 *APS*, i, 378, 398. For recent comment, see H. L. MacQueen, 'The laws of Galloway: a preliminary survey', in R. D. Oram and G. P. Stell, eds., *Galloway: Land and Lordship* (Edinburgh, 1991), 131–43. MacMares *judex* witnesses No. 3.

20 *Chron. Melrose*, 54. Certainly Alan's administration had to have the capacity to deal with large sums of money; in particular, the use of the Gallovidian army by the English crown as mercenary troops (with Scottish royal approval) may help to account for this apparent bureaucratic precocity: cf. *CDS*, i, nos. 529, 533, 540; *Pipe Roll 14 John* (London, 1955), 154.

local steward or bailiff who had oversight of the manor of Kippax in Yorkshire [Nos. **55, 57**]; but we know from other sources that Lauderdale and Cunningham were each administered for Alan by a baronial officer styled a sheriff[21] – though the apparent 'newness' of the sheriff's office should not be taken for granted. The most appropriate venue for formal meetings between the lord and his vassals was evidently a session of his honorial court, referred to explicitly in No. **60** (concerning Cunningham). Study of the witness-clauses shows that a nucleus of trusted advisers accompanied the lord as he moved about, so that (for example) knights of Galloway might appear with him in Lauderdale or Cunningham. As regards the lord's clerical household, for Alan's period of lordship the charters and other records supply the names of twelve personal clerks, including Prior William of St Mary's Isle.[22] That three of the twelve, Masters Adam of Thornton, Robert of Edenhall and William of Kilkenny, had received an academic education argues for business practices of some efficiency. In fact the Oxford-trained Kilkenny entered English royal service in the 1230s, became chancellor of England, and ended his career as bishop of Ely (1255–6).[23] Richard the clerk, whose services were secured by beneficing him at Troqueer in Galloway, produced at least two of Alan's charters [Nos. **32, 35**]. Scribes were also expected to draw up on Alan's behalf not merely administrative mandates in the form of letters patent [Nos. **55, 57**], but private letters to the king of England.[24]

There is, of course, much that the *acta* fail to illuminate. But, above all, this collection contributes to our understanding of the interaction between Scotland's west-coast 'Celtic' periphery and its east-coast Anglo-Normanised core. In the recent historiography of Galloway a sceptical view has gained ground concerning the degree of 'integration' achieved. In Richard Oram's assessment, for example, Galloway's exposure to foreign influences was carefully regulated by the ruling family, and their impact was localised, leaving a vast hinterland that remained firmly part of Gaeldom. Oram therefore stresses 'the shallowness of the changes', emphasises the continued reality of regional particularism, and suggests that 'too much attention has been devoted to change ... rather than to the levels of continuity which underlie the documentation'.[25]

21 G. W. S. Barrow, *The Kingdom of the Scots* (London, 1973), 298–9 (for the sheriff of Lauder); *Carte Monialium de Northberwic*, ed. C. Innes (Bannatyne Club, 1847), no. 28 (for Andrew sheriff of Cunningham, 1204 × 1228).

22 *CDS*, i, no. 754.

23 D. E. R. Watt, *A Biographical Dictionary of Scottish Graduates to AD 1410* (Oxford, 1977), 170, 298, 531; A. B. Emden, *A Biographical Register of the University of Oxford to AD 1500* (Oxford, 1957–9), ii, 1048–9. It cannot escape notice that while Kilkenny served as King Henry III's chancellor, Philip Lovel held office as English royal treasurer. Lovel, who became treasurer in 1252, was previously one of Roger de Quincy's leading followers, serving as steward of his English estates, supporting him in Galloway, and acquiring an interest at Leuchars in Fife: Simpson, '*Familia* of Roger de Quincy', 108, 110–11; idem, 'Acts of Roger de Quincy', Texts, no. 153.

24 PRO, Chancery Miscellanea, C47/22/9(1), and Special Collections, Ancient Correspondence, SC1/3/147 (text badly damaged and often illegible). These letters from Alan to Henry III, calendared in *CDS*, i, nos. 754, 890, have been excluded from the collection, as has reference to the charter, now lost, by which Alan and other barons of Scotland pledged themselves in Jun. 1220 to support Alexander II's oath to marry Henry III's sister: ibid., no. 762.

25 R. D. Oram, 'A family business? Colonisation and settlement in twelfth- and thirteenth-century

Admittedly the main pressure for charters was from new religious houses and incoming families. Such records thus give only one part of the story and, notoriously, their stereotyped vocabulary can in itself distort contemporary realities. In the present case, as has already been indicated, they barely touch on the rich and enduring 'Celtic' contribution made to the fabric of lordship; and they undoubtedly ignore or gloss over the fact that in many respects Galloway remained a semi-independent region with its distinct identity and outlook. As Grant Simpson has put it, 'Scottish clerks worked in a tradition which was Anglo-Norman in origin and their ... inclinations ... were to suit their descriptions of Scottish conditions to the language of their charters, to iron out the differences rather than elaborate upon them.'[26]

Nevertheless, we must not go to the extreme of denying the force of the changes in social ethos and political orientation to which this collection of *acta* appears to provide incontrovertible testimony. Of vital significance to the issue of integration is the Galloways' willingness to adopt the new manners and modes of Scottish courtly society, and on this score it is rewarding to consider more fully what the charters can tell us. The processes involved were not straightforward and, most importantly, there were complicated responses to the expanding power of the Scottish state. Yet Roland's and Alan's adoption of the style 'constable' (in its various forms) emphasised their elevated status in the Scots king's household; by the same token, it underscored the nature of the transformation that had by then taken place in the family's assumptions and aspirations. More specifically, the charters help to illuminate the far-reaching importance of its enthusiasm for European monasticism in bridging the socio-cultural divide between Galloway and the Scottish royal heartlands.[27] We see, too, that the Galloways were by no means averse to forging close links with the east-coast aristocracy through intermarriage, including an alliance with the Abernethies hitherto ignored by the family historians [No. **65**]. The attestation-clauses of Uhtred's acts reveal that a significant component of his court came from the local Gaelic-speaking elite, and the appearance of his foster-brother Gillecatfar highlights one of the key ties of clientage in the kin-based society; but we also discover that the native nobility was already beginning to lose its place in the pecking order to Englishmen or Anglo-Normans [Nos. **3**, **6**, **9**, **10**, **12**]. The surviving *acta* of Roland and Alan are even more striking in this respect, for it was quite abnormal for members of the native community to attest at all, even when charters were issued in Galloway itself. Of course, this does not mean that Galloway's kindreds were politically insignificant, still less that Uhtred's successors simply abandoned native culture.[28] Quite apart from other

Galloway', *SHR*, lxxii (1993), 111–45; quotations at pp. 126, 141. Cf. also R. D. Oram, 'Bruce, Balliol and the lordship of Galloway: South-west Scotland and the Wars of Independence', *TDGAS*, 3rd ser., lxvii (1992), 29–47.

26 Simpson, 'Acts of Roger de Quincy', 210.

27 Cf. K. J. Stringer, 'Reform monasticism and Celtic Scotland: Galloway, *c*.1140–*c*.1240', in E. J. Cowan and R. A. McDonald, eds., *Alba: Celtic Scotland in the Middle Ages* (East Linton, forthcoming).

28 Alan naturally used Gaelic when he renamed a burn in order to clarify the marches of Holm Cultram's grange at Kirkgunzeon [No. 50].

considerations, innovation did nothing to change the fact that their military power and prestige depended in large measure on the co-operation of Galloway's traditional elites, and in consequence some regard had clearly to be paid to native sensitivities and interests.[29] Nonetheless, the charter evidence does suggest that the lord's household had become a focal point of Anglo-Norman influence;[30] and those on whom – we may reasonably suppose – Roland and Alan chiefly relied for counsel and companionship often had strong affiliations with eastern Scotland.[31] Another manifestation of this kind of 'Anglo-Norman supremacy' is found in a much neglected source, the seals used by the family to authenticate its *acta*.[32] With a symbolic as well as a utilitarian function, they were a central means of articulating senses of identity. Uhtred's seal bears the impression of a greyhound [No. **10** and *Plate 2*]; but very different from this traditional imagery was the design chosen by Roland. Although no example of his seal survives, a description of *c*.1700 is sufficiently detailed to show that he selected an overtly 'feudal' motif [No. **29**]. Thus he proclaimed his power and standing by depicting himself as a mounted knight wielding a sword; and the description fits broadly with the attributes of Alan's seal – save that Alan had on its reverse a small counterseal which he called his *secretum*, and whose main use was probably as a privy seal on personal letters [Nos. **58–9**].[33]

Another key point is that this collection enables us to judge more carefully how far the processes of 'modernisation' were kept under the family's direct control, and how far they were interwoven with the policy and influence of the Scots crown. If Uhtred seems on one level to have shunned royal Scotland and gravitated towards English Cumbria, it is clear from the documentation that even in his day the family's patronage network was far from self-contained [Nos. **3, 4, 10–14**]. In fact the Galloways' regular dealings with monasteries loyal to Scottish royal interests is one of the central features of the collection as a whole, and since those dealings often gave the government valuable links with the south-west, Galloway was in consequence drawn more firmly within the orbit of its power.[34] Similarly, Oram's emphasis on the importance of Cumbria as a source for lay colonists in Galloway needs to be qualified by the important

29 Stringer, 'Periphery and core', especially 84.

30 Oram, 'A family business?', 134, correctly indicates that very few of Roland's and Alan's *acta* illuminate society in the core of the lordship of Galloway west of the Urr Water; yet his attempts to downplay the significance of Anglo-Norman representation are weakened by the blanket assumption that 'different personnel are employed as witnesses in different contexts', so that (as he has characterised Alan's entourage) 'the circle of men moving around him changed with whatever portion of his vast inheritance he was in at any given time'. This is true only up to a point. Most tellingly, followers in Galloway did in fact travel with the lord outside the province as members of his personal retinue, but on such occasions only Uhtred's household can be found to have contained native Gallovidian supporters.

31 Cf. Stringer, 'Periphery and core', 99–101, 112–13.

32 The quotation is from G. W. S. Barrow, 'Witnesses and the attestation of formal documents in Scotland, twelfth–thirteenth centuries', *Journal of Legal History*, xvi (1995), 7.

33 For a full description of Alan's seal, with photograph, see Stringer, 'Periphery and core', 108–9. As regards Uhtred's seal, I am most grateful to Alan Borthwick, who has scrutinised it with the aid of a high-powered microscope, and reassured me that in identifying the animal concerned as a greyhound I have not let my imagination run riot.

34 Stringer, 'Reform monasticism'.

consideration that five of those who had gained feus in the province by *c.*1200 were certainly or very probably major tenants-in-chief of the king of Scots [Nos. **13, 25–6, 35**].[35] We also learn that the links between Galloway and north-west England often followed routes opened up by the Scots crown and well used by the Morvilles themselves [Nos. **10, 18, 26, 28, 53**]. Finally, a more comprehensive understanding of the Galloways' experiences is facilitated by the bringing together of *acta* for all their Scottish territories within a single series. There is no better way of reminding ourselves of their status from 1196 as more than just lords of Galloway, and of the importance of the wealth and prestige they drew from their association with the Scottish court. At once 'Celtic' chieftains and leading feudatories of the crown, Roland and Alan held powerful new positions enabling them to play a prominent role in Scottish society at large – to the extent that Galloway itself lost some of its focal significance in their affairs. In brief, their fortunes depended on the ability to exploit both traditional and non-traditional sources of social and political authority. Such an accommodation did not involve the replacement of one set of cultural loyalties by another; but successful adaptation to east-coast values did mean the giving up of some elements of the family's separate identity, not least the desire for political autonomy and the right to oppose the monarchy at will. Change, however, brought benefits as well as costs; and thanks to the Galloways' surviving *acta* we are left with a clearer picture of the complex processes of give and take whereby the various regional elites in early medieval Scotland were gradually assimilated into a single Gaelic-Anglo-Norman magnate class.

[35] See further Stringer, 'Periphery and core', 99–101, 112–13. Thus: Walter of Berkeley (d. *c.*1193), his successor Enguerrand de Balliol, Gilbert son of Richer, Gilbert's son Adam, and Ivo de Vieuxpont. It is also significant that Berkeley served as chief chamberlain of William I for some twenty years from *c.*1171; while his predecessor and successor in this key royal office, Philip de Valognes (d. 1215), was closely associated with the Galloways through his tenure of Torpenhow in Cumberland [No. 10].

* * *

## *Acta* of the Lords of Galloway to 1234

**1** *Fergus king of the Gallovidians *(rex Galwitensium)* grants to the Knights Hospitallers the land of Galtway [in Balmaclellan, Kirkcudbrightshire]. [*c.*1140 × 1160]

SOURCE. W. Dugdale, *Monasticon Anglicanum*, ed. J. Caley *et al.* (London, 1817–30), vi, 838.
COMMENT. Fergus would not have been styled 'king' after Malcolm IV's conquest of Galloway in 1160. The land concerned has been identified as Galtway in Kirkcudbright parish; but see now Brooke, 'Fergus', 55ff.

**2** *Fergus grants to Holyrood Abbey the Isle of Trail [i.e. St Mary's Isle] and the lands and churches of Dunrod and Galtway [all in Kirkcudbright]. [*c.*1160]

SOURCE. *Holyrood Liber*, nos. 25, 49, 73 (= No. **31** below).
COMMENT. Fergus may have issued separate charters concerning these gifts. According to the Holyrood Chronicle, the *villa* of Dunrod was given when he took the habit of a canon of Holyrood in 1160: Lawrie, *Annals*, 56. See *RRS*, i, no. 230; ii, no. 39, for royal confirmations and a grant of royal protection.

**3** Uhtred grants in alms to Holyrood Abbey the church of *Colmanele* [i.e. Urr, Kirkcudbrightshire], with the chapel of St Constantine and one ploughgate of land, and a tenth of all his cain, pleas and game between the rivers Urr, Nith and Cluden. [12 May 1161 × *c.* Jun. 1164]

Hiis testibus . Mac Mares . Judice . Gillecatfar . Collactaneo vchtredi . Gillecrist . mac . Gillewinin . Mactheuel . Daniel fil*io* Erlenuine .

SOURCE. *Holyrood Liber*, no. 23 (printed from the original charter *penes* Lord Panmure in 1840, but now lost).
PRINTED. As above.
COMMENT. The church of *Colmanele* was confirmed to Holyrood by Pope Alexander III on 29 Jul. 1164: *Holyrood Liber*, 169. This charter (cf. also No. 6) therefore shows that Uhtred had gained control of Desnes Ioan (between the rivers Urr and Nith) earlier than is suggested in R. D. Oram, 'Fergus, Galloway and the Scots', in Oram and Stell, *Galloway: Land and Lordship*, 126–7. William I's confirmation, though no longer extant, has a mention in *Holyrood Liber*, no. 81 (omitted from *RRS*, ii). In Bishop Ingram of Glasgow's confirmation, *Holyrood Liber*, no. 52 (1164 × 1174), the chapel is called St Constantine's of Edingham. D. Brooke, 'The deanery of Desnes Cro and the church of Edingham', *TDGAS*, 3rd ser., lxii (1987), 48–65, deals with this former mother-church or minster and its extensive *parochia*. The second witness Gillecatfar, who also attests Nos. 9, 12, is described as Uhtred's foster-brother (*collactaneus*). The scribe's use of this rare word is noted in *Dictionary of Medieval Latin from British Sources, Fascicule II C* (London, 1981), 377; but *collactaneus* is there confusingly linked with Gillecrist MacGillewinin.

**4** *Uhtred grants to Holyrood Abbey the churches of Kirkcudbright and Tongland [Kirkcudbrightshire]. [12 May 1161 × *c.* Jun. 1164]

SOURCE. *Holyrood Liber*, nos. 49, 73 (= No. 31).
COMMENT. Each church may have merited its own charter. Both were confirmed to Holyrood by Pope Alexander III in Jul. 1164. William I's confirmation is *RRS*, ii, no. 39 (probably 1165 or 1166).

**5** *Uhtred confirms to Holyrood Abbey the land of Dunrod [in Kirkcudbright]. [12 May 1161 × 20 Sep. 1164]

SOURCE. *RRS*, i, no. 230.
COMMENT. Cf. *Holyrood Liber*, no. 25. Latest possible date supplied by source.

**6** Uhtred and his heir [unnamed] grant in alms to St Peter's Hospital, York, for the souls of, among others, King David of Scotland one ploughgate of land and a toft in *Creuequer* [i.e. Troqueer, Kirkcudbrightshire]. Uhtred also exhorts all his men and friends to protect the brothers and their possessions, and to assist them whenever necessary. [12 May 1161 × *c.*1164; possibly 1164]

[a]Hujus donationis hij sunt testes: Christianus Galwalensis episcopus, Eueradus[b] abbas de Holmcultram, Robertus prior eiusdem loci, Willelmus celerarius, Robertus archid*iaconus* de Carl', Robertus arch*idiaconus* de Galwathea, Hubertus de Vallibus, Robertus fil*ius* Trute vice*comes* et Ric*ardus* frater eius, Lohlan fil*ius* Huddredi, Petrus del Teillol, Ricardus de Chenai, Ricardus de Heriz, Robertus clericus de Eboraco, Radulfus fil*ius* Ricardi, Willelmus de Lacressuner, Hudardus de Hodelma, Gilla Chad, Gilla Mor, Radulfus clericus de Card', Ricardus de Eboraco, Simon frater Radulfi clerici, Willelmus de Briscou, Robertus Dunbredan.

SOURCE. PRO, Charter Roll 35 Edward I, C53/93, memb. 8 = *A*. PRO, Chancery Miscellanea, C47/22/4(8) = *B*.
PRINTED. *Calendar of the Charter Rolls* (London, 1903–27), iii, 91–2 (from *A*), whence R. C. Reid, ed., *An Introduction to the History of Dumfries by Robert Edgar* (Dumfries, 1915), 218–19. *CDS*, ii, 422 (English summary of *B*).
NOTES. [a] From *A*. [b] Sic.

COMMENT. The seventh witness Hubert de Vaux, lord of Gilsland (Cumberland), died in *c.*1164: *The Lanercost Cartulary*, ed. J. M. Todd (Surtees Soc., 1997), 2. It is possible (but by no means certain) that since the charter was addressed to Bishop Christian of Whithorn – though Troqueer lay in Glasgow diocese – it was issued during the short vacancy at Glasgow after Bishop Herbert's death in 1164. William I's confirmation, incorporating a grant of protection, is *RRS*, ii, no. 103 (1165 × 1170). The large Cumberland contingent in the witness-list, including both the sheriff (Robert son of Truite) and the archdeacon of Carlisle (who acted as head of the diocese in the 1160s), strongly suggests that this act was executed in a session of the county court at Carlisle (cf. also No. **9**). G. W. S. Barrow, 'The pattern of lordship and feudal settlement in Cumbria', *Journal of Medieval History*, i (1975), 129, comments on the distinctly 'royal' tone adopted by Uhtred, especially in the charter's mode of address: to Bishop Christian and 'the abbots, priors and all his responsible men ... of his whole land'. For other endowments secured by St Peter's Hospital in southern Scotland, see K. J. Stringer, 'A twelfth-century "Scottish" charter concerning Yorkshire', *Yorkshire Archaeological Journal*, lxi (1989), 35–7.

*7* Uhtred, with the consent of his heir Roland, grants to Holm Cultram Abbey [Cumberland] the toun of Kirkgunzeon [Kirkcudbrightshire] in feu-ferme by its right marches, with one saltworks outwith its marches in a convenient place, and pasture for pigs, free of pannage, in all his demesne woods; to be held for an annual rent of £6, half at Easter and half at Martinmas, for as long as the monks wish to hold it. They have given Uhtred ten merks as a gift, to be returned with interest if, after three years, the land does not suit them and they want to surrender it. [12 May 1161 × *c.*1170]

Notum[a] sit omnibus tam presentibus quam futur*is* quod ego Huctredus filius Fergus consensu Rolandi heredis mei dedi et concessi Deo et beate[b] Marie de Holmcoltran[c] et monachis ibidem Deo seruientibus villam que dicitur Kyrkegunni[d] in[e] feodifirmam per rectas diuisas suas cum omnibus pertinenc*iis* suis, videlicet in bosco, [f]in plano, pratis et pascuis, in aquis et molendinis, moris, mussis[f] et mariscis; et vnam etiam salinam concedo eis extra diuisas in opportuno sibi loco, et pasturam porcis eorum sine pannagio[g] per omnes siluas meas de dominico meo, vt teneant libere et quiete ab omnibus seruiciis et consuetudinibus vniuersis pro vj libris annuatim mihi et heredibus meis persoluend*is* quamdiu ill*is* placuerit predictam terram tenere de me et heredibus meis, tribus libris ad Pascha[h] et tribus ad festum[i] sancti Martini. Decem autem marcas dederunt mihi in donacione ita tamen vt si ill*is* predicta terra tribus annis expletis displicuerit et eam dimittere uoluerint, reddam ill*is* predictas marcas cum bono. Seruicium autem reg*is* Scocie ego et heredes mei acquietabimus.[j] Teste[k] episcopo Galweie[l] Christiano,[m] et cetera.

RUBRIC. *A* and *B*: Carta Huctredi fil*ii* Fergus (in red). *C*'s rubric is stained and illegible.

SOURCE. CRO, Carlisle, Dean and Chapter Muniments, Cartulary of Holm Cultram, p. 99 = *A*. BL, MS Harleian 3911, fo. 106v = *B*. BL, MS Harleian 3891, fo. 85r = *C*. Text above from *A*, with some variants of *B* and *C* noted.

PRINTED. *Holm Cultram Reg.*, no. 120 (English summary of *A*).

NOTES. [a] Blue initial flourished in red, *A*; red initial, *B*, *C*. [b] sancte, *C*. [c] Hom', *B*. [d] Kirkewynny, *B*; Kyrgunny, *C*. [e] ad, *B*. [f–f] et plano, in pratis et pascuis, aquis et molendinis, moris, mustis, *B*; et plano, pratis et pascuis, piscacionibus et aquis, et molendinis, moris et mossis, *C*. [g] pasnag', *B*, *C*. [h] Pasca, *B*, *C*. [i] festiuitatem, *C*. [j] *B* concludes here with warr'. [k] T', *C*. [l] Galwidie, *C*. [m] Cristino, *C*.

COMMENT. Holm established a grange at Kirkgunzeon soon after this agreement; but Uhtred deprived the monks of part of the estate and granted it to Walter of Berkeley: *Holm Cultram Reg.*, no. 133; No. **13**. On the outbreak of the Galloway uprising in 1174 they may have been ejected altogether; by *c.*1190, however, they had apparently been fully reinstated (Nos. **15**, **25**).

**8** *Uhtred grants to Holm Cultram Abbey one saltworks in Colvend [Kirkcudbrightshire], all easements of wood [from] the port of Urr to *Polstursheuid* [i.e. the source of the New Abbey Pow], rights of way, and harbours. [12 May 1161 × *c*.1170]

SOURCE. *RRS*, ii, no. 88.
COMMENT. The source is William I's confirmation of a charter issued by Uhtred to supplement No. 7 and of a chirograph, also lost, unless it be the agreement between Holm and Dundrennan Abbey summarised in *Holm Cultram Reg.*, no. 133.

**9** Uhtred, with the consent of his son and heir Roland, grants to Richard son of Truite the whole land of *Lochenelo* [i.e. Loch Kindar *alias* New Abbey, Kirkcudbrightshire] by its right marches, in feu and heritage, for one knight's service. As long as Uhtred has to render cain from *Cro* and *Desense Ioan*, Richard shall give him eight pounds of silver yearly, half at Whitsunday and half at Martinmas, to free himself of all service and customary dues to the king of Scotland and to Uhtred and his heirs; but whenever Uhtred is released from the burden of cain, Richard shall hold by the service of one knight. He is to possess the land with all its appurtenances and liberties, including churches (*monasteria*), mills, saltworks, sand-dunes (*harene*), the hunting of all beasts of the chase, harbours, and the broods or eyries of hawks and all other birds. [12 May 1161 × Aug. 1173, possibly 1166 × 1172]

his testibus christiano episcopo . Roberto archid*iacono* suo . Gilleberto capell*ano* ioh*anne* nepote suo . thoma clerico de torpenneu . Roberto clerico uicecomitis . roberto filio tructe . Bernardo flandrensi Willelmo [ ][a] Nichol*ao* nepotibus suis adam nepote . Roberti filii tructe . Roberto filio sungeue . Radulpho clerico de carl' . dauid filio teri /nor/[b]manno obside . nicholao filio d*aui*d augustino fratre suo . hiuone de stoches . Willelmo filio remboldi herberto filio hugonis maraschaldi . Willelmo de cantelu . andrea de dunfrees henrico filio hodardi . Willelmo clerico de louchamaban . Simone fratre ricardi marchaldi gille catphara . Gilleberto filio suo . Gillemore albanac . Gille cohel . Mactierne[c] cum multis alijs .

ENDORSED. No endorsements.
DESCRIPTION. 10.6" (26.8 cm) top and bottom x 5.5" (13.9 cm) left-hand side, 6.5" (16.6 cm) right-hand side. Fold, depth varies between 0.8" (2 cm) and 1.2" (3.1 cm). Sealing: on a tag through double slits; seal gone. Hand: relatively formal charter hand. The scribe wrote at speed, and had to correct several errors. The use of capitals and punctuation is eccentric; text ruled in pencil.
SOURCE. Original charter, CRO, Carlisle, Lowther Medieval Deeds, D/Lons/L5/1/S1.
PRINTED. F. W. Ragg, 'Five Strathclyde and Galloway charters', *CWAAS Trans.*, new ser., xvii (1917), 218–19 (with a rather inadequate translation and a poor photograph), reprinted in *TDGAS*, 3rd ser., v (1918), 249–50, whence *Wigtownshire Chrs.*, pp. xix–xx (English summary, with four witnesses inadvertently omitted).
NOTES. [a] Though Ragg prints et, this is not what the scribe wrote, which appears to be que. [b] Interlined and marked for insertion by a caret. [c] Ragg prints Macherne, wrongly.
COMMENT. *Wigtownshire Chrs.*, p. xxi, and Oram, 'A family business?', 125–6, assume that the money due was additional to knight service; the text suggests sequential obligations. Presumably issued before the outbreak of Anglo-Scottish warfare in Aug. 1173, by which date Robert son of Truite, the seventh witness, was in any case probably dead: J. Boorman, 'The sheriffs of Henry II and the significance of 1170', in G. Garnett and J. Hudson, eds., *Law and Government in Medieval England and Normandy* (Cambridge, 1994), 274. Though this charter may provide another potential example of the use of the county court at Carlisle for business concerning Galloway (cf. No. **6**), it is perhaps significant that in this instance Robert is not styled sheriff. Moreover, he did witness in a private or semi-official capacity in Scotland, and it is possible that the occasion was the session of William I's court at Lochmaben in Annandale recorded in *RRS*, ii, no. 80 (probably 1166 × 1172), whose attestors include Robert as well as Uhtred, Roland and Bishop Christian of Whithorn. The last heads the witness-list above, and note also that William the clerk of Lochmaben occurs towards its end. The donee, Robert's brother, was a prominent member of the Cumberland gentry. He was apparently expelled from Loch Kindar no later than 1174 (cf. Nos. **15**, **27**); and he

(or his son and namesake) participated in John de Courcy's conquest of Ulster: S. Duffy, 'The first Ulster plantation: John de Courcy and the men of Cumbria', in T. B. Barry *et al.*, eds., *Colony and Frontier in Medieval Ireland* (London, 1995), 19. Richard Masculus (Maule), another member of John de Courcy's following in Ireland, had links with Richard de Morville and Roland: K. J. Stringer, 'The early lords of Lauderdale, Dryburgh Abbey and St Andrew's Priory at Northampton', in Stringer, *Nobility*, 59, n. 44. The by-name of the last witness, Gillecohel Mactierne, evokes 'that obscure class of "young nobles" found in Brittany and, elusively, in the highlands of Scotland': Barrow, 'Witnesses', 10.

**10** Uhtred and his wife Gunnilda daughter of Waltheof, with the consent of their heir Lochlan [Roland], grant in alms to Holyrood Abbey the church of Torpenhow (*Torpennoth*) [Cumberland]. [1164 × *c.* May 1174]

His testibus . Galfrido abbate de dunfermeliN . Osberto abbate de Jedeuurde . Aluredo abbate de striueliN . Gillemure mac blancard . Gillemure albanach . Gilleberto mac gillefiN . Serlone . Bernardo . Ricardo bertha burgensibuS .

ENDORSED. Uctredus (on the seal-tag, in hand of text). Donacio ecclesie de torpennoth (xii cent.). de torpennoc. (xiii cent.). Torpenev. (on the seal-tag, xiii cent.). 186 J. Scott (xvi–xvii cent.). Also modern numeral endorsements.

DESCRIPTION. 7.3" (18.5 cm) top, 7.4" (18.8 cm) bottom x 3.1" (7.9 cm) left-hand side, 3.3" (8.4 cm) right-hand side. Fold, average depth of 0.9" (2.3 cm). Sealing: on a tag through single slits. Seal in natural wax varnished dark brown; almost entire with fair impression; diameter 2.0" (5.2 cm). It displays a greyhound standing with the head turned and facing to sinister; certainly not a lion as was suggested in NLS, Walter Macfarlane's Collections, MS Advocates 35.2.4(ii), fo. 120r–v. The legend reads + [SIGILLV]M VCHTR[EDI] FILII FERGVS. Hand: upright charter hand, characterised by its neatness and regularity; text ruled in ink. See *Plate 2*.

SOURCE. Original charter, NAS, Dalhousie Muniments, GD45/13/233.

PRINTED. *Holyrood Liber*, no. 24, whence *St Bees Reg.*, p. ix, n. 1.

COMMENT. Not confirmed by Pope Alexander III in Jul. 1164. Gunnilda was the sister of Alan son of Waltheof, lord of Allerdale (Cumberland), who during David I's occupation of northern England had given Torpenhow to Uhtred on their marriage – one of several grants made by him to the Scots king's supporters: *St Bees Reg.*, no. 498. Torpenhow had passed in unrecorded circumstances to William I's chamberlain Philip de Valognes by 1178, and Philip's daughter Sibyl (d. 1222) regranted the church to the Yorkshire priory of Rosedale: *Pipe Roll 24 Henry II* (London, 1906), 126; Barrow, *Anglo-Norman Era*, 136; Dugdale, *Mon. Angl.*, iv, 318.

**11** *Uhtred grants to Holyrood Abbey the church of Twynholm [Kirkcudbrightshire]. [1164 × *c.* May 1174]

SOURCE. *Holyrood Liber*, nos. 49, 73 (= No. 31).

COMMENT. Not confirmed by Pope Alexander III in Jul. 1164.

**12** Uhtred grants in alms to Holyrood Abbey for the souls of, among others, King David, his son Henry, and King Malcolm [IV] the church of St Bridget of Blaiket [in Urr] with one ploughgate of land. [9 Dec. 1165 × 2 Feb. 1174]

Uchtredus filius feregus . Omnibus sancte matris ecclesie filijs salutem ; Sciant omnes tam posteri quam presentes . me dedisse 7 inperpetuam elemosinam concessisse pro salute anime regis dauid . 7 filij eius henrici . 7 Malcolmi regis . 7 patris mei feregus . 7 antecessorum meorum . ecclesie sancte crucis de edenesburch . 7 canonicis ibidem deo seruientibus . ecclesiam Sancte Brigide de Blachet cum una carrucata terre . 7 omnibus rectitudinibus suis 7 eisiamentis . scilicet . in piscationibus . in nemore . 7 in plano . in aquis . 7 pratis . 7 cum communi pastura . Uolo itaque ut predicti canonici prefatam ecclesiam cum omnibus adiacentijs suis 7 pertinentijs . liberam 7 quietam 7 ex omni exaccione solutam teneant . sicut aliqua ecclesia in tota Laudonia liberius 7 quietius tenetur 7 possidetur . His testibus . Rodberto archid*iacono* . Salomone decano . Malbec decano . Helia clerico episcopi . Ingeranno capell*ano* episcopi . Radulfo sacerdote de lintune . Gillechatfar . Gillecrist MacGillewinne . Daniele filio Herlewini[a]

ENDORSED. Huctredus. (xii cent.?). [Confirmatio?] de Blacet (on the seal-tag, xii–xiii cent.). De Blaked (xiii cent.). Grant to the church of Holy Cross (xviii cent.).
DESCRIPTION. 7.5" (19 cm) top, 7.7" (19.6 cm) bottom x 2.5" (6.3 cm) left-hand side, 2.6" (6.6 cm) right-hand side. Fold, average depth of 0.5" (1.4 cm). Sealing: on a tag through single slits; only the upper lengths of the tag remain; seal missing. A tie, cut to within 1.1" (2.7 cm) of the left-hand edge of the top of the fold and 0.3" (0.7 cm) deep at the stub, has been torn off and lost. Hand: idiosyncratic charter hand, angular and inelegant; text ruled in ink, with two superfluous lines below. See *Plate 3*.
SOURCE. Original charter, NAS, Logan Charters, GD141/1/no. A.
PRINTED. P. H. M'Kerlie, *History of the Lands and their Owners in Galloway* (Edinburgh, 1870–9), v, 287 (with numerous errors). H. E. Maxwell, 'The Logan charter', *Archaeological and Historical Collections relating to the Counties of Ayr and Wigton*, iv (1884), 55 (translation, with engraving).
NOTE. [a] Herlewine, with the final e marked for deletion and i written above.
COMMENT. Not confirmed by Pope Alexander III in Jul. 1164, and the *pro anima* clause surely indicates a date after Malcolm IV's death. The witness-list agrees very closely with that of *Holyrood Liber*, no. 52, the confirmation by Bishop Ingram of Glasgow (1164–2 Feb. 1174), and both deeds were no doubt executed simultaneously. William I's confirmation has a mention in ibid., no. 81 (omitted from *RRS*, ii).

**13** *Uhtred grants to Walter of Berkeley part of the toun of Kirkgunzeon. [*c.*1170?]

SOURCE. *Holm Cultram Reg.*, no. 120a.
COMMENT. This act alludes to Walter's infeftment in the lordship of Urr. It infringed the rights of Holm Cultram Abbey (No. 7), and the source shows that on Holm's petition William I ordered a fresh perambulation of Kirkgunzeon's marches which found in the monks' favour (× 1174). After some delay, Walter reinstated them, as his tenants (No. 25). He served as William I's chamberlain, and held knights' feus of the crown in Roxburghshire and Angus: Barrow, *Anglo-Norman Era*, 102–3, 174.

**14** *Uhtred grants to Holyrood Abbey the churches of Barncrosh [in Tongland], Kelton, Kirkcormack [in Kelton] and St Andrew [of Balmaghie, all in Kirkcudbrightshire]. [*c.*1173?]

SOURCE. *Holyrood Liber*, nos. 49, 73 (= No. 31).
COMMENT. These churches, previously belonging to Iona Abbey, were the subject of an independent (but perhaps contemporary) grant to Holyrood by William I, a striking instance of direct royal intervention in Galloway's affairs: *RRS*, ii, no. 141 (1172 × 1174). See further A. Macquarrie, 'Kings, lords and abbots: Power and patronage at the medieval monastery of Iona', *TGSI*, liv (1984–6), 356–7.

**15** Roland grants in alms [sic] to Holm Cultram Abbey the toun of Kirkgunzeon in feu-ferme by specified marches as freely and fully as he and Uhtred held it, one saltworks in Loch Kindar with pasture for four oxen, pasture for 500 pigs, free of pannage, in all his demesne woods from 29 September to 30 November, easements in his wood in Preston [in Kirkbean] and Loch Kindar, convenient harbours throughout his land, and rights of way between them and the grange [of Kirkgunzeon] for the monks and their men, livestock, carts and packhorses; all to be held for an annual rent of £10, half at Whitsunday and half at Martinmas. Warrandice. [*c.*1176 × *c.* Mar. 1185]

Notum[a] sit omnibus tam presentibus quam futur*is* quod ego Rolandus filius Huctredi dedi et[b] concessi in perpetuam elemosinam Deo et sancte Marie de Holm' et monachis ibidem Deo seruientibus ad feodi[c] firmam villam que dicitur Kyrkegumi[d] cum omnibus pertinenc*iis* suis, scilicet per has diuisas: per viam que ducit a ponte Polatkertin usque ad Crosgileultan et inde per uiam directam usque ad Cloenchonethro et inde descendendo per riuulum qui uocatur Grenethfalde sicut ipse riuulus currit in aquam que exit de Lochartur et sicut Polnechauc cadit in ipsam aquam ad pedem de Lochartur et a Polnehauc usque in[e] Muninuch et a Muninuch per summitatem montis supra[f] Glasteri indirectum usque Poldereduf et ita in transuersum ab illo loco usque ad ortum Poldereduf et sicut Poldereduf cadit in magnam aquam que currit inter Culwen et Boelewinni et ita descendendo usque ad aquam que currit inter Blareguke et Haclthetofte et ita ascendendo per ipsam aquam sicut currit per medium alnetum vsque ad magnam mosam[g] et per transuersum ipsam mosam[g] vsque ad Polneheruede et sicut Polneheruede cadit in Polchillebride et sicut Polchillebride cadit in Dufpole et ita ascendendo contra aquam vsque ad Polatkertyn, ita scilicet libere et plenarie sicut pater meus Huctredus et ego Rolandus melius et plenius tenuimus, cum omnibus pertinenc*iis* suis infra predictas diuisas in bosco [h]et plano, in pratis et pascuis, in piscacionibus[h] et aquis, tam in fluuiis quam in marinis, in stagnis et molendinis, moris et mussis[i] et mariscis. Et vnam salinam dedi eis extra predictas diuisas in Locchendelo et ligna sicut necessarium est eis ad tenendam illam[j] salinam, et ibidem pasturam quatuor bobus, et pasturam quingentis porcis sine pannagio[k] per omnes siluas de dominio[l] meo singul*is* annis a festo sancti Michael*is* vsque ad festum sancti Andree, et aysiamenta nemor*is* mei in Prestona et in Lochildela vsque ad Pollesteresheued' materie et lignis et ceteris rebus necessariis domui de Holmo ad suos proprios vsus, et portus qui eis fuerint vtiliores et viciniores per totam terram meam, et vias et semitas sine disturbacione ad eund*um* et redeund*um* a portubus mar*is* ad grangiam et de grangia ad mare sibi et hominibus suis et catall*is* suis et carettis et summagiis suis. Hec omnia predicta et prenominata habebunt et tenebunt predicti monachi de me et heredibus meis in perpetuam elemosinam, libere et quiete ab omnibus seruiciis et consuetudinibus et exaccionibus[m] et omni terreno seruicio et auxilio[n] ad me vel[o] ad heredes meos pertinente, pro x libris annuatim persoluendis[p] mihi et heredibus meis, scilicet[q] quinque ad Pentecosten et quinque ad festum sancti Martini. Et ego et heredes mei faciemus totum seruicium domini reg*is* inde plenarie. Et warantizabimus[r] eis omnia predicta contra omnes homines in perpetuum.[s] Hiis testibus[t] Christino Candide Case episcopo, et cetera.

RUBRIC. *A* and *B*: Carta Rolandi filii Huctredi (in red). *C*'s rubric is illegible.

SOURCE. CRO, Carlisle, Cartulary of Holm Cultram, pp. 99–101 = *A*. BL, MS Harleian 3911, fos. 106v–7v = *B*. BL, MS Harleian 3891, fo. 85r–v = C. Text above a collation of *A*, *B* and *C*, with *A*'s readings normally preferred (see also under Comment).

PRINTED. *Holm Cultram Reg.*, no. 121 (English summary of *A*).

NOTES. [a] Red initial flourished in blue, *A*; red initial, *B*, *C*. [b] *A* omits et; supplied from *B*, *C*. [c] feudo, C. [d] Sic in *A*, where Kyrkegunni was probably intended. [e] ad, *C*. [f] *A* omits supra; supplied from *B*, *C*. [g] mussam, *B*. [h–h] in plano, pratis et pascuis, piscacionibus, *C*. [i] mustis, omitting et, *B*; mosis, *C*. [j] ipsam, *C*. [k] pasnagio, *B*, *C*. [l] dominico, *B*, *C*. [m] *A* omits last two words; supplied from *B*, *C*. [n] axilio, *A*. [o] et, *C*. [p] soluend', *B*. [q] *A* omits scilicet; supplied from *B*, *C*. [r] warrantizabimus, *B*, *C*. [s] *B* breaks off here with etc. [t] *A* ends here; the remainder from *C*.

COMMENT. See also No. 7. Confirmed by Pope Lucius III on 2 May 1185: *Holm Cultram Reg.*, no. 50a; Dugdale, *Mon. Angl.*, v, 598. Most of the place-names in *A* have variant forms in the other texts. Few have real significance, but note Kirgewynny, *B*; Kirkewynnyn, *C*. Though almost all the names of the boundary-marks have failed to survive, R. C. Reid, 'The early ecclesiastical history of Kirkgunzean', *TDGAS*, 3rd ser., xiv (1926–8), 203–8, learnedly argues that the circuit, carefully excluding Walter of Berkeley's lands (cf. No. 13), corresponds very closely to the modern parish boundary. The charter's wording indicates an act of restitution, the implication being that the monks had been ejected from Galloway in 1174. See in addition *Scotia Pontificia: Papal Letters to Scotland before the Pontificate of Innocent III*, ed. R. Somerville (Oxford, 1982), nos. 98–9.

**16** *Roland grants to the Knights Hospitallers in England the land of *Artun* and the land of *Hirtun* [i.e. Girthon, Kirkcudbrightshire?] in Galloway. [*c*.1176 × 1192]

SOURCE. *Holyrood Liber*, no. 54.
COMMENT. Latest possible date supplied by source, a charter of Brother Alan, prior of the Hospital in England, confirming the lands concerned to Holyrood Abbey for an annual rent of 40s.

**17** Roland grants in alms to Melrose Abbey one saltworks in Preston [in Kirkbean] with pasture for six cows, six oxen and one horse, one full toft and croft for building a house, and easements in the wood of Preston to fire the boiling pan. Warrandice. Witnesses [omitted]. [*c*.1176 × 1196]

SOURCE. BL, MS Harleian 3960, fo. 95v.
PRINTED. *Melrose Liber*, i, no. 65.
COMMENT. Roland is not styled constable.

**18** *Roland grants to Thomas son of Cospatric the lordship of Colvend. [*c*.1176 × 1196]

Witnesses: Alexander and Gilbert sons of Cospatric, and Thomas and William sons of Gilbert.

SOURCE. *An Accompt of ... Estates and Families in the County of Cumberland ... by John Denton, of Cardew*, ed. R. S. Ferguson (CWAAS, Tract Series, 1887), 35.
COMMENT. By 1196 Colvend had apparently been split between Thomas and Roger Masculus: *St Bees Reg*., no. 60. Thomas (d. *c*.1201) was lord of Workington (Cumberland), founder of Shap Abbey (Westmorland), and a tenant of the honour of Kendal under his kinsman William II of Lancaster, whose sister Avice, wife of Richard de Morville, was Roland's mother-in-law: H. M. Colvin, *The White Canons in England* (Oxford, 1951), 168–9; Stringer, 'Lords of Lauderdale', 47. No evidence supports the suggestion in Oram, 'A family business?', 130, that Uhtred had granted Colvend to Cospatric (son of Orm), and Thomas's appearance in Galloway is probably best explained by Morville connections. Roland and Alan received regular support from Thomas's family: his brother Alexander (see also Nos. **29**, **42**); his brother Gilbert (see also Nos. **21**, **32**, **35**, **42**, **44**, **53**), who held Southwick next to Colvend (*Holm Cultram Reg*., nos. 131–2); his son Patrick of Colvend (No. **52**), on whom see G. S. H. L. Washington, *Early Westmorland M.P.s, 1258–1327* (CWAAS, Tract Series, 1959), 24–6; and his nephew Patrick of Southwick (No. **59**). They seem to have witnessed for the Galloways mainly in northern England and Galloway itself, but sometimes in Cunningham and Lauderdale. The family was also represented in Roger de Quincy's 'outer circle': Simpson, '*Familia* of Roger de Quincy', 109, 119.

**19** *Roland confirms to Holyrood Abbey grants made by Fergus and Uhtred. [*c*.1176 × Nov. 1200]

SOURCE. *Holyrood Liber*, no. 73 (= No. **31**).

**20** *Roland grants to Kelso Abbey [unspecified] property in the diocese of Whithorn [i.e. Galloway west of the Urr]. [*c*.1176 × Nov. 1200]

SOURCE. *Kelso Liber*, ii, no. 468.

**21** Roland grants in alms to St Bees Priory [Cumberland] one saltworks in Preston [in Kirkbean] with all easements of wood belonging to the saltworks, a full toft in Preston for building a house, and pasture for four oxen, four cows and one horse; also leave to cut timber in his demesne wood for the monks' own uses and the building works of their church. [*c*.1185 × 1196]

Test*ibus* Jacobo decano, Gilberto fil*io* Gospatric,[a] Rob*erto* de Port, Rad*ulfo* de Luuetot', Johanne presbitero, Laurenc*io* fil*io* Orm, Rog*ero* Masculo, Walt*ero* clerico, Durando clerico, Rob*erto* clerico, Willelmo fil*io* Petri, et multis alijs.

SOURCE. BL, MS Harleian 434, fo. 35v.
PRINTED. *St Bees Reg.*, no. 62.
NOTE. [a] *St Bees Reg.* prints Gospatricii, wrongly.
COMMENT. Given on the same occasion as *St Bees Reg.*, no. 60, a grant to St Bees by Roger Masculus of one saltworks in Colvend. Roland and eight of the above witnesses attested Roger's charter, as did Thomas de Colville, constable of Dumfries, and Robert son of Simon, who held the feu of Kirkconnell in Troqueer (Nos. 23, 47). Since Gilbert son of Cospatric was another landowner in Galloway and James *decanus* served as dean in Galloway, these acts were possibly executed there, or in the sheriffdom court of Dumfries. Thomas de Colville first appears in Scottish royal service in 1185: *RRS*, ii, no. 263.

**22** *Roland grants to the priory of St Mary's Isle the church of Eggerness [*alias* Kirkmadrine, in Sorbie, Wigtownshire] with its lands and teinds, and two ploughgates of land in the toun of Eggerness; also a tenth of the food, drink, wax, tallow and all other provisions supplied to his residence at Kirkcudbright. [1186 × *c.*1193]

SOURCE. *RRS*, ii, no. 293.
COMMENT. Latest possible date supplied by source, William I's confirmation. This is the earliest record of Galloway's only Augustinian monastery, a daughter-house of Holyrood Abbey.

**23** Roland grants in alms to Holm Cultram Abbey for the souls of, among others, King David and the king's heirs one saltworks in Southerness [in Kirkbean] and a fishery at a convenient place between *Polben* and Southwick [in Colvend] outwith Robert son of Simon's land; also one acre of land for building a house, common pasture for twelve cows with their calves, one bull, four oxen and two horses, all necessary easements in his wood to supply the saltworks and fishery, and right of way to and from the grange of Kirkgunzeon. Warrandice. [*c.*1190 × 1196]

Sciant[a] omnes tam presentes quam futuri quod ego Rollandus[b] filius Huctredi[c] dedi et concessi et hac presenti carta mea[d] confirmaui Deo et[e] sancte Marie de Holmo et monach*is* ibidem Deo seruientibus in liberam, puram et perpetuam elemosinam vnam salinam in Salternes et similiter vnam piscariam inter Polben et Suithayc[f] vbi eiis[g] commodius fore viderint, excepta terra Roberti filii Symon*is*, et vnam acram terre vbi poterint[h] suam mansionem edificare, et communem pasturam duodecim vaccis cum suis vitul*is* et vni tauro et quatuor bobus et duobus equis, et omnia necessaria aysiamenta tam de bosco meo ad predictam salinam sustinendam quam ad[i] prefatam piscariam, et viam liberam ac quietam inter predictam piscariam et prenominatam salinam et grangiam suam de Kyrkegunni[j] eundo et redeundo sine omni impedimento. Hec omnia dedi et concessi pro anima D*aui*d reg*is* et heredum suorum et pro anima patris mei et matris mee, et cetera, libere et quiete ab omni seculari seruicio et terrena exaccione. Hanc igitur elemosinam ego Rolandus et heredes mei predictis monach*is* contra omnes homines warantizabimus[k] in perpetuum.[l]

RUBRIC. *A* and *B*: Donacio Rollandi filii Huctredi (in red). *C*'s rubric is illegible.
SOURCE. CRO, Carlisle, Cartulary of Holm Cultram, p. 104 = *A*. BL, MS Harleian 3911, fo. 109v = *B*. BL, MS Harleian 3891, fos. 85v–6r = *C*. Text above based on *A*, with some variants of *B* and *C* noted.
PRINTED. *Holm Cultram Reg.*, no. 128 (English summary of *A*).
NOTES. [a] Blue initial flourished in red, *A*; red initial, *B, C.* [b] Roland', *B, C.* [c] Uctredi, *C.* [d] mea precedes presenti, *C.* [e] *A* omits et; supplied from *B, C.* [f] Suthaik', *C.* [g] eis, *B, C.* [h] poterunt, *C.* [i] *C* has atque for quam ad. [j] Kirkguny, *B*; Kirkewinni, *C.* [k] warrantizabimus, *B*; *C* ends here with warr', etc. [l] *B* adds etc.
COMMENT. Confirmed at Roland's request by Bishop Jocelin of Glasgow (1174–99): *Holm Cultram Reg.*, no. 135. Not confirmed, however, by Pope Lucius III in May 1185, or by Clement III in 1190: ibid., no. 268; Dugdale, *Mon. Angl.*, v, 600–1. The *Polben* entered the Nith estuary near the marches between Kirkbean and New Abbey: *RRS*, vi, no. 235. Robert son of Simon, Roland's tenant for Kirkconnell (in Troqueer), was himself a benefactor of Holm: *Holm Cultram Reg.*, no. 149.

**24** *Roland grants to Glenluce Abbey [unspecified] property. [*c.*Jan. 1191 × Nov. 1200]

SOURCE. *Wigtownshire Chrs.*, 57.
COMMENT. The date of foundation for Glenluce, established by Roland as a daughter-house of Dundrennan Abbey, is 21 Jan. 1191/2.

**25** Roland confirms in alms to Holm Cultram Abbey the land it held of Walter of Berkeley, chamberlain of the king of Scotland, by specified marches, with those liberties contained in Walter's charter. [*c.*1193? × 1196]

Sciant[a] presentes et[b] futur*i* quod ego Rollandus[c] filius Huctredi[d] concessi et hac presenti carta mea[e] confirmaui Deo et sancte Marie de Holm' et monachis ibidem Deo seruientibus terram quam tenuerunt de Waltero de Berkeley[f] camerar*io* reg*is* Scocie per rectas diuisas has, scilicet sicut magnum iter[g] quod uenit de ponte de Pollatkertin et extendit se vsque in Letegilultan et sicut predictum iter extendit se ad quercum crusiatam[h] scilicet[i] proximam Cloenchonethro[j] et ita inde sicut vallis quedam se extendit in nemore vsque ad quamdam sicam et sic descendendo per ipsam sicam vsque in Poladkertin et sic descendendo per Poladkertin vsque ad prenominatum pontem de Polladkertin, in liberam, puram et perpetuam elemosinam adeo libere, pure et quiete et solute sicut aliqua elemosina liberius,[k] quietius et melius potest dari, teneri et possideri in regno Scocie, cum[l] libertatibus illis que continentur in carta Walteri de Berkelay, prout carta[m] ipsa testatur[n] et confirmat.[o] Testibus hiis.

RUBRIC. *A*: Carta Rollandi fil*ii* Huctredi (in red). *B*: Item carta Rolandi fil*ii* Hucredi (in red). *C*'s rubric is illegible.
SOURCE. CRO, Carlisle, Cartulary of Holm Cultram, p. 101 = *A*. BL, MS Harleian 3911, fos. 107v–8r = *B*. BL, MS Harleian 3891, fo. 86r = *C*. Text above based on *A*, with some variants of *B* and *C* noted.
PRINTED. *Holm Cultram Reg.*, no. 122 (English summary of *A*).
NOTES. [a] Blue initial flourished in red, *A*; red initial, *B*, *C*. [b] tam presentes quam, *C*. [c] Roland', *B*; Rol', *C*. [d] Uctredi, *C*. [e] mea carta, *C*. [f] Berkelaye, *B*; Berkelai, *C*. [g] *C* continues etc. ut supra in proxima carta (i.e. Walter of Berkeley's charter) and omits the marches specified. [h] cruciatam, *B*. [i] et, *B*. [j] Cloencheneterro, *B*. [k] *C* adds et. [l] *C* adds omnibus. [m] *A* and *C* omit carta; supplied from *B*. [n] *C* concludes here with etc. [o] *B* ends here.
COMMENT. See also No. 13. The phrase *terram quam tenuerunt de Waltero* points to a date after Walter's death in *c.*1193 (*RRS*, ii, 6). For his charter, see *Holm Cultram Reg.*, no. 123; for William I's confirmation of it, *RRS*, ii, no. 256 (probably *c.*1180 × 1190); and for the boundaries, Reid, 'Kirkgunzean', 208, n. 28.

**26** Roland constable[a] of the king of Scots grants [sic] in alms to Dryburgh Abbey the church of St Fillan of Great Sorbie (*Maior Sowrby*) with adjacent land, as the charter of Ivo de Vieuxpont, the donor of the church, bears witness, saving the right of the parson, W. de Valognes. Witnesses [omitted]. [Aug. 1196 × Nov. 1200]

SOURCE. NLS, MS Advocates 34.4.7, fo. 26r.
PRINTED. *Dryburgh Liber*, no. 77.
NOTE. [a] confrater in source.
COMMENT. Ivo issued two deeds recording his grant of this church, one addressed generally, the other to Roland as *dominus suus*; his gift was also confirmed by Bishop John of Whithorn (1189–1206), the appropriation to take full effect on the death of another incumbent, John the chaplain, later archdeacon of Galloway: *Dryburgh Liber*, nos. 75–6, 78, 80. A close kinsman of the Morvilles, Ivo had presumably been infeft in Sorbie by Roland. He was also Roland's vassal in Lauderdale, a landowner in Westmorland, and a prominent tenant of the honour of Leicester; his chief estate, however, was Alston in the Liberty of Tynedale, held under the Scots crown. See further Stringer, 'Periphery and core', 113.

**27** Roland of Galloway, constable of the king of Scots, grants in alms to Kelso Abbey one saltworks in Loch Kindar (*Lochkendeloch*) with easements in his wood to fire the boiling pan, pasture for four oxen and one horse, and one messuage and a curtilage. He takes the monks and their men residing in Loch Kindar under his firm peace and protection. [Aug. 1196 × Nov. 1200]

Hiis test*ibus* R. abbate de Mailros, G. priore, Hug*one* capellano et clerico reg*is*, Hug*one* capellano meo, Gaut*ero* clerico meo, Henr*ico* de Sancto Claro, Alano de Thirlestano, Petro de la Haga, Alexandro de Cressewell', Gilberto de Morewill', Alano de Clapham'.

SOURCE. NLS, MS Advocates 34.5.1, fos. 102v–3r.
PRINTED. *Kelso Liber*, i, no. 254.
COMMENT. Most of the lay witnesses held knights' feus in Lauderdale, which perhaps suggests a session of the lord's court at Lauder.

**28** Roland constable of the king of Scots and his wife Helen [de Morville], with the consent of their heir Alan and their other heirs, confirm in alms to Furness Abbey [Lancashire] all the pasture of Selside and Birkwith [in Horton in Ribblesdale, Yorkshire, West Riding], as in the charter of Avice of Lancaster, wife of Richard de Morville, by these marches: viz. from the top of Ingleborough [in Ingleton] by the upper ridge of *Langhals* to the top of *Norhlaghals*,[a] thence by the spinney that goes up opposite the face of *Norhlaghals*,[a] thence to the hermit's house.[b] [Aug. 1196 × Nov. 1200]

Hiis test*ibus* domino Johanne Candide Case episcopo, domino Nicholao abbate de Dundrainan, Thoma fil*io* Gospatrici, et cetera.

SOURCE. BL, MS Additional 33244, fo. 124r–v.
PRINTED. *The Coucher Book of Furness Abbey*, ed. J. C. Atkinson and J. Brownbill (Chetham Society, 1886–1919), II, ii, 337.
NOTES. [a] *Furness Coucher Bk.* prints Norhlanghals, wrongly. [b] Here the cartulary scribe has etc. vt supra, i.e. as in Avice of Lancaster's charter (*Furness Coucher Bk.*, II, ii, 335–6): viz. thence by the Mossdale Beck to the earl of Richmond's forest, thence across to Cold Keld Gill on Cam Fell, thence to Stanpapan [lost], thence through the middle of Green Field [in Buckden] to Thueregille [lost], thence to the River Ribble, thence to Erdolfgile [lost], thence to Sulber, thence to the head of Crummack [in Austwick], thence by the path from Horton to the four ash trees at the head of Clapdale [in Clapham].
COMMENT. Most of the names in this set of bounds are identified in A. H. Smith, *The Place-Names of the West Riding of Yorkshire*, vi (English Place-Name Society, 1961), especially 218ff. Avice, Helen's mother, was the daughter of William I of Lancaster, lord of Kendal. On her marriage to Richard de Morville, a large estate in Lonsdale and Ribblesdale, in the honour of Mowbray, had passed into Morville hands; but tenurial security was undermined by the long-standing rivalry between the Mowbrays and the Stutevilles. In *c.*1189 Richard and Avice had granted the pasture of Selside and Birkwith to Furness Abbey for 300 marks 'to acquit our land of Lonsdale from the hands of William de Stuteville'; subsequently William renounced all his claims against Roland and Helen in respect of Burton in Lonsdale and its appurtenances: Stringer, 'Lords of Lauderdale', 47–8; *Furness Coucher Bk.*, II, ii, 334–6; *Curia Regis Rolls* (London, 1922– ), i, 380.

**29** Roland constable of the king of Scots grants [sic] *in mariagium* to Alan de St Clair and his wife Matilda of Windsor, and the heirs of their bodies, that land given to them by William de Morville: viz. by *Mosburne* [i.e. the Hillhouse Burn] downstream to *Langild* [i.e. the Kelphope Burn], thence upstream to the source of *Langild*, thence to the marches of Lothian towards Lammer Law [in Yester, East Lothian]. [Aug. 1196 × Nov. 1200]

Roll' filius Vhtredi Const*abularius* Reg*is* Scottorum Omnibus hominibus et amicis suis presentibus et futuris Salutem Sciatis me dedisse et concessisse et presenti carta mea confirmasse alano de Sancto claro et Matilde de Windesoure Sponse Sue et heredibus eorum qui ex eis exient . illam terram quam Willelmus de Moruilla eis dedit tenendam de me et heredibus meis In Mariagium . silicet[a] . sicut Mosburne descendit In langild . et langild In ascendendo . usque ad caput de langild . et de capite de langild usque ad diuisas de laodonia uersus lamberlauwe Hiis Testibus . Herberto decano de glescu . Alexandro filio Cosp*atricii* . Gilleberto de vmframuilla . alano de clepha*m* Thom*a* anglico . Willelmo fil*io* Rogeri . Jacobo de Ros alexandro de Neho' . Waltero et Ethelredo clericis MeiS

DESCRIPTION. Anderson's engraving (see Source) shows no tag or seal; but a transcript of this charter, *c.*1700, in NLS, Father Richard Hay's Collections, MS Advocates 34.1.9(ii), fo. 139r–v, has the following note: 'The seal therunto appended was of white wax, representing on the one side ane armed man, with ane naked sword in his hand a horseback. The horse coverd also with armour haveing chevrons on the pans, sutch we have seen att the carousels.' Hand: fluent cursive court hand.

SOURCE. *Selectus Diplomatum et Numismatum Scotiae Thesaurus*, ed. J. Anderson (Edinburgh, 1739), plate 81 (engraving of the original charter, *penes* Charles Sinclair Esquire of Herdmanston in 1739, but now lost).

PRINTED. As above.

NOTE. [a] Sic.

COMMENT. Matilda of Windsor was probably a niece of Avice of Lancaster, the mother of William and Helen de Morville: cf. *Records relating to the Barony of Kendale*, ed. J. F. Curwen (CWAAS, Record Series, 1923–6), i, 386–7. The property lay in upper Lauderdale above Carfrae (in Channelkirk), where William had already granted or confirmed a knight's feu to Henry de St Clair (Sinclair), who had previously been infeft in Herdmanston (East Lothian) by Richard de Morville: Barrow, *Anglo-Norman Era*, 129. See also A. Allan, *History of Channelkirk* (Edinburgh, 1900), 404–6, though Allan appears to have been mistaken in his identifications of *Mosburne* and *Langild*. As the witnesses include the dean of Glasgow and two Cunningham tenants, James de Ros and Alexander de Néhou (No. 39), the business was possibly done in Cunningham.

**30** Alan constable of the lord king of Scots grants in alms to Kelso Abbey, in exchange for the revenue the monks used to have in Galloway, five ploughgates of land in *Vlfkelyston'* [i.e. Oxton in Channelkirk] in Lauderdale, all common easements of the toun, and a mill if they wish, with leave to construct a mill-pond on his land if necessary. They remit their claims to the revenue and to all arrears from Uhtred's time onwards. They absolve the souls of Roland and Uhtred and admit them to the benefits of their church; similarly, they receive Alan, his mother[a] and all their heirs, ancestors and successors into their fraternity. They are to hold their alms by those marches perambulated by Alan and responsible men: viz. from Overhowden (*caput del Holdene*) by the Howden Burn downstream to Dere Street, by Dere Street northwards to *Fuleforde*, [and] by Samson's marches to the Leader Water; thence by the Leader straight up to the east end of Oxton, thence by the south road up to Dere Street, excluding the tofts and crofts of William of Collielaw and Richard son of Geoffrey, thence by the same road southwards to the cross, thence westwards as the crosses have been placed and the ditches dug to the road from Howden, thence by that road to Overhowden. [Jan. 1201 × 1205, possibly × 25 Sep. 1201]

Hiis test*ibus* domino Joh*anne* episcopo Candide Case, domino Hug*one* capellano, magistro Ad*a* persona de Laweder, Thoma de Colewill', Henr*ico* de Ferlint', Petro de Haga, Alexandro de Hecford', Waltero Anglico, cum multis aliis. Teste etiam capitulo Kalchoens*i*.

SOURCE. NLS, MS Advocates 34.5.1, fo. 98r–v.

PRINTED. *Kelso Liber*, i, no. 245.

COMMENT. William I's confirmation, *RRS*, ii, no. 448, supplies the later date-limits, and shows that Helen de Morville issued her own charter, now lost, concerning this business. For the marches, see R. P. Hardie, *The Roads of Mediaeval Lauderdale* (Edinburgh, 1942), 88–9. Kelso's entitlement to revenue in (eastern?) Galloway probably originated in prince David's grant of a tenth of the cain of cattle, pigs and cheeses from that part of Galloway held by him in Alexander I's reign: *RRS*, i, no. 131. Payments had presumably fallen into arrears as a result of Uhtred's rebellion in 1174. The appearance of the whole chapter of Kelso as witnesses shows that the agreement was concluded at Kelso Abbey, where Alan and his kin would have been formally admitted to fraternity by a solemn ceremony in the chapter-house. The third witness Master Adam (of Thornton), who served as Alan's clerk, also attested for Alan in Galloway, Lauderdale(?) and Cumbria (Nos. **35**, **44**, **52–4**). To the details given on his career in Watt, *Scottish Graduates*, 531, and Stringer, 'Periphery and core', 92, can be added his occurrences as parson of Lauder under Richard de Morville: *Melrose Liber*, i, nos. 95, 107. Note also that an Adam de Torneton' witnessed a grant by William Masculus to the monks of Holy Island of lands in Tweedmouth (Northumberland) in *c.*1200: Raine, *North Durham*, Appendix, no. 687.

**31** Alan constable of the lord king of Scots grants [sic] in alms to Holyrood Abbey all that Fergus and Uhtred gave and confirmed by their charters. By Fergus's gift: the whole of Dunrod [in Kirkcudbright] with its church, free of all cain and conveth. By Uhtred's gift: the churches of St Cuthbert of *Denesmor* [i.e. Kirkcudbright], Tongland, Twynholm (*Twenham*) and Urr (*Colmanele*) with the chapel of St Constantine and one ploughgate of land; the church of St Bridget of Blaiket (*Blakhet*) [in Urr] with one ploughgate of land, and the churches of *Locheletun* [i.e. Kelton], Kirkcormack [in Kelton], St Andrew [of Balmaghie] and Barncrosh (*Balnecros*) [in Tongland]. Grants also to the canons easements in all his demesne woods and forests, with leave to take timber and all necessities for their own uses, and quittance of pannage for their pigs. The canons are to hold all the above as the charters of Fergus, Uhtred and Roland bear witness. Witnesses [omitted]. [Jan. 1201 × 1218, probably × 1206]

SOURCE. *Holyrood Liber*, no. 73. (The source of the printed text has not been traced. Inferior copies are in NLS, MS Advocates 35.4.16, fos. 139v–40r, and MS Advocates 35.2.4(ii), fos. 121r–2r.)

PRINTED. As above.

COMMENT. Probably issued simultaneously with *Holyrood Liber*, no. 49, a general confirmation for Holyrood in similar terms by Bishop John of Whithorn (1189–1206), executed at Whithorn Priory in Alan's presence; certainly no later than 1218, when the church of Tongland was annexed to Tongland Abbey on its foundation: I. B. Cowan, *The Parishes of Medieval Scotland* (Scottish Record Society, 1967), 198. Holyrood also armed itself with a royal confirmation of its churches in Galloway in *c.*1209: *RRS*, ii, no. 485. The church of Galtway, originally granted to Holyrood by Fergus (No. **2**), had been reassigned as part of the endowment of the priory of St Mary's Isle: Cowan, *Parishes*, 72.

**32** Alan lord of Galloway, constable of Scotland, quitclaims to Roger de Lacy, constable of Chester, and his heirs the advowson of the church of Kippax [Yorkshire, West Riding]. [Jan. 1201 × 1 Oct. 1211; possibly 1205]

Hijs Test*ibus* . Eustacio de Vescy . Roberto Walensi . Willelmo de bello monte . hugone despensario . Thoma fratre suo . Gilberto fil*io* Cospatric . Radulfo de Campania . Ricardo clerico de creuequor litterarum scriptore . 7 multis aliis .

SOURCE. Original charter, PRO, Duchy of Lancaster, Cartae Miscellaneae, DL36/1/10.

PRINTED. Stringer, 'Periphery and core', Appendix (A), no. 2 (with full description and note on dating). *CDS*, i, no. 553 (English summary).

COMMENT. See also Nos. **55**, **57**. Eustace de Vescy, William I's son-in-law, was lord of Alnwick and Malton. The next four witnesses were members of Roger de Lacy's retinue. Both Gilbert son of Cospatric and Ralph de Campania held feus in Galloway; but the venue was possibly in Yorkshire. The important manor of Kippax, in the honour of Pontefract, formed part of the dowry of Alan's first wife, a daughter of Roger de Lacy. Their daughter Helen became the first wife of Roger de Quincy, who in her right had taken control of Kippax and the rest of her mother's *maritagium* by 1233: K. J. Stringer, 'A new wife for Alan of Galloway', *TDGAS*, 3rd ser., xlix (1972), 49–55.

**33** *Alan grants to the church of St Cuthbert of Kirkcudbright that part of Sypland [in Kirkcudbright] held by Kineth. [Jan. 1201 × 7 Jan. 1210]

SOURCE. *RRS*, ii, no. 489.
COMMENT. Latest possible date supplied by source, William I's confirmation.

**34** *Alan grants to the church of St Oswald the Martyr of Kelton thirty-two acres of land in the territory of Kelton. [Jan. 1201 × 7 Jan. 1210]

SOURCE. *RRS*, ii, no. 489.
COMMENT. Latest possible date supplied by source, William I's confirmation.

**35** Alan constable of the Scots grants [sic] to Adam, son of Gilbert the dispenser, Airdrie [in Kirkbean] by those marches by which Gilbert held it of Roland, in feu and heritage, for the tenth part of one knight's service. The land is to be free of multure, and Adam's corn shall be ground at Alan's mill of Preston immediately after the corn already in the hopper, unless Alan's own corn or church corn is waiting. [Jan. 1201 × 7 Jan. 1210]

Hiis testibus Hen*rico* fil*io* comit*is* D*aui*d, Thom*a* fratre meo, Gilbert*o* fil*io* Cospatricij, Thoma [ ],[a] Willelmo de Mara, Radulfo[b] de Campan*ia*, Alex*andro* de Derwentwater, Willelmo Olifard, Ada de Thore', Ric*ardo* clerico presentium[c] scriptore.

SOURCE. NAS, Register House Charters, RH6/308 (notarial copy of 15 Mar. 1443/4).
PRINTED. Stringer, 'Periphery and core', Appendix (A), no. 1 (with note on dating).
NOTES. [a] Illegible in source. [b] Raduff' in source. [c] presensium in source.
COMMENT. The *scriptor* was presumably the same man as Richard the clerk of Troqueer, who wrote No. **32**. Both charters are also witnessed by Gilbert son of Cospatric and Ralph de Campania; and in this instance at least, a session of Alan's court in Galloway may be indicated. For Adam's lands outside Galloway, the chief of which was his tenancy-in-chief at Kilbucho (Peeblesshire), and for his ties with the Comyns, Grahams, Hays and Stewarts, see Stringer, 'Periphery and core', 100. His father Gilbert (son of Richer), infeft by Walter son of Alan (d. 1177) at Tarbolton (Ayrshire), was a regular witness of William I's *acta*, almost certainly a crown vassal, and just possibly dispenser of the royal household.

**36** *Alan grants to Soutra Hospital one ploughgate of land called *Fulwidnes* [lost, in Channelkirk]. [Jan. 1201 × 11 May 1214]

SOURCE. No. **52**.
COMMENT. Latest possible date supplied by source. *Fulwidnes* can possibly be identified with the modern farm at Threeburnford (NT 469522): Allan, *Channelkirk*, 564ff; Hardie, *Roads of Mediaeval Lauderdale*, 91, 94. In *c*.1220 Dryburgh Abbey remitted to Soutra all teinds and dues owed to the mother-church of Channelkirk from *Fulewithnis ad Wedelford*, in Channelkirk parish, for one pound of pepper and one pound of cumin yearly, payable at Roxburgh fair: *Dryburgh Liber*, no. 187; *Midlothian Chrs.*, 11–12.

**37** Alan constable of the king of Scots confirms in alms to Melrose Abbey the grant made by his mother, Helen de Morville, of land in the territory of *Gillebecchistun* [i.e. Harehope in Eddleston, Peeblesshire] by the marches specified in her charter. Warrandice. Witnesses [omitted]. [Jan. 1201 × 4 Dec. 1214]

SOURCE. NLS, MS Advocates 34.4.11, fo. 56v.
PRINTED. *Melrose Liber*, i, no. 84.
COMMENT. See also No. **38**. Helen's charter is *Melrose Liber*, i, no. 82. The cartulary scribe entitled

it *De Noua Terra*, to which was added in a later (xv-cent.?) hand *que dicitur Harhope*. Eddleston was originally held by Richard de Morville at ferme of the bishopric of Glasgow for fifteen years from 1170; but the bishops lost control of the property until *c.*1235, when it was returned by Alan's heirs. Their surrender did not affect Melrose's right: C. Innes *et al.*, eds., *Origines Parochiales Scotiae* (Bannatyne Club, 1851–5), i, 212–14; J. W. Buchan, ed., *A History of Peeblesshire* (Glasgow, 1925–7), ii, 445ff.

**38** Alan grants [sic] in alms to Melrose Abbey all that land in the territory of *Gillebeccokestun* contained within these marches: viz. from the top of Wide Hope Shank (*Widhope*)[a] by the middle of the slope eastwards to the old fort (*uetus castellarium*) [on Harehope Hill], thence across country to *Carelgiburne* [i.e. the Crailzie Burn], thence between the arable land and the moor to the Harehope Burn, thence downstream to its confluence with *Withopeburne*[b] [i.e. the Meldon Burn], thence by *Withopeburne*[b] upstream to the top of Wide Hope Shank. Grants also common pasture in the territory of the toun for 700 sheep with their lambs up to two years old, or as many wethers, forty cows and one bull with their calves up to two years old, forty oxen and eight horses, and four sows with their piglets up to three years old. All this is given in exchange for Simon de Beaumont's land in Cunningham, which Alan's uncle, William de Morville, in his last will bequeathed to the monks. They remit all claim to that land, and absolve the souls of William and Roland. Warrandice. Witnesses [omitted]. [Jan. 1201 × 4 Dec. 1214]

SOURCE. NLS, MS Advocates 34.4.11, fos. 56v–7r = *A*. BL, MS Harleian 3960, fo. 73r–v = *B*.
PRINTED. *Melrose Liber*, i, no. 83 (from *A*).
NOTES. [a] Widhop, *B*. [b] Witopburn, *B*.
COMMENT. Though Alan is not styled constable, this text presumably belongs after Roland's death and is later than No. 37, the necessity for a supplementary charter no doubt being explained by a redefinition of the boundaries, for the marches specified are rather different from those in Helen de Morville's charter. William I's confirmation is *RRS*, ii, no. 449. On the old fort (NT 196445), see *Peeblesshire: An Inventory of the Ancient Monuments* (Royal Commission on the Ancient and Historical Monuments of Scotland, 1967), i, 118–20. Melrose's difficulties over the land in Cunningham apparently arose because William de Morville had died in possession. On the invalidity of death-bed bequests of land, see M. M. Sheehan, *The Will in Medieval England* (Toronto, 1963), especially 269–74.

**39** Alan constable of Scotland confirms to Dryburgh Abbey that half-ploughgate of land in the territory of Giffen [in Beith, Ayrshire] granted in alms by Alexander de Néhou, with the liberties and marches specified in Alexander's charter. Corroboration. Witnesses [omitted]. [Jan. 1201 × *c.* 2 Feb. 1234]

SOURCE. NLS, MS Advocates 34.4.7, fo. 67v.
PRINTED. *Dryburgh Liber*, no. 228.
COMMENT. Alexander's charter is *Dryburgh Liber*, no. 226. Abbot Thomas of Dryburgh subsequently granted this land to his clerk Richard, also Alan's chaplain, for 4s. yearly, payable on the feast of St James at Roxburgh fair: ibid., no. 229. On the Néhous and their association with Alan's Morville predecessors, see Barrow, *Anglo-Norman Era*, 79 and n. 105.

**40** Alan constable of Scotland confirms to Dryburgh Abbey and the mother-church of Channelkirk (*Childinch'*) one toft and croft in *Samsonschel'* [i.e. Shielfield in Lauder] with the other lands granted by Henry son of Samson, as Henry's charter justly bears witness. Corroboration. Witnesses [omitted]. [Jan. 1201 × *c.* 2 Feb. 1234]

SOURCE. NLS, MS Advocates 34.4.7, fo. 53r.
PRINTED. *Dryburgh Liber*, no. 180.
COMMENT. Henry son of Samson de Logis issued two charters for Dryburgh concerning his grants in *Samsonschel'*: *Dryburgh Liber*, nos. 176–7. On the identification of this shieling site (NT 511513), see Hardie, *Roads of Mediaeval Lauderdale*, 85–6. The church of Channelkirk had been given to Dryburgh by Hugh I de Morville: *RRS*, ii, no. 65.

**41** *Alan grants or confirms to Glenluce Abbey [unspecified] property. [Jan. 1201 × *c.* 2 Feb. 1234]

SOURCE. *Wigtownshire Chrs.*, 57.

**42** Alan constable of the king of Scotland confirms in alms to St Andrew's Priory, Northampton, one ploughgate of land of his demesne in Lauderdale granted by his mother, Helen de Morville, as her charter bears witness. [Jan. 1201 × *c.* 2 Feb. 1234]

[a]Hiis testibus Gilberto filio Co[spat*ricii*, Alex*andro* fil*io* Cosp*atricii*], Willelmo de la Mare, Thom*a* Anglico, Radulfo de la Ch[am]paygn', Jacobo decano, Hug*one* capellano, Ad*a* capellano, Waltero et Ethereldo clericis meis et aliis.

SOURCE. BL, MS Royal II B.ix, fo. 103r–v = *A*. BL, MS Cotton Vespasian E.xvii, fo. 255r = *B*.
PRINTED. Stringer, 'Lords of Lauderdale', Appendix, no. 7 (collation of *A* and *B*).
NOTE. [a] From *A*, save where damaged.
COMMENT. Roland, who died at Northampton, was buried in St Andrew's Priory. The land concerned was in Newbigging (in Lauder), and in 1243 the monks leased it in perpetuity to Dryburgh Abbey for an annual rent of two merks. See Stringer, 'Lords of Lauderdale', 52, 55, 68–9. Helen's charter is ibid., Appendix, no. 6. Three witnesses, Gilbert son of Cospatric, Ralph de Campania and James the dean, were associated with Galloway, where this act may have been executed.

**43** *Alan grants to St Andrew's Priory, Northampton, three merks yearly from the ferme of Redpath [in Earlston, Berwickshire], 20s. from the ferme of *Langeld* [lost, in Lauder], and half a merk from the ferme of *Grombelau*, half at Martinmas and half at Whitsunday. [Jan. 1201 × *c.* 2 Feb. 1234]

SOURCE. Simpson, 'Acts of Roger de Quincy', Texts, no. 39; Stringer, 'Lords of Lauderdale', Appendix, no. 8.
COMMENT. For *Langeld*, see No. 56.

**44** Alan lord of Galloway and constable of Scotland grants in alms to St Bees Priory one merk of silver yearly from his chamber, until he assigns one merk's rent in land or spiritualities, half at Whitsunday and half at Martinmas. Corroboration. [Jan. 1201 × *c.* 2 Feb. 1234]

Hijs test*ibus* Alano fil*io* Ketelli, Alan*o* de Camerton', Gilbert*o* fil*io* Gospatrici, Rob*erto* de Haueringt', Willelmo de Mara, Randulfo de Campania,[a] Alexandro fil*io* Adam, Michaele capellano, Alexandro de Stainburn, magistro Thoma, magistro Adam de Thorn'[b] clerico nostro.

SOURCE. BL, MS Harleian 434, fo. 26v.
PRINTED. *St Bees Reg.*, no. 42.
NOTES. [a] Preceded by Caude (Cande?) in source. [b] *St Bees Reg.* prints Thorn in error.
COMMENT. Four witnesses, Alan son of Ketel, Alan of Camerton, Robert of Harrington and Alexander of Stainburn, were landowners in west Cumberland, where this charter may have been issued. Specific references to a magnate's chamber are still rare at this date, even in contemporary English record: cf. D. Crouch, *William Marshal: Court, Career and Chivalry in the Angevin Empire* (London, 1990), 168–9.

**45** *Alan confirms to Alan of Clapham two and a half husbandlands held by Alden de Langhald in the toun of Addinston [in Lauder], as the charter of William de Morville bears witness. [Jan. 1201 × *c.* 2 Feb. 1234]

SOURCE. *APS*, vii, 153.
COMMENT. From a xvii-cent. list of charters, made for the earl of Lauderdale, concerning Whalp Law, Soonhope and other places in Lauder parish. Alan of Clapham (Clephane), a Yorkshireman, hailed from the Morville lordship of Lonsdale and occurs as Alan's sheriff of Lauder in 1203: Barrow, *Anglo-Norman Era*, 83 and n. 123. He is probably identical with Alan son of Uhtred the

priest of Clapham, beside Ingleborough, who in *c.*1190 granted to Furness Abbey two bovates of land in Clapham, on the abbey's agreeing to admit him as a monk in his old age or infirmity: *Furness Coucher Bk.*, II, ii, 299–300, 306–7. A Walter of Clapham attested for Alan's brother Earl Thomas of Atholl in a Cunningham context: *Newbattle Reg.*, no. 27.

**46** *Alan grants to Alan of Clapham [blank] Struther [in Lauder] by its right marches. [Jan. 1201 × *c.* 2 Feb. 1234]

SOURCE. *APS*, vii, 153.

**47** Alan constable of Scotland confirms to Durand son of Christian all the land of Mabie and *Achencork'* granted by Robert son of Simon in his feu of Kirkconnell [in Troqueer], by specified marches, to be held as Robert's charter bears witness. Corroboration. [Jan. 1201 × *c.* 2 Feb. 1234]

Omnibus[a] hoc scriptum visur*is* vel auditur*is*, Alanus fil*ius* Rolandi Scoc' constabular*ius*, salutem. Noueritis nos concessisse et hac presenti carta nostra confirmasse Durando filio Christini totam terram que vocatur Mayby et Achencork'[b] quam ei dedit Robertus fil*ius* Symon*is* infra feodum suum de Kyrkconeuel[c] integre cum omnibus pertin*entiis* suis, scilicet per has diuisas:[d] scilicet per Carepoll' vsque ad Locisfernam et de Locisfernam vsque ad Altaladi, vsque Polleos, vsque Polleroth, vsque Garpol, et de Garpol vsque Furan Gilbanan et de Furan Gilbanan vsque Polingouir, vsque Locangre ad quercus que habent cruces et de quercis ill*is* vsque ad semitam que iacet iuxta dom*um* Gillek' et de illa semita vsque ad riuulum qui currit iuxta hostium Gillecoln' filii Patin[e] et de illo riuulo vsque ad Locisfernam vt cadit in Locisfernam. Habend*am* et tenend*am* sibi et heredibus suis cum omnibus pertin*entiis* suis et libertatibus, in boscis et planis, in pratis et pascuis, in aquis et molendinis, in stagn*is*, in mussis et mariscis[f] et in omnibus aliis aysiamentis, libere,[g] quiete, plenarie et honorifice prout carta dicti Roberti filii Symon*is* dicto Durando facta melius purportat et testatur, saluo nobis et heredibus nostris seruicio nostro. Et in huius rei testimonium huic scripto sigillum nostrum fecimus apponi.[h] Hiis t*estibus*, et cetera.

RUBRIC. *A* and *B*: Confirmacio Alani filii Rolandi Durando facta (in red). C's rubric is illegible.

SOURCE. CRO, Carlisle, Cartulary of Holm Cultram, p. 113 = *A*. BL, MS Harleian 3911, fo. 115v = *B*. BL, MS Harleian 3891, fo. 92v = *C*. Text above from *A*, with some variants of *B* and *C* noted.

PRINTED. *Holm Cultram Reg.*, no. 142 (English summary of *A*).

NOTES. [a] Red initial flourished in blue, *A*; blue initial, *B*; red initial, *C*. [b] Aghencork', *C*. [c] Possibly Kyrkeoneuel, *A*; Kirkoneuill', *B*, *C*. [d] *C* continues que nominantur in proxima carta supra (i.e. Robert son of Simon's charter) and omits the marches specified. [e] Pantin, *B*. [f] marissis, *B*. [g] *C* adds et. [h] *B* breaks off here with etc.; *C* ends with apponit', etc.

COMMENT. The boundary survey cannot now be reconstructed in any detail, but the circuit seems to have embraced the western part of Troqueer parish between Lochaber Loch (*Locisfernam*) and the middle reaches of Crooks Pow. Robert's charter, specifying a reddendo of one merk yearly, is summarised in *Holm Cultram Reg.*, no. 148. Durand subsequently granted the land to Holm Cultram Abbey: ibid., no. 143 (a defective abstract).

**48** *Alan grants to William of Lynn land in Perth. [Jan. 1201 × *c.* 2 Feb. 1234]

SOURCE. *Scone Liber*, no. 80.

COMMENT. The land concerned was attached to the constable's office. According to *Scone Liber*, no. 89, another prominent burgess of Perth, Richard of Leicester (on whom see Duncan, *Kingdom*, 492), was joint beneficiary.

**49** *Alan grants to Vivian de Mulineys [Molyneux], in exchange for his land of Collielaw [in Channelkirk], land in Saltoun [East Lothian] for his homage and service. [Jan. 1201 × *c.* 2 Feb. 1234]

SOURCE. *Midlothian Chrs.*, 27.

COMMENT. On Vivian, a Morville follower imported from Lancashire, see Barrow, *Anglo-Norman Era*, 82, 187–8. Note also that according to genealogical notes, *c.*1636, by Roger Dodsworth, Richard de Molyneux (d. *c.*1320) of Sefton (Lancashire) quitclaimed to his son Thomas his right in Little Saltoun and in all the other property in Scotland once belonging to Vivian de Molyneux, whose heir Richard was: Oxford, Bodleian Library, MS Dodsworth 61, fos. 4r–v, 14r. In 1236 × 1241 Vivian endowed Soutra Hospital with all the land in Saltoun given to him by Alan, for the salvation of the souls of Roland and Alan, his lords: *Midlothian Chrs.*, 27.

**50** Alan constable of Scotland grants in alms to Holm Cultram Abbey that land disputed between them, by specified marches. Warrandice. [1209 × *c.* 2 Feb. 1234]

Vniuersis[a] sancte matris ecclesie filiis, et cetera, Alanus filius Rolandi Scoc' constabularius, salutem in Domino. Nouerit vniuersitas[b] vestra[c] nos concessisse, dedisse et hac presenti carta nostra confirmasse Deo et beate Marie et domui de Holm' et monach*is* ibidem Deo seruientibus terram illam de qua inter nos et eosdem monachos quondam fuit contencio, scilicet per has diuisas: a loco vbi Grenefaude[d] cadit in aquam que exit de Lochartur,[e] ascendendo per eandem aquam vsque ad locum illum ubi eadem aqua exit de Lochartur et ita ascendendo per ipsam Lochartur vsque ad quemdam paruum[f] riuulum qui cadit in Lochartur ex parte australi, qui riuulus de nouo a nobis propter prehabitam contencionem uocatus est Pollenchosnewa,[g] ascendendo per eundem[h] riuulum quamdiu manifeste se demonstrat vsque ad locum vbi prius se bifurcat et inde indirectum vsque ad Munenemuch[i] et a Munenemuch[i] per easdem diuisas que nominate sunt in carta patris nostri Rolandi. Tenend*am* et habend*am* integre cum suis pertin*entiis* de nobis et heredibus nostris in liberam, puram et perpetuam elemosinam, libere et quiete et solute ab omni seculari seruicio, consuetudine et exaccione. Et nos et heredes nostri warantizabimus[j] eisdem monach*is* hanc donacionem contra omnes homines inperpetuum.[k] His testibus Waltero Candide Case episcopo, et cetera.

RUBRIC. *A* and *B*: Carta Alani filii Rollandi (in red). *C*'s rubric is illegible.

SOURCE. CRO, Carlisle, Cartulary of Holm Cultram, pp. 105–6 = *A*. BL, MS Harleian 3911, fo. 110r–v = *B*. BL, MS Harleian 3891, fo. 87r = *C*. Text above a collation of *A* and *C*, with *A*'s readings normally preferred.

PRINTED. *Holm Cultram Reg.*, no. 130 (English summary of *A*).

NOTES. [a] Blue initial flourished in red, *A*; red initial, *B*, *C*. [b] vniuersita, *A*. [c] nostra, *C*. [d] Grenefade, *C*. [e] Loghartur here and throughout, *C*. [f] *A* and *B* omit paruum; supplied from *C*. [g] Pollencosnewa, *B*; Polenchosnewa, *C*. [h] *A* and *B* omit eundem; supplied from *C*. [i] Munenemuche, *B*; Munnenemuth, *C*. [j] warrantizabimus, *B*; *C* concludes here with warr', etc. [k] *B* ends here with T', etc.

COMMENT. Walter, Alan's chamberlain, became bishop of Whithorn in 1209. This charter apparently redefines the bounds of the north-east part of Kirkgunzeon parish between the Lawston Burn (*Grenefaude*) and Lotus Hill (*Munenemuch*): cf. Reid, 'Kirkgunzean', 205–6 and n. 15. Of special note is the fact that, to clarify the marches, Alan renamed a burn flowing into Loch Arthur because it had changed its course. Its new name, *Pollenchosnewa*, seems to be for *pol(l) an choise nuadh* = 'burn with a new foot or exit', a suggestion I owe to Geoffrey Barrow.

**51** *Alan confirms to the Knights Templars 123 acres of land outside the covert of the park of Whissendine [Rutland]. [*c.*1212?]

SOURCE. *Curia Regis Rolls*, vii, 189; *CDS*, i, no. 576.

COMMENT. The manor of Whissendine, in the honour of Huntingdon, formed part of the Morville inheritance. It subsequently passed to Nicholas de Stuteville (d. 1233), lord of Cottingham (Yorkshire), on his marriage to Alan's sister. See K. J. Stringer, *Earl David of Huntingdon, 1152–1219: A Study in Anglo-Scottish History* (Edinburgh, 1985), 114, 130, 184, 233–4.

**52** Alan constable of Scotland grants to Kelso Abbey, for a quitclaim of all its right in the ploughgate of land called *Fulwidnes* [lost, in Channelkirk] which he gave in alms to Soutra Hospital, 8s. yearly from William of Hartside and his heirs or successors from the land which belonged to Gillefalyn in Oxton (*Vlkilleston'*), half at Whitsunday and half at Martinmas, and one toft and croft in the east part of Oxton on the river-bank, which Roger son of Ailif held. Corroboration. [5 Aug. 1213 × 11 May 1214]

Hiis test*ibus* domino A. abbate de [Melros][a] Catenensis[b] ecclesie electo, domino Petro de la Haga, domino Rad*ulfo* de Campania, domino Roberto de Ros', domino Willelmo de la Mare, domino Viuian*o* de Mulynaus, domino Will*elmo* de Geuelest', domino Patricio de Culwen', magistro A. de Thornenton', domino Ric*ardo* et domino Helya capellanis et aliis.

SOURCE. NLS, MS Advocates 34.5.1, fos. 98v–9r.
PRINTED. *Kelso Liber*, i, no. 246.
NOTES. [a] Omitted in source. [b] *Kelso Liber* prints Catanensis, wrongly.
COMMENT. Abbot Adam of Melrose was elected bishop of Caithness 5 Aug. 1213 and consecrated 11 May 1214: *Chron. Melrose*, 57–8. On *Fulwidnes*, see No. 36. William de Morville had confirmed to William of Hartside all the land held by Heden and Hemming in Hartside (in Channelkirk) east of the road from Stow to Dere Street, to be held of Soutra Hospital in feu and heritage: NAS, RH6/12. The witness-list brings together knights from Lauderdale (Peter de la Haya, Vivian de Molyneux), Galloway (Ralph de Campania, William of Gelston, Patrick of Colvend), and Cunningham (Robert de Ros).

**53** Alan constable of Scotland confirms to John son of Laurence of Newbiggin and his heirs three parts of the land between the Trout Beck and the marches of [Temple] Sowerby and between the king's highway to Carlisle and the River Eden, with the tofts and crofts between Whelp Castle and the mill, and one toft and croft on the other side of the road, altogether making up one carucate of land in Kirkby Thore [Westmorland], to be held of the successors of Waltheof son of Gamel as Waltheof's charter bears witness; also the moiety of Hillbeck [in Brough] granted by Thomas of Hillbeck to Robert the steward of Appleby with his sister Dionisia, to be held of the successors of Thomas as Thomas's charter bears witness. [*c.* Jun. 1216 × *c.* Oct. 1217]

His Testibus . .E. de Ballielo Ric*ardo* Gernun . Gilberto fil*io* Cospatricii Ric*ardo* de Leuingt' Rad*ulfo* de Campanio . A. de Wigetona . Rog*ero* de Bello Campo . Rad*ulfo* de feritate Eudone de Carll' . Rob*erto* de castello kairoc . Rad*ulfo* daencurt . thoma fil*io* Rand*ulfi* . Magistro . A. de thorentona Thoma de kent thoma de Morlund . Willelmo de Warh*er*cop . N. de morlund . Rog*ero* de Loncastre . Wigano de saunford . Joh*anne* d[e ][a]mebi . Thoma de tibai . W. fil*io* Hamonis de [H][a]ellebec . Simone de uenacione et Aliis .

SOURCE. Original charter with fragment of seal, CRO, Kendal, Crackanthorpe Muniments, WD/Crk/A1428/M–48.
PRINTED. Stringer, 'Periphery and core', Appendix (A), no. 3 (with full description, note of other printed texts, and photograph).
NOTE. [a] Hole in parchment.
COMMENT. On the political significance of this act, which shows that Alan annexed the former Morville lordship of North Westmorland during the Anglo-Scottish war of 1215–17, see Stringer, 'Periphery and core', 90–2. The venue was in Cumbria, perhaps Appleby, and three tenants in Galloway attest (Enguerrand de Balliol, Gilbert son of Cospatric, Ralph de Campania).

**54** Alan constable of Scotland/of the Scots[a] confirms to St Peter's Hospital, York, one ploughgate of land and a toft in Troqueer (*Creueqr'*)[b] granted by lord Uhtred, as Uhtred's charter justly bears witness. Corroboration. [1218 × Aug. 1222]

[c]Hiis testibus domino Waltero Candide Case episcopo, domino Galfrido abbate de Dundranin, domino Elia abbate de Tungeland', domino Johanne archidiacono, domino Durando officiali, domino Matheo[d] decano, magistro Ada de Thornet', Thoma de Cancia, Thoma persona de Creuequer, Ric*ardo* persona de Culewen, Martino persona de Kirkecuthbrith, magistro Geruasio de Sumeruile, magistro Thoma et aliis.

SOURCE. PRO, C53/93, memb. 8 = *A*. PRO, C47/22/4(8) = *B*.
PRINTED. *Cal. Charter Rolls*, iii, 92 (from *A*), whence Reid, *History of Dumfries*, 219 (English summary). *CDS*, ii, 422 (English summary of *B*).
NOTES. [a] Scot' constab', *A*; Scott' constab', *B*. [b] *Cal. Charter Rolls* prints Croveqr', wrongly. [c] From *A*. [d] *Cal. Charter Rolls* prints Mattheo.
COMMENT. See No. 6. Tongland Abbey, whose abbot witnesses, was founded in 1218. Abbot Geoffrey of Dundrennan attended the Cistercian General Chapter in Sep. 1222, and died on his way home at Auberive Abbey, near Dijon: *Chron. Melrose*, 75–6.

**55** *Alan issues letters patent (*litere patentes*) ordering the men of his fee to obey Herbert de Arches as his bailiff [of Kippax]. [Jun. 1220?]

SOURCE. *Curia Regis Rolls*, xi, no. 1092.
COMMENT. See Nos. **32**, **57**. After the war of 1215–17 Alan secured restoration of his lawful English estates while in attendance on Alexander II during the meeting with Henry III at York in Jun. 1220: *CDS*, i, nos. 755, 762–3. Herbert's Yorkshire tenancies are dealt with in *Early Yorkshire Charters*, iii, ed. W. Farrer (Edinburgh, 1916), 257–8. He or his father and namesake had visited Scotland by *c*.1185 in the retinue of Earl David of Huntingdon, whose daughter Alan married in 1209: Stringer, *Earl David*, 255.

**56** Alan constable of Scotland grants to Kilwinning Abbey and Dryburgh Abbey all that portion held by Master Andrew of Moray in the parish of the church of Lauder: viz. the teinds of Trabrown (*Treburn'*), of Pilmuir, of the land of Walter Hostiarius, of Martin's land, namely Whitlaw, of *Langelt*, of the land of Uhtred de Langelt, of *Hailisespeth'*[a] [i.e. Allanbank], of Samson's land, namely *Todlaw*, of Addinston (*Aldenistoun'*), of Whalp Law (*Welpelaw*), of Lylestone (*Lyolstoun'*), and of Burncastle; to be held of Alan and his heirs for the good of peace. Corroboration. Witnesses [omitted]. [1222]

SOURCE. NLS, MS Advocates 34.4.7, fo. 28r–v.
PRINTED. *Dryburgh Liber*, no. 85, whence 'Collections towards a history of the monastery of Kilwinning', *Archaeological and Historical Collections relating to the Counties of Ayr and Wigton*, i (1878), 132.
NOTE. [a] *Dryburgh Liber* prints Hailisepeth in error.
COMMENT. On 9 Jul. 1221 Pope Honorius III appointed judges-delegate to settle the dispute between Kilwinning and Dryburgh over Lauder church; in 1222 they reported that both abbeys, with Alan's advice and consent, had agreed to share Master Andrew's portion: *Dryburgh Liber*, no. 84. The confirmation charter of Bishop William Malvoisin of St Andrews (1202–38) shows that Alan was in fact a party to the dispute, and that it also involved the advowson: ibid., no. 86. The identifiable place-names lie above Lauder, on either side of the Leader Water; for the identification of *Hailisespeth'* with Allanbank, see ibid., no. 88. Master Andrew, who probably owed his portion to Alan's patronage, became bishop of Moray in 1222. See further Watt, *Scottish Graduates*, 407.

**57** *Alan issues letters patent (*litere patentes*) sanctioning whatever Herbert de Arches did concerning the knight's fee in Swillington [Yorkshire, West Riding] and Preston [in Kippax] when he was his steward [sic]. [*c*.1223]

SOURCE. *Curia Regis Rolls*, xi, no. 1092.
COMMENT. The source is the record of a court case, 1223, in which Walter of Pattishall, son of King John's senior judge Simon of Pattishall, accused Herbert of unlawfully seizing his land at Swillington as an escheat and distraining his men for rents and aids. Herbert defended the action on grounds of special authorisation from Alan, whose attempts to assert his local supremacy as

lord of Kippax (cf. Nos. **32**, **55**) conflicted with Walter's claim that his interests in the neighbourhood belonged to the Luterel fee.

**58** Alan constable of Scotland grants to Hugh of Crawford the land of Munnoch [in Dalry, Ayrshire] by these marches: viz. from that place where the white stones are which is called *Swynissete* up eastwards by the right marches between Cunningham and Largs to the burn which falls from Caldron Hill (*Kalderunh*), thence downstream to its confluence with the Caaf Water, thence by the Caaf Water downstream to the marches of the land of Norman the stud-keeper (*equiciarius*), thence by those marches across westwards to the Munnoch Burn, thence upstream towards the north to *Swynissete*. Hugh and his heirs are to hold the land with all its easements and liberties, saving stags, hinds, roe-deer and young hawks, for an annual rent of one unmewed sparrowhawk payable on 15 August. Warrandice and corroboration. [*c.*1225]

Hijs testibus . Domino Waltero fil*io* alani . Domino . InGelRamo de balliolo . Domino . dunechano de karrich . Domino . Willelmo de brus . Andr*ea* . de loudun . Rob*erto* de Ros . alex*andro* . de neuh' . hug*one* . de . ardrossan . ada . de hormishoc . Ricardo capellano . Symone . clerico . Radulfo . de clift' . 7 aliiS .

SOURCE. Original charter with seal and counterseal, Glasgow, Strathclyde Regional Archives, Floyer-Acland Muniments, TD826/1.

PRINTED. Stringer, 'Periphery and core', Appendix (A), no. 4 (with full description, note on dating, and photograph).

COMMENT. Hugh was a cadet of the Flemish family based at Crawford John in Upper Clydesdale. The composition of the witness-clauses strongly suggests that Nos. **58–61** were executed in a single session of Alan's honorial court in Cunningham. Though members of the Cunningham gentry predominate, Galloway is represented by Enguerrand de Balliol, William of Gelston and Patrick of Southwick. In *c.*1228 Hugh of Crawford was one of three 'knights of Cunningham' who attested for Enguerrand de Balliol in Galloway: *Holyrood Liber*, no. 70. Roger of Crawford, probably Hugh's nephew, appears in a Galloway context in 1262: ibid., no. 81.

**59** Alan constable of Scotland grants to Hugh of Crawford the land of Crosbie [in West Kilbride, Ayrshire] to be held heritably with all the easements and liberties that any knight has in Alan's whole *tenementum*, saving stags, hinds and young hawks, for an annual rent of one unmewed sparrowhawk payable on 15 August, and provision of the forinsec service due from one ploughgate of land. Warrandice and corroboration. [*c.*1225]

Hijs testibus domino . Ingelramo de balliol' . Domino Willelmo de brus . Domino erchebaut de duueg*las* . Domino Willelmo de Geuelist' . Domino patricio de suthayc . Domino andr*ea* de loud*un* . domino Rob*erto* de log*an* . Domino Rob*erto* de Ros . hug*one* de ardrossan . Al*ano* de ros . Ric*ardo* capellano . Rob*erto* de stubhil . yuoloto paruuo[a] . Willelmo fil*io* cospat*ricii* . Willelmo de Mauecestria . Et AlijS .

SOURCE. Original charter with seal and counterseal, Mount Stuart, Isle of Bute, Marquess of Bute's Muniments, Loudoun Charters, no. 3.

PRINTED. Stringer, 'Periphery and core', Appendix (A), no. 5 (with full description).

NOTE. [a] Sic.

**60** Alan constable of the Scots confirms to Hugh of Crawford and his heirs the third part of the toun of Stevenston [Ayrshire] sold to Hugh for forty merks of silver by Margaret daughter of Adam Loccard, who has resigned her right to it *per lingnum et baculum* in Alan's court. Margaret has also renounced her right to the church of Irvine [Ayrshire] and, as a woman of full age and in lawful ownership, has for greater security given to Hugh her charter of quitclaim in King Alexander's court. The land is to be held of Alan for the third part of one knight's service, as Margaret's charter justly bears witness. [*c*.1225]

Hiis Testibus . Ada . de loudun . Roberto de Ros . Arthuro de Ardrossan . Roberto de logan . Alex*andro* . de Neuh' . Andrea de loud*un* . Ricardo de Wintonia Roberto fil*io* ledmeri . Alano de Ros . Hugone de ardrossan . Ricardo de Cuningham . Ada de ormeshoc . et Aliis .

SOURCE. Original charter, Mount Stuart, Loudoun Charters, no. 4.
PRINTED. Stringer, 'Periphery and core', Appendix (A), no. 6 (with full description).
COMMENT. Like the Crawfords, the Loccards (Lockharts) were prominent in the Flemish colonisation of Clydesdale: see most recently L. Toorians, 'Twelfth-century Flemish settlements in Scotland', in G. G. Simpson, ed., *Scotland and the Low Countries, 1124–1994* (East Linton, 1996), 8. Hugh also secured the tenancy of John of Samuelston in Stevenston in exchange for lands in Cousland (West Lothian): Stringer, 'Periphery and core', 111. On the significance of this charter for 'interaction of the lord's court with the king's', see H. L. MacQueen, *Common Law and Feudal Society in Medieval Scotland* (Edinburgh, 1993), 45.

**61** Alan constable of Scotland grants to Alan de Ros all the land of Fairlie [in Largs, Ayrshire] by these marches: viz. from the Kel Burn where it falls into the sea upstream to its confluence with the Clea Burn, thence by the Clea Burn upstream towards the south to its source, thence by the valley beneath a certain craig across southwards to the source of *Pollroch* [i.e. the Fairlie Burn], thence downstream to the sea. The land is to be held in feu and heritage as anyone most freely and fully holds of the donor for habergeon service (*per servitium haubergelli*), with all easements and liberties, saving stags and hinds, by providing in the expedition of his army (*in expeditione exercitus nostri*) one young man with a habergeon, and by paying the aids due from one ploughgate of land. Corroboration. [*c*.1225]

[a]Hijs testibus domino Ingelramo de Baliolo, Reiginaldo de Crauford, Rogero de Bellocampo, Andrea de Loudun,[b] Richardo de Winchestra, Hugone de Crauford, Will*elmo* fil*io* Lambert*i*, Thom*a* de Cancia, Joanne de Crauford, Ric*ardo* capellano, Hug*one* de Ardrossan, Simone clerico, Rad*ulfo* de Clifton[c] et alijs.

SOURCE. NLS, Sir James Balfour's Collections, MS Advocates 15.1.18, fo. 75r (xviii-cent. copy) = *A*. NAS, Deeds Warrants, RD12/40/942 (12 Dec. 1700) = *B*.
PRINTED. Stringer, 'Periphery and core', Appendix (A), no. 7 (from *A*, noting some variants of *B*).
NOTES. [a] From *A*. [b] Loride in source. [c] Aitton in source.
COMMENT. Alan or other members of the Ros family, established in Cunningham by the Morvilles, witnessed Nos. 29, 52, 58–60, two of which concern Lauderdale. The importance of this charter as evidence for the blending of 'Celtic' and 'feudal' notions of military service was first noted by Barrow, *Anglo-Norman Era*, 140.

**62** *Alan grants to his illegitimate son Thomas [unspecified] lands. [*c*.1228 × *c*. 2 Feb. 1234]

SOURCE. *CDS*, v, Part II, no. 162.

**63** Alan constable of the Scots grants to Melrose Abbey, in exchange for the land of Carsphairn (*Keresban*) [Kirkcudbrightshire] which the monks have given to him by their charter, his whole waste of Lammermuir (*Lambremor*) [Berwickshire]. If they farm the waste, they may build ditches, hedges or dykes to enclose their corn-fields and meadow-land. Warrandice. [*c*.1230]

Hiis Testibus . Thoma de kent . Radulfo de cliftun clericis nostris . Bernardo de Rippeleye . Ricardo Mautalent . Alano de seint cler . Willelmo de Hertesheueth . Henrico de la hage . Ingeramo gurle . Gilberto de thirsi . et Multis aliis .

ENDORSED. de pastura de Lambermor (xiii cent.). R. (xiv–xv cent.?). 17 J. Scott (xvi–xvii cent.). Also modern numeral endorsements.
DESCRIPTION. 10.2" (26 cm) top, 10.1" (25.8 cm) bottom x 4.3" (11.1 cm) left-hand side, 4.7" (12 cm) right-hand side. Fold, average depth of 0.9" (2.1 cm). Sealing: on a tag through double slits and a slit in the crease; seal missing, though the tag still bears its shadow. A tie has possibly been cut off at the top left-hand corner of the fold. Hand: rounded court hand of distinctly ceremonious appearance; text begins with a large elaborately decorated initial. See *Plate 4*.
SOURCE. Original charter, NAS, Melrose Abbey Charters, GD55/227.
PRINTED. *Melrose Liber*, i, no. 227.
COMMENT. Alan's charter was confirmed by Alexander II in 1233, × 11 Sep.: *Melrose Liber*, i, no. 228. Carsphairn, an outlier of the barony of Dalmellington (Ayrshire), had been leased by Thomas de Colville to the Cistercians of Vaudey Abbey (Lincolnshire), who in 1223 had transferred the land to Melrose in perpetual ferme: ibid., nos. 192–3, 195. See further D. Brooke, 'The Glenkens 1275–1456: Snapshots of a medieval countryside', *TDGAS*, 3rd ser., lix (1984), 52, though some particulars are garbled. Most of the lay witnesses were members of the Lauderdale tenantry. The chief exception, Bernard of Ripley, held an estate in Galloway at Kirkandrews (in Borgue): Simpson, '*Familia* of Roger de Quincy', 119.

**64** Alan constable of Scotland/of the Scots[a] grants in alms to Melrose Abbey lands in the territory of Lauder contained within these marches: viz. from *Fairforde* up to *Staincros*, thence up to the marches of Wedale [*alias* Stow, Midlothian], thence by the road on the march between Wedale and Lauderdale to *Alewentisheuete*,[b] thence by the marches between Wedale and Lauderdale to the road on the march between Brown Rig (*Burnerig*) and Lauder Common (*Leuedeparc*), thence by that road down to the stone cross, thence across country to the cross at the head of *Fulewithenis* [lost, in Channelkirk], thence by the road to the south hard by *Harlaw* until it comes opposite Muircleugh (*Morclou*),[c] thence by the burn downstream to *Standenburne* [i.e. the Lauder Burn], thence upstream to the marches of Threepwood (*Threpuude*) [in Melrose, Roxburghshire], to include Threepwood with all the liberties Alan has there. Warrandice. [*c*.1230]

Hiis test*ibus* Thoma de Kent, Radulpho de Cliftun', clericis nostris, et cetera.

SOURCE. BL, MS Harleian 3960, fo. 36v.
PRINTED. *Melrose Liber*, i, no. 79.
NOTES. [a] Scot' constabularius in source. [b] *Melrose Liber* prints Alewentisheude, wrongly. [c] *Melrose Liber* prints Morclow.
COMMENT. Entitled by the cartulary scribe *De Alewentchawis*, i.e. Allanshaws in Melrose (NT 491438), this charter was confirmed by Alexander II on 4 Aug. 1233 (*Melrose Liber*, i, no. 229), and is probably contemporary with No. **63**, also attested by Thomas of Kent and Ralph of Clifton as chief witnesses. It represents a further concession to Melrose Abbey concerning the respective rights of the monks and the lord of Lauderdale in the royal forest between the Gala and Leader Waters. On the background, see J. M. Gilbert, *Hunting and Hunting Reserves in Medieval Scotland* (Edinburgh, 1979), 250–3; on the bounds, Hardie, *Roads of Mediaeval Lauderdale*, 82–3.

**65** *Alan grants to Hugh of Abernethy, his kinsman (*consanguineus suus*), the lands of Oxton [in Channelkirk] and Lylestone [in Lauder] in feu and heritage. [*c*.1230]

SOURCE. NAS, Transcripts etc. of Royal Charters, RH1/1 (photograph of original charter of confirmation by Alexander II, 18 Mar. 1233, *penes* Lord Amherst of Hackney in 1905, but now lost).
COMMENT. Hugh (d. *c*.1291) was a younger son and the eventual heir of Laurence son of Orm (d. *c*.1245), last lay 'abbot' of Abernethy (Perthshire). Their kinship with the earls of Fife is well known, but not their kinship with the Galloways. The account in *Scots Peerage*, vii, 398–9, misses the point that this no doubt stemmed from Laurence's wife Dervorguilla, though her precise relationship with Alan is uncertain. Note also that Laurence had appeared in Roland's company by 1196: No. **21**; *St Bees Reg.*, no. 60. Important details on Hugh's later career are provided in G. W. S. Barrow, *Kingship and Unity: Scotland, 1000–1306*, 2nd edn (Edinburgh, 1989), 137–8.

# 17

# Acts of Lordship: The Records of Archibald, Fourth Earl of Douglas

*Alexander Grant*

The fourth earl of Douglas (1400–24) is one of the most powerful, famous and colourful magnates in medieval Scottish history. He is also probably the best documented, for complete or virtually complete texts of ninety-two of his *acta* survive (not counting diplomatic letters and precepts of sasine), along with notes of twenty-three others. This documentation provides an essential basis for the kind of full-length study that was pioneered by Grant Simpson's work on Roger de Quincy.[1] Considerations of space preclude that here, but an initial step is offered, by presenting a Calendar of Earl Archibald's surviving charters and related documents,[2] together with an introductory commentary.

Archibald was born in about 1370, and succeeded his father in the Douglas title and estates at around Christmas 1400.[3] Highlights of his career include marrying Robert III's eldest daughter in about 1390; seizing the earldom of March from its renegade earl in 1400; assisting in the fatal imprisonment of the duke of Rothesay in 1402; leading a Scottish army to disaster at Humbleton Hill, also in 1402; fighting for his Percy captors in their defeat at Shrewsbury in 1403; establishing himself (after returning from England on broken parole in 1407) as the dominant power across southern Scotland; heading the 'Foul [foolish] Raid' on northern England in 1417; being made duke of Touraine in 1424 as a reward

1 G. G. Simpson, 'An Anglo-Scottish Baron of the thirteenth century: the acts of Roger de Quincy, earl of Winchester and Constable of Scotland' (University of Edinburgh, unpublished PhD thesis, 1965); G. G. Simpson, 'The *Familia* of Roger de Quincy, Earl of Winchester and Constable of Scotland', in Stringer, *Nobility*, 102–30.

2 I.e. the 92 full or nearly full texts, the notes of the other 23, and 14 precepts of sasine. There are also five documents issued *to* the earl; but his extensive diplomatic correspondence is not dealt with here. Thus this is not an absolutely exhaustive study; and, indeed, I would not claim that every one of Douglas's surviving charters, etc., is included, for while the holdings in the National Archives of Scotland and the National Library of Scotland have been searched, muniment collections still in private hands have not. That the Calendar is as complete as it is owes much to the kindness of Alan Borthwick and Michael Brown, who brought several Douglas documents to my attention; my warmest thanks to them both. But despite its shortcomings, the Calendar probably constitutes the largest set of *acta* for any one medieval Scottish noble. By comparison, there are 81 surviving texts for Roger de Quincy, and 91 (of which 55 are full texts) for David, Earl of Huntingdon: Simpson, '*Familia* of Roger de Quincy', 123 n. 1; K. J. Stringer, *Earl David of Huntingdon, 1152–1219: A Study in Anglo-Scottish History* (Edinburgh, 1985), 212. Moreover, a high proportion of those concern lands in England, not Scotland.

3 Until recently, the only specific accounts of the fourth earl's life were in *Scots Peerage*, iii, 157–63; *Dictionary of National Biography* (Oxford, 1917), v, 1168–71; and, most fully, Fraser, *Douglas*, i, 360–94. But a thorough modern study is now available, in chs. 5–10 of M. Brown, *The Black Douglases: War and Lordship in Late Medieval Scotland, 1300–1455* (East Linton, 1998). This was published, however, after the present essay was written, and only minor revisions to take account of it have been possible. For other recent views of the fourth earl, see the passages on him in S. Boardman, *The Early Stewart Kings: Robert II and Robert III* (East Linton, 1996), and in chapter 9, above, by Alastair Macdonald.

for bringing a Scottish army to France; and dying later that year in the crushing defeat at Verneuil. The highlights (or low-lights?) are mostly military, and it is as a mighty warrior that he is best known, in characterisations by William Shakespeare and Sir Walter Scott.[4] But in fact, as Ranald Nicholson put it, he 'clattered his way through history from one lost battle to another' – losing an eye at Humbleton, a testicle at Shrewsbury, and his life at Verneuil![5]

For all his military failures, the fourth earl was an able politician, for example constantly outmanoeuvring his great Scottish rival George Dunbar, Earl of March, even though March really was an outstanding general. Douglas excelled in particular at selling himself as a warlord: to Robert III and the duke of Albany in 1400–2; to the Percies after Humbleton; to Henry IV after Shrewsbury; to Duke John the Fearless of Burgundy, who retained him in 1412; to Henry V of England, who retained him in 1421; and to Charles VII of France, in whose service he died fighting *against* the English and Burgundians! His main selling-point is obvious. In 1421 he promised Henry V 200 knights and squires and 200 mounted archers,[6] which was a military retinue on a par with those of most English magnates. Earlier, in 1412 he promised John of Burgundy no fewer than 4,000 men-at-arms and archers (at the duke's expense) when required – and actually obtained a reciprocal undertaking that John would come in person to Scotland with 300 men-at-arms whenever Douglas needed him![7] The impression of his power that Douglas must have given Duke John was no doubt much the same as he would have given Charles VII in 1423 – that he could raise a full-scale army. And in the latter case, at least, it was not hyperbolic boasting: the force which he recruited in Scotland and led to annihilation at Verneuil probably consisted of several thousand men.[8]

*

That Earl Archibald could promise – and manage – to recruit on this scale is related, of course, to the extent of his lands and his following. He possessed a vast amount of land, including four (and for a time five) great 'provincial' lordships plus twenty-seven other baronies. It was one of the largest territorial complexes ever seen in Scottish history.[9] Moreover, much of it was held with the vice-regal powers of regality.[10] There were huge swathes of property in south-western Scotland, very significant estates in Lothian and the eastern Borders (especially Lauderdale), and considerable amounts of land in northern

4 William Shakespeare, *Henry IV* part I; Walter Scott, *The Fair Maid of Perth* (1st edn, Edinburgh, 1828).

5 Nicholson, *Scotland*, 288; *Chron. Bower* (Watt) viii, 48–9, 58–9.

6 T. Rymer, *Foedera* (London, 1704–35), x, 123–4.

7 R. Vaughan, *John the Fearless* (London, 1966), 260; Brown, *Black Douglases*, 215, 225 n. 22.

8 Scottish forces at Verneuil probably numbered about 2,500 men-at-arms and 4,000 archers (ibid., 216–17), but that includes the force recruited and led by Albany's son the earl of Buchan.

9 It would have been rivalled only by the MacDonald Lordship of Isles, to which the earldom of Ross was added in the 15th century. The Douglas lordships and baronies are mapped, *inter alia*, in A. Grant, 'Baronies, lordships and earldoms in the early fifteenth century', in P. G. B. MacNeil and H. MacQueen, eds., *Atlas of Scottish History to 1707* (Edinburgh, 1996), 206–7.

10 All the original Douglas estates (a regality since 1354); Annandale (a regality since *c.*1322); Sprouston (a regality since Alexander III's reign); and, controversially, Galloway, where the fourth earl and his successors apparently exercised regality powers, although those were not included in his father's grants of that province.

and north-eastern Scotland. Most of it was inherited from his parents, who had combined three main sets of territory: the original Douglas lands and those bestowed by Robert I on 'the Good Sir James', which had gone to Archibald's father in 1389 by virtue of the Douglas entail; the lordship of Galloway, which his father had acquired himself; and the estates of the Murrays of Bothwell, Petty and Drumsargard, which had gone to his mother, Joanna Murray. Here is a perfect demonstration of how inheritance, entail and marriage could, under favourable circumstances, bring together a huge amount of property. It should be noted, however, that in this case the bringing together had been done in previous generations, and that the fourth earl's own marriage to the king's daughter did not give him any land.

The notes of the lost Great Seal Register record a royal grant of the entailed Douglas estates to 'Archibald Douglas son to the earl of Douglas' **[131]**,[11] so Archibald received the main part of his inheritance shortly before his father's death, though the latter presumably kept the liferent.[12] He also replaced his father as March Warden. That was possibly at the same time (4 June 1400) as Robert III made him keeper of Edinburgh Castle for life **[130]** and let him take over the earldom of March at the expense of the disaffected Earl George; his father was over seventy, and was perhaps already known to be dying. After Archibald actually became fourth earl of Douglas, however, only two more grants to him of land in Scotland are recorded, and of these one is simply an exchange with his mother **[132]**. The other is a crown grant of the lordship of Annandale, surrendered by the earl of March in 1409 following his return to Scotland **[133]**; though with March's restoration Douglas lost control of the landsof the earldom of March itself. In general, therefore, with the major exception of Annandale, the fourth earl did not acquire his estates himself; he inherited them.

Therefore – unlike with many of his contemporaries – the interest of his property documents lies not in his acquisition of land but in what he did with it.[13] This is the subject of the great majority of his *acta*: ninety-two of the 113 documents calendared below (not counting precepts of sasine) deal with land transactions. What they demonstrate immediately is that Douglas hardly ever alienated land completely. There are only eleven exceptions.[14] With three **[105–7]**, however, the beneficiaries were Douglas's daughter and son-in-law; here jointures were being established as part of the marriage-contract, and if the marriage failed to produce descendants, the lands were to revert to the earl or his heirs. Three more appear to have been to his brother James, the future seventh earl **[100, 103, 104]**.[15] Thus there were only five permanent and outright alienations: Cortachy and Lintrathen baronies **[101, 108]**, Douglas's main possessions in the sheriffdom of Forfar;

11 References in this form are to the numbered items in the Calendar, below, pages 254–74.

12 Brown, *Black Douglases*, 91, suggests 1398 for this transaction, but it is impossible to be sure.

13 In what follows, the general points about Scottish tenurial practices at this time are based on A. Grant, 'The Higher Nobility in Scotland and their Estates, *c.*1371–1424' (University of Oxford, unpublished DPhil thesis, 1975), 186–210.

14 Four resignations of land to the crown for transfer to a new owner, and two grants where the recipient replaced the earl in possession of the land in question.

15 In the absence of the actual charters, it is impossible to be certain that these grants were outright alienations; but that is implied by James I's subsequent charters: *RMS*, ii, nos. 38–40.

Nether Calderwood in the Lanarkshire barony of Kilbride [**51**]; Clerkington near Edinburgh [**115**];and Eskdalemuir, where superiority was transferred to the tenant, Melrose Abbey [**59**]. Otherwise, whatever the transaction, Douglas always maintained his superiority over the land in question.

Twenty-one of the remaining eighty-two property documents deal with transfers of land made not by the earl but by his 'feudal' tenants. Of these, ten were charters [**40, 43, 47, 50, 52, 65, 74, 75, 81, 93**] granting properties which had been resigned to the earl as overlord by their previous owners; some were transfers within a particular family, others no doubt were sales of land.[16] The other seven were 'inspections' confirming grants made by his 'feudal' tenants [**23, 25, 49, 62, 70, 86, 89**]. He also made four confirmations of charters issued by his predecessors [**4, 58, 69, 110**]. These documents all seem fairly routine, but it must be remembered that the earl could veto such conveyances, and would have charged for his charter or confirmation. And once his charter or confirmation was issued, he had to warrandise his tenant's conveyance, while any dispute over the recipient's tenure would have to have been heard before him. Two of the confirmations of old charters [**58, 69**] concerned Melrose Abbey's share of Bemerside, in Lauderdale, which the laird of Bemerside claimed; Douglas dealt with the case as superior lord [see **57**], and his confirmation charters ratified its outcome in the abbey's favour. This is one way in which 'feudal' overlordship still mattered, to lord and tenant alike, in early fifteenth-century Scotland.

Next, there are nineteen transactions in which what changed was not the actual ownership of land but the terms by which it was held of the earl. In ten cases the change of tenure took place by means of a fresh grant following the tenant's own resignation. Six of these simultaneously regranted lands in Annandale to Simon Carruthers [**34–9**]. Why Carruthers obtained these regrants is unclear. His original title may have been uncertain or challenged, and since the transactions were made in the earl's Annandale justice-ayre, they perhaps resulted from a lawsuit; also, since Carruthers was the earl's squire, there may have been a patronage element. With the four other regrants following resignations, good lordship is more evident. The purpose of two of them [**63, 92**] was probably to convert the tenure to blench farm, which was advantageous to the tenant;[17] with the other two [**33, 91**], it was to enable the lands to be inherited by their owners' illegitimate children, in default of legitimate heirs of the body.

Such acts of good lordship, however, did not always require a resignation and regrant. Those same illegitimate children also benefited from straightforward charters which had much the same effect: in one case [**60**] the father had already died, and so Douglas was granting land which had escheated; in the other two [**64, 71**] direct grants were made which included tailzies to the illegitimate children (these may have been conveyances of Douglas's own property, but it is impossible to be sure). Also, two charters [**54, 73**] appear to have granted deceased fathers' lands to their illegitimate sons, though that is not spelled out precisely. Then there is one more conversion of tenure to blench farm, not by resignation

16 Brown, *Black Douglases*, tends to assume Douglas's own initiative in such transactions (e.g. William Hay's acquisition of land in Galloway [47]: ibid., 116, 171); but that cannot be taken for granted.

17 For blench farm tenure, see below, pages 244–5.

and regrant but simply by the earl's letter patent [**6**], 'on account of the tenderness' which Earl Archibald had for the beneficiary, William Sinclair of Hermiston. The other three transactions which changed the terms of tenure are *sui generis*. One (made after the earl of March's return to Scotland) states that although the land of Wedderburn belonging to Douglas's squire David Home lay within the earldom of March, it was to be held of Douglas until the earl died, and only then was the superiority to revert to the earl of March [**87**]. The second is a grant to Douglas's niece Egidia and her husband the earl of Orkney, in jointure, of Herbertshire barony (Stirlingshire) [**20**] – which (although the charter does not say so) had been held by Egidia's father. And by the third, Sir James Douglas of Dalkeith received Buittle, Preston and Borgue (in Galloway), all in regality [**11**]; although ostensibly this is a property transfer, Buittle, Preston and Borgue were already held by the lord of Dalkeith, and so the actual purpose of the charter was to give him the regality rights. Regality rights were similarly given to Melrose Abbey with respect to the territory of Eskdalemuir, though in this case Douglas's superiority was alienated to the abbey [**59**]. These two creations of regalities are the most striking of all Earl Archibald's acts of patronage (though both Douglas of Dalkeith and Melrose Abbey did already have royal grants of regality over most of their other estates).

Forty-two of Earl Archibald's property documents remain to be considered. The great majority look like fairly ordinary grants of land, to be held of the earl and his heirs 'in feu and heredity' (or in 'free alms' in the single instance of a grant to the Church [**78**]) – though with seven notes of charters [**94–7, 102, 111, 113**] there are insufficient details for the nature of the transactions to be determined. In a few cases [**84, 88, 112**], the lands are expressly said to have come to the earl through escheat or forfeiture. In most of the others, the lands are simply *terras nostras*, and there appears to be no obvious reason for not taking that at face value. With these transactions, therefore, Douglas was almost certainly conveying his own property – though, since he invariably retained the superiority – not alienating it altogether.

The thirty-five transactions which can be analysed fall into three distinct groups. The first consists of five early grants, dated 1401 or 1402, to Sir John Montgomery [**1**], Sir John Swinton [**2, 3**], Sir William Cranston [**5**], and Sir John Edmonston [**7**]. Those to Swinton and Cranston were dated at Dunbar, and may have been rewards for backing the earl's seizure of the earldom of March; that is particularly likely in the case of Swinton, who was a major figure in Lothian, and who was actually given land within that earldom. More broadly, these men all had long-term Douglas links: Montgomery and Edmonston had fought at Otterburn in 1388 with the second earl, whose widow Edmonston married; Swinton had married the first earl's widow, and was thus the second earl's stepfather; and Cranston's father had received land from the first earl.[18] The connections, however, seem to be more with the first and second earl than with the third. Perhaps, therefore, the grants suggest that after succeeding his father, Earl Archibald was recreating the broad Douglas affinity which had

[18] Boardman, *Early Stewart Kings*, 150; *Scots Peerage*, iii, 153, 157; *RMS*, i, no. 638.

backed the second earl in the years up to Otterburn. Certainly the second earl's aggression towards England was echoed by the fourth earl – who in 1402 led his followers to defeat, captivity, and in Swinton's case death, at Humbleton Hill.[19]

The repercussions of Archibald's own capture at Humbleton are visible in the second group of transactions. To begin with, there are eight documents relating to three hypothetical grants, or wadsets. One is a charter of Glenken in Galloway to Sir Alexander Gordon [**82**], which was to be void if, within three months of returning to Scotland (presumably from his English captivity), Douglas gave him fifty-five gold nobles and twenty merklands; the latter are probably represented by the grant to Gordon of Shirmers in Balmaclellan barony in 1408 [**22**]. The second is a nineteen-year wadset of Dunberny in Methven barony, made in 1407 to his squire James Dundas in return for money given to the earl [**14**]; it was secured on two charters purporting to convey Dunberny permanently [**9, 15**], and may have been redeemed in 1417 when Dundas was granted Easter Blairmucks, in Bothwell barony [**53**].[20] The third, again dated 1407, is the earl's agreement that, in return for 240 merks, Sir John Edmonston should hold Tulliallan in Strathearn directly of the earl of Strathearn for nineteen years [**17**], with the security of an outright grant to that effect [**8**].[21] This was redeemed in 1415 when, following Edmonston's death, his heir had an acknowledgement that the 100-merk relief of Tulliallan had been paid, and received a wadset of land for the other 140 merks from one of Douglas's close followers [**48, 49**]; it looks like a transaction hastily arranged to restore Douglas's superiority over Tulliallan. These three wadsets are no doubt connected with financial obligations resulting from the earl's captivity in England: Dundas was with him in London, while Edmonston and Gordon were two of his hostages. Douglas was clearly short of ready cash, and had to dispose of land. But in these cases he did so initially in the form of wadsets; only later, with respect to Gordon and Dundas, did he grant land permanently.

Five other conveyances appear to have been for similar reasons: certainly the grant of the Halls of Airth (Stirlingshire) to Sir William Crawford in 1409 in return for keeping Edinburgh Castle during Douglas's captivity [**27**]; probably the grant of Hawick barony to his kinsman and hostage Sir William Douglas of Drumlanrig in 1407 [**19**]; and possibly the three other land grants from this period, namely ten merklands in Lauderdale to his squire Henry Haliburton in 1407 [**16**], part of Smailholm barony to his squire Robert Pringle in 1408 [**24**], and 'Drumgrey' in Amisfield barony to William Johnstone, also in 1408 [**21**]. Two further grants in 1407 probably come into this category as well: the regality rights (mentioned above) for Sir James Douglas of Dalkeith, and a 40-merk annuity for Sir Herbert Maxwell, heir to Caerlaverock [**12**], which was payable until he got £20-worth of land (perhaps Greenan in Galloway).[22] Both Douglas

19 Boardman, *Early Stewart Kings*, ch. 5 and pp. 246–7, 267–73; Brown, *Black Douglases*, 95–106.

20 Though there is a note [**113**] of the fifth earl's confirmation of grants by the fourth earl to Dundas of Dunberny, Blairmucks, and (interestingly), Tulliallan; unfortunately, no details survive.

21 The date of the charter [**8**] is given as Edinburgh, 10 July 1403, but (*pace* Boardman, *Early Stewart Kings*, 270, and Brown, *Black Douglases,* 105) that seems impossible. The likelihood is that the true date was July 1407.

22 Maxwell held Greenan of the earl in 1419 [**63**], and may have received it initially sometime after 1407.

of Dalkeith's heir and Maxwell himself were hostages for the earl. All these grants may have been to clear off financial obligations, and so could count as sales. On the other hand, most of the recipients were described as the earl's kinsmen or squires, and so can be regarded as members of his affinity; while several had performed valuable services during his captivity. The grants can therefore also be seen as being in return for services rendered – especially, in the case of his hostages, for (presumably) having to ransom themselves or their heirs after the earl broke his parole. Sir James Douglas of Dalkeith, for instance, had to pay 1,000 marks sterling to ransom his grandson.[23]

The third group consists of the seventeen remaining conveyances. Two of them [**98, 99**] granted Douglas's lands in the north of Scotland (chiefly the old Murray of Petty estates) to his brother James, probably sometime before the end of 1408; as well as fraternal endowment, the aim was probably a geographical rationalisation of the Douglas estates.[24] The others are later, no earlier than 1414 in the case of those which are dated, and can perhaps be considered as the earl's normal grants of land, after the obligations caused by his captivity had been redeemed. None of these grants was very extensive, and the recipients were not particularly important. Nevertheless, they mostly appear to be acts of patronage on Douglas's part, and are perhaps the most typical examples of it. They include grants to the earl's 'familiar' and squire Michael Ramsay [**45, 61**], to his kinsman Archibald Hepburn (a cadet of the family of Hailes) [**67**], to his kinsman and squire William Towers [**55**], and to his squires David Murray [**72**], William Cockburn [**79**] and Gilbert Grierson [**83–5**]. Here, again, the earl was bestowing land upon men who clearly belonged to his affinity. And that is probably true, too, of the grant to George Rutherford [**112**]: although no relationship is mentioned in the document as it survives, there are other indications of Rutherford's links with Douglas.[25] There are, in fact, only two cases of grants to laymen who did not have any evident connection with the earl: those to Simon Hannay and William Bell [**42, 88**].

The three other grants in this group are to recipients who were not laymen. One gave the land of Gilkerscleuch, in Crawfordjohn barony (Lanarkshire), to Douglas's long-serving clerk and 'chancellor', Mr Alexander Cairns, provost of Lincluden [**90**]. Another was the earl's only grant of land to the Church, Cruggleton and Poltoun in west Galloway to Whithorn Priory, in December 1423 [**78**]. The third was a much more secular – and remarkable – transaction, in favour of his mistress, Christian Ramsay [**68**]. In 1421 she received the Lothian estates of Ballincrief and Gosford for life, and after her death they were to go to 'the eldest son begotten or to be begotten by us and Christian by mutual intercourse', failing whom, 'to the second, third and subsequent children similarly begotten'. Such gifts of property to mistresses are uncommon. This one appears particularly

23 *Rot. Scot.*, ii, 205; it was not achieved until 1412, five years after the earl's 'escape'.

24 And also perhaps to remove James Douglas from Lothian, where he was notoriously aggressive during the earl's captivity, especially in 1406 when he attacked and killed David Fleming at Longhermiston (see Boardman, *Early Stewart Kings*, 294–6). Note that in 1407 the fourth earl was establishing good relations with Henry Sinclair, Earl of Orkney and lord of Roslin [**20**], who had been Fleming's co-leader at Longhermiston.

25 He witnessed two of the earl's charters [**45, 87**]; and later his heir Robert was squire to the fifth earl of Douglas [see **112**].

poignant, for Douglas had been badly wounded in the testicles at Shrewsbury in 1403, and is not known to have had children thereafter; the phrase 'begotten or to be begotten' seems to indicate that in 1421, when he made the grant, he believed Christian was pregnant – mistakenly, it would appear. Interestingly, the earl's 'familiar' Michael Ramsay (who worked for Douglas on the other side of the country, in Annandale) had a wife called Christian. If she were the same woman, that might explain an unusual phrase in Douglas's grant of Howthat in Annandale, dated 1419: it was to be held in jointure by Michael and Christian Ramsay, and then by the heirs of their bodies 'procreated by legal and mutual intercourse', with reversion to Douglas if they begot no heirs [**61**]. Michael had Howthat in return for holding Douglas's stirrups once a year during the earl's life; if his wife was the earl's mistress, this charter leaves a somewhat unpleasant impression.

*

Twenty-one documents with concerns other than land remain to be considered. Seven involved offices. Two appointed bailies for Tulliallan [**18, 44**]; these are the only surviving appointments of the numerous local officers which, as the precepts of sasine [**116–29**] indicate, Douglas would have had throughout his estates. By the others, Alexander Home became the earl's depute as keeper of the lands of Coldingham Priory [**10**]; Sir Herbert Maxwell was made hereditary steward of Annandale [**28**]; and after Maxwell's death in 1420, he was in effect replaced by Michael Ramsay, who was made keeper of Lochmaben Castle and chancellor and chamberlain of Annandale for life [**66, 76, 77**].[26] Those more significant offices were accompanied by annuities: £80 a year for Ramsay, £20 a year each for Home and Maxwell. And among the remaining *acta* are three straightforward grants of annuities: one of 40 merks had already been given to Maxwell [**12**]; one of £40 went to the earl of Mar [**31**]; and one of £20 went to Andrew Raeburn, a monk of Kilwinning Abbey [**109**].[27]

Finally, there are eleven documents which can only be categorised as miscellaneous. Two, a receipt and the letter about Melrose Abbey's lawsuit [**48, 57**], are a reminder of the many mundane and ephemeral documents that the earl must have issued. By two others, Douglas gave up the £100 fee due to him as keeper of the lands of Coldingham, though he kept the office itself [**41, 46, 134**].[28] Others are more significant, especially two indentures with the Governor, the duke of Albany: one arranged for Douglas's daughter to marry Albany's son, the earl of Buchan [**30**]; the other is the famous Albany–Douglas agreement of 1409, that they would support each other mutually and that disputes between them and their affinities should be settled by their councils' arbitration [**26**]. The latter is one of the few items in the *acta* that really illustrates Douglas's power and prestige in southern Scotland; it is on a par with the grants of regality that he made [**11, 59**]. There are also some individual reflections of his status. In 1407, on behalf of his kinsman Sir William Hay, sheriff of Peebles, he confirmed

26 These could not have been 'to balance Maxwell's local authority' (Brown, *Black Douglases*, 175).

27 Raeburn perhaps represented Douglas at Coldingham, along with Alexander Home.

28 In 1413 and 1414. After that, Alexander Home's payment as Douglas's depute was paid directly by Coldingham Priory, but at only £10 Scots: *Coldingham Corresp.*, no. XCIX. Andrew Raeburn's annuity out of Douglas's payments from Coldingham was also continued [**46**].

letters of David II empowering the sheriff of Tweeddale or Peebles to lead the men of the sheriffdom in war [**13**]; this unusual confirmation of a royal grant was presumably because Douglas was hereditary military leader of the middle Borders, including Peeblesshire.[29] The fourth earl was also justiciar south of the Forth, and, as such, in 1411 gave letters of remission to James Dundas and eight others, pardoning them for 'cruel rapine' done to husbandmen of 'the Isle of Bathgate' [**32**]; there was the usual requirement that the complainants had to be satisfied, but nevertheless the fact that Dundas was one of Douglas's squires raises the question of whether the earl was abusing his position. Another aspect of Douglas's lordship is evident in a precept of 1418, again on behalf of William Hay, ordering the earl's officers in Galloway west of the Cree to make sure that Hay received the rents due from his lands of Auchquhone [**56**]; Douglas had granted the property to Hay following its resignation by Sir John McCulloch [**47**], and it appears that the transaction was being challenged, perhaps by McCulloch's heirs. In this case, Douglas's lordship may not have been so mighty, at least in west Galloway.[30] His acknowledgement of a 100-merk debt to Sir William Fraser in 1410 is another illustration that things did not always go Douglas's way; whether or not this was connected with the earl's 'escape' from England is unclear, but £52 of it was soon paid off [**29**]. Lastly, there is the final document Douglas issued in Scotland: a letter dated 6 February 1424 declaring his special affection for Melrose Abbey, and telling his eldest son to maintain its privileges [**80**]; this is reminiscent of two of Robert I's last documents, which were similarly on behalf of Melrose,[31] though it is impossible to know if Douglas had forebodings of his death in France.

Most of these twenty-one *acta* – the grants of feed offices and annuities, the actions for members of the affinity, and the declaration of protection for Melrose – typify the main concepts of the late medieval lordship that used to be characterised as 'bastard feudalism'. Its language is also there, most obviously in the grant of Herbert Maxwell's annuity [**12**], where Douglas promised 'to supowelle and defende the forsayde Syr Harbarte in all his ryghtwys cause, als we awe to our man and our kosyn'. That is a perfect statement of 'bastard feudal' lordship. On the other hand, Maxwell's 40-merk annuity was only to be paid until he received £20-worth of land. Such a proviso was common in late medieval Scottish annuities, and generally no land was actually given; but here (as already suggested) the annuity may have been replaced by a grant of the land of Greenan, in Galloway [see **63**]. And, more generally, one of the most striking points about the fourth earl's *acta* is how the grants involving money – the feed offices and annuities – are utterly outweighed by grants of land.

Yet that does not mean that the simple conveyance of land was the chief concern of Douglas's transactions. The frequency of grants to men who were called his

29 *RMS*, i, App. I, no. 123. Hay was already sheriff of Peebles in 1387 (*ER*, iii, 167), and so was not appointed by the fourth earl; thus this is not an example of Douglas usurping the Governor's authority, as stated in Brown, *Black Douglases*, 115.

30 For a different analysis, see Brown, *Black Douglases*, 116, 172, where the 'distress' to be levied becomes 'harrying', and the 'wasting' of the land (? by illicit grazing) becomes 'devastation'.

31 *RRS*, v, nos. 379, 380.

kinsmen or squires will have become apparent. Indeed, across the whole range of the earl's grants to laymen,[32] no fewer than three-quarters (65 out of 86) were made on behalf of his kinsmen or squires: twenty-nine to kin, thirty-two to squires, and four to men who were both kin and squires. Furthermore, over half these grants (45 out of 86) were stated to have been made in return for service of some kind; by far the commonest phrase is 'for service done and to be done'.[33] The main element in the fourth earl's *acta* consisted of grants of land in feu and heredity to his followers in return for service.

In that case, Douglas's grants might seem to belong more to the tenurial world of the twelfth and thirteenth centuries rather than to that of the fifteenth; in traditional terminology, they appear 'feudal' rather than 'bastard feudal'. But they are significantly different from typical twelfth- and thirteenth-century charters. The term 'homage' hardly ever occurs: while Douglas almost invariably maintained his superiority over whatever land he granted, and generally stated that service was to be done, he was rarely concerned to stipulate the performance of homage.[34] And, even more importantly, although the majority of his grants were said to be in return for service, the formal military service *reddendo* of the standard 'feudal' charter was never explicitly demanded. Admittedly, in eleven charters [**1, 27, 35, 38, 39, 47, 60, 73, 83, 88, 91**] the recipient owed 'the usual service' (normally *servicia debita et consueta*), by which standard military service was probably – though not axiomatically – intended. Conversely, there are thirty grants of land in 'blench farm', by which both the formal military service and the 'feudal incidents' which went with it (essentially those of relief and wardship) were waived, and instead a symbolic 'blench' (i.e. blank) render had to be provided once a year if asked for: generally a penny, but also, in Douglas's charters, a harrier [**2**], a greyhound [**3**], a pair of spurs [**6, 20**], an arrow [**19**], a red rose [**33**], and the holding of the earl's stirrups [**45, 61**]. In addition, in ten cases [**21, 22, 24, 42, 43, 55, 64, 71, 85, 87**] land was granted to be held simply for suit of court once a year (or in three charters three times) to one of Douglas's seigneurial courts; as with blench farm, this was to take the place of all other obligations. While the fourth earl granted much land to be held of him in return for service, for the most part he did not impose traditional 'feudal' service and incidents.

Two reasons for this may be suggested. First, for the recipient the cancellation of relief, wardship and other incidents was a valuable privilege, and hence a grant in blench farm or for suit of court was a significant piece of patronage. This is neatly demonstrated in Douglas's letters of 20 January 1402 [**6**], which stated that while William Sinclair of Hermiston had held Carfrae in Lauderdale from the earl for homage and service, suit of court, ward, relief and marriage, now, 'on account of the tenderness which we have for the said William, and not without cause, we ... grant Carfrae ... in blench farm', for the

32 I.e. all the *acta* except the confirmations, the resignations to and the indentures with Albany, the grants to the Church and to Mr Cairns, a receipt, and the grant to his mistress.

33 And with several of the other grants there are no full texts. Hence a stipulation of service was probably even more common in the earl's charters than the statistics indicate.

34 It only appears in seven grants [**2, 3, 9/15, 28, 35, 54, 85**]. This contrasts strikingly with contemporary royal charters, which almost invariably required homage.

token render of a pair of spurs each year if required. Second, although it might have seemed disadvantageous for the earl to cancel the formal 'feudal' military obligation, that was strictly limited by law – classically, to forty days' knight-service – and inflexible. Late medieval lords wanted something more flexible: that their men should simply do whatever was asked. That was presumably the intention behind Douglas's grants in blench farm or for suit of court, which waived the limited formal 'feudal' service, but maintained the earl's position of lordship and normally stipulated that unspecified service was to be done. Thus the traditional concepts do not apply to them: they are neither 'feudal' nor 'bastard feudal', but somewhere in between.[35]

*

In the *acta*, names of 167 individuals associated in one way or another with the fourth earl of Douglas are to be found. One hundred and fifty-two of them were laymen, all presumably from the landowning classes; two were women (Douglas's mistress Christian Ramsay [**68**], and Elizabeth Stewart of Girthon [**60**]); and thirteen were clergy. All the names and their associations with the earl are shown in *Table 4* (on the following three pages). The most common association is, of course, as a charter witness. There are fifty-one sets of witnesses in the *acta*,[36] providing in all 117 individual names (probably).[37] The number of occasions on which these individuals witnessed is given in the first column of the table. Next, a special association is revealed by seven English lists of proposed hostages for the earl, made between 1406 and 1408 when he was negotiating visits to Scotland, ostensibly to arrange his ransom.[38] Twenty-two possible hostages were named, and the second column shows the frequency with which each was proposed. Then there is the association derived from kinship. In the *acta*, no fewer than forty-seven people are described as Douglas's kin: two sons, a brother, a nephew, and forty-three who were called *consanguineus*, or 'kinsman';[39] they are noted in the third column. The fourth column notes various non-kinship links: the thirty-three men described as the earl's squires (*scutifer* or *armiger*); one 'man', one (Albany) with whom there was a bond of alliance, two other 'allies', and one 'familiar'; fourteen of the earl's officers (ranging from his depute as keeper of Edinburgh Castle to numerous local bailies); one creditor; and his 'chancellor', secretary, and two of his clerks. Finally, the fifth column indicates the associations derived from the earl's grants –

35 And note the inconsistency of practice in the charters to Simon Carruthers [**34–9**].

36 Fifty-seven of Douglas's charters have witness lists, but two of them are dated 20 Oct. 1401 [**2, 3**], and six are dated 4 Dec. 1411 [**34–9**]; since the present analysis is really of the number of times men were in the earl's company, each of these two sets of witnesses has been counted only once.

37 It is not always possible to be certain about the identification of witnesses who have the same names.

38 The lists are in English safe-conducts: *Rot. Scot.*, ii, 177, 180–2, 186; *CDS*, iv, nos. 707, 736, 752. Those named were not necessarily sent, however; the earl did not actually make seven visits to Scotland. Note that in the case of Sir James Douglas of Dalkeith (junior), the proposed hostage was either him or his son and heir.

39 *Consanguineus* is rendered 'kinsman' rather than 'cousin' – Sir Herbert Maxwell of Caerlaverock was 'our belovyde kosyn' [**12**] – because of the modern tendency to restrict the term 'cousin' to first cousins. In *Table 4*, the earl of Buchan's marriage to Douglas's daughter is recognised, though in the *acta* he is always called *consanguineus*.

*Table 4. The Affinity of the Fourth Earl of Douglas*

| | Witness | Hostage | Kinship | Link | Grant |
|---|---|---|---|---|---|
| **A. 'INNER CIRCLE': DOUGLASES** | | | | | |
| Sir Archibald Douglas | 3 | 6 | heir | squire | |
| Sir James Douglas | 2 | 6 | son | | |
| James Douglas of Balvenie | 9 | 2 | brother | | land |
| Sir William Douglas of Nithsdale | 9 | 2 | nephew | | |
| Sir William Douglas of Drumlanrig | 6 | 4 | kin | | land |
| *Archibald Douglas of Cavers* | – | 1 | | | |
| Sir James Douglas of Dalkeith | 5 | | kin | | regality |
| *Sir James Douglas of Dalkeith (jun)* | 3 | 6 | | | |
| *Sir Henry Douglas* | 1 | | | | |
| **B. 'INNER CIRCLE': OTHERS** | | | | | |
| Sir William Borthwick of that ilk | 27 | 2 | kin | | (? land) |
| *William Borthwick (jun)* | 5 | | kin | squire | |
| *David Borthwick* | – | | | squire/office | |
| *Robert Borthwick* | 1 | | kin | squire | |
| Sir William Hay of Loquhariot | 15 | 2 | kin | (office) | land |
| Sir John Seton of that ilk | 15 | 5 | kin | | land |
| Sir William Crawford of the Farm | 12 | | kin | office | land |
| *Robert Crawford* | 2 | | | | |
| *John Crawford* | 1 | | | | confirm. |
| Sir John Sinclair of Lethrig | 11 | | kin | | |
| Sir John Edmonston of that ilk | 8 | 2 | kin | | land |
| *William Edmonston* | 4 | | | squire | |
| *Archibald Edmonston* | 1 | | | | |
| *David Edmonston* | 1 | | | | |
| Sir John Forrester of Corstorphine | 8 | | kin | | land (resig.) |
| Alexander Home of Dunglass | 7 | | | ally/squire | office |
| *David Home of Wedderburn* | – | | | squire | (land) |
| Sir Thomas Murray of Cockpool | 7 | | kin | | land |
| *David Murray* | – | | | squire | land |
| *John Murray* | 4 | | kin | | |
| *George Murray* | – | | | | confirm. |
| Adam Hepburn of Hailes | 6 | | | squire | |
| *Archibald Hepburn* | – | | kin | | land |
| *Sir Patrick Hepburn of Hailes* | 1 | | | | |
| James Dundas of that ilk | 5 | | | squire | land |
| Sir William Muirhead | 5 | | | | |
| Sir John Herries of Terregles | 4 | 3 | kin | | |
| *Sir Robert Herries* | 2 | | kin | | |
| Robert Ramsay of Dalhousie | 4 | | kin | squire | |
| *Alexander Ramsay of Dalhousie* | 2 | | | | |
| Sir Alexander Gordon of Stichill | 3 | 1 | | | land |
| *Robert Gordon* | – | | | squire | (land) |
| Sir John Montgomery of Ardrossan | 3 | 5 | | | land |
| Sir William Sinclair of Hermiston | 3 | 5 | | | (land) |
| *John Sinclair of Hermiston* | 1 | | | | |
| *William Sinclair* | 4 | | | squire | |
| Sir Simon Glendenning | 2 | 6 | | office | |
| Sir William Graham of Kincardine | 2 | 2 | kin | | land |
| *Thomas Graham* | 1 | | | squire | |
| Sir Herbert Maxwell of Caerlaverock | 2 | 3 | kin | man/office | annuity/land |
| *Sir Robert Maxwell of Caerlaverock* | 2 | | kin | | |
| *Sir Herbert Maxwell of Conheath* | 1 | | | | |
| Walter Haliburton of Dirleton | 2 | 1 | | | |
| *Fergus Haliburton* | 1 | | | | |
| *Henry Haliburton* | 1 | | | squire | land |
| Robert Pringle | 4 | | | squire | land |
| *George Pringle* | 1 | | | squire | |

| *Table 4 (continued)* | | | | | |
|---|---|---|---|---|---|
| | **Witness** | **Hostage** | **Kinship** | **Link** | **Grant** |
| C. EARLS | | | | | |
| Robert Stewart, Duke of Albany | 1 | | kin | bond | |
| *John Stewart, Earl of Buchan* | 2 | 2 | son-in-law | | |
| Alexander Stewart, Earl of Mar | 2 | | kin | | annuity |
| George Dunbar, Earl of March | 1 | | kin | | |
| *Sir Gavin Dunbar* | 1 | | kin | | |
| George Douglas, Earl of Angus | 1 | | kin | | land |
| Henry Sinclair, Earl of Orkney | 4 | 1 | kin | | land |
| Alex. Lindsay, heir to Crawford | – | 1 | | | |
| D. 'OUTER CIRCLE' | | | | | |
| Sir William Stewart of Castlemilk | 4 | | kin | | |
| Hugh Campbell of Loudon | 3 | | | | |
| Sir John Cockburn | 3 | | | | |
| *Sir William Cockburn of Skirling* | 1 | | | office | |
| *William Cockburn (of Langton)* | – | | | squire | land |
| Sir William Cranston of Denholm | 3 | | kin | | confirm. |
| *Sir William Cranston of that ilk* | – | | | | land |
| *John Cranston of that ilk* | – | | | squire | |
| Sir Thomas Somerville of Carnwath | 3 | | | | |
| Sir John Swinton of that ilk | 3 | | kin | | land |
| *David Swinton* | – | | | office | |
| Sir William Abernethy | 2 | | | | |
| Sir Walter Bickerton | 2 | | | | |
| *Richard Bickerton* | 1 | | | | |
| *William Bickerton* | 1 | | | | |
| William Crichton of that ilk | 2 | | | | |
| *Robert Crichton (of Sanquhar)* | – | | | office | |
| John Durant | 2 | | | squire | |
| Robert Livingstone | 2 | | | | |
| Sir Fergus McDowell | 2 | | | office | |
| *Uchtred McDowell* | – | | | office | |
| George Rutherford | 2 | | | | land |
| Thomas Turnbull | 2 | | | squire | |
| John Akersan | 1 | | | | |
| Sir John Bothwell | 1 | | | | |
| Sir John Carlyle | 1 | | kin | | |
| John Caverhill | 1 | | | | |
| *Thomas Caverhill* | – | | | | (land) |
| Sir William Colville | 1 | | | | |
| Herbert Corry | 1 | | | squire | |
| Simon Dalgleish | 1 | | | squire | |
| Michael Davidson | 1 | | | | |
| *William Davidson* | – | | | office | |
| Walter Dempstar | 1 | | | | |
| James Erskine | 1 | | | | |
| Sir David Fleming | 1 | | | | |
| Thomas Fotheringham | 1 | | | | |
| Egidius of Gebilston | 1 | | | | |
| Patrick Herring | 1 | | | | |
| Sir Humphrey Jardine | 1 | | kin | | |
| Adam Johnstone | 1 | | | | |
| *William Johnstone* | – | | | | land |
| Sir John Keith | 1 | | | | |
| Sir Thomas Kirkpatrick | 1 | | kin | | |
| Sir Robert Lauder of the Bass | 1 | | | | |
| *John Lauder* | 1 | | | | |
| *Robert Lauder* | 1 | | squire | | |

| *Table 4 (continued)* | | | | | |
|---|---|---|---|---|---|
| | Witness | Hostage | Kinship | Link | Grant |
| Sir William Liddel | 1 | | | | |
| Sir William Lindsay of Byres | 1 | | | | |
| *Sir Walter Lindsay* | 1 | | | | |
| Sir Robert Logan of Restalrig | 1 | | | | |
| *Simon Logan* | 1 | | | | |
| Sir Thomas McCulloch | 1 | | | | |
| Sir Robert Maxwell of Calderwood | 1 | | kin | | (land) |
| Sir John Mowbray | 1 | | | | |
| Robert Stewart of Lorn | 1 | | | office | |
| *Sir John Stewart of Lorn* | – | | kin | | |
| *Alexander Stewart* | – | | kin | squire | (land) |
| Sir William Stewart (? of Jedworth) | 1 | | | | land |
| Thomas Porter | 1 | | | squire | |
| David Annand | – | | | office | |
| William Bell | – | | | | land |
| John Cairns | – | | kin | squire | (land) |
| Simon Carruthers of Mouswald | – | | | squire | (land) |
| Thomas Corbet | – | | | | confirm. |
| Thomas Forman | – | | | office | land |
| William Fraser of Philorth | – | | kin | (loan) | |
| Gilbert Grierson | – | | | squire/office | land |
| Richard of Hangingside | – | | | office | |
| Simon Hannay | – | | | | land |
| James Heriot of Niddrie | – | | | ally/office | |
| *John Heriot* | – | | | squire | (land) |
| 'Macgyewe' | – | | | office | |
| Sir Robert Maitland | – | | | | (land) |
| William Meldrum | – | | | office | |
| *Thomas Meldrum* | – | | | office | |
| Sir Adam Mure of Hershaw | – | | | | (land) |
| *Alexander Mure* | – | | | squire | (land) |
| Patrick Ogilvy of Auchterhouse | – | | kin | | (land) |
| *Walter Ogilvy of Lintrathen* | – | | | | land |
| John Park | – | | | | land |
| Christian Ramsay | – | | mistress | | land |
| Michael Ramsay | – | | | familiar/squire | land/office |
| William Stevinston | – | | | | (land) |
| Sir John Stewart of Girthon | – | | kin | | (land) |
| *Elizabeth Stewart* | – | | kin | | (land) |
| William Towers | – | | kin | squire | land |
| James Gledstanes | – | | | office | |
| Andrew Ascot | – | | | office | |
| Thomas 'Makilqwod' | – | | | office | |
| E. CLERGY | | | | | |
| Mr Alexander Cairns | 17 | | kin | chancellor | land |
| MrWilliam Foulis | 10 | | | secretary | |
| Matthew Geddes, rector of the Forest | 7 | | | | |
| Mr James Fawside | 4 | | | clerk | |
| Eliseus, Bishop of Galloway | 2 | | | | |
| Alexander, Bishop of Caithness | 1 | | | | |
| James, Prior of St Andrews | 1 | | | | |
| Robert Feuer | 1 | | | clerk | |
| James Hallsyde | 1 | | | | |
| Mr Andrew Henry | 1 | | | | |
| Mr John Merton | 1 | | | | |
| Mr Patrick Young | 1 | | | | |
| Andrew Raeburn, monk | – | | | | annuity |

mostly land grants,[40] but also grants of office, annuities and regality, and confirmations on behalf of his tenants.

From these names, a good idea of the personnel and shape of Earl Archibald's affinity can be obtained. To begin with, a version of the methodology first applied to Scotland by Grant Simpson should be used. This focuses on charter witnesses, assigning them to 'inner' and 'outer circles' of the affinity according to the frequency with which they occur.[41] So far as the fourth earl of Douglas is concerned, it may be suggested that the twenty men who witnessed about 10% or more of his charters – that is, five or more – can be thought of as belonging to his inner circle.[42] The actual individuals are named in *Table 4*, which is organised essentially on the basis of charter witnesses. Its arrangement, however, does not quite accord with the frequency of witnessing, for two other factors have been taken into account. First, the hostage lists also indicate those who were presumably close to the earl, at least in the mid-1400s. Comparison of the first two columns shows that there is a fair correspondence between the proposed hostages and the frequent witnesses; but the earl's agnatic relatives, especially his sons, are clearly more prominent in the hostage lists, and several men who were infrequent witnesses are also featured in them. Because of this, the earl's Scottish kin have been collected together at the beginning of the table, and almost all the proposed hostages have been included within the probable inner circle, irrespective of how often they witnessed.[43] Second, several of Douglas's witnesses died before the earl himself, and in some cases their successors are also found as witnesses. That suggests that, to a certain extent, the affinity might have operated as much on a family as on a personal basis. Therefore, throughout the table, individuals with the same surname who definitely or probably belonged to the same immediate family have been grouped together, and those whose collective appearances on witness lists come to five or more have been added to the likely inner circle.[44]

The result is that, while the concept of inner and outer circles certainly appears valid for the fourth earl of Douglas's affinity, the likely inner circle finishes up as being larger than it would have been on a strict basis of counting witnesses – perhaps, indeed, too large. But the three other columns in *Table 4* seem to support the analysis. Out of twenty-six groupings of landowning families assigned to the inner circle (counting the earl's sons and brother as one), seventeen were his kin, seventeen included men who were his squires (plus in one case, his 'man') or important officers, and eighteen received grants (mostly significant ones) from him. Taken together, the combinations of the different kinds of association revealed in the first two sections of *Table 4* indicate that the men listed there probably constituted the main part of the earl's affinity. At the

40 Brackets denote cases where land is known to have been held of, but not acquired from, the fourth earl. Where an individual received several grants, only the most significant is noted.

41 Simpson, '*Familia* of Roger de Quincy', 105–9.

42 Compare ibid., 107, where those who are witnesses in at least 6 out of 81 full texts (a slightly lower percentage) are assigned to the inner circle. The full breakdown of Douglas's witnesses is as follows: 1 witnessed on 27 occasions; 1 on 17; 2 on 15; 1 on 12; 1 on 11; 1 on 10; 2 on 9; 2 on 8; 3 on 7; 2 on 6; 4 on 5; 9 on 4; 10 on 3; 20 on 2; and 58 on only 1.

43 The exceptions are the earls of Buchan and Orkney, and the heir of the earl of Crawford;

44 But in some cases, especially those of the Sinclairs, identifications are only conjectural.

very core, there would have been his sons;[45] his brother James of Balvenie (the future seventh earl); and the three who were surely his closest associates, Sir William Borthwick of that ilk, Sir William Hay of Loquhariot and Sir John Seton of that ilk. After them, there were his other Douglas kin – Sir William Douglas of Nithsdale,[46] Sir William Douglas of Drumlanrig,[47] and the two Sir James Douglases of Dalkeith[48]– together with Sir William Crawford of 'the Douglas Farm' near Rutherglen, who was not proposed as a hostage because he was looking after Edinburgh Castle on the earl's behalf. Alongside these, the inner circle would have contained a number of other prominent barons like Sir John Montgomery of Ardrossan, the Maxwells of Caerlaverock and the Ramsays of Dalhousie; the bureaucrat Sir John Forrester of Corstorphine;[49] Sir John Edmonston, husband of the second earl's widow (and hence brother-in-law to Robert III and the duke of Albany); and various nobles of rather lesser status. Among the latter was certainly William Sinclair of Hermiston, towards whom, the earl said, he had good cause for tenderness [**6**] – a sentiment that could probably have been applied to all those listed in the first two sections of *Table 4*. Finally, the clerical element should be remembered. To facilitate the complex analysis of the landowners who made up the bulk of the affinity, its clerical element is given in a separate section, at the end of the table; but Mr Alexander Cairns, Mr William Foulis, and Matthew Geddes, rector of the church of the Forest, can all be assigned to the inner circle also.

If that is an approximation of the earl's inner circle, what of the outer? It must be stressed that every single person listed in *Table 4* was not necessarily a member of the earl's affinity; far from it.[50] That applies particularly to the magnates brought together under the heading of 'earls'. Their connections with Douglas were more as equals than as members of the affinity; the earl of Mar's annuity [**31**] was probably a reward for 'favours' (*beneficium*) rather than service.[51] Only Henry Sinclair, Earl of Orkney can reasonably be counted within the affinity, and he, perhaps, comes into the fringe of the inner circle.[52] Similarly,

45 Though his younger son, James, was left as a hostage in England for several years after 1408, while his heir, Archibald, was campaigning in France in 1419–23.

46 His father, also called Sir William of Nithsdale, was an illegitimate son of the third earl, and hence the fourth earl's half-brother. But (*pace* Fraser, *Douglas,* i, 358–9 and *Scots Peerage*, iii, 164) the younger Sir William was not his father's heir, and so must also have been illegitimate; this is proved by the fact that Henry Sinclair, Earl of Orkney, who was married to his legitimate sister Egidia [see 20], was 'lord of Nithsdale' in 1411 and 1419, during the younger William's lifetime: R. A. Hay, *Genealogie of the Sainteclaires of Rosslyn* (Edinburgh, 1835), 59, 60.

47 He and his brother Archibald, of Cavers, were illegitimate sons of the second earl.

48 Heads of the main legitimate cadet branch of the house of Douglas.

49 Son of the great Edinburgh merchant Adam Forrester, he was also a frequent witness of the duke of Albany's charters as Governor, deputy chamberlain from 1406, keeper of the Great Seal from 1420, and chamberlain from 1424.

50 Cf. Simpson's remark that 'those who witnessed once or twice only are insignificant for the present purpose': '*Familia* of Roger de Quincy', 107. But see also the following paragraph; and, of course, note those with clear ties to the earl who nevertheless did not witness at all.

51 Cf. Brown, *Black Douglases*, 109–10; note that Mar witnessed for Douglas in England in 1406 [**9**].

52 Despite his kinship with the fourth earl, George Douglas, Earl of Angus (illegitimate son of the first earl of Douglas) seems not to have been part of the affinity, and was a probable rival: Brown, *Black Douglases*, 87–92, 99, 101–4. He was captured at Humbleton and died shortly after; his son the second Douglas earl of Angus (born 1398) had no ties with the fourth earl at all.

among the clergy, the bishop of Galloway, who had been provost of Lincluden, probably had the earl's patronage; but the bishop of Caithness and the prior of St Andrews, who both witnessed the grant of regality to Melrose Abbey [**59**], may not have been linked to him at all. And the same can surely be said about some, at least, of the occasional lay witnesses included rather arbitrarily under the heading 'outer circle'. Sir David Fleming, for instance, belonged to the king's affinity, not Douglas's – and indeed in 1406 was killed in the battle with the earl's brother James at Longhermiston.[53] When Sir Herbert Maxwell of Conheath was a witness, it was to a charter for Sir Herbert Maxwell of Caerlaverock [**63**], and no doubt he was his namesake's follower. Thomas Fotheringham witnessed two grants to Patrick Ogilvy, one from Douglas [**40**] and one from Walter Ogilvy; presumably he was an Ogilvy man.[54] Being an occasional witness does not necessarily denote a member of even the outermost circle of the earl's affinity.

On the other hand, it is striking how many of the occasional witnesses were the earl's kin, or his squires, or his officers, or had land from him. Moreover, the affinity certainly included men who are not known to have witnessed any of his charters, such as the well-rewarded familiar and squire Michael Ramsay. Among these, some of the bailies and other officers seem obscure, in particular 'Macgyewe' (no first name is given) who worked for him in west Galloway [**56**]; they probably had no direct connection with the earl. But those who were expressly called his squires or recognised as his kin surely did, and would have enjoyed respectable places within at least the wider affinity.

*

That raises, finally, the question of the affinity's structure.[55] One of the most remarkable features of the *acta* is the number of Douglas's squires – thirty-three of them. Their periods of personal attendance on the earl were no doubt fairly limited, but nevertheless they were clearly a prominent part of the affinity. Some, like Robert Ramsay, Adam Hepburn, Alexander Home, James Dundas and Simon Carruthers were fairly significant landowners. Others belonged to baronial houses: Douglas's own son and heir; Alexander Stewart of Lorn; William, David and Robert Borthwick; William Cockburn; William Edmonston; Henry Haliburton; and Robert Lauder. But most of them probably came from lesser landowning families. In general, these squires look like junior members of the affinity, in status just as (mostly) in age. More than half of them, however, were from families who may be considered part of the earl's inner circle, and

53 Boardman, *Early Stewart Kings*, 295–6.

54 *RMS*, ii, no. 113. Fotheringham also witnessed for the second earl of Angus: Fraser, *Douglas*, iii, no. 64.

55 Note that the *acta* do not illuminate personal relationships within the affinity. It is Walter Bower who tells us that in 1416 Sir William Crawford – a faithful and well-rewarded adherent according to the *acta* [esp. **27**] – was actually besieged by Douglas in Edinburgh Castle: *Chron. Bower* (Watt), viii, 86–7, 190. An English source shows Sir James Douglas of Dalkeith's grandson being left for years as a hostage in England: *Rot. Scot.*, ii, 205. A Flemish source describes how in 1413, after Douglas was charged with piracy *en route* to Flanders, he abandoned two knights as sureties in Bruges while he went on to Paris: Vaughan, *John the Fearless*, 260. Thus Douglas's lordship may not have been so good at times for the affinity's individual members – and by the 1420s some of the loyalties may have been wearing thin: see Brown, *Black Douglases*, 116–17. Here, however, the discussion is limited to the evidence provided by the *acta*.

Home, Hepburn, Dundas and the younger William Borthwick were probably particularly close to him.

Unfortunately, 'our squire' is the only term used frequently to denote a lord–man relationship with Douglas; no similar terminology was used for the more senior members of the affinity. Thus when the squires moved up in military rank, they were merely listed with other knights; the phrase 'our knight' never appears. On the other hand 'ally', later a common general term for members of an affinity,[56] does occur twice, once in a context suggesting higher status: James Heriot of Niddrie was the earl's *confederatus* or ally, while his son John was Douglas's squire [75].[57] Normally, however, Douglas probably thought of his more important followers simply as his 'men' – a fundamental term of lordship which may be taken for granted in the Latin texts, but does appear in one of the rare vernacular documents, when Sir Herbert Maxwell of Caerlaverock was described as 'our man and our kosyn' [12].

The significant point about Maxwell's description, however, is that he was the earl's 'kosyn' as well as man, and it is as 'our belovyde kosyn' that he was initially addressed. Now in that kin relationship, Maxwell was one of many – but, as *Table 4* shows, hardly any were Douglases. The earl's sense of kin, as revealed in the *acta*, was not agnatic; almost all the links were cognatic, through various female relatives. In some cases, especially with Albany and the earls, the designation was perhaps merely a courteous acknowledgement of kinship. But for most of the others it may have been more significant. 'The question why men made bonds of maintenance and manrent ... can ... be answered in a single sentence: they made their bonds to become as kinsmen to one another.'[58] If that is so, and if bonds of manrent and earlier 'feudal' ties were designed to replicate the obligations of kinship,[59] then when the fourth earl of Douglas described so many men as his kin, he was perhaps stressing that with them he had the strongest and oldest link of all. At the very least, there is the concept of a huge kinship group headed by the fourth earl – but unlike later kindreds extending far beyond those who had the earl's own name. This is a second remarkable feature of the fourth earl's affinity.

A third feature should be emphasised, too. The last column of *Table 4* shows that a very considerable number of the families listed held land from the fourth earl of Douglas: forty-two out of ninety-three (not counting the 'earls' and clergy). Thus the affinity had a strong tenurial side, as has already emerged from discussion of the earl's charters. It is particularly clear with respect to the inner circle families: a tenurial relationship is revealed by the *acta* in seventeen out of twenty-six cases (not counting Douglas's sons). Half, indeed, received land grants from the earl, and there were also the grants of regality, annuity, and significant office; his inner circle did very well out of him. Moreover, the surprising absence of any recorded grants to the Borthwicks, the earl's closest followers, is probably

56 J. Wormald, *Lords and Men in Scotland: Bonds of Manrent, 1442–1603* (Edinburgh, 1985), 90.

57 The other ally was Alexander Home, 'our lufit squyer and allie' [10]; does that denote a former squire, perhaps, or a superior one?

58 Wormald, *Lords and Men*, 76.

59 Ibid.

explained by the fact that the Borthwick muniments were lost in the seventeenth century;[60] but in the 1470s they possessed the lands of 'Colilau' and 'Bourhous' in the former Douglas lordship of Lauderdale,[61] and this almost certainly derived from a grant by an earl of Douglas, probably the fourth earl. The fourth earl's affinity, especially the inner circle, may have consisted essentially of kinsmen and squires, but it was consolidated by the granting and tenure of land.[62]

Finally, the affinity's geography is also significant. To judge by their estates, the main Douglas spheres of interest would have been in the south-west and in the central Borders. This is reflected to a certain extent in the affinity, with the likely inner circle, for instance, including seven south-westerners (Douglas of Nithsdale, Douglas of Drumlanrig, Crawford, Murray, Herries, Montgomery and Maxwell) and three Borderers (Gordon of Stichill, Glendenning and Pringle). They are, however, outweighed by men from Lothian, twelve of whom are in the inner circle (Douglas of Dalkeith, Borthwick, Hay, Seton, Sinclair,[63] Forrester, Home, Hepburn, Dundas, Ramsay, Sinclair of Hermiston, and Haliburton), and at least a further dozen probably in the outer circle.[64] This is a point that has been stressed elsewhere.[65] Like the second earl before him, the fourth earl was leader of the men of Lothian, especially in the absence of the earl of March.

It has, indeed, been convincingly suggested that Douglas's main sphere of influence centred on Edinburgh, with his command of Edinburgh Castle being the focus of his power.[66] Certainly the place-dates of his *acta* indicate that Edinburgh was where he spent most time: there are sixty-eight separate place-dates, of which thirty-six are Edinburgh, while the next most frequent are Bothwell and Lochmaben, at only five times apiece. That said, the Douglas estates in Lothian should also be taken into account. Although not so vast as his south-western territory, they included the extensive lordship of Lauderdale and the adjoining barony of Heriotmuir.[67] As lord of Lauderdale, Douglas was a close neighbour of the Lothian members of his affinity, especially his Douglas kin at Dalkeith, the Borthwicks at Borthwick, and the Hays at Loquhariot. Moreover, land in Lauderdale was held by the Borthwicks (see above), the Sinclairs of Hermiston [**6**], the Haliburtons [**16**],[68] David Home [**50**], David Murray [**72**], the Lauders,[69] and the Maitlands [**93**]. Lauderdale, as much as Edinburgh, probably

60 'The direct line of the original peerage family died out in 1674, and the location of the muniments of that family is unknown': note in the NAS Inventory of Borthwick of Borthwick Muniments, GD350.

61 *RMS*, ii, no. 1130. They also held land of the earls in Strathaven barony, Lanarkshire: ibid., ii, no. 40.

62 For a more detailed analysis of the fourth earl's lordship, with which I mostly agree, see Brown, *Black Douglases*, 166–80. Note that, as Brown stresses, the relationships which the fourth earl consolidated with grants of land did not necessarily endure under the fifth earl.

63 Or so I assume; I have not identified Sir John Sinclair of Lethrig, but he no doubt belonged to either the Roslin or the Hermiston Sinclairs.

64 Namely the earl of Orkney, Cockburn, Swinton, Abernethy, Crichton, Livingstone, Herring, Lauder, Lindsay of Byres, Logan, Heriot, and Maitland. There are doubtless others as well, but identification of the lesser figures is very difficult.

65 Brown, *Black Douglases*, 164, 175–8.

66 Boardman, *Early Scottish Kings*, 311; Brown, *Black Douglases*, 164, 175–8.

67 Granted by Robert I to 'the Good Sir James': *RMS*, i, no. 2; Fraser, *Douglas*, iii, no. 289. The Lauderdale/Heriotmuir territory came to within about a dozen miles of Edinburgh.

68 Also, the first earl had given land in Lauderdale to John Haliburton: Fraser, *Douglas*, iii, no. 334.

69 The 1st earl gave land in Lauderdale to Alan Lauder: *RMS*, i, no. 376.

provided the basis for the fourth earl's power in the south-east, and was perhaps the crucial part of his entire territorial complex. And as lord of Lauderdale, he was following in the footsteps of Roger de Quincy a century-and-a-half earlier – in vastly different political circumstances, though perhaps not quite such different social ones. Given the context of the present volume, that is the most appropriate note on which to conclude this discussion of Earl Archibald's *acta*.

* * *

## *Acta* of the Fourth Earl of Douglas: A Calendar[70]

### DATED TEXTS[71]

**1** Charter to Sir John Montgomery of Ardrossan, for service done and to be done: of Dunlop in Cunningham barony (AYR);[72] to John, his heirs and assigns; of Douglas and his heirs; for the usual service; with warranty. Witnesses: Sir David Fleming; Sir John Swinton; Sir John Edmonston; Mr John Merton, provost of Bothwell; William Hay; William Sinclair; Patrick Herring. At Bothwell, 4 July 1401.

SOURCE. NAS, Reg. Ho. Chrs., RH6/207; Fraser, *Douglas*, iii, no. 344.

**2** Charter to his kinsman Sir John Swinton, for homage and service done and to be done: of Cranshaws [BRK]; to John and the heirs of his body; failing whom, to John's illegitimate son John and the heirs-male of his body; then to John's illegitimate son Alexander and the heirs-male of his body; then to David Swinton and the heirs-male of his body; of Douglas and his heirs; in blench farm, for one harrier a year at Dunbar Castle; with warranty. Witnesses: Sir Patrick Hepburn; Sir John Edmonston; Sir William Borthwick; William Hay; William Sinclair; Walter Bickerton; William Muirhead; Mr Alexander Cairns. At Dunbar Castle, 20 October 1401.

SOURCE. NAS, Swinton Charters, GD12/16.
COMMENT. John Swinton junior was given sasine of Cranshaws in 1412 [111]. But some time before 1422 George, Earl of March recognosced it into his own hands: GD12/20; the above charter was subsequently confirmed by George Dunbar (junior), Earl of March, 7 Apr. 1425: GD12/23.

**3** Charter to Sir John Swinton, for homage and service done and to be done: of Pitcox, in Dunbar, Lothian; to John and the heirs of his body; failing whom, to John's illegitimate son Alexander and the heirs-male of his body; then to David Swinton and the heirs-male of his body; of Douglas and his heirs; in blench farm, for one greyhound a year at Dunbar Castle; with warranty. Witnesses: Sir Patrick Hepburn; Sir Robert Lauder; William Sinclair; Walter Bickerton; William Crawford. At Dunbar, 20 October 1401.

SOURCE. NAS, Reg. Ho. Chrs., RH6/210; Fraser, *Douglas*, iii, no. 345.

70 The texts in this Calendar have been heavily summarised, and comments have been kept to a minimum. Where MS references are given, the texts have been found in or checked against the original documents; otherwise they have been taken from the printed sources stated.

71 Including texts that can be dated to within a year.

72 For sheriffdoms, the system of abbreviation used in *Chron. Bower* (Watt) has been employed, except that EDB, HAD and LIN denote the sheriffdom of Edinburgh and the constabularies of Haddington and Linlithgow within it, and that Kirkcudbright (KCB) was then a constabulary within the sheriffdom of Dumfries. Square brackets are used when no sheriffdom is given in the actual text.

**4** Confirmation of a charter by Dervorguilla, Lady of Galloway: of the church of 'Kyraem' [Kirkholm, WIG], in Galloway; to Sweetheart Abbey; in free alms. The confirmation is for the souls of his father Archibald third Earl of Douglas, himself, Margaret his wife, and all his ancestors and successors; with warranty. Witnesses: George Douglas, Earl of Angus; Henry Sinclair, Earl of Orkney; Sir John Swinton; Sir John Edmonston; Sir John Herries; Sir Robert Maxwell (kinsmen);[73] Eliseus, provost of Lincluden; Mr Alexander Cairns, rector of the church of the Forest; William Muirhead. At Lincluden [no date; *c.*1401].

SOURCE. Fraser, *Carlaverock*, ii, 417.
COMMENT. Douglas is styled lord of Dunbar, which indicates a date *c.*1401. Mr William Cairns is not yet provost of Lincluden, which dates this before No. **5**.

**5** Charter to Sir William Cranston of that ilk, for service done and to be done: of Nether Crailing (ROX) (except demesne lands and mill); to William, his heirs and assigns; of Douglas and his heirs; in blench farm, for one penny a year; with warranty. Witnesses: Sir James Douglas of Dalkeith; Sir John Montgomery; Sir John Seton; Sir John Edmonston; Sir William Borthwick; Mr Alexander Cairns, provost of Lincluden; Walter Haliburton; Thomas Somerville; Hugh Campbell. At Dunbar Castle, [no date, *c.*1401].

SOURCE. Fraser, *Douglas*, iii, no. 374: inspection by Archibald Douglas, Earl of Wigtown, 20 Sep. 1419.
COMMENT. 'At our castle of Dunbar' indicates that the original charter was issued in *c.*1401.

**6** Letters for William Sinclair of Hermiston: stating that William holds Hermiston in Lauderdale in blench farm, and Carfrae in Lauderdale for homage and service, suit of court, ward, relief and marriage; now, 'on account of the tenderness which we have for the said William, and not without cause, we ... grant Carfrae also in blench farm'; both lands are to be held by William and his heirs in blench farm, for a pair of spurs each year at Lauder Castle. At Dunbar, 20 January 1402.

SOURCE. NAS, Yester Writs, GD28/249A; *Yester Writs*, no. 56; HMC, *Milne-Home Rep.*, no. 591.

**7** Charter to Sir John Edmonston of that ilk, for service done and to be done: of Douglas's fortalice in his land of Tulliallan (PER); to John, his heirs and assigns; of Douglas and his heirs; in blench farm, for one penny a year; with warranty. Witnesses: Sir John Swinton; Sir William Stewart; Sir William Borthwick; William Hay; John Murray (kinsman); Mr Alexander Cairns; John Sinclair; Fergus Haliburton; William Crawford. At Edinburgh, 21 May 1402.

SOURCE. NAS, Cardross Writs, GD15/332; Fraser, *Douglas*, iii, no. 346.
COMMENT. Tulliallan was in the earldom of Strathearn, and Douglas held it of the earl. This grant was confirmed by Earl Patrick of Strathearn on 1 Apr. 1410 (Fraser, *Douglas*, iii, no. 358).

**8** Charter to his kinsman Sir John Edmonston of that ilk, for service done and to be done: of Douglas's lands of Tulliallan, in Strathearn regality (PER); to John, his heirs and assigns; of Douglas and his heirs, so long as Douglas and his heirs do the full usual service to the earl of Strathearn; otherwise to be held directly of the earls of Strathearn; with warranty. Witnesses: Sir John Seton; Sir William Abernethy; Sir William Hay; Sir William Borthwick; Walter Haliburton; John Sinclair; John Lauder; William Crawford; Robert Pringle; William Cranston. At Edinburgh, 10 July 1403 [*sic*].

SOURCE. NAS, Cardross Writs, GD15/333.
COMMENT. The charter's date must be wrong, because July 1403 saw Douglas's participation in the Percy rebellion against Henry IV of England; the battle of Shrewsbury was fought on 21 July. The place-date might be mistaken, but the list of witnesses is incompatible with a charter issued in England. Probably the true date is 1407 (note that Hay was not a knight in 1406, but was in 1407 [**9**, **13**]); but '*tercio*' is written clearly, though perhaps in a different hand. One possibility is that

73 I.e. all those named before '(kinsmen)' are called *consanguinei* of Earl Archibald.

the formal charter was written later, from a draft in which Roman numerals were used for the date; a clerk might accidentally have confused '*iii*' and '*vii*'. (I am grateful to Alan Borthwick for assistance with this charter.) Cf. Nos. **9**, **14**, **15**, **17**. The actual grant of Tulliallan was confirmed by Earl Patrick of Strathearn on 1 Apr. 1410 (Fraser, *Douglas*, iii, no. 358).

**9** Charter to James Dundas, for service and homage: of Dunberny [in Methven barony], (PER): to James and his heirs; of Douglas and his heirs; in blench farm, for one penny a year at Bothwell Castle. Witnesses: Alexander Stewart, Earl of Mar; Sir Walter Lindsay; Sir William Cockburn; Sir John Sinclair; Sir Walter Bickerton; William Cranston; William Hay; Robert Crawford. At London, 20 September 1406.

SOURCE. NLS, MS Adv. 80.4.15, p. 146, no. 1.
COMMENT. But see Nos. **14**, **15**.

**10** Letters, in Scots, to 'our lufit squyer and allie' Alexander Home, appointing him depute to Douglas as keeper of the lands and rents of Coldingham Priory; and granting £20 Scots a year from Douglas's annual pension of £100 Scots from Coldingham, so long as Douglas keeps that pension. At London, 28 October 1406.

SOURCE. *Facsimiles of the National Manuscripts of Scotland* (London, 1867–71), ii, 47; Fraser, *Douglas*, iii, no. 298; Raine, *North Durham*, appendix, no. CXLVIII.
COMMENT. Douglas presumably had been bailie, or keeper, of Coldingham since about 1401. In Durham the earl's pension was later described as 'the gret fee of c marks': *Coldingham Corresp.*, no. CXXXIV. Douglas surrendered the fee in 1413 and 1414 [**41**, **46**], after which Home received £10 Scots directly from Coldingham Priory for being 'sub-bailie': ibid., no. XCIX. [See also No. **134**].

**11** Charter to Sir James Douglas of Dalkeith: of Buittle barony, Preston barony, and Borgue, in Galloway; to James and his heirs; of Douglas and his heirs; all in regality, with pleas of the crown; in blench farm, for one penny a year; with warranty. Witnesses: Archibald Douglas (eldest son); James Douglas (brother); Sir John Montgomery; Sir William Douglas of Nithsdale (nephew); Sir William Borthwick; Mr Alexander Cairns (clerk). [No place or date; *c.* 2 February 1407.]

SOURCE. *Morton Reg.*, ii, no. 215.
COMMENT. Date from precept of sasine [**119**]. James Douglas already held these lands: *Morton Reg.*, ii, nos. 83, 200–1.

**12** Bond (in Scots) to 'our belovyde kosyn' Sir Herbert Maxwell, son and heir of Sir Robert Maxwell of Caerlaverock; agreeing to pay Herbert and his heirs 40 merks Scots a year; until Douglas grants Herbert or his heirs £20-worth of land in Clydesdale, Nithsdale, or Galloway, within the next two years; 'alswa we oblych vs to supowelle and defende the forsayde Syr Harbarte in all his ryghtwys cause, als we awe to our man and our kosyn'. [No place, before Whitsun]; 1407.

SOURCE. Fraser, *Carlaverock*, ii, 417–18.

**13** Inspection and confirmation, on behalf of Sir William Hay of Loquhariot, sheriff of Peebles: of letters of David II to Patrick Fleming; appointing Fleming hereditary sheriff of Tweeddale [i.e. Peebles], and authorising him to lead the men of the sheriffdom in war. [No witnesses; no place]; 20 May 1407.

SOURCE. NAS, Yester Writs, GD28/44; *Yester Writs*, no. 44; Fraser, *Douglas*, iii, no. 349.
COMMENT. David II's original letters are dated 8 Sep. 1346: *RRS*, vi, no. 108. It is not known whether Hay was an heir of Patrick Fleming.

**14** Letters to his squire James Dundas, granting tack and wadset of Dunberny, in Methven barony [PER]; to James for the next 19 years; for a certain sum of money already paid by James to Douglas. At Edinburgh, 16 July 1407.

SOURCE. NLS, MS Adv. 80.4.15, p. 146, nos. 2, 3.
COMMENT. But see Nos. **9**, **15**.

**15** Charter to James Dundas, for service and homage: of Dunberny [in Methven barony], (PER): to James and his heirs; of Douglas and his heirs; in blench farm, for one penny a year at Bothwell Castle. Witnesses: William Douglas (nephew); Mr Alexander Cairns; Matthew Geddes, rector of the church of the Forest; Sir William Crawford; Sir William Muirhead; Sir John Sinclair; Sir Thomas Murray; Thomas Somerville; Hugh Campbell of Loudon; Robert Pringle; Robert Crawford. At Edinburgh, 16 July 1407.

SOURCE. NLS, MS Adv. 80.4.15, pp. 146–7, no. 4.
COMMENT. But see Nos. 9, 14.

**16** Charter to his squire Henry Haliburton: of 10 merklands in Merton in Lauderdale; to Henry and his heirs; of Douglas and his heirs; in blench farm, for one red rose a year; with warranty. Witnesses: Sir William Hay; Sir William Borthwick; Sir William Crawford; John Caverhill; Thomas Turnbull; Robert Lauder; Simon Dalgleish (squires)[74]. At Edinburgh, 2 August 1407.

SOURCE. NAS, Scott of Harden (Lord Polwarth) MSS, GD157/260.

**17** Letters for Sir John Edmonston of that ilk: granting tack of Tulliallan, in Strathearn, for 19 years; for 240 merks Scots, paid by John to Douglas in his great need; to be held for the next 19 years directly of the earl of Strathearn. At Edinburgh, 2 August 1407.

SOURCE. NAS, Cardross Writs, GD15/334.
COMMENT. Confirmed by Earl Patrick of Strathearn, 1 Apr. 1410 (Fraser, *Douglas*, iii, no. 358).

**18** Letters for Sir John Edmonston of that ilk: appointing him bailie of Tulliallan. At Edinburgh, 2 August 1407.

SOURCE. NAS, Cardross Writs, GD15/335.

**19** Charter to his kinsman Sir William Douglas of Drumlanrig: of Hawick barony (ROX); to William and the heirs of his body; in place of Douglas ('*a nobis*') and his heirs; in blench farm, for one arrow a year, payable to Douglas and his heirs; with warranty. Witnesses: Archibald Douglas (eldest son); Sir Herbert Maxwell; Sir Simon Glendenning; Sir Alexander Gordon; Sir John Seton. [No place or date; probably shortly before 24 October 1407.]

SOURCE. Fraser, *Buccleuch*, ii, no. 22: inspection by the Governor, 24 Oct. 1407.
COMMENT. Despite the phrase '*a nobis*', the blench farm was payable to Douglas and his heirs, and in 1427 and 1450 retours of Hawick stated that it was held of the earls of Douglas (ibid., ii, nos. 28, 45).

**20** Charter to his kinsman Henry, Earl of Orkney, for aid and counsel: of Herbertshire barony (STL); to Henry and his wife Egidia (Douglas's niece) jointly, and the heirs of their bodies; with reversion to Douglas and his heirs; of Douglas and his heirs; in free barony; in blench farm, for a pair of white spurs a year; with warranty. Witnesses: James Douglas (brother); Sir John Edmonston; Sir Robert Logan; Sir John Forrester; Sir William Borthwick. At Edinburgh, 17 November 1407.

SOURCE. Fraser, *Douglas*, iii, no. 351.
COMMENT. Herbertshire was granted by the third earl of Douglas to his illegitimate son, William Douglas of Nithsdale, and his wife Egidia, Robert II's daughter Egidia (ibid., no. 338); their daughter, the heiress to Herbertshire, was the Egidia of this charter. The William Douglas of Nithsdale who was the fourth earl's nephew and a frequent witness of his charters was an illegitimate son of this William; see above, note 43.

74 This denotes those specifically called 'our [i.e. Douglas's] squires'.

**21** Charter to William Johnstone, for service done and to be done: of 'Drumgrey' in Amisfield barony (DMF); to William and his heirs; of Douglas and his heirs; for one suit a year to the head court at Douglas, in place of all other obligations; with warranty. Witnesses: James Douglas (brother); Sir William Douglas of Nithsdale (nephew); Sir James Douglas of Dalkeith; Sir William Hay; Sir William Borthwick; Sir William Crawford; Mr Alexander Cairns; Matthew Geddes, rector of the church of the Forest; Thomas Turnbull; Alexander Home. At Edinburgh, 24 May 1408.

SOURCE. Fraser, *Annandale*, i, no. 18; Fraser, *Douglas*, iii, no. 353.

**22** Charter to Sir Alexander Gordon of Stichill: of Shirmers, etc., in Balmaclellan barony, Galloway (KCB); to Alexander and his heirs; of Douglas and his heirs; for one suit a year to the head court of Balmaclellan barony, in place of all other obligations; with warranty. Witnesses: James Douglas (brother); Sir William Douglas of Nithsdale (nephew); Sir John Herries of Terregles; Sir Robert Maxwell of Caerlaverock; Mr Alexander Cairns; Matthew Geddes, rector of the church of the Forest. At Edinburgh, 28 May 1408.

SOURCE. NAS, Reg. Ho. Chrs., RH6/219; Fraser, *Douglas*, iii, no. 354.

**23** Inspection and confirmation of a charter by his brother James Douglas (of Abercorn), to William Fraser (Douglas's kinsman): of lands in Aberdour barony (ABD). [No witnesses.] At Edinburgh, 28 October 1408.

SOURCE. Fraser, *Frasers of Philorth*, ii, 221–2; *Aberdeen-Banff Ills.*, ii, 377–8; Fraser, *Douglas*, iii, no. 355.
COMMENT. James Douglas's charter is dated 5 Oct. 1408; witnesses include the earl of Douglas, Sir William Borthwick and William Borthwick junior.

**24** Charter to his squire Robert Pringle, for service done and to be done: the eastern part of Smailholm barony demesne (ROX); to Robert and his wife Isabella, in jointure, and the heirs of their bodies; failing whom, to the heirs of Robert's body; failing whom, reversion to Douglas or his heirs; of Douglas and his heirs; for three suits a year to the barony's chief courts, in place of all other obligations; with warranty. [No witnesses.] At Tinnis, 16 November 1408.

SOURCE. NAS, Scott of Harden (Lord Polwarth) MSS, GD157/75: inspection by James II, 2 Mar. 1452.
COMMENT. Tinnis is in the Yarrow valley, in Ettrick forest.

**25** Inspection and confirmation (as *custos* of Annandale), of a charter by Thomas Corbet, to his son John: of 'Lymidilnes', etc., in Annandale; to John and his heirs; of the chief lord of the fee. [No witnesses.] At Lochmaben, 24 November 1408.

SOURCE. HMC, *Portland Rep.*, ii, 2; BL, Add. Ch. 76705. A transcript, NLS, MS Adv. 34.1.10, pp. ii–iii, is wrongly dated 25 Nov. 1411. (I am grateful to Alan Borthwick for assistance with this document.)
COMMENT. Douglas did not formally acquire Annandale until Oct. 1409 [133].

**26** Indenture (in Scots) between Robert Duke of Albany and Archibald Earl of Douglas, for mutual friendship and kindness, with reciprocal promises of support and security against everyone except the king, and with procedures for settling disputes between them, their families, and their men, by means of arbitration on the advice of their councils. If Albany becomes king the bond (which involves equality in status) will lapse, but kindness and friendship will continue. The bond will extend to Robert Stewart of Fife and Walter Stewart of Lennox [Albany's grandsons], and to Archibald and James Douglas (Douglas's sons), if these agree so to be bound. [No witnesses.] At Inverkeithing, 20 June 1409.

SOURCE. NAS, Reg. Ho. Chrs., RH6/223; Fraser, *Menteith*, ii, 277–80; *ER*, iv, p. ccix; Fraser, *Douglas*, iii, no. 300.

**27** Charter to Sir William Crawford, for his service in keeping Edinburgh Castle while Douglas was in England: of the Halls of Airth, etc. (STL); to William and his heirs; of Douglas and his heirs; for the usual service; with warranty. Witnesses: James Douglas (brother); Sir James Douglas of Dalkeith; Sir John Montgomery; Sir John Seton; Sir William Muirhead; Mr Alexander Cairns; Matthew Geddes rector of the church of the Forest. At Edinburgh (after Douglas's escape from his enemies of England), 20 August 1409.

SOURCE. NAS, Reg. Ho. Chrs., RH6/225; Fraser, *Douglas*, iii, no. 356.
COMMENT. Confirmed by Robert, Duke of Albany, Governor, in charter dated 2 Aug. 1409 [which must be an error]: Fraser, *Elphinstone*, ii, no. 11.

**28** Charter to Sir Herbert Maxwell, for his homage and service: of the office of steward of the lordship of Annandale; to Herbert and his heirs; of Douglas and his heirs; with the right to keep £20 from the proceeds of each steward's court, and all amercements of 18 shillings and less. [No witnesses.] At Linlithgow, 8 February 1410.

SOURCE. NAS, Gt. Seal Reg., C2/3, no. 153; *RMS*, ii, no. 242: inspection by James II, 6 Aug. 1440.

**29** Letters for his kinsman Sir William Fraser of Philorth: stating 100 merk obligation to William; with promise to pay this sum by 1 November 1410. At Edinburgh, 10 July 1410.

SOURCE. *Aberdeen-Banff Ills.*, iv, 85–6.
COMMENT. There is a note that 'ane and threttie pundis' was paid to William at Lochmaben, and that another 'ane and twenty pundis' was paid subsequently.

**30** Indenture (in Scots) between Robert Duke of Albany and Archibald Earl of Douglas, for the marriage of Albany's son, John Stewart, Earl of Buchan, to Douglas's daughter Elizabeth. Douglas is to grant John and Elizabeth 200 merks-worth of land, namely Stewarton and Ormsheuch in Cunningham barony (AYR), plus other lands if need be; to John and Elizabeth jointly, and to the heirs of their bodies; failing whom to John and the heirs-male of his body, with reversion to Douglas and his heirs. The transfer is to be made by Douglas's resignation to Albany as Governor for a crown grant to John and Elizabeth. The countess of Douglas is to give up her jointure rights in Stewarton and Ormsheuch; if not, full compensation is to be paid from the rents of Douglas's baronies of Bothwell, Strathaven, Drumsargard and Carmunnock. The earl of Buchan is to grant Elizabeth 200 merks-worth of land for her life. [No witnesses.] At Perth, 21 July 1410.

SOURCE. NAS, Fraser Charters, GD86/9; Fraser, *Menteith*, ii, 281–3; Fraser, *Douglas*, iii, no. 359.

**31** Charter to Alexander Stewart, Earl of Mar, for his service and favours (*beneficium*) done and to be done: of an annuity of £40 Scots from Bothwell barony (LAN); to Mar, his heirs and assigns; of Douglas and his heirs; until Mar is granted land worth £40; with warranty. [No witnesses.] At Perth, 22 July 1410.

SOURCE. NAS, Mar and Kellie Muniments, GD124/1/423; HMC, *Mar and Kellie Suppl. Rep.*, 15: inspection by the Governor, also dated 22 Jul. 1410.

**32** Letters of remission, by Douglas as justiciar south of the Forth: to James Dundas, John Spence, John Spence junior, Richard Bisset, Alan Lawson, Nicholas Cairns, Adam Spence, James Meldrum, John Auld; for their part in the 'cruel rapine' done to the husbandmen of the Isle of Bathgate and Turbay; on condition that the complainants are satisfied. In the justice-ayre at Edinburgh, 20 January 1411.

SOURCE. NLS, MS Adv. 80.4.15, p. 159, no. 2.

**33** Charter to his kinsman Sir Thomas Murray, for service done and to be done: of Ruthwell in the lordship of Annandale; resigned by Thomas; to Thomas and the heirs of his body; failing whom, to Thomas's illegitimate sons Gavin and Charles, in turn, and the heirs-male of their bodies; failing whom, to Thomas's illegitimate brothers David and Patrick, in turn, and their heirs-male; failing whom, to Thomas's cousin Robert, and his heirs-male; failing whom, to the heirs-general of Thomas's father; of Douglas, etc., lords of Annandale; in blench farm, for one red rose a year; with warranty. [No witnesses.] At Lochmaben, 20 July 1411.

SOURCE. NAS, National Register of Archives (Scotland), 776, survey of Earl of Mansfield's Muniments, 2nd ser., bundle 1835, no. 3. (I am grateful to Alan Borthwick for details of this charter.)

**34** Charter to his squire Simon Carruthers, for service done and to be done: of Mouswald, etc., in Annandale; resigned by Simon in the Annandale justice-ayre at Lochmaben; to Simon and his heirs; of Douglas, etc., lords of Annandale; in blench farm, for one penny a year; with warranty. Witnesses: James Douglas (brother); Sir William Graham; Sir William Douglas of Nithsdale; Sir William Douglas of Drumlanrig; Sir William Hay; Sir William Borthwick; Sir John Carlyle; Sir Humphrey Jardine; Sir Thomas Murray; Sir Robert Herries (kinsmen). At Lochmaben, 4 December 1411.

SOURCE. HMC, *Drumlanrig Rep.*, i, no. 110; Fraser, *Douglas*, iii, no. 363.

**35** Charter to his squire Simon Carruthers, for service and homage done and to be done: of Hoddom, etc., in Annandale (DMF); resigned by Simon in the Annandale justice-ayre at Lochmaben; to Simon and his heirs; of Douglas, etc., lords of Annandale; for the usual service; with warranty. Witnesses: James Douglas (brother); Sir William Graham; Sir William Douglas of Nithsdale; Sir William Douglas of Drumlanrig; Sir William Hay; Sir William Borthwick; Sir John Carlyle; Sir Humphrey Jardine; Sir Thomas Murray; Sir Robert Herries; Sir William Stewart (kinsmen). At Lochmaben, 4 December 1411.

SOURCE. NAS, Crown Office Writs, AD1/33; noted in HMC, *Drumlanrig Rep.*, i, no. 110, and Fraser, *Douglas*, iii, no. 363.

**36** Charter to his squire Simon Carruthers, for service done and to be done: of Hetlandhill, in Dalton forest, Annandale; resigned by Simon in the Annandale justice-ayre at Lochmaben; to Simon and his heirs; of Douglas, etc., lords of Annandale; in blench farm, for one penny a year; with warranty. Witnesses: James Douglas (brother); Sir William Graham; Sir William Douglas of Nithsdale; Sir William Douglas of Drumlanrig. At Lochmaben, 4 December 1411.

SOURCE. HMC, *Drumlanrig Rep.*, i, no. 110 (1); Fraser, *Douglas*, iii, no. 363 (1).

**37** Charter to his squire Simon Carruthers, for service done and to be done: of Logan in Moffat parish, Annandale; resigned by Simon in the Annandale justice-ayre at Lochmaben; to Simon and his heirs; of Douglas, etc., lords of Annandale; in blench farm, for one penny a year; with warranty. Witnesses: James Douglas (brother); Sir William Graham; Sir William Douglas of Nithsdale; Sir William Douglas of Drumlanrig; Sir William Hay; Sir William Borthwick; Sir John Carlyle; Sir Humphrey Jardine; Sir Thomas Murray; Sir Robert Herries (kinsmen). At Lochmaben, 4 December 1411.

SOURCE. HMC, *Drumlanrig Rep.*, i, no. 110 (2); Fraser, *Douglas*, iii, no. 363 (2).

**38** Charter to his squire Simon Carruthers, for service done and to be done: of Middlebie, etc., in Annandale; resigned by Simon in the Annandale justice-ayre at Lochmaben; to Simon and his heirs; of Douglas, etc., lords of Annandale; for the usual service; with warranty. Witnesses: James Douglas (brother); Sir William Graham; Sir William Douglas of Nithsdale; Sir William Douglas of Drumlanrig; Sir William Hay; Sir William Borthwick; Sir John Carlyle; Sir Humphrey Jardine; Sir Thomas Murray (kinsmen). At Lochmaben, 4 December 1411.

SOURCE. HMC, *Drumlanrig Rep.*, i, no. 110 (3); Fraser, *Douglas*, iii, no. 363 (3).

**39** Charter to his squire Simon Carruthers, for service done and to be done: of Dornock, in Annandale; resigned by Simon in the Annandale justice-ayre at Lochmaben; to Simon and his heirs; of Douglas, etc., lords of Annandale; for the usual service; with warranty. Witnesses: James Douglas (brother); Sir William Graham; Sir William Douglas of Nithsdale; Sir William Douglas of Drumlanrig; Sir William Hay; Sir William Borthwick; Sir John Carlyle; Sir Humphrey Jardine; Sir Thomas Murray (kinsmen). At Lochmaben, 4 December 1411.

SOURCE. HMC, *Drumlanrig Rep.*, i, no. 110 (4); Fraser, *Douglas*, iii, no. 363 (4).

**40** Charter to his kinsman Patrick Ogilvy, for service done and to be done: of Pitleys in Lundie barony (FOR); resigned by John Brown of Midmar; to Patrick and his heirs; of Douglas and his heirs; in blench farm, for one penny a year; with warranty. Witnesses: George, Earl of March; Henry, Earl of Orkney; Sir William Borthwick (kinsmen); Mr James Fawside (clerk); Walter Dempstar; Thomas Fotheringham. At Edinburgh, 27 September 1412.

SOURCE. NAS, Gt. Seal Reg., C2/2, no. 113; *RMS*, ii, no. 112: inspection by James I, 2 Aug. 1428.

**41** Letters for Coldingham and Durham Priories, surrendering the annual pension or fee due to Douglas as bailie of Coldingham Priory, but reserving the office itself for life. At Edinburgh, 5 October 1413.

SOURCE. Raine, *North Durham*, appendix, no. CLXIX.
COMMENT. See Nos. 10, 46, 109, 134.

**42** Charter to Simon Hannay: of Sorbie, etc. (WIG), Galloway; to Simon and his heirs; of Douglas and his heirs, lords of Galloway; for one common suit of court to Wigtown. Witnesses: Eliseus, Bishop of Galloway; Sir William Douglas (nephew); Sir John Herries; Sir Herbert Maxwell of Caerlaverock; Sir Alexander Gordon; Sir Fergus McDowell; Mr Alexander Cairns (chancellor); Hugh Campbell; Egidius of Gebilston; John Crawford; John Akersan. At Wigtown, 12 February 1414.

SOURCE. NAS, Register of Acts and Decreets, 1st ser., CS7/430, fo. 286v: transumpt made during a case before the Lords of Council and Session, 4 Mar. 1630. (I am grateful to Alan Borthwick for details of this charter.)

**43** Charter to his squire and kinsman Alexander Stewart, son of Sir John Stewart of Lorn (his kinsman), for service done and to be done: of Grandtully, etc., in the *abthania* of Dull (PER); resigned by John Stewart; to Alexander and the heirs-male of his body; failing whom, to John Stewart and his heirs; of Douglas and his heirs; for three suits a year to Douglas's courts of Grandtully, held at 'the Courthill' (which Douglas keeps, for his courts); and for the usual service owed to the lord of the *abthania* of Dull. [No warranty clause.] Witnesses: Robert, Duke of Albany; John Stewart, Earl of Buchan; Robert Stewart of Lorn; Sir William Borthwick (kinsman). At Stirling, 30 March 1414.

SOURCE. Fraser, *Grandtully*, i, no. 5; Fraser, *Douglas*, iii, no. 366.

**44** Letters appointing James Heriot bailie of Tulliallan. [No place], 30 March 1414.

SOURCE. NAS, Cardross Writs, GD15/336.

**45** Charter to his familiar Michael Ramsay, for service done and to be done: of 10 merklands of Nether Sypland (KCB), in Galloway ; which Douglas previously granted Michael for life, and which Michael resigned; to Michael and his heirs; of Douglas and his heirs; in blench farm, for holding Douglas's stirrups once a year; with warranty. Witnesses: Archibald Douglas (eldest son and squire); Sir William Douglas of Drumlanrig; Sir William Liddel; Sir John Sinclair; Sir Thomas Murray; Robert Ramsay; William

Borthwick junior; William Edmonston; George Rutherford. At Lochmaben Castle, 7 July 1414.

SOURCE. NAS, Gt. Seal Reg., C2/2, no. 65; *RMS*, ii, no. 70: inspection by James I, 3 Jan. 1427.

**46** Letters for Coldingham and Durham Priories, surrendering the annual pension or fee due to Douglas as bailie of Coldingham Priory, but reserving the office itself for life, and also reserving the annuity of £20 granted out of his fee (without the prior of Coldingham's consent) to Andrew Raeburn, monk of Kilwinning. At Edinburgh, 27 June 1414.

SOURCE. Raine, *North Durham*, appendix, no. CL.
COMMENT. See Nos. 10, 41, 109, 134.

**47** Charter to his kinsman Sir William Hay of Loquhariot, for service done and to be done: of Auchquhone (WIG), in Galloway; resigned at Lincluden by Sir John McCulloch; to William and his heirs, of Douglas, etc., lords of Galloway; for the usual service; with warranty. Witnesses: Henry Sinclair, Earl of Orkney; Sir William Douglas of Drumlanrig; Sir William Borthwick; Sir John Mowbray; Sir John Sinclair; Adam Hepburn; Robert Livingstone; Robert Pringle; William Edmonston; William Sinclair; Mr James Fawside (secretary). At Edinburgh, 28 September 1414.

SOURCE. NAS, Yester Writs, GD28/47; *Yester Writs*, no. 47; Fraser, *Douglas*, iii, no. 367.

**48** Letters to David Edmonston: acknowledging the payment of 100 merks relief, for Tulliallan, etc. At Edinburgh, 31 July 1415.

SOURCE. NAS, Cardross Writs, GD15/338.
COMMENT. Clearly only the fortalice of Tulliallan was held in blench farm (cf. Nos. 7, 8); and see above, page 240.

**49** Inspection and confirmation of a wadset by Sir William Sinclair of Hermiston, to David Edmonston of that ilk: of Carfrae mains, toun and mill, Lauderdale; for 140 merks. [No witnesses.] At Edinburgh, 31 July 1415.

SOURCE. HMC, *Milne-Home Rep*., no. 592.
COMMENT. William Sinclair's wadset is dated 31 Jan. 1414; and see above, page 240.

**50** Charter to his squire David Home, for service done and to be done: of 'Bayherdlands' in Douglas's lordship of Hutton (BRK); resigned by Marjorie Harcarse; to David, his heirs and assigns; of Douglas, etc., as lords of Hutton; in blench farm, for one penny a year. [No witnesses.] At Edinburgh, 23 March 1416.

SOURCE. HMC, *Milne-Home Rep*., no. 2.

**51** Charter to his kinsman Sir Robert Maxwell of Calderwood, for his service and counsel: of Nether Calderwood, in Kilbride barony (LAN); to Robert, his heirs and assigns; '*a me*' [i.e. Douglas], of the baron of Kilbride and his heirs; as Douglas and his predecessors used to hold the lands; with warranty. [No witnesses.] At Edinburgh, 31 May 1416.

SOURCE. Fraser, *Pollock*, i, no. 27.
COMMENT. Here it is clear that the territory was alienated completely. The baron of Kilbride was Sir James Stewart of Kilbride, illegitimate son of Robert III.

**52** Charter to John Cairns: of Gilkerscleuch, in Crawfordjohn barony (LAN); resigned by Mr Alexander Cairns, John's uncle; to John and his heirs; of Douglas and his heirs; in blench farm, for one penny a year; no warranty. Witnesses: Sir William Borthwick; Sir [*sic*] Adam Hepburn; Sir William Colville; Sir John Cockburn; Robert Ramsay of Dalhousie; William Borthwick junior; Mr William Foulis (clerk). At Edinburgh, 4 August 1416.

SOURCE. NAS, Gt. Seal Reg., C2/3, no. 145; *RMS*, ii, no. 255: inspection by James II, *c*. 8 Dec. 1440.

**53** Charter to his squire James Dundas, for service done and to be done: of Easter Blairmucks, in Bothwell barony (LAN); to John and his heirs; of Douglas and his heirs; in blench farm, for one penny a year; with warranty. Witnesses: Sir John Seton; Sir William Borthwick; Sir William Hay; Sir John Sinclair; Robert Ramsay; Adam Hepburn; William Borthwick junior; Alexander Home; Thomas Graham (squires). At Edinburgh, 27 February 1417.

SOURCE. NAS, Gt. Seal Reg., C2/3, no. 32; *RMS*, ii, no. 119: inspection by James I, 24 May 1429.

**54** Charter to his squire Alexander Mure, son of Sir Adam Mure, late of Hershaw and Drumboy, for homage and service done and to be done: of Hershaw and Drumboy, in Strathaven barony (LAN); to Alexander and his heirs; of Douglas and his heirs; as Adam Mure held the lands; with warranty. [No witnesses.] At Edinburgh, 13 November 1417.

SOURCE. NAS, Reg. Ho. Chrs., RH6/249A.

**55** Charter to his kinsman and squire William Towers of Cramond, for service: 'Knokfubill', etc., in Bothwell barony (LAN): to William, his heirs and assigns; of Douglas and his heirs; for three suits a year to the chief courts at Bothwell, in place of all other obligations. Witnesses: Sir James Douglas of Dalkeith; James Douglas (brother); Sir William Borthwick; Sir William Crawford; Sir William Cranston of Denholm (kinsmen); Robert Ramsay of Dalhousie; William Borthwick junior; Robert Borthwick (squires and kinsmen); Mr William Foulis, rector of Cambuslang (secretary). At Edinburgh, 20 November 1417.

SOURCE. HMC, *7th Report, App.*, 728, no. 5.

**56** Precept (in Scots) to Robert Crichton and 'Macgyewe', officers west of the River Cree: stating that Sir William Hay is not receiving his rents from his lands of Auchquhone, in Galloway; therefore they are instructed to take charge of the lands, impose distress on those who are wasting them with grazing ('eting'), levy the rents, and send the proceeds to Hay. At Edinburgh, 18 February 1418.

SOURCE. NAS, Yester Writs, GD28/52; *Yester Writs*, no. 52; Fraser, *Douglas*, iii, no. 371.

**57** Letters on behalf of Melrose Abbey: stating that the lands disputed between Melrose Abbey and the laird of Bemerside have been set at pledge by Douglas; they are to stay in Melrose's hands while the case is dealt with. At 'Edybredschelis' [Selkirk], 13 May 1418.

SOURCE. *Melrose Liber*, ii, no. 541.

**58** Inspection and confirmation of a charter by Thomas Randolph, Earl of Moray, to Melrose Abbey: of the lands of Bemerside. [No witnesses.] At 'Edybredschelis' [Selkirk], 10 July 1418.

SOURCE. *Melrose Liber*, ii, no. 542.

**59** Charter to Melrose Abbey: of regality rights over Eskdalemuir, in Douglas's regality of Eskdale (ROX); in free alms; in place of Douglas and his heirs ('*a nobis*'); for prayers for the abbey's patrons; with warranty. Witnesses: Alexander, Bishop of Caithness; James, Prior of St Andrews; Sir John Seton; Sir William Borthwick; Sir John Bothwell; Alexander Home; James Dundas (squires); Mr William Foulis (secretary). At Edinburgh, 16 January 1419.

SOURCE. *Melrose Liber*, ii, no. 512; Fraser, *Douglas*, iii, no 57.
COMMENT. Inspection by Archibald, Earl of Wigtown, 10 Dec. 1422: ibid.

**60** Charter to his kinswoman Elizabeth Stewart: of Cally, in Kirkcudbright constabulary (DMF), that belonged to her late father Sir John Stewart of Girthon; to Elizabeth and her heirs; of Douglas and his heirs; for suit to the three head courts of Kirkcudbright, and the usual service; with warranty. Witnesses: Alexander, Earl of Mar;

John, Earl of Buchan; Sir John Seton; Sir William Borthwick; Sir Robert Maxwell (kinsmen); Alexander Home; James Dundas (squires). At Edinburgh, 6 February 1419.

SOURCE. NAS, Broughton and Cally Muniments, GD10/16; Fraser, *Douglas*, iii, no. 373.

**61** Charter to his familiar Michael Ramsay, for service done and to be done: of Rammerscales, etc., in the lordship of Annandale; which belonged to William son of Henry; to Michael and his heirs; of Douglas and his heirs. Also includes grant to Michael Ramsay and Christian his wife: of Howthat in Dalton forest, Annandale, which belonged to Roger of Lochirmos; to Michael and Christian jointly, and the heirs of their bodies 'procreated by legal and mutual intercourse'; with reversion to Douglas if they beget no heirs; of Douglas and his heirs; in blench farm, for holding Douglas's stirrups once a year during the earl's life, and subsequently for one penny a year; with warranty. [No witnesses.] At Edinburgh, 10 May 1419.

SOURCE. HMC, *6th Report*, *App.*, 710, no. 5; Fraser, *Douglas*, iii, no. 387; *RMS*, ii, no. 71: inspection by James I, 3 Jan. 1427.
COMMENT. Michael Ramsay's wife Christian may well be the Christian Ramsay of No. **68**.

**62** Inspection and confirmation of a charter by William Cranston of Denholm to his son and heir Thomas, of Nether Crailing in Bothwell [*sic*] barony (ROX). Witnesses: Sir William Hay; Sir William Borthwick; David Edmonston; William Borthwick junior. At Edinburgh, 20 September 1419.

SOURCE. The Hirsel, Home Muniments, Box 94/1. (I am grateful to Alan Borthwick for details of this charter.)
COMMENT. This William Cranston is not the same as the Sir William Cranston of that ilk, to whom Nether Crailing was granted *c*.1401 [**5**], because the latter was dead by 4 Nov. 1413 [**123**]. The *Scots Peerage* account (ii, 586–7) is inaccurate.

**63** Charter to his kinsman Herbert Maxwell of Caerlaverock: of Greenan (KCB), in Galloway; resigned by Herbert; to Herbert, his heirs and assigns; of Douglas and his heirs; in blench farm, for one penny a year; with warranty. Witnesses: Sir Herbert Maxwell of Conheath; Adam Johnstone; Mr Andrew Henry, rector of Glenholm; Michael Davidson; Mr William Foulis (secretary). At Lochmaben, 18 December 1419.

SOURCE. Fraser, *Carlaverock*, ii, 420–1.

**64** Charter to his kinsman Sir Thomas Murray, for service done and to be done: of 'Layk' (KCB) in the lordship of Galloway; to Thomas and his heirs-male; failing whom, to Thomas's illegitimate sons Gavin, Charles, Lancelot, Florence, Herbert and John, in turn, and the heirs-male of their bodies; of Douglas, etc., lords of Galloway; for suit to the Easter head court of Kirkcudbright; with warranty. [No witnesses.] At 'Bewic', 20 October 1420.

SOURCE. NAS, National Register of Archives (Scotland), 776, survey of Earl of Mansfield's Muniments, 2nd ser., bundle 1835, no. 4: inspection by James, 9th Earl of Douglas, 13 Dec. 1452. (I am grateful to Alan Borthwick for details of this charter.)

**65** Charter to William Stevinston and Edane his wife: of Stevinston in Bothwell barony (LAN); resigned by William's father John Stevinston; to William and Edane jointly and the legitimate heirs of their bodies; with reversion to John Stevinston and his heirs-general; of Douglas and his heirs; with the cancellation of the relief of 13s. 6d. normally due from the land. [No renders, no warranty clause.] Witnesses: Sir James Douglas of Dalkeith; Sir John Seton; Sir William Borthwick; William Foulis, secretary. At Edinburgh, 1 December 1420.

SOURCE. NAS, Gt. Seal Reg., C2/4, no. 38; *RMS*, ii, no. 364: inspection by James II, 26 Jun. 1450.

**66** Indenture (in Scots) with his squire Michael Ramsay: appointing Michael keeper of Lochmaben Castle for life; which Michael must maintain for Douglas and his heirs, in peace and war, against everyone; for an annual fee of £80 Scots and the land of Usebyfeld; and also appointing Michael keeper of the water and chamberlain of Annandale for life. Witness: Mr Alexander Cairns. At Lochmaben, 3 February 1421.

SOURCE. NAS, Gt. Seal Reg., C2/3, no. 57; *RMS*, ii, no. 143: inspection by James I, 8 Jan. 1430.

**67** Charter to his kinsman Archibald Hepburn, brother of Adam Hepburn of Hailes: of Flemington, in Drumsargart barony (LAN); to Archibald, his heirs and assigns; of Douglas and his heirs; in blench farm, for one penny a year; with warranty. Witnesses: James Douglas (son); Sir John Seton; Sir John Forrester of Corstorphine; Sir John Sinclair of Lethrig; Sir John Cockburn; Adam Hepburn of Hailes; John Sinclair of Hermiston; Alexander Ramsay of Dalhousie; William Crichton; Simon Logan; Richard Bickerton; James Erskine; William Bickerton. At Edinburgh Castle, 12 March 1421.

SOURCE. NAS, Gt. Seal Reg., C2/3, no. 144; *RMS*, ii, no. 254: inspection by James II, 8 Dec. 1440.

**68** Charter to Christian Ramsay: of Ballincrief and Gosford, in Lothian; to Christian, for life; and after her death, to the eldest son begotten or to be begotten by Douglas and Christian by mutual intercourse; if he dies, then to the second, third and subsequent children similarly begotten; with reversion to Douglas and his heirs; of Douglas and his heirs; as Douglas and his predecessors held the lands; with warranty. [No witnesses.] At Edinburgh, 20 April 1421.

SOURCE. Fraser, *Douglas*, iii, no. 60: inspection by the Governor, Duke Murdach of Albany, 26 Oct. 1421.
COMMENT. Inspection by Archibald Douglas, Earl of Wigtown, 6 Mar. 1423: Fraser, *Douglas*, iii, no. 380. See also No. 61.

**69** Inspection and confirmation of a charter by Thomas Randolph, Earl of Moray, to Melrose Abbey: of the lands of Bemerside. Also statement by Douglas of the boundaries of the lands. [No witnesses.] At 'our manor of Edybredschelis' [Selkirk], 15 September 1421.

SOURCE. *Melrose Liber*, ii, no. 543.

**70** Inspection and confirmation of a charter by John Crawford to Douglas's kinsman and squire John Cairns: of Cultis (WIG), in Galloway. Witnesses: Mr Alexander Cairns; Alexander Home; James Dundas; George Pringle (squires); Mr William Foulis (secretary). At Edinburgh, 20 October 1421.

SOURCE. NAS, Agnew of Lochnaw Muniments, GD154/1; *Wigtownshire Chrs.*, no. 133.
COMMENT. John Crawford's charter is dated 30 Sep. 1419.

**71** Charter to his kinsman Sir Thomas Murray, for service done and to be done: of Arbigland (KCB) in Galloway, to Thomas and his heirs-male; failing whom, to Thomas's illegitimate sons Gavin, Charles, Lancelot, Florence, Herbert and John, in turn, and the heirs-male of their bodies; of Douglas, etc., lords of Galloway; for suit to the Easter head court of Kirkcudbright; with warranty. Witnesses: Sir James Douglas of Dalkeith; Sir John Seton; Sir Thomas Somerville; Sir John Forrester; Mr William Foulis, secretary. At Bothwell, 29 November 1421.

SOURCE. NAS, National Register of Archives (Scotland), 776, survey of Earl of Mansfield's Muniments, 2nd ser., bundle 1835, no. 5. (I am grateful to Alan Borthwick for details of this charter.)

**72** Charter to his squire David Murray, for service done and to be done: of Newton in [illegible] barony, regality of Lauder; to David and his heirs; of Douglas, etc., lords of Lauder. Witnesses: Sir John Seton; Sir John Forrester; Sir Thomas Murray (kinsmen); Mr William Foulis, secretary; Mr Patrick Young. At Bothwell, 30 November 1421.

SOURCE. NAS, National Register of Archives (Scotland), 776, survey of Earl of Mansfield's Muniments, 2nd ser, bundle 1835, no. 6; damaged, and partly illegible. (I am grateful to Alan Borthwick for details of this charter.)

**73** Charter to his squire Robert Gordon: of half of Bordland, etc., in Balmaclellan barony (KCB); which belonged to Robert's father Alexander Gordon; to Robert and the heirs of his body, failing whom his brother William and the heirs of his body; of Douglas and his heirs; for the usual service; with warranty. [No witnesses.] At Threave, 1 July 1422.

SOURCE. NAS, Reg. Ho. Chrs., RH6/296; Fraser, *Douglas*, iii, no. 401: inspection by Margaret, Dowager Countess of Douglas, 12 Apr. 1437.

**74** Charter to John Cairns and Elizabeth his wife: of Carsluith, in Kirkdale parish (KCB), resigned by John's uncle, Mr Alexander Cairns; plus the neighbouring land of Strothans; to John and Elizabeth jointly, and the heirs of their bodies; failing whom, to John's heirs general; reserving liferent to Mr Alexander Cairns; in blench farm, for one penny a year; with warranty. Witnesses: Sir John Seton; Sir John Cockburn; James Dundas; Alexander Home; Mr William Foulis; Robert Feuer (clerks). At Wigtown, 20 November 1422.

SOURCE. NAS, Gt. Seal Reg., C2/3, no. 145; *RMS*, ii, no. 255: inspection by Margaret, Dowager Countess of Douglas, 10 Oct. 1425; from inspection by James II, *c.*1440.

**75** Charter to his squire John Heriot ('*armigero nostro*'), son of his ally James Heriot of Niddrie Marischal ('*confederati nostri*'): of Trabroun in Lauder regality (BRK); resigned by Walter Ogilvy of Lintrathen; to John, his heirs and assigns; of Douglas and his heirs, lords of Lauder; in blench farm, for one penny a year; with warranty. Witnesses: Sir James Douglas of Dalkeith; Sir John Seton; Sir John Forrester; Adam Hepburn; William Crichton; Alexander Ramsay of Dalhousie; Mr William Foulis, rector of Cambuslang (secretary). At Edinburgh, 18 July 1423.

SOURCE. NAS, Scott of Harden (Lord Polwarth) MSS, GD157/371.
COMMENT. Inspection by Archibald, Earl of Wigtown, 2 Dec. 1423, and by James I, 18 Jan. 1425: *RMS*, ii, no. 13.

**76** Letters (in Scots) for his squire Michael Ramsay, appointing Michael to the offices of keeper of Lochmaben Castle, and chancellor and chamberlain of Annandale; and authorising him to hold courts and punish offenders. At Lochmaben, 22 November 1423.

SOURCE. NAS, Gt. Seal Reg., C2/3, no. 57; *RMS*, ii, no. 143: inspection by James I, 8 Jan. 1430.

**77** Letters (in Scots) for his squire Michael Ramsay, authorising him to levy revenues (mostly in chalders of meal) for his own use from certain churches in Galloway; and giving him the small customs of Galloway, and fishing rights in Annandale; to be held for the rest of Michael's life. At Lochmaben, 22 November 1423.

SOURCE. NAS, Gt. Seal Reg., C2/3, no. 57; *RMS*, ii, no. 143: inspection by James I, 8 Jan. 1430.

**78** Charter to Whithorn Priory: of Cruggleton and Poltoun (WIG), in Galloway; in free alms. Witnesses: Sir James Douglas (son); Sir John Seton; Sir John Sinclair; Sir Thomas Murray; Alexander Home; James Dundas; John Murray. At Bothwell, 6 December 1423.

SOURCE. NAS, Gt. Seal Reg., C2/3, no. 1; *RMS*, ii, no. 12: inspection by James I, 25 Oct. 1424.
COMMENT. Douglas's countess, Margaret, made a similar grant on 27 Mar. 1424: ibid.

**79** Charter to his squire William Cockburn, son of Sir Alexander Cockburn of Langton, for service done and to be done: of the two touns of Curmannock in Curmannock barony, plus Aldirston etc. in Bothwell barony (LAN); to William and the heirs of his body; failing whom to his brother Patrick and his heirs-general; of Douglas and his heirs; in blench farm, for one penny a year; with warranty. [No witnesses.] At Bothwell, 10 December 1423.

SOURCE. NAS, Gt. Seal Reg., C2/3, no. 146; *RMS*, ii, no. 256: inspection by James II, 5 Jan. 1441.

**80** Letters to Archibald Douglas, Earl of Wigtown (eldest son) and the rest of his sons and friends: declaring Douglas's special affection for Melrose Abbey; stating that it is free of all impositions, and does not owe attendance at March Days and other external courts; and granting it Douglas's special protection. At Edinburgh, 6 February 1424.

SOURCE. *Melrose Liber*, ii, no. 507.

## UNDATED TEXTS

**81** Charter to his kinsman Sir William Crawford, for service done and to be done: of Douglas Farm (near Rutherglen, LAN); resigned by John Towers; to William, his heirs and assigns; of Douglas and his heirs; in blench farm, for one penny a year; with warranty. Witnesses: Sir James Douglas of Dalkeith; Sir John Edmonston; Sir William Hay; Sir William Stewart of Castlemilk; Sir William Muirhead; Mr Alexander Cairns; Matthew Geddes, rector of the church of the Forest. [No place or date; presumably September 1406 × October 1409.]

SOURCE. NAS, Reg. Ho. Chrs., RH6/226: inspection by the Governor, 11 Mar. 1410.
COMMENT. William Hay is a knight, which gives a date after 19 Sep. 1406 [**9**]; but Douglas is not styled lord of Annandale. This virtually repeats a charter of the third earl, dated 21 May 1400 (Fraser, *Douglas*, iii, no. 342), but adds the destination to 'assigns', which allowed Crawford to alienate the land if he wished.

**82** Charter (wadset) to Sir Alexander Gordon of Stichill: of the New Forest of Glenken (DMF), in Galloway. If Douglas grants Alexander land worth 20 merks Old Extent and pays him 55 gold nobles within three months of returning to Scotland, this charter will have no effect. Otherwise, the New Forest is to be held by Alexander and his heirs; of Douglas and his heirs; in free forest. Witnesses: Henry Sinclair, Earl of Orkney; Sir William Douglas of Drumlanrig; Sir John Seton; Sir William Sinclair; Sir Simon Glendenning. [No place or date; probably before 22 May 1408.]

SOURCE. Fraser, *Douglas*, iii, no. 357.
COMMENT. The date is obviously before Douglas's 'escape' from England, and doubtless before the grant of Shirmers to Gordon on 22 May 1408 [**22**], which was probably the stipulated grant of 20 merklands.

**83** Charter to his squire Gilbert Grierson: of Meikle Dalton etc., in Annandale (DMF); to Gilbert and his son William and the latter's heirs-male of the body; failing whom to Gilbert's heirs-general; of Douglas, etc., lords of Annandale; for suit to the head court at Lochmaben every Easter, and for the usual service; with warranty. Witnesses: Sir Gavin Dunbar; Sir William Borthwick; Sir William Crawford; Sir John Sinclair (kinsmen); Adam Hepburn; William Edmonston; Henry Haliburton; William Sinclair (squires). At Edinburgh [no date; after October 1409].

SOURCE. HMC, *6th Report, App.*, 710, no. 3; Fraser, *Douglas*, iii, no. 362.
COMMENT. Douglas is styled lord of Annandale, indicating a date after 2 Oct. 1409 [**133**].

**84** Charter to his squire Gilbert Grierson: of the liferent of Meikle Dalton etc. (DMF); which was forfeited by Thomas Corbet, because he dared to infringe the sasine of the infeftment of these lands given to Gilbert by Douglas; to Gilbert for life, and then to his son William and the latter's heirs-male of the body; failing whom to Gilbert's heirs-general;

of Douglas, etc., lords of Annandale; with warranty. Witnesses: Sir William Borthwick; Sir John Forrester; Sir William Crawford; John Murray; Mr James Fawside (clerk). [No place or date; after October 1409.]

SOURCE. HMC, *6th Report, App.*, 710, no. 4.
COMMENT. Douglas is styled lord of Annandale (and it is presumably later than No. **83**).

**85** Charter to Gilbert Grierson, for homage and service: of Drumgewane (KCB) in Galloway; to Gilbert and his heirs; of Douglas and his heirs; for suit to the annual Easter head court of Kirkcudbright sheriffdom. Witnesses: Sir William Douglas of Nithsdale; Sir John Herries of Terregles; Sir William Douglas of Drumlanrig; Sir Thomas Kirkpatrick; Sir Robert Herries (kinsmen); Mr Alexander Cairns; Herbert Corry; John Durant; Thomas Porter (squires). [No place or date; after October 1409.]

SOURCE. Fraser, *Douglas*, iii, no. 382: inspection by Margaret, Dowager Countess of Douglas, 9 Apr. 1425.
COMMENT. Douglas is styled lord of Annandale.

**86** Inspection and confirmation of a charter by his brother James Douglas (of Abercorn), to Patrick Reedie Ramsay: of Drumwhindle, in Aberdour barony (ABD). Witnesses: James Douglas (brother); Sir William Hay; Sir William Borthwick; Sir William Crawford (kinsmen); Mr Alexander Cairns; Matthew Geddes, rector of the church of the Forest. [No place or date; after October 1409.]

SOURCE. *Aberdeen-Banff Ills.*, ii, 375–6.
COMMENT. Douglas is styled lord of Annandale. James Douglas's charter is dated 31 Oct. 1408; witnesses include the earl of Douglas, Sir William Borthwick and William Borthwick junior.

**87** Charter to his squire David Home of Wedderburn, for service done and to be done: of Wedderburn, in the earldom of March (BRK); to David and his heirs; of Douglas while he is alive, and after Douglas's death of George Dunbar, Earl of March, and his heirs; for one suit to the chief court of Lauderdale each year, and after Douglas's death for whatever service Douglas owed to the earl of March. [No warranty.] Witnesses: Sir William Hay; Sir William Borthwick (kinsmen); Robert Pringle; George Rutherford; William Sinclair. [No place or date; presumably October 1409 × 28 February 1414.]

SOURCE. HMC, *Milne-Home Rep.*, no. 1.
COMMENT. The date is probably after the reconciliation with the earl of March, but before March's inspection of this charter, dated 29 Feb. 1414 [*sic* – but 1414 was not a leap year!]; also inspection by James I on 19 Apr. 1431: NAS, Gt. Seal Reg., C2/3, no. 106; *RMS*, ii, no. 189.

**88** Charter to William Bell, for service done and to be done: of Kirconveth or 'le Flemynglandis', in Annandale; which escheated to Douglas when John Carruthers, who was illegitimate, died childless; to William and his heirs; of the lord of the lands of Luce; for the usual service; with warranty. Witnesses: Sir John Edmonston; Sir William Graham; Sir William Borthwick; Sir John Forrester; Sir William Crawford; Sir Thomas Murray (kinsmen). [No place or date; presumably October 1409 × 30 March 1414.]

SOURCE. NAS, Gt. Seal Reg., C2/2, no. 78; *RMS*, ii, no. 85: inspection by James I, 6 Mar. 1427.
COMMENT. Douglas is styled lord of Annandale; the inclusion of Sir John Edmonston among the witnesses gives a date of before 30 Mar. 1414 [see **124**].

**89** Inspection and confirmation, as lord of Lauderdale, of a charter by George Murray of Halton, to John of Duddingston, burgess of Edinburgh: of 'Achincleuch' in the barony of Halton. Witnesses: Sir William Borthwick; Sir John Sinclair of Lethrik; Sir Henry Douglas; Robert Livingstone; William Edmonston; Mr James Fawside (secretary). [No place or date; presumably after October 1409, and possibly before March 1414.]

SOURCE. NAS, Elibank Muniments, GD32/3/2.
COMMENT. Douglas is styled lord of Annandale; the witnesses to Murray's original charter (GD32/3/1) include Sir John Edmonston, which dates it to before 30 Mar. 1414 [see **124**].

**90** Charter to Mr Alexander Cairns, provost of Lincluden, for his good services: of Gilkerscleuch, in Crawfordjohn barony (LAN); to Alexander, his heirs and assigns; of Douglas and his heirs; in blench farm, for 1d. a year; with warranty clause. Witnesses: James Douglas (brother); Sir William Douglas of Nithsdale (nephew); Sir William Douglas of Drumlanrig; Sir William Stewart of Castlemilk; Sir William Crawford; Sir Thomas Murray. [No place or date; presumably October 1409 × 4 August 1416.]

SOURCE. NAS, National Register of Archives (Scotland) 2177, survey of Hamilton Muniments, bundle 515; noted briefly in HMC, *Hamilton Rep.*, no. 129. (I am grateful to Alan Borthwick for details of this charter.)
COMMENT. Douglas is styled lord of Annandale; Cairns transferred the lands to his son on 4 Aug. 1416 [**52**].

**91** Charter to his kinsman Sir John Stewart of Girthon, for service done and to be done: of Barlay (Kirkcudbright sheriffdom), in Galloway; resigned by John; to John for his life, and then to his illegitimate daughter Elizabeth, and the heirs of her body, with reversion to Douglas and his heirs; of Douglas and his heirs; for the usual service; with warranty. Witnesses: Sir William Douglas (nephew); Sir Thomas McCulloch; Sir Fergus McDowell; Sir Alexander Gordon; Sir John Keith; Mr Alexander Cairns (clerk and kinsman); John Murray; William Sinclair; John Durant. At Wigtown, [no date; presumably October 1409 × 6 February 1419].

SOURCE. NAS, Broughton and Cally Muniments, GD10/11; Fraser, *Douglas*, iii, no. 360.
COMMENT. Douglas is styled lord of Annandale; John Stewart of Girthon was dead by 6 Feb. 1419 [**60**].

**92** Charter [damaged] to his 'beloved and special' Thomas Caverhill, for service: of lands in Roxburghshire; [possibly resigned by Thomas]; to Thomas and his heirs; of Douglas and his heirs; [apparently in blench farm]. Witnesses: John Forrester of Corstorphine; Archibald Edmonston [and others]. At 'le Ernhuch', 31 May [no year; presumably after October 1409].

SOURCE. NAS, Cranston of Gorehouse Papers, GD134/3, p. 5: notarial transumpt, 1443 × 4, of confirmation by Archibald, fifth Earl of Douglas; damaged, and only partly legible, because much has been eaten by rodents. (I am grateful to Alan Borthwick for deciphering what remains and giving me the details.)
COMMENT. Douglas is styled lord of Annandale.

## NOTES OF TEXTS

**93** Note of charter to Sir Robert Maitland: of Thirlestane and the demesne lands of Lauder, in Lauder[dale] and Heriotmuir lordship; resigned by Robert's father John; to Robert and his heirs; of Douglas and his heirs; in blench farm. At Dunbar, 28 April 1401.

SOURCE. *APS*, vii, 159: note of inspection by Robert III.

**94** Note of charter to George Douglas, Earl of Angus: of Cortachy barony (FOR). [*c.* 12 July 1402.]

SOURCE. HMC, *Hamilton Rep.*, no. 128: the precept of sasine [**117**].
COMMENT. The subsequent transfer of Cortachy to the earl of Atholl [**101**] would probably have followed on the resignation of the barony by the earl of Angus.

**95** Note of charter 'by Archibald earl of Douglas, etc., to William Graham of Kincardine, [of] the lands of Logyachray. Stirling[shire]'. [Presumably before Humbleton, 14 September 1402.]

SOURCE. *RMS*, i, App. II, no. 1937.
COMMENT. This is a charter of the fourth earl, because William Graham was not lord of Kincardine until after May 1400: *Scots Peerage*, vi, 213–16.

**96** Note of charter 'By Archibald earl of Douglas, son in law to the king, to William Stewart of Teviotdale or of Jedworth, the lands of Abercorne and castle thereof [LIN], blench.' [Before Humbleton, 14 September 1402.]

SOURCE. *RMS*, i, App. II, no. 1962.
COMMENT. William Stewart was executed shortly after Humbleton. Brown, *Black Douglases*, 91, dates this grant to 'late October 1398'; it is unclear why.

**97** Note of charter to Walter Ogilvy: of 'Cordabow' etc. in Lintrathen barony (FOR); to Walter and his heirs; of Douglas and his heirs. [Before 20 November 1406.]

SOURCE. *RMS*, i, no. 876: confirmation by the Governor, 20 Nov. 1406.

**98** Note of charter to James Douglas of Balvenie (brother): of Avoch, Eddirdour, Strathdearn and Brachlie baronies (INV); of Boharm barony, Balvenie in Mortlach barony, and Conveth (BNF); and of Aberdour and Rattray baronies (ABD); to James and his heirs; of Douglas and his heirs. [Presumably before 1408.]

SOURCE. NAS, Gt. Seal Reg., C2/2, no. 47; *RMS*, ii, no. 43: confirmation by James I, 18 Apr. 1426.
COMMENT. James Douglas granted lands in Aberdour in 31 Oct. 1408 [**23, 86**].

**99** Note of charter to James Douglas of Balvenie (brother): of Petty barony, one-third of Duffus and Alvah-shire, and Douglas's lands in 'le Thayndomeis' in Kilmalemnock (ELG); and of Even, etc. (INV); to James and his heirs; of Douglas and his heirs. [Probably about the same date as No. **98**.]

SOURCE. NAS, Gt. Seal Reg., C2/2, no. 53; *RMS*, ii, no. 49: from confirmation by James I, 11 May 1426.

**100** Probable grant to James Douglas (brother), by means of resignation to the Governor: of the lands and castle of Abercorn [LIN], perhaps as a barony. [Before October 1408; probably about the same date as No. **98**.]

SOURCE. NAS, Gt. Seal Reg., C2/2, no. 34; *RMS*, ii, no. 38: grant by James I of 'the lands of the barony of Abercorn and the castle of the same' to James Douglas of Balvenie on 7 Mar. 1426, following the latter's resignation. James Douglas was styled 'of Abercorn' in 1408 [**23, 86**], and so it must have been given to him by the fourth earl [cf. **96**] (as stated by Brown, *Black Douglases*, 178), by means of resignation and grant (otherwise the earl's charter would have been confirmed, as in Nos. **98, 99**).

**101** Note of resignation to the Governor, Robert, Duke of Albany: of the land of Cortachy barony (FOR); for Albany's grant to Walter Stewart, Earl of Atholl; to Atholl, his heirs and assigns; of the crown; in free barony; for the usual service. [*c.* 22 October 1409.]

SOURCE. *RMS*, i, no. 910: Albany's charter, dated 22 Oct. 1409.
COMMENT. This was probably resigned to Douglas by the earl of Angus [**94**].

**102** Note of charter to John Seton, his kinsman: of 'Altham' (ROX). Witnesses: Sir William Lindsay of Byres; Sir William Hay; Sir William Abernethy; Sir John Edmonston; Sir William Borthwick. At Edinburgh, 4 March 1410.

SOURCE. *A History of the Family of Seton during Eight Centuries*, ed. G. Seton (Edinburgh, 1896), 845.

**103** Probable grant to James Douglas of Balvenie (brother), by means of resignation to the Governor: of the barony of Strathaven (LAN); reserving superiority of the tenancies to the earl. [Probably after 1410.]

SOURCE. NAS, Gt. Seal Reg., C2/2, no. 36; *RMS*, ii, no. 40: grant by James I of the barony of Strathaven (except for the tenancies, which were reserved to the fifth earl) to James Douglas of Balvenie on 7 Mar. 1426, following the latter's resignation. Since James Douglas held this barony before Mar. 1426, it was probably given to him by the fourth earl (as stated by Brown, *Black Douglases*, 178), by means of resignation and grant (otherwise the earl's charter would have been confirmed, as in Nos. **98**, **99**); but the fourth earl appears still to have been lord of Strathaven in 1410 [see **30**].

**104** Probable grant to James Douglas of Balvenie (brother), by means of resignation to the Governor: of the lands of 'Hesyldoun' and 'Grenburn' in Stonehouse barony (LAN). [Possibly same date as No. **103**.]

SOURCE. NAS, Gt. Seal Reg., C2/2, no. 35; *RMS*, ii, no. 39: grant by James I of 'Hesyldoun' and 'Grenburn' in Stonehouse barony to James Douglas of Balvenie on 7 Mar. 1426, following the latter's resignation. Since James Douglas held these lands before Mar. 1426, they were probably given him by the fourth earl (as stated by Brown, *Black Douglases*, 178), by means of resignation and grant (otherwise the earl's charter would have been confirmed, as in Nos. **98**, **99**).

**105** Note of resignation to the Governor, Robert, Duke of Albany: of Stewarton and Ormsheuch, in Cunningham barony (AYR); for Albany's grant to John Stewart, Earl of Buchan and Elizabeth, Douglas's daughter, jointly, and the heirs of their bodies; failing whom, to Buchan's heirs-male of the body; with reversion to Douglas; to be held of the Stewards of Scotland; for the usual service. [*c.* 2 May 1413.]

SOURCE. *RMS*, i, no. 945: Albany's charter, dated 2 May 1413.
COMMENT. This and the next two transactions follow from No. **30**.

**106** Note of resignation to the Governor, Robert, Duke of Albany: of 'Trabeath', in the earldom of Carrick (AYR); for Albany's grant to John Stewart, Earl of Buchan and Elizabeth, Douglas's daughter, jointly, and the heirs of their bodies; failing whom, to Buchan's heirs-male of the body; with reversion to Douglas; to be held of the earls of Carrick; for the usual service. [*c.* 6 November 1413.]

SOURCE. *RMS*, i, no. 947: Albany's charter, dated 6 Nov. 1413.

**107** Note of resignation to the Governor, Robert, Duke of Albany: of Dunlop, in Cunningham barony (AYR); for Albany's grant to John Stewart, Earl of Buchan and Elizabeth, Douglas's daughter, jointly, and the heirs of their bodies; failing whom, to Buchan's heirs-male of the body; with reversion to Douglas; to be held of the Stewards of Scotland; for the usual service. [*c.* 24 November 1413.]

SOURCE. *RMS*, i, no. 946: Albany's charter, dated 24 Nov. 1413.

**108** Note of charter to Walter Ogilvy: of the lands of Lintrathen barony (FOR); to Walter and his heirs; [probably] of the crown, in place of Douglas. [No place or date: before 15 June 1414.]

SOURCE. NAS, Airlie Muniments, GD16/3/6: confirmation by the Governor, 15 Jun. 1414.

**109** Note of grant (by Douglas and his council *in hac parte*) to Andrew Raeburn, monk of Kilwinning Abbey: of an annuity of £20 Scots out of the proceeds of Coldingham Priory [i.e. Douglas's fee as bailie]. [No place or date: before 27 June 1414.]

SOURCE. Raine, *North Durham*, appendix, no. CL [see **46**].

**110** Note of confirmation of a charter by William, first Earl of Douglas, to John Carmichael: of Overton of Carmichael, in the earldom [and barony] of Douglas (LAN). At Edinburgh, 10 October 1414.

SOURCE. NAS, National Register of Archives (Scotland), 243, survey of Earl of Hyndford's muniments: Inventory of writs of Hyndford estates, bundle 1, no. 3. (I am grateful to Alan Borthwick for these details; he tells me that the charter may be in a collection of Hyndford writs awaiting cataloguing in NAS, but it has not been located.)

**111** Note of charter to John Park, for service done and to be done: of Gilbertfield, in Drumsargard barony, in Lauder regality [*sic*]; to John Park and Janet Chisholm, and their heirs-male. Witnesses: Sir William Hay; Sir William Borthwick; Sir William Stewart of Castlemilk; Mr Alexander Cairns; Matthew Geddes; James Hallsyde (parsons). [No place or date; after October 1409.]

SOURCE. HMC, *Hamilton Rep.*, no. 130 (7).
COMMENT. Douglas is styled lord of Annandale.

**112** Note of charter to George Rutherford: of Nether Chatto, etc., in Sprouston regality (ROX); which had been forfeited by Tassy Chatto, who died in the king of England's faith; of Douglas and his heirs. [No place or date; after October 1409.]

SOURCE. NLS, MS Acc. 7750/1/3 (Rutherford of Egerton): confirmation by Archibald, fifth Earl of Douglas, to his squire Robert Rutherford. (I am grateful to Alan Borthwick for details of this charter.)
COMMENT. Douglas is styled lord of Annandale.

**113** Note of charters to James Dundas: of Dunberny (PER) [cf. **15**], Easter Blairmucks (LAN) [cf. **53**], and Tulliallan (PER). [No places or dates.]

SOURCE. NLS, MS Adv. 80.4.15, p. 148, no. 8: confirmation by Archibald, fifth Earl of Douglas.
COMMENT. There is no other record of a grant of Tulliallan to James Dundas.

**114** Note of charter to Thomas Forman: of Hutton in Sprouston regality (BRK: *sic*). [No place or date.]

SOURCE. NAS, Gt. Seal Reg., C2/2, no. 70; *RMS*, ii, no. 84: inspection by James I of a charter by Archibald, fifth Earl of Douglas, granting Hutton to Thomas Forman's son, Adam, who stated that it had been given to his late father by the fourth earl of Douglas.

**115** Note of grant to Sir John Forrester, probably by means of resignation to the Governor or the king: of the lands of Clerkington (EDB). [No place or date.]

SOURCE. NAS, Gt. Seal Reg., C2/2, no. 17; *RMS*, ii, no. 7: grant by James I erecting various lands, including Clerkington which his 'brother' Archibald, Earl of Douglas had resigned, into the barony of Liberton, on 10 Jul. 1424.

## PRECEPTS OF SASINE

**116** Precept of sasine: of Cranshaws (BRK); for Sir John Swinton; addressed to David Swinton. At Dunbar, 10 October 1401. [See **2**.]

SOURCE. NAS, Reg. Ho. Chrs., RH6/209; Fraser, *Douglas*, iii, no. 343.
COMMENT: Note that, unusually, the precept of sasine predates the charter (dated 20 Oct.).

**117** Precept of sasine: of the barony of Cortachy (FOR); for George Douglas, Earl of Angus; according to Douglas's charter; addressed to David Annand. At Edinburgh, 12 July 01402. [Cf. **94**.]

SOURCE. HMC, *Hamilton Rep.*, no. 128.
COMMENT. The precept of sasine is the only evidence for this grant.

**118** Note of precept of sasine: of Kenmure in Galloway; for Alexander Gordon of Stichill, as son and heir of his late father Robert Gordon. At Threave, 24 January 1403.

SOURCE. *Scots Peerage*, v, 100.
COMMENT. No source for this is given in the *Scots Peerage*.

**119** Precept of sasine: of regality rights over Buittle barony, Preston barony and Borgue, in Galloway; for Sir James Douglas of Dalkeith; addressed to Sir William Cockburn of Skirling, Sir Fergus McDowell, Gilbert Grierson, and Thomas Forman. [No place], 2 February 1407. [See **11**.]

SOURCE. *Morton Reg.*, ii, no. 216.

**120** Precept of sasine: of Dunberny (PER); for James Dundas; addressed to William and Thomas Meldrum. At Edinburgh, 16 July 1407. [See **15**.]

SOURCE. NLS, MS Adv. 80.4.15, p. 147, no. 6.

**121** Precept of sasine: of Pitcox; for John Swinton, as son and heir of his late father, Sir John Swinton; addressed to Richard of Hangingside, bailie of Douglas's 'barony of Dunbar'. At Edinburgh, 10 October 1407.

SOURCE. NAS, Reg. Ho. Chrs., RH6/217; Fraser, *Douglas*, ii, no. 350.
COMMENT. Cf. Nos. **3**, **122**. Note the five-year timelag between John Swinton junior's sasines of Pitcox and of Cranshaws.

**122** Precept of sasine: of Cranshaws (BRK); for John Swinton, as son and heir of his late father, Sir John Swinton; addressed to Douglas's squire David Borthwick. At Edinburgh, 10 August 1412.

SOURCE. NAS, Swinton Charters, GD12/19.
COMMENT. Cf. Nos. **2**, **121**.

**123** Precept of sasine: of £20-worth of land in Sprouston regality [ROX]; for Douglas's squire, John Cranston, as heir of his late father, Sir William Cranston of that ilk, to whom the land was granted heritably; addressed to James Gledstanes, Douglas's bailie of Sprouston regality. At Edinburgh, 4 November 1413.

SOURCE. Fraser, *Douglas*, iii, no. 365.

**124** Precept of sasine: of Tulliallan, etc.; for David Edmonston, as heir of his late father, Sir John Edmonston; addressed to James Heriot, Douglas's bailie of Tulliallan; following inquest and retour made by the former bailie, Robert Stewart of Lorn. At Stirling, 30 March 1414. [Cf. **44**, **48**.]

SOURCE. NAS, Cardross Writs, GD15/337.

**125** Precept of sasine: of 'Auchquhone' (WIG), in Galloway; for William Hay of Loquhariot: addressed to Uchtred McDowell, sheriff of Wigtown. At Edinburgh, 6 October 1414. [See **47**.]

SOURCE. NAS, Yester Writs, GD28/48; *Yester Writs*, no. 48; Fraser, *Douglas*, iii, no. 368.

**126** Precept of sasine: of Grandtully, etc.; for Alexander Stewart; addressed to Andrew Ascot, Douglas's bailie *in hac vice* in the *apthania* of Dull. At Stirling, 8 March 1415. [See **43**.]

SOURCE. Fraser, *Grandtully*, i, no. 6.

**127** Precept of sasine: of Hershaw, etc.; for Alexander Mure; according to Douglas's charter; addressed to William Davidson, Douglas's sergeant and bailie. At Edinburgh, 13 November 1417. [See **54**.]

SOURCE. Fraser, *Douglas*, iii, no. 370.

**128** Precept of sasine: of regality rights over Eskdalemuir; for Melrose Abbey; addressed to Simon Glendenning, Douglas's bailie of Eskdale. At Edinburgh, 16 January 1419. [See **59**.]

SOURCE. Fraser, *Douglas*, iii, no. 58.

**129** Precept of sasine: of Greenan; for his kinsman Herbert Maxwell; addressed to Thomas 'Makilqwod', Douglas's officer in Glenkenstan. At Edinburgh, 20 March 1420. [See **63**.]

SOURCE. Fraser, *Douglas*, iii, no. 375.

## GRANTS TO THE FOURTH EARL OF DOUGLAS

**130** Note of Great Seal letters of Robert III, to Archibald Douglas: granting him 200 merks a year for life, as keeper of Edinburgh Castle. [No place], 4 June 1400.

SOURCE. *ER*, iii, 515.

**131** Note of charter of Robert III, to 'Archibald Douglas son to the earl of Douglas', and [presumably] his wife Margaret, daughter of Robert III: 'of the lordship of Douglas and regalities of the forest of Etrik, Lauderdaill and Romannoch, and all the rest in general, with a taillie'; [presumably on the resignation of his father the third earl of Douglas and reserving the latter's liferent]. [No place or date; before 24 December 1400.]

SOURCE. *RMS*, i, Appendix II, no. 1817.
COMMENT. The third earl of Douglas probably died on or about 24 Dec. 1400.

**132** Charter of Joanna, [Dowager] Countess of Douglas, to her son Archibald, [fourth] Earl of Douglas: of her lands of Cranshaws (HAD: *sic*); in exchange for £10-worth of land of the Halls of Airth; to Douglas and his heirs of Joanna and her heirs; for the usual service. Witnesses: Sir Robert Stewart of Innermeath; William Muirhead; Patrick Murray; Robert Melville (Joanna's chaplain). At Bothwell, [no date; *c*. 6 February 1402].

SOURCE. NAS, Swinton Charters, GD12/14.
COMMENT. Date from precept of sasine: GD12/15; cf. Nos. **2**, **27**.

**133** Charter of Robert, Duke of Albany, Governor, to Archibald, [fourth] Earl of Douglas: of the lordship of Annandale; resigned by George, Earl of March, and his son George Dunbar; to Douglas and the heirs-male of his body; failing whom, the earl of March and his heirs; of the crown; in regality, with pleas of the crown; for the usual service. Witnessed. At Haddington, 2 October 1409.

SOURCE. *RMS*, i, no. 920.

**134** Letters of John, Prior of Durham Cathedral Priory, and John, Prior of Coldingham, appointing Archibald, [fourth] Earl of Douglas, 'our soverayn bailie and governor' of the lordship and lands of the house and barony of Coldingham [BRK]; with full powers to administer it, on their behalf. At Durham, 1 May 1414.

SOURCE. *Coldingham Corresp.*, no. XCVIII.
COMMENT. Douglas had already been bailie, or 'keeper of the lands and rents' of Coldingham Priory since before 1406 (presumably since 1401) [**10**]. This is a reappointment without a fee, following the earl's surrender in Oct. 1413 of the £100 Scots (or 100 marks sterling) fee which he had received for the office [**41**]; note the second surrender of any fee in June 1414 [**46, 109**].

# 18

# Recreating the Urban Past

## *E. Patricia Dennison*

It was Grant Simpson who, with other members of the Medieval Archaeology Committee of the Society of Antiquaries of Scotland in 1972, gave a timely warning: Scotland was in danger of destroying the remnants of one of its significant heritages – its historic towns.[1] The repository of evidence for them, it was argued, was not merely the documentary source, but also the archaeological inheritance. The former was in relatively safe hands, but the latter was under threat. Redevelopment and upgrading of the townscape, essential though they might be, were wiping out centuries of Scotland's past. Since then, the committee's words have not gone totally unheeded. Townscape management has increasingly exhibited an awareness of the need for conservation along with the necessity for change. Central and local government bodies have committed a level of funding, not only to protect the archaeological heritage, but also to monitor necessary development and raise public awareness of the value of irreplaceable facets of historic burghs.[2]

There has, at the same time, been a shift of emphasis in the academic approach to urban studies. The traditional, constitutional and legalistic, assessment of burghal institutions has, to some extent, been replaced by a methodology that sees towns more simply – as places where people lived, worked and communicated. As such, they were vibrant, living organisms which expressed themselves not merely through their charters, liberties and political organisations, but also through the skills and handicrafts, the religion and values, and the built environments of their inhabitants. There is a wealth of source material which provides an insight into the lifestyles of these inhabitants. The most crucial source, for the historian, is documentary evidence. The other chapters in this volume discuss, and rely heavily upon, written sources. Written sources, however, often fail to reveal the full scope of town life. The historian must, therefore, turn to other evidence too. It is the remit of this paper to consider the other source materials which the historian may use to supplement that essential core of documentary evidence.

Archaeology is one such tool, used either in conjunction with historical evidence, or, if this latter is not available, within an informed historical perspective. We are, to cite only one example, virtually totally dependent on archaeology in assessing the nature or extent of pre-urban settlement. Prehistoric shell middens and evidence of neolithic farmers and bronze age metallurgists, in

1 G. G. Simpson, *Scotland's Medieval Burghs: An Archaeological Heritage in Danger* (Edinburgh, 1972). The other members of the committee were Nicholas P. Brooks, Stewart H. Cruden, William A. Dodd, A. A. M. Duncan, John Gerrard, Geoffrey Stell, Eric Talbot and Frank P. Tindall.

2 Historic Scotland and The Royal Commission on the Ancient and Historical Monuments of Scotland should in particular be mentioned.

the form of stone, copper and bronze axeheads, and wooden dug-out canoes in Glasgow; mesolithic remains of shell-fish overlaid with bronze-age pottery, flint and stone artefacts of the neolithic and bronze age and ceramics, possibly of the bronze age, in Dundee; and a bronze age cist in Jedburgh – are firm indications that the siting of a medieval town was not usually random and confirm that many medieval urban settlement sites had been favoured by man for centuries.[3] For later periods too archaeology is an invaluable tool for the historian. The Roman presence in Scotland is sketchily documented and physically evidenced by structural remains of walls, fortifications and marching camps. But it is solely from archaeological finds in the Kirkcaldy area, for example, that evidence exists of a Roman presence in that region, which may imply that pre-urban Kirkcaldy was used as a ferry terminal for Roman militia crossing the Forth.[4] Ultimately, the putative identities of the Roman Apardion and Aberdeen, and of Rerigonium and Innermessan too, can only be proven or discredited by archaeological evidence.[5] And excavations of early native centres, such as Traprain Law, have revealed strong proto-urban characteristics which raise serious questions for the urban historian of the origins of urbanisation in Scotland.[6]

Even when documentation becomes more copious, historians face certain difficulties. Early charters and burgh laws, such as *Leges Burgorum*, *Assise Regis Willelmi* and *Statute Gildae*, are virtually the sole documentary sources for early burghs.[7] While they offer an insight into early burgh organisations, they are deficient when used as sources to comprehend lifestyle. Burgh charters were formal, legal documents, often repeated one from the other; and early burghal legislation tells us how people were intended to live, not how they did, in fact, conduct their lives. With regard to settlement patterns, for example, the archaeological discipline has already provided invaluable information on the early burghs. In Perth and St Andrews, for example, the size of burgage plots, intensity of activity in backland sites and street development have all been monitored. Elsewhere, it is known that some early burghs, such as Hamilton and Selkirk, shifted their focus from the original urban nucleus. It is suspected that others, such as Dunfermline and Aberdeen, did likewise; but firm evidence for this is not available in the documentary sources and can, in all probability, come only from archaeology.[8] In addition, artefactual remains in towns confirm

3 S. J. Stevenson and E. P. D. Torrie, *Historic Glasgow: The Archaeological Implications of Development* (Scottish Burgh Survey, 1990), 33, 42; E. P. D. Torrie, *Medieval Dundee: A Town and its People* (Dundee, 1990), 17; A. T. Simpson and S. J. Stevenson, *Historic Jedburgh: The Archaeological Implications of Development* (Scottish Burgh Survey, 1981), 22.

4 E. P. Dennison Torrie and R. Coleman, *Historic Kirkcaldy: The Archaeological Implications of Development* (Scottish Burgh Survey, 1995), 11.

5 E. P. Dennison and J. Stones, *Historic Aberdeen: The Archaeological Implications of Development* (Scottish Burgh Survey, 1997), 11; E. P. Dennison and R. Coleman, *Historic Stranraer: The Archaeological Implications of Development* (Scottish Burgh Survey, 1995), 12.

6 B. Dicks, 'The Scottish medieval town', in G. Gordon and B. Dicks, eds., *Scottish Urban History* (Aberdeen, 1983), 34–5.

7 See *Ancient Laws and Customs of the Burghs of Scotland*, ed. C. Innes (Scottish Burgh Records Soc., 1868).

8 The work of Scottish Urban Archaeological Trust, the Archaeological Unit of Aberdeen District Art Galleries and Museums, GUARD, Headland Archaeology and Kirkdale Archaeology should be particularly noted.

the patterns of external and overseas trade which have been established by documentary sources such as customs rolls, port books, Exchequer Rolls and the Sound Toll Register. Artefacts have, however, a perhaps greater significance: they may be the sole information available on the inland trading activities of towns. For many urban centres the domestic manufacturing and finishing process, allied to internal trade, was their life-blood and may have been of greater significance to the average town than the more fully documented external trade. It would be difficult, without the archaeological resource, to reach a meaningful understanding of the town's symbiotic relationship with its rural neighbours, its dependent hinterland and beyond.[9]

It is probably in assessments of urban material culture that archaeological evidence is most required. Detailed knowledge of, for example, medieval house structure is virtually impossible to glean from the historic source. One might note the construction method of 'frist and panning' in the burgh records of Selkirk, Stirling and Dunfermline;[10] but precisely what this was, has to be left to intelligent guesswork. Excavations in Perth, Aberdeen, Linlithgow and elsewhere have provided an insight into the exterior framework of primitive urban dwellings and also into the standards of living within. Clothing and personal possessions appear in the documentary source, in inventories and testaments and as disputed pawned objects in burgh court records, but archaeological finds provide further information on textiles, both home-made and imported, and on such details as the fastenings and overall design of clothes and the workmanship of jewellery.[11] Paleobotanical studies in, for example, Glasgow, and evidence from the cesspits and middens of several towns, have given a clearer picture of the medieval diet.[12] Information about meat, fish, bread, ale and dairy products, for example, is fulsome in the historic sources. Less so is the collection of berries – raspberries, brambles, wild cherries, elderberries, blaeberries and rowans – and edible herbs such as henbane, and the trapping of wild game, which archaeological evidence has shown to be an important supplement to the diet.[13]

Also, when assessments are made of health and life expectancy the archaeological resource is most useful. Although documentary sources refer to 'pest', 'grangore' or 'gore' and leprosy, and although the use of purging powders, evidenced historically from the late sixteenth century, is a clear indication of parasitic infection, such references alone do not reveal a full picture of medieval disease. Research on skeletal remains has, however, transformed knowledge not

9 See R. M. Spearman, 'Workshops, materials and debris – evidence of early industries', in M. Lynch *et al.*, eds., *The Scottish Medieval Town* (Edinburgh, 1988).

10 'Protocol Book of John Brydin, 1530–37', in *Selkirk Protocol Books, 1511–1547*, ed. T. Maley and W. Elliot (Stair Soc., 1993), D 14; *Extracts from the Records of the Royal Burgh of Stirling*, ed. R. Renwick (Glasgow, 1887–9), 52; *The Burgh Records of Dunfermline*, ed. E. Beveridge (Edinburgh, 1917), 149, 174, 305.

11 See, e.g., J. A. Stones, ed., *A Tale of Two Burghs* (Aberdeen, 1987), 32; J. A. Stones, ed., *Three Scottish Carmelite Friaries: Aberdeen, Linlithgow and Perth* (Edinburgh, 1989), 158–9.

12 Scottish Urban Archaeological Trust, College Goods Yard, High Street, Glasgow, 1983–4; W. E. Boyd, 'Botanical fossils from medieval and post-medieval Glasgow', *Glasgow Archaeological Society Bulletin*, xxii (October 1986).

13 Stones, *Tale of Two Burghs*, 30; P. Holdsworth, ed., *Excavations in the Medieval Burgh of Perth* (Edinburgh, 1988), 27.

only of overall standards of health but also of specific illnesses, such as spina bifida, tuberculosis, arthritis and amoebic dysentery. Such work has additionally provided provisional data to estimate average sizes of men and women and even, by dental assessment, given clues to age of weaning.

For the historian, the archaeological resource is, then, of prime importance. The evidence from excavations may be used to reinforce historical data and, on occasions, offers an insight into early urbanisation at a period when written sources are deficient. There remain only two mild caveats: publication time scales in the archaeological world have until recently proved frustratingly slow; and archaeological findings have been, in certain cases, assessed without an adequate understanding of the historical background. There is, however, clear indication, as in the historical milieu, of a re-thinking, and many archaeologists are now increasingly conversant with the need to apply the historians' techniques alongside their own. Historians can benefit also from this cross-fertilisation.

A full application of historical and archaeological resources is at its most successful when worked, if not totally within a framework of the geographical and geological perception, at least with an awareness of the effect of natural phenomena on the unnatural built environment. Early urban settlement, in particular, was determined by such factors. The four basic essentials were security from human and other predators and shelter from the elements; firm, dry ground for building; a local food supply; and ready access to drinking water. The last was probably the most important and all first settlement sites would be found beside a stream or river, although urban settlement could shift from its early site once wells were dug. In Dundee, for example, wells, such as the Lady Well and the Cross Well, were sunk at the junction of impermeable igneous rock with the permeable Devonian sedimentary series, the Lower Old Red Sandstone.[14] In Dunfermline the Causagait or High Street, probably not the original nucleus of the town, was laid out along a spring line;[15] and in Aberdeen, a probable shift of focal point could be made to the Broadgait/Castlegait area, an open space, ideal economically and physically for a market where, although ill-endowed with streams, wells might be sunk.[16]

Failure to assess adequately the nature of the terrain could sometimes lead to disaster. The Nethertoun, the first site of Hamilton, or Cadzow as it was originally called, was in an area close by the Clyde and liable to flooding, as it is to this day. If Cadzow was to survive it needed to transfer to higher ground. This had been effected by the mid-fourteenth century.[17] Hence, in all probability, the development of the Hietoun, medieval Hamilton. Perth was to lose its royal

14 S. J. Stevenson and E. P. D. Torrie, *Historic Dundee: The Archaeological Implications of Development* (Scottish Burgh Survey, 1988), i, 89.

15 J. Masterton, 'A study of growth patterns and the changing cultural landscape of a Scottish town' (1962; unpublished typescript available in Dunfermline Central Library).

16 E. P. D. Torrie, 'The early urban site of New Aberdeen: a reappraisal of the evidence', *Northern Scotland*, xii (1992), 1–18.

17 *APS*, ii, 59; *Registrum Episcopatus Glasguensis* (Bannatyne and Maitland Clubs, 1843), i, 282, no. 310. This is discussed in further detail in D. Pringle, 'Cadzow Castle and the castle of Hamilton: an archaeological and historical conundrum', *Chateau Gaillard*, xv (1992), 279; and in E. P. D. Torrie and R. Coleman, *Historic Hamilton: The Archaeological Implications of Development* (Scottish Burgh Survey, 1996), 14.

castle in 1210 to flooding and that was never to be replaced. And, although without archaeological or documentary evidence it is not certain where precisely urban settlement was originally concentrated at Glasgow, thanks to the charting of the early medieval flood plain by geographers, the area near the confluence of the Camlachie Burn and the Clyde can be discounted as one of intense, early settlement.[18] Natural harbours, at Montrose and Inverkeithing, fording points, at Perth, Alloa and Glasgow, crossroads of trading routes, at Cumnock and Hamilton, are merely further examples of the relevance of geographical factors to early settlement sites.

The morphological development of the medieval town can best be understood within its geographical and geological context. The linear expansion of Dundee, for example, was determined by natural factors: dolerite ridges and swampy ground to the north and the Tay to the south were not conducive to building in the Middle Ages.[19] Edinburgh, founded on a ridge with a steep northern slope bounded by a loch and, from the twelfth century hemmed in on the east by another burgh, Canongate, would in the first instance inevitably extend south and south-west to the Cowgate and Grassmarket.[20] Kirkcaldy High Street is a graphic illustration of urban man's response to his physical environment. Experienced either on foot or viewed from above (see *Plate 5*), its curving form appears to be somewhat perverse, until a close analysis of pre-determining geological and geophysical features reveals that this medieval street, very logically, followed the line of the cliff-like raised beach which initially prevented expansion inland. This physical phenomenon gave the further effect of truncated burgage plots west of the street, compared to the east side, from which burgage plots ran down to the Forth.[21]

An important further research tool is cartographic evidence. The earliest set of maps available for Scotland is that of Timothy Pont, either in manuscript or adapted into Blaeu's *Atlas of Scotland* (Amsterdam, 1654). Pont's drawings, made in the latter decades of the sixteenth century, display an admirable precision. The storeys of castles and large buildings, for example, are often indicated by a series of horizontal slashes. Where it is possible to verify his interpretation, there is an amazing accuracy. Sometimes a minute examination of a highly-enlarged Pont drawing reveals apparently hidden features. St Mary's Church in Dundee, for example, is topped in the maps with faint lines that strongly suggest that the sixteenth-century structure was surmounted, not with a cape house, as at present, but with a crown, much in the style of that at King's College, Aberdeen.[22] Urban historians benefit not only from Pont's portrayal of significant town structures, but they also gain a vivid impression of the scatter of sixteenth-century towns: sparse in the West and the Highlands, but clustering on the east coast and in the Lothians. Whatever niggling discussions modern historians may wish to indulge in regarding what precisely constituted 'a town',

18 A. Gibb, *Glasgow: The Making of a City* (London, 1983), 12.
19 Torrie, *Medieval Dundee*, 53.
20 Simpson, *Scotland's Medieval Burghs*, 16.
21 Torrie and Coleman, *Historic Kirkcaldy*, 7–8.
22 I have benefited greatly from the ideas of, and discussions with, Charles McKean.

it is very clear that a town was at least readily recognisable to sixteenth-century man!

Town plans, such as those of John Wood drawn in the early nineteenth century and later ordnance survey maps, can be an invaluable source, indicating the lay-out of towns before major twentieth-century developments destroyed earlier remnants. There are, of course, limitations with such evidence. A degree of stability in the urban form has to be assumed and this may be confirmed only by other source material, documentary or archaeological. Given this caveat, town plans can still shed considerable light on early towns. Adopting Conzen's view of the innate conservatism of the urban fabric and following his method of stripping the town plan of its modern accretions, it is possible in many cases to reconstruct the medieval or early town plan, on the valid assumption that the street pattern is the element of the town plan that is most persistent. Perhaps one of the most readily recognisable features on a town plan is market repletion, a clustering of development on a previously open space, sometimes revealing an earlier market area. The town plans of Inverkeithing and Haddington, to name merely two, show graphically this secondary use of open areas once urban land for building had reached a premium.

Many Scottish burghs were quite deliberately and formally laid out, for example Glasgow by Ranulf of Haddington and St Andrews by Mainard the Fleming, who had probably taken part in the planning of Berwick. Often, although not always, the Scottish plan was a single street with back lanes. These back lanes might in due course become developed, forming a more complex town plan and in some cases creating a grid pattern, as in Crail and Perth. Typically, running back in a herringbone pattern from the main street were the burgage plots. Burgh records reveal that a close watch was kept on the maintenance of street alignment and burgage plot boundaries by officials (the liners). This respect for tradition resulted in a degree of territorial continuity; and it is therefore often possible, bearing in mind amalgamations and subdivisions, to work out the medieval width of plot frontages from nineteenth-century cartographic sources. Archaeologists have shown that in the relationship between plots and abuttals, for example a river at Ayr or a back lane at Selkirk or Elgin, continuity may be the norm. However, other factors may have affected plot sizes. In Aberdeen archaeological evidence has shown that reorganisation and regularisation of toft boundaries caused changes in toft frontage size.[23] These fluctuating plot boundaries are not revealed in the cartographic sources. Corner sites and plots accessible on more than one frontage in particular were vulnerable and their past development is unpredictable without a full documentary resource. Major disasters could also produce large disturbances to territorial boundaries. Fire, the ever-present hazard in the medieval town, could devastate the urban fabric. Although man's memory and sense of property, so fully recorded in the burgh records, along with stone foundations to wooden buildings, might ensure rebuilding to the old land measurements, this cannot always be assumed. Accepting such limitations, however, the cartographic

[23] J. Murray, ed., *Excavations in the Medieval Burgh of Aberdeen 1973–81* (Edinburgh, 1982), 25, 78.

resource is one that should not be underestimated. It has, for example, been shown by archaeological evidence that an assessment of plot frontage sizes in New Row, Dunfermline, based on cartographic evidence, was accurate;[24] and Perth's frontages of twenty feet, according to archaeological excavations, accord with nineteenth-century ordnance survey plans.[25]

Phases of development of the town plan may on occasion also be revealed by plan analysis. The case of St Andrews is a prime example, where innovatory assessments of a Scottish town map, in conjunction with documentary evidence, have brought a remarkable insight into the early lay-out of the burgh and extensions and adaptations thereafter.[26] Interestingly, more recent archaeological work in the Swallowgate/Castle area has brought to light unknown and undocumented structures abutting the original line of the thoroughfare.[27] This reinforces the view that a town plan, even one as early as the *c.*1580 Geddy 'Bird's eye view' of St Andrews, shows what is present at the time of illustration, and takes no account of what may once have existed but later disappeared from the townscape. To cite only one further example: John Wood's plan of Hamilton detailed and excellently surveyed though it may have been (see *Plate 6*) can take no account of the wholesale demolition over the previous thirty years of the medieval burgh, as witnessed, for example, in Thomas Barn's plan of 1781 (see *Plate 7*). A town plan is a statement in time and, as such, is limited.

This highlights the necessity for a wider-ranging, interdisciplinary approach. There are, for example, a number of visual resources available to the historian. Early engravings and paintings, in spite of artistic licence, can offer insights into past land use. Slezer's work in particular merits attention. For Dunfermline, documentary sources offer a clear picture of a quite exceptional use of water power in the west end of the town from the fifteenth and sixteenth centuries. A flagged water system was channelled from the Town Loch in the north, supplying power for the Collier Row mill *en route*, and then fed southwards while being supplemented by sewers, drains and street gutters. The records then lose the water source when it disappears into the Dunfermline Abbey lands. The conjecture that the source passes through the abbey lands to the south of the Maygate has now been supported by archaeological evidence; but the theory that the supply then re-emerges from the abbey lands via a mill dam, from whence it supplied a further two mills, is graphically given substance when one notes this same mill dam and the first of the two southerly mills on one of Slezer's seventeenth-century engravings (see *Plate 8*).[28] In Dundee also there has been uncertainty and considerable discussion as to whether the East Port of the town was removed when a later encircling wall surrounded the town. The

24 Archaeological work undertaken by John Lewis, Scotia Archaeology; cartographic research by E. P. Dennison.

25 Archaeological work undertaken by Scottish Urban Archaeological Trust; see also R. M. Spearman, 'The medieval townscape of Perth', in Lynch, *Medieval Town*, 55–8.

26 N. P. Brooks and G. Whittington, 'Planning and growth in the medieval Scottish burgh: the example of St Andrews', *Transactions of the Institute of British Geographers*, ii (1977), 278–95.

27 J. Lewis, 'Excavations at St Andrews, Castlecliffe, 1988–90', *PSAS*, cxxvi (1996), 612–17.

28 E. P. D. Torrie, 'The Gild of Dunfermline in the Fifteenth Century' (University of Edinburgh, unpublished PhD thesis, 1984), 130–2.

evidence, however, is readily available in Slezer's view of Dundee from the east: it was not demolished.

Eighteenth- and nineteenth-century illustrations can tell much about the built form of the contemporary and earlier town. While in Scotland there is little of the calibre of the Flemish School to assist a study of the townscape, the Scottish source material merits close attention. A nineteenth-century view of Kirkcaldy from the north (see *Plate 9*) gives an interesting slant on the problem of the truncated burgage plots on the west side of High Street, referred to above. Over the centuries the occupants dug their way into the abutting cliff, until ultimately lengthy, terraced plots ran back from the dwellings on the street frontage. In some cases this may, still, be witnessed to this day on the ground. Nineteenth- and, on occasion, early twentieth-century photographs can also tell much about the urban form prior to major industrialisation and modern redevelopment. In some cases photography is the only visual evidence. Nothing of Roxburgh, abandoned in 1400, remains standing. Aerial survey is at present the sole reinforcement to the documentary evidence. Archaeological investigation of that location is clearly essential.

The ideal visual resource is obviously the standing evidence. Virtually intact burghs, such as Kintyre and Culross, are not the norm, although both of these have strong statements to make on the Scottish urban built fabric and form. Remnants of the townscape may remain, however, in less obvious a guise. The street alignment and lie of burgage plots in such towns as Haddington, Elgin and St Andrews retain much of their medieval character, and pockets of such remnants may be found in many historic towns. Medieval and early modern buildings have not survived prolifically, but those that do may offer considerable information, as long as it is borne in mind that numerous alterations and additions have been made over the centuries, including, in many cases, both horizontal and vertical subdivisions. Dwellings such as Provand's Lordship in Glasgow, Mar's Wark in Stirling and the 'John Knox House' in Edinburgh are well known; but to these should be added, for example, the less prestigious, but equally significant Gardyne's House in Dundee and 339–343 High Street in Kirkcaldy, both of which offer an insight into quality merchant housing in east-coast burghs.

A further source, occasionally somewhat shunned by professional historians, is oral tradition. Placed within an informed historical context, however, important pieces of information may emerge which add to the overall, and detailed, picture of an individual town. In a study of Stranraer, for example, the precise dating of the completion of a house in the town's suburbs was felt to be important, but elusive. The matter was resolved when a local resident retold the family tradition of a forebear pursuing his apprenticeship as a joiner. While working on the final stages of this property, panelling a reception room, he and his co-workers were brought the news that Britain had won the Battle of Waterloo.[29] Oral tradition might also have provided assistance to a reconstruction of the demolished Nethertoun of Hamilton. An old man, who in his youth had

29 Torrie and Coleman, *Historic Stranraer*, 54.

been a servant on the Hamilton estate, remembered the vestiges of the defunct settlement and in autumn could trace the alignment of buildings in the earlier fading of the grass above the stone foundations. He died in the early years of this century and, with him, the nineteenth-century evidence.

Apparently less significant, but in fact sometimes telling, can be place- or street-names. These may not be the sole clue to an extinct feature, but can often help to pinpoint a particular site or structure. Charterhouse Lane in Perth is a reminder of the nearby Carthusian monastery founded in 1426; Castlegate in Aberdeen is the roadway leading to the long-extinct castle; and the numerous Tannery Rows, Port Streets and Mill Streets speak for themselves, as do the Little Irelands and the Dublin Streets. Back Rampart Street in Stranraer is an interesting reminder of the significance of the geophysical setting of all historic towns: the Back Rampart was a hill to the west of the town, and for centuries its physical dominance formed a natural boundary to the western limits of the townscape.

As academics trained to adopt an interpretative approach rather than a rigid acceptance of apparent facts, many historians are aware of that indefinable resource – intuition. This is a facility not always understood by those with a more scientific background; but, by the same token, some historians may recognise the merits of scientific research and its relevance to historical work. Historians are increasingly conversant with the scientific appraisals utilised by archaeologists, such as dendrochronology; but perhaps too rarely does urban history avail itself of the growing corpus of research findings on, for example, climatology or the evidence of spore samples from micro-bores.[30] Biologists, for example, are beginning to challenge what historians have accepted about epidemic disease and reassessments of the life-style of rats, particularly in sickness and the last day before death, call into question many accepted truths about the virulence of 'pest'.[31] Geophysics, using resistivity and magnetronomy, have already opened new doors; and research systems such as ultra-sound technology, X-rays and the like may also add greatly to our understanding of the built environment.

Grant Simpson was correct in warning that Scotland was 'far behind the rest of Europe in the archaeological study of our early towns'.[32] We have made great progress in the last two decades, but much has been lost irredeemably over the same period through unmonitored development. Fresh public money has been injected into urban research, but continuous effort will be needed if this initiative is not to be wasted; the level of government funding for such research requires to match developmental pressure. This paper would like to suggest, however, that historians have many other resources that could, and should, be tapped to gain a fuller comprehension of the urban past. Historical methodology must be based on the 'documentary and archaeological evidence' which, the Committee argued, would 'build a new kind of picture ... a picture which will

30 In particular, the work of D. Whittington, University of St Andrews.

31 G. Twigg, 'Plague in London: spatial and temporal aspects of mortality', in J. A. I. Champion, ed., *Epidemic Disease in London* (London, 1993), 1–17.

32 Simpson, *Scotland's Medieval Burghs*, 12.

be less institutional and more realistic';[33] but in an age of almost bewildering progress in technological support systems, the research findings of other disciplines are also readily available. These may be used not only to supplement the documentary resource, but also to interpret the urban past in a manner which makes the past comprehensible not only to academics but also to the layman. It was the contention of the Medieval Urban Archaeology Committee that 'very few Scotsmen [were] aware that in many of our ancient towns and cities valuable historical information [was] being destroyed every day'.[34] Townscape management, at central and local levels, is sometimes increasingly sensitive to this although it at times lapses into an inappropriate, or even crass, imagined 'heritage'. The committee continued, 'The man [sic] in the street has come to appreciate the value and interest of archaeology for the study of distant eras ... But he has hardly yet realised that the street on which he walks may conceal equally vital information about more recent and more comprehensible times.'[35] How much progress have we made here?

33 Ibid., 11.
34 Ibid., 7.
35 Ibid., 11.

# Index

This index is selective rather than exhaustive. Places in the United Kingdom are designated by pre-1973 counties; those abroad by modern countries. Kings and Popes are indexed by Christian name; abbots, priors, bishops, archdeacons, canons, dukes and earls are indexed according to their territorial designations.